Hinduism Beliefs & Practices

RELIGIOUS HISTORY AND PHILOSOPHY

The Sussex Library of Religious Beliefs & Practices

This series is intended for students of religion, social sciences and history, and for the interested layperson. It is concerned with the beliefs and practices of religions in their social, cultural and historical setting. These books will be of particular interest to Religious Studies teachers and students at universities, colleges, and high schools. Inspection copies available on request.

Published

The Ancient Egyptians Rosalie David
The Bhagavad Gita: A text and commentary for students Jeaneane Fowler
Buddhism Merv Fowler
Chinese Religions Jeaneane Fowler and Merv Fowler
Christian Theology: The Spiritual Tradition John Glyndwr Harris
Gnosticism John Glyndwr Harris
Hinduism Jeaneane Fowler (published 1997, compact 192-page edition)
Hinduism: Beliefs & Practices (Major Deities and Social Structures), expanded edition
Hinduism: Beliefs & Practices (Religious History and Philosophy), expanded edition
Hindu Goddesses Lynn Foulston
Humanism Jeaneane Fowler
Islam David Norcliffe
The Jews Alan Unterman
The Protestant Reformation: Tradition and Practice Madeleine Gray
Sikhism W. Owen Cole and Piara Singh Sambhi
T'ai Chi Ch'üan Jeaneane Fowler and Shifu Keith Ewers
Zen Buddhism Merv Fowler
Zoroastrianism Peter Clark

Forthcoming

You Reap What You Sow: Causality in the Religions of the World
Jeaneane Fowler

Published and of related interest

Chanting in the Hillsides: Nichiren Daishonin Buddhism in Wales and the Borders
Jeaneane Fowler and Merv Fowler
An Introduction to the Philosophy and Religion of Taoism: Pathways to Immortality
Jeaneane Fowler
Perspectives of Reality: An Introduction to the Philosophy of Hinduism
Jeaneane Fowler
World Religions: An Introduction for Students Jeaneane Fowler, Merv Fowler, David Norcliffe, Nora Hill and Diane Watkins

Hinduism Beliefs & Practices

RELIGIOUS HISTORY AND PHILOSOPHY

Volume II

Jeaneane Fowler

SUSSEX
ACADEMIC
PRESS
Brighton • Chicago • Toronto

2 4 6 8 10 9 7 5 3 1

First published 2016 in Great Britain by
SUSSEX ACADEMIC PRESS
PO Box 139
Eastbourne BN24 9BP

and in the United States of America by
SUSSEX ACADEMIC PRESS
Independent Publishers Group
814 N. Franklin Street, Chicago, IL 60610

and in Canada by
SUSSEX ACADEMIC PRESS (CANADA)

British Library Cataloguing in Publication Data
A CIP catalogue record for this book is available from the British Library.

Library of Congress Cataloging-in-Publication Data
Fowler, Jeaneane D., author.
Hinduism beliefs & practices : v. II Religious history and philosophy / Jeaneane Fowler.
pages cm
Previously published: 1997.
Includes bibliographical references and index.
Volume I – ISBN 978-1-84519-622-6 (pb : alk. paper)
Volume II – ISBN 978-1-84519-623-3 (pb : alk. paper)
1. Hinduism. I. Title.
BL1202.F68 2014
294.5—dc23

2014005777

MIX
Paper from responsible sources
FSC® C013056
FSC www.fsc.org

Typeset and designed by Sussex Academic Press, Brighton & Eastbourne.
Printed by TJ International, Padstow, Cornwall.

Contents

Preface and Acknowledgements

I was delighted to have been given the opportunity to extend my 1997 introduction to Hinduism in the *Beliefs and Practices* series to the present two volumes. The expansion of content has provided a deeper understanding of Hinduism, and the inclusion of other areas that were absent from the 1997 book. In Volume I, I explored Hinduism through a mainly phenomenological approach, looking at the social structures that underpin many of the religious themes of multi-faceted Hinduism and studied the rise and popularity of major deities. The emphasis here was very much on *living* religion that included ways of worship, life-cycle rites, temples and pilgrimage. Volume II has a more philosophical tone that replaces the second part of the 1997 book, and has, with the advantage of a longer text, facilitated a more detailed study of this complex religion. I was pleased also to have the space to explore the hymns of the medieval devotional poets, a study that was absent from the 1997 book. I am grateful to Anthony Grahame and the team at Sussex Academic Press for their support of the original book and for giving me the opportunity to expand on that in the present two volumes.

The team at Chepstow library has been invaluable in acquiring texts for the present volume in particular. Annie Lloyd, Shirley Ayres, Deborah Mundil-Williams, Diane Sullivan, Sarah Delahunty and Sallyanne Powell have been efficient and very helpful, as has been Catherine Macdonald, the Resources Officer in Monmouth. Sadly, the campus of the University of Wales, Newport, where I worked for so many years as head of Philosophy and Religious Studies and later as an Honorary Research Fellow, has now been relocated and absorbed in the more distant University of South Wales. That has made the service provided by the team at Chepstow Library, which is close to my home, an invaluable one. I would encourage students to use the inter-library loan services that libraries provide and for which I am very grateful.

My husband, Merv, worked with me at the University for many years in the same subject area. His knowledge of Hinduism is sound and he lectured on Hindu religion and philosophy, especially the *Upaniṣads* for many years. He has been an invaluable help in reading all of the present text and has made many useful suggestions and highlighted where there could be changes that would aid clarification. I am grateful to him for the time taken to do this and for his continued support in the writing of this book and for those that have preceded it. Finally, I owe considerable gratitude to Mr Kartik Hariharan, Consultant Orthopaedic Surgeon in South Wales, United Kingdom, for the dialogues on Tamil poetry in which we engaged. He gave me something rare that cannot really be expressed in the written word; his *inspiration* and *passion* for the poetry of Mānikka Vācakar is indelibly placed in my memory and it is he who provided the impetus and fascination for the study of the devotional poets in this present volume.

Wentwood
New Year 2016

Every being dwells on the very brink of the infinite ocean of the force of life. We all carry it within us: supreme strength – the plenitude of wisdom. It is never baffled and cannot be done away, yet is hidden deep. It is down in the darkest, profoundest vault of the castle of our being, in the forgotten well-house, the deep cistern. What if one should discover it again, and then draw from it unceasingly? That is the leading thought of Indian philosophy.

Heinrich Zimmer

The mind sees everything through its veil of interpretation. It never sees a thing directly, but always through a glass, darkly. The direct experience is possible only when the veil of the mind's interpretation is rent asunder. But to remove mind's veil of interpretation is to render mind, mindless. It is indeed true that only when the mind becomes mindless that man can come to that direct experience where alone the Secret of Life is communicated to him.

Rohit Mehta

. . . the soul knows more than the mind can understand, and it would be a tragic mistake to kill the soul with the tools of the mind.

John Koller

One becomes what one chooses to be, in the end.
Thus persons are different from one another.
Good and evil and that grey between them
Determine our own blend of suffering.
. . . God is a vast jig-saw puzzle of which we are
Mere tiny bits. Grasp him whole and the pieces all fit.

Tukārām

AND NOW MAY GOD, Soul of the Universe,
Be pleased with this my offering of words.
And being pleased may he give me
This favour in return.
That the crookedness of evil men may cease,
And that the love of goodness may grow in them.
May all beings experience from one another
Friendship of heart.
May the darkness of sin disappear.
May the universe see the rising of the Sun of Righteousness.
Whatever is desired, may it be received
By every living being.
And may the Supreme Being be worshipped
For ever and ever.

Jnanadeva

Introduction

This current book is the second of two volumes on Hinduism, a religion better termed "Hinduisms" given the many streams that have fed into its present phenomena. In the introduction to Volume I, I likened exploring Hinduism to putting together parts of a jigsaw puzzle. The topics with which I dealt in the first volume were the *Major Deities* (Śiva; the divine as female; Viṣṇu; Kṛṣṇa and Rādhā), and the scriptures associated with them, and *Social Structures* (class and caste; stages of life; ritual worship and life-cycle rites; women; sacred times and places). Such topics supplied some of the pieces of the "jigsaw" of Hinduism. Here, in this companion volume, I add two further perspectives, *Religious History* and *Philosophy*. Since Hinduism is a religion that is so diverse, multi-layered and culturally and religiously complex, the "jigsaw", in my view, can never be completed, and the further one journeys into the vastness of the expressions of Hinduism, the more one realizes the full picture will remain ever evasive, ever concealed. But that is the attraction of the study of Hinduism. However, the same complexities of "Hinduisms" that were highlighted in the introduction to Volume I obtain also in this companion volume. Importantly, each volume is an *Introduction*, which is to say that no prior knowledge is necessary for the reading of either, and each stands independently of the other, though the material included is complementary.

Volume II is designed as an introduction to the development of the religious expressions within Hinduism from earliest times. While traditions are explored from as far back as pre-Āryan times in the fascinating ancient civilization that existed in India and present Pakistan a few thousand years BCE, later expressions of religion and philosophy that began early Hindu traditions are gleaned from its sacred texts. My approach in this volume is to present a more philosophical viewpoint rather than the more phenomenological one of Volume I: greater depth has informed exploration of the scriptures and the interpretation of those scriptures by some of the philosophical schools that have influenced Hinduism to the present day. As in Volume I, I have confined the study of Hinduism to India, though it is to be found in other parts of the world such as Africa, the West Indies and Indonesia, as well as in so many countries in which Hindu migrants have made their homes.

The present book divides into two major areas, having historical and scriptural themes in the first and devotional Hinduism in the second. The former deals with prehistoric India, the scriptures and theories that informed historical Hinduism, and then the influential schools that gleaned their theories from those scriptures. Chapter 1 visits the ancient Indus civilization, a civilization forgotten and buried beneath the alluvial deposits of northern India and Pakistan and a civilization so great that it could rival the better-known

Mesopotamian civilization of the same time frame of the third millennium BCE. Unearthed at the Indus sites is evidence of ancient signs or symbols, inscriptions of a kind that have perplexed epigraphers since their discovery. This chapter, then, examines the archaeological discoveries in the environs of the Indus valley and elsewhere in a fairly chronological scheme. It also examines the signs and symbols that give us some understanding of the nature of the civilization, including the pictorial images on the many seals. The overall purpose here is to draw from the evidence some indicators of the religion or religions that informed these ancient beginnings of settled life in India and Pakistan.

Chapter 2 explores the thorny question of the appearance of the Āryans in northern India followed by the important scriptures of the Āryans, the four *Vedas*. From these, especially the *Atharva Veda*, I have tried to glean something of the interface between the Indus civilization and the *Vedic* period of the Āryans – an exploration that needed meticulous searching for evidence of popular and tribal customs hidden in the texts. My main purpose here, as in chapter 1, is to extract the religious ideas and the early concepts of deity that pervade these ancient scriptures. Chapter 3 also deals with the concept of *Veda*, "knowledge" or "wisdom", but in the context of the more mystical scriptures that comprise the *Upaniṣads*, known by the definition *Vedānta*, because they come "at the end of the *Vedas*". Again, it is the more developed concepts of deity that concern me in this chapter.

Chapter 4 turns to one of the important schools that were influenced by the *Vedānta*, Advaita Vedānta, one of the six orthodox schools of philosophy in Hinduism. It was important enough to remain influential in Hinduism to the present day. Here, in this chapter, we leap forward in time to the eighth–ninth centuries CE to examine the theories of the founder of the school, Śaṃkara. It is his concept of deity, and his view of the nature of the soul and the world that occupy the content of this chapter. Chapter 5 takes up two other orthodox schools of Hindu philosophy, Sāṃkhya and its complementary system of classical Yoga. While Saṃkhya today is barely evident in Hinduism, its theory of the unified nature of matter has been a major influence in the many centuries that followed its inconsistent beginnings. Yoga needs no introduction to the modern and post-modern world for it is endemic in it. But the complexities of its earlier classical theories, especially its quite brilliant analysis of the nature of the self and the means to free the self from the shackles of egoistic involvement in the world, are ones that I have explored in some depth.

I move then in chapter 6 to the second area of study, devotional Hinduism, beginning in this chapter with that well-known text, the *Bhagavad Gītā*. Here, I have taken a thematic approach analysing the concept of God, creation, the nature of the liberated Self and the ordinary, worldly self. This chapter also examines the themes of *dharma*, the different paths to God and the concept of liberation in the *Gītā*. It is a chapter based on an earlier work of mine, *The Bhagavad Gita: A text and commentary for students*[1] which examines the text verse by verse and gives a full introductory synopsis of the *Vedic* and *Vedāntic* influences on the text, the nature, date and historicity of the text as well as its authorship, translators and commentators. Space has not allowed me to do any more than sketch a brief outline of these areas in chapter 6.

Devotional Hinduism is a vast area of study and there has been much field research that has complemented the translations of the hymns of the great poets, saints and mystics who were the foundations of popular monotheistic devotion to a personal God. Chapters

7 and 8 deal with these foundations and I have confined myself here to exploring, in the main, the hymns of the medieval Vaiṣṇava saints in chapter 7 and those of the Śaiva saints in chapter 8. As an introduction to these poets, I have discussed such devotion, *bhakti*, in considerable detail at the beginning of chapter 7. In chapter 7, also, I have included the qualified non-dualism of the great devotional Vaiṣṇava theologian and philosopher, Rāmānuja. His school of Viśiṣṭadvaita Vedānta I have discussed fully in *Perspectives of Reality: An Introduction to the Philosophy of Hinduism*[2] and the interested reader will find more detailed exploration of this orthodox school of Hinduism there, in addition to chapters on Advaita Vedānta, Sāṃkhya, and classical Yoga. The final chapter, chapter 9, is the conclusion to the book and draws together the evidence for a unity that underlies the apparent diversity and plurality that exemplifies our existence in the world.

For both volumes, I decided to use diacritical marks for the transliteration of Sanskrit, mainly because they are an aid to pronunciation. I have included a *Glossary of Sanskrit Terms* at the end of the book but with one difference from the first volume. Place names for the Indus civilization rarely appear with diacritical marks and so I decided not to use them for this chapter. To bring the remainder of the book in line with this first chapter, and since this second volume can be read independently of the first, no diacritical marks will appear on place names throughout: "Tamil Nāḍu", therefore, will be simply "Tamil Nadu". Additionally, I decided to leave some of the famous names of the *bhakti* tradition in their popular forms; thus, Tulsīdās, Tukārām and Sūrdās. Similarly, some of the names of the Tamil poets I have simplified as, for example, "Sambandar" for Tamil "Campantar". Sanskrit pronunciation will be dealt with in the context of the Sanskrit *Glossary* at the end of the book, but since Tamil scarcely features throughout, I have not burdened the reader with Tamil pronunciation. Extensive *Notes* are supplied for each of the chapters at the end of the book, as well as detailed suggestions for *Further Reading* and a comprehensive *Index*.

To iterate a comment I made at the end of the *Introduction* in the first volume, "Hinduism" is not something to be encompassed in a few books. It is a religion that incorporates many religions, many expressions of spirituality and perplexing varieties of religious praxis: whatever depths the student explores, there will always be more to fathom. Hinduism is a religion of all possibilities and the study of it will always be a journey but never an arrival at the whole unless the ultimate aim of liberation is realized. Georg Feuerstein says something similar when he points out that the mind has a vast spectrum of consciousness that allows for equally vast potentials of human existence. He writes: "We can either become congealed on one particular level, or we can broaden out and learn to master other sectors of this enormous keyboard, to explore the different dimensions of reality, or at least open ourselves to them."[3] It is exactly the "different dimensions of reality" that Hinduism offers the student and the individual interested in exploring its rich traditions and their outcomes in daily living. At its deepest levels there is a search for what is ultimate. The quest of the ancient seers of the *Upaniṣads* expressed that search with the words: "From the unreal lead me to the real! From the darkness lead me to the light! From death lead me to immortality!"[4] The ultimate search for the real as opposed to the unreal is one that led to the experience of Brahman – that which is permanent, unchanging, eternal and intransient. The world we know is, in comparison, "unreal" because it is subject to change, to the intransience of the life and death of all things so that nothing in it can be ultimately real. The experience of an *ultimate* reality is an emergence into the light of real knowledge from the darkness of ignorance, the enlightenment of liberation from a world of life and death – this last in Hinduism a perpetual cycle through age after age. Hinduism has so many pathways towards the goal of what is ultimate reality and an almost infinite number of deities that aid the search. Alain Daniélou made a very pertinent point when he said: "We may be nearer to a mental representation of divinity when we consider an immense number of different gods than when we try to stress their unity; for the number one is in a way the number farthest removed from infinity."[5] In other words, divinity cannot be confined to one perspective, one religious viewpoint. And as Daniélou says: "The more insights we can get, the more aspects of the Divine we can perceive, the more we see of divinities beyond the different aspects of the universe, the more elements we can assemble to build up some conception of the origin of things, of the destiny and purpose of life, the nearer we are to understanding something of what divinity is."[6] A study of Hinduism, I believe, offers all these possibilities. Ultimately, Hinduism is a mirror of all the many ways in which the human being can approach God.

1
The Indus Civilization

There are many great ancient civilizations that are well-known from history and travel books: some are also studied in schools and colleges throughout the world. The remains of them are still to be seen by travellers even though time has erased their inhabitants and descendants. Imagine, then, a long lost civilization whose structural remains vanished along with the memory of it. Hidden deeply beneath alluvial soils and the scattered settlements of generation after generation of habitation in northern India and Pakistan, laid the remains of an incredible civilization about which those who dwelt on the surface were totally oblivious. It was a civilization that could have rivalled any other in ancient times, including that of Mesopotamia with which it shared time in the third millennium BCE. While hints of its existence were attested in the nineteenth century, it was not until the nineteen twenties of the last century and the decades that followed that excavations revealed a remarkable and expansive forgotten culture, though that was not before British railway engineers had plundered much of the ruins of one of its major cities, Harappa, for the building of their railways. Today, new sites are still coming to the light of day and bear witness to the extent of this great civilization, now known as the Indus civilization, given its concentration around the Indus River and other rivers of northern India and Pakistan.

Archaeological explorations

Despite the advanced nature of this civilization, there is no real writing system by which we are able to assess its culture. Archaeology has had the lone task of building information from the excavated remains and the artefacts that have been found at the plethora of Indus sites. Important as such artefacts are they cannot project with certainty into the realms of ideas and thoughts, into abstractions and theories about life. This makes my purpose in the present chapter difficult because, exciting as these archaeological discoveries are, it is the *religion* of the ancient people that walked the streets of the Indus towns and cities in which I am mainly interested. Archaeologists often have a tendency to let their imaginations and excitement belie the facts. Troy Organ makes the rather amusing point that "the British archaeologists find citadels, the Germans find palaces, the French temples, and the Americans kitchens",[1] and we are often at the mercy of their excitable ideas, controversies about finds, and competitive constructs. The presence of a decipherable script would make the study of ideas an easier matter, but without it, it is necessary to tread warily amongst the maze of hypotheses that abound regarding the ancient Indus religion. Nevertheless, our post-modern world has become much more technological, scientific and specialist. Fields such as archaeo/palaeo-climatology, archaeo/palaeo-botany, zoo-archaeology, geo-archaeology and geomorphic studies, satellite remote sensing imagery, sedimentology, palaeo-environmental studies, the use of multispectral scanners for scanning landscapes and ancient river beds, alongside the more usual carbon-dating processes and up-to-date thermo-luminescent dating all serve to make the available information about the Indus civilization much more reliable in the present day. Nevertheless, as we shall see in what follows, the forces operative on the Indus civilization were fluid and the changing patterns of growth and decay, of expansion and contraction, evolution and involution, left diverse traces for archaeologists to fathom.

Since my purpose in this chapter is to suggest areas of religious praxis, it will not be within my remit to examine closely the expansive archaeological nature of the Indus civilization. Nevertheless, the setting of such religious praxis is an important indicator of what one might expect of religious ideas and so will be needed in some way as a backdrop. Rita Wright's comment that when we examine Indus religious ideologies, "we enter into one of the most complex and poorly understood aspects of the Indus civilization",[2] is a point that needs to be borne carefully in mind as we proceed, for most of the ideas about ancient Indus religion can only remain hypothetical, suggestive but not definitive, and gleaned from tablets of stone but not written in them. At best, there are misty windows that provide clues; though there is all too often no agreement as to what is viewed on their other side.

At this point I think it apposite to mention some of the terms that apply to the Indus civilization. Given its original provenance in archaeological terms as the Indus Valley, it is sometimes referred to as the Indus Valley civilization, though we now know that it was by no means confined to the valley of the Indus River. Since the first city to be excavated was Harappa, the term Harappan civilization is sometimes used synonymously with Indus civilization. I must point out, too, that the word *civilization* does not carry with it quite the same nuance of meaning of present times. Yet, deriving from the Latin term for city, *civitas*, we would expect the civilization to have many cities and towns and, indeed, it did. The city of Harappa demonstrates this aspect of "civilization" very well, though it should not be thought that the Indus civilization began at Harappa or even centred on it. There is, too, in the nature of "civilization" a certain degree of large-scale homogeneity in that there is a linking of many of its aspects under that singular term, though it is wise not to eschew the many divergences. We should expect, too, a "civilization", as Gregory Possehl put it, "to relate to the cultural aspect of life and to historically long-lived cultural traditions":[3] We should, thus, expect some clear signs of continuity in culture: indeed, continuity will be a crucial aspect in how we view this civilization in respect of its legacy to Hinduism if, in fact, there is any. It is common practice to divide the phases of the Indus civilization into at least three. These three are:

- Early/Pre-/Proto-Indus, Pre-Harappan or Pre-Urban
- Mature or Urban
- Late Indus, Post-Urban, Late Harappan, Degenerate Harappan

Geographically, we now know that the Indus civilization spread well beyond the valley of the River Indus. Indeed, the fertility provided by other riverine locations was essential for the spread of its towns and cities. Five tributaries fed the great Indus River in the Punjab and what is now known is that there were other rivers, too, along the fertile plains of which many towns and settlements were situated. The ancient Sarasvati River, for example, no longer exists, but was once a mighty river in its own right, flowing parallel to the Indus. Today, it is the mostly dry Ghaggar-Hakra river bed. But in the distant past the people of the Indus cities and towns had to live intimately with the rivers that supported their success as a culture – a culture that remained unique, despite extensive trade well beyond its own borders. What I want to do now is explore briefly the roots of that culture in the long centuries before the beginnings of the Indus civilization.

Roots of the Indus civilization

Long before any hints that a civilization would emerge in the Indus Valley and beyond, pastoral and farming communities peppered the extensive lands, particularly in Sind, and the Ghaggar-Hakra River in Rajasthan and Cholistan, each community with its own particular culture. Many of the peoples were hunter-gatherers. These Palaeolithic small communities relied on their environment for game such as wild sheep, goats and cattle, antelope and birds, but they also relied on fish and a variety of plants. As hunter-gatherers, they would have had to move seasonally where food was available, but it was possible for some to remain fairly geographically stable where environmental factors permitted. Here we have our first glimpses of possible religious praxis permanently painted on rock surfaces as far back as ten thousand years ago. Jane McIntosh comments on these: "There are scenes of dancing men, dressed in loin cloths and often wearing streamers on their legs, arms and heads, who move together in a long line or execute complicated individual steps, either singing to accompany themselves or accompanied by musicians."[4] Significantly, in the light of what we shall explore later in this chapter, animals, especially in the hunt, feature vividly on such paintings. Terracotta figurines of females may hint at some concept of deity in female form. As peoples moved from Palaeolithic to Neolithic times, they began to domesticate animals and plants for food. Many of these hunter-gatherer groups later settled into a farming village culture, way back in about the seventh to sixth century BCE in areas such as Baluchistan, though the stage was later elsewhere and not uniform. This Neolithic stage is dated to about 7000–4300.[5] Pottery was mainly handmade, and figurines of humans and bulls suggest to Asko Parpola a fertility cult of some kind,[6] but evidence is thin to stretch to such a conclusion. The more nomadic hunter-gatherer groups continued alongside these more settled communities in a symbiotic relationship that was repeated over millennia: despite the variations in the cultures of the different groups of Palaeolithic, Mesolithic and Neolithic cultures, they are all ancestors of the Indus civilization.[7] While there must have been considerable migratory movement both of large and small groups, as Possehl pointed out, "autochthonous change is the dominant theme revealed by excavation".[8]

Sometime in the fifth millennium BCE, as the Neolithic phase passed to Chalcolithic, some village settlements grew in size spreading on the fertile plains of the rivers. The inhabitants of these larger sites were able to construct mud-brick houses, work with copper and bronze and make their well-decorated pottery on wheels. They may even have begun to develop a little trade.[9] As settlements grew in size, by the fourth millennium BCE, skilled craft work is attested, some workshop produced, and pottery wares became more complex. But there was much variation and diversity given the climatic seasonal changes and vastness of the river plains. However, there must also have been a good deal of interaction and overlapping of cultures, none particularly dominating, but these disparities, while remaining, seemed to give way, in time, to some fundamental similarities. The ways in which different groups disposed of their dead – a factor to which I shall return at many points below since such praxis illuminates religious ideas of afterlife – is one facet that seems to have retained its divergent character. Continuity in evolving and developing settlement is exemplified magnificently at a site called Mehrgarh and it is worthwhile pausing to explore this phenomenon and discover what it can tell us about religion.

Mehrgarh

Mehrgarh is in the Bolan Valley, at the foot of the Bolan Pass[10] in the Kachi plain of Baluchistan in what is now Pakistan. The special factor about Mehrgarh is the continuity of settlement there right through from Neolithic times up to the Bronze Age of the Indus civilization with continued occupation at all its excavated levels. Gregory Possehl graphically highlighted this factor when he wrote: "The Subcontinent has been raided and invaded, conquered and colonized on many occasions throughout the 9,000 years of history involved here, but the strength of the established cultural traditions has always proved to be as powerful and enduring as the customs brought by new peoples."[11] I shall want to search for these cultural traditions at other sites but Mehrgarh is such a good example of the changing yet enduring fabric of ideas throughout incredible expansion into mature settled life. Excavations at Mehrgarh have been described as, "the most momentous discoveries in subcontinental archaeology",[12] and illustrate that the Indus civilization had its roots in Indian soil. Braj Basi Lal offers the forceful point that "even as far back as the seventh millennium BC the Indian subcontinent had started laying the foundation of its own cultural evolution".[13] It seems the patterns for the Mature Indus civilization were already emerging at this very early phase.[14] Thus, it will be here, in the lowest strata of remains at Mehrgarh as far back as 7000 BCE that we can begin our journey of discovery into the religious ideas that not only predated historical Hinduism but predated even the Indus civilization by a good three-thousand years. We can divide the phases of development according to the archaeological periods thus:[15]

- Period I circa; 7000 to circa; 5000 or 4800 BCE
  IA Neolithic aceramic (pre-pottery)
  IB Neolithic ceramic

- Period IIA circa; 4800–4300 BCE Chalcolithic
- Period IIB circa; 4300–4000 BCE
- Period III circa; 4000–3200 BCE
- Period IV–VII Pre-Indus/Pre-Mature 3200–2600 BCE

In the Neolithic Period I, the transition from hunting to herding animals, the domestication of cattle and cultivation of crops took place, though hunting and gathering would have existed alongside the more domesticated productivity as probably the mainstay of existence. Inhabitants lived in mud-brick houses divided into a few rooms. They did not make pottery but had places for storage perhaps for the barley they cultivated as well as some wheat, and they used stone tools. Their burial customs at this time provide our first glimpse of a belief in an afterlife, for the dead were buried close by, in between the houses of the settlement. Stone tools were left in the graves, also jewellery made with shells, turquoise, lapis lazuli and similar, and bangles made from conch shells. Clearly, we find the beginnings of craft work at this early phase. Occasionally, young goats were buried. Such evidence suggests that there was a belief that life continued in the hereafter in much the same manner as before death. The evidence of remains of young goats indicates that they had begun to domesticate them. Examination of the skeletal teeth from these graves demonstrates that the inhabitants were of mixed races and some think they had affinities with present South and South-East Asian peoples.[16] As the centuries rolled by, the dependence on hunting and gathering decreased, and domestication of cattle, sheep and goats increased[17] along with the cultivation of cereals and the transition to a ceramic culture with the making of hand-made pottery.[18]

Period II attests to cotton seeds – the earliest ever known – and it was a phase when village communities developed into steady pastoral and farming groups that expanded the size and number of sites. Pottery came to be wheel-made, homes larger with some up to ten rooms in size,[19] and crafts more developed – all indicative of continuity from Period I, but with change alongside consolidation. There must have been some interaction with more distant lands judging by the extension of craft-work involving lapis lazuli and turquoise. As the previous Neolithic phases passed into the Chalcolithic stage, such handicrafts became more specialized particularly with the use of copper and bronze. The wheel-turned pottery was now a red ware on which were painted black designs. Period III was a time of rapid change: there were technological developments in tools and greater specialization in crafts with the use of copper and gold. Pottery seems to have been mass produced and standardized, wheel-turned and fired in kilns. It was sometimes painted with a stylized bull motif. The size of settlements was such that they were in the transition stage between villages and towns. It may have been population growth that necessitated Mehrgarh moving location to a distance away that facilitated its growth, judging by the remains of pottery that are spread over a much larger area at this second location. In any event, there seems to have been some kind of disruption of the population about 4500 BCE.[20] Skeletal remains from this phase suggest that there was some influx of people from the Iranian plateau.[21] There was, however, no interruption in the continuity of culture. Copper seals constructed for the marking of produce are first dated to this period. Large storage places suggest that granaries may have been constructed to house surplus grain.

The remaining periods see continued growth, Period IV with refined pottery mass produced and, importantly, terracotta seals that were the forerunners of those of the Indus civilization. Small terracotta female figurines – important enough to be dealt with separately below – were also found at this stage. Urbanization, with the growth of towns and growing wealth supported by trade characterized the later phases. Houses were tightly packed next to each other in lanes[22] and there does not appear to be any planning as to their siting. This sign of population growth was, in later phases, concomitant with provincial expansion and a growing interrelation with wider communities, particularly within the Indus Valley. Mehrgarh would have been one of a large number of settlements, some of which were small or large villages, others small towns, all with interconnected trading outlets and networks both of short and long distances. At these later stages from IV onwards, we pass to the important Pre-Indus stage, the long but important phase that demonstrates how Mehrgarh transformed itself into a notable provincial town. Graffiti etched on pottery suggest to some the beginning of writing in the Pre-Indus phases.[23] By the time Mehrgarh was concurrent with the Mature Indus civilization in about 2600 BCE, its continuity ceased with influences evident from elsewhere,[24] but excavations there have demonstrated admirably the development of indigenous peoples from hunter-gatherers to town inhabitants.

Indications of religion at Mehrgarh

No written records from the phases at Mehrgarh provide any information about the religious ideas of the people who lived there during the thousands of years of occupation. All that can be gleaned must be done so from archaeological excavations of material structures and items. Such material evidence that may give us a glimpse of religious praxis are the burial customs, which tell us something about beliefs in afterlife, and figurines, which are of particular interest.

Burials

In Period I, human burials were in pits with the body flexed, the arms bent at the elbows, the hands up to the head and the knees bent with the feet up to the seat.[25] Young goats, sometimes as many as five, were interred with the body. Perhaps they were there so that the deceased could begin a new life in the hereafter, a point suggested also by evidence of the use of baskets, probably filled with food. Tools buried with the dead are also suggestive of a belief that individuals carried on the same kind of existence post-death. What is particularly of note is the jewellery that was buried with the body – necklaces, pendants, bangles, anklets, belts, rings and beads. Even at this early period, some graves bore traces of turquoise and lapis lazuli that must have been imported from distant regions through trade. Males, too, were buried with jewellery, though more frequently with stone axes and the like, and one grave, probably belonging to a craftsman, had extensive tools.[26] Jonathan Kenoyer points out that occasionally, young children were buried with more elaborate jewellery than adults,[27] though others think that generally there were actually fewer artefacts found in the graves of children.[28] The emphasis on jewellery is one that pervades pre-historic and historic Hinduism to the present day. It is a symbol of status and was probably no less so in ancient pre-Indus contexts.

Period I as a whole has revealed 320 burials: as many as 150 of them have been discovered at levels associated with Period IB. Here, they were interred in a surrounding low-brick casement, a burial chamber. Occasionally there were two or more humans buried in the same grave, earlier remains having to be squashed to one end to facilitate later ones. To enable this, a part of the funerary wall had to be removed and then filled again after the addition of a new corpse. There is also evidence of the disarticulated bones of a few individuals being collected, probably after being exposed to the elements, and given a collective secondary burial.[29] Some suggest in this case that the deceased may have died elsewhere, at a distance, the bones being taken back to the ancestral home.[30] Importantly, burial customs varied during Periods I and II. Some graves were devoid of any contents other than the skeleton, but at the other end of the scale, some contained much more elaborate and costly items, suggestive of higher status. Interestingly, too, bodies were placed in an east–west orientation, the head facing south, suggestive, perhaps of some astral significance. While some burials were still in a simple pit, those in the burial chambers might be wrapped in leather or some kind of shroud.[31] Red ochre applied to the shrouds suggests some ritual idea essential to the burial.

The practice of burying individuals with costly ornaments and items for a future existence did not, however, increase with time; for in Chalcolithic times and later, burials were simplified and very little was placed in the graves, despite the increasing wealth and expertise in craft production.[32] What the earlier burials show is that there was surely some differentiation between the wealthy and not-so wealthy – an inevitability of increasing trends towards stabilized settlements – but we do not get the same kind of differentiation in the later Periods, though minor personal ornaments were still found in some graves. By Period III, the burial chambers had disappeared, but the skeletons were placed with the skulls on a brick "pillow" though, as earlier Periods, in an east–west orientation. Red ochre was no longer used. If children were buried with artefacts in earlier periods, this was not the case in Period III and child burials were separated from those of adults. The custom of burying animals with the dead was discontinued.

So what can we glean from these early burial practices that sheds light on religious belief? Clearly, there is a belief in afterlife, especially in the earliest Period. The amount and type of grave goods suggests that life after death was conceived of as a tangible existence that was the same as the previous life. Therefore, the same kind of status in life would follow into death, with plenty of ornamentation to secure it. The woman was sometimes buried with a spindle, and the male with the tools of his trade. The goats might have supplied sustenance or perhaps a source of income. But there is also disparity in burial practices that might suggest variations in religious beliefs about the afterlife.

Figurines

Perhaps the most important indicator of religious beliefs is to be found in the many figurines, though we can only speculate about their purpose. Some are more than eager to give them a cultic significance, others a simply pragmatic one and Possehl puckishly wrote of the tendency to see them as mother goddesses: "In our own culture this would be akin to thinking of every Barbie doll as a representation of a goddess, an object of ritual and religious adoration."[33] The truth probably lies somewhere between these two extremes. It is interesting that the figurines found are mostly broken, and it seems deliberately so, for they were often found in refuse sites. Their provenance in the vicinities of homes may suggest some domestic function, perhaps for home ritual or magical praxis. The main excavator at Mehrgarh, Jean-François Jarrige, noticed holes running through them, suitable for small twigs to pass through, and that may be suggestive of sympathetic magic.[34]

Most of the clay figurines were of females and while some of them may simply have been dolls, none, as far as I know, were found in the graves of children, which might suggest another purpose for them other than toys. In the earliest Periods at Mehrgarh these female figurines were simply made but they were coated with red ochre, the same that is associated with some burials, and were also presented as large-hipped and very full-breasted, perhaps associated with ideas of fertility. Decorative adornment was clearly important also. The figurines were not very large, the largest being mainly about ten centimetres with some a little bigger, and the smallest ones of just 1.5 centimetres which would have been useless as dolls. They were seated or standing and the arms and legs were minimally represented. Interestingly, they disappeared from Period III, when bull figurines became prolific. This, in itself is important, since it may be suggestive of forms of animal worship, the bull being the symbol of power and virility. We shall come across this concept much later in the Mature Indus civilization.

It is not until Period IV that clay female figurines re-emerge with elongated heads, legs attached separately, no arms, and large hips and breasts accentuated by very narrow elongated torsos and heads. Additional representations of jewellery were added. The overall impression is that there is little that is in proportion with a real woman's figure. The elongated shapes suggest that they could be held very easily in the grasp of the hand or between the fingers, the legs being joined together to enhance the long rod-like effect, and these features might, I think, suggest some ritual significance. By Period V, the figurines were more refined, the clay from which they were made of better quality and the figures were fired at high temperatures. The highly accentuated hips and breasts remained a feature, leaving the torso disproportionately thin and elongated. Indeed, the waist was excessively tiny in comparison to the bulging breasts and enormous hips, the latter enhanced by the legs being joined together. Facial aspects were now detailed but what are especially striking were the hairstyles, which were quite incredible and surely indicative of status in either a secular or religious context. Perhaps this was reflective of a new stage of urbanization and wealth. Many of these later female figurines were seated figures. These figurines and those of later Periods are composite in the sense that a basic bodily shape was added to, especially with jewellery. Female figurines were extensively ubiquitous in these later stages of life at Mehrgarh.

Subsequent centuries of the third millennium at Mehrgarh witnessed a greater refinement and sophistication of female figurines. The lavish and spectacular hairstyles became simplified, though jewellery more evident, and some of these figurines had paint applied to them. It was clearly an important aspect of social life. Sometimes female figurines were found to be holding infants in their arms and they were found not only at Mehrgarh but throughout the Indus network of sites. It is likely that, by this time, they were mass produced.

How much credence can be given to the suggestion that these female figurines had something to do with religious praxis? To begin with, the excessive accentuation of breasts and hips must surely have had some links with a concept of fertility. Reproduction was probably important and, while I do not think that evidence can suggest a mother goddess in the singular (and certainly not a Mother Goddess in the upper case), the representations of female images as appearing wholly fertile might suggest at least some form of domestic objects felt to promote fertility in women and, perhaps, protection in the success and process of conception and birth. This was not an age when life expectancy was very high, and the fertility of women would have been exigent. And how important was the fanciful hair? If any of these figurines were representative of divinity in female form, the elaboration of the hair would have been important, as it must have been for the better off amongst the women of society. But we should not see all female figurines as indicative of divine images. A heavily-coiffured female figurine from another site is shown kneeling and kneading bread, indicative that female figurines also represented daily living and, at least in this case, the hairstyle has nothing to do with goddess features.

Despite the occasionally slim evidence for female figurines as sometimes representative of goddesses or as items involved in sympathetic ritual magic, in the very late Period VII of Mehrgarh male figurines begin to emerge, evidenced by the depiction of their genitalia and, of course, by their lack of breasts. Significantly, these male figurines were mass produced and became far more evidenced than female ones, even to the extent that a male figurine holding a baby was found but not one with a woman in the same pose. Perhaps this represented a shift to a male-orientated religious thinking, with male virility and power coming to the fore. The earlier male figurines were also highly coiffured or had fantastic headdresses probably marking their status, though such hairstyles of men gradually declined. Male figurines were prolific at other sites, too, and this point is important. While I have concentrated on Mehrgarh for the simple reason that it is an excellent example of the continuity of development and evolution, there are many, many other sites that exhibit the same stages of development at different times, though the continuity is far less pronounced. Continuity is important because it demonstrates the ways in which the Indus civilization itself developed. However, Mehrgarh began to decline by about 2600 BCE, and the continuity here ceases, with changes in culture that probably reflect external influences.

Early civilization in northern India and Pakistan

I turn now to the rise of the great Indus civilization centred on the rivers of northern India and Pakistan. The River Indus, the ancient Sindhu, lends its name to the civilization that grew up on its banks and the fertile plains of other rivers. A hymn of the *Ṛg Veda* is devoted to extolling it:

> The singer, O ye Waters in Vivasvān's place, shall tell of your grandeur forth that is beyond compare. The Rivers have come forward triply, seven and seven. Sindhu in might surpasses all the streams that flow. . . .

> Flashing and whitely-gleaming in her mightiness, she moves along her ample volumes through the realms, most active of the active, Sindhu unrestrained, like to a dappled mare, beautiful, fair to see.[35]

The number of excavated sites in this area and beyond is considerable, and many more remain to be found. To date, there are over a thousand that have come to light, some small of about fifty hectares and some as much as a hundred hectares in size.[36] There are thousands of sites if those further afield in, for example, Afghanistan are included. River valleys offered immense scope for uninterrupted evolution and stabilization for many centuries. When excavations were undertaken at two major sites, Mohenjo-daro in Sindh and Harappa in the Punjab, as Lal poignantly puts it, the discoveries "threw back, with a single stroke, the antiquity of Indian civilization from the fourth century BC to the third millennium BC".[37] One of the reasons why Mehrgarh is such an interesting site is because it demonstrates the growth of settlement that is indigenous to India, and that in itself suggests that we do not have to look beyond India for the origins of the people of the Indus civilization, though it is a hotly-debated issue. Nevertheless, the inhabitants were diverse and came from hunter-gatherer traditions, fishing traditions, merchant people, and small settlements, but in most respects, they were biologically interrelated.[38] The vast alluvial plains set the provenance for the development of larger and larger settlements and yet, the expansive territories allowed for some diversity of traditions. Possehl offered the following pertinent comment: "The forces of communication, diffusion, homogenization, and regional unity are in constant, dynamic tension with local forces of parochialism and the need for group identity and solidarity. All of these forces are real and in some ways contradictory."[39] I think this is a very important point, for it contradicts those comments about the Indus civilization being a rather boring, monotonous and over-systematized phenomenon, and it will be seen that, at points of religion, there is a rich variety of custom. The archaeological evidence and the physical remains of the inhabitants of this huge area with thousands of sites speak to diversity within an overall continuum in a unified system.[40] There would also have been people who remained on the edge of the Indus civilization, retaining their long-established cultures and traditions. What we are looking at are emerging networks of diverse peoples who mutually coexist. We would have to accept, however, that in the distant aboriginal past, different types of people would have made up the very first settlers in South Asia, a factor evident in the different features that still remained in the inhabitants of the Indus and beyond at the time of the Indus civilization.[41]

If we now append dates to the three phases of the Indus civilization that I gave earlier in this chapter we have the following, with the addition of a Transitional Period between the Early and Mature phases and bearing in mind that there would be variation from site to site and considerable overlap between phases:

- Early Indus Period 4000–2600 BCE
- Transitional Period 2600–2500 BCE
- Mature Indus Period 2600–1900 or a little later BCE
- Late Indus Period 1900–1300 BCE

Early Indus Period

The Early/Pre-/Proto-Indus or Early/Pre-/Proto-Harappan phase witnessed a change from regional, local patterns of living and a move to a more unified pattern of existence, exemplified by, for one thing, a more standardized pottery, the Kot Dijian, which is synonymous with the Early Indus developing stage of the Indus civilization. The growing size of settlements and the interaction and trading between them seems to have brought about a convergence of cultural traditions, though there were still some variations in pottery and cultural patterns. Certainly, technical skills increased, as did trade, metal work, economic activity and artistic craft. The number of settlements had increased considerably and some new ones sprang up. The pottery was marked, indicative of private ownership and decorated stamp seals had the same purpose. Kenoyer describes the period as "formative urbanism"[42] and the overlapping of sites meant a movement towards larger and larger settlements that were almost towns. Two famous sites where excavations were early and extensive earned the civilization the title Indus *Valley* civilization, since Mohenjo-daro is in the lower Indus Valley and Harappa in the upper. But sites extend far, far beyond the Indus Valley and the greater concentration of sites is in Cholistan, clustered around what was once the Sarasvati or Hakra River in Pakistan.[43] The outpost trading site of Shortughai in North-East Afghanistan, and sites in the north of the Ganges and Yamuna Rivers as well as in Gujarat exemplify the vast area over which this civilization was to spread.[44] In the Early Indus phase, it was around the Ghaggar-Hakra valley in Cholistan that settlements were clustered. In this long early phase, a process of cultural and economic change was taking place with a move to uniformity, but excavations and discoveries at so many sites now indicates that there was diversity, too. Yet, a certain degree of interrelation to manage the capricious nature of flood waters was exigent for economic growth and there was probably a symbiotic relationship between the settled communities and those beyond. The settlements were clustered, and Possehl was of the view that the open spaces beyond such settlements were occupied by nomadic pastoralists,[45] indicative, again, of the variety of peoples who made up this huge and ancient cultural environment and of the mutual dependencies of urban and pastoral peoples. Hunter-gatherers probably continued to exist alongside the growing settled communities, providing some of the latter's subsistence and means of transport of some materials.[46] Scenes on Mature Indus seals show that hunting remained an important part of Indus life throughout its duration and farming would also have been a continuing occupation for many.

Excavations at Mehrgarh, Amri, Kalibangan and Lothal have revealed that the settlements held people who were diverse but, nevertheless, indigenous to India and they remain so into the following phases. Yet, important to the early development were the crossings of trade routes, and it was at such places that settlements were established and the interaction between communities was entrenched. It was also necessary for settlements to develop where there was less danger of flooding yet greater agricultural and trade possibilities. Inevitably in the period of growth, houses became more substantial and complex, defence walls were built, wheeled carts transported produce, tools became more specialized and craft specialization refined. It was surely population growth that brought about the transition of settlements into towns. Thus, the Early Indus phase developed over the centuries to the point where it became a civilization.

Indications of religion in the Early Indus Period

When exploring any evidence for religious ideas during this Early Indus Period, I must point out that, with no evidence of writing, such "indications", as I have put it, must remain speculatively suggestive and by no means certain. However, to begin with, the terracotta female figurines that are a feature of many, many previous centuries are still to be found at most of the sites, which might suggest a continuation of belief in female divine beings – though I doubt a *single* mother goddess – or such a belief alongside notions of fertility. They decline in number as the Early phase comes to an end. What seemed to emerge instead was the prominence of the buffalo – such a symbol of male virility and strength. The horns of the buffalo are found painted on pottery and this suggests to Bridget and Raymond Allchin that the symbol is representative of a Buffalo deity.[47] Sometimes the whole head of the buffalo is to be seen and sometimes, too, the horns have a plant growing between the horns, especially *pīpal* leaves. Similarly, depiction of a bull's head and horns have been found on pottery, again, with a *pīpal* seeming to grow out of the middle of the horns. Allchin and Allchin write: "It seems reasonable to infer that there were already certain associations of buffaloes and cattle with a horned deity or deities, and that they anticipate the horned deity of the Mature Indus religion."[48] Many clay figurines of bulls have also been found. This seems to me to herald the beginnings of a certain reverence for powerful male animals in the Mature Period. Whether we can posit a bull or buffalo deity or deities at this stage, I think, is less certain.

Asko Parpola has identified the fish design on Early Indus pottery as a symbol of a god of waters. The fish, he says "is one of the most powerful motifs of the Early Harappan painted pottery. It seems that in (Early) Harappan religion, the god of the waters and fertility, having the fish as his emblem and symbol, occupied a central position."[49] I shall delay taking up Parpola's point until I examine the religious ideas that emerge in the Mature Indus Period, where his thesis about the fish deity will re-emerge. Leaving aside a fish deity for the moment, what we are left with, then, was a declining emphasis on female figurines for whatever purpose they were used – and it seems to me that they were likely to have involved some kind of domestic religious or magical ritual – and a rising emphasis on masculinity represented by the bull and buffalo. Both seem to incorporate ideas of fertility.

The Transitional or Intermediate Period

Between the Early and Mature Indus Periods, there was a hiatus and it seems that it may have been a time of intense upheaval. There is a burnt layer at Kot Diji, a thick level of ash and charcoal at Gumla, burning at Amri and extensive burning at Nausharo, as well as displacement of strata at Kalibangan suggestive of an earthquake.[50] It seems, too, that there was a dramatic change of locations of sites, a desire to start afresh, of what Possehl described as "qualities of renewal, of people cutting their ties with older Early Harappan settlements and seeking fresh, different places to establish themselves and their new way of life and civilization".[51] When new settlements were built, they were done so with a great degree of uniformity in their designs and orientation suggestive of, to use Wright's phrase, "the widespread adoption of a new ideology".[52] There was a good deal of overlap between the Late, Early and Mature Indus phases with different sites earlier or later in date, but there also seems to be a simultaneous development of the Mature phase. Nevertheless, such considerable change came about with its roots in the Early Period itself and was an indigenous process with no extraneous invasions or migrations from outside the regions. In a way, it was an urban revolution of its own making, a phenomenon that resulted from so many stages in previous centuries and a phenomenon that bears every sign of continuity between its different stages at all sites. Yet there were developed differences in pottery, even though there was at first an overlap between old and new styles. There was a large-scale use of bronze, systematic architecture, and a host of other features that we shall see below. All these must have been generating in the Early Period but reached their fruition in the Mature. Something, too, must have been generating the kind of unity of purpose of planning, productivity: to date, there is a great deal more that needs to be known about the ideological changes that took place in the Transitional Period that brought about such a great ancient civilization. The Transitional Period was probably a short phase – only about a hundred years or so – but it was a dramatic and important one. It seems, too, that the very first signs of the Indus "script" emerged during this Transitional Period.[53] Overall, continuum at individual sites blossomed into a shared continuum of a highly civilized pattern of living.

The Mature/Urban Indus civilization

The Mature Indus Period is what Braj Basi Lal termed "a perfect Bronze Age".[54] After the hiatus of the Transitional Period, it seems it was preferred to build the towns and cities of this civilization on virgin locations. The great city of Mohenjo-daro was one such site, but other places like Harappa had continuous occupation from earlier times. However, the overall picture is one of the abandonment of the old for the building of the new: it was a fresh start for many towns and cities. It is remarkable that these towns and cities were constructed similarly from location to location and with all the aspects of "civilized" life that characterized the Indus civilization. This desire for new and fresh may have been the reason why some sites were completely destroyed by fire and many were levelled and rebuilt anew. That, it seems to me, must suggest a powerfully organized social or political force that instigated such wholesale renewal *internally* to the Indus Valley areas: again, it was an indigenous change. The process of change from Early to Mature was, nevertheless, variable in date and not all locations underwent radical change from their own traditions. What is certain is that such sites increased considerably in number so that the extent of the Indus civilization is far greater than its earlier phases with locations mainly in the plains and located all over the Punjab; in Haryana; Sindh; northern Rajasthan; western parts of Uttar Pradesh; extensively in Gujarat; in North-East and South Baluchistan; the North-West Frontier Province; in Jammu; and in Kashmir – in all, over a million square miles, an area larger than today's Pakistan, western Europe and each of the other ancient civilizations of Mesopotamia and Egypt. Cholistan in Pakistan saw a particular rise in the number of sites in the Mature Period – indeed, they more than doubled – and the most prolific sites were on the plains of the old Ghaggar-Hakra River system, so much so that it would be more correct to speak of the Ghaggar-Hakra civilization than the Indus civilization. It was the riverine systems that provided the fertile land necessary to support each settlement and the management of water was a key feature of the whole civilization. Interesting, indeed fascinating, as this whole civilization is, it is beyond the remit of this chapter to dwell on aspects that are secular rather than religious, but I think it is important to set the scene, the backdrop, against which religious aspects can be placed.

Cities and towns

While two major cities are well known, Mohenjo-daro and Harappa, a few other major cities have also come to light, but I shall, in the main, concentrate on the former two that have been so well excavated over such a long period, were the first to be excavated, and which were by far the largest. The pattern of building was by no means invariable, but cities and towns were generally uniformly constructed with a grid of streets often surrounded by walls that were not so much for defence as protection against flooding. The uniformity of planning at Mohenjo-daro and Harappa suggest a rigid imposing of building style, but subsequent excavations elsewhere have demonstrated that such uniformity was not a feature of the Indus civilization as a whole. Cities and towns were about 250 kilometres apart and some housed as many as 40,000 inhabitants, so they were not so close as to be devoid of variable cultures and yet sufficiently linked to have an overarching ideology of city planning and cultural identities in productivity and trade. Were they, then, independent city states, each in its own right? If so, their individual identity was nevertheless part of a culturally and ideologically larger network. Uniformity of building construction, much art, craft, trade and economy rather suggests there may have been a single state, though I think this is unlikely, given the vast nature of the Indus civilization. There is no archaeological evidence to suggest an overall state that unified all the towns, cities and village settlements, and there is certainly no evidence for what might be called an "empire" as some suggest.[55] We do not know whether the uniformity of the Mature Indus was forcefully imposed or willingly adopted. What is remarkable is the manifestation in these towns and cities of a standardized civic authority that resulted in a high standard of living.

Many though not all cities and towns were laid out in the same pattern with fairly straight streets arranged in accordance with the cardinal directions that divided up the whole in something of a grid-like pattern, the main street being broad with narrower ones branching off.[56] What seems to have been an important raised mound area and a less important lower level characterizes the larger sites. Some sites had a number of such mounds, sometimes walled, and since the buildings and houses located on them were often larger than those elsewhere, it is assumed that they housed important individuals or were specially constructed for important reasons. However, larger buildings can be found that were not on such mounds and, conversely, mounds may also have remains of many small buildings, so such divisions by no means obtain at all sites. It has become customary to call the remains of such mounds "citadels", though since it is a rather value-judged word that presupposes the idea of a fortress and defence, which is not uniformly correct, I prefer to use the simple term "mound", though not denying the significance that they may suggest in the context of the surrounding area. Perhaps the buildings on these mounds had ritualistic significance or perhaps they were the seats of administration; we simply do not know. Buildings were of baked bricks or mud bricks, and houses were generally constructed to a standard size. Houses were well-constructed around a courtyard, were sometimes two- or three-storeyed, often spacious, and decorated with designs. The houses had bathrooms, lavatories, good drainage, wells and a good deal of privacy from the lanes outside.

There was a unique standardized system of weights and measures throughout the Indus lands based on binary numbers and a decimal system. Even the bricks were of standard size. Trade was extensive, much expanded in the Mature Period though, as was seen earlier in this chapter, already extant in the previous Periods. Trade was undertaken to Mesopotamia and Central Asia with outposts at places like Shortughai in Afghanistan that I mentioned above as just one of the outposts for trade links. Precious stones and many such luxury goods were a particular trading commodity and merchants developed travel by sea to take goods to Mesopotamia and other places, where Indus merchant seals have been found. It is possible that at Lothal near present-day Ahmadabad in Rajasthan not far from the Gulf of Cambay, which is an inlet of the Arabian Sea, was possibly a substantial port with a "dock" of 216 x 37 metres, though its identity as such is often disputed and it is sometimes seen simply as a very large water tank. If the latter, it is *extremely* large. Technology and economic output expanded with an extension of animal husbandry, farming, crop production, fishing, and what has been described as "small" art, finely crafted, "small, elegant art and sophisticated craft technology".[57] Gold and silver, bronze and semi-precious stones were worked by specialist craftsmen in workshop locations and jewellery maintained its importance from earlier times but was exquisitely crafted. Bead-making by specialist artisans displayed particular sophistication. Evidence suggests that women wore a considerable amount of jewellery, no less in these ancient times than in the present. It was probably a sign of status then as now.

While there were variations from site to site, a good deal of uniformity characterized the Indus civilization. The earlier excavators were eager to stress this, especially since Mohenjo-daro and Harappa were several hundred kilometres apart and yet displayed the same characteristics of city building. To them, the Indus civilization suggested monotony, though subsequent excavations of other sites have changed this view. So any later excavations have disproved such extensive homogeneity between all the sites though, in my view, we are still left with an invasive cultural tradition that characterized the several hundred years – a brief span in contrast with other civilizations – of the Mature Indus civilization. Pottery style, for example, is particularly uniform, with few exceptions. But variation in living is evident even at Mohenjo-daro and Harappa and it was probably environmental factors that brought about the necessity for this.[58] Diversity certainly obtained in the cultures of the Indus civilization. Alongside the towns and cities, such diversity is exemplified in the animal husbandry, village life, farming, fishing, even hunting and gathering – all coexisting with the urban culture.

We do not know why such civic standardization existed. There is plenty of evidence for "small" art, but not a great deal for larger structures. Nothing has been found that might suggest the remains of a palace, or a temple, though as far as the latter is concerned, that does not surprise me given the criteria necessary for a temple and its late arrival in

Hinduism.[59] No burials of some great figure exist and there is nothing to suggest any uniformity of religious praxis in the form of religious buildings. While every effort seems to have been undertaken for the welfare of its citizens, there is little to raise a few of them to any high profile. Perhaps such civic standards were maintained by groups of people rather than one individual, and no need was seen for an overarching political or theocratic control vested in one person. Possehl termed the civilization "a faceless sociocultural system"[60] and, indeed, this is exactly what it seems to be. We have no means of establishing any political structures for the Indus civilization, though from the evidence of artefacts, there does seem to be some differentiation of class with a higher class able to afford refined material possessions, better amenities and larger houses, and more elite areas of living have been found at some sites.[61] Some burials occurred with a greater number of grave goods than others though all in all, there seems to be less evidence for extremes of wealth and poverty than one would normally associate with "civilized" living.

Fortifications might be indicative of some kind of political divide, but evidence of fortified settlements for the purpose of defence is less tangible than once thought and many may have served the purpose of protection from flooding or as civic, social or manufacturing division of inhabitants. As to the so-called "citadels" understood as "fortresses", some may have been defence fortifications but, as that at Harappa, many are flood defences.[62] There are no indicators of warfare amongst the Indus towns and cities and people lived as much outside the urban complexes as inside. The indigenous nature of the Indus civilization as *sui generis* and indigenous probably necessitated no fears of warfare with extraneous enemies. This was a civilization that set out to cultivate rather than to conquer and I think we can eschew the idea of war and conquest accompanying the Mature Indus civilization.[63] Before exploring the religious artefacts of the Mature Indus civilization, I want to look briefly at the two major cities of Mohenjo-daro and Harappa.

Mohenjo-daro and Harappa

Mohenjo-daro (sometimes Moenjo-daro) and Harappa were two of the most important cities of the Indus civilization and, given their situation on the fertile plains of the Indus, epitomized the Indus civilization. I want to leave discussion of religious aspects related to these two cities until later but some mention needs to be made of them at this point. Possehl described Mohenjo-daro as "the epitome of all Mature Harappan settlements"[64] and added that it "symbolically represents a good deal of what it meant to be Harappan",[65] as well as being "arguably the most impressive, best-preserved Bronze Age city in the world".[66] As the largest of all the Indus sites, having had possibly up to forty thousand inhabitants, it was the most important and is now a World Heritage site. The Sindhi name means "Mound of the Dead", a Sindhi descriptor for an ancient site. It was a key location for river transport, with Harappa to the North near the mountains and Dholavira to the south-west near the sea. It was a virgin site planned freshly from nothing and must have risen rapidly, but its earliest levels are not accessible because of the rise of the water level: several metres still lie mysteriously unknown under sub-soil water. Flooding, indeed, was a constant threat to the ancient city and necessitated the building of mammoth platforms to protect it and keep it above the flood level. Such platforms formed the foundations for whole areas or single buildings. Mohenjo-daro is the only city to have used baked bricks for nearly all its buildings, though some were constructed in wood. It was particularly well laid out, other towns and cities not reaching the same standard of its precision of street and lane plans, spaciously varied houses, sewage disposal and bathrooms, hundreds of wells – some shared between two or three houses and some for each house – workshops and latrines. Planning and execution of its construction in the ancient past, particularly its water-engineering and drainage system, must have been a colossal undertaking and nothing anywhere compares to it in the contemporary ancient world.

Mohenjo-daro had two major mounds (so-called "citadels"), one in the west that was higher, though smaller, than another larger and lower one in the east. It seems to have had higher and lower areas, the latter also having a number of small mounds that probably also served as foundations. Lest it be thought that the higher areas were for the elite and the lower areas for ordinary people, such a suggestion is overridden by the presence of very large, spacious houses in the lower area and one very large building that is unlikely to be residential, though to suggest its identification as a temple or palace is considerably overstretching the evidence. We do not know what purpose these mounds served and in some cases, houses on them at many sites were no different to those in "lower" areas though, as we shall see below, the smaller mound at Mohenjo-daro has the unique remains of what is called the Great Bath and other structures that I shall examine below in the context of religion. Such mounds, if they were important, are not situated at the heart of the settlement, though gateways into them often seem to have been impressively constructed. While an overall ruler seems unlikely yet general civic standards very high, the variation in size of houses, amenities, and the kind of artefacts found suggest that there was some differentiation of status between the inhabitants, though not necessarily spatially. A large building on the same mound as the Great Bath with many rooms and probably having had wooden columns has been identified as possibly a granary or, more probably, a great hall:[67] there are similar structures at Harappa and Lothal. Another building on the same mound has often been described as a "college", and many writers add "of priests". The layout suggests a number of rooms of the same shape and size, and the proximity to the Great Bath suggests the building had something to do with bathing, but to assign it to priests is, in my view, stretching the evidence once again.

Unlike Mohenjo-daro, Harappa has continued occupation from the fourth millennium to Pre-Mature and Late Indus Periods:[68] it was not constructed on virgin territory, nor was it the same size as Mohenjo-daro, but it seems to have been a major economic centre. Harappa was strategically placed in the North, in the now Pakistani western Punjab and was an ideal centre for the management of trading resources through the mountains, particularly since it had an established history prior to the Mature Indus Period. Like Mohenjo-daro, Harappa had its walled mounds, beyond which were residential and craft areas: one of these is more imposing than the others. In the Mature Period, the city grew to having a population of somewhere between 25,000 and 30,000.[69] There was no suggestion of higher and lower areas at Harappa but there were a number of walled mounds, the highest of which has been heavily plundered and little can be stated about it. Again, there are fortifications around the mounds though how much so for defence is questionable.

An impressive building on one of the mounds is thought to have been a granary and with some assurance given what have been identified as threshing platforms nearby.[70] There were far fewer wells at Harappa, but its bathrooms were impressive, efficiently built for drainage, and each house had a private latrine. As at Mohenjo-daro, drainage of waste was efficiently planned. In short, the civic amenities at Harappa were of a high standard.

The Indus inscriptions

To date, Indus inscriptions from the Mature Period have not been convincingly deciphered: where some have ventured far in attempting to do so, their hypotheses are fervently challenged by others, and Possehl wittily wrote: "Decipherment is an art; unfortunately, in the case of the Indus Civilization, an art not yet perfected."[71] Despite a substantial number of sources containing the signs – about five thousand – the inscriptions are all very short. Over two thousand come from Mohenjo-daro, the remainder from over fifty other sites. Of these inscriptions most are no longer than four or five characters, some have just two. They occur on seals, a few seal impressions, copper and bronze objects, small rectangular copper tablets found at Mohenjo-daro, pottery, stone, ivory and bone objects, amulets and bangles, tools, weapons, a long inscription of ten signs found at Dholavira, and the longest inscription of twenty-six characters found at Mohenjo-daro on two terracotta bars. The main sources of the inscriptions are square stamp seals made mainly of steatite and, again, mainly found at Mohenjo-daro: overall, it is Mohenjo-daro and Harappa that provide us with the bulk of examples.

What we do not have are any other manuscripts offering much longer texts. Some, like Asko Parpola insist that there must have been many and that they were written on perishable materials.[72] Others point out that this is an argument from silence and that no writing equipment has come to life anywhere.[73] The inscriptions were used throughout the Indus settlements – part of that uniformity that characterizes the Mature Period – and must have been generating in the previous phase though at a more simplistic level. Simple markings on pottery existed in the Pre-Indus Period, especially at Harappa, and continued in the Mature phase, developing perhaps in the Transition Period. But, like the towns and cities of the Indus civilization, the inscriptions suddenly appear in their full forms in which we now have them dated to about 2600 BCE, and became universally accepted and adopted, with no regional variations. And, surprisingly, the signs on the inscriptions remained the same throughout the five- or six-hundred years of the Mature Period, with no hint at any evolution. Moreover, the signs on the inscriptions are unique and to relate them to any other system is tenuous.

There is absolutely no agreement amongst scholars about the number of signs: they amount to three or four hundred and a good many are attested only once, but there appear to be variations of some. These are too few for the script to be logo-graphic and too many for it to be alphabetic. Some, as we shall see below, may have a religious meaning. This may be true of the "jar" sign U, which has two small dashes outside the tops of both its arms, and which is the most prolific sign, occurring over a thousand times. Another repeatedly used sign is II. Asko Parpola terms each sign a grapheme and believes the signs to be logo-syllabic[74] homophones that follow strict rules of order.[75] Others find the signs to be totally non-linguistic and perhaps religious symbols.[76] The intricacies of the debates surrounding the signs and, indeed, whether it is a "script" at all, I must leave for the reader to glean from elsewhere. A few extra points must suffice. The signs are written from right to left and sometimes the next line is read from left to right (boustrophedon). As to the possible language, some have attempted to root it as a kind of pre-*Vedic* Sanskrit[77] influenced by Proto-Elamite,[78] (which is also written from right to left) and Dravidian, the major proponent of this last being the Finnish scholar Asko Parpola.[79] Steve Farmer, Richard Sproat and Michael Witzel are the foremost of those who reject any form of literacy for the inhabitants of the Mature Indus settlements or even the presence of the Indus symbols as a script. In their view, had the Indus civilization been literate, "it would be the only known literate society in the world, ancient or modern, that did not produce texts of significant length somewhere on durable materials".[80] Interesting from my remit in the present chapter is that these authors believe some of the symbols represented deities. They write of the purpose of the symbols: "Their most likely function, as suggested by Near Eastern parallels, was to associate individuals, families, clans, offices, cities, festivals, or professions, etc., with specific gods or their celestial correspondents, partly for identification purposes and partly to draw down whatever magic was accessible through those god's symbols."[81] Steve Farmer is adamant that "Indus signs were symbolic and mythological in character – not linguistic."[82] Whatever the nature of the inscriptions, they represented official signs that were universally recognized, constructed by specialists, and must have had some economic and administrative purpose judging by their association with goods. But inscriptions on gold and personal ware suggest that it may well have been the wealthy that used the inscribed objects.

Seals and sealings

A prolific number of mainly square, inscribed, stamp seals have been found dated to the Mature Period of the Indus civilization. Steve Farmer cryptically states: "We find a higher level of standardization in Indus seals than in *any* other known 3rd-millennium civilization."[83] That fact is indicative of the extent of uniformity throughout the whole of the Indus lands. They were probably means of identification and ownership, but the provenance of each one is often difficult to ascertain given that they could have been scattered for all kinds of reasons. When they were pressed on a soft surface such as clay, they left an impression, which is the "sealing", a kind of signature. Fewer of these have been found in comparison to the seals themselves. Most sealings have been found in Gujarat at Lothal, which may have been a port, and most of the seals – over two thousand – were found at Mohenjo-daro where, it seems, every dwelling must have had one. Many broken seals were found, suggesting perhaps that once they had served their purpose they were deliberately destroyed,[84] though they seem to have been designed for long-term use. The uniformity of the symbols on them suggests, too, that they were probably for trading purposes and belonged perhaps to merchants, ruling officials, perhaps kinship groups or "guilds". Parpola even suggests that the inscriptions on the seals might have been proper names.[85] Farmer thinks the majority were connected with agriculture[86] and this certainly seems to be the overall impression concerning their purpose. The reverse of the seal had on it a small boss so that it could be held between the fingers and it is possible that many were used as amulets, especially given their prolific provenance in almost every building at Mohenjo-daro. Most had loops or rings on the backs, indicative, perhaps, that they could be worn on a thread. They were mainly made of steatite (soapstone), though occasionally of agate and they were quite small (about 1.9 to 3.2 centimetres). One seal found at Harappa is twice the size of the usual seals and bears the longest inscription of thirteen characters. Whoever engraved these seals, usually with an inscription and/or a scene generally with one animal, must have been very skilled. They were carved in reverse so that the sealing would come out the right way, and once finished they were fired in order to harden them.

Indications of religion in the Mature Period

We must turn now to explore the vestiges of religious belief and praxis that can be gleaned from the major artefacts discovered throughout the vast expanse of what is known as the Indus civilization, though we know that it extended well beyond the Indus riverine systems. Bearing in mind the fact that the inscriptions on Indus artefacts have not been definitively deciphered, I have to point out that for any analysis of religious beliefs during the Mature phase of five or six-hundred years, I can only present broad ideological strokes without fine details. While uniformity of economic and civic control seemed to be evident in the Indus civilization, we should not, I think, assume that there was religious unity and that the same beliefs permeated the vast lands of the civilization. I want to approach the religious evidence thematically, rather than examine evidence from different sites, and it is the theme of purification that I want to explore first.

Purity and purification

We have seen that bathing facilities were a prominent feature of cities and towns, and the separation of pure water from polluted waste seems to have been paramount in the planning of settlements. I think that this was not just a need to supply a civic amenity, but that it also had a purification function. Kenoyer suggests that since many of the houses at Mohenjo-daro and Harappa had private wells, there may have been present some idea of avoiding pollution.[87] Was this a hint at ritual bathing as some writers suggest?[88] A magnificent and sophisticated structure at Mohenjo-daro has been called the Great Bath. It was set apart from ordinary buildings of the city, though the "granary" is next to it, high on the western mound, away from the lower town – indicators, in addition to its sheer size, suggestive of some kind of ritual function. Possehl commented: "Thus, whoever conceived of Mohenjo-daro as a totality was intelligent enough to use two dimensions, separateness and height, to symbolically set apart the functions and functionaries of whatever went on within the precincts of the Mound of the Great Bath."[89] It is a major watertight construction about 12 by 7 metres that is sunk below the level of a surrounding pathway. Another strategic building to the north has eight rooms with bathing platforms suggestive that purification there was necessary before entering the Great Bath. Alongside the Great Bath is another impressive building that could have been the residences of religious functionaries of some kind. It would not seem unreasonable, then, to imply that the Great Bath had some kind of ritual function linked with purification. The Great Bath was unique to Mohenjo-daro, so the city may have been a centre for certain rituals, or it may have had a religious system of its own. Some suggestions of bathing rituals may be evident from the site of Kalibangan,[90] and I have already said that some think the massive rectangular structure at Lothal was a bathing tank rather than being connected to a port. At Dholavira, too, the remains of a small tank for bathing purposes has been discovered.[91] I do not think we can go as far as to say that the Indus peoples had a "reverence" for water, nor do I think that a strong link between Mature Indus and historic Hindu praxis involving purification is a valid conclusion, but it is not beyond the evidence to see some kind of ritual purification to have been centred at the Great Bath of Mohenjo-daro.

Figurines

We have seen earlier in this chapter how figurines, especially female figurines, were a significant feature of the artefacts that emerged from the site of Mehrgarh. They are no less a feature of the Mature Indus civilization. Generally, figurines were not just of humans but were also of animals, and many figurines portray ordinary, daily pastimes and were clearly not connected to any religious activities. Many were crudely hand formed; others well-crafted.[92] My interest here is in those that might have had a cultic significance. The extensive number of female figurines, which predominate at all sites, is indicative to some that worship of a mother goddess was rife[93] but, as I have said a few times before, I think we must be cautious of over-emphasizing a mother goddess, particularly in the singular. Let me just say that I think it more likely that there was some emphasis on the fertility and fecundity of women and their reproductive powers: some figurines, for example, are crafted nursing an infant. But I do not think it inappropriate to project such notions of fertility to an ideological level of domestic veneration of female divinities in the plural or, at the very least, superstitious magical praxis, the domestic nature emphasized especially by the crudely-crafted terracotta figurines in an otherwise generally highly technical nature of the Mature Indus Period. Notably, female figurines are portrayed with added, appliqué jewellery, sometimes heavily so, a factor that surely survives in India through all the ages down to the present day as a symbol of status for women. On such figurines, the elaborate, usually fan-shaped headdresses (or hair) of earlier times prevail and the higher the headdress and the more elaborate it is, probably the higher the status.[94] What is interesting is that the headdresses of some of these more decorated figurines at Mohenjo-daro and Harappa are pannier- or cup-shaped at the sides and may indicate that they held burning oil in ritual practice.[95] One such elaborately-ornamented figurine has two "cups" each side of the head, with blackish, soot-like traces inside. Others also have been found with traces of black residue.[96] This surely suggests some kind of ritual use. If they were used ritually, then there must have been some division of religious praxis between those who used the rougher models and those who possessed the more carefully crafted ones. The prolific number of female figurines found, and yet their absence from portrayal on more specialized craft such as seals, further implies that they were a feature of the domestic scene and not the corporate one.[97] However, I must iterate that there is no evidence at all for a "Great Mother-Goddess", though this is accepted by some.[98]

While female figurines predominate, there are also male figurines easily distinguished by their genitalia (occasionally ithyphallic) and the lack of the accentuated shape of the female body. Some are, like the female figurines, also ornamented. One terracotta male figurine from Mohenjo-daro has a face both at the front and the back of the head. The fact that some male figurines may have had V-shaped, rounded or curled horns represents at the very least an indication of power and virility and perhaps some indication of divine status. Human male figures wearing a horned headdress with buffalo horns occur on pottery and a terracotta cake and, as we shall see below, this horned headdress is a feature of characters on seals. In my view, it is a symbol of virility and power and, without anticipating too much of what I want to discuss below, is indicative of divine status. Many of these male figurines are represented in the same standing posture, which also suggested to some that they were divine images.[99] Another interesting feature of some of these male figurines is that they sit with their knees drawn up and their arms around their knees or at the sides of their lower legs. While this may seem a fairly relaxed pose, it matches the same one on some seals where it seems clear that the figure is in the pose before a god. This hunched pose, then, may well be a ritual posture. Another such posture is seen as ritualistic by Clark: "Another type of male figurine sits with legs extended straight in front of the body and arms raised in front of the chest with hands clasped together, probably a posture of devotion or prayer."[100] Some figurines appear to be androgynous or cross-dressers, but without any characteristics to suggest links to fertility.

Sculptures

Ancient civilizations usually leave behind massive monuments as evidence of their grandeur – palaces, temples and sculptures of the major figures of the civilization, both divine and human. While some have been eager to find evidence of temple remains at Indus sites, the evidence is so slim as to be really non-existent and I think we can rule out any vestiges of the existence of temples in the Indus civilization.[101] However, there is a building named House 1 in the lower town of Mohenjo-daro that is unusual in that, unlike other buildings, it has no well and its design is rather different from anything else at the site. It is also a very large building and other artefacts found *in situ* there – stone sculptures, unicorn seals, terracotta figurines, pots and jewellery – suggest to some that they may have been votive offerings.[102] But there is no tangible context in which to place any of these objects. While Mohenjo-daro is unique with its Great Bath, it would seem unreasonable to assume that House 1 could be identified as a temple given that no evidence has conclusively suggested such a building existed at other sites. What is particularly unusual is that, also unlike other areas of the city, stone sculptures were discovered in House 1. Some stone sculptures of males, mostly in fragments, have been found at Mohenjo-daro and it is not unreasonable to assume that they may have represented important people in the city, perhaps ancestors or clan members, especially since they have been found in larger, non-residential buildings, but I do not think it necessary to give them cultic significance.

One stone figure that is sometimes linked with cultic activity or royal status, or even both, has been called the "priest-king" and is dated a little later than the Mature Period at Mohenjo-daro. The sculpture is a white steatite statue of a majestic looking figure, finely crafted and detailed on all sides. The lower part is lost, so that all that remains is the torso, which is about 17 centimetres high and it was probably a seated figure. A cloak is thrown over one shoulder and is decorated with trefoils and single and double circles, and the face shows a meticulously groomed beard. Some believe that the eyes are half closed and focusing on the tip of the nose in a "yogic" and meditative aspect and, hence, conclude that this is a sacred figure,[103] but this is fanciful since the eyes are not actually sculpted in but merely deeply chipped out. A narrow band around the head holds in place a circular ornament in the middle of the forehead and the same is found on the upper right arm. Another similar male head made of sandstone has also been found at Mohenjo-daro,[104] but since it is not exactly the same, suggests that it portrays a different and real individual. Despite the majestic, austere appearance of the so-called "priest-king", I doubt that the figure represents either priest or king but is probably a rich merchant or the like, especially since it was found in a residential area, albeit in a large building suggestive of affluence. Farmer, in fact, thinks it is Central Asian and, therefore, not Indus at all.[105] Two holes under each ear are indicative of an ornament or maybe a headdress. Had it been the latter, we would have been in a better position to ascertain the status and nature of the figure.[106]

Animals

When we come to the whole spectrum of animals in the Indus civilization, I think it really is possible to move from the speculative to the concrete in saying that they had religious and cultic significance. It is interesting that in the various mediums in which animals are portrayed, they are almost always male, and symbolic, as we shall see, of power, virility, strength and also fertility. The female figurines may have been connected to domestic beliefs of female fertility, but the animals are indicative of male fertility and power. Bull figurines were common in the Pre-Indus and Mature Indus Periods and many were probably toys. There were also figurines of the rhinoceros, elephant, tiger, humped zebu and humpless bull, water buffalo, antelope, as well as domesticated animals, small creatures like rabbits and squirrels, and even fish. Many of the animals in the Indus world were wild, untamed and fierce and it is possible that some kind of sympathetic magic may have been practised as protection from, or conquest of, them.[107]

Of particular interest are the composite animals that appear as figurines and on seals. Combinations of animals with three heads of different animals are found particularly on seals and it would not be unusual to see the horns of a buffalo on the cheeks of an elephant.[108] Even more interesting are the composite human and animal figures and here, horns seem to represent the epitome of power. One rare such female/animal composite figure has a human torso, an animal's body, a long tail and claws. It is shown in battle with a horned tiger.[109] Other female figurines may also have horns. Several attachable horns have been discovered at Harappa,[110] and humans with the curved horns of the water buffalo are often found on pottery. Even animals like the tiger are portrayed with horns. Clearly, the demarcation between human and animal is a blurred one, for many composite forms are combinations of human and animal. What I think we have here is a symbiosis between humans and animals, an interaction and interrelation of power and strength that may be indicative of at least veneration of male animals, if not worship. At the very least, some animals seem to have been given a kind of sacred status. Early Indus figurines were worn as amulets,[111] which may have been some form of apotropaic protection. A seal from Chanhu-daro shows a bull engaging in sexual intercourse with a female, perhaps indicative of some kind of fertility ideology.[112] These are all inferences of possible ritualistic activity that informed Indus life.

The many seals found throughout the Indus lands are the major source for depictions of animals. Most seals had on them a single animal (invariably facing right) and, given the small size of the seals, the craft work was exceptional. McIntosh writes: "Here, the artists were able to create miniature masterpieces: menacing rhinoceroses, short-horned bulls and water buffaloes with their heads down and one horn raised, majestic zebu bulls standing in calm contemplation. These are beautifully observed portraits of animals, true not only to the anatomical detail but also to the spirit of the beasts."[113] At Mohenjo-daro it was particularly the zebu bull that was featured and since it is rare on seals elsewhere, it may have been a symbol of the city.[114] On some seals, multiple creatures are joined together to form one single creature. Perhaps different animals were identifiable with different locations. Indeed, Kenoyer suggests: "Although this combination animal may represent various attributes merged into one creature for some special ritual, it could also symbolize the joining together of several clans in a commercial or political treaty."[115] It is likely that animal sacrifice took place and there seems to be some evidence of this at Kalibangan with what have been identified as "offering pits".[116] There is also a terracotta cake that seems to show an animal being taken for sacrifice.[117] There is only one piece of evidence for human sacrifice, with a human head seemingly offered to a deity on a steatite seal,[118] though I shall return to this seal (M-430/1186/DK 6847) in the context of ritual procession below, but conclusive evidence of a human head is rather slim. This is rather insufficient evidence to suggest that it was widespread practice but Farmer notes the excavation of severed human skulls with few body bones, along with bones of animals, outside the city walls of Harappa.

Much has been made of an object placed in front of unicorns and sometimes other animals. It has been described as anything from a feeding trough to a sacred brazier or a stand for ritual offerings. However, feeding troughs are generally depicted as shallow basins and have been excavated, but the "ritual stand", as I shall call it, is much more intricately designed and, while one has never come to light in excavations, it is always depicted on seals with unicorns. A terracotta tablet from Mohenjo-daro shows a processional scene in which such a ritual stand is carried aloft, indicative that it is more than likely to have had some cultic significance. It has also been found on faience tablets and carved in ivory.[119] The suggestion that it was a filter for the production of *soma*, a hallucinatory beverage made by *Vedic* priests during sacrificial ritual, I find far-fetched: there is nothing to connect this Indus practice with *Vedic* ritual in the several hundred years preceding the presence of the Āryans in India. The likelihood that an offering was being made to the represented animal on such seals is not without some credence, particularly given the prolific representation of one in front of unicorns and since the ritual stand is usually under the animal's nose. Farmer has the attractive idea that the stand represents a *pīpal* tree and it does seem that in some cases fruit may be suspended from the bottom part. As we shall see below, trees are a sacred phenomenon in Indus religion.[120]

The animal that features more than any other is the unicorn. If Kenoyer is right in thinking that animals represent clans, then the unicorn must be representative of the largest and he thinks it is a sign of the most powerful clan.[121] They are, indeed, prolific on seals and as figurines, but they were all different and not standard. Seals bearing a unicorn have been found throughout Indus lands and the majority of seals from Mohenjo-daro have the unicorn on them. Almost half of those found at Harappa also have unicorn figures. Frequently, the unicorn is depicted with a collar and a *pīpal*-designed blanket around the shoulders. Many identify it as the humpless bull, which is also often placed before a ritual stand. Was the portrayal of the animal an artistic convention in that a second horn is hidden by the first? It was certainly not so on figurines. In an interesting article, Gautama Vajracharya identifies a single-horned animal, the *ṛśya*, not as a deer or antelope, as most scholars believe, but as a single-horned creature. He claims that animals on the Indus seals are so very well-portrayed with attention to details and differences, that it would be uncharacteristic to misrepresent them. The single horn is artistically curved and ribbed, the neck is long and not at all like that of a bull, and the overall view of Vajracharya is that the unicorn existed. There are also references to the *ṛśya* in *Vedic* literature.[122]

A few other seals are noteworthy for their portrayal of animals. An impression of a cylinder seal from Kalibangan shows two warriors in battle against each other with spears, but each has one hand held by a goddess with a headdress, who transforms into the same figure but with the body of a tiger. A seal was also found in the same place, showing a tiger-bodied goddess with the horns of a goat.[123] On another seal from Harappa a female, probably a goddess, grapples with two tigers standing on hind legs either side of her, while she has them by their throats. It is a powerful image, enhanced by the elephant below the scene.[124] All the animals that feature in Indus art, it seems to me, are indicative of virility, power, fertility, strength, that either have to be conquered or symbiotically accessed.

Sacred trees

There is considerable evidence that trees were sacred in the Indus lands. The *pīpal* or *aśvattha* tree, especially, is found as a decoration with its heart-shaped leaves at all times from the pre-Indus periods through to the present day, and I see no reason why this natural phenomenon should not have remained a continuous sacred object, since it was ever-present. Occasionally, it is the acacia tree that is featured. In one tablet, a figure of indeterminate sex is seen protecting acacia trees from humans who are trying to uproot them.[125] Then, the next scene places a tiger on the ground and a figure seated in the tree that is now safely in the earth. As Wright comments: "The tiger looks back with a quizzical gaze (not rage in any event) at the individual gesturing in the tree",[126] and the whole hints at a symbiosis between animal, tree and human or deity. Where a figure appears within or on the tree, or under an arch of *pīpal* leaves, the character certainly seems to be a tree deity. On a terracotta tablet from Harappa, such a deity stands beneath an arch of *pīpal* leaves with a branch issuing from the centre of the head. The arms are covered with bangles – a feature, as we shall see below, often indicative of deities. This feature of a figure underneath such an arch is associated particularly with Harappa, whereas at Mohenjo-daro, the figure stands in the midst of the tree.[127]

Deities are certainly to be identified by headdresses, but so are humans who are participators in ritual proceedings and it is by no means always certain which is which. While headdresses are of different types, they are usually horned or horned with plants emerging from the centre. On one seal, two unicorns' necks and heads are shown emerging from a *pīpal* tree. It is not impossible that this represents some combination of male and female, though I would be very reticent indeed to connect such a notion with the divine male and *śakti* energies that I dealt with in Volume I.[128] Projecting Indus ideas right through into historical Hinduism without taking into account the several-hundred years of a lacuna between the two is to make a grave and mistaken leap in all but a few examples.[129] All we can say is that for the Indus civilization there was a close relationship and interaction between humans, male animals, deities and trees but I think it likely that veneration of female forces would have been especially prevalent at the popular level of life and that this veneration is endemic to all periods of pre- and historic Hinduism.

Three of the characters amongst the signs are of special interest here. On a tablet (M-478) from Mohenjo-daro, reading from right to left, the first character is clearly a tree, the second is the U-shaped pot I mentioned in connection with the symbols above, and this is being held by a third character who is kneeling down and offering the pot to the tree. A fourth character is simply four straight lines, IIII. Even a simplistic interpretation could hardly avoid assessing this as a ritual act, and it seems that the IIII probably signifies four of whatever was offered or the fourth time it was offered. Were such tablets vouchers for offerings in religious ritual as Farmer suggests?[130] It is an attractive idea and the sequence of the kneeling figure before the tree is also found on other inscriptions. From earlier times, designs on pottery combined plants of the *pīpal* tree with the horns of the bull or buffalo and this is a particular combination that has some cultic significance when ornamenting figures on seals and tablets in the Mature phase. Given the sacred nature of trees like the *pīpal*, figures in trees may, thus, be representative of deities: they have been found not just at Mohenjo-daro and Harappa but also at Kalibangan and Chanhu-daro.[131] The emphasis on trees and animals may also intimate that Indus religion was centred outdoors, which may be one reason why religious buildings were not found. Nature in its animate and inanimate forms seems to have been at the centre of the religion.

Deities

I have mentioned female deities in connection with trees and plants and that seems to be the milieu in which they emerge in the Indus world, as well as perhaps in some of the figurines at a domestic level. The wearing of horns appears to be usual for both male and female deities as, also, a large number of bangles. Such horned deities appear not just on seals but on terracotta cakes, as the image of a horned deity found at Kalibangan.[132] One seal (M-305), in particular, found at Mohenjo-daro has been the most widely discussed. I am going to name it the *horned power figure*, but it is unfortunately more widely known as "Proto-Śiva", suggestive that this is the precursor of the deity Śiva, a hypothesis that is widely iterated and widely criticized and was first highly publicized by the great excavator of the Indus civilization, Sir John Marshall, in the nineteen-thirties. It was a view that was much repeated. The Allchins are happy to state that this seal deity and the same image on a few others is to be linked with Śiva and write: "These show him seated in a Yogic posture, upon a low throne flanked by wild goats, and wearing a great buffalo-horned head-dress; he is ithyphallic, he has perhaps three faces, and he is surrounded by jungle creatures – a veritable Lord of the Beasts. In several instances he has a sprouting plant emerging between his horns. Every one of these features can be found in the descriptions of the Śiva of later times."[133] The image of this deity is widely known and even features on the front covers of many books. I want to examine some of the features of this iconic deity in some detail since they are not, in my view, as straightforward as they may once have seemed.

The horned power figure/the so-called "Proto-Śiva"

The posture of the figure on this seal and on the few other pieces on which he is found is fairly unique to Indus artefacts. It is in a seated pose, legs wide and knees bent with the heels brought up together in the groin. The multiple-bangled arms – ten or eleven bangles on each arm – are stretched out on each side with the hands resting on the knees. On each arm, three of the bangles are larger than the rest. The low seat or dais on which the figure is seated seems to have bovine feet. The seated position is similar to later *yogic* seated positions and was prefigured on earlier pottery.[134] However, if there were elements of disciplined *yogic*-type praxis in the Mature Indus Period, we have no means of knowing and I do not think that such slim evidence should provoke any connections with the later Śiva as the supreme ascetic. Any suggestion that the eyes of the figure are directed downwards to the tip of the nose as in *yogic* meditation is ridiculous given the small size of the seal and the amount of material the crafter included: the eyes could not possibly be anything more than small marks. The seal is about three and a half centimetres square and into that small space is fitted considerable detail below the seven characters in the inscription at the top.

The horned headdress is magnificent with wide curved and ribbed horns stretching out each side that probably equate with the water buffalo, though it may represent a bull. A plant is at the centre of the horns and is fan-shaped. I fail to see any resemblance to a three-pronged trident here that was later associated with Śiva, but the feature of horns/plant as a headdress I have already indicated above is well-established in the Mature and Pre-Indus Periods and I think has ritual significance. The animals surrounding the figure – all of which appear on other seals – are a buffalo, an elephant, a rhinoceros and a tiger and at his feet are two creatures that look like deer or antelopes, notably all wild animals. Since Śiva was known sometimes as Paśupati, "Lord of Creatures", some make a further connection between the Indus deity and Śiva here. But Śiva was connected with domesticated cattle. Hiltebeitel linked the animals on the seal with the vehicles of various Hindu deities, especially the buffalo and the Goddess Durgā,[135] though Durgā is not an early deity as I pointed out in Volume I,[136] and there is a long span of centuries through which a link between the two could be made.[137]

The figure is reputed to be ithyphallic and many who see the figure so find a further connection with the Hindu deity Śiva, whose *liṅga*, nakedness, and myths about his phallus have been linked with the horned god – erroneously in my view. In fact, around the figure's waist is a belt or girdle and the so-called erect phallus appears to be simply the tassel of the belt (in which case, the figure could be female). The dichotomy between testicles and tassels seems to have been noted by Hiltebeitel.[138] Where the figure appears naked on other seals (M-305, M-1181), I am inclined to think that the figure has no more than stylized genitalia; Farmer describes the genitalia of the figure on one of these seals (DK 12050) as a "double tree-branched phallus".[139]

The face of the figure is a strange one that hardly bears the features of a human and some have suggested that the figure has three heads -- again, prefiguring Śiva, for those who wish to press such a hypothesis. The face is long, the eyes high-set and the nose remarkably long if it were a human. I am inclined to see it as bovine, and if the horns are of the water-buffalo, it may suggest that it is a stylized face of a buffalo. However, since a buffalo is one of the creatures surrounding it, it may well be a bull. The face of probably the same figure on other seals and tablets is less clear. Something also none too clear are the three heads that the figure is supposed to have. The markings on the side of the head could easily be those of the buffalo and not extra faces. In her excellent article, Doris Srinivasan described these so-named extra faces as "lateral projections consisting of a long pointed flap over horizontal strokes",[140] and finds them bull-like. Since "bovine features have been subtly integrated into the face",[141] we probably have a deity with a bovine face and a human body. Indeed, as Hiltebeitel commented: "It takes an act of will" to agree with three heads and identify this figure as anticipating Śiva.[142]

The figure on the seal is not unique and where it occurs elsewhere kneeling figures either side suggest that it is being venerated – rather strong indicators of its nature as a deity. The horned headdress and bangles are missing from the figure on a faience tablet from Mohenjo-daro but it is flanked by kneeling figures behind each of which is a cobra. Other examples of kneeling figures either side have also been found at Harappa. When the figure appears on other seals, he is seated on the same kind of dais on two of them and on another he is seated on the ground. He appears again on a less-clear terracotta amulet from Mohenjo-daro and on terracotta tablets from both Mohenjo-daro and Harappa.[143] In all, this is, I believe, a deity of power, virility, austerity, fertility and majesty.

I have a good deal of sympathy for Possehl's comment: "There is ultimately no proof for the contention that this figure is a god, but the look of the figure elicits an irresistible conclusion for me – it is a god because it looks like a god!"[144] I must add that there are many indicators in the figure that suggest it is a deity for this, indeed, is a figure with an immense aura of austere power. Srinivasan puts this superbly: "The bovine power is symbolized by the horns; the *yogic* power is symbolized by the posture. Together they coalesce to convey the superior power possessed by this prehistoric deity."[145]

Ritual scenes

Occasionally we have a glimpse of ritualistic practice and this is the case with one particular seal that conveys a surprising amount of detail in addition to a little narrative. The setting for such detail is always, it seems to me, nature, the natural environment, involving the creatures and supernatural beings that were believed to inhabit it. This is an outdoor religion so it is not too surprising that no remains of religious buildings have been found. Where figures kneel or process, the context is likely to be cultic. The seal (M-430/1186/DK 6847) from Mohenjo-daro is described by Wright as "one of the most evocative narratives in Indus imagery".[146] There are two lines to this seal. In the top line, reading from right to left as it would be in a sealing, an anthropomorphic deity with a horned headdress that has a plant in the centre stands within a *pīpal* tree. The hair of the figure seems to be a long braided plait, and the arms are clearly and heavily covered with bangles. The second image is, as far as I can determine, a low stool, though it has been identified in some cases as a human head that has been sacrificed to the deity – if so, the only evidence for human sacrifice. Then, there is a human-like figure, towards whom the deity in the tree looks. This figure also has a horned headdress with *pīpal* leaves in the centre, braided hair and a human body. It is kneeling, one knee low and the other raised and both hands are stretched out in front of it towards the figure in the tree in a respectful gesture. The face is strange and does not appear to be human. Behind this kneeling figure is an animal with the horns of a goat, and with heavy folds of skin down its chest. Kenoyer describes it as a "giant ram".[147] Perhaps it is this that is the sacrifice. On the second line, facing left as if they are following the creature and one behind the other are seven human figures, each with what appear to be single-horned headdresses, each with a long braid and they could be male, but to me appear female. Each of these seven figures is a little different from the others. Again, I am not happy about linking these seven with mythical use of seven in Hindu mythology, such as the seven *ṛṣis*, or the seven *Mātṛkās* that we met in Volume I in the context of *Śakti*,[148] though there may be merit in seeing the number as being of astronomical significance, perhaps the Pleiades.[149] Seven figures are occasionally found on other seals, so the number is probably significant. The inscription contains the sign of a fish (this time with a dot inside), which Parpola has argued via the Dravidian languages is indicative of deity and star at the same time.[150] Parpola, however, makes the deity on the seal female and identifies her, again via the Dravidian languages, as the star and goddess Rohiṇī.[151]

Processions feature on some terracotta tablets where individuals are carrying ritual symbols, and where there are depictions of animals. Terracotta masks may be a feature of such ritual: some are miniature and we have no context in which to place them, though it is likely that they were used in performances of some kind. Their small size suggests that they may have been used as talismans or amulets. Such masks were not designed for humans, but would perhaps have been attached to puppets. Clark comments: "As an amulet or a symbolic mask, it may represent the practice of magic or ritual transformation in Indus society."[152] Similarly, attachable horns have been found at Harappa that may have served some ritual purpose.[153] The wearing of amulets must have been prolific and, certainly, many of the seals could have been worn as such. Amulets are often associated with apotropaic magic, serving to ward off evil forces: while we have no textual evidence to suggest their usage, I think they may have been a pronounced feature of popular religion.

The most often used symbol of the inscriptions is, as stated earlier the jar, U (though with two bars at the top of each arm). We can surmise that this carried an offering and it is interesting that the symbol develops into a man carrying one each side at each end of a yoke, generally called "The Water Carrier". The fish, too, is a prolific sign, so may indicate that fish were offerings, carried in the water jar, particularly by the Water Carrier.[154] And since straight lines IIII appear alongside, this may be indicative of the number of offerings. In some cases, stars are portrayed in the same inscription of the Water Carrier or with a fish, and Parpola believes that Indus religion was conducted according to astronomical features with deities having astral aspects.[155] That is, of course, if the connection between the "script" and Dravidian languages is a valid one. But given that Indus city plans were set out according to the cardinal directions, ritual offerings may also have been connected with calendrical mapping.[156] The remains of what appears to have been a sun disc have been found at Dholavira on the island of Kadir in Kutch, a site that has had occupation from about 3000 BCE, so pre-dating the Mature phase of the Indus civilization. The disc is a large circle with a domed top and remains of spokes. The spoked wheel had not been invented at that time, so the spokes on the disc are more likely to represent the rays of the sun. The sign also features on a terracotta tablet.[157] A large area of open space has been found at Dholavira, which suggests to some the possibility of a ritual or ceremonial "stadium". If it was for ritual practice, it would be unique as far as excavations have gone thus far into the Indus culture. Other such areas are also there, though they could have had a political rather than a religious purpose.

We have, then, glimpses of ritual offerings and perhaps, as Parpola suggests, mass-produced tablets on which such signs occurred and that were tokens of votive offerings. Indeed, as was seen above, we know that offerings were made to deities and to trees.[158] One ritual symbol that is ancient to the Indus culture is the swastika. It has been found on sealings from Lothal and became very popular, particularly on square button seals that may have been worn as ornaments or used as buttons. The swastika is portrayed turning counter-clockwise when stamped. When the Indus civilization declined, the elaborate seals gave way to simpler-designed ones without any "script", and the swastika became one of the most popular of the designs. It is a clear example of a symbol with continuous meaning in pre-historic and historic Hinduism, indeed, to the present day.

Ritual praxis, therefore, seems to have involved a widespread veneration of nature deities – animals and trees – for their power, strength and virility on the one hand and perhaps a more domestic nature of practice in the homes involving female figurines with a focus on fertility and protection. This may suggest less uniformity than the Indus culture is normally credited with, and a difference between what may have been an official cult and a domestic one. However, there seem to have been overall emphases on the symbiosis of human and animal life, of the power of deities in the natural world around, and the representation of deities in concrete and not abstract forms. Humans are part animal, animals are part god or goddess and deities are part human and animal in a supernatural integration of the conceived different worlds that do not seem to be separate from each other. While I am reticent to equate many of the practices at this pre-historic time with those of historic Hinduism, especially with the beginning of the latter in *Vedic* religion, I think it highly likely that the emphasis on nature, fertility and the power of certain animals outlasted the Indus civilization and filtered through to historic times.

Liṅgas and *yonis*?

Some objects have been found that excavators and others have identified as phallic objects and have seen here the origins of the *liṅga* of Śiva in historic Hinduism. Most of them are small though a few are much larger. Some of these may have had general usage in games, as pestles and such things: those that are conical in shape, I think, have no connection with phalluses at all. Some of the larger ones have now been shown to be for architectural structures as stabilizers for poles. Others are almost certainly phallic, though George Dales argues incisively against a widespread cult of the phallus in Indus culture.[159] Even if phallic representations were present, I do not think the connection between them and Śiva is convincing: the association of Śiva with the *liṅga* was a much later development, and not evidenced in his *Vedic* precursor as Rudra. The fact that many of these objects were found in very secular places is also suggestive that they were not for cultic use. As to *yonis*, these are the female generative organ in which the *liṅga* of Śiva is placed in the Śiva–*Śakti*, male–female, synthesis of Hinduism, as was seen in Volume I.[160] Again, I think the leap from the Indus culture to such a synthesis is misguided. Heavy ringstone bases have been found at Dholavira and these seem as if they housed wooden pillars. This may suggest similar usage for smaller ringstones as Kenoyer believes.[161] Nevertheless, some of the smaller ringstones are beautifully made and decorated, indicative that they may have had considerable value and importance, and a round, shallow depression on the upper surface certainly intimates that something was meant to stand on top.[162] Indeed, one example of the cone and ringstone has been found at Kalibangan. Perhaps there is disparate usage between the large examples and the smaller decorative ones.

Fire-altars

In the southern part of one of the mounds at Kalibangan, excavators have discovered what some have called "fire-altars", a row of seven rectangular or oval pits on top of a mud-brick platform and sunk into the ground. A flight of steps led to each platform. Several other such platforms were also found but only one with an altar. Terracotta cakes were found in it and traces of ash and charcoal. The remains of a faceted clay stele were found in each pit, which Parpola has no difficulty in regarding as *liṅgas*, though I doubt they had any phallic significance. Were these platforms places where sacrifices occurred? On one of the other platforms the bones of cattle as well as antlers were found in a separate pit beside the altar, but no animal bones have been found in the pits themselves.[163] Similar structures were found in the east of the site. Many of the houses, or certainly parts of the lower town beyond the mound also seem to have had the same kind of structures, but similar ones found at Nausharo suggest that there were no sacrifices in the domestic sphere. Fire altars have been tentatively attested elsewhere, at Rakhigarhi, Banawali, Amri, Vagad and Nageswar and one at Lothal, though the identification as fire-altars is rather pressing the evidence.[164] Bathing structures have been found near the altars. If these structures were part of the ritual ceremonies at Kalibangan, it suggests that there were differences in the way religion was communally conducted in the Indus lands, just as the Great Bath was unique to Mohenjo-daro.

At Lothal, too, it is possible that such fire altars existed. A hole for a post was found at the altar and it must have been wooden as opposed to the clay ones at Kalibangan. A terracotta ladle on which there were smoke stains suggests it may have been used in some kind of ritual using fire, though it would be stretching evidence to suggest that this had any connection with the pouring of libations over the *liṅgas* of Śiva as in later Hinduism. And if fire was used in Indus rituals, I see no reason either to link such supposed fire rituals with *Vedic* praxis. Again, the leap in years from the end of the Indus civilization to the *Vedic* period is too extensive to suggest such continuation.

Death and afterlife

Possehl commented on "how elusive the Indus treatment of the dead is to us",[165] and what seems to be apparent is a good deal of variation in ways of disposing of the dead on the rare occasions that cemeteries have been found. If there was uniformity in many aspects of cultural and religious ideas in the Indus civilization, it seems that individualized group praxis informed ideas about death and the life hereafter. If there is some synonymy with religious beliefs about life and ensuing death, then I can only suggest that at the level of clans and kinship ties, there may well have been significant variations in religious praxis and ritual at the local and domestic levels. Archaeology has not found homogeneous gene pools in the Indus lands but multi-ethnic variations. What is certain is that there *was* a belief in an afterlife of some kind and perhaps different kinship/ethnic groups had different ideas about it. We saw that at Mehrgarh grave goods decreased over time and this seems to have been the custom in the Mature Period: grave goods were not, generally, lavish. Throughout the Mature Period, however, we find considerable variety between the different sites, again, I think, reflecting a multi-ethnic society in which family and kin customs and beliefs would prevail over wider cultural concerns. In most cases, the dead were buried outside the settlements but the paucity of evidence of cemeteries might suggest that the dead were cremated, especially given the size of populations in the largest settlements. The cemetery excavated at Kalibangan, for example, had only ninety bodies despite about a thousand residents.[166] The main sources for information about customs of disposing of the dead come from Harappa and two cemeteries in particular, R-37 and H, the latter being dated to the Late Period. R-37, however, has yielded the remains of two-hundred individuals.

In the Mature phase, burial was the main means we know of by which the dead were laid to rest. This was in extended inhumation in a deep rectangular or oval grave, the body stretched out on its back with the head placed mainly north–south with the head at the north, though at some sites the body was placed on an east–west axis as in Pre-Indus times. Some bodies were laid on the side and flexed. Pottery was placed in, or buried under, the graves and sometimes the body was ornamented. Such grave goods usually intimate that there was a belief that they were needed in a post-death existence. This kind of burial was the custom at Harappa in Cemetery R-37, and also at some of the graves at Kalibangan, though there the body was placed in the north–south position and large numbers of pots, usually at the heads were placed in the graves. Ornaments on the bodies of males and females, especially shell bangles for women, were frequent, but not usually excessive. Many female skeletons were found with stone amulets around the neck – a symbol, perhaps, of a married woman like the *tali* worn by Hindu married women today, or to ward off evil forces. Some women were buried with mirrors. Pottery found in graves varied in size but some exquisitely crafted pieces have been found. Since the amount of grave goods varied, we should probably infer that the more goods the higher the status that would be transferred to the hereafter. There is no evidence of what, if anything at all, was placed in the pots, even food, though it is likely that sustenance for the hereafter would have been thought of. At Harappa, flat plates that had signs of use were also evident in the graves and many pointed-based goblets were found scattered at the surface, hinting that some funeral feasting, perhaps accompanied by ritual, took place.[167] Animal bone remains sometimes occurred and suggest that meat was being provided for the life beyond.[168] Those buried at Cemetery R-37 at Harappa were of the same genetic group and seem to have been members of the same clan or kinship group, one that may have been disposed to this particular type of burial. Individuals were sometimes buried on top of each other and I rather think that such a practice indicates that a whole clan may have believed it could meet together in the life after death. Kenoyer comments: "This pattern suggests that the burial ground itself was possibly a sacred place".[169]

At Harappa an (originally wooden) coffin was discovered with the body having been wrapped in a shroud of reeds. The deceased individual was an elderly male who must have had some standing in the community for he was ornamented with more than three-hundred beads, a few of which were rare. This would almost certainly be a case of burial of a high-ranking individual. Other such coffins have been unearthed, though the wood from which they were made is long gone. A few other men were also buried with valuable possessions. Interestingly, very few seals and few figurines have been found in graves, so if someone had a personal seal, it was not generally taken to the next life. Nor were the tools of a man's trade buried with him, suggestive that the belief in an afterlife did not quite match the life lived. Women, too, could be placed in a wooden coffin and one has been found with as many as thirty-seven pots, indicative that she must have been a woman of some standing.[170]

Some graves were chambers made of bricks and at Rakhigarhi a chamber was constructed with a brick-vaulted roof for the deceased before being covered with soil. Some Kalibangan graves were set out in an orderly manner six or eight at a time, indicative of the care and ritual surrounding death. At Kalibangan, pots were buried, but no traces of bones were found inside them, though other pottery was. Similar urns were found at Mohenjo-daro and Harappa with pottery, ash and bones within, but no human bones. Several hundred of these were discovered at Harappa – over two hundred such urns with no human bones within. Possehl depicted them as "post cremation" urns, but they contained animal not human bones, pots, terracotta toys, cereal grains along with ash and charcoal. Possehl also added that they contained some seals.[171] A whole row of fifty-four such urns has been found at Harappa. But, again, since no human remains have been found in these urns, in what way they are linked with burial is difficult to discern. Many pots have been found which would have contained nothing at all. It is possible these and the urns were commemorative rather than associated with burial: empty pots in circular pits at Dholavira and Kalibangan have been described by McIntosh as "cenotaphs", perhaps an apt point here.[172] It is interesting that at Kalibangan at least three different methods of disposing of the dead were contemporaneous – the burials in an oval or rectangular pit as at Harappa; pot burials, as they are called, in circular pits but without skeleton remains, though it seems unreasonable to term them "burials"; and similar pot burials but with grave goods and no skeletal remains, the "cenotaphs" mentioned above.[173] It is possible that, occasionally, for some reason someone died at a considerable distance and that burial was not appropriate and had to be accommodated by a commemorative pot or urn.[174] Each type at Kalibangan is given separate space in the cemetery so clearly the burial customs suggest that different groups had different ideas about the ways in which preparation for afterlife was conceived of and, it seems to me, this must give some indication that there were different religious beliefs in the domestic and kinship groups of the Indus civilization. Nevertheless, the excavated cemeteries at any site show only a fraction of what must have been the entire population, and it remains a mystery as to how the massive remainder of the population were treated at death.

Sometimes a male and female were found in the same grave. At Lothal three such double burials have been discovered. Any suggestion that the remains of a woman and man in the same grave prefigure the late Hindu custom of the *satī* committing ritual suicide is stretching evidence to unreasonable limits given the time lapse between. In any case, remains in double graves are sometimes of the same sex.[175] This suggests more kinship ties in burial practices with members of the same group or clan sharing the same grave.

The bones of some deceased beings were collected and buried in pits. There are a few examples of fractional burial at Mohenjo-daro and Harappa, when bones have been gathered and placed in a basket. In this case, the dead body had probably been exposed to the elements and the remaining bones then buried. Possehl noted in such cases of fractional burial that there could be a mixture of bones of different adults or adults and children. There is a little evidence for cremation, the usual situation in which bones may be gathered after burning but at Mohenjo-daro a few people were cremated and the bones then buried. Five clear cremations have been credited unequivocally at a small site west of Kalibangan on the now dry Sarasvati at Tarkhanwala Dera.[176]

The Late/Post-Urban Period

We come now to the time when the Indus civilization declined into a Post-Urban or Post-Mature Period. Some divide this into Late Harappan and Post-Harappan or Post-Urban, though I want to deal with them together for the purpose of exploring religious ideas. The Late Period is still referred to as the Indus civilization but it is a stage when the civilization was in decline at a number of sites. However, whereas some places declined and eventually became abandoned, as in the Indus and mid-Hakra Valleys, other settlements were expanded in the Yamuna-Ganges region, in Saurashtra and the upper Ghaggar-Sutlej. But instead of the cultural homogeneity of the Mature phase, we find a growth of local traditions and a relapse to rural-based lifestyles. Many call the phase "Degenerate", for most that we understand by Indus civilization came to be abandoned. The uppermost stratum of Mohenjo-daro, for example, dated to about 1900–1800 BCE, showed degeneration from the once proud and organized city to haphazard dwellings made of odd and broken bricks. There is some evidence that the use of female figurines continued in the domestic situation,[177] but since the inscriptions that were once endemic in the Indus civilization disappeared, there is no evidence for religious ideas to be gleaned from them and a valuable source is lost.

In the previous section I explored the nature of burial at Harappa from excavation reports of Cemetery R-37. The other main cemetery at Harappa (though there are others) is dated to the Late Period (Level II) and Post-Urban Period (Level I) and is Cemetery H. The discoveries at this cemetery are interesting in that they bear witness to the changes that took place as the Indus civilization slipped into degeneration. Harappa is an interesting site in that it was not completely abandoned, underwent considerable change but, at the same time, continued with Mature praxis. Change in pottery occurred, for example, but alongside the Mature Harappan style for some time,[178] and while seals, the use of weights and measures and the Indus script disappeared, other technologies developed there.[179] When we look at burial practices, we find some of the pottery used in the graves to be of a different type to that used in the Mature period.

In Level II were earth burials. One area of such burials was in the eastern part and the other in the western area of the settlement and the patterns of burials were different in both – again, indicative of regional differences of belief even in one settlement. In the eastern area the bodies were left complete and while some were supine, others were flexed to the left and placed northeast to southwest or east–west. In a very few cases, fractional burials or simply the haphazard burial of the bones of the deceased were found in the eastern section. The western area was different. There were no burials in earth though there were some fractional burials at the edge of the cemetery area, where bones had been collected and buried with pottery.[180]

In Level I, above the earth burials, the main method of disposing of the dead was by fractional, secondary burial in pots and here human pot remains were found unlike at R-37 and elsewhere in the Mature period. It seems the bodies were exposed to the elements and the remaining bones then placed in the pots. The pots could contain the bones of more than one individual, sometimes several, and some also had animal bones, bones of birds and rodents in them as well. No jewellery or personal grave goods were put into the pots. As Wright remarks: "The pots are small and the method of placing bodies into the vessels seems a bit unpleasant."[181] Indeed, in many cases a remarkably large number of bones may be crammed into just one pot. Possehl offered the following rather humorous remark: "It is also clear that whoever gathered the bones together to deposit them in the pots probably did so in a place rich in human remains, possibly with many individuals all decaying together. They seem to have paid more attention to simply gathering bones than they did to finding precisely those person(s) they came to fetch."[182]

Kenoyer notes that in the Hindu *Gṛhya-sūtras* so much later, instructions are given on how to collect bones after exposure or burial and place them in a pot with a lid before burying them.[183] This may suggest that some regional customs of disposing of the dead survived the centuries to become a more common practice. In Level I, much of the pottery was plain but some depicted highly-stylized animals like antelopes and peacocks, though, interestingly, the U-shape similar to the Indus sign is evident on one piece,[184] and *pīpal* leaves and stars remain. So different is this pottery in shape and decoration from what was found earlier that it is now known as Cemetery-H Ware and it was widely distributed far beyond the settlement of Harappa.

At Mohenjo-daro once the demise of the city was well under way the dead were thrown in deserted areas or houses. One group of deceased individuals – thirteen adults and a child – were thrown into one house at different times and other such groups of bodies were found casually disposed of, but with no signs of violence having caused their deaths. What a contrast in disposing of the dead to what we saw in the Mature period! There is no evidence of burials at Mohenjo-daro in the last days of occupation there. Two important points can be extracted from these late forms of disposing of the dead. The first is that they are far less ritualistic and careful; indicative, I would think, of a change in religious emphasis, perhaps even a more casual approach to religion and death. The second point is that underlying differences in how the dead are disposed of suggests modes emergent probably from kinship groups as opposed to general cultural principle, concomitant with variation in beliefs. I rather think such variations in beliefs at family and clan level were probably always there during the centuries of the Mature Period, but were subordinate to the overall homogeneity of the Indus culture.

The demise of the Indus civilization

As civilizations go, the Indus civilization did not last long, just six or seven hundred years. Importantly, the demise was not a uniform one. In some cases it was abrupt and the settlement was abandoned; in others the process was slower. What we do know for certain is that the old claim of the archaeologist, Sir Mortimer Wheeler, that Mohenjo-daro met its end with extreme violence at the hands of invaders is simply not true. The skeletons that were found in stairwells and other places in the city show that they died at different times: they were merely discarded in empty places as the city passed to a degenerate phase: there was no massacre. Nor was there an Āryan invasion to account for the change in culture that we find with *Vedic* Hinduism, for the Āryans came much later. The whole process of the demise lasted from about 1900–1300 BCE, but in many cases, centuries shorter, from 1900–1800 BCE: the Āryans came on the scene somewhere between the mid and late second millennium, long after the Indus civilization had ceased to function. I must leave the prickly question of the origins of the Āryans to the beginning of the next chapter, but we can safely exclude any idea of a massive invasion by them. What is more likely is that there were permeating migrant movements that gradually infiltrated different areas, but these did not cause the decline of the Indus civilization.

So what did cause the Indus civilization to decline and cease to be with very few vestiges of its great culture? There is no one answer to this question because different factors informed different settlements. But one cause that seems to have had the proverbial domino effect is the breakdown of the whole infrastructure of Indus culture as a whole. City structures were no longer as well-planned and the high standard of living declined. There seems to have been a breakdown in the prior order of things, which rather intimates that there was a concomitant political and civic breakdown not just in the local sense but throughout the Indus lands. Communication, interchange and interaction between settlements then became more difficult. The distinctive seals of the Indus gave way to ones with geometric designs and the usual depictions on them, along with the signs, vanished. Trade declined, crafts and skills deteriorated, the production of crops was less civically controlled and more the responsibility of small family groups. There may have been overcrowding and disease as civic amenities like sewage and water systems declined. Possehl almost suggested that the Indus civilization lost its heart: "That is, the fatal flaw was centrally, and most importantly, sociocultural in nature; not flood, avulsion, drought, trade, disease, locusts, invasion, or any other of a myriad of "natural" or "outside" forces. A failed Indus ideology is here proposed to be the sociocultural flaw."[185]

Possehl may well be right about the failure of the ideology at some point, but certain natural changes may have influenced that breakdown. Theories as to why the demise occurred occupy the specialists of a wide range of archaeological subjects. Environmentally, we know that there were significant changes in the courses of rivers on which the Indus economy was based. Hydrographic changes with a change in rainfall causing the drying up of rivers in some cases and flooding in others, with excessive river-silt deposition at times, took their toll on settlements. The ancient Sarasvati River that once freely flowed dried up. Those specializing in aspects like climate change argue to and fro as to whether such a factor contributed to the demise. Others suggest deforestation and similar ecological considerations to supply answers. It is highly likely, too, that tectonic activity affected the course of rivers and that earthquakes would have been a fairly frequent phenomenon in the Indus lands. What is certain is that there was a considerable shift of populations to the Gangetic valley and other areas and it is likely that there is no one answer why the Indus civilization declined and disappeared without trace. One or two factors may have been the cause at one place and another or others elsewhere. We know, for example, that there was flooding at Mohenjo-daro and that the site was temporarily abandoned before re-settlement was attempted. Likewise, at Harappa the usual pattern of living was disrupted and then renewal attempted, but nowhere do we find any rebuilding and resettlement in the same vein as the earlier Mature Period. Many communities reverted to pastoralism and the great craft workshops along with the expertise of those who worked in them vanished from what were formerly the greatest cities. In a way, the peoples of the Indus civilization did not disappear along with the seals and inscriptions, the weights and measures, the civic order and so on; they simply shifted and adapted. They were not wiped out by something or someone else, they continued, some with vestiges of their skills and lives in newer, smaller settlements in newer places further South; others reverting to pastoralism like their very ancient ancestors. For some, the transformation was gradual, for others, abandonment was exigent. It was a process of change and transition that piece by piece took away the structure that was the Indus civilization leaving in its wake soon-forgotten cities.

2
The *Vedas*

Historical Hinduism begins with the written scriptures of the *Vedas* and there is a gap of several hundred years between the Indus civilization and the arrival on the scene of the Āryans, who were responsible for those scriptures. The Āryans were "nobles", or, rather appropriately, "Good Guys", as Wendy Doniger terms them,[1] at the very least, an elitist people who maintained and were united not so much by race as by a particular culture that was underpinned by their scriptures, the *Vedas*. Exactly who they were is the subject of heated debates, the traditional view being that they were a nomadic people or group of tribes that came from the steppes north of the Caucasus from where they migrated in several directions. This traditional view of their origins is challenged again and again, and it is wise to bear in mind the words of Edwin Bryant here when he says that "much of the evidence associated with the Indo-Āryans, whether philological, linguistic, or archaeological, can prove to be extremely malleable if one is prepared to consider it from different perspectives. It can thus be construed in sometimes diametrically opposed ways by scholars approaching the issue with differing presuppositions and expectations."[2] It is not within my remit to deal with the lengthy debates surrounding this issue, but some exploration of the interface between the Indus civilization and the historical *Vedas* is, I think, essential. What *is* certain, as was seen in the concluding part of the last chapter, is that there was no "invasion" of the Āryans that overthrew the peoples of the Indus civilization: there simply is no evidence for this at all.

Origins of the Āryans

From linguistic evidence, many believe that the ancestors of the Āryans came from original Indo-Europeans, some of whom may even have been present in the Mature Period of the Indus civilization.[3] The branches of the Indo-Europeans are numerous, and their migrations were far and wide, taking place somewhere in the fourth millennium BCE.[4] Their geographical diversity is exemplified by linguistic cognates to *Ārya* such as *Irān* and even the Gaelic word for Ireland, *Eire*. One of these branches, the Indo-Iranian tribes, eventually divided to become Indo-Iranians and Indo-Āryans, the latter being those responsible for the *Vedas*,[5] but the origins and migrations of both groups remain elusive, even though there are clear linguistic cognates in both languages.[6] The picture is not at all clear as Michael Witzel says only too well: "At the present stage of research, neither the exact time frame, nor the exact trail, nor the details of the various movements of the speakers of Indo-Iranian and Indo-Āryan are clear."[7] The Āryans were highly likely to have been a composite group, their migrations accumulating additional tribes that added to the muddle surrounding their origins. Inevitably, as peoples migrated to new areas, admixture of racial stocks, tribes and languages was bound to have occurred.

The ancestral language of the Indo-Āryans is regarded by most as Proto-Indo-European, sometimes written as just PIE. One branch of PIE went West, the other East to form the Indo-Iranian branch. It is from this latter that Indo-Āryan is believed to derive. It would be difficult to deny that, linguistically, the language we have in the *Vedas*, Old Indo-Āryan or Sanskrit, is close to Old Iranian. Indeed, the Old Iranian text, the *Avesta*, and the Sanskrit texts of the *Vedas* have remarkable similarities of language and culture. These links I shall point out as we proceed. In Michael Witzel's view, the ancestral language of the Āryans "became *Indianized* and has grammatically *innovated after* its arrival in the Panjab". But he adds: "Exactly how the IA [Indo-Āryan] *spiritual and material culture* of the archaeologically still little traced Indo-Aryan speaking tribes was introduced, that is still an open and very much debated question."[8] Thus, it is almost impossible to say exactly how the Āryan religion that I shall be exploring below in this chapter came about. From a different viewpoint, there are non-Indo-Āryan terms that occur in the earliest *Vedic* texts. These are foreign words that refer to flora and fauna, agriculture, dancing, music and to names of people, places and tribes. Such terms are related to popular living not to the higher echelons of *Vedic* society.[9] Witzel suggests that some of these words were indigenous to the Punjab area and predated the Indo-Āryan people.[10] Thus, it might be posited that some strata of the Āryans were actually indigenous and incorporated through what Fritz Staal described as "multiple processes of reciprocal acculturation".[11]

So how much credence should be given to the idea that the Indo-Āryans were in the Indus region during the Late Harappan Period? Witzel notes the synonymy between Cemetery H burial motifs on urns that have a small human portrayed inside a painted peacock and the *Vedic* idea of birds containing the souls of ancestors.[12] Others see some synonymy between the *Vedic* domestic fire rituals and the fire altars at Kalibangan.[13] What we do know is that the Indo-Āryans used a grey painted pottery, Painted Grey Ware or simply PGW, as it is known, and that serves to identify them and their whereabouts to a certain extent. But their presence in the Late Harappan Period is not generally accepted and it would be difficult to ascribe these flimsy synonymous features to the Āryans *per se* as opposed to indigenous praxis that was later absorbed in the Āryan fold. I shall have more to say on this below.

A wholesale immigration of Indo-Āryans into the North of India is to be ruled out. Their religious ideas are different, as we shall see, from the Indus civilization that we saw in chapter 1. The diversity and fluidity of Āryan nomadic movements, their acculturation, accommodating of, and synthesis with, the other cultures they met, must have been of such a nature that the resulting cultural pattern they present to us in the *Vedas* has some disparate aspects as much as coherence. But they certainly accumulated sufficient numbers and influence to become a dominant presence. However, it would be naïve to think that the religious culture conveyed to us in their written scriptures was the only religion practised in that ancient time. For masses of others, we have little idea of their religious beliefs and praxis. The Indo-Āryans who present their religious culture in the *Vedas*, while a mixed lot, created the division between those who accepted the *Vedas* and those who did not. But we should not search for major discontinuity in this process: it seems to me that it was more a question of gradual change and synthesis, a suggestion that biological data generally supports.[14]

Thus far, it would seem that the Āryans were not indigenous to India, their origins stretched over the plains from the Ukraine to the east of Kazakhstan, but their ancestral stocks became widely dispersed. There is some synonymy between the old Hurrian language of the kingdom of Mitanni in upper Mesopotamia and early Sanskrit, even the same names of deities, and both cultures shared an interest in horses and chariots.[15] Asko Parpola notes that the Mitanni aristocracy had Āryan names, and Āryan deities featured in their treaties that date to the fourteenth century BCE,[16] though the main language was Hurrian. It seems, then, that there was a language that might be termed "Mitanni Vedic".[17] Another area of interest is the Bactria-Margiana Archaeological Complex (abbreviated to BMAC), of Afghanistan, Central Asia; its mature phase dated to about 2100–1900 BCE. Parpola believes that Indo-Iranians flooded the BMAC and from there moved down into the Indus Valley in the Late Harappan Period between 2300 and 1500 BCE.[18] Steve Farmer also cites a superb example of a late seal from Mohenjo-daro that has an Indus inscription on one side and a BMAC bird icon on the other.[19] But the BMAC is likely to have been a very mixed cultural phenomenon, so its people are not, *per se*, identifiable as Indo-Āryans.[20] In Parpola's view, it was the BMAC peoples in Bactria with their forts and fortified villages that feature as the enemies of the Āryans in the *Vedic* texts.[21] If Indo-European peoples infiltrated the BMAC – and it needs to be pointed out that the BMAC peoples were not Indo-European according to some[22] – their cultures were lost at that point. All that can be said is that somewhere in the second millennium BCE small groups of Indo-Āryans, perhaps from the BMAC, infiltrated the Indus regions. There were probably many such movements of peoples from the end of the Indus civilization to the beginning of historical Hinduism in 600 BCE. And just as the Indus civilization consisted of multi-ethnic groups, so the Āryans, too, were of mixed tribes. As Doniger puts it: "Hybridity defies binary oppositions and understands reality as a fluid rather than a series of solid separate boxes."[23]

However, many Indian authors – especially those with a political agenda – wish to make pre-Hinduism thoroughly indigenous in origin. Satya Swarup Misra, for example, posited Sanskrit as the parent language, the date of the *Ṛg Veda* to be as early as 5000 BCE, and the Indus civilization a *continuation* of *Vedic* culture, not following it by several hundred years. For Misra, the Indo-Iranians and Indo-Āryans were both indigenous to India.[24] Vishal Agarwal claims that there is no evidence at all in the *Vedas* to suggest the Āryans migrated into India.[25] Braj Basi Lal argues that there were no "little" invasions either,[26] and that the *Ṛg Vedic* homeland was north-west India, Pakistan and extensive areas of Afghanistan.[27] Koenraad Elst also argues from a linguistic viewpoint that there were no invasions or migrations of Indo-Āryans into India, that the Indo-Āryans were autochthonous and that the European origin is specious.[28]

So what evidence is there from the *Ṛg Veda* that suggests the Āryans were a new cultural presence in India? Much is written of their enmity with the *Dāsyas* or *Dasyus*, an elusive group of people or peoples that fuel one way or another the debate about the Āryans. Edmund Leach, in arguing against any Āryan invasions conveys the *Dasyus* to mythology.[29] Parpola, on the other hand, thinks the *Dasyus* were Āryan nomads who migrated to the BMAC in Late Indus times. He thinks that another wave of Āryans then followed who were the Āryans of the *Ṛg Veda*, both *Dasyus* and Āryans having different religious cultures but eventually coalescing. In Parpola's view the Āryan battles against the *Dasyus* refer to the settlement of the two Indo-Āryan strands in the BMAC,[30] later to fuse in *Vedic* culture. In the *Ṛg Veda*, the Āryans described the *Dasyus* as dark, often taken to mean that they were dark-skinned, though it could have been a description of their "dark" beliefs as opposed to the enlightened beliefs of the Āryans,[31] so the references may be more concerned with differentiation of culture – Doniger's "Good Guys" – rather than race.[32] The important point here is that the Āryans and the *Dasyus* may not have been different races, though Witzel believes the *Dasyus* were held by the Āryans to be "foreigners".[33] Once again, however, we should not be tempted to think that the *Vedic* Āryans were a homogeneous group. There must have been pre-existing tribal groups that were absorbed into the Āryan fold as well as many that stayed outside it. Indigenous Dravidians are also highly likely to have been part of the Āryan acculturation process.[34]

Were the people of the Indus civilization part of this acculturation? The Āryans were mainly a post-Harappan phenomenon, especially since they were, unlike the people of the Indus civilization, distinctly non-urban. But there may well have been some kind of cultural interaction between the Harappan people and the Indo-Āryans, enough, as Laurie Patton suggests, to lead to "major changes in religious, material, and linguistic life that led to what we now call the Vedic culture".[35] Kenneth Kennedy, too, thinks that there may well have been some elements of the Indus civilization that survived into *Vedic* times, citing the fire altars at Kalibangan, noted above, and at Lothal and their possible link with *Vedic* deification of fire.[36] And Doniger says rather pertinently: "The Indus civilization may not have simply gone out like the flame of a candle or, at least, not before lighting another candle."[37] Thus, there are surely some indicators of earlier religious life stretching into the *Vedic* period that, with careful scrutiny, we may well find. It is not unreasonable to suggest that there could have been some overlap between the Indus civilization and the oral traditions of the *Ṛg Veda*.[38] It seems to me, however, that there is little to connect the Indus civilization and *Vedic* society *as cultures*: there is a good deal that is new and different in *Vedic* religion, but interaction between the newcomers and the settled indigenous inhabitants along with concomitant acculturation must have been evident, though the Āryans with their horses and chariots, their fire rituals and male deities, became predominant as far as we can tell from *Vedic* texts.

One factor that is highly disputed is the question of the horse. Was it known before the Āryans, or can its presence only be attributed to the Āryans? Those who wish to claim that the Āryans are indigenous to India have to find the presence of the horse there from ancient times. Claims that it was present in the Indus Valley before the second millennium are spurious and it is notable that the horse was not depicted on seals or occurred in the form of terracotta images, despite the claims of some to force a horse image on one or two very unclear artefacts, or to identify a wild ass as a horse.[39] Lal, however, is adamant that there is ample evidence of the presence of the horse in the Mature Indus civilization, in order to strengthen his view of the Āryans as autochthonous.[40] It is clear, however, that the presence of the chariot in *Vedic* hymns is a characteristic of Āryans and not of the Indus civilization. The Āryans clearly reflect an Iron-Age culture and their introduction of iron late in the second millennium BCE is likely to have been one of the major factors leading to their supremacy. Āryan characteristic pottery, too, the Painted Grey Ware, is not known in northern India until 1100–300 BCE, coincident with Āryan incursions. The overwhelming evidence, it seems to me, suggests that Indo-Āryans came from outside India and not from indigenous communities.

Crucial to the indigenous or immigrant status of the Āryans is the dating of the oldest of the *Vedic* texts, the *Ṛg Veda*. Its contents suggest a date of somewhere in the second half of the second millennium BCE, though established Iron-Age Āryan society in India is likely to have been after 1000 BCE and probably in the middle of the first millennium BCE, well after the demise of the Bronze-Age Indus civilization. A long period of oral tradition predated the written text of the *Ṛg Veda* but, while some authors want to project it back to the fourth or fifth millennium BCE,[41] the general consensus of opinion is that it is much later than this and certainly later than the demise of the Indus civilization. On the other hand, Edmund Leach believes that the *Ṛg Veda* is no earlier than 400 BCE and that its archaic language is simply a device to authenticate the text as ancient.[42] Contrary to this, however, is the linguistic evidence that I noted above and the language connections of the *Ṛg Veda* with both the Hurrians and with Old Iranian, which give a timescale of somewhere before 800 BCE.[43] A reasonable date for the bulk of the hymns is generally agreed on as somewhere between 1500–1300 or 1200 BCE, and allowing for considerable oral tradition, perhaps 1900–1300 BCE.[44] Later parts of the *Ṛg Veda* stretched down to about 900 BCE and the whole *Vedic* period to about 600 BCE. One factor that helps date some parts is the River Sarasvati, which is hailed as a mighty river in the *Ṛg Veda*. However, it dried up at the beginning of the second millennium BCE, and that seems to suggest that some parts of the *Ṛg Veda* that mention the river are earlier than 1900 BCE. As a composite text, with preceding oral traditions, we should reckon with variable dating for its hymns.

The four *Vedas*

Vedic religion provides us with a journey to the spiritual past of an ancient era, where we can discover the earliest spiritual thought, and have an opportunity to traverse time to the dawn of Indian history, "the point of departure of all the doctrines of classical India".[45] The extensive literature that represents the *Veda* as a whole has been justifiably termed by Ainslie Embree as "one of the most magnificent achievements of the human spirit in any place or time".[46] Later *Vedic* literature will be dealt with in the following chapter, chapter 3: here, I want to concentrate on the four *Vedas* as products of early Āryan religion. With these ancient texts, especially with the earliest, the *Ṛg Veda*, the language is so archaic as to provoke considerable ambiguities in translations. The *Vedas* are also sufficiently archaic to become highly obscure and yet are regarded as immensely sacred. Wilhelm Halbfass comments on such a paradox: "For the 'reality' of later Hinduism, they seem to be nothing more than a distant, barely recognizable echo of a different world."[47] And yet, as Halbfass goes on to say, "an idea and vision of the Veda emerges not only as a focal point of Hindu self-understanding, and a center for the precarious unity and identity of the tradition, but also as a prototype for its inner variety and potential universality".[48] Whatever the obscurities of the literature, and the adaptations and acculturation through synthesis of tribal movements, the phenomenon of *Vedic* religion and culture spread throughout most of India and became the defining foundation of Hinduism.

The four *Vedas* began as oral compositions that were regarded as sacred. They were ultimate Truth that "was a powerful, active, and transformative force".[49] These words of William Mahony are particularly apt, since the very words of the *Vedas* were believed to have a causative effect within the world around and the world of the deities, as we shall see. The word *veda* means "knowledge" and that knowledge is of a dynamic Truth, what John Koller describes as "sounds of wisdom issuing from the very heart of existence itself".[50] The spectrum of the *Veda* covers *mantras* or collections of hymns called *Saṃhitās*, and related *Brāhmaṇas*, *Āraṇyakas* and *Upaniṣads*, but it is just the *mantras*, the *Saṃhitās* that will concern us for the moment. It is these *mantras* that are generally referred to as *Veda*. The hymns were the property of hereditary families of priests who belonged in all probability to different tribes or clans in different localities, each with a family name that was handed down with their respective hymns. This was the beginning of the different *Vedic* schools or branches. A long period of oral tradition – perhaps as long as a thousand years – preceded the written texts that are dated well after the entire *Vedic* period, the sacred nature of the hymns being such that to write them down would have been a polluting action. It would be difficult to maintain, then, that the *Vedas* are *script*ure: they were never meant to be written. Early Āryans were, in any case, illiterate, but they, as their descendants down through time, remained entirely faithful to the original oral compositions. As Doniger puts it, referring to the oldest *Veda*: "The *Rig Veda* was preserved orally, but it was frozen, every syllable preserved for centuries, through a process of rigorous memorization. There are no variant readings of the *Rig Veda*, no critical editions or textual apparatus. Just the *Rig Veda*."[51] When all the orally transmitted *Ṛg Vedas* came to be written down, they were perfect matches. As Arthur Macdonell commented almost a century ago, "the text of the Rigveda has been handed down for 2,500 years with a fidelity that finds no parallel in any other literature".[52]

As the property of elitist family priests, the *Vedas* were recited in an archaic Sanskrit unknown to the populace or outsiders. They were not collected together into a composite text until about 800–500 BCE. It is this old language that has most similarities with the Indo-European and Indo-Iranian languages.[53] Later, it would develop into the classical Sanskrit of the epics and other scriptures. Essentially, the *sounds* and *syllables* of the *Vedas* were believed to represent reality and were appropriately "the thread of sound that wove the sacrifice together" as Thomas Hopkins put it[54] since Sanskrit *saṃskṛta* means "well-made". Because the *Vedic mantras* had such a long era of oral transmission, those that were eventually committed to written form were probably not the entire collection, just those that were most suited to ritual were included.[55] Indeed, ritual became the *raison d'être* of the entire collections. By the time they were written down, the individual hymns were quite disparately dated with centuries separating the oldest from the newest.

Mantras were the key to *Vedic* ritual: they were the magic formulae by which anything could be assured, from the rising of the sun each morning to the need of a charm to ensure the love of a woman. The four *Vedas* – *Ṛg*, *Sāma*, *Yajur* and the later *Atharva* – all served such a purpose as well as offering praise to a large number of deities. Each was a *saṃhitā*, a "collection", literally a "put" (*hita*) "together" (*sam*) of hymns suited to the different nature of each *Veda*. All are *śruti*, "heard", by ancient sages and are respected as ultimate Truth. It is this factor that lifts the *Vedas* from the purely magical to the spiritual level, a factor that justifies John Keay's description of the hymns as "pearls of descriptive verse from poetry's remotest past".[56]

The *Ṛg Veda*

The *Ṛg Veda*, "Knowledge of Verses or Praises", is the oldest of the four *Vedas*; indeed, the other three have much material in them that is taken directly from the *Ṛg*. All the hymns in this collection are centred on ritual, especially the vibratory *sound* of the *mantras*, the hymns being regarded as sacred speech that is chanted, sung or recited. Its era is believed to belong to a historical Golden Age. The *Ṛg Veda* is regarded as *the Veda* far outweighing the other three in importance. Macdonell called it "the oldest literary monument of the Indo-European languages"[57] and Sarvepalli Radhakrishnan and Charles Moore described its 1,017 hymns as "the outpourings of poetic minds who are struck by the immensity of the universe and the inexhaustible mystery of life".[58] There is, indeed, in the *Ṛg Vedic* hymns a tantalizing balance between magic and spirituality, between propitiation and praise and between public ceremony and individual fervour. The verses of the *Ṛg Veda* are divided into ten "books", more literally "circles", *maṇḍalas*, some books being much older than others. The oldest books are 4–6, the latest, 1 and 10, the latter being the latest of all.[59] As we shall see, these latest books will provide the more speculative and philosophical aspects of *Vedic* religion. The ninth book is devoted entirely to one theme, the deity *Soma* and the hallucinatory beverage of the same name. This suggests that all the hymns related to *soma* were gathered together from all the *Vedas* and presented in one *maṇḍala*. The hymns are the works of many authors, poets that composed them during their nomadic wanderings, and handed them down within their tribes. Traditionally, the hymns were composed by famous seers[60] though they were in reality the product of many hands within many tribal families. However, books 2 to 7 have a homogeneity that may suggest they came from the same family tradition.[61] In the *Ṛg Veda*, hymns were arranged so that they praised each deity in turn: all those for Agni, for example, occur first. The latest book, book 10, contains hymns devoted to marriage and funeral rituals, though other *saṃskāras*, life-cycle rites, are not featured.

Sāma Veda

Sāma Veda is the "Knowledge of Chants", a musical arrangement of the *Ṛg Veda*. Staal thought that the melodies may have predated the verses since the words do not always fit the melody. He believed, too, that the melodies may also have accompanied another language.[62] The chants were believed to be extraordinarily powerful and Staal suggested that some were particularly pertinent to the alien and dangerous areas of the forests, as opposed to villages, a point that for him is possibly indicative of an indigenous provenance akin, perhaps to the BMAC language.[63] Whatever the origins of the *Sāma Veda* chants, the exactitude of syllable, sound and musical note, became pivotal to the cause–effect processes of ritual.

Yajur Veda

The *Yajur Veda* is separated into the four collections that constitute the *Black Yajur Veda*, now associated with southern India and the single collection of the *White Yajur Veda* that became associated with the North. The *Yajur Veda* embodies ritualistic power and ritualistic exactitude. Such ritual took place in a temporary sacred area with three altars, one at the west, which was a circular altar on which offerings were cooked, thus, the domestic altar. To the east was a square altar on which the cooked food was placed, usually in fire. Then, facing south was a semi-circular altar in between the other two. Since the south was seen as a dangerous and harmful direction, this last altar protected the ritual and its priests. The ritual area was the speciality of the priests of the *Yajur Veda* who chanted or muttered *yajus*, ritual formulas, believed to be responsible for the efficacy of the ritual ceremonies.[64] The *Black Yajur Veda* has a mixture of *mantric* poetry and prose, as well as explanatory discussions about ritual, whereas the *White Yajur Veda* is more orthodox in following the *Ṛg Veda* with poetic *mantras*.

The *Atharva Veda*

For the purposes of the section that follows on the interface between the Indus civilization and the era of the Āryans, it is the *Atharva Veda* that supplies us with a good deal of information, albeit concealed within its pages. It is a book of spells and incantations, on the one hand steeped in magic and on the other, the probable beginnings of medical experimentation and knowledge. It also has some remarkable philosophical elements. It is written in poetry and prose, and there are two divisions: one, the elder, is the *Paippalāda*, the name of its founder being derived from the *pīpal* tree, and the younger is the *Śaunaka*. The *Atharva Veda* was originally excluded from the other *Vedas*, perhaps because of its different content, but also because it was compiled later. Even just a glance at the contents of this *Veda* demonstrates the extent of the magical spells for use in all sorts of situations in life that have nothing to do with religious thought other than there may be a deity addressed who is believed to make a spell efficacious. References to iron suggest that the texts cannot be any earlier than 1100 or 1000 BCE when iron was introduced into northern India and we are looking at a date of around 900 BCE for its composition. Nevertheless, some parts may be more ancient and it is likely to have reflected the more popular beliefs that circulated for a very long time. Sarvepalli Radhakrishnan thought the "weird" religion of the *Atharva Veda* to be older than the *Ṛg Veda* itself, though its written composition was much later.[65]

What we find in the *Atharva Veda* are pronounced beliefs in demons and evil spirits, which are surely indicative of old tribal beliefs endemic amongst the populace for centuries. As Surendranath Dasgupta pointed out, the teeming accounts of witchcraft "derived from an immemorial antiquity".[66] Renou, too, thought that the very primitive ritual contained in the *Atharva Veda* may have existed alongside the more orthodox ritual or pre-existed it.[67] As Michael Witzel comments: "Because of its focus on small non-Śrauta rituals, the AV [*Atharva Veda*] is an irreplaceable source for the material culture, the customs and beliefs, the desires and sorrows of everyday Vedic life" and he, too, believes that some of the old sorcery rites may be older than the *Ṛg Veda*.[68] The "cloud of minor and indistinct evils", as Renou termed them,[69] are clearly what occupy the fears and religious praxis of the ordinary populace. Balanced with these more primitive ideas are the mystical elements that juxtapose and interconnect existence and non-existence through rather brilliant metaphysics intuited by the visionary poets. Late poems such as 10:8:44 and 10:2:23 give us a glimpse of the *ātman* as the essence of all things – a foundation principle of Hinduism. The *Brāhmin* attached to the *Atharva Veda* became the priest who oversaw the whole ritual conducted by the priests of the other *Vedas*, a point that elevated the *Atharva Veda* in line with the first three.

Across the *Vedas*, particularly the first three, there is considerable repetition, but there are also considerable repetitions in the *Ṛg Veda* itself, and the development of the *Vedas* is a complicated process.[70] Staal pointed out wisely that the *Vedas* are not a unit: "Their riches and deficiencies are due to a great variety of people of different backgrounds and origins, living in different regions and interacting during an extended period of time."[71] It is important to reflect on the wide origins of the *Vedic* material both geographically, tribally and in time. One thing is clear, the *Vedas* reflect a masculine world, patrilineal descent and patriarchal dominance. Although there are some hymns by women, the overall picture is of male predominance. The *Vedic* male was pragmatic about his needs – cattle, health, wealth, a wife and happiness:

> Our thoughts bring us to diverse callings, setting people apart: the carpenter seeks what is broken, the physician a fracture, and the Brahmin priest seeks one who presses Soma. . . . With his dried twigs, with feathers of large birds, and with stones, the smith seeks all his days a man with gold. . . . I am a poet; my Dad's a physician and Mum a miller with grinding-stones. With diverse thoughts we all strive for wealth, going after it like cattle.[72]

While these words may suggest a level of involvement of the ordinary individual, the elitism of *Vedic* ritual excluded much of the populace.

The *Vedas* were the product of creative imagination that stretched into the realms of ritual, causative theories and cosmic theories. Much of the material is enigmatic – deliberately so, since priestly schools had contests to ascertain the best contributory revelations in poetic compositions. But *Vedic* ritual, for all its obscure meaning and archaic language, has survived to the present day in the performance of life-cycle rites, and *Brāhmin* daily prayers are still the same as they were in ancient times. As Dasgupta put it: "Thus in short we may say that in spite of the many changes that time has wrought, the orthodox Hindu life may still be regarded in the main as an adumbration of the Vedic life, which had never ceased to shed its light all through the past."[73]

The interface between the Indus civilization and the *Vedic* period

Is there, then, any religious legacy of the Indus civilization that is taken up by *Vedic* religion? To begin with, I think inferred links between the Indus civilization and *later* Hinduism are forced and somewhat spurious in most cases. As the communities lapsed back into village-based farming and herding alongside nomadic lifestyles, nature with its blessings and vicissitudes must have been foremost in the minds of the ordinary people and local traditions must have prevailed to some extent, though becoming synthesized with those of others from time to time. It is at the popular level that I think some continuity of religious cultures was probably maintained and I hope to highlight some instances of such in the pages that follow. However, these village peoples were illiterate: unlike the Āryans who brought their orally-transmitted hymns, we have little to assign to popular village religious cultures. Excavations in the Swat Valley, the furthest northern area of the Late Indus Period, have revealed graves containing female terracotta figurines.[74] Terracotta bull figurines turn up on the Malwa plateau and Maharashtra[75] as well as male and female terracotta figurines that become prolific during the Iron Age.[76] One figurine combines a female with a bull,[77] suggestive, perhaps, of the fertility praxis we saw in the Indus civilization. If the Indo-Āryans filtered into the Indus areas over a long period of time, some cultural synthesis is likely between the two and that may well be present in the hymns of the *Vedas*. Archaeology, at present, has little to tell us of these intervening years and it is to the inferences supplied by the *Vedic* texts that I want to turn to glean some idea of the interface between the two.

The *Ṛg Veda* contains a considerable number of agricultural terms. These do not seem to be native Dravidian[78], and may have arisen from post-Indus agricultural villages.[79] Pre-Āryan customs must surely have survived well into the historical period in northern India, infusing the *Vedas* with non-Āryan elements. Witzel has listed a large number of non-Indo-Āryan names in the *Ṛg Veda* suggestive of a "thorough mix" of different speakers in the period of Āryan acculturation.[80] In contrast to post-Indus agriculturalists, early Āryans were nomadic or semi-nomadic, possibly moving from settlement to settlement.[81] Interaction with more settled agriculturalists would have been present but also some distinction between Āryan tribes and indigenous tribes. Witzel is certain of "early interaction and amalgamation of the immigrant Aryan civilization . . . and the preceding Indus civilization and its local, village level continuants:"[82] indeed, the Āryans would have been partially dependent on the agricultural village products. I think we can safely say that there was an element of acculturation in the several hundred years' interface between the Harappan civilization and *Vedic* Hinduism, an acculturation that must have included many different tribal elements, many linguistic admixtures and much genetic inter-mixing. Ethnic and racial distinction do not seem to have been present in the Āryan people either before their entry into northern India or immediately after it. The indigenous tribes must have contributed some of their own influences to *Vedic* religion. The names of some indigenous tribes and families gave themselves to *Vedic* schools, the language of the *Vedas* being adopted as a secondary language by such indigenous tribes.[83] Tribal alliances are attested in the *Ṛg Veda* and those alliances would have been accompanied by a blending of deities, of priestly activities, ritual activities with their *mantric* powers, and an adoption of Āryan rituals by indigenous tribal kings concomitant with an increasing tendency to separation of Āryan and non-Āryan.

Tribal religion is the key to understanding the interface between the Harappan civilization and the *Vedic* period and there are strong hints of such in the *Atharva Veda*. Some of the material in this text reflects the customs of small tribal groups and clans. Many tribes were connected with creatures like the fish and bird as totemic symbols of their clans[84] and while it would be stretching evidence too far to make firm links, we know that the emphasis on animals in the Indus civilization was endemic. In the Indus civilization, animals were associated with power: the tiger, especially, must have continued to be a symbol of strength of the type that could defeat foes. Snakes were partly deified and partly demonized, and the belief that the glance of a snake was tantamount to evil, was probably very ancient. Vṛtra, the demon serpent of the *Ṛg Veda* who prevents creation – a myth to which I shall return below – symbolized evil and chaos but there is no evidence of snake worship *per se* in the *Ṛg Veda*. The bull that featured so widely on Indus seals is also used as a descriptor of many *Vedic* deities – Agni; Soma; Indra, the "mighty bull"; Kāma, the god of desire; Dyaus; Rohita. The sun is often hailed as the heaven-conquering bull and, here, as the One:

> They adorned him even as he climbed upward.
> Self-luminous he moves, dressed in brilliance.
> That is the bull's – the divine being's – mighty form:
> consisting of all forms, he bears immortal names.[85]

The hymn refers to the "primordial bull", a reference to its strength, power, virility and majesty as divine characteristics but, importantly, to the primordial progenitor, the One, from which all becomes manifest. Bulls were also sometimes sacrificed, as they were on the Indus seals, but while endemic in pre-Hinduism and *Vedic* Hinduism (and even in modern times), there were changing perceptions of their characteristics and roles and they do not seem to have been worshipped as independent creatures. Cows were not featured at all in the Harappan culture, whereas they are mentioned more than bulls in the *Vedic* texts.

Evidence for popular religion is hard to find but by no means impossible. While there are hymns to a great many established *Vedic* deities there are some remarkable references in the *Ṛg Veda* to the deity, the *kṣetriya-pati*, of a cultivated field (4:57:1–4), and the goddess of the furrow, *Sītā* (4:57:5–6). There is also reference to a god of the home, *vāstoṣ-pati* (7:54), verses for ploughing, for wealth from cattle, for safety of cattle, and even hymns for the tools of one's trade (1:28:5–6). Such references are likely to refer to ancient popular praxis in religion, the kind of religion that was essential in the day-to-day living of ordinary village folk that could well have been pre-Āryan. Later *Vedic* texts have many popular sayings introduced by "they say . . ." and the like.[86]

A clear aspect of Indus religious praxis that was maintained was the veneration of trees. Trees featured on Indus seals with a cultic significance, and were clearly often divine or housed the figure of a deity. The *pīpal* tree, especially, has remained connected with religious activity in popular belief right through to post-modern times. Indeed, one of the two schools of the *Atharva Veda* takes its name from the *pīpal* tree. While the tree appears in the later official cult, it is likely to have been maintained at the local village level from Indus times. I think this was likely to have obtained at the popular level, but there is no evidence in the *Ṛg Veda* that trees were venerated *per se*, though *apsaras*, celestial nymphs, are occasionally said to dwell in trees and there are some trees named in the *Ṛg Veda* that probably reflect popular religion.[87] The *pīpal* is linked with the deity Varuṇa in 1:24:7, and there is a reference to the "holy fig-tree" in 1:135:8. The *aśvattha* tree is mentioned frequently in the *Atharva Veda*. Whether nomadic and pastoral or settled and agricultural, forests, with their wild animals and dangers would have been a continued threat to ordinary people. In a rather beautiful *Ṛg Vedic* hymn to the goddess of the forest and the wild, *Āraṇyānī*, the softness of the forest by day is contrasted with its dangers at night when all kinds of strange things are imagined (10:146). Because the goddess rests at night, it is then when the demons and forest beasts emerge.[88]

Dark and evil forces were surely in the backdrop of popular minds right through from Harappan times to the present day. Demons, evil spirits, ogres and anti-gods plagued the lives of individuals and communities from time to time. Many of these dark forces may well have been the gods of enemies of the Āryans on occasions, especially the *Dasyus*. Fear of evil monsters of the forest must have been endemic and engendered much religious superstition. The *Atharva Veda* abounds with spells against demons believed to cause all kinds of maladies to human and beast. The priests of the *Atharva Veda* were steeped in knowledge of charms and magical practices for the benefit of the upper echelons of society but the beliefs that underpin the praxis, I believe, are likely to stem from long-accepted folk religion. Magic has been defined by Jamison and Witzel as referring to "ritual activities that have private, well-defined ends – to win the love of a woman, to cure an illness, to harm an enemy",[89] to which can be added ritual to offset inimical forces. There is abundant evidence of black and white sorcery in the *Atharva Veda* and magical practices were likely to have been the product of centuries of habit handed down for generations in the popular mind, eventually absorbed into *Vedic* orthodox religion, and controlled as a result by specialist priests. Even the later portions of the *Ṛg Veda* contain hymns that are really spells for mundane as well as more serious matters, though these are exceptions to the general spirit of the *Ṛg Veda*. I think the *Atharva Veda* reflects popular religious sentiment rather well and Keith pertinently commented that texts like the *Atharva Veda* reveal that India of the time "was one in which magic and religion were inextricably blended".[90] Much of *Vedic* ritual could be described as magic in that the priests were attempting to control forces that were supernatural by their ritual words and actions. Some of the sorcery rites of the *Atharva Veda* may predate the *Ṛg Veda*[91] though they are presented in a literary form that post-dates it.

Alongside the sorcery is the witchcraft presided over by official priests, but it is obvious from the *Atharva Veda* that unofficial tribal witchcraft was widely practised, which the orthodox priests, the *atharvans*, castigated in no uncertain terms. This, too, it seems to me, must have stemmed from ancient praxis among the ordinary populace, praxis that may have been, in many cases, longstanding and endemic. There are hymns that seek to weed out the barbarian sorcerers[92] with destruction for those found. Invectives from white sorcerers against black sorcerers pepper its pages. Max Müller over a century ago wrote in his introduction to his translation of the *Atharva Veda*: "Even witchcraft is part of the religion; it has penetrated and has become intimately blended with the holiest Vedic rites; the broad current of popular religion and superstition has infiltrated itself through numberless channels into the higher religion that is presented by the Brahman priests, and it may be presumed that the priests were neither able to cleanse their own religious beliefs from the mass of folk-belief with which it was surrounded, nor is it likely that they found it in their interest to do so."[93] Folk belief is almost invariably very old and my point here is that it would have been present during the Indus period itself and in the interface between the Indus civilization and the *Vedic* period.

A belief in demons and goblins obtained widely in popular belief and pervades the *Vedic* texts and much subsequent literature. Such beings feature widely in the *Atharva Veda* and there are charms against them to counteract possession and get rid of them. Demons personified death, dark powers, palpable evil, inimical forces and terror. They had to be appeased or sent back to their abode through magical charms. Again, we have a very ancient belief here. Perhaps the fact that they were often believed to be part human and part animal reflects some remains of Indus beliefs. In the *Ṛg Veda* we hear a great deal of the class of demons known as *Rākṣasas* who could appear as animals or birds or as grotesque humans and were ready to cause disease and terror, particularly at night. They tried to sabotage sacrifices and were often associated with the souls of the dead who had not passed on in the proper manner. That many of these demons were local, indigenous and non-Āryan is not improbable.[94]

The *Atharva Veda* has many spells that include the use of amulets against such harmful creatures and forces, and also for the benefit of ordinary living. As was seen in chapter 1, seals were often in the form of amulets to be worn by an individual. These may have had some protective aim, and those cited in the *Atharva Veda* certainly did so. Lead amulets were recommended against demons, with appropriate priestly spells (1:16; 2:9), and there were amulets for success and good fortune (1:29; 6:129); for long life (1:35; 19:32); for protection and thwarting evil (2:4; 4:10; 5:28; 19:30; 19:36); against witchcraft (2:12; 8:5); for prosperity (3:5; 19:31); for successful pregnancy (6:81); against illness (6:126); against rivals (10:3; 19:28); in short, for all manner of things in life. Some amulets were kept in the home "as a guest" (10:6:4), suggestive that they were believed to have a living force of their own. Usually cast with a particular deity in mind in order to make the spell potent, the force contained in an amulet is exemplified in the following verse from 19:46: "In this amulet [are] a hundred and one heroisms; a thousand breaths in this unsubdued one; a tiger, do thou attack all our rivals; whoso shall fight against thee, be he inferior: let the unsubdued one defend thee."[95] The amulet is seen here to contain a living essence. Lest we should relegate such practice totally to the realms of primitive superstition – and there are certainly strong elements of this – there is much here that in giving essence to natural phenomena, paved the way for juxtaposed pantheistic views of the world in other *Vedic* texts.

One interesting legacy of the Harappan civilization on *Vedic* India was the use of bricks for fire-altars. Doniger suggests that when the *Vedic* people started to make bricks for their altars, they did so with a level of sophistication that suggests they may have been influenced by the remnants of peoples from the Indus civilization whom, we know, were excellent in the making of bricks for their buildings.[96]

Nature itself would have been of key importance to pastoralists and agriculturalists alike. The wheel as a possible symbol of the sun was found on some Indus seals and this seems to have survived into *Vedic* times.[97] Indeed, the miracle of the sun rising each morning was a key feature of *Vedic mantras* and was associated with a number of deities, as will be seen below. Unlike the urban Harappan culture, *Ṛg Vedic* people were pastoral and semi-nomadic for a long period, though the move to more settled agricultural life took place, particularly with the overpowering of indigenous people and the taking of their land, which saw an increase in village settlement. Kinship groups were united by the early term for village, *grāma*, and consisted of a few families grouped together with their wagons and herds: these groups occasionally remained in temporary settlements. The move to agricultural settlement prompted some hymns of the *Atharva Veda* to be devoted to pleas to deities for successful ploughing, richness in grain, and cattle always remained the sign of wealth for the semi-nomadic and settled Āryans who were adept at cattle rustling! It was the indigenous peoples who gave their knowledge of agriculture to the semi-nomadic Āryans, judging by the non-Āryan agricultural terms present in the *Ṛg Veda*, probably along with the deities associated with agriculture that I noted above. Water and appropriate rains were essential and hymns reflect this continuing need. The *Atharva Veda* has many hymns addressed to the waters, requesting blessings[98] and the *Ṛg Veda* also has many myths associated with water and rain. Thus we have the scenario in which the Āryans are to be placed in northern India. They appear to have existed alongside indigenous tribes some of whom entered the Āryan fold and many who did not.

The Āryans were not originally numerous but they were united by their culture, language and religious traditions despite the fact that they were tribes of mixed races. Perhaps it was this underlying unity that helped to make them eventually dominant. They were illiterate but retained their religious culture meticulously through oral transmission. Their cows and cattle were their wealth and their success in stealing as many as possible considerable. References to horses and chariots would also point to a reason for success, though Staal raises the intriguing suggestion that horses and chariots may have been imported "*through their minds*" as an oral memory of their pre-Indian traditions.[99] Despite the famous hymn in the *Ṛg Veda* that includes the origins of the four classes there is no evidence for class in the early *Vedic* period. There were ruling tribal chiefs, which is the only sense in which the term *kṣatriya* was used; priests, *purohits*, who served the clan leaders through sacrificial ritual and perpetuated *Vedic* religion; those who were ordinary *Vedic* tribal members; and then all those who were not in the *Vedic* fold. The *āśrama* system of the stages of life was not in place in the early *Vedic* period, though its embryonic form was developing for childhood, student and householder. The amalgamation of clans and tribes into larger coalitions like that of the Kurus, which took place in the Middle and Later *Vedic* age, strengthened the Āryan presence and its spread. It was this amalgamation of the tribes that made the gathering together of the collections of *Vedic* texts possible, and that engendered divisions of priests for the important ritual to maintain the new culture. Concomitantly, some of the lesser tribal deities declined in favour of those of the more powerful coalitions and consolidated kingdoms. This backdrop was one of aggression of Āryan against Āryan as much as Āryan against non-Āryan.

The *Vedic* poets

The *Vedas* are part of the *śruti* tradition, *śruti* meaning "heard" or "hearing". Those who heard these hymns cognized and perceived them in the depths of their being. They were *ṛṣis*, "seers", and at the same time *kavis*, "poets", and "sages", proponents of Truth at the foundations of reality. Many of the hymns were composed by *ṛṣis* long before the movements into India and the Indo-Iranians also had their poetic tradition as the hymns of their *Avesta* show. It was an art characteristic of both with some overlaps of deities and metres. *Ṛṣis* were close to the gods and, as Govind Pande rather beautifully put it, "the two are linked in a common wavelength. The gods are themselves seers and priests, sacrificers and artificers. It is only through the nearness of the human priest to the divine that the former becomes a seer, privileged for the moment to participate at the human level in the cosmic process of the manifestation of Truth."[100] Thus, the creative energies of the deities were synonymous with the creative poetry of the *ṛṣis*. The deities addressed in the hymns attended the ritual ceremonies and the poets competed with each other in presenting their compositions not just to the gods but also to their patrons. The hymn of the poet was a *bráhman*, a prayer, a formulation or composition of ultimate cosmic Truth appropriate for the nature of the ritual and the deity, though perceived inwardly and voiced metrically. As Mahony puts it: "The successful poet thereby linked the human community to the divine world".[101] It was frequently the power behind nature that was the subject of their poetry – the forces that made the world as it is and the truths that lay beneath the phenomena of physicality. The *ṛṣis* explained the inexplicable, gave words to the indescribable and articulated ultimate and eternal Truths beyond the realities of ordinary existence. A hymn to Indra in the *Ṛg Veda* expresses this birthing of a *ṛṣi*'s poem:

> To Indra from the heart the hymn proceedeth, to him Lord, recited, built with praises;
> The wakening song sung forth in holy synod: that which is born for thee, O Indra, notice.[102]

Importantly, the *ṛṣis* were believed not to have composed the hymns themselves but to have heard them "from the mysterious depths of timeless reality", as Mahony beautifully puts it.[103] It was the revelation by the *ṛṣi* that was new, not the hymn itself. And yet, as Mahony also says, the *ṛṣis* heard the poems "then carved and reshaped them, nursed them, moved them about, adorned them, separated them, and put them back together again in a different arrangement".[104] But the hymns were accepted as timeless, self-existent before the creation of the world and even, at times, before the gods. The hymns were believed to be a blend of visionary experience and linguistic creativity and the outcome was a spirituality that at times reached superlative heights, particularly in the later *Vedic* period. The kind of intuitive knowledge attributed to the *ṛṣis* paved the way for the search for ultimate Truth and Knowledge and the path of knowledge that characterized the end of the *Veda*, the *Vedānta*. From a purely poetic viewpoint, Radhakrishnan so poignantly said of the *ṛṣis*: "They knew what it was to love nature, and be lost in the wonders of the dawn and the sunrise, those mysterious processes which effect a meeting of the soul and nature."[105]

The cosmic law: *Ṛta*

The hymns of the *ṛṣis* were founded in the rhythmic power behind the universe, the cosmic power or energy that made all things what they are and how they act. This is *ṛta*,[106] the cosmic law, cosmic Reality and Truth (*satya*) of the universe. It is an immensely important concept because it is the foundation of later Hindu philosophy that witnessed the development of the foundation of the world as the Brahman that informs all things, and the development of the principle of *dharma*, what is right for all aspects of creation. *Dharma* is a term that is sometimes used in the *Ṛg Veda* for the kind of right conduct that assists in sustaining cosmic harmony mainly through ritual (e.g. 7:88:5). *Dharma* is primarily mainly connected with *ṛta* in those hymns in which it occurs. Mahony describes *ṛta* rather well when he says:

> Looking out over the earth's broad expanse, up into the skies and the heavens above them, Vedic poets saw a powerful and mysterious play of being. The sun rose in the morning seemingly out of nothing, emerging from enveloping darkness, bringing form to a formless world and impelling creatures to begin the new day; the heavy clouds gathered and, punctured by lightning, dropped their rain onto the earth; as if following some invisible guide, cows returned from their pasture each day to be milked. Based on the principle of *ṛta*, the world in all of its complexity revolved like a cosmic wheel.[107]

The cosmic law of *ṛta* is what binds the universe together, interconnecting and sustaining all things. It is the Truth by which the *ṛṣis* sang their hymns and that which underpins movement of the sun and moon, of creatures and humans, of seasons, rains and so, says Mahony, "suggests both a correctness or smooth compatibility of things as well as the principle of balance and integrity that gives foundation to that compatibility".[108] It is *ṛta* that creates harmony and proper processes of change and transformation so it is a dynamic principle that continually operates. *Ṛta* is thus, as Jamison and Witzel so aptly describe it, "an active realization of truth, a vital force which can underlie human or divine action".[109] It is this *active* dimension of *ṛta* that is so important here and in this sense it means "the natural course of things", deriving from a Sanskrit root *ṛ* meaning "go, move", though perhaps in a straight, fixed and especially regular manner.[110] And all is subject to it, even the gods and goddesses, and demons and goblins.

To me, *ṛta* is *Vedic* thought at its most powerful and intrinsically meaningful for progression to great philosophical thought. It was a transcendent principle that was yet dynamically operating in and sustaining the world. *Ṛta* supplies ethical dimensions to the *Vedic* hymns with right paths of integrity for humans as much as right paths for the setting and rising of the sun or the order of the seasons, the gently blowing winds, the generous milk from cows and the sweetness of the fruits of trees and of plants.[111] The world was believed to be structured according to *ṛta* and each entity had a unique role within it. To act according to *ṛta* was to create balance and harmony in one's own life, in communal life, in the environment, in relationship with the gods and in all dimensions of existence. Its opposite, *anṛta*, was tantamount to chaos, to what is unreal, which is why it was important to follow the course of *ṛta*. As harmonious rhythm and balance between all entities, *ṛta* was especially relevant between human and divine and it was priestly *Vedic* ritual that effectuated and perpetuated the natural rhythms and active presence of *ṛta* in the world, so sustaining the universe for gods and men. *Ṛta* was an integrating natural law from which the priests acquired their powers just as the gods got theirs. The sacrificial ritual supported *ṛta* and sustained it, too, reciprocally making possible the ordered natural processes by the ordered processes of the ritual. As we shall see below, without the ordered priestly ritual it came to be accepted that *anṛta*, chaos, would ensue.

The interconnection created by *ṛta* hints of a unity behind all existence. *Ṛta* certainly provided an underlying unity for all the deities whose powers stemmed from it but it also provided unity between human and deity experienced through ritual and expressed by the ancient seers. Mahony accepts an interconnected totality that informed *Vedic* religion, "an encompassing whole in which everything exists in an interconnected totality; It is a seamless universe rather than a disjointed multiverse".[112] Yet, as we have seen from the hymns of the *Atharva Veda*, there was also a this-worldly side to *Vedic* religion in a need for the basic things of life – health, long-life, wealth, success in battle. These wishes are evident in the *Ṛg Veda*, too, and when we look at some of the deities – I have Indra in mind – we shall find balance and harmony, indeed morality, somewhat lacking at times. Nevertheless, interconnection gives us an underlying foundation of spirituality in early *Vedic* thought, a fullness and wholeness to the way the cosmos was organized. In this way, *ṛta* paved the way for the more explicit interconnection of the macrocosm and microcosm in later thought. I think *ṛta* is certainly the precursor of the Absolute, Brahman, the abstract unitary foundation and mysterious hidden power of the universe that sustains all. Concomitant with this development, too, was the priestly power in the *bráhman*, the prayer that through the musical chants of the priests reached to *ṛta*, and was synonymous with it, making *bráhman* the causal law of the universe. Both ideas pre-empt the later developed ideas of Brahman as Absolute. One of the more philosophical sections of the *Atharva Veda*, 10:8, reflects these ideas. Verse 27 depicts this superbly:

> You are woman. You are man.
> You are boy, and young girl, too.
> When old, you lean on a staff as you totter.
> When born, you reveal your face in all directions.
>
> He is their father, and also their son.
> He is the largest and the smallest of them.
> He is the one god, who has entered into the mind:
> The firstborn, yet even now within the womb.[113]

The *Vedic* conception of reality was one of what was true and life-affirming, *sat*, and its opposite of chaos and death, *asat*. It was a sense of being and non-being that is found in the later hymns of the *Ṛg Veda*. But reality extended to abstract forces in the natural world, as Witzel comments: "The Vedic Indian regards any force of nature (such as wind), good or bad luck, illnesses, feelings and even abstract notions like revenge as living, personified powers."[114] Within the ideas of unity posited by some hymns, reality was, on the whole, multiform, but interconnected, "an immense symbiosis of being".[115] There were three worlds, the heavenly, the earthly, and the intermediate space between the two and sometimes each of these was divided into three. There was also another model of that which was seen and that which was hidden or that which was manifest and that which was not – a concept that develops in the later hymns and that moves towards the idea of an ultimate Reality that is the One, from which all that is manifest emanates. That which was manifest is often described as just one quarter of ultimate Reality as in *Ṛg Veda* 1:164:45–6.

Birth, growth, decay and death were part of the laws of *ṛta*. *Vedic* people accepted a Heaven that was a sensuous improvement of life on earth for those who had maintained the correct sacrifices – a world of sun and light; joy; cool breezes as opposed to the Indian heat; good eating of milk, *ghī* and honey; drinking of *soma* (of which, more below); music and singing; life with the gods and the Fathers; and plenty of women for the patriarchal *Vedic* men: if the soul left the body at death, the individual was surely reunited with the body in Heaven. The occasional distinction between body and soul seems to be an early one and may pre-date the *Ṛg Veda*.[116] Hell was much less defined in the *Ṛg Veda* and seems to have been dark abysses. The *Atharva Veda* and *Brāhmaṇas* describe it as a dark place from which no one could return and those sent to it were evil doers, sorcerers (especially female), goblins (again, especially female) and murderers. Whether in Heaven or Hell, the fate of individuals appeared to be an immortal one. There was no concept of reincarnation in the *Vedas* and the later horror of death after death in life after life is left for the *Brāhmaṇas*.

The path to an afterlife was by way of the *Fathers* (*pitṛ*). These were ancient priestly ancestors who had founded the human race or, in some cases, the Fathers were simply the totality of the dead. Like gods, they were regarded as immortal and so ritual was focused on them as on the gods and they could bestow favours on mortals. Yama, the first to die, features in much subsequent myth and is regarded as living with the Fathers, or in Heaven, or controlling the land of the dead as its lord. On the other hand, Fathers may be separated from the gods and the "way of the Fathers" after death became inferior to the "way of the gods". What is clear is that the treatment of the dead was important not only for their subsequent afterlife but also for their relationship with those still living, though it was demons and ogres that were more feared than the dead at this stage. However, the *Vedic* poets were never really certain about the post-death experience. In *Ṛg Veda* 10:14–18, for example, all sorts of fates occur – a return home (in Heaven) with a glorious body; a plea to the god of fire, Agni, not to destroy the body completely because it would be needed; dispersal of the body parts; and burrowing in the earth. Whether cremated or not, the soul went to Heaven but it was not the hereafter on which the *Vedic* individual concentrated: he ("she" does not really figure) wanted a hundred years of living in a happy existence. The *Ṛg Veda* seems to have favoured cremation, though burial was by no means rare and may have been the earlier custom.[117] The burial hymn of *Ṛg Veda* 10:18:11 has the words: "Open up, earth; do not crush him. Be easy for him to enter and to burrow in. Earth, wrap him up as a mother wraps a son in the edge of her skirt."[118] In cremation, the deity Agni burned the body and conveyed the soul to the Fathers: he also took funeral offerings to the gods.

Later hymns of the *Ṛg Veda* move to a philosophical level that found the origin of all things as One. The most famous of these is the *Nāsadīya*, the Creation Hymn of 10:129. I can only give a few verses here, though the whole hymn is truly magnificent:

1. There was neither non-existence nor existence then; there was neither the realm of space nor the sky which is beyond. What stirred? Where? In whose protection? Was there water, bottomless deep?

2. There was neither death nor immortality then. There was no distinguishing sign of night nor of day. That One breathed, windless, by its own impulse. Other than that there was nothing beyond.

The hymn continues to sing of darkness hidden by darkness and a life force covered by emptiness from which heat, *tapas*, and desire, *kāma*, became the primary motivators to manifest existence. And then, the last two verses raise both philosophical doubt and intense speculation, "piling up paradoxes" as Wendy Doniger puts it:[119]

6. Who really knows? Who will here proclaim it? Whence was it produced? Whence is this creation? The gods came afterwards, with the creation of this universe. Who then knows whence it has arisen?
7. Whence this creation has arisen – perhaps it formed itself, or perhaps it did not – The One who looks down on it, in the highest heaven, only he knows – or perhaps he does not know.[120]

The hymn has been described as: "The most important in the history of the philosophy of India" and "the finest effort of the imagination of the Vedic poet".[121] The development of *ṛta* as the dynamic transformative power behind all into a mysterious transcendent that is the unity, the One, from which all emanates is truly metaphysically brilliant at this early stage of Hinduism. It represents the dawn of true philosophical and metaphysical enquiry. It is not the only hymn that speaks of That One,[122] but it is the most magnificent in its indication of a primal Cause that is beyond space and time, beyond all manifestation, beyond even the gods. We cannot even label it a search for monotheism for there is no hint of theism in the hymn at all, simply a search for the hidden power that lay behind all phenomena, beyond all dualities, beyond even all thought. Mysore Hiriyanna described it as "the quintessence of monistic thought" and justifiably commented: "We are here on the threshold of Upaniṣadic monism."[123] The poets who composed such hymns experienced not just the interconnection of all things but the underlying unity of them, a harmony of existence that stemmed from a mysteriously hidden, transcendent Reality, description of which they knew no one could ever attempt to master.

Sacrificial ceremony: *Yajña*

Yajña, the ritual of offerings to deities, was at the heart of *Vedic* religious praxis. It was the activation of the principle of *ṛta* in the cosmos in such a way as to maintain the cause–effect processes of nature that brought order to the world, day to follow night, seasons to be rhythmic: *yajña* aligned with the pulse of the universe, and in doing so, ensured its continuation. Koller translates *yajña* as "sacrificial celebration" because the *Vedic* hymns celebrated the powers of the deities and the ability of humans to share in that power.[124] Coming from the root *yaj*, the term means "to honour", "to venerate" and "to offer". All the hymns of the *Ṛg Veda* were hymns for ritual recited by priests and the recipients were the various deities who were invited to attend, given a comfortable seat, were sung to and given food and drink – the offerings of the *yajña*. It was a developing process and texts subsequent to the *Ṛg Veda* delineate meticulously how ritual should be conducted but even in the *Ṛg Veda* we can see *yajña* becoming more formalized. Correctly performed, *yajña* brought rewarding effects. Since *yajña* is cognate with Iranian *yasna*, and a number of terms in *Vedic* ritual as well as the titles of priests are similar also, we can assume that *yajña* was not entirely an Indian phenomenon. It was probably also not a uniform practice in the early *Vedic* period because there were different families with different hymns, metrical arrangements and traditions. Elitism coloured the ceremonies because it would have been the rulers and those rich enough to finance sacrifice who would be the recipients of *yajña*'s rewards.

Vedic ritual was not conducted in temples but in the open air – a necessary corollary of an originally nomadic and semi-nomadic people. Thus, a ritual area would not be the same from one ceremony to the next: patrons of the sacrifice from far and wide necessitated different places for conducting it. Neither were there any icons of the deities though some were anthropomorphically described. Since ritual was not conducted in one designated space, the implements of ritual were simple and Jamison and Witzel believe that they were made anew each time.[125]

Ritual action was *karman*, that action by which specific results could be brought about, so aiding the gods, an individual, and the community. Does this have characteristics of magic? In the sense that a ritual action was believed to produce a required result, it would seem so. There is certainly an abundance of magical practice in the *Atharva Veda* and there must have been elements of it too in the more public expressions of ritual. But as Robert Zaehner commented, no incongruity should be seen in this since "the cultic act creates a magical rapport with the entire cosmos".[126] Keith was unequivocal that the ritual was sympathetic magic – "one of the most obvious and undeniable facts in the whole of the Vedic sacrifice", he wrote, though he concurred that the magical element may sometimes have been secondary.[127] *Mantras* were used for both blessings and curses but I think we should also remember the cosmic function of the ritual, the underlying *ṛta* that transcended pure magic, and the mystical gems that pepper the *Vedas* suggest magic was not always to the fore. While ritual propitiated demons as much as deities and remains of the sacrifice were often offered to demons to get rid of them, the symbolism generally accompanying ritual had deeper meanings in uniting microcosm and macrocosm, and in accepting the interconnection of the divine and human worlds.

Yajña was based on the rule of cause and effect: when ritual was conducted, a particular effect happened. As Witzel says: "Nothing is without cause to the Vedic Indian; it is the cause for the existence of a particular entity, its origin and true nature that the Vedic magician wants to find out in order to influence it."[128] *Ṛta* ensured the smooth operation of the cause–effect process. Reciprocity was the major feature of the process in that the priests offered praise and thanks to the deities but, critically, offerings were given in meticulous ritual for the receiving of divine favours, whether mundane, as for wealth; needful, as for the avoidance of death, disease and famine; success against enemies; or cosmic, as for the rebirth of the sun each day. Deities received their praise and nourishment in turn for their favours. Ritual was, thus, pragmatic and utilitarian and conducted in a spirit of exchange. In fact, Keith saw this as "the fundamental fact of the whole Vedic religion".[129] However, Koller lifts the seemingly mundane purpose of *yajña* to a whole new level in claiming that *yajña* was a returning of existence to its cosmic source from where it was renewed and recreated. Such ritual allowed the divine power to pervade nature, humanity and the deities in order to maintain existence, a "participatory act through which human beings create and maintain their existence in the world", making *yajña* "the loom on which the fabric of the universe is woven".[130] At a metaphysical level, too, *yajña* maintained being and existence so that non-being and chaos were kept at bay and light triumphed over darkness. At the same time, *yajña* interconnected the world of humanity with that of the divine and ensured that deities carried out their respective functions without causing harm. If magic informed much ritual, some of the aims of *yajña* were creatively philosophical, a participation in *ṛta* as the energies of the cosmos, a "metaphysical and causative bond between cosmic realms" as Mahony puts it.[131] A harmonizing function underpinned *yajña* so maintaining balance and unity between the microcosmic and macrocosmic worlds and acting as a means to structure reality and a means to engage in and perpetuate the process of creation. Some, at least, of the *Vedic* hymns have this higher purpose.

The priests who conducted *yajña* were experts in their field – one mistake could be enough to turn creation to chaos. Their lineage was ancient and, like some of the rituals, is mirrored in the Iranian *Avesta*.[132] The *Vedic* hymns were entirely priestly orientated and each of the four *Vedas* had its increasing number of specialist priests with specific functions during ritual.[133] Their professional skills alongside elaboration of ritual gradually increased and they might travel widely to offer their services to patrons. Since ritual praxis was hereditary amongst families of priests, their profession became exclusive[134] and if harmony was the intention of the whole *yajña* it did not prevent competition and rivalry between the different priests. As seen earlier in this chapter, too, the priests gradually incorporated the customs of popular beliefs, so extending the compass of their influence.

A key aspect of *Vedic* ritual was the hallucinatory drink, *soma*, which was also the name of a god. It seems to be an Indo-Iranian phenomenon also, called *haoma* in the *Avesta*. Its name means "pressed drink", and it was meticulously prepared by the priests and drunk in order to heighten consciousness into ecstasy. The identity of the plant from which it was processed is uncertain. It seems to have been found in mountainous regions and has been variously identified with *ephedra intermedia* (which is a desert plant), or the *fly agaric* mushroom (which does not grow in northern India). It was burned on the sacrificial fire as the most prestigious offering to the gods, the offering *par excellence*. It was carried by the god of fire, Agni, and was believed to give the gods their immortality, power and strength. Those permitted to drink the remnants after it had been poured onto the fire were also believed to be blessed with immortality. A whole book of the *Ṛg Veda* is devoted to *soma*, suggestive that all the hymns referring to it in the *Vedas* were collected together in this book.

Another key aspect of *yajña* was fire and, again, specialist priests were associated with fire in Indo-Iranian traditions. Fire was the central medium of ritual, and was that by which offerings could be transformed and taken to the deities. The simplest fire offering was the *agnihotra* in which milk and *ghī* were offered twice each day – once in the morning and again in the early evening – at the domestic and priestly ritual, though such offerings varied for the domestic fire. Fire in the domestic scene did not go out, but was rekindled each morning and the priests would take from it the fire necessary for more public ritual. It was a major duty of a householder and his wife to keep this fire perpetually burning. Fire served the double purpose of reaching the gods and of keeping evil forces away. Three basic fires were central to the cult corresponding to the three altars that I mentioned earlier. They were constructed for the occasion of the ritual but not permanently located. Sacrificial offerings apart from *soma* – *ghī*, honey, milk, curds, seeds, grains, barley and rice cakes, nuts and fruit – were placed on the sacred fire though, occasionally, animals such as goats, sheep, cows or horses were sacrificed. If an animal was sacrificed, it was tied to a sacrificial post (*yupa*), which was a sacred ritual implement in the time of the *Ṛg Veda*. Rites accompanied every sacrifice and were mainly requests to the deities rather than praises or thanks, though both these last were features of some hymns.[135] Cooked food was transformed into smoke and an aroma, which were taken to the deities by Agni, where the offering was consumed leaving the remains on Earth as the "leftovers" to be eaten by the priests and mortals. Again, we have reciprocity of exchange, food for the deities in exchange for rewards for the participants in the sacrifice. Evidence for human sacrifice is slim; where it is documented, it seems the victim was set free and only used symbolically: indeed, this may have been the case with some animals, too.[136] A horse sacrifice, the *aśvamedha* was one conducted by a ruler who wished to extend his kingdoms. The horse was allowed to roam freely for a year and protected, after which it was sacrificed and the lands on which it ventured taken by the king. Sacrificial offerings also accompanied the new and full moons and seasonal times.

The complexities of *yajña* are too intricate to deal with in a chapter of this nature; the symbolism of the *yajña* is immense, a point conveyed only too well by Mahony when he says: "The *yajña* was the universe in miniature: in it played all the forces and dynamics that pulled the world apart and, more important, put that world back together again."[137] It was seen to be enveloped in danger but necessary, hence the attention to sacred sound and language, to appropriate times, and meticulous observation in the unifying of microcosm and macrocosm in order to recreate the world anew. The greater the danger and the more exigent *yajña* became, the more ritual became elaborated with divisions between domestic and public rites and powerful priesthoods related to major political alliances. Later texts like the *Brāhmaṇas* reflect this increased complexity making *yajña* even more enigmatic but central to religious praxis.

Creation

Vedic poets were inspired to contemplate on the beginnings of the world and the origin of the gods but their views were all different. Given the long timescale of composition of the *Ṛg Veda* and the different priestly family traditions, there are different ideas of creation not only in this text but across all the *Vedas*. Later hymns provide us with more philosophical material that has to be placed alongside more primitive views. The creative force was something of a magical entity to which the poets, for the most part, attempted to give some concrete description. The tenth book of the *Ṛg Veda*, in particular, provides us with a number of these attempts. I have already included the *Nāsadīya* of **10:129** where the origins of the world were taken beyond even existence and non-existence. Others that are of interest in the *Ṛg Veda* are the following:

1:32 is a famous myth that sees the world created by the god Indra. A number of gods were associated with creation and Viṣṇu's three strides that I dealt with extensively in

Volume I is a good example.[138] But just as Viṣṇu measured out the cosmic regions with his strides, so Indra, too, is accorded the same function. But it was Indra's battle against the demon Vṛtra that epitomized the battle for light and existence over darkness and chaos. The name Vṛtra comes from the root *vṛ*, which has basic meanings of resistance and obstruction or covering up of something.[139] Did the Indra-Vṛtra myth arise from the obstructions caused to the migrating Āryans by their enemies, Indra being the warrior god who symbolized and realized success against them? Vṛtra was, indeed, called a *Dasyu* and the theory is not without some justification. Vṛtra was a demonic serpent that obstructed the waters of life (perhaps the rains) that were pent up on the mountains by his coiled body, or entrapped in his belly according to some versions. Indra in an intensive battle slew the serpent with his thunderbolt and released the waters and forces of life, permitting the creation of the world, and of light – the sun, the sky and the dawn – from darkness. The myth can be taken as symbolic of creation from potentialities held in non-existence (*asat*) with Indra as the force behind existence (*sat*), releasing those potentialities and all manifest phenomena in the waters of life. On the other hand, it may be indicative of the coming of life-giving rains from the melting mountain snows, or the release of the rains from dark, foreboding clouds since it was a repeated action of Indra, not just an action in time.

1:185 asks which of Heaven and Earth was the earlier. Heaven, Dyāvā or Dyaus, and Earth, Pṛthivī, are depicted as the originators of the world in several hymns of the *Ṛg Veda*. Dyaus (compare Gk. Zeus) was an ancient sky deity that may well go back to the Indo-European era. He is Father Sky, Dyaus Pitṛ. Earth, the fecund and fruitful Mother was impregnated by the Father, so suggesting the union of the two as Dyāvapṛthivī, followed by their subsequent separation in order to form Heaven/Sky and Earth. With Dyaus and Pṛthivī we have perhaps the earliest concept of creation that considerably pre-dates the *Ṛg Veda*, a point supported by an offering to the pair before ploughing and, therefore, connected with popular religion and agriculture, probably from a very early time.[140] The two deities were said to have created the gods but also, paradoxically, to have been created by them. "Together", wrote David Kinsley, "they represent a wide, firm realm of abundance and safety, a realm pervaded by order (*ṛta*), which they strengthen and nourish."[141] They may be depicted as one androgynous being, as separate male and female, or even as two sisters. Dyaus is never mentioned unless it is with his dual Pṛthivī whereas she appears independently, especially in the *Atharva Veda*. Dyaus and Pṛthivī are immortalized in the marriage vows: "I am the sky and you are the earth", representing the inseparability of a wedded couple. Neither had sufficient characteristics to remain prominent and Dyaus, though having a creative role here, was eclipsed by Varuṇa as a rising deity. Pṛthivī, however, is still featured in some aspects of Hinduism today.

3:31 has the god Indra rending open a cave in which cows were enclosed. Wendy Doniger interprets this myth on a number of levels, as expressive of successful Āryan cattle raids; birth from the womb; rains after drought; finding and creating the rays of the sun after darkness.[142]

10:10 rejects the origin of the world in the combining of Yama and Yamī, the brother and sister of Iranian mythology but occasionally in the *Ṛg Veda* we find the idea of primeval incest as the origin of the world – an original male and female that must have seemed thoroughly logical to all ancients.

10:71 and **72** find Bṛhaspati, also occasionally identified as Brahmaṇaspati ("Lord of Prayer")[143] and Vācaspati, as the originator of speech and prayer and thence of the ritual sacrifice and the sounds of the ritual. He was at once the divine priest as Bṛhaspati, and the prayer of the priest as Brahmaṇaspati and the one that enabled ritual to be effective. **10:72** is an interesting creation hymn because it explores a number of creative sources rather than being definitive about one. Alongside existence emerging from non-existence, *sat* from *asat*, we find Brahmaṇaspati firing and smelting creation like a blacksmith. According to this hymn, too, Aditi, the non-existent, gave birth to the earth and sky and, paradoxically, she gave birth to Daksa, who was also her father, and she had seven main sons. In 10:13:4, Bṛhaspati is identified as the sacrificed cosmic Puruṣa of the *Puruṣa-sūkta* hymn, which I shall examine below, and so was a late god. In a mythical creative scene, Bṛhaspati was said to have released life-giving cows from caves in the mountains (2:23:18 and 4:50:5) – a symbolic action that brought light from darkness. In the name Brahmaṇaspati, we have the forerunner of the later Brahman as the ultimate Reality, but beyond the *Ṛg Veda*, this god ceased to have any identity.

10:81 and **10:82** posit a divine architect, Viśvakarman, "All-Maker" as a sacrificial divine being who crafted the universe. He was a sculptor, or a blacksmith smelting the world, or even a carpenter, though despite such anthropomorphic characteristics, he was unfathomable. It was he who separated Heaven and Earth but how he created remains a mystery, though his own volition seems to have begun the process. In 10:82, he seems to have preceded even the One. Thus, in this late hymn, he seems to be projected as the most superior of the gods, though he also arose from the world egg that floated on the waters of chaos. He was omnipotent and the gods were dependent on him for their names and, therefore, characters. He was sometimes identified with Brahmaṇaspati and, later, with Prajāpati.

10:90 is the famous *Puruṣa-sūkta* that is often cited as providing the origin of the four classes.[144] It is obviously a late hymn, since the *Ṛg Veda* has no concept of the four classes other than this hymn. It was the sacrifice of a gigantic cosmic man that brought about all aspects in the created world. The concept of a sacrificed giant man/divine being was probably an old one going well back to Indo-European times.[145] What is particularly interesting about the hymn is that the created world was only one quarter of the sacrificed Puruṣa. The other three quarters were concealed, risen upwards. It was a pantheistic concept of a transcendent creature part of which is the whole world, enough so to make the universe part of the divine body. The divine and human worlds were intimately connected, indeed unified. Hopkins makes the valid point about such connection that it united realities, which suggests that knowledge of one provides knowledge of others "since they are linked by systematic identities".[146] The interrelation of *Vedic mantras* and chants both emerging from Puruṣa, then being presented back to the primal sacrificed being through ritual is a splendid example of the reciprocity behind all sacrifice. The belief that the microcosm was a mirror of the macrocosm and that the sacrifice on Earth was the same as the original divine sacrifice united Heaven and Earth in a profound way by replicating the original creative sacrifice in *yajña*: it also reinforced the importance and effectiveness of sacrifice on Earth as the legitimate and correct religious pathway in *Vedic* experience.

10:121 posits an unknown creator, "Who", or *Ka* in Sanskrit, as an attempt to speculate on the originator of the universe. This creator was called Hiraṇya-garbha, "Golden Womb" or "Golden Germ", a "Golden Embryo". It is he who made the dome of the sky, separating it from the earth with its intermediate space and creating the waters on Earth. It is the waters that become pregnant with all things. The whole tone of the hymn, however, is one addressed to Hiraṇya-garbha as an unknown god, though right at the end of the hymn he is also identified as Prajāpati, the "Lord of Creatures". Prajāpati, while relatively unimportant in the *Ṛg Veda* where the name is only mentioned five times, became increasingly central as a creator god. He is identified as Puruṣa in the *Brāhmaṇas* where he is a sacrificial being that is reconstituted and made whole, just as creation has to be made whole through *yajña*. Thus, Prajāpati became a personification of ritual sacrifice.[147] The title Prajāpati was one given to a number of deities in earlier hymns but was later elevated to become the name of a supreme god, the creator and preserver of all gods and creatures.

10:125:7–8 assigns the source of creation to the goddess Vāc, the goddess of speech, who originated in the heavenly waters, created all creatures and was the means by which all was interconnected.

10:130 sees creation as a woven sacrifice by which the sacrificed cosmic Puruṣa created the world as the warp and weft of a cloth.

10:190 finds heat, *tapas*, as the source of creation. From it was born *ṛta* and Truth, *satya*. *Tapas* here was essentially the *energy* of creation, the dynamic force that burst out and made creation possible. From *tapas* came night, the waters, the year, sun, moon, heaven, earth, the sky and light. In 10:129:3 we find *tapas* emerging from the One: "In the beginning, darkness was obscured by darkness; all was water, indiscriminate. Then, stirring, that which was hidden in the void – the One – emerged through *tapas*."[148] Cosmic *tapas* became replicated in sacrificial ritual and in the kind of ascetic fervour that could produce immense power not only for the gods, but also for mortals.

All these varied accounts of creation were underpinned by the sacrifices that were believed to perpetuate creation. The gods themselves sacrificed and so human beings, too, were expected to do the same in order to participate in the divine world and the created universe. The cosmic law that was *ṛta* ensured the connective balances between sacrificial ritual and the divine world, both sustaining the universe and recreating it each time *yajña* was performed to establish Truth and order as opposed to death and chaos. *Yajña* was the medium for the continuation of existence, conducted according to the imaginations of the seers who visualized the depths of Reality, leaving the priests to articulate their hymns in perpetual ritual that ensured the continued renewal of creation.

Vedic deities

The deities that were to become central to Hinduism barely feature in the *Vedas*. I dealt with them in Volume I – Viṣṇu, Śiva and the Śāktism that elevated the divine in female form[149] – and it is not my intention to deal with these deities here. *Vedic* deities were the focus of *yajña* in the early period but became secondary to it as time went on. Some deities were physically and anthropomorphically portrayed though at the same time their essence and nature tended to be more important than their physical forms. Hiriyanna termed this "incomplete personalization".[150] This is an important point in that the lack of concrete definition made possible more philosophical trends concerning the concept of deity in the later *Vedic* period. The deities were *devas*, "shining, luminous ones" and they symbolized for the most part, though not exclusively so, natural forces like thunder, lightning, rain, the dawn, fire, wind, the sun and also such things as speech and creativity. Nevertheless, they were projections of mortal personalities so they ate, drank, quarrelled, fought, and were capable of being kind or vengeful, but as powerful beings that influenced the lives of humans they were to be propitiated. There was an intimacy between deities and humans that stemmed from reciprocal interaction based on needs, and deities were often referred to as "father" or "brother" suggestive of reciprocated fondness. Some of the *Vedic* deities had a long pre-history, some being even Indo-European in origin. Importantly, deities did not necessarily remain the same in nature during the evolution of their identities and they were in many ways unified despite their diverse qualities. All were linked to sacrificial ritual, to *yajña*, and were dependent on it in the same way that mortals and the manifest world were dependent on the deities. There are all kinds of myths about how the gods came into being but most of them make deities a secondary stage in the creative process. We must reckon, too, with different tribes having different gods and amalgamation of tribes affecting the status of some of the gods: some disappeared and others rose to greatness. Some had to earn their immortality or have it granted by other deities.

The existence of so many deities might suggest that *Vedic* religion was polytheistic. If it was in any way polytheistic it was no ordinary polytheism. We do not find a divine hierarchical family and clear demarcations and rankings of personalities amongst the deities. A deity may be supreme in one instance and insignificant in another: when supreme, there are hints of monotheism, though this was never developed fully in the *Vedas*. *Vedic* worshippers saw no contradiction in focusing on one deity and temporarily neglecting others. Some have accepted *henotheism* (or *kathenotheism*) as an appropriate term for such a tendency, or a "kind of serial monotheism".[151] There are hints, too, of the unity of the gods in a kind of monism. *Ṛg Veda* 1:164:46 states: "They call it Indra, Mitra, Varuṇa, Agni, and it is the heavenly bird that flies. The wise speak of what is One in many ways; they call it Agni, Yama, Mātariśvan."[152] However, the plurality of the universe was generally accepted by the *Vedas*; there may have been interconnection between the divine and human realms but there was not total monism. There is, in fact, not one system of belief that can be attributed to the *Ṛg Veda*, but what is certainly there is the foundation for the development of monism that was to come with the *Vedānta*, the end of the *Veda*.

The move towards a unity of deities was the result of a search for the creative power that caused the gods to exist. Given that deities could be joined together in a fused, assimilative nature with similar or the same functions at times, it was not difficult to view all the deities as part of the same fundamental power. This tendency hints occasionally at pantheism as in *Ṛg Veda* 3:64:8, for example, which states: "One All is Lord of what is fixed and moving, that walks, that flies, this multiform creation."[153] Here, the reality behind all was a unity that informed everything. We have seen, too, the panentheism suggested by the *Puruṣa-sūkta* hymn where the reality of the sacrificed primal being was greater than all he created. The move towards unity and a "One" divine neuter from which all the deities emanated was enhanced by the blurred distinctions between the deities and by the fluidity of their functions and natures. In *Ṛg Veda* 2:1, Agni the god of fire is identified with the gods Indra, Viṣṇu, Brahmaṇaspati, Varuṇa, Aryaman, Rudra and even with the collective group of *Maruts*. At other times, Indra is the greatest of all the gods and takes on their identities more than any other deity. In 2:3–7 he is identified with as many as twelve gods and five goddesses. Inevitably, given the functions of the deities as personifications of aspects of nature, there would have been overlapping of those connected with rain and storm, with lightning and thunder, and at the same time, they may be sufficiently impersonal for distinctions to blur: Agni as fire, for example, was connected with lightning and with the sun. There was also an interconnection and interdependency of the deities and each, at times, had to submit to another. Such characteristics of *Vedic* deities readily show that polytheism is not *per se* easily used as a designation for *Vedic* gods and goddesses and this fact allowed a certain levelling of all the deities to take place, a characteristic that encouraged speculation on the Source behind them that emerged as "That One". Multiplicity became underpinned by unity, a philosophical move also made possible because of the thin level of anthropomorphism ascribed to deities: indeed, some were simply no more than abstract names.

The deities were characterized mainly in three groups corresponding to the three levels of reality of celestial (as Dyaus, Varuṇa, Mitra, Viṣṇu, Sūrya, Savitṛ, Pūṣan, Uṣas and Rātrī), sky or atmospheric (deities of the natural world like Indra and Vāyu and the *Maruts*), and terrestrial (as Pṛthivī, Agni and Soma). Between them, the deities fashioned the heavens and the earth and were the hidden forces behind all nature, though *ṛta* informed their natures and their manifestations in nature. It was the *ṛṣis* who were able to visualize their inner natures and one of their great achievements was to avoid the kind of intense anthropomorphic description of the deities that solidified and petrified their natures, preventing evolution of the concept of deity. Nevertheless, as projections of the human mind, the deities ate the same foods as humans, wore radiant garments, rode in chariots and were often formed like humans. On the other hand, the tongue of Agni was flame, the arms of Sūrya, the sun deity, rays of light. While the deities provided answers to natural phenomena, they were not confined to them, remaining too fluid and blurred to be over-specified as nature deities. They also had characteristics of power, luminosity, wisdom, that were general to all gods and that overarched their associations with nature. Their relationship with humanity was a mainly benevolent one supplying the daily needs of *Vedic* man from the pragmatic to the cosmic.

Opposing the *devas* were the *asuras*, demons, those that obstructed light, life and creation. The term *asura* is cognate with Old-Iranian *ahura* and may even be Indo-European and an ancient term for a deity.[154] Since the epitome of deity in the *Avesta* is the highest deity, Ahura Mazdā, *asuras* were once not demons but gods. Indeed, in the *Ṛg Veda* we sometimes find a deity depicted as both *deva* and *asura*. Be that as it may, in time – and for no clear reason – Hindu *devas* (Iranian *daevas*) became gods, and *asuras* became demons in contradistinction to Iranian tradition where Ahura Mazdā became the sole God/*ahura* and all other deities sank to the level of demons/*daevas*. Occasionally in the Hindu texts the distinction between gods and demons is blurred, especially since the demons could, at times, behave more morally than the gods and the morality of the gods could on occasion be wanting. By the time of the *Atharva Veda*, however, the *asuras* were generally assigned to the realm of demons that battled continually against the gods. There may be some connection between the derogatory use of *asuras* as a synonym of *Dasyus* and *Dānavas*, both these last being enemies of the Āryans. The *Dānavas* were sons of Danu, a demoness, and their leader was Vṛtra, so they were associated with chaos, constraint, obstruction and death. They were in opposition to the *Ādityas*, sons of Aditi who were forces of light, life, vitality and liberating experience. The constant battles between *devas* and *Ādityas* on the one hand and their enemies, the *Dasyus*, *Dānavas* and their like, pervades Hindu mythology to the present day.

Gods

To do justice to the plethora of *Vedic* deities would need more space than I have here. I shall, therefore, give only a brief indication of the major gods and, later, goddesses, the latter being far fewer in number. I have deliberately excluded any discussion of Rudra and Viṣṇu who appeared at length in Volume I.[155] What I want to do now, therefore, is highlight the main deities, for the most part those that are featured in the *Ṛg Veda*.

Indra

Of all the gods, Indra is the one praised the most by the seers in the two hundred and fifty hymns dedicated entirely to him. He is also mentioned in many others. The name is variously derived: a root "to swell" may refer to his bringing forth the swelling waters in creation (10:121:9); or "to shine", may refer perhaps to the self-luminous nature of Indra; the name may mean "Lord" or "King", since Indra is the King of the gods. He may be an ancient deity, since a demon of the same name is found in the Iranian *Avesta*, demoted, perhaps, from the status of a god, and Michael Witzel thinks he may go back as far as Indo-European or earlier.[156] Epithets of the god are bountiful, referring to his power; greatness; wisdom; his role in creation; his defeat of the *Dasyus* and enemies of the Āryans; his warrior strength and skill; and his acquisition of booty as a culture hero. Indra personified the Āryan warrior with his strength, manliness, his quaffing of *soma* and his sexual prowess with women for whom he bestowed fertility. His creative power is epitomized in the slaying of the demon Vṛtra, but Indra also accomplished things through power of the mind

(1:165:10), with energies expanding out from his own self to create forms: indeed, he was able to take any form at will. There is occasionally the idea that Indra uses his special mysterious power of *māyā* to become multiform in the world (3:53:8 and 6:47:18), giving us another early concept of the plurality of the world emanating from a single source.

Indra was associated with life-giving rains and the thunderbolt, the *vajra* (probably lightning), so he was clearly a god of the atmosphere but the most important and prestigious of such gods and, given his warrior nature, probably the most anthropomorphized, the *Ṛg Veda* being replete with descriptions of him. Thus, he had a humanized corporeal form, though a gigantic belly so that he could drink one or several lakes of *soma*. Later texts will portray him as having a horrendous hangover! If he ate, it was the bull or buffalo that he best liked. Perhaps it was his anthropomorphic character that made him on occasion the only *Vedic* deity to be immoral: he killed his father, for example, after stealing his *soma*, and he was quick to become angry, even with his fellow gods. On the other hand, we might see such actions as symbolic of the renewal of creative life at the time of the spring rains and the overcoming of any dark elemental forces. Indra was an advocate of truth and, therefore, began to usurp the control Varuṇa had over cause and effect and the laws of the universe as *ṛta*. Clearly, this was a god who was cosmic and earthly. He was cosmic in that he brought the potential for creation into being, and he was of such stature that Heaven and Earth would not even fit around him as a girdle. At times he was portrayed as begetting the sun and the dawn and as creating their pathways. Yet he was earthly as a vegetation god in that he brought the rains necessary for fertile growth and agricultural prosperity, and he overcame drought: *Vedic* peoples certainly had need of a god of rain. Indra was earthly, too, because as a kind of culture hero he supported warriors in battle against non-Āryans and was with them on the battlefield: Keay rather aptly calls him the "bellicose and bloodthirsty Mars of the Aryan pantheon".[157] On a softer side, he was father, mother and brother to his worshippers and could be jovial and very human, being generous and compassionate to those who reached out to him. Indra was an archetypal hero, an earthy god and the destroyer of foes, both human and demon without the niceties of correct behaviour. He fulfilled Āryan needs for rain and success in battle by fair means or foul.

As priestly roles in the sacrificial rituals became more and more intense and more meticulous, the gods directly associated with sacrifice retained their importance, whereas a god like Indra, though he continued to receive sacrifices, became more peripheral, perhaps, too, because a belligerent and bellicose god was less needed in more settled times. Since he was a god of warriors – of *Kṣatriyas* – he was less acceptable in time to the *Brāhmin* elite and so declined in prestige, to be replaced by other gods pertinent to other needs. However, unlike many of the *Vedic* gods, Indra was entrenched in many myths and his mythological persona continued throughout Hinduism's long history, primarily as a rain god and as ruler of Heaven, even though his role was supplanted by Viṣṇu. Indra served a specific purpose for the Āryans as Bhattacharji aptly comments: "Indra's power lies in his being the culture-hero of the Vedic Aryans. They needed a god in whom they could project their aspirations and experiences, a god who symbolized their national dreams. They created Indra in their own image, and he grew with them in stature and power. Thus Indra appears as the national hero-god of the *Vedic* Aryans. He shares their experiences and is a pioneer of the advancing hordes of the Aryans. But simultaneously with his mundane career he symbolizes the cosmic creator."[158]

Agni

Agni, the god of fire, was probably an ancient god that pre-dated the Āryans given the importance of fire in the sacrificial rituals, and the cognates English *ignite* and Latin *ignis*, suggestive of an Indo-European origin, though he is not featured in Indo-Iranian sources. It was Agni that transported offerings to the gods. Essentially, Agni was a terrestrial god but he had cosmic functions also and moved between Heaven and Earth as much as *vice versa.* His terrestrial character was exemplified in his epithet as Vaiśvānara, "pertaining to all men", for no one can avoid fire in its domestic setting or in sacrificial ritual, but as Agni, he represented cosmic and terrestrial roles. Since the sun provides heat, he was associated with it and with lightning, but he dwelt also intimately at the hearth of the home as the friend of the household. There are different accounts of his birth but three main myths depict the origins of Agni; from two sticks rubbed together, the upper being the male and the lower female; from waters where he emerged from an embryo, a point that makes him also associated with clouds; from Heaven, where he was the rays of the sun. He is the second most important deity in the *Ṛg Veda* and it is hymns to Agni that open that text.

Like other deities, Agni was the destroyer of dark forces and demons and he was often petitioned against enemies on the one hand, or for blessings on the other. But it was his inner essence that attracted the *Vedic* poets, his divine energy and power that was present in all forms of heat and fire. The miracle of Agni was that he could be visibly present in so many places and in so many forms simultaneously. He provided vital energy for life, not only in the rays of the sun, but he was believed to be present in food and, thus, in the process of combustion by which food is transformed within the human being to form vital energy. When he burned a sacrificial offering of any kind, he changed it from gross form to subtle spiritual substance that was able to be transported to and sustain the gods. Because he was so ubiquitous, Agni was a unifying and interconnecting force in the universe and it was he that united the divine and human worlds like no other deity, interceding between gods and men to bring positive effects. Agni was the role model for the priests: just as they were the intermediaries for worshippers so Agni was the intermediary for the priests. Agni sometimes brought the deities to the sacrifice and at other times conveyed the sacrifice to them: in this way, he was a messenger between priests and gods. Another of his roles was to burn up the bodies of the dead, so releasing the soul for a life with the Fathers: again, he was an intermediary here, transforming in order to unify.

There is a sense in all the functions of Agni that he made things right; he maintained true causes and effects, what is right, or *dharma*: indeed, Agni was said to be the firstborn of *ṛta*. His ubiquitous nature was enhanced by his birth from sticks, which made him present in all wood, and his connection with waters made him present in all plants because of the streams and rivulets that pepper the earth. He traversed Earth, atmosphere and skies with ease, and was omnipresent in the three, linking them and shaping himself to become all forms of fire and heat. Since fire illuminates, Agni could see all, know all and connect all. Zaehner pointed out that Agni united dualities for he was ancient and yet young; mighty and yet humble at the hearth of the home; immense in size and yet very small, "uniting within himself the opposites in a manner that was later to become utterly characteristic of Hindu thought".[159] As both fire and the deity within it, Agni continuously vibrated between the two, something Laurie

Patton ascribed to "the genius of Vedic poetry":[160] indeed, Agni, it seems to me, is the most profound of all the *Vedic* deities, especially since he is the one that lasts through time. Agni was the centre between dualities, the centre of the sacrifice and the centre, the navel, of the earth as priest of the deities and the central and pivotal deity of the priests. He was brightness and yet blackness in forest fires, the sun in the day and the moon at night, the giver of form in life but he was also the devourer at death – truly, a god that united dualities. His presence is still believed to be there today in many rituals and especially in life-cycle rites.

Soma

Soma was a terrestrial god, he who gave his name to the intoxicating and invigorating *soma* juice used during ritual both as an offering to the gods and to heighten the consciousness of the priests and sacrificers. Just as Agni was fire, so Soma was the juice or, more pertinently, the plant, though Agni was less tied to the natural phenomenon of fire, while Soma's presence was more confined to the complicated process of pressing *soma.* The god did, however, have some wider function in connection with the liquidity of streams and rains that were likened to the liquid juice and so he was often associated with water as the essence of waters. Soma roared or bellowed like a bull, a simile believed to reflect the trickling of the pressed *soma* juice. Since Indra was the greatest drinker of *soma* of all the gods, Soma's character was often aligned with the warrior aspect of Indra. And since both Soma and Agni had to be present at the sacrifices, they were also concomitant with each other, "Soma is the fiery fluid and Agni the fluid fire" as Doniger puts it.[161] Sometimes connected (and later identified) with the moon, which itself was also connected with plants and immortality, Soma was the source of immortality and of the consciousness and spiritual inspiration that wins it. His nature was such that he was scarcely anthropomorphized and epithets of the god had as much to do with the plant *soma* as the deity. Hence, the yellowness of the juice or plant made Soma like the sun that streamed from Heaven.

Varuṇa

The nature and origins of the celestial King of the gods, Varuṇa, are somewhat mysterious. While scarcely venerated singly and not featuring widely in the hymns of the *Ṛg Veda*, Varuṇa was, nevertheless, an extremely important deity, at least in the early *Vedic* period. He was an awesome god in the *Ṛg Veda*, one before whom humility was essential and Bhattacharji believed that in this god there was something of a "primitive monotheism" because of his supreme nature.[162] His name may be derived from a root *vṛ*, suggestive of covering, encompassing or enveloping,[163] and what he encompassed was the whole of the earth as a celestial sky god and also cosmic law, *ṛta.* Varuṇa was the guardian of *ṛta* (though there were occasions when he himself offended it, being somewhat mischievous of nature). Essentially, he was associated with the cause and effect and rhythm of all things: he caused the rivers to flow, the sun, the moon and the stars to shine, cows to have milk, horses to have speed, and wind (his breath), to rustle the trees. When two plotted in secret, Varuṇa was there as the third. All this was done by *māyā*, the concealed, mysterious, supernatural and extraordinary power by which he caused all things to be in the right place and to function properly. The laws of the universe were put in place by him and could not be altered: he held sky and earth apart and set the sun in its pathway. Varuṇa saw everything, from the flight of a bird, the wink of an eye, and the paths of ships at sea, to the actions of deities and humans and so he was the god that controlled morality and punished or rewarded according to good or evil actions. The sun was his eye and saw all, though he had many other spies.

Yet Varuṇa was a compassionate god who could forgive, and many of the hymns that mention him do so in connection with forgiveness for some misdemeanour (like cheating in gambling), or even confession for some transgression or carelessness that is unknown to the worshipper. There are strong similarities with Iranian Ahura Mazdā, suggestive that Varuṇa was a very ancient god, though there are no myths associated with the latter. Both are given the title *Asura*,[164] and the Greek sky god Ouranos, with whom his name is cognate, suggests an Indo-European origin. Parpola believes he was the main god of the *Dasyus*.[165] Since he was associated with the *ṛṣi* Vasiṣṭha, Varuṇa may well have been the god of that clan.[166] Varuṇa had few anthropomorphic characteristics, though he lived in a celestial palace and dressed in golden garments as befitted his status as monarch of gods and men. He had a thousand eyes, which were probably the stars – also his spies – but he attended the sacrifices, sitting on the special grass provided for the deities. Although Varuṇa was a celestial god, he was also a god of the celestial waters and, thus, of rain. Later, he became associated with waters in general as lord of waters. His connection with the sea suggested to Parpola that he was associated with fish and aquatic creatures.[167]

I said earlier that political affiliations between tribes correlated with the rise and demise of deities. This seemed to be the case with Varuṇa and in 10:124 of the *Ṛg Veda* an explicit statement of preference for Indra rather than Varuṇa is given by the seer of the hymn – an open transference of allegiance that measured the decline of Varuṇa. In this late book of the *Ṛg Veda* he barely appears and Indra becomes by far the greater, leaving the once monarch of men and gods in obscurity and, where evident, he lapsed into a darker, even malevolent, god more associated with punishment and sub-normality than beneficence. It may well have been the case, as Bhattacharji suggested, that the lofty and passive nature of Varuṇa gave way to a more dynamic and engaged god like Indra when the Āryans needed to fight and destroy their enemies, or just steal their cattle.[168]

Other gods

A few other gods need mention here. One is the celestial god Mitra, a god often combined with Varuṇa who appears to have adopted many of the characteristics and functions of this ancient god. Only one hymn (3:59) is dedicated to Mitra in the *Ṛg Veda* despite his long pre-history. He is clearly to be linked with the Iranian god Mithra both possibly connected with light and the sun. Mitra is also associated with contracts, alliances and agreements between individuals, tribes and clans, and vows between people – in short, truth in all its mundane applications. There is a correlation, too, between Iranian Ahura and Mithra and *Vedic* Varuṇa and Mitra. Less severe than Varuṇa, Mitra was the friend of *Vedic* people despite his role in assisting Varuṇa in upholding *ṛta*. If Varuṇa and Mitra were once associated with the natural element of the sun, neither remained a nature deity exclusively, which is a good reminder that *Vedic* deities cannot be solely described as nature gods. The two were, however, responsible for the sun rising according to some hymns (e.g. 4:16). It is mainly together that they were invoked in numerous *Ṛg Vedic* hymns, though there are a few hundred instances where Mitra is mentioned alone. The *māyā*, mysterious power, of these two gods combined was considerable, stretching in every direction. Since Varuṇa was connected with the waters, together, he and Mitra were invoked to bestow rain, soaking the ground for pasture and creating the clouds that brought rain, free-flowing rivers and streams. As time went by, just as Varuṇa became only lord of the waters, so Mitra, too, declined and became little more than a name.

Many gods were associated with the sun. Two, in particular, I want to mention here, Savitṛ and Sūrya. These celestial gods were clearly personifications of aspects of nature and were not at all anthropomorphized. They may have had slightly different functions at times, golden Savitṛ being the life-giving rays of the sun especially at dawn and sunset, and Sūrya being the sun itself, that which, rising itself, impelled action on Earth. Sūrya is sometimes described as a bird in flight, a white steed, a bright gem or a wheel but his most natural descriptor was as an eye that saw all and knew all. This was a gracious god that gave life and health, driving away sickness and evil and he was frequently associated with other gods. Savitṛ had a similar role. The *Gāyatrī -Mantra* of the *Ṛg Veda* (3:62:10) is recited each day by devout Hindus when beginning and ending the day: "Let us meditate on the lovely splendour of the god Savitṛ; may he inspire our thoughts." Thus, Savitṛ inspires the first ritual of the day as well as human consciousness and motivation. Savitṛ, too, was besought to take away people's transgressions, to revivify, keep rivers on their true courses and he was believed to rule the waters and winds. Like Sūrya, Savitṛ, whose name means "inciter", "stimulator", sends the motivation for action, but perhaps more so than Sūrya. It is easy to see how the functions of the two gods overlapped and how they could also combine with other gods.

A clear atmospheric nature god was Vāyu, the god of wind. This free-roaming god was associated with winds and storms and so had some connections with Indra: the two are sometimes featured riding together in a great chariot across the skies, and like Indra, he was a *soma* drinker and first to drink at the sacrifice. Since his name occurs in the Iranian *Avesta*, he was probably an ancient deity. Another wind god was Vāta, who was less anthropomorphically presented than Vāyu and was more the element of wind and its sheer force, but Vāta was also the breath of the gods. He was also connected with healing. It was he that was believed to make red streaks across the sky.

Another semi-god with Iranian connections was Yama, the ruler of the dead. As the first of men, he was the first to die, just as Iranian Yima in the *Avesta*. Two dogs guarded the post-death path corresponding to the four of Yima in the *Avesta*. The first mortal to die, he was able to gather the departed souls who came after him – a positive note, though he became increasingly king of the dead in later texts and judge of the deeds of mortals, separating them for either Heaven or Hell. There is no hint of this kind of retributive thinking in the *Ṛg Veda*. Whereas he began as a lord of paradise, he became lord of an underground realm and while beginning as a mortal, he became immortal. In 10:14 of the *Ṛg Veda* is a funeral hymn asking Yama to come and guide the deceased to the Fathers, the forefathers and ancestors of the living. The presence of this god is a clear indication of the concept of life continuing in some form after death, a concept that became more developed in the *Atharva Veda*.

The gods had an architect, engineer and divine sculptor, Tvaṣṭṛ, who designed such things as Indra's thunderbolt and his own iron axe and that of Brahmaṇaspati. He made the goblets from which the gods drank *soma* and was sometimes presented as the creator who fashioned the world. He became the god that created in the womb, fashioning an embryo in humans and animals. A deity that features much in later myths was Kāma, the god of love and desire. Aside from the erotic character that the god was eventually given, desire was also seen as a creative energy, a primal impulse from which all sprang, as in the *Atharva Veda* 19:52:1. The celestial solar god Pūṣan, "Prosperer", was a guide for all beings but especially travellers for he protected them on journeys. Something of a pastoral god, despite his solar nature, he looked after cattle and their owners. If cattle were lost, Pūṣan would be implored to find them and bring them home. For the man tilling the soil, he made furrows straight, so this god was responsible for successful cultivation, a characteristic that linked him, as so many gods, with rain. He was a generous god and slightly anthropomorphized with braided hair, a beard and no teeth!

Gods and divine beings were sometimes grouped together collectively. Such were the *Aśvins*, "Horsemen", twin, youthful, horse-headed, solar gods who rode through the sky and bestowed good fortune on Earth below. They were present, too, in the *Avesta*, and were probably pre-*Vedic*, even Indo-European. They were helpful to beings, curing illnesses and getting humans out of difficulties. They are another good example of gods who have little to do with nature and natural forces but were associated with mundane agriculture, health and long life, though they were sometimes connected with dawn and dusk. They must have been very popular with ordinary folk and they are mentioned many times in the *Ṛg Veda* as helpers of mortals, particularly as divine physicians. They had a lot to do with honey, which they loved – even their skin was of honey – and they poured out honey for bees and people. They are invoked during the marriage ceremony in the hope of a fruitful union. In short, the *Aśvins* offered help in multiple ways but according to myth were rather too mundane at first – too close to humankind, especially farmers and cattle breeders or anyone in distress – to be allowed at the sacrifices, until they were reconciled by Indra.

A large group (at least twenty-one but sometimes a hundred and eighty) of divine or semi-divine beings that feature in many hymns of the *Ṛg Veda* are the *Maruts*, atmospheric beings that were also mentioned by their other name, *Rudras*. I dealt with these in Volume I in connection with Rudra/Śiva who was said to be their father.[169] They were associated with some good things, milk, honey, rains and good-will. But they were mainly destructive storm gods under the control of Rudra, though their connection with storms, thunder and lightning made them also Indra's companions. And just as Indra was an Āryan warrior, so they, too, were youthful warriors, a "commando group"[170] that spurred Indra to victory. They were boisterous and revealed themselves in the spectacle of the thunder storm and their spears that were lightning, but they were playful and mischievous and liked to sing (the noise of the wind, but also hymns of praise). They were golden bright, shone brilliantly and were fiery (lightning), their main function being seen in the dark thunderclouds that preceded rain, so they were important, like many gods, in providing the waters necessary for fertility of the land and general existence. They had the supportive nature of Indra, but when linked with Rudra they could be a source of evil and display great anger, roaring like Rudra, destroying the sacrifice and being inimical to human and animal life.

Another group of divine beings were the *Ādityas*, sons of Aditi, lists of whom vary, though they were originally seven or eight in number.[171] Major deities as Varuṇa and Mitra are listed among them and like both, the *Ādityas* saw all the good and evil deeds committed by humankind. Another of the group was Aryaman, whose name containing Ārya is suggestive of social customs, clanship and marriage. Others were Bhaga, Dakṣa and Aṇśa and the god of journeys, Pūṣan. The *Ādityas* were kindly beings, protecting those who appealed to them with a good life and prosperity, but punishing their foes. Since they were all associated with light and brightness, they may well have represented stars.[172] The *Ādityas* were continually in battle with the *Dānavas* in post-*Vedic* times, the *Dānavas* having come from the line of Diti, "constricted, bound", the antithesis of the bright, unbounded Aditi.

Popular amongst the general populace must have been *apsaras* and *gandharvas*, the former being connected with water, perhaps symbolizing streams, clouds and mists and the moving atmospheric phenomena that labelled them as dancers for the gods. They were not confined to their watery elements and could mix with men, only to abandon them later, as well as their offspring. They were nymphs and the mistresses of the *gandharvas*, the latter being strange half-human, half animal creatures, though occasionally graceful men, who had considerable control over *soma*. Both *apsaras* and *gandharvas* may have had more affiliation with tribal religions that were not Āryan, speaking to the darker sides of daily life. The *apsaras* could take on any form, could seduce the pious and be very promiscuous. They and their strange accomplices, the *gandharvas*, were somewhat feared. It is interesting that both were thought to stand in trees, reminiscent of the tree deities of the Indus seals, and the *Atharva Veda* 4:37:4 seems to reflect this thought, along with the fear with which they were viewed.[173] Since both are involved with marriage rites, they may well have had a role in fertility.

Goddesses

In comparison to the number of gods in the *Vedas*, goddesses are minimalized. Many goddesses have names simply derived from their spouses and little else to say about them. This has led many authors to dismiss all but a few as unimportant and insignificant. Tracy Pintchman has put a better perspective on these shadowy females of the *Vedic* divine world by saying that they "help lay the foundation for later formulations of the Great Goddess as *prakṛti* and *śakti*".[174] We do not find the dominant, powerful image of the divine in female form that I addressed in Volume I in the form of Dūrga and Kālī as a Great Goddess, or even the dual gentle and terrible aspects of goddesses such as Pārvatī.[175] The portrayal of female divinity in the *Vedas* is of the gentler and benevolent kind. I want to single out four that I think are the most important and add a few details of some others.

Aditi

A hymn of the *Artharva-Veda* (7:6) describes Aditi, the mother of the *Ādityas*, as Heaven, atmosphere, father, son, all gods, five races, what is born and what is to be born. She is referred to as a great mother, with mighty authority, and an expansive and protecting nature. She is well-preserving earth, and the unenvious sky with the wide atmosphere as her lap. Her name, meaning "boundless" is suggestive of infinity and of the hidden infinite expanse that stretches everywhere throughout the cosmos. It is this hidden characteristic that made Aditi an abstract deity and closely associated with the cause–effect rhythms of *ṛta* but, at the same time, she was immanent in all things, indicative of a pantheistic nature of the goddess – no small point, I think, in *Vedic* doctrine, and indicative of the philosophical concept of deity to come. There are no hymns in the *Ṛg Veda* totally dedicated to her, but she is invoked frequently and mentioned in it many times in association with other deities. She could release people from the effects of wrongdoing, in other words, bestowing the freedom that pervades her character. In time, she will become a synonym for Earth but earlier references align her with the luminous brightness of the boundless expanse of the sky. The mother aspect of Aditi sometimes lends her the descriptor of a cow that gave nourishing milk but as mother, she was never a consort of a male god and the descriptor of a nurturing cow providing sustenance for humankind was one of the few features she was given. As such, too, she bestowed happiness and longevity and protected those who besought her. As Earth, she was also associated with fertility and vegetation.

Uṣas

The dawn was praised in the exquisite and auspicious goddess, Uṣas. The hymns to her are full of beauty, "dazzling lyricism",[176] describing her as a lady of light. There are many hymns and references to her in the *Ṛg Veda*:

> Dawn arrives, shining – like a lady of light –
> stirring all creatures to life . . .
> Dawn's light breaks the shadows.
> Her face turned to all things across this wide world,
> she rises in splendour, enwrapped in bright clothes.
> Shining in golden colors, dressed with rays of light,
> she guides forth the day like a cow leads her calves.[177]

Uṣas drove away the darkness of the night, sometimes metaphorically depicted as yoking up her tawny cows or horses to drive across the sky lighting it with sunlight of many colours. She awakened humankind to happiness and the optimism of the day to come, looking into the eyes of everyone and inspiring all, especially the poets though, it seems, she awakened beings to what their natures allowed them to do (*Ṛg Veda* 1:13). She was invoked in ritual before the birds began their morning song or, sometimes, she awakened the worshippers so that morning sacrifices to the gods could take place. But each day, beings grow older, so she wore away their lives, even though she bestowed on them riches. Thus, she was asked for long life since she was the controller of time. We have here, I think, something of the positive and negative dualities that were to be the hallmark of many of the later goddesses both great and minor. By rhythmically recurring, she followed *ṛta*, the cosmic law that ensured she was there at the beginning of each day for eternity, for she was reborn each morning. Since she preceded the sun, she was often linked with sun gods like Sūrya or with the sacrificial fire of the early morn that was Agni. As a thorough nature goddess, she was not destined to survive in anything but name beyond the *Ṛg Veda.*

Sarasvatī

As a goddess of waters and, especially of rivers, Sarasvatī was a deity that remained throughout the history of Hinduism and I featured her in Volume I as an important goddess of learning favoured by students.[178] She began in the ancient *Vedas* as a gracious goddess who bestowed wealth, vitality, treasures, fertility, progeny, immortality and good things. In one hymn of the *Ṛg Veda* (6:61:11–12), it is Sarasvatī who is said to pervade all creation – Earth, atmosphere and the celestial heavens – presenting a powerful image of a *Vedic* goddess. It was in her role as the inspirer and inciter of all eloquent and harmonious speech that she became associated with learning, music and the arts, but harmony was and still is a main attribute of this attractive goddess. Her name is that of the greatest river of the Indus Valley. This was a divine river and she was its goddess in the *Ṛg Veda*, though the river dried up leaving little other than its mark on ancient myth and history and a goddess who metamorphosed into a gracious, benevolent and permanent favourite. Waters as a divine entity in *Vedic* mythology were in essence, feminine, and Sarasvatī was the divine power in them all. Divine water (*ap*) nourishes, cleanses, purifies, heals, maintains life and makes fertile, and it was an important feature through the period of the Indus civilization as well as in subsequent eras. Given these propensities of water, Sarasvatī was occasionally characterized as a goddess that nurtured like a mother, protecting her progeny. Waters, *ap*, have so many forms and all of them have positive, female qualities. In creation myths, waters often feature as the medium for creation as in *Ṛg Veda* 10:121:7–8 where they are the place in which the womb for life produces Agni and the gods. While occasionally Sarasvatī is linked with the god Brahmā, she is normally a virgin goddess whose purity in today's world is represented by her youthful beauty, her white attire and her gracious form.

Vāc

Speech, *vāc*, was personified in the goddess Vāc a goddess of some importance given the central role that prayer and praise of deities had in *Vedic* life, and the fact that it was her voice, sounds and rhythms that, as Sarasvatī with whom she was sometimes identified, inspired the seers. As such, Vāc was one of the few goddesses central to ritual sacrifice. The spoken word for *Vedic* people had a power beyond anything ordinarily imaginable: it was a power of consciousness of the thing spoken of and an intimate knowledge of it. The whole of *yajña* was based on this principle. As Mahony puts it: "Vedic sages not only saw the divine; they also heard it, and they sang what they heard."[179] The seers heard what others did not, understanding the hidden reality of sounds. Sound was one medium by which the world was created and as Mahony says superbly: "Understood in this way, the cosmos was a poetic work of art, for it was, itself, a universal poem."[180] Since *yajña* was the means to ensure the continuation of creation, to recreate over and over again, the sounds that flowed from Vāc could be said to come from an ultimate Reality, a One, behind all the multiplicity and diversity of form. Vāc was the creator of all through sound and yet transcended her creation (by three-quarters) lending to her nature a grounding Reality that was ultimate. From her flowed an unending syllable that allowed the universe to exist (*Ṛg Veda* 1:164:42) and gave order to chaos. She was the mysterious power that made possible hearing, seeing, touching and transferring such sense experience into words. Vāc, who later merged with Sarasvatī, was connected with the primordial waters, where *Ṛg Veda* 10:125 states she originated. This goddess is, I think, significant for the later introspection that searches for an ultimate Reality, especially in the idea that each being dwelt within her, though they did not know it (*Ṛg Veda* 10:125:4), as well as her identity with *ṛta* as a singular source of all things (*Ṛg Veda* 1:164). Her more tangible gifts to *Vedic* people were strength, food and light as sustainer and mother to gods and men. Thus, as Kinsley said of her: "She is, then, more than a kind of artificial construct, a personified abstract."[181] Again, as other goddesses, she was sometimes described as a celestial cow that bestowed the finer inspirations of poets and priests.

Other goddesses

A few other goddesses need some mention here. Pṛthivī or Bhūmi we have already met in the context of creation and her association with Dyaus and there is little else in the *Ṛg Veda* to single her out other than one hymn. But her connections there (5:84) were extended beyond Earth to the atmosphere, where she caused rain from swelling clouds, sometimes as lightning. As Earth, she supported the weight of the mountains and the trees of the forest, and encouraged the fertility of the soil through her many streams. At a few other points in the *Ṛg Veda* Pṛthivī as Earth is the Mother, just as Dyaus is Father and, as such, she is described as both kind and gracious (10:18:10). The *Atharva Veda* (12:1) has a particularly beautiful, long hymn devoted to Pṛthivī where she is mistress of what is and what is to be and a goddess in her own right. There it is said that Pṛthivī created the ocean and rivers, food and agriculture and enlivened whatever breathed and stirred. She kept waters flowing according to their correct courses and made pleasant the hills and snowy mountains. In her role as Mother, mortals were born from her as were creatures. She gave the perfume to flowers and plants, provided herbs, and gave essence to all things. The seasons were her making, the day and night and the years: in short, she was presented as the womb of all manifest matter. Unlike her partner Dyaus, Pṛthivī has been venerated through the long years to the present day. She is especially associated with women's vows, *vratas*, where her nature as nurturing mother is pre-eminent.

The star-studded night sky was the eyes of the goddess Rātrī clothed in the blackness from where she gazed on all around her. *Ṛg Veda* 10:127 tells us that she was immortal, conquering darkness with her lights, driving away the thief and wolves, and guiding beings to safety. She guided all things to rest – the birds to their roosts and humans to their homes – until Dawn, her sister Uṣas, arrived. Both these sisters were daughters of Heaven and Rātrī as Night was not necessarily a dark goddess but was a luminously sparkling one. It was her stars that were the main focus not the blackness on which they were studded. Yet Rātrī had her darker side (*Ṛg Veda* 1:122:2; 10:172:4) that somewhat pre-empted the later dual nature of the Śākta goddesses that I examined in Volume I.[182] This more negative side represented the starless night that was dreaded by those unprotected in it; the gloom and barrenness and hostile forces that *Vedic* people associated with the night.

One goddess that was dark was Nirṛti: the total opposite of *ṛta*, she embodied utter darkness, dissolution, annihilation, death and chaos and was connected with all kinds of inimical forces – decay, decrepitude, dire need, anger, old age. She was considered a sufficient threat for rituals to include the colour black and a good deal of magical and superstitious praxis to offset her sinister presence, or sickness and death of which she was the cause. Women who had not borne a son were believed to be possessed by her. Abstract concepts could also become deified. Faith, Śraddhā, was also personified as a goddess and was formally respected in sacrificial ritual. Other abstract concepts such as Devotion, Favour and Bounty were also deified. The superstitions surrounding the goddess Nirṛti are indicative, it seems to me, of a primitive indigenous tribal culture that is likely to pre-date the Āryans. She faded into insignificance with the rise of the dark Great Goddesses, but localized village goddesses often echo her nature in the darker sides of their characters.

No aspects of nature or life were omitted from divine activity in *Vedic* life. There is even a short hymn in the *Atharva Veda* (7:49) to the spouses of gods, though they are merely named in the feminine form of their male husbands. Just in case any deities were omitted, we find Viśvedevas, "All-gods", celebrated in about forty complete hymns of the *Ṛg Veda*. There may, I think, be a deeper meaning in this collective term that united deities in a kind of Oneness, an idea enhanced, perhaps, by one hymn (6:51:9), in which these collective deities were said to dwell in the singular principle of *ṛta*. And in another hymn to Viśvedevas (1:89), while many of the deities are actually named, it seems, in the final verse that they were all reduced to One as Aditi. As Hiriyanna commented on this unifying aspect of Viśvedevas, "it implies a consciousness of the harmony of purpose underlying the workings of nature".[183] Many of the deities of the *Ṛg Veda* were destined to fade into insignificance in later times: others rose to the fore to fulfil new religious and social needs. The Great Goddess, for example, is not to be found in the *Vedic* texts and was, at that time, still to emerge.

Concluding remarks

This chapter has journeyed a long way from the interface between the Indus civilization, through the long intervening years to the *Vedic* religion and its understanding of all aspects of life as divine activity. Some deities became permanent characters in Hinduism: Indra is a good example of such a god, though his character declined and he became a figure in myth. Sarasvatī is a good example of a goddess whose character changed but who became popular in Hinduism to the present day. Others faded totally into insignificance and some, as Rudra and Viṣṇu, hardly feature in the *Vedas* but become two of the great Gods of Hinduism. Of concepts that link right through the whole of the ancient pre-historical and early historical periods, water in all its forms, but especially rain, is venerated, as is light with its life-giving properties, and fire as a form of light and a medium of sacrifice. The mainstay of *Vedic* religion as *yajña* became critically important, so much so that the priestly actions became the cause–effect mediums for all possibilities, a fact that led the deities to become almost manipulated by the priests and part of a backdrop to developing Hinduism. As to *Vedic* religion *per se* it would have to be admitted that its language and praxis are now regarded as somewhat archaic, even though it is maintained in life-cycle rites and special rituals. But the status of the priests that was so enhanced and became so specialized during *Vedic* times was a lasting legacy.

From a philosophical point of view, the *Vedas* have all the seeds of what was to come. Hiriyanna put this point well when he had this to say about *Vedic* religion: "It signifies a conviction that the visible world is not in itself final and that there is a reality lying hidden in it. It is also at bottom seeking after an explanation of observed facts, implying a belief that every event has a cause; and to believe in the universality of causation is perforce to believe in the uniformity of nature."[184] These are ideas that will come to fruition in the later *Vedic* and post-*Vedic* periods, as we shall see in the chapters that follow. Study of this very early period with its pendulum swings between wide extremes offers a privileged view into ancient thought. In Radhakrishnan's words: "We find a freshness and simplicity and an inexpressible charm as of the breath of the spring or the flower of the morning about these first efforts of the human mind to comprehend and express the mystery of the world."[185] Hinduism still considers the *Vedas* as the foundation of its religious consciousness and self-identity. All that we have studied in this chapter has shaped the Hinduism of today in some form or another. Doniger aptly calls this a "fusion and bricolage".[186] Hints, influences, nuances, shades of many aspects of religious and social living have been added to the melting pot of the many Hinduisms that we have today, some ingredients being clear, others melded and transformed. It is this last sense of transformation of *Vedic* concepts that I want to explore in the next chapter, the end of the *Veda* or *Vedānta*.

3
Vedānta

The latest of the *śruti* literature comes at the end of the *Vedas* and is called just that, *Vedānta* (*Veda* and *anta* "end"). The particularly speculative and mystical nature of much of the literature that comprises the *Vedānta*, the *Upaniṣads*, tends to separate it from the rest of *śruti* literature though the content is far from systematic. While broadly philosophical, the thought contained in the *Upaniṣads* is too experiential in nature to be reasoned philosophy. Early *Upaniṣads* were written at a time when new ideas challenged the old ritualism or sought to view that ritualism in different ways. The search for an ultimate Reality and essence that underpinned all existence was the specific quest of much *Upaniṣadic* thought, and we see in it the ways in which the sages wrestled with that search. Some of the most ancient *Upaniṣads* represent the oldest attempt of humankind to provide a philosophical explanation of the universe, of ultimate Reality, of the nature of the self and the purpose of humankind. The *Bṛhad-āraṇyaka Upaniṣad* expresses this quest in the inspiring words: "From the unreal lead me to the real, from darkness lead me to light, from death lead me to immortality."[1] *Vedānta* also means end of the *Vedas* in the sense of fulfilment and consummation of the *Vedas*, a final teaching: the *Upaniṣads* brought out what was considered the real meaning behind *Vedic* ritual through the pursuit of true knowledge. The *Chāndogya Upaniṣad* (3:5:4) put it thus: "These, clearly, are the very essence of the essences, for the essences are the Vedas and these are their essence. These are, moreover, the immortal nectar of nectars, for the nectars are the Vedas, and these are their nectar."[2] Since the *Upaniṣads* are the only literature pertaining to the *Vedānta* the two terms are synonymous. The importance of *Upaniṣadic* thought in the development of Hinduism is enormous, for it contains most of the seeds of the developed concepts that we associate with Hinduism today – belief in the Absolute of Brahman, concepts of *karma*, *saṃsāra*, *mokṣa*, *dharma*, *ātman* in relation to Brahman and both monistic and theistic developments are just some of the most fundamental.

Relation to the four *Vedas*

Despite the rather different nature of the *Upaniṣads* in relation to the *Vedas*, it has to be remembered that the material of both form the *Veda* or "knowledge" that is *śruti* literature. So while the *Upaniṣads* develop the ideas of the *Vedas* beyond their ritual formalism they should not be seen as isolated from them. Indeed, the subject of *Vedic* ritual is endemic throughout most of the major *Upaniṣads*. The early chapters of the *Chāndogya*, a text associated with the *Sama Veda*, clearly uphold *Vedic* ritual chanting – the "High Chant" as Patrick Olivelle translates *udgītha*,[3] though analogies of aspects of the *Vedas* with manifest phenomena including the human body, its breath and sense functions widens the significance of the chants. *Vedic* deities are linked to the chant, too, clearly recognizing the importance of the *Vedas* as foundational to *Vedāntic* thought. Nor do the *Upaniṣads* disregard the basic *Vedic* proximate goals of man such as wealth, progeny, cattle and a wife, and the kinds of mundane charms that we saw in the last chapter in the context of the *Atharva Veda* continue through the *Upaniṣads*. In short, there is plenty of ritual for worldly aims in the *Upaniṣads*. But it is the more speculative aspects of the *Vedas* that are particularly emphasized in the *Vedānta*: the efficacy of *Vedic* ritual was not rejected, nor were the gods with which it was involved, it was just that there was a search for the Reality that informed them, and a performance of ritual *within* the mind and the body. This was a significant change in that there was transference of overt ritual into internalized mental correlations – a crucial point that informs most *Upaniṣadic* thought. As Thomas Hopkins says of such mental sacrifice: "The performer was thus raised in power and importance to the level of the sacrifice itself. A person of advanced training and knowledge became a creator in his own right; like the Brahman priest he could meditate on the meaning of the sacrifice, search out its hidden truths, and control the universe by the power of his mantras alone."[4] What these words suggest is a significant concentration on the nature of the self and the individual rather than corporate ritual. While both *Veda* and *Vedānta* correlated ritual with the cosmos, the *Vedas* did so externally and the *Upaniṣads* internally.

The fact that the *Upaniṣads* were attached to the *Brāhmaṇas* shows that they were regarded not only as ancient as them but, also, as being in their own way connected to, and explicative of, *Vedic* ritual. The nature of the monotheistic trends of the *Vedas*, I believe, set the stage for a unique development of a totally transcendent Absolute.[5] But, while the philosophical search in the *Vedas* for a Reality behind the deities and existence is extended in the *Upaniṣads*, also evident is a new and profound interest in the nature of the true self. Yet even this inquiry is prefigured to a certain extent in the panentheism of *Vedic* hymns such as the *Puruṣa-sūkta*, in which the self, as all in life, is an emanation of the divine sacrificial being, Puruṣa.[6] The synthesis of these two aspects – Reality and the self – is the particular genius of the *Vedānta*. And in the nature of the inquiry into Reality and self, and the fusion of the two, more introspective and meditative approaches (*upāsanas*) to the *Vedas* were adopted: such trends began in the *Brāhmaṇas* and *Āraṇyakas*, so it is advisable not to divorce the *Upaniṣads* from them. Stephanie Jamison's and Michael Witzel's comment is therefore important in this context: "The Upaniṣads then do not represent a break with the intellectual tradition that precedes them, but rather a heightened continuation of it, using as raw material the religious practices then current."[7]

The *Upaniṣads*

The *Upaniṣads* reflect a long period of compilation preceded by oral tradition. Dating is precarious: in fact, as Olivelle aptly comments, "in reality, any dating of these documents that attempts a precision closer than a few centuries is as stable as a house of cards".[9] The earliest of them are likely to be the *Bṛhad-āraṇyaka* and the *Chāndogya* dated to the seventh or sixth centuries BCE,[10] pre-dating the Buddha, while the latest date to the early centuries CE and even later. About a dozen of the few hundred *Upaniṣads* are the earlier, older, classical *Upaniṣads* that are generally considered to be the most important and have been termed by one writer as "the flower of Vedic thought".[11] A rough estimate of the dating of these principal canonical *Upaniṣads* is as follows.[12] The specific *Veda* to which each is attached is added in parentheses.

Bṛhad-āranyaka (White *Yajur Veda*) and ***Chāndogya*** (*Sāma Veda*)
(prose) 7th to 6th centuries BCE

Taittirīya (Black *Yajur Veda*), ***Aitareya*** (*Ṛg Veda*) and ***Kauṣitaki*** (*Ṛg Veda*)
(prose) 6th to 5th centuries BCE

Keṇa (*Sāma Veda*), ***Kaṭha*** (Black *Yajur Veda*), ***Īśā*** (White *Yajur Veda*), ***Śvetāśvatara*** (Black *Yajur Veda*) and ***Muṇḍaka*** (*Atharva Veda*)
(verse) late centuries BCE

Praśna (*Atharva Veda*) and ***Māṇḍūkya*** (*Atharva Veda*)
(prose) early CE

Some, such as the *Bṛhad-āranyaka* are long, while a *Upaniṣad* such as the *Māṇḍūkya* has only twelve verses.

The meaning of "*upaniṣad*"

The usual translation of the word *upaniṣad* is "sitting close to", presumably a *guru*, in order to hear the wisdom of one who had cognized the truths of the universe. The pupils, *chelas* or *śiṣyas*, sat around the *guru* listening to his teachings and engaging in dialogue with him. The *Upaniṣadic* literature contains a considerable amount of such dialogue between disciple and *guru* and the translation "sitting close to" is therefore an apt one. However, the word *upaniṣad* is a compound one, and the roots that compose it can have a variety of meanings. R. N. Dandekar, for example, suggested a meaning "placing side by side" or "equivalence, correlation", and this would reflect the *Upaniṣadic* theme of equating all things in life as of one fundamental essence.[13] Attractive, too, is the interpretation put forward by Alain Daniélou of a meaning "near approach" to the Absolute, Brahman. This, indeed, would reflect a major trend of *Upaniṣadic* thought.[14] Then, again, the *Upaniṣads* are essentially *esoteric*, hidden or secretive teachings that were only for the initiated, and some disciples had to wait patiently for many years before they were deemed worthy by their teachers to receive knowledge. Paul Deussen, therefore, saw the word *upaniṣad* as denoting the idea of "secret", or "secret teaching", "that which is hidden", *rahasya*.[15] Balancing the secret nature of the teachings, however, is the fact that public debates were frequently the scenarios for their presentation, usually at royal courts. But some teaching had to be done "in private" if a truly secret teaching, a true *upaniṣad*, was about to be divulged.

If something deep had to be taught, teacher and inquirer went apart in secret, though they may have begun discussion in the public arena. However, the teacher–pupil relationship and the forest/wilderness settings for instruction would, I believe, endorse a predominance of secretive and exclusive discourse.[16] The proponent of Advaita Vedānta, Śaṃkara, took the basic meaning from the root *sad*, "to loosen, reach" or "destroy" with the idea of loosening or destroying the ego and ignorance, both of which prevent knowledge of the Absolute and Reality. This is a topic that I shall explore in the following chapter, chapter 4. All these meanings reflect the particular theses of their commentators but, collectively, they highlight well the nature of the speculative ideas of the *Upaniṣads* in meanings that are characterized by a certain overlap of thought.

Composition of the *Upaniṣads*

The early *Upaniṣads* were, as I have said above, one strand of the composite *śruti* literature, but their very nature made them more suitable for the meditative recluse than the worshipping householder. For this reason, they overlap considerably with the *Āranyakas*, the forest traditions, the same more philosophically reflective tenor informing them both. This is seen in the title of the early *Upaniṣad*, the *Bṛhad-āraṇyaka*, a text that is associated with one branch of the *Yajur Veda* and is also the concluding part of the *Śatapatha Brāhmaṇa*. Clearly delineated differences between the *Upaniṣads*, the *Brāhmaṇas* and the *Āranyakas* are simply not there: there is more of a merging together and an overlapping of ideas at the edges.[17] Knowledge imparted in the *Upaniṣads* was probably added to over time, the original teaching being quite brief but profound, and this was then overlaid by the related discourse that took place. One *Upaniṣad* may contain a number of such formulas, which may or may not be contradictory one with another. The composition of the *Upaniṣads*, therefore, is very varied, containing old ideas alongside new ones, the ideas of one teacher alongside those of another, and expositions on the teachings of many *gurus*, so that they end up bafflingly heterogeneous and the record of many varied traditions. They are, as Surendranath Dasgupta said, "collations or compilations of floating monologues, dialogues or anecdotes",[18] or some are simply "flashes of thought" as Mysore Hiriyanna put it.[19] Like the *mantras* of the four *Vedas* they were considered to be timeless and authorless, so the name of each of the early *Upaniṣads* is not derived from a compiler or author, but is the title of an old *Vedic* school or branch (*śakhā*). Each of these schools would have been connected with one or more of the *Upaniṣads* but, in time, the *Upaniṣads* became associated with all schools. Since a good deal of material is common to a number of *Upaniṣads*, it is likely that the compilers drew on the same already existing teachings in bringing together the content of a particular *Upaniṣad*, and earlier ones were used by compilers of later *Upaniṣads*. Further, later ideas may well have been inserted into earlier texts. However, some of the *Upaniṣads* feature sages of great repute such as Uddālaka Āruṇī and Yājñavalkya, and it is likely that these were the original teachers of the ideas associated with them. Most of these teachers would have been of the *Brāhmin* class, but *Kṣatriyas*, especially kings, also seem to have contributed to the philosophical teaching, occasionally to the extent that they are depicted as instructing *Brāhmins*. Some of the debate that entered the *Upaniṣads* would have been conducted in royal courts, famous philosophers being summoned by kings to compete in religious discourse. Tradition, however, retains anonymity of *śruti* literature as essential to the belief in its timeless nature, yet suggests an overall priestly transmission and development. Indeed, we must reckon, I think, with the fact that the Absolute was given a neuter term, Brahman, alongside the masculine *Brāhmin*, so connecting Absolute and priest in a lasting way.

Content of the *Upaniṣads*

From the wide dating and varied composition, then, the content of the *Upaniṣads* is, itself, philosophically varied, and does not reflect homogeneous ideas. Many different solutions are offered to the metaphysical questions raised about the nature of the self, ultimate Reality, knowledge and the nature of the divine, and some texts may be more interested in one of these aspects than in others. The material is sufficiently varied even in one *Upaniṣad* to contain contradictory ideas in this exploration, though they are similar in that they deal with religious experience and spirituality in all its variety. Hiriyanna put it thus: "There are great, almost insurmountable, difficulties in deciding what exactly is the teaching of the Upaniṣads in certain important respects."[20] How far this is true will be exemplified in later chapters when I examine the widely differing philosophies that have the *Upaniṣads* as their foundation. Ultimately, the *Upaniṣads* were based on *Vedic* texts, so that any part of the considerable *Vedic* material could be taken up for discourse, philosophical analysis and discussion. As will be seen, a prominent message of the *Upaniṣads* is a monistic one, but this is by no means the only one in the melting pot of philosophical ideas that informed them.

Intuitive knowledge: *Jñana*

The *Upaniṣads* deal with a quest for Truth that can only be known intuitively and not empirically. They are not, claimed Dasgupta, "reasoned statements, but utterances of truths intuitively perceived or felt as unquestionably real and indubitable, and carrying great force, vigour, and persuasiveness with them".[21] They represent a journey of the inner self rather than the mind, and a quest to find the nature of the self and the means to its liberation from a world of change, finitude and transience. The journey was not to be undertaken by the ordinary person who was necessarily bound to the world. Rather, it was a journey for the initiated, those who already displayed the capabilities of heightened consciousness and intuitive understanding. It was a spiritual journey. It would be to such individuals that the *gurus* would expound their teachings. Such emphasis on intuitive knowledge and understanding in the *Upaniṣads* classifies them as *jñāna-kāṇḍa*, the "knowledge portion" of the *Vedic* material as a whole, as opposed to the ritual-action portion, the *karma-kāṇḍa* of the four *Vedas* and *Brāhmaṇas*. Each supplied a different route to the ultimate goal: *jñāna-mārga*, the path of knowledge; *karma-mārga*, the path of works and actions. Most *Upaniṣads* accepted the *Vedas* as authentic and, therefore, the ritual, *karman*, that they endorsed, though they sought to deepen the meaning of ritual into more esoteric themes especially by symbolically equating aspects of ritual with those of the cosmos and the body. Nevertheless, a text like the theistic *Upaniṣad*, the *Muṇḍaka*, which was connected to the

Atharva Veda, eschewed all forms of *Vedic* ritual as lower knowledge (*aparā vidyā*) in favour of a higher knowledge (*parā vidyā*) of God as Absolute, even calling those who continued sacrificing "imbeciles" (1:2:10). The rejection of ritual and emphasis on knowledge here meant a focus on ascetic disciplined lives of renunciation in forests for its proponents, who claimed to follow true *Vedānta*. In contrast, in the later *Śvetāśvatara* there is something of a symbiosis between the old *Vedic* deities and the ritual they supported and the transcendent, personal God.

As all *śruti* literature, the *Upaniṣads* are considered to be *sanātana*, timeless, and that is why they can only be known intuitively and not in the context of the empirical and finite world. Cognized or "seen" by ancient sages with the heightened consciousness necessary to receive direct revelation, they represented the kind of knowledge that needed comparable levels of consciousness in order to understand them. That is why a *guru* was so fundamental to the imparting of such wisdom, and why only the chosen few were initiated and taught. Some *gurus* required many years of austerities from would-be initiates before initiation. Indeed, Deussen's interpretation of the word *upaniṣad* as "secret", noted above, reflects well the secrecy attached to the knowledge, and its deeply esoteric nature. We should not, then, expect *Upaniṣadic* thought to be consistently clearly articulated, for the *Upaniṣads* often dealt with their material symbolically and were meant as formulas around which a good deal of oral discourse was necessary.

Reality in the *Upaniṣads*

Dealing with the spiritual search for Reality, the *Upaniṣads*, generally, are idealist rather than realist. That is to say they deal with the knowledge experienced deep in the self, and to some extent the mind, rather than with knowledge acquired by the senses. The teaching they contain rests on such experiential foundations and builds on it with metaphors, attractive analogies and parables. The search for a Reality that is ultimate lies at the heart of the *Upaniṣads* and later Hindu philosophy, and I believe Klaus Klostermaier is to the point when he says: "Reality is the term that stands at the centre of all the endeavour of Indian philosophy, the differentiation between the obvious and the real, the conditional and the essential, the apparent and the true."[22] That search for Reality that was ultimate, however, led to very different speculations. In chapter 5, I shall be examining the philosophical system of Sāṃkhya in which the reality of matter and the Reality of spirit are separate and there are a number of passages in the later principal *Upaniṣads* that reflect this view. A thread that is common to most of the principal *Upaniṣads* is the acceptance of the world as a changeable reality at the root of which is a changeless Reality that is the fundamental basis of all: the phenomenal world can have no independent reality apart from this basis. But this is not to say that realism barely features in the *Upaniṣads*. Olivelle points out the "diversity of goals that their authors pursue, chief among which are food, prosperity, power, fame, and a happy afterlife. There are rites to secure greatness, to win a woman's love, to harm the lover of one's wife, to ensure pregnancy, to guard against pregnancy, to assure a safe childbirth – the list can go on".[23] So the *Upaniṣads* have their mundane themes as much as their celebrated flights of metaphysical thought. Indeed, Laurie Patton points out that: "Philosophical ideas for which the Upaniṣads are so famous are linked to crafts, such as pottery and weaving; and luxuries, such as garlands and perfumes, become major images. Courtly images, such as food and drink and singing and music, are crucial for the new Upaniṣadic perspective."[24] Even a sage and teacher as the one in the *Taittirīya Upaniṣad* (1:4) expresses his wish to be prosperous with sheep and cattle, flocks of students, and to be famous among men.

Nevertheless, it is the search for a unified Absolute Reality that is a major theme of the *Upaniṣads*, a search resulting in the articulation of knowledge that is both ultimate and infinite. The very fact that the *Upaniṣadic* sages asked: "From the unreal lead me to the Real" is indicative that some differentiation between the world of the senses and Reality that was ultimate had to be made. At the same time, the exploration of both realities was part of the search and, in the spirit of the *Upaniṣads*, there was also a trend to relate the two to each other in a harmonious whole. But while the two were explored relationally, there seemed to be no desire to make the manifest world with its plurality of forms unreal. Indeed, Reality emerged as that which informed the apparent plurality of all things and it is this thread of thought that pervades *Vedāntic* literature. There are some passages which, as in the *Vedas*, suggested that the ultimate Reality behind the universe was elemental – Air, Water, Fire, Ether. Other early ideas suggested *prāṇa*, "Vital Breath", *manas* "Mind", or the Sun. But what emerged as the main thought in the *Upaniṣads* was the *unified* nature of Reality that underpinned all and remained changeless in all the transience and finitude of existence. It was a Reality that was beyond the senses, a Reality unknowable by ordinary means and yet, since it informed all life and was its fundamental essence, it was intimately present in all things. Nothing could exist outside it and all things took their *raison d'être* from this ultimate Source. So all the souls of existence and the whole of the physical universe were unified in one Reality.

However, as I said above, an *underlying* Reality that is ultimate and changeless suggests that the phenomenal world that we observe, and which is subject to change, is comparatively unreal – either having no reality at all or having a lesser reality. The *Upaniṣads* can support both these concepts though little of the former. They also support a more pantheistic or monistic view of reality, that is to say, the identification of the whole of the cosmos with ultimate Reality, without suggesting a Source that transcends the cosmos by preceding it. There are also theistic threads in the *Upaniṣads*, particularly in the later principal ones, but the main current that unites them is monism, the belief that Reality is one single principle in which all things are at one with, and identical to, another, and all are identical to the ultimate Reality that is their Source. Yet, broadly, these types of belief are united by an *emanationist* view of reality. That is to say, the world is considered, in some way, to have *come forth* from the ultimate Source and to have that ultimate Source as its fundamental essence. As we shall see below, the *Chāndogya* develops this cause–effect view with the Absolute, Brahman, as the ultimate Cause and the world as the effects that emanate from Brahman, just as all things clay come from clay. Like the clay at source, Brahman is the essential Reality from which all named forms occur – a *transformation* of the Cause into effects. Brahman reveals itself in the whole of creation by such transformation of itself though, for much *Upaniṣadic* thought, remains concealed. The link between each entity in the universe and its Source is therefore a profound one, but can be viewed very differently. The *Upaniṣads* and the philosophical schools that base their premises on them seek to answer this particular problem among the many metaphysical questions they raise. Later *Upaniṣads* pick up the term *māyā* from earlier *Vedic* sources and project a more illusory meaning to it, seeing matter as "illusory power", and "the illusionist as the great Lord",[25] but for most, *māyā* is simply "power", though there is no singular meaning given it throughout the *Upaniṣads*. Even so, it is logical to presume that a Reality that is *ultimate* must be in some ways different from that of the transient world. Wendy Doniger puts it thus: "The pluralistic world has a secondary, illusory status in comparison with the enduring, real status of the underlying monistic being."[26] It is to that "underlying monistic being" that I now want to turn.

Brahman

The ultimate Reality, the Source from which all emanates, the unchanging Absolute, as I noted above, is termed *Brahman*.[27] Heinrich Zimmer termed it with some justification, "the most important single concept of Hindu religion".[28] The word *bráhman* was originally associated with "prayer", "sacred utterance", or "utterance of Truth" in the *Vedas*. Indeed, the *Vedas* as sacred utterance are in totality a *bráhman*. The related word *Brāhmanas* denotes the commentaries that pertain to the sacred prayers and devotions of the priests. The divine *Brahman* was a kind of philosophical shift in emphasis of the word, an internalizing of it, and a reflection of the *power* behind the efficacy of prayer and sacrificial ritual. Nevertheless, Brahman as a term does not lose its connection with sound since a synonym of Brahman is the syllable *Oṃ*, a syllable uttered before ritual and a sacred utterance in the same way as a *bráhman* in the earlier sources. Although it is a difficult word to pin down, many suggest Brahman derives from the root *bṛh* "to burst forth", or "to grow, increase",[29] reflecting, perhaps, the emanation of Brahman into the universe as the Ground of all being, as well as the unlimited nature of Brahman. Some suggest a meaning "to be strong".[30] The concept of Brahman as ultimate Reality in the *Upaniṣads* was the result of a long search, which the *Upaniṣads* sometimes reflect with imperfect and inadequate postulations that were eventually cast aside. Brahman was the culmination of a search for the Real behind all things. While ideas such as breath, wind, space, eternity, pure consciousness, gained some credence for a while, they were independently unsatisfactory in finding something true and ultimate that was sufficiently profound and infinite, transcending all. Something or no-thing beyond logical reasoning and inquiries of the mind was necessary.

Whatever Brahman was or was not, as a neuter noun, "It" was mainly felt to be beyond the conceptions of human imagination, "in the dark, great, unmeasured zone of height beyond height, depth beyond depth".[31] It was more the essence behind all, that which was behind breathing, sight, hearing and was the thinking behind thinking (*Bṛhad-āraṇyaka* 4:4:18). In the *Bṛhad-āraṇyaka*, Yājñavalkya had to respond to profound questioning by the clever thinker, Gārgī, notably a woman, indeed, "the feistiest woman in the Upanishads" according to Doniger.[32] Yājñavalkya said of Brahman: "Verily, that Imperishable, O Gārgī, is unseen but is the seer, is unheard but is the hearer, unthought but is the thinker, unknown but is the knower. There is no other seer but this, there is no other hearer but this, there is no other thinker but this, there is no other knower but this!"[33] In the Īśā *Upaniṣad* it says: "It moves – yet it does not move. It's far away – yet it is near at hand! It is within this whole world – yet it's also outside this whole world."[34] It was a Reality, the Real, *satya*, that was indescribable, though could be experienced in the deepest part of the self: something in the depths of the ancient *Upaniṣadic* sages *knew* that it was the highest expression of Reality. Radhakrishnan expressed this superbly:

> The word suggests a fundamental kinship between the aspiring spirit of man and the spirit of the universe which it seeks to attain. The wish to know the Real implies that we know it to some extent. If we do not know anything about it, we cannot even say that it is and that we wish to know it. If we know the Real, it is because the Real knows itself in us. The desire for God, the feeling that we are in a state of exile, implies the reality of God in us, though we cannot tell what it is. All spiritual progress is the growth of half-knowledge into clear illumination. Religious experience is the evidence for the Divine. In our inspired moments we have the feeling that there is a greater reality within us, though we cannot tell what it is.[35]

These words epitomize admirably the fundamental link between the deepest self and the Reality that is ultimate, that is Brahman, the Source of all being, whose manifestation or emanation in the universe gives the cosmos a degree of reality. The *Taittirīya Upaniṣad* says of Brahman: "That from which these beings are born; on which, once born, they live; and into which they pass upon death – seek to perceive that! That is *brahman*."[36] For much *Upaniṣadic* thought, the Cause and Source of the universe, Brahman, is both the active generator of all things and yet is also the passive and unmoved Absolute. Pervading all, Brahman is yet unaffected by all and though the Source of space and time, and of cause and effect, Brahman is beyond both. The *Kena Upaniṣad* says of the totally transcendent Brahman: "Sight does not reach there; neither does thinking or speech. We don't know, we can't perceive how one would point it out."[37] Since Brahman is beyond the limitations of human conception and is a neuter principle, an "It" rather than a he or she, the term "God" is therefore often inapplicable to Brahman. Brahman also transcends the dualities and differentiations in existence. It is not this as opposed to that, light as opposed to dark, good as opposed to evil, and so on. Brahman is *neti neti* "not this, not this".

Brahman is, thus, an abstract principle beyond human comprehension and empirical knowledge. It is *Tat*, simply "*That*", Absolute, and unknowable in the ordinary sense of the word. And yet it is the Source of all because everything emanates from it, is sustained by it, and returns to it. Brahman, therefore, is both Unmanifest and devoid of qualities (*nirguṇa*) and yet manifest in the universe and therefore with qualities (*saguṇa*). *Upaniṣadic* thought is inclined to focus on both these aspects at times. The *nirguṇa* Brahman is mostly depicted in negative terms – Immovable; Imperishable; Invisible; Immortal; Intangible. The Unmanifest and manifest aspects of Brahman are not different, but simply two aspects of Reality, two sides of the same coin – unity in diversity. But the degree to which the world is considered as real will vary, for any linking of the essence of divinity with a world of change and finitude is problematic. This would suggest that Brahman is changeable in its manifest form, and what is subject to change is impermanent and not Absolute. Even if the changing world were considered to be illusionary, that illusionary nature must *also* emanate from Brahman. Conversely, if all form, *rūpa*, is the manifestation of Brahman it must also be real, and because each form has an intrinsic identity given to it through *nāma*, "name", common sense will suggest it is real. These questions of the degree of manifestation of Brahman in the world, alongside the degree of reality ascribed to the world, are two important issues that are dealt with in the philosophical schools.

Related to these difficult questions is also the degree to which Brahman, as the Unmanifest Source of the manifestation of cause–effect processes in the universe, is also bound in those causes and effects. How can effects like you and me, and all other effects in the universe, emanate from the ultimate Cause of Brahman without Brahman, too, being effect as well as cause, and subject to the same changes that bring about effects? Are the changes that occur in the manifestations of Brahman, that is to say in each *rūpa* in existence, only apparent and not real changes, like clay that can become a pot, a jar, a plate and so on? Or are changes from cause to effect *real* changes in every way, so that the effect is something new? These are issues on which the *Upaniṣads* touch, but which, again, the schools of philosophical thought took up more earnestly.

Impersonal and personal Brahman

The two aspects of Brahman – *nirguṇa* and *saguṇa* – gave rise to two different views of Brahman: both feature in the *Vedānta*. The *nirguṇa* Brahman remained the indescribable and impersonal Absolute to which no qualities could be given – a perspective particularly eveident in the *Bṛhad-āraṇyaka Upaniṣad* – but the *saguṇa* Brahman was a more personalized aspect of Brahman, manifested in the forms of deities like Rudra, and referred to as Īśvara "Lord". The impersonal is sometimes referred to as higher Brahman, and the personal form lower Brahman. The distinction between the two is often blurred in the *Upaniṣads*. The *nirguṇa* view of Brahman is of an Absolute in which all dualities cease to exist, it is a "no-thing", a "non-entity" and that is one reason why no attributes or qualities can be assigned to It. Any differentiation between this and that fails to understand the nature of ultimate Reality that is *neti neti*, "not this, not this" or "not so, not so". So Reality here is non-differentiated, that is to say, when we differentiate between this and that we obscure the Real that is not one or the other. The *nirguṇa* Brahman is therefore essential Reality and ultimate knowledge. It is "*That*" from which all springs and so is the ultimate subject in which all knowledge is subsumed as object so that the two are one. Chandradhar Sharma profoundly wrote, "the Absolute is the Existence of all existences, the Truth of all truths, the Reality of all realities".[38] This indicates clearly the *ultimacy* of Brahman, without which, nothing in existence can obtain.

The *saguṇa* Brahman is that aspect of Brahman that is more involved in the manifestation of the universe, that which allows the universe to come forth, that sustains it and that draws it back into itself. The transcendent, *nirguṇa* Brahman may still remain the indescribable force that underpins the *saguṇa* aspect but a more personal Brahman emerges from such a concept and this finds expression in an *Upaniṣad* such as the *Kena* where Brahman makes himself visible to the gods. It is the *saguṇa* Brahman that may more easily be given the term "God" and the personal pronoun "he" or "him". The *saguṇa* Brahman is like clay that gives rise to many articles, the ultimate essence from which all is produced and can be reduced. Like the clay it is the fundamental and *real* nature of the effects or forms that come from it.

Similarly, as we shall see below, Brahman is the reality that informs the self, and is the real Self that acts as the "inner controller", the *antaryāmin*, of each being. Thus, the nature of Brahman as ultimate Reality, as the foundation of the cosmos, whether *nirguṇa* or *saguṇa*, permits a substantial degree of reality to the phenomenal world and the creatures and beings that inhabit it. Differentiation and plurality in the physical world need not be separated from their Cause resulting in apparent dualities and plurality in an overall unity.

The distinction between the *saguṇa* and *nirguṇa* Brahman in the *Upaniṣads* is not always clear, for they are really two aspects of a single Reality – an undifferentiated unity that becomes the differentiations of the world. The creative power that brings this about is more readily depicted as God, as *Īśvara*, in theistic *Upaniṣads* where *Īśvara*, the Lord, is the all-knowing and all-pervading subject, who has the world as its created object, and in whom all knowledge is held. In the *Bṛhad-āraṇyaka* alongside the idea of an Immense Being that breathes out existence (2:4:10), is *akṣara*, "imperishable" (3:8), a term used to describe that which weaves together all phenomena, past, present and future. While some *Upaniṣads* favour an impersonal Absolute that is without qualities (*nirguṇa*), without form (*nirākāra*) and indescribable, it is mainly the later principal *Upaniṣads* that favour a personal Brahman with qualities (*saguṇa*), with form (*sākāra*) as Īśvara. Both can be united as one, and for some, *Īśvara* is the means of focus on the impersonal Brahman beyond the personal.

Where Brahman is personalized, it is sometimes featured as the cosmic Puruṣa, who is responsible for creation, as we shall see below. Or, Brahman is referred to as Self, Ātman, and the foundation of all existence. Such ideas were evident in the *Śatapatha Brāhmaṇa* (10:6:3), indicative, again, of the overlapping thought in the two genres of sacred literature. In the latest of the principal *Upaniṣads* the more personalized God bestows his grace whereby a true Self deep within the ordinary self is revealed. The *Kaṭha Upaniṣad* puts it thus: "Without desires and free from sorrow, a man perceives by the creator's grace the grandeur of the self."[39] Such a personalized Brahman provides space for theistic devotion, devotion to a personal God as the controller and sustainer of the universe. The later *Kaṭha*, *Īśā*, *Śvetāśvatara*, and *Muṇḍaka* principal *Upaniṣads* are all infused with some theistic thought, what Olivelle describes as "probably the earliest literary products of the theistic tradition".[40] It is these later principal *Upaniṣads* that tend to incorporate concepts of an omnipotent, omniscient and indwelling God. The *Īśā*, for example, opens with the words: "This whole world is to be dwelt in by the Lord".[41] The Hindu deity Rudra features in such a way in the *Śvetāśvatara Upaniṣad*, but not exclusively theistically, for the impersonal *nirguṇa* conception of Brahman is still evident. But where theism is overt there is a clear understanding that devotion to God is *the* means to liberation, which can only mean a dualistic relationship between individual and divine. Indeed, in the *Śvetāśvatara* there is evident the idea that human beings are providentially controlled, and the divine grace of God is available only to the devout worshipper. This is far removed from an impersonal, *nirguṇa* view of divinity. Yet, while the focus of attention is on the personal *Īśvara* as Brahman manifest, the supreme nature of the Lord as Brahman is never lost. So such theism is not a major current in *Upaniṣadic* thought. Even in a theistic *Upaniṣad* as the *Śvetāśvatara* the idea of One behind the plurality and diversity of the universe is still to be found. The immanence of the "person", God, identified as Rudra in this *Upaniṣad*, is said to fill the whole world, indicative of the profound interconnection between the world and the divine. Rudra as "that immense

Person" is said to be higher than Brahman in the *Śvetāśvatara*, but is still referred to as "Lord". The *Bhagavad Gītā* takes up many of these thoughts in its portrayal of Kṛṣṇa as we shall see in chapter 6. Given its theistic nature, the *Śvetāśvatara Upaniṣad* sees creation as a result of the grace of God (3:20). However, the unity with, and pervasiveness of, God in manifest existence is maintained in the same way as with the totally transcendent Absolute of earlier *Upaniṣads*. Such unity is beautifully expressed in the following verses of the *Śvetāśvatara Upaniṣad*:

> You are woman; you are man; you are boy or also a girl. As an old man, you totter along with a walking stick. As you are born, you turn your face in every direction.
> You are the dark blue bird, the green one with red eyes, the rain-cloud, the seasons, and the oceans. You live as one without a beginning because of your pervasiveness, you, from whom all beings have been born.[42]

In grand theistic style, the final chapter of the *Śvetāśvatara Upaniṣad* refers to the "highest Great-Lord among lords, the highest God among gods, the highest master among masters, the God beyond the highest as the adorable Lord of the universe".[43] The idea that this God can be adored is the central tenet of theistic devotion.

In the *Muṇḍaka Upaniṣad* God is the imperishable Brahman from which the diversity of life emerges and to which it returns. However, ascetic life and knowledge in this *Upaniṣad* are insufficient to realize Brahman for there is some suggestion in this text, too, that God *chooses* him whom he will free and permit entry to his "Brahman abode" (3:3–4). Nevertheless, despite the theistic nature of God, which might suggest a duality between God and man, even in this *Upaniṣad* unity prevails and the fusion of *nirguṇa* and *saguṇa* aspects of Brahman into a single unity is maintained. Such unity also characterizes liberation: "When a man comes to know that highest *brahman*, he himself becomes that very *brahman*."[44]

Ātman

Brahman is sometimes referred to as Ātman, Self, that which exists in its own Self without another. The same word, *ātman*, is also used for the inner Self of the human being. Much of the material in the *Upaniṣads* is concerned with the nature of the self, and *ātman* becomes important in depicting both the living being that we know, including the body, its senses, and that which is born and dies but, also, a deeper unchanging aspect of the self that I have hinted at above and that some might here call "soul", or better, *S*elf. It is the latter that seems to me the clearer term in order to avoid western connotations. Some of the questions that were raised above concerning the relation of the changeless Brahman to the cause–effect processes as the manifestations of Brahman in the universe, are answered by this key *Upaniṣadic* concept of *ātman* as Self. *Ātman* is likely to be derived from the root *an* "to breathe" and, by extension therefore, suggestive of the breath of life that animates human beings.[45] The *Bṛhad-āraṇyaka* refers to the *ātman* at one point as that which unifies the breath and the body as a living being.

But even here the *ātman* is described as "the real behind the real" (2:20), and though this is probably referring to the self as motivator, instigator and inner controller of the body, it is easy to see how it could also mean an inner essence as soul or Self. Indeed, the *Bṛhad-āraṇyaka Upaniṣad* as a whole has a tendency to explore the inner nature of things as a "real" beyond "vital functions" of the tangible self. Such a "real", in the same way as Brahman, is *neti neti*, "not this, not this" (*Bṛhad-āraṇyaka* 2:3:6), and since it is beyond name and form, it is indescribable, albeit in the *Kaṭha Upaniṣad* (1:2:20) it is smaller than the smallest, yet larger than the largest. Thus, like the *nirguṇa* Brahman, the *ātman* came to be accorded the same indescribable Reality that is immensely precious. "This innermost thing, this Self (*ātman*) – it is dearer than a son, it is dearer than wealth, it is dearer than everything else."[46] We can certainly see in the *Bṛhad-āraṇyaka* evolving concentration on *ātman* as the real Self. The inner *ātman* gradually became differentiated from body, mind and other external phenomena.

The *Upaniṣads* spend a good deal of time analysing the nature of breath from both technical and religious perspectives, so breath relates to the ordinary self as well as the inner Self. The *Taittirīya Upaniṣad* (2:3:1), in fact, says that Brahman should be worshipped as the life-breath. It seemed natural to suppose that the *ātman*, too, was the vital breath of the self and responsible for conveying all the functions of life with it when it finally left the body at death. The *ātman* as the true Self resides, according to the *Upaniṣads*, in the "cavern of the heart". "As vast as the space here around us is this space within the heart, and within it are contained both the earth and the sky, both fire and wind, both sun and the moon, both lightning and stars. What belongs here to this space around us, as well as what does not – all that is contained within it."[47] The interconnection – indeed, unity – of the Self with all phenomena is clear here and in many other passages such as the following from the *Bṛhad-āraṇyaka Upaniṣad*: "The Self has entered this body, this dense jumble. If a man finds him, recognizes him, he's the maker of everything – the author of all! The world is his – he's the world itself!"[48] In short, the Self is the universe and the universe is Brahman so the Self is also Brahman. It was a fusion of microcosm and macrocosm, the five senses correlating with the five elements and five deities and the *ātman* that is the inner controller and spiritual centre of being correlating with Brahman, the Ground of all being. Paul Younger is right, I think, in claiming that the *Upaniṣadic* doctrine of the self is more elaborate than that in any other tradition: "Man", he says, "is a microcosm in himself. He contains all the elements that make up the world as well as a series of spiritual levels that contain in various measures the divine life itself."[49]

The *ātman* is the real Self, what Radhakrishnan depicted as "what remains when everything that is not the self is eliminated".[50] Since breath was seen as the essential element of life – the *essence* of life without which human beings cannot exist – it was a short step to seeing the *ātman* as the *essence* of the self, the fundamental and *real* part of the self that underpinned the personality. Thus a transfer from *breath* to *essence* took place in the usage of the word. The *Bṛhad-āraṇyaka* depicts the *ātman* as pure Consciousness (*cit*) that is different from ordinary subject–object consciousness, and also as Bliss (*ānanda*). The *ātman* is the *still* part of the self, the deepest part of the self that transcends the phenomenal world and is the eternal core of each person. This incredibly profound and remarkable doctrine posits the inner Self as the totality of Reality.

The idea of the hidden essence of the *ātman* as infinitesimally tiny and yet immeasurably expansive is expressed many times in the *Upaniṣads*. This, from the *Śvetāśvatara*, describes the *ātman*, here referred to as *jīva*, as such: "When the tip of a hair is split into a hundred parts, and one of those parts further into a hundred parts – the individual soul (*jīva*), on the one hand, is the size of one such part, and on the other, it partakes of infinity."[51] In transcending the phenomenal world, the *ātman* is not subject to its processes. As the later *Upaniṣad*, the *Kaṭha* states: "The wise one – he is not born, he does not die; he has not come from anywhere; he has not become anyone. He is unborn and eternal, primeval and everlasting. And he is not killed, when the body is killed".[52] The *ātman* simply *is*, unmoved and unchanging like the self in deep sleep. The whole idea here is one taken up by Kṛṣṇa in the *Bhagavad Gītā*, which I shall examine in detail in chapter 6.

So how could this *ātman* be experienced? Control of desires and of reactions to senses were the immediate goals. Such control was likened to a chariot and its driver in the third chapter of the *Kaṭha Upaniṣad*. The correlations are as follows:

- The self = the rider
- The body = the chariot
- The intellect = the charioteer
- The mind = the reins
- The senses = the horses
- Sense objects = pathways

Just as horses need to be controlled, so should the senses be. If senses *are* controlled, then the horses obey by means of the reins, just as the mind needs to rein in reactions to senses. Reaction to sense stimuli causes obscuring of the *ātman*. Therefore, while to pursue knowledge and not ignorance may seem a logical path and a worthwhile goal, even the desire for knowledge is inimical to experience of the *ātman* because it is still desire.

Thus, the *ātman*, while interpreted differently, came to be thought of as the permanent aspect of the self. To realize this ultimate Self, to experience the reality of it, became the goal. And this experience would transform the egoistic self into one devoid of the usual conceptions of "I" and "mine", for the *ātman* was pure and unconnected with the transient processes of life. It was the *ātman* that became conceived of as the substratum of all real knowledge about the world and, as the ultimate and real aspect of the self, needed no validation for its existence.

Brahman-*ātman*

The particular brilliancy of the *Upaniṣads* was the synthesis of Brahman and *ātman*. It was a fairly logical conception that, if Brahman was the unchanging and permanent but indescribable Absolute Reality that underpinned all existence; and the *ātman* was the fundamental, real and permanent part of the self, then they were conjoined by their particular reality and permanence. Madeleine Biardeau described the *ātman* as the "'human' correlate of the Absolute",[53] and this is a very important point in the understanding of *Upaniṣadic* thought. Since all in the universe was believed to have emanated from Brahman, then at least the fundamental *essence* of all things must be equated either wholly or partially with Brahman. Once *ātman* had shifted its meaning to "essence" then not only human beings but also all things in existence, animate and inanimate, were believed to contain this same essence that was Brahman. So at the deepest levels of life there is a fundamental and permanent Reality that runs through all things – *ātman*, which is Brahman. This, indeed, is the monism so typical of much *Upaniṣadic* thought, by which all is one and each entity in the universe is identical to Brahman. Brahman and Ātman/*ātman* may have originated as separate etymological ideas but the evolution in their nuances of meaning resulted in their synonymy.

It is this equation of *ātman* = Brahman that was the major discovery of *Upaniṣadic* thought, and that really provided the answer to so many of the philosophical questions that a search for Reality and Truth had engendered. The sages had at last emerged from the unreal to the real, from darkness to light and found a path from death to immortality. Two different concepts had become synthesized in a unique way that would provide a basis for much philosophical thought in the centuries to follow, and provided, with some modifications, the core of much Hindu religious belief. Hiriyanna went as far as to say: "The enunciation of this doctrine marked the most important advance in the whole history of India's thought. It introduced almost a revolution in the point of view from which speculation had proceeded till then."[54] The microcosmic world of humankind had become intimately equated with the whole of the macrocosm because of the presence of *ātman* in all things. The inner Self became projected out into cosmic identity and unity with all phenomena and equated with the permanent substratum of Reality which was its divine Source. Each human being was, thus, identical to another, identical to the cosmos and identical to Brahman. Whether or not the *Upaniṣads* equated the *ātman* with Brahman totally or partially, the interconnection between ritual and cosmos of the *Vedas* was raised to a whole new level: the interrelation of *ātman* and Brahman united microcosm and macrocosm in fundamental totality. But whereas ritual was the key in the *Vedas* to experience that connecting energy, knowledge became the key in *Upaniṣadic* thought and the Self as the agent of that knowledge.

Monism

Monism, the idea that everything in the cosmos is one, became the characteristic philosophy of the *Vedānta*.[55] Differentiation between this and that, and the recognition of dualities in the universe, occur only because of ignorance (*avidyā*). But not only is everything in the cosmos one, each entity in it *is* Brahman – not a *part* of Brahman as in pantheistic or panentheistic belief, but totally identical with Brahman. And just as Brahman is indescribable and beyond human conception so the *ātman* is also beyond any empirical analysis; it, too, is indescribable and can only be experienced by the kind of deep, intuitive knowledge that penetrates to the hidden Reality in the depths of the self. Monism is hinted at in the *Bṛhad-āraṇyaka Upaniṣad* 1:4:10 in the words: "In the beginning this world was only *brahman*, and it knew itself (*ātman*), thinking: 'I am *brahman*'. As a result, it became the Whole."[56] Knowledge of this, the verse says, makes men, gods and seers whole too, that is to say, becoming the Wholeness, the All, Completeness, Perfection that is Brahman.[57] The equating of the Whole or the All with the *ātman* is clear in the words: "When, however, the Whole has become one's very Self (*ātman*), then who is there for one to smell and by what means?"[58] The verse asks the same for sight, hearing, greeting, thinking and perception, indicative of the non-duality pertaining to the real *ātman*. The *Bṛhad-āraṇyaka* 2:5, especially, links the essence of all things – earth, water, fire, wind, sun, moon, lightning, thunder, space, *dharma*, humanity and the self with "the Whole" and ends with the statement: "This *Brahman* is without a before and an after, without an inner and an outer. Brahman is this Self (*ātman*) here which perceives everything" (2:5:19).[59] Similarly, the *Chāndogya Upaniṣad* (3:14:2–4) refers to the Self that lies deep within the heart, smaller than a grain of seed but larger than all the worlds put together, and containing the whole world: "It is Brahman", the text says, and the speaker, Śāndilya, states that after death "That (Brahman) I will become."

Tat tvam asi

Of the many parts of the *Upaniṣads* that express such identity of *ātman* and Brahman it is the expression *Tat tvam asi*, "That you are", of the *Chāndogya Upaniṣad* that epitomizes this identity. Indeed, Wilhelm Halbfass referred to this specific text as "one of the most seminal texts in the history of Indian thought".[60] The story behind these words is that of Śvetaketu, a young boy who, at the age of twelve, embarked on his period of study with a *guru*. When he returned twelve years later at the age of twenty-four, somewhat conceited and arrogant with the amount of knowledge he had acquired, his father, Uddālaka Āruṇī, asked him whether he had requested from his *guru* that instruction "by which the unhearable becomes heard, the unperceivable becomes perceived, the unknowable becomes known?"[61] It is to the *ātman* and its identity with Brahman that Uddālaka was referring. But Śvetaketu did not know, and could not see how such a question could be answered. His father explained that just as there is one substance like clay from which all things made of clay come, so there is one Being from which the world of not-being is derived. But the example of clay was an easy one and Uddālaka directed his son to more subtle ideas. He asked his son what he could see when he cut the fruit from a *nyagrodha* tree in half. When it revealed the tiny seeds, his father asked him to cut one of the seeds in two and again say what he can see. This time Śvetaketu had to admit that he could see nothing, yet he knew that something within the seed must cause it to grow to the mighty *nyagrodha* tree. Uddālaka was directing his son to the idea of the *essence* of things which, while hidden, we know to be present, and from there to the subtle essence of Brahman as the *ātman* in all things. He told his son:

> My dear, that subtle essence which you do not perceive, verily, my dear, from that very essence this great *nyagrodha* tree exists. Believe me, my dear.
> That which is the subtle essence, this whole world has for its self. That is true. That is the self. That art thou [*tat tvam asi*] Śvetaketu.[62]

Like air in a jar that is the same as the air outside it, the *ātman* in the self is identical to the cosmos and its Source, the Ground of all being that is Brahman. And like honey that comes from the pollen of many plants and trees, when each being merges in Brahman all sense of distinction and individuation is lost. Or, as salt becomes invisible when dissolved, so the essence that is Brahman remains invisibly the essence and Reality of each being and, as the statement *tat tvam asi*, "*That* you are", emphasizes, the Self and Brahman are identical.

Such is the core monism of the *Upaniṣads* but while monism may be a major trend in the *Upaniṣads*, the more theistic *Upaniṣads* like the *Īśā*, which posits the personal Brahman, still maintain the Brahman-*ātman* synthesis and the unity of all: "When a man sees all beings within his very self, and his self within all beings, It will not seek to hide from him."[63] Then, says the *Īśā*, there can be no confusion and sorrow. This *Upaniṣad*, especially, stresses the need to transcend dualities but continues to claim Brahman as Supreme Lord. While *tat tvam asi* is perhaps the quintessential statement, or "great saying", *mahā-vākya*, of identity with Brahman, the *Bṛhad-āranyaka* (1:4:10) also contains another, "I am Brahman", and the *Māṇḍūkya* (1:2) "this *ātman* is Brahman". Again, however, we should not think that monistic identity of Brahman and *ātman* is the only relationship between the two that is present in the *Upaniṣads*, remembering that sometimes, the Brahman and *ātman* relationship is still an identity but a qualified one in that Brahman as ultimate has an *essential* Reality that transcends the whole created universe even though Brahman infuses that creation. We shall see this in the section on creation below.

Yoga

With the interrelation of *ātman* and Brahman, and breath as the living essence of life came a trend to correlate microcosmic breathing and parts of the body with the macrocosm itself, sometimes not with Brahman but with natural phenomena – the sun, moon, wind, dawn, fire and so on. Such thought was clearly an influence on the development of *yoga*. The *Kaṭha Upaniṣad* 6:10–11 specifically defines *yoga* as the stilling of the five senses and the mind so that no thinking takes place and the senses are totally controlled, "for Yoga is the coming-into-being, as well as the ceasing-to-be",[64] in other words, identity with the Real and loss of the unreal. The *Śvetāśvatara Upaniṣad* is clearly influenced by *yoga* and speaks of the necessity of "yoking" thoughts and the mind, referring even to the straight body as the best position for practice. Chapter 2 of this *Upaniṣad* deals also with *yogic* breathing techniques, the best places for their practice, with restraint and with right attitudes of mind – all aspects that were taken up by classical Yoga.

Reincarnation

The idea of reincarnation came into the *Vedic* texts gradually. The *Vedas* had a general conception of the self surviving death and, in the main, joining the Fathers, the ancestors, or perhaps being assigned to a less well-articulated Hell. The Fathers of the *Vedas* were divine beings who enjoyed immortality amongst the gods. We find no hint of reincarnation in the *Vedas*[65] and just a few in the *Brāhmaṇas* with the pessimistic idea of repeated deaths. The *Śatapatha Brāhmaṇa* (14:9:1) dealt with the concept in more depth and with the idea of retribution for one's actions but especially a second death in the afterlife. Perhaps, as Wilhelm Halbfass suggested, this idea of re-death, of dying again at the end of a post-death existence preceded and influenced ideas of rebirth.[66] But rebirth was not to be prized. As the *Maitrī Upaniṣad* put it: "In such a world as this, what is the good of enjoyment of desires? For he who has fed on them is seen to return (to this world) repeatedly."[67] Each rebirth was likened to being a frog in a waterless well.

The *Upaniṣads* were much more concerned with the fate of the self after death than earlier texts and explored ideas of a self that reincarnated on Earth, though theories about the pathways to rebirth were various. An *Upaniṣad* such as the *Kauṣītaki* dealt almost exclusively with the fate of the self after death and the complex pathway to rebirth. Some of the deceased became immortal in the realm of the gods but the Fathers were no longer immortal but reborn. It is to their realm that most were destined to go. The *Vedas* accepted the superiority of those who carried out the correct prescribed rituals: these were "the good" among men and those who were destined for a pleasant post-death experience. The *Upaniṣads* took this basic thought to a wider level in correlating the quality of afterlife with the nature of the pre-death existence and a subsequent rebirth. There was, too, the pragmatic question of why the place to which one went after death, *Vedic* Heaven, or the realm of the fathers did not fill up with the many dead? The *Bṛhad-āraṇyaka Upaniṣad* (6:2:2) posed such a question and explored rebirth as an answer with a moral cause–effect basis as its cause.[68] The process of how beings returned was variously described: one theory stated that while those with knowledge proceeded on the path of the gods, the *deva-yāna*, to Brahman via the sun, those without it wended their way by the path of the ancestors, *pitṛ-yāna*, from smoke eventually to reach the moon. There, they were consumed by Soma and returned via space, wind, smoke, thunder-cloud, rain, vegetation, food for men, semen and the womb of a woman to be reborn – a recycling process.[69] Some differentiation between those who carried on sacrificial ritual in the villages and increasingly urban settlements and those who dwelt in the wilderness and forests seems to have informed the idea of reincarnation, the sacrificers being reborn, but the wilderness dwellers reaching Brahman and release. The term that became widely accepted for rebirth, *saṃsāra*, appears for the first time in the *Kaṭha Upaniṣad* (3:7), which is not one of the earliest principal *Upaniṣads*. Here, it was the fate of those who had no right knowledge and who were impure. Reincarnation came to be generally accepted in Indian thought by the sixth century BCE, though with some exceptions.

The basic idea informing rebirth is the cause–effect concept of *karma*.[70] It was an idea that emerged initially in the *Brāhmaṇas*[71] and was preceded even earlier by the cause–effect aspects of *ṛta*, and ritual action, *karman*, in the *Vedas*. While the concept emerged more tangibly in the *Upaniṣads*, according to the *Bṛhad-āraṇyaka Upaniṣad* (3:2:13) knowledge of *karma* was an *upaniṣad*, a secret teaching, and it was not articulated fully until the later classical *Maitrī Upaniṣad* (1:3–4). The *Bṛhad-āraṇyaka Upaniṣad* defines *karma* succinctly: "A man turns into something good by good action and into something bad by bad action."[72] The law of cause and effect suggests that a person has to be reincarnated in order to reap the results – negative and positive – of the accumulation of all his or her actions in life or even in previous lives. And since physical and mental actions are taking place in every waking moment of life, the effects that have to bear fruit necessitate countless lifetimes. So at death it is only the body that ceases to exist, while the subtle accumulated *karma* of one's existence in the present and past lives continues into the next. Each individual, then, creates the specific personality that will accompany him or her in the next existence and the sorrows and joys that are the fruits of actions in past existence(s). The following often quoted analogy depicts the process in the context of increasingly improved existences: "As a caterpillar, when it comes to the tip of a blade of grass, reaches out to a new foothold and draws itself onto it, so the self (*ātman*) after it has knocked down this body and rendered it unconscious, reaches out to a new foothold and draws itself onto it."[73] The *Chāndogya Upaniṣad* is more specific: "Now, people here whose behaviour is pleasant can expect to enter a pleasant womb, like that of a woman of the Brahmin, the Kṣatriya, or Vaiśya class. But people of foul behaviour can expect to enter a foul womb, like that of a dog, a pig, or an outcaste woman."[74] Being reborn as an insect or some such creature was not excluded, nor was being born into a "stationary" condition, that is to say, as inanimate (*Kaṭha* 5:7). Just as gold is melted down to form a new object, so a new body is made from the psychic residues of an old one, though the *Bṛhad-āraṇyaka* makes it clear that the dispelling of ignorance is necessary for an improved rebirth.

The doctrine of *karma* involves what Younger describes as "a patient determination to remove the chaff which hides the kernel of truth".[75] Each moment of life, and each action of body and mind, contributes to the journey. As Younger also says: "man is somewhere in the garden of God, but he has yet to make his way to the source of life."[76] The *Śvetāśvatara* (5:11–12) makes it clear that the intentions, the actions of body and mind, desires and even food and drink create the various kinds of conditions of the next life. In other words, a being *chooses* the qualities of the next life while in the present one. The situation is clear: re-death is the fate of those who do not know the immortal, unborn Self (*Bṛhad-āraṇyaka Upaniṣad* 4:4:17–20), and of those who see diversity not unity of the Self and Brahman. The Self is not affected by actions at all, and so is not affected by negative or positive *karmic* action. And Brahman, too, is removed from all facets of evil: Brahman is the Source of cause and effect but it is the choices of beings that make good or evil causes in this or past lives leaving Brahman free from any immediate causal connections. But nothing can exist without the unchanging divine essence within, so the passive *ātman* accompanies each rebirth of a being.

Yet there are plenty of contradictions in the theory of *karma* informing rebirth. Some, for example, are said to atone for the sins of their fathers and there were also ideas of the father handing on his personality at death to his son. It seems, too, from the *Kauṣītaki Upaniṣad* (1:4) that Brahman could be realized by an individual who still had both good and evil *karma*.[77] Doniger points out, too, that with increasing urbanization, extensive trade and acquisition of wealth, *karma* came to be accepted by many as merit that was realized as increased property and material aggrandisement in this life as well as the next.[78]

The empirical self

In the *Ṛg Veda* (1:164:20) we find an image of two birds in a tree. One eats voraciously moving from branch to branch. The other is still and passive and is simply the observer. The self that we know in life, the ordinary self, is the active bird and is completely different from the inner Self, the inner *ātman*, the passive bird. The *Muṇḍaka Upaniṣad* (3:1:1) picks up the same analogy referring to the close nature between the two, yet the delusion of the active bird in comparison to the grief-dispelling, spotless nature of the other. The self that we know is the egoistic personality that operates in the world from the self-consciousness of individual psyche. Our view of the world is based on our likes and dislikes, our positive and negative responses to our environment, our aims, drives, genetic make-up and interaction with others and the world at large. The sum total of our personality to date is sometimes termed the *jīva* "that which breathes", from the root *jīv* "to breathe". It is the biological, psychological and social personality that enjoys, suffers, acts, thinks, breathes, makes choices between this and that, and is subject to the experiences mediated by the five senses – all in contrast to the pure *ātman* that is the still, non-active, subtle and real Self that combines with the *jīva* as a *jīvātman*. While *jīvātman* can sometimes mean just a living being, as such it is the *jīvātman* that is subject to reincarnation, the *jīva* carrying *karma* as the active bird above, and the *ātman* being the inner, passive observer without which a being cannot exist. Reincarnation, or *saṃsāra*, occurs because the *jīvātman* accumulates both positive and negative *karma* as a result of its actions in mind, speech and body. The *Chāndogya Upaniṣad* 8:2 is interesting in that it suggests man reaps his desires by his *intentions*, he conjures up the kind of world he desires, whether this is Brahman-focused or not. It is the intention of desire that makes the man rather than the fulfilling of it.

Each individual then is, as Sharma put it, "a mixture of the real and the unreal, a knot of the existent and the non-existent, a coupling of the true and the false".[79] It is mainly to the false and unreal world that the *jīvātman* leans, and not to the subtle, eternal, real Self within. The only way that the *ātman* in life can be experienced is by transcending the "other" self, the *jīva*, and by transcending the dualities of life to experience the unity behind it. The inimical inhibitors of this are desire and aversion – our negative and positive responses to the multitude of stimuli in life – and the egoistic self that they create. Desires are the root reason for rebirth: "One who hankers after desires in his thoughts, is born here and there through his actions" states the *Muṇḍaka* (2:2:2).[80] A. L. Herman translates this verse as: "He who desires desirable things and broods upon them is born again because of that desire."[81] The idea of *brooding* here is particularly graphic, indicative of ways in which desires take hold and drive the individual well before they hatch into right or wrong action. Even desires for good – especially the desire for good *karma* through correct sacrificial ritual in order to enjoy a life in Heaven after death – are the result of ignorance since, as the *Muṇḍaka* says (1:2:5–10), once good *karma* expires in Heaven, rebirth with repeated old age and death will follow.

So desires fuel existence but, "when they are banished, those desires lurking in one's heart; then a mortal becomes immortal, and attains *Brahman* in this world."[82] At the deepest level, subject–object differentiation, the dualities of life, desire, aversion, ego, *jīvātman* and sense perceptions are all dissolved. All is passively still, like a rippleless lake. The *Bṛhadāranyaka* (2:4:12) puts this succinctly in the sage Yājñavalkya's response to a question posed by his clever, inquiring wife: "For when there is a duality of some kind, then the one can smell the other, the one can see the other, the one can think of the other, and the one can perceive the other. When, however, the Whole has become one's very Self (*ātman*), then who is there for one to smell and by what means? Who is there for one to hear and by what means? Who is there for one to think of and by what means? Who is there for one to perceive and by what means?"[83] What these words suggest is the transcending of subject–object differentiation for pure subject – and that pure subject is Brahman. That pure subject is a unified consciousness that unites all dualities.

It is the ego, *ahaṃkāra*, which causes the *ātman* to be obscured like layers of dust on a mirror. *Ahaṃkara* does not feature widely as a term in the *Upaniṣads*, but becomes highly developed in later philosophical traditions. The responses we make to all the stimuli in life, desiring one thing and rejecting another – whether that be physical objects or mental thoughts – create our egos and the kind of personal *karma* that must bear fruit in the future – hence the necessity for reincarnation. So if the ego can be lost, all that is left is the pure Self, *ātman*, and for this to happen, the individual has to be less involved with the dualities of the phenomenal world, and overcome desire (*kāma*). According to the *Muṇḍaka Upaniṣad* (3:2:2) "He who entertains desires, thinking of them, is born (again) here and there on account of his desires. But of him who has his desire fully satisfied, who is a perfected soul, all his desires vanish even here (on earth)."[84] Fully satisfied desire is Brahman-focused, and those who gain perfection by ridding themselves of passions "enter into the All" that is Brahman (2:2:5), attain the divine Puruṣa like rivers flowing into an ocean (3:2:8), and become Brahman (3:2:9). The problem is that the *jīvātman* does not usually *want* to stop desiring this and that – the world is so attractive. According to the sage Yājñavalkya in the *Bṛhad-āraṇyaka* (4:4:5), it was a common saying that: "A person is made up simply of desire."

Because the personality self is so keen on being involved in the world, detachment from it was something that had to be cultivated, but only in those who were prepared to undergo the rigorous pursuit of it. There were a number of groups devoted to ascetic practices, wanderers outside of, and antagonistic to, the *Vedic* fold. The ascetics within the Vedic fold were different for, in the main, they did not turn away from *Vedic* ritual, but sought to reinterpret it. Yet they were similar to the less orthodox ascetics in their pursuit of detachment from worldly issues. Through detachment (*vairāgya*) the slow process of eradication of desire and ego could take place. Being involved in the phenomenal world was rooting oneself in *avidyā* "ignorance", for ultimately real knowledge is that rooted in the *ātman* that is Brahman. This was the kind of knowledge by which a person experienced the unity of his or her self with all other animate and inanimate things in the universe. *Avidyā*, on the other hand, made all the dualities of life important, feeding the ego with desires and aversions, and engendering a false sense of separateness from all other beings and things. Through *avidyā* it was believed that the world was all there was to reality; it deluded the mind into believing that there was no need to search for the Real. And so, the *Upaniṣads* teach, humankind suffers and is subject to *saṃsāra*. As the *Bṛhad-āraṇyaka Upaniṣad* 3:5:1 puts it of the one with true knowledge: "he is the one who is beyond hunger and thirst, sorrow and delusion, old age and death. It is when they come to know this Self that Brahmins give up the desire for sons, the desire for wealth, and the desire for worlds, and undertake the mendicant life. The desire for sons, after all, is the same as the desire for wealth, and the desire for wealth is the same as desire for worlds – both are simply desires."[85] The Self transcends all desires and trains the sense faculties to operate without involvement with their objects.

Creation

As was seen in chapter 2, the *Vedas* contained – even in one *Upaniṣad* – a variety of theories concerning creation. Such variety also characterizes *Upaniṣadic* ideas of creation but, as I have pointed out earlier, there was a search also for the absolute beginning. Sometimes, Prajāpati, who emerged in the *Vedas* and evolved in the *Brāhmaṇas*, was presented as the sacrificed Puruṣa from which all phenomena emerged. One idea in the *Bṛhad-āraṇyaka Upaniṣad* (5:5:1) was that waters were the originators of the real, *satya*, and it was the real that created Brahman as Prajāpati from whom, in turn, the gods were created. In the *Chāndogya Upaniṣad* (2:23:2), Prajāpati is said to have "incubated" the worlds and the *Vedas*. Or elsewhere in the *Chāndogya* (4:17:1–3), Prajāpati is said to have extracted the essences of the three worlds while they were incubating – fire from the earth, wind from the middle regions and sun from the sky: these formed the triple *Veda*. This deity, Prajāpati, was unlike other *Vedic* gods in that he evolved in such a way as to be far superior: he more readily approached transcendence as Creator similar to the idea of Brahman, especially in the *Brāhmaṇas*. He features in different creation myths in the *Upaniṣads*.

Thus, the concept of a Puruṣa, a being that existed at the beginning and that figured in the *Ṛg Veda*, emerged also in the *Upaniṣads*. Another creation myth in the *Bṛhad-āraṇyaka* (1:4:1) states that this first being shaped like a man was simply an "I" (*ātman*) without any other until "I" expanded, split, and formed male and female. Their copulation brought forth not only humans but the male and female of all species. A little later in the same text (4:6 and 11), creation is described as from the mortal Brahman, who created the gods and immortals, but then became inferior to them. And yet, it was this Brahman as Puruṣa that was the vital aspect of all things, the breath of breathing, the sight of seeing and so on, but it is the *totality* of the different essences of all things that the *Bṛhad-āraṇyaka Upaniṣad* describes as *ātman*. It was this *totality* that paved the way for a more explicit monism and identity of Brahman with the essence of all. Similar to the concept of an "I" that created was a Self, an *Ātman* in the *Aitareya Upaniṣad* (1:1–3). Here, the creator was alone and created through volition. Into that creation by fiat he brought floods above the sky, stars, Earth, waters on Earth, and then a cosmic man from the waters, the parts of whom formed the gods as keepers of the worlds. The gods became linked with the different parts of that cosmic man. Then man was formed and the Source, Ātman, entered man to unify all and link microcosmic man with the macrocosm of the universe.

Since water is ubiquitous, is present in a variety of forms, and is essential for all life, man's essential being as water seemed logical to the ancients. Water was associated with the moon, which was seen as the source of rain and believed to be the place where the moisture from a deceased person on a funeral pyre rose and was collected. That moisture made another life possible unless the deceased passed through the door of the moon to freedom from rebirth. Such was one idea amongst many. The *Śvetāśvatara Upaniṣad* (1:1:2) notes many different views of creation – from Nature, Time, the elements, fate, Puruṣa – but also posits Ātman as the ultimate Source.

Food was seen as a source of all creatures in the *Taittirīya Upaniṣad* (2:2:1). They were born from food, survived on food and returned into food when they died. This *Upaniṣad* states that Brahman should be the food of men, suggestive that food was more than a gross product to the ancient mind, for it was the source of life. Ideas of food in some form or other pervade the *Upaniṣads*. Death, presumably in the sense of darkness, but in personified form, is found as the source of creation in the *Bṛhad-āraṇyaka* (1:2). From the mind of his formless self came first his body, then water, foam that solidified to form Earth, fire from his essential heat and then Death split up his body to become other manifestations. Fire was posited as a source of creation also in the *Bṛhad-āraṇyaka Upaniṣad* (6:2:9–14), which saw the created world as the sky, rain cloud, the world below, man, and woman – the five-fire doctrine by which each of these five aspects represented a cosmic sacrifice. The firewood, flames, embers, smoke and sparks from the fires represented different manifest phenomena.

Other ideas were more philosophical. The *Taittirīya* also emphasized that Brahman was pure Bliss, *ānanda*, and that such Bliss was the true nature of the Self when its outer levels had been peeled away. The whole world, animate and inanimate, came into being from Brahman mainly through *tapas*, heat. In the *Bṛhad-āraṇyaka* (1:4:10), where Brahman and *ātman* are identical, Brahman was the only original existent that knew itself as Ātman. It was from this Source that all originated. This *Upaniṣad* includes among its many creation theories the idea that the world consisted of material entities each of which was given name, form and function, with Brahman as their Source. Other more philosophical ideas of creation usually focused on whether existence (*sat*) or non-existence (*asat*) was the source of creation. The *Chāndogya* explores such ideas particularly well, but not consistently. At one point (3:19), non-existence produced "*That*" as existence and, in turn, an egg, then division of the egg into gold forming the heavens, and silver forming the earth. All things emerged from this egg. The idea of existence stemming from non-existence is found also in the *Taittirīya Upaniṣad* (2:6:1). This text is more explicitly panentheistic in that Brahman pre-existed creation, emitted the whole world through *tapas*, heat, and then, importantly, entered into it, becoming *sat*, existence, including all its distinct phenomena, but also *tyat*, what is indistinct, "the distinct and the indistinct, the resting and the never resting, the perceived and the non-perceived, the real (*satya*) and the unreal (*anṛta*)".[86] There was a tendency, then, to view Brahman as both the efficient and material cause of the world, especially in those parts of the *Upaniṣads* that reflect an emanationist concept of its existence. The successive creations from Brahman > space (ether) > air > fire > water > earth > plants > food > man were clearly indicative of the original Source, Brahman, being the material cause of the world. But in chapter 6 of the *Chāndogya*, the sage Uddālaka tells his son that non-existence as the creative source is impossible since what exists cannot come from what does not exist. For Uddālaka, the beginning of the world was the Existent, the One, and nothing else. From this One, who decided to become many, came heat, fire or energy; from heat came water (fluidity) and from water came food (solidity). These three combined and were infused by the Existent to begin the process of individuation of forms that were given different names. Here, all creation is indivisibly One.

Yet it is Brahman and Brahman as Ātman that emerged in the *Upaniṣads* as the innovative Source of creation. Generally, the more firmly evolving concept in the *Upaniṣads* is of Brahman as the ultimate Source of all and the world as emanating from that Source: "As a spider sends forth and draws in (its thread), as herbs grow on the earth, as hair (grows) on the head and the body of a living person, so from the Imperishable arises here the universe."[87] And in the same *Upaniṣad*, the *Muṇḍaka*, "This is the truth. As from a blazing fire, sparks of like form issue forth by the thousands, even so, O beloved, many kinds of beings issue forth from the immutable and they return thither to."[88] The *Muṇḍaka* more than any other *Upaniṣad* features the emanationist view of creation with the effects that are the world being transformations or modifications of the ultimate Cause that is Brahman. In much *Upaniṣadic* thought such as this, Brahman has an essential nature that transcends the world and the *ātman* that unifies all beings. The sparks are of the same nature as the fire, but are not the fire as cause. I particularly like John and Patricia Koller's idea of *sharing* here: "Each person shares his or her deepest being (*Ātman*) with all other beings. One need only know this Self to know all."[89] To know the Self is to know all manifest reality and that reality is One. But though the Self may be ultimately united with Brahman, it is not depicted as Creator and, therefore, total identity seems evasive. The idea of sharing is indicative of identity with other phenomena, particularly beings, but the *ātman* here remains a *part*, a spark, a thread, but it seems to me not the Source itself. That Source pervades but transcends the universe in the *Muṇḍaka*. Relevant here is Robert Charles Zaehner's comment on Brahman: "It pervades all things, yet is other than what it pervades."[90] The Self is a spark of the Absolute just as are all phenomena, bestowing reality to all that is manifest. In Younger's words: "The Transcendent does not actively create the world, but rather allows the world to evolve as a screen of activity veiling the truth of the Absolute. As man comes to understand himself and the world around him the veil fades from view and only the Transcendent One remains."[91] Thus, the means to liberation may be founded in intuitive knowledge but the realization of Brahman is essentially *experiential*.

What seems clear from many parts of the *Upaniṣads* is that while the *ātman* is identifiable in some way with Brahman, Brahman remains that which exists above and beyond all manifestation – a panentheistic tendency where Brahman is immanent in creation but transcends it. Such concepts exist alongside the monistic trends elsewhere, while additionally, Brahman is also sometimes the pantheistic totality of all things. The concept of Brahman transcending the whole of creation is exemplified in the *Śvetāśvatara* (3:2 and 5:3), where Brahman is repeatedly drawing back all beings into himself at the end of time. The image of a spider mentioned above, emitting its threads and drawing them in again, has the same suggestion of recreation. Such a conception is purely panentheistic: Brahman is All but that totality is not in itself Brahman for Brahman is greater than All.

The means to ultimate Reality

From what has been said it is easy to see that knowledge, *jñāna*, was the key to liberation, especially since its opposite, ignorance, was that which concealed the *ātman*. It was a means particularly emphasized by the sage Uddālaka. Knowledge was praised as the means to the world of the gods from the time of the earliest *Upaniṣads* such as the *Bṛhad-āraṇyaka* (1:5:16). Unlike the *Vedas* that were the *karma-kāṇḍa*, or ritual-action portion, of *śruti* literature, the *Upaniṣads* were the *jñāna-kāṇḍa* or knowledge portion. The *chelas* who attached themselves to *gurus* for the purpose of acquiring knowledge were searching for a spiritual, meditative path of intuitive knowledge rather than knowledge of anything in the material world. But it was a difficult path, one that even the god Indra took over a hundred years to perfect. It was to be undertaken only by the most dedicated of pupils, many of whom became wandering ascetics, turning away from ritual, the householder stage of life and the necessity for sons and wealth, though the *Chāndogya* (8:15) ends with the path of action, of a householder, as a legitimate means to the world of Brahman. Indeed, the path of action, that is to say of good works, is not eschewed by the *Īśā Upaniṣad*: "Always performing works here one should wish to live a hundred years. If you live thus as a man, there is no other way than this by which karman (or deed) does not adhere to you."[92] Since the tone of this *Upaniṣad* is theistic, "performing works" here means dedicating all actions to God. It would, then, be a mistake to think that the ascetic pathway to liberation pervades the *Upaniṣads* to the exclusion of normal social life: asceticism *per se* was not seen as an essential means to liberation in the earliest *Upaniṣads*.

Given the esoteric and secretive nature of the material in the *Upaniṣads*, there must have been very few who proceeded to the end goal. Those who were attracted to the path sat at the feet of their *gurus* to hear Truth and, through a process of critical analysis and discussion, proceeded to a second stage of intellectual knowledge and conviction of what had been heard. But it was the *practical* realization of wisdom, the third stage, which was the goal, that is to say, the inner, meditative and experiential cognition of the *ātman* that was all important. These three stages represented a period of faith, of understanding and of Brahman-realization respectively. But knowledge of Brahman was difficult to achieve: Brahman is always there though unknown, like gold treasure that remains hidden under the feet of countless passers-by. Thus, the *Chāndogya Upaniṣad* (8:4 and 5) advocated a life of celibacy in order to realize the *ātman* within. According to the *Aitareya Upaniṣad* (3:3), knowledge is the eye of everything and is Brahman. And in the *Chāndogya*, meditation on the syllable *Oṃ* in its three sounds of *a*, *u* and *m*, is meditation equated with "I am the All".[93]

Considering the intuitive nature of the knowledge that has to be acquired, meditation or *yoga* provided the means. When the mind is pulled away from its attractions to the sense stimuli of the environment then it can become calm and still and receptive to the inner experience of direct knowledge that is independent of the senses. *Yoga* provided the techniques by which the mind and intellect could be stilled and made more receptive to the deeper kind of knowledge that is ultimate. The practice of austerities, *tapas*, was an important means of developing the spiritual at the expense of the physical. It should be remembered that it was non-attachment of the ego to the stimuli of the world that was the aim; this was denial of the self and not necessarily the denial of the world *per se*. It was detachment of the self as opposed to attachment of the self. Yet it was easier to control the self when it was withdrawn from the world than when bombarded by the sense stimuli of daily existence. The *Kaṭha Upaniṣad* amalgamated many of the concepts explored in earlier *Upaniṣads* – the transcendent Absolute; Brahman in the impenetrably deepest self, mysteriously hidden in the cave of the heart; the meditative path for its discovery; the abandonment of dualities for true knowledge. These more concise formulations developed into the systematic philosophies of orthodox schools, a number of which I shall explore in later chapters. These philosophies delineated ideologies for both the impersonal and personal Brahman, mostly using the *Upaniṣads* as their starting point. The *Kaṭha Upaniṣad*, indeed, returns us to the secretive nature of an *upaniṣad* that is suited only to the wise, who know that Brahman is:

> The changeless, among the changing,
> the intelligent, among intelligent beings,
> the one, who dispenses desires among the many;
> The wise who perceive him within themselves,
> they alone, not others, enjoy eternal happiness.[94]

Liberation

While the pathways to liberation in the *Upaniṣads* are various, and the final release remains always a tension between an immortal life in Heaven – even in Brahman's palace, according to the *Kauṣītaki Upaniṣad* – and identity with Brahman, to lose the egoistic perceptions of the world, the dualities which that perception engenders, and the desires that create the ego, are the goals of *Upaniṣadic* thought. Here, the liberated individual knows the Self that is in himself and sees all things as identical to that Self – a thought picked up in the *Bhagavad Gītā*. It is a *liberation*, a release, from all that restricts, binds, and holds humans in ignorance but particularly release from the rounds of death and rebirth. The term for such liberation is *mukti*, later *mokṣa*,[95] and it seems from the evidence of the *Upaniṣads* that it could be experienced in life. The early *Vedic* idea of liberation, as we saw in the last chapter, was that at the end of one existence the soul of the good would be recompensed in Heaven and the soul of the evil punished in a dark abode, a somewhat undeveloped Hell. The later *Upaniṣadic* idea of reincarnation is sometimes combined with this concept, so that an individual is believed to go on experiencing the results of *karmic* action accumulated in life in the context of some heavenly or hellish abode, only then to be reborn in order to reap the fruits of other positive and negative *karma*.

While articulated differently throughout the *Upaniṣads* and, indeed, in later philosophies based on them, liberation is not something that can be "reached" or "acquired". Since the *ātman* is already there as the fundamental essence of the self it is there to be experienced. But a certain amount of knowledge is necessary to reveal it, not, as we have seen, empirical knowledge, but deep, intuitive knowledge that is, like the *ātman* itself, indescribable. But it is liberation that brings the realization of *ultimate* knowledge, the unity with the cosmos that makes all sense of "I" disappear. The diversity of the world vanishes in the ultimate knowledge of the unity of all things and the identity of the *ātman* with Brahman is realized. The ultimate goal is to become the Self, *ātman*, of all beings, just as the unfailing divine breath informs all animate and inanimate phenomena (*Bṛhad-āraṇyaka Upaniṣad* 4:4:23). Subject–object differentiation is lost and all is One. It is like polishing a dusty mirror to see the Self as it really is.

But, as I pointed out above, it would be wrong to assume that the only perspective of liberation in the *Upaniṣads* is that of monistic identity with Brahman for there are many times when the more dual pantheistic, occasionally panentheistic, and overtly theistic perspectives of liberation are to be found. In this last, there is a more intimate and personal relationship with the divine. The degree of identity with the divine will vary, but the overall impression is one that supports the belief *ātman* = Brahman, stemming from the *nirguṇa*, monistic view of the indescribable Absolute. Identity with Brahman permits a state of liberation that is depicted as *sat* "Truth" or "Being" (as opposed to the non-being of the changeable and finite world), *cit* "Pure Consciousness", and *ānaṇda* "Bliss". Liberation is not necessarily self-extinction, but the degree to which self-identity is lost will depend on the particular conception of the Absolute Brahman. To say that this cannot be personal in the *Upaniṣads* would be misleading, and an *Upaniṣad* like the *Kaṭha* even suggests that it is by the *grace* of the supreme Self that the *ātman* can be realized.[96] The *Kauṣītaki Upaniṣad* (3:8) even hints at predestination with Brahman as the inner controller, "the one that makes those people perform good actions whom it wants to lead up from these worlds and makes those people perform bad actions whom it wants to push down from these worlds".[97] Perhaps the *Śvetāśvatara Upaniṣad* (11:12) has the same thought in mind when it refers to "the overseer of action" or the one who apportions qualities to individuals (5:5) and similar. Where a personal Brahman is accepted then monism is lost for a panentheistic view of the relationship of the world and the individuals in it to the divine. This is evident in, for example, parts of the *Śvetāśvatara Upaniṣad*, yet even in this theistic *Upaniṣad* the impersonal Brahman is by no means absent.

In the *Muṇḍaka Upaniṣad* (3:2:8–9) we find the ultimate expression of liberation:

> As the rivers flow on and enter the ocean
> giving up their names and appearances;
> so the knower, freed from name and appearance,
> Reaches the heavenly Person, beyond the very highest.
>
> When a man comes to know that highest Brahman, he himself becomes that very Brahman . . . He passes beyond sorrow, he passes beyond evil. Freed from the knots of his heart, he will become immortal.[98]

Zaehner's comment here was rather apt: "How to realize this eternal soul and how to disengage it from its real or imaginary connexion with the psycho-somatic complex that thinks, wills, and acts, is from the time of the Upanishads onwards the crucial problem facing the Hindu consciousness."[99] Finally, the *Upaniṣads* present us with a riddle for those who follow the path of knowledge to liberation – he who thinks he knows Brahman does not, though he who says he does not know, *does*.

4
Advaita Vedānta

I turn now to other expressions of the *Vedānta* as they occurred in the philosophical schools that came into being many centuries later. Here, I want to concentrate on one of those schools, Advaita Vedānta, leaving the interpretations of the *Upanisads* by other philosophical schools for later chapters. Advaita Vedānta is a school that has been, and still is, of considerable influence and is the most well-known system of Hindu belief in the West as well as the East. While it has had many expressions, it still obtains in one form or another in the monastic traditions of Hinduism and has absorbed numerous lay followers. Three fundamental questions pervade its philosophical inquiry, *What is the nature of Brahman?*, *What is the relation between the Absolute Brahman and the self?* and *What is the relation between the Absolute Brahman and the world?* It is the nuances of responses to these questions that serve to distinguish the various branches of Vedānta schools in general, and that have given rise to a prolific amount of philosophical literature within the various strands of Vedānta, both original in content and as commentaries on the works of others. Advaita Vedānta is just one of the six orthodox schools of philosophy, *darśanas*, accepted by Hinduism. *Darśana* means "to see, gain sight of" and this may be meant empirically as when one is having sight of a deity in a temple or intuitively through spiritual experience. Here, the term is linked with the latter and meant philosophically and epistemologically.

Background to the school

The schools of Vedānta, as the name suggests, are based heavily on the literature of the end of the *Vedic* period, the *Upaniṣads*, which provided the content of the previous chapter and which form the "knowledge portion", *jñāna-kaṇḍa*, of the *Vedic* corpus. One of the most important proponents of the Vedānta tradition was Śaṃkara, who lived in the eighth century CE, and the teachings related to him have witnessed centuries of impact. The *Upaniṣads*, as we saw in chapter 3, put forward a thoroughly (if somewhat inconsistently) articulated concept of a transcendent Absolute as Brahman, and how Brahman might be known. It was these facts that made Śaṃkara's Vedānta essentially a path of knowledge – a knowledge that revealed ultimate Consciousness and Reality. It was a search for the true Self, like the *Upaniṣads*, and came to be viewed by its proponents as the superior path to that of ritual action in the performance of religious duty. As a non-dualist, an *advaitist* (*a* = not, *dvaita* = dual), Śaṃkara believed that both ritual and knowledge portions of the *Veda* were aimed at different people. There was nothing in the *karma-kaṇḍa*, the ritual portion, to suggest that it would bring someone to liberation, though it could prepare a person for the kind of moral restraint that underpinned the path of knowledge, and could be effected for the purpose of specific results. But, as far as Śaṃkara was concerned, no action could bring about liberation, only knowledge. Therefore, the actions of the *karma-kaṇḍa* were bound to be seen by Śaṃkara as inferior to the *jñāna-kaṇḍa*. It is from this point of view that we can begin a study of Śaṃkara's Advaita Vedānta.

In basing teachings very firmly on the content of the *Upaniṣads*, all strands of Vedānta rely on the same, traditional, foundational material, concentrating on the nature of Brahman and the Self. Vedānta schools are based on three major sources, the *Upaniṣads*, the *Brahma-Sūtras*,[1] which was a systematization of the philosophical teachings of the *Upaniṣads*, reputedly by Bādarāyaṇa possibly in the last few centuries BCE, and the *Bhagavad Gītā*. There was no need for Śaṃkara to gather together the respective strands of philosophical thought about the path of knowledge to provide the basis of his teachings, for the material was already in place. While he systematized and elaborated on some ideas, it was not the aim of Śaṃkara to depart from what was revealed Truth. He believed, however, that those texts that dealt with the identity of Brahman and *Ātman* were superior to all others in the *Upaniṣads* and there is certainly evidence of "revealed Truth" being only that which was in line with his *advaitist* view. And yet, as far as Śaṃkara was concerned, the truth to those three questions that I mentioned above could barely be ascertained by reason and rational debate – though Śaṃkara used both in his refutation of the theories of other schools – for Truth transcends any thought process and is of a different reality. Truth is radically different from any kind of epistemological reality and reason and is ultimately experientially realized.

Yet, as we shall see, the complexities of the relation of Brahman to the self on the one hand, and to the world on the other, inevitably required differences in perspectives. Some Vedānta schools are absolutist. That is to say the underlying philosophy is based on the acosmic, *nirguṇa*, Brahman of the *Upaniṣads*. Others are theistic, resting their cases on the *Upaniṣadic* cosmic, *saguṇa*, Brahman as a describable God. These differences are well exemplified in the major branches of Vedānta with the proponents of Śaṃkara, Rāmānuja and Madhva as the major schools, Rāmānuja and Madhva founding theistic branches of Vedānta. This chapter, however, is concerned with *advaita* Vedānta, that is to say with the strictly non-dual approach. Within such an approach Śaṃkara aimed to refute the doctrines of the other schools that he felt had no support in the *Upaniṣads*. At the same time, of course, he had to demonstrate that his own interpretations were correct – and that often meant dealing with some very inconsistent material in the *Upaniṣads* themselves. A primary aim was to interpret the *Upaniṣads* as a single and coherent philosophy concerning Brahman. But four great sayings, *mahā-vākyas*, from the *Upaniṣads* informed Śaṃkara's core views. These are:

- Brahman is Consciousness, *prajñanam Brahma* (*Aitareya Upaniṣad* 3:5:3)
- I am Brahman, *aham Brahmāsmi* (*Bṛhad-āraṇyaka Upaniṣad* 1:4:10)
- That you are, *tat tvam asi* (*Chāndogya Upaniṣad* 6:8:7)
- This Ātman is Brahman, *ayam Ātmā Brahma* (*Bṛhad-āraṇyaka Upaniṣad* 2:5:19).

What we find, then, in the traditions of Advaita Vedānta, is an acceptance of the traditional monism of the *Upaniṣads* and Śaṃkara was the great proponent and traditional founder of the school.

Śaṃkara's name is frequently found suffixed with *ācārya*, "great spiritual teacher", a title subsequently given to all Advaita Vedānta *gurus*, especially those who are leaders of monasteries. Although the thinker mostly associated with Advaita Vedānta, there were several others of like-minded thought that preceded him,[2] and there are likely to have been other ideas along the same lines amongst other groups[3] and a "variety of philosophies" that went by the name Vedānta.[4] We must reckon, too, with influences from other philosophical schools, especially Sāṃkhya, but also even heterodox Buddhism, particularly its Mahāyāna strands.[5] While Śaṃkara's dates have been traditionally accepted as 788–820, some modern views are inclined towards a longer life for Śaṃkara and an earlier dating of about 700–750.[6] Gauḍapāda was responsible for the earliest known exposition of *advaita*, "non-dualism", in his *Gauḍapāda-Kārikā*. This was a commentary on the *Māṇḍūkya Upaniṣad*. So much of his teaching pre-empts that of Śaṃkara that it is clear his influence on the latter was considerable. Indeed, Gauḍapāda's pupil, Govinda, was Śaṃkara's own teacher, so the three were participants in a similar school of thought.

There are many varying accounts of Śaṃkara's life, especially at different monasteries associated with him but generally, according to tradition, Śaṃkara was a *Brāhmin* and was born in Kāladi in southern India, though traditions about him are pan-Indian. He became a *saṃnyāsin* at an early age. In his mature life, he is said to have been the founder of four *maṭhas* or monasteries, having been a prolific traveller.[7] His commentaries seem to suggest that Śaṃkara was a worshipper of Viṣṇu in the form of Nārāyaṇa.[8] This is a term for Viṣṇu that contains the word for human, *nāra*, and is indicative of the manifestation of the divine in the human – a concept close to Śaṃkara's thought, but from a lower level of reality of the phenomenal world, as we shall see. Other traditions see him in the Śaiva religion, though there is nothing in his writings to connect him with the worship of Śiva. Those works that do so are doubtfully authentic.[9] We must also reckon with a substantial amount of hagiographic material surrounding the life of Śaṃkara.[10] But, while not strictly atheist,[11] he was primarily non-theistic: his beliefs were rooted in one ultimate Reality of Brahman, a Reality so ultimate that it denied the world as we know it. His greatness and prestige have stood the tests of the ages, his theology and qualities being depicted rather well by Sengaku Mayeda: "Penetrating insight, analytical skill, and lucid style characterize Śaṅkara's works. He cannot be called a particularly original philosopher . . . but it has to be remembered that in India it is not originality but fidelity to tradition which is the great virtue. He was an excellent exegete, with an approach to truth which was psychological and religious rather than philosophical. . . . He was really not so much a philosopher as a pre-eminent religious leader and a most successful religious teacher."[12]

But there is little to suggest that his views were original. He was not an innovator. As Rasvihary Das remarks: "For Advaitism truth has been already found and recorded in the

Upanishads. What is left for Advaitic philosophy to do is to defend this truth against hostile criticisms and make it generally acceptable to our understanding by removing from our mind all doubts about it."[13] Śaṃkara was thus a prolific critic of the views of other schools – both unorthodox and orthodox – especially of orthodox schools that he felt fell short of a correct interpretation of *śruti* literature.[14] But despite such emphasis on correct interpretation much of his terminology is "recklessly used" to quote one author.[15] This is a factor that is not without its problems in analysing his views. Nevertheless, while he has had many critics, Śaṃkara was a remarkable philosopher, the more so if his life was really so brief.

General features of the school

Śaṃkara eschewed all sense of duality between subject and object, and between Self and divine. In a way, this reduces all to one essence and is monistic, but the negative term *non-dual*, *advaita*, is possibly more appropriate for it contains no sentiment of *parts* of one unity and no plurality whatsoever. In other ways, "one" is dual to two or many,[16] and Śaṃkara, being true to *Upaniṣadic* thought, takes the principle of Reality beyond any definition. In this sense his non-duality is absolute (*kevala advaita*), and to maintain it he had to deny the reality of the world in any ultimate sense. This necessitated some bifurcation of *Upaniṣadic* teaching that was, on the one hand, non-dual and, on other hand, seemed to separate Brahman from the world and the self. It is such division of *Upaniṣadic* thought into two kinds – core teaching related to ultimate Reality and the acosmic, *nirguṇa*, Brahman, and supportive teaching related to the lower reality of a cosmic, *saguṇa*, Brahman – that is the key to the understanding of Śaṃkara's theories. I think we would have to reckon with this as a dual view of things, the enlightened one, and the unenlightened one. And this dual perspective of things underpins Śaṃkara's views of knowledge, the self, the world, causality and the divine – all concepts that I shall develop below. Since there are few who could perceive things from the enlightened level, he was forced to give much space to the unenlightened one. He had to teach *as if* the world is real, *as if* cause–effect exists, *as if* there is a self that was bound and transmigrated, *as if* there is a describable God. Ultimately, none of these obtains, but Śaṃkara cleverly applied the theory to the *śruti* texts themselves, which, to him, also contained supportive material that spoke *as if* dualities exist. This dual perspective, then, needs to be kept in mind in the pages that follow, for it seems to me as fundamental to Śaṃkara's position as his *advaitist* viewpoint.

Reality: The Advaita view of the world

Behind all the apparent plurality of the universe, Śaṃkara believed there is an underlying Reality. This we can call *Existence*, *Being*, *sat*, or Brahman. It is the common substratum or essence that runs through all things as *Ātman*,[17] but all such things are only an apparent, and not real, modification of it. Everything, therefore, is *really* this same essence. This formless, infinite and indivisible essence that is Brahman is the only Reality. In the *Bṛhad-āraṇyaka Upaniṣad* 1:4:10 we find the words "I am Brahman", on which, Śaṃkara says of Brahman: "I am all, always pure, enlightened and unfettered, unborn, all-pervading, undecaying, immortal, and imperishable."[18] Brahman as pure Existence, pure Being, is self-illuminating Consciousness. For Śaṃkara, reality is not some modification of Reality but Reality itself. It is not the clay pot, but the "clayness" that informs the pot that is real: the clay seems to have different forms, but its reality of clayness stays the same. Similarly, Existence or pure Being *seems* to become diverse, but it is the ultimate Reality of all things, the "things" only being of an apparent reality. Thus, "I" as a perceiver am really pure Consciousness, and "that" which I perceive is also pure Consciousness. So "I" and "that" are really the same, and cannot be said to exist apart from that essence and sameness in any real or ultimate sense. The Reality of "me" and the Reality of the world are both the same, and this Reality is identified as Brahman, so establishing the non-dualism of all things.

Reality, then, is something that *is*, that *exists* throughout all existence: it pervades and persists in all things. It is pure Subject, pure Consciousness, devoid of objects. In Śaṃkara's words: "As I am devoid of the life principle, I do not act. Being without intellect, I am not a knower. Therefore I have neither knowledge nor nescience, having the light of Pure Consciousness only."[19] Pure, subjective Consciousness is self-illuminating, and all-expansive, unlike ordinary consciousness that is limited, fluctuating and subject–object orientated. Pure Consciousness has a thorough "autonomy of status", as Debabrata Sinha puts it.[20] What is not real neither pervades all things nor persists in one or more things, and the phenomenal world that we know falls into this category. Reality, R. N. Dandekar summarized, is: "that which is one without a second, which is not determined by anything else, which is not sublated[21] at any point of time, which transcends all distinctions, to which the familiar categories of thought are inapplicable, and which can be only intuitively realized."[22] His description admirably fits many of the *Upaniṣadic* statements about Brahman: Reality is Brahman, and since it pervades all things, then all things are identical in their pure Being to Brahman. Reality as Brahman is Absolute and unchangeable and exists in itself without being caused. Śaṃkara depicted it thus:

> The highest [*Brahman*] – which is of the nature of Seeing, like the sky, ever-shining, unborn, one alone, imperishable, stainless, all-pervading, and non-dual – That am I and I am forever released. Om.
>
> I am Seeing, pure and by nature changeless. There is by nature no object for me. Being the Infinite, completely filled in front, across, up, down, and in every direction, I am unborn, abiding in Myself.
>
> I am unborn, deathless, free from old age, immortal, self-effulgent, all-pervading, non-dual; I am neither cause nor effect, altogether stainless, always satisfied and therefore [constantly] released. Om.[23]

While all this suggests that the world is to some extent unreal, Śaṃkara did not go as far as to say that it doesn't exist *at all*. For Śaṃkara, ultimate Reality cannot be contradicted by any other knowledge, but everything we "know" in the ordinary world, that is to say, empirical knowledge, could be contradicted at some point, so such knowledge is, at the very least, of a lesser reality. Any knowledge that can be contradicted later is not knowledge of the truth. Truth/Reality for Advaita Vedānta remains uncontradicted in the past, present and future and in all instances. So what we have here in the world is a different kind of reality. Nevertheless, we can see that the world exists, and we operate in it according to that perception of its "reality"; we believe what we see. If there were no reality at all, then there would be no value in any thought, for our minds would have nothing external to which they could relate. Śaṃkara accepted such pragmatic realism and a sort of partial reality of the world: it is *empirically* true but not *ultimately* true, so things can exist but are not real, resulting in a paradoxical unreal order of reality. We distinguish between objects, and we certainly know the difference between the illusory objects of a dream and those in our experience when we are awake. But, just as the world we know when we are awake is a different level of reality than the world of our dreams – even though the latter may be the cause of "real" emotions – just so the pervasive Reality of Brahman is of a different level to the reality of the world. But this pervasive level of Reality that is Brahman is such that we can hardly call the lesser reality of the world "reality" at all. Śaṃkara preferred to describe the world as of the nature of *vivarta*, "appearance" or "apparent change". Just like clay can be changed in appearance to be a plate or a pot, but is *really* clay, so Brahman, ultimate Reality, "appears" to be the forms of the phenomenal world. In fact, the change is not a *real* one at all. Reality doesn't become transformed into something else, and the things of the world do not evolve into their present states. All things are simply apparent changes but not *real* changes; it is in this sense that they are illusory.

So Śaṃkara has to accept some kind of "apparent" reality in which beings dwell and objects seem to exist – an unenlightened view of reality. From his commentary on the *Brahma-Sūtras* (2:1:14), Śaṃkara seems to have had no objection to regarding the world as real "for the time being". His commentary on the *Bṛhad-āraṇyaka Upaniṣad* (4:4:6), also suggests that objects exist for others when they are not being perceived by me.[24] Pragmatically, the world needs to be accepted as real even if it is ultimately false. Reality, whether from the enlightened or the unenlightened perspective is Consciousness / Knowledge / Intelligence / Awareness. It can be ultimate, absolute, pure and objectless, or it can be empirical consciousness of objects, subject to change and apparent only. Between these two kinds of reality there is what William Indich terms "a radical ontological discontinuity",[25] that is to say, they are totally dissociated from one another. Brahman is subjective Consciousness, the world is objective and unconscious – they cannot be the same. In the lower consciousness that belongs to the world, there is always contradiction, finitude and contingency. Raphael pointedly states: "Reality, fragmented into indefinable and fleeting phenomena, does not guarantee the stability and certainty of knowledge, but leaves it a prey to gnawing relativism, incapable of determination."[26] But the world and ordinary selves are not totally unreal like the horns of a hare; they are simply not ultimately real like the *Ātman* that is Brahman. Being neither real nor unreal, they have a vague reality because they exist only in so far as, as yet, they have not been contradicted by a greater Reality. It is in this sense that they are illusion. Such phenomena are what Bina Gupta terms "empirical existents", the whole world of names and forms, beings and subject–object distinctions.[27] These may produce illusory realities but are not *total* illusions in the sense of the horns of a hare. They are understood to be real for pragmatic reasons – just as a rope that appears to be a snake produces the appropriate reactions. Ignorance, nescience, is the cause of such illusion. So the world must be taken as real until the time when ultimate

Reality dawns. In the meantime, as Chandradhar Sharma put it: "Thought reigns supreme in the empirical realm and its authority cannot be questioned here, otherwise the entire empirical life would be exploded."[28] Thus, the vague and apparent reality of the world lies somewhere between absolute Reality and absolute non-reality. This leaves us with three distinct and disparate levels of reality:

- *Sat*: Reality that is absolute, ultimate and pure, and that cannot be contradicted by any other experience, knowledge or reality – *sat* is, in other words, Brahman.
- *Mithyā*: something that is illusory in the sense that it is neither real nor unreal. Thus, it is appearance – the phenomenal world of the senses, and of ordinary selves, which can be contradicted by a higher reality.
- *Asat*: unreal illusory impossibilities like the horns of a hare or the child of a barren woman. Strictly speaking, these cannot really be contradicted because they can never exist in the first place.[29]

Between these levels of reality there can be no relation.

The world, then, is not an effect that is any different from its cause: it is not a transformation of its cause but a rather unreal *superimposition* (*adhyāsa*) of names and forms on what is a substratum of Reality. What we live in is a world of illusory phenomena to which we give names, and to which we cling in the belief that they are real. It is the path of knowledge that leads one away from such an illusion to the ultimate level of Reality that is Brahman. *Ultimate* Reality is not open to any contradiction, but other levels are. When we wake up from a dream, we realize that what was so real in the dream was unreal. But since the things we dream about are the things we experience in waking existence, then waking existence must, to some extent, contain the same images as dreams, and so must be partly unreal too. When we wake up to ultimate Reality, we will then know that the experiences we had in the waking world are also unreal. Ultimate Reality is just Consciousness alone – Consciousness not operating at all, and not reflected in anything else: ordinary consciousness is consciousness *of* something whether in dreams or in the waking world.

As an orthodox *Brāhmin*, it was necessary for Śaṃkara to present some sort of provisional reality that would endorse and retain the *Veda*, though recognizing that ultimate Reality transcended anything in the material universe, even the *Veda*. So the important question of the relation between the infinity of the divine and the finitude and change of the world and selves had to be answered in two ways by Śaṃkara. First, he stated that pure Consciousness, that is to say the Absolute, is the only Reality, in comparison to which all else is impure consciousness, erroneous and illusory. Secondly, he used the analogy of the *reflection* of the pure Consciousness of the Absolute in the mind and intellect of each individual, like the moon or sun reflected on the surface of water, to account for selves and their perspectives of an apparent world. Śaṃkara saw all selves as characterized by "limiting adjuncts" (*upādhis*), making them apparent manifestations in an apparent world of subject–object differentiation. His theory *separates* the ultimate Reality that is Absolute from the finitude of the world, from transmigration, suffering, evil, pain, joy – in short, from the whole manifest universe. How far this is a dual perception masquerading as *advaitism* I shall leave to the reader to judge, and I think Keith Ward's opinion here is to the point when he says: "It remains unclear how a perfect and self-sufficient reality could give rise to a world of illusion and desire; and it remains unclear what is meant by the 'limiting adjuncts' which seem in some way to be part of Brahman, even though Brahman is simple and without parts."[30]

Śaṃkara's concept of Brahman

It would be worth pausing here, I think, to reflect on Śaṃkara's understanding of Brahman as the ultimate *nirguṇa* Absolute and Reality, for his teaching here is diametrically different from his concept of God as the *saguṇa* Brahman. The *nirguṇa* Brahman is the ultimate focus of Śaṃkara's being, "the polestar to which he orients all his philosophical and religious endeavor".[31] Brahman, as the ultimate Reality of pure Existence is the essence that runs through all things. It is unchanging, unlike the change that characterizes the world of appearances. So each time a particularity of the phenomenal world is perceived or experienced in some way, it is but an apparent form. It is only the essence of it that is pure Existence, pure Reality, Brahman. Importantly, this absolute Reality, being itself unchanging, doesn't *do* anything. It doesn't change itself into the world, doesn't create the world as an efficient cause of it, and in contradistinction to much *Upaniṣadic* thought, it doesn't emanate out into the world. And yet Brahman is the manifest essence in all things without any modifications of itself, just as clay does not modify itself to become the clay of pots but simply *is* the substance of the pot. The most important factor to arise from this is the total identification of the essence of the self, the *Ātman* with Brahman. I shall deal with this concept of the self in a separate section below.

Brahman, then, is not the differing forms that appear in the world, or the different selves that inhabit it. Brahman is the same essence that underpins them and informs them. All the apparent forms of the world are incorrectly superimposed on this *Being* that is Brahman. The real conception of the Absolute, Brahman, is of a totally *nirguṇa* principle, a "no-thing" that transcends all description and all analysis, and that can be only intuitively experienced – in line here with so much *Upaniṣadic* thought. Supreme Reality is beyond the world as we know it and yet is the only means by which the world can be known. Being *nirguṇa*, "without qualities", Brahman cannot be a substance of any kind and there can be no differentiations of nature in Brahman. The nature of Brahman, if at all it can be depicted, is Truth, Reality, pure Being, Existence or *sat*, pure Consciousness, which is *cit*, and Bliss, which is *ānanda*, the three, *saccidānanda*, depicting the essence of the *nirguṇa* Brahman, though these are in no way qualities. As pure Consciousness, Brahman is pure awareness, pure subject. Unlike ordinary consciousness, however, the Consciousness of Brahman is independent of any object whatsoever. It is never the object of another consciousness, nor does it have objects that it is conscious of, and it is not the object of its own Consciousness. It is the differentiation between this and that, consciousness of dualities in the world around us, which makes our consciousness, our knowledge, always object-centered. Nevertheless, the self has consciousness only by reason of its essence that is the same pure Consciousness that is Brahman – a sullied consciousness that involves itself in the world of appearances and apparent reality with its subject–object dualities. And so the self gets lost. When the

Self loses such dualities, it becomes Brahman, for it *is* Brahman, and it is, at the same time, the essence of all things in the universe. There is a good deal here that reflects the division of spirit and matter of the school of Sāṃkhya as we shall see in the next chapter.

The famous words of the *Chāndogya Upaniṣad*, *tat tvam asi*, "That you are" depict the Self, the *Ātman*, as identical to Brahman, and Advaita Vedānta is true to this teaching. Brahman as Absolute is without parts, which means that the Self, the *Ātman*, cannot be a part of Brahman, but must either be or not be Brahman. Since Brahman is also, according to the *Veda*, "One without a second", there cannot be a Self that exists secondarily to Brahman. When this truth is realized the world of appearances no longer has any reality, just as the dream has no reality in the waking world.

Māyā and *avidyā*

What we need to turn our attention to now is not the ultimate Reality that is Brahman and the true Self, but the world, its "unreality", and its illusory nature that is known as *māyā* – "the warp and woof of the world of appearances".[32] If the world is a lower level of reality from the ultimate Reality of Brahman, and sufficiently so to give it an "unreality" and make it of the nature of "appearance", how, then, did it come into being? Why should we have a world at all? And why should the real Self or *Ātman* not be so readily perceptible? The answer the Advaitin gives to the first of these questions is the rather unsatisfying one that the world has always been so. The *Upaniṣads* accepted mainly that existence was one, and that the plurality we normally know of in the world is a mistaken view, though the world was real. Śaṃkara went further and said that the world itself is illusory though, at times, it is not really clear whether the world does exist or whether it is total illusion: since it is real (in essence) and unreal (in appearance) it has an ambiguous reality that could go one way or the other. If the world is simply "appearance", even though appearance is a wrong perception, it is not *absolutely* unreal. After all, a mirage may well be the result of incorrect perception, but some kind of appearance of known existents occurs. Again, the associated phenomena are called by Śaṃkara "limiting adjuncts" (*upādhis*), like the vision of water that is projected on the heat rays in the desert, and like the worldly sense realities that are imposed incorrectly on Brahman. Thus, as Arvind Sharma neatly defines *upādhi*, it is "the limitation, owing to mental imposition, of infinity by finitude, of unity by multiplicity. It results in the seeing of the Infinite by, and through, limitations or conditions that do not properly belong to the Infinite."[33]

Nevertheless, from the unenlightened view Śaṃkara, as in *Upaniṣadic* thought, accepted that the world exists timelessly in its cycles of manifestation and dissolution. Thus, illusion is timeless. It is a fact that is accepted rather than logically worked out. As far as the second question is concerned – why we have a world – there is a tension of meaning between answering it totally negatively and suggesting that the world doesn't exist at all but is merely an illusion or, by depicting it as a lower level of reality that has only an apparent existence, like the apparent existence of the world of the dreamer, albeit that in such an apparent world pragmatic empirical knowledge can relate causes to effects and make sense of the whole plurality of forms. But in both cases it would have to be asked who or what creates the illusion and who or what creates the dream? So pressing was this question that some Vedāntins made Brahman the substance from which the appearances of the world came into being – a material cause.[34] If *māyā* as illusion or the power of illusion is created by Brahman then Brahman is, in a way, the efficient cause of it, and if it is given any kind of reality – even a "lower" one – then Brahman is a material cause also. Brian Carr believes that Śaṃkara accepted the *nirguṇa* Brahman as the origin of the world of experience and, therefore, that Brahman as efficient and material cause of the world was fundamental to Śaṃkara's thought.[35] It is in his commentary on the *Brahma-Sūtras* that Śaṃkara clearly states that Brahman is both the material and efficient cause of the world by a kind of projection of Power Consciousness. But then he refutes that view as one from nescience, in particular, because no modification of Brahman ever takes place to form the world. What we see, once again, are the "limiting adjuncts", appearances, that have no fundamental reality but, nevertheless, are sometimes said to be present by the power inherent in Brahman and sometimes occur "by some inherent power of its own" as Keith Ward puts it,[36] though this smacks keenly of duality. Perhaps Arvind Sharma is right when he says that: "Metaphysically, *māyā* is that mysterious power of Brahman" and epistemologically, *māyā* is ignorance."[37] As far as I can see, this nature of Brahman as cause must apply only to the *apparent* reality of the world so that Brahman is the origin, as Carr says, "only in the sense that it merely apparently transforms into the diversity contained in our experience".[38] Since the effect has to be identical to the cause, as we shall see below, ordinary experience, which is so different, cannot be real.[39] The tension between *māyā* as the power of Brahman or as the nescience of the world is a formidable philosophical problem.

What we can say of *māyā* is that it is the principle of illusion; it is that which obscures unified Reality. But, while it is beginningless and endless, in itself it has no reality. It acts as a kind of veil over the real essence of things, the *Ātman*, and represents error in true perception, though in this lower level of reality it seems reason and rational thought have their place. As such, it is very close in meaning to ignorance, *ajñāna* or *avidyā*. Indeed, as far as Śaṃkara was concerned, these terms were synonymous. *Māyā* is not seen as something that opposes Reality and, therefore, as something dualistically juxtaposed to Brahman. It is, like ignorance, a misconception, a lack of the appropriate knowledge of Reality. We cannot say *why* ignorance occurs, or what it really is. We only know that it obscures the truth and real knowledge, and lasts only as long as the truth is not perceived. So, just like ignorance, when illusion is removed and the truth is realized, it ceases to exist. Illusion or ignorance cannot affect truth; just as Brahman is not affected in any way by the *māyā* of the world. Thus, *māyā* "is not conceived as utter non-being, but only as deficient in being".[40]

The inscrutable nature of the term *māyā* is reflected in the *Ṛg and Atharva Vedas* where it was used in the sense of supernatural power. But it was not a prominent feature of the *Upaniṣadic* texts, where it was more implicit than explicit in their thought. There, too, it tended to be used in the sense of a mysterious power. It eventually came to mean something like "magic" and the kind of illusory effects that can be produced by magical skill, and Śaṃkara wrote of *māyā* in the same sense as magic. Just as the performer of the Indian rope trick hypnotizes his audience *en masse* so that everyone thinks there is someone climbing up the rope, so the power of illusion, ignorance or nescience traps each individual in a phantasmagorical world of magic, albeit one in which there seems to be an interrelation of causes and effects. Śaṃkara equated the power of the Absolute to create the illusion of the world with the power of the magician to delude his audience without any effort. In both the truth is hidden, and yet is evident for the enlightened. And the world is no more real than the figure at the top of the rope in the Indian rope trick: it only appears to be so by the deluded. However, just as the vision of the figure at the top of the rope cannot exist without the magician, so the illusory world cannot exist without the existence of the Absolute. As Śaṃkara said: "The magician himself is in no way affected in past, present or future by the magic display he has spread forth by his hypnotic power (māyā), as it is nothing real. And in just the same way, the supreme Self is unaffected by the magic display of the world of transmigratory experience (saṃsāra-māyā)."[41]

The illusory nature of the world of appearance, the world of names and forms, is essential for a truly non-dualist philosophy. For if the world is accepted as real then so is its impermanence, its change, its constant cause–effect processes, and the reality of all this has to be the same Reality as Brahman. This would necessitate Brahman being changeable itself – at least in terms of the world that is composed of It – and if Brahman is changeable then it would have to be asked what causes the change? Then we are into the quest for a cause beyond the cause *ad infinitum*. But if the world is a kind of illusion it has no effect on the ultimate nature of the Reality of Brahman, the unity of Reality is safeguarded, and there is no duality of cause and effect. Nevertheless it is, I think, an unsatisfactory solution that resorts to a mysterious manifestation of an illusory power that exists indefinitely (and therefore is permanent!) without original cause. It leaves us begging the question of how pure and real Existence can appear to be manifested as a plurality of different forms. Das concurs: "Advaitism is unsatisfactory as philosophy mainly on account of its self-contradictory notion of *maya* which defies all logical treatment."[42] While *māyā* serves to explain the apparent nature of the world, it lacks substance on the one hand, and is not a quality on the other. We are left, I think, with the problematic idea of Brahman as its ontological cause.

One partial solution to the nature of *māyā* lies in the separation from, and yet relation between, *māyā* and ignorance, *avidyā* or *ajñāna*. *Avidyā* is ignorance or nescience. It was a term widely used in the *Upaniṣads* where it designated the opposite of knowledge, *vidyā*. Gupta believes that for Śaṃkara "it is a kind of psychic defilement, a 'natural' propensity to err, seed of the whole world, and generates attachment from a psychological perspective".[43] Clearly it was a fundamental principle in Śaṃkara's thought, though here, too, as Karl Potter comments, Śaṃkara sometimes "confesses inability to explain the mysterious ways of *avidyā*",[44] and Śaṃkara seems to use the term interchangeably with *māyā*. If *avidyā* is the general ignorance in human perception of the world, while *māyā* is the apparent result of that perception – the illusory world in which the effects of the perceptions are worked out – it would solve some of the issues, and I do not think that this would do any violence to Śaṃkara's general position. He is not clear in his use of the terms but at least positing ignorance as the individual perception of a dual and differentiated world would make *māyā* its concomitant result – an illusory world of perceived effects. *Avidyā* is, thus, endemic to human nature, and illusion, *māyā*, the collective superimposed experience that makes up our view of the world. Gupta says something of this sort when she sees *māyā* as cosmic and *avidyā* as individual ignorance.[45]

Clearly, ignorance is not something usually imposed from without, but is inherent in the self; it is one's own fault. Śaṃkara said: "Everything comes from nescience. This world is unreal, for it is seen by one who has nescience and is not perceived in the state of deep sleep."[46] Here, there is no cause of error other than *individual* false perceptions of reality. Thus, as Das comments, "we cannot think of an impersonal ignorance, of ignorance which belongs to nobody. Ignorance is not a self-subsistent entity".[47] Ignorance has a power, a *śakti*, to maintain illusion, and it is this that keeps the world processes in existence – albeit in cycles of evolution and involution. Yet it is not real because it is contradicted by correct knowledge, and is not completely unreal because of its power to maintain the illusion that is the world. But it is, I think, ignorance rooted in individual misconceptions that maintains the power of illusion.

Avidyā, wrote Radhakrishnan graphically, is "the force that launches us into the dream of life", and "the mental deformity of the finite self that disintegrates the divine into a thousand different fragments".[48] In this case, the *Ātman*, too, becomes falsely conceived of as involved in the world, through ignorance. Thus, as Surendranath Dasgupta pointed out: "We not only do not know what we ourselves really are, but do not also know what the world about us is."[49] But ignorance is illusion in the sense that it is a veil that hides Reality. It is in this sense that illusion is unreal; it isn't really there, but is just a mind blockage, a refusal to see Reality. The pure Consciousness, the *cit* of the true *Ātman* is there, and the ignorance of the mind is the veil, the illusion, that hides it. Thus, all life is lived in ignorance. In the words of Vivekananda,

> ignorance is the great mother of all misery, and the fundamental ignorance is to think that the infinite weeps and cries, that it is finite. This is the basis of all ignorance – that we, the immortal, the ever pure, the perfect Spirit, think we are little minds, we are little bodies. It is the mother of all selfishness. As soon as I think I am a little body, I want to preserve it, to protect it, to keep it nice, at the expense of other bodies. Then you and I become separate.[50]

Like the rope that is perceived as a snake through ignorance of the real nature of the rope, the world of forms is seen as real through the same kind of ignorance that blinds the individual to *sat*, the pure Being that is Brahman in all things. It is a projection or *superimposition* of something that is unreal on what is real – the medium of which is ignorance. Śaṃkara called this *adhyāsa*, "illusory superimposition". Of it he said: " This whole [universe] is qualification, like a beautiful ornament, which is superimposed [upon *Ātman*] through nescience. Therefore, when *Ātman* has been known, the whole [universe] becomes non-existent."[51] Such superimposition, *adhyāsa*, at a simpler level is the apparent presentation to one's consciousness of the nature of something seen previously onto something else, like apparent water superimposed on the desert sand that is a false perception on a real one; or superimposition of the figure of a man on a post. Śaṃkara gives many examples all leading to the point that the ordinary self superimposes on itself a reality that only the *Ātman* that is Brahman has. The problem here, of course, is that whether mistaken identity or not, the phenomena of, say, post and man could both be said to exist, suggestive that the world is not by any means unreal, though it can be falsely interpreted. However, it seems the three concepts of *māyā*, *avidyā* and *adhyāsa* inform the whole world of appearance and the kind of lower reality that it has.

Knowledge[52]

Eliot Deutsch and Rohit Dalvi make a very interesting comment about knowledge in the Indian context in that "the acquisition of knowledge is not looked upon as a gradual *discovery* of it, but as the gradual *recovery* of it".[53] Knowledge for Śaṃkara is synonymous with consciousness and is of two kinds. Real knowledge, real consciousness, is the pure Consciousness of the enlightened state. The other kind of knowledge or consciousness is that of the unenlightened state. Real knowledge is the "higher knowledge", *parā-vidyā*, which is Brahman-realization. Unenlightened knowledge is "lower knowledge", *aparā-vidyā*, the knowledge of the phenomenal world. This was a distinction put forward in the *Muṇḍaka Upaniṣad* (1:1:4). Indich describes the higher knowledge as "a fully autonomous state of being in which the identity of the all-pervading consciousness underlying the apparently distinct subject, object and means of knowledge is realized".[54] As we have seen above, however, the lower knowledge is not absolutely unreal; it is simply unreal in relation to *parā-vidyā*, higher knowledge. Indeed, as Radhakrishnan commented: "If not, Śaṃkara's elaborate and even passionate discussion of the lower knowledge will border on the grotesque."[55] Here, then, is a tension between knowledge and ignorance with the nature of the latter philosophically tainted with a kind of reality that does not obliterate it altogether.

Knowledge, *vidyā* – of the deep intuitive type – is critical to the soteriological quest of Advaita. It is the opposite of *avidyā*, ignorance, which is completely dispelled once true knowledge is acquired. This pure Knowledge or pure Consciousness is passive. So it is not an action, and it has no object; it simply *is*. Thus, "no *action* can remove *avidyā*; the only thing that can remove *avidyā* is knowledge, and knowing is not an act".[56] Pure Consciousness is Self-knowledge and transcends all dualities that are normally associated with knowledge. It is knowledge that *is* the *Ātman*, in which subject and object are one. Śaṃkara said: "Thus, with concentrated mind, one should always know everything as *Ātman*. Having known Me to be abiding in one's own body, one is a sage, released and immovable."[57]

From the unenlightened view, Śaṃkara conceded that knowledge/consciousness is that *of* something. It must have an object. However, the intellect, ego and mind, *antaḥ-karaṇa*, is a limited consciousness that is affected by the physical self, the body and the particular dispositions of the egoistic self. How can it have a *true* perception of what it sees, when it is so limited? No object can reveal itself, it has to be revealed by the subjective consciousness of a perceiver, so it is known only by the level of consciousness that perceives it. And that level of consciousness is not pure, unless it is the pure Consciousness of the liberated Self. When knowledge is knowledge *of*, that is to say is focused on an object, it is always *aparā-vidyā*, "lower knowledge" even if the object of knowledge is Brahman. As Chandradhar Sharma says: "Thought cannot reveal Reality; it necessarily distorts it".[58] What we perceive is done so with the limitations of our empirical consciousness and, when pure Consciousness is realized in the state of liberation, it will contradict all our knowledge and perceptions from the limited consciousness that we once had: thus, our present knowledge must be illusory. There is a distinct difference between pure Consciousness and the objects that are in the world. The outward *forms* of objects are simply superimposed on pure Consciousness like images on a screen, and they are dependent on the screen, the pure Consciousness, for their manifestation. We shall see a similar idea in the Sāṃkhya perception of reality in the next chapter. But, just like the images on the screen, the objects of consciousness have no real existence, they are limited in existence, unlike the infinite pure Consciousness that is all-pervading. In comparison to pure Consciousness, then, such objects, such forms, have no reality, and the empirical self that perceives them is living in a deluded state ignorant of its own true identity:

> The states of the mind, the intellect, and the sense-organs, which are aroused by actions, are illumined only by Pure Consciousness as a jar, etc., are illumined by the sun.
> Since this is so, the Knower, which illuminates the notions [of the intellect] by Its own light, and of which they are the objects, is called the agent of those notions [of the intellect] only by the deluded.
> [Only to the deluded], therefore, is [It] also all-knowing since [It] illuminates everything by Its own light. In like manner, as [It] is the cause of all actions, *Ātman* is all-doing.
> The *ātman* thus described is [the *ātman*] with adjuncts. [But] the *Ātman* without adjuncts is indescribable, without parts, attributeless and pure; neither mind nor speech reaches It.[59]

Thus, the self that says "I know this", and "I know that" is deluded because the real *Ātman* is *passive* Consciousness. It is devoid of any object of knowledge that creates duality between subject and object. But as long as the self is unenlightened it will be involved with the world of objects. Chandradhar Sharma put this well when he wrote: "The tragedy of human intellect is that it tries to know everything as an object. But whatever can be presented as an object is necessarily relative, and for that very reason unreal. The knower can never be known as an object. Ultimately there is no distinction between the true knower and pure knowledge."[60] Thus, Śaṃkara said, "he who has fallen into the rivers of births and deaths can never save himself from them by anything else but knowledge".[61]

Śaṃkara's view of knowledge, then, is twofold. It is an acceptance of false knowledge for the pragmatic existence of unenlightened beings on the one hand, but this knowledge is to be retracted on the other in the enlightened state by *pure* Knowledge devoid of objects. It is the superimposition (*adhyāsa*) of objects – name and form – on the pure Consciousness that is *Ātman*, that binds the self to transmigration. Radhakrishnan rightly commented: "That particular application of adhyāsa which inclines us to break up the nature of one absolute consciousness into a subject–object relation results from the very constitution of the human mind,"[62] and: "The reality of an ordered world exists only for mind and in terms of mind."[63] Śaṃkara's view, then, is that our slavery to sense perception, and our ego-involvement with what we experience, cause us to impose differentiation and duality on a non-dual Reality. However, it seems to me that while oneness of the universe is a respectable hypothesis and a philosophically viable proposition that even the *Upaniṣads* supported, the non-existence of the world of cause and effect is, I think, not at all viable, which is why Śaṃkara had to posit the "lower" knowledge of the world as opposed to none at all.

An important point here is that Śaṃkara accepted testimony in the form of *śruti* as the primary, indeed only, means by which knowledge of ultimate Reality could be developed, because this was the only source dedicated to providing evidence that Brahman and *Ātman* are one.[64] Śaṃkara said: "There is no other attainment higher than that of *Ātman*, for the sake of which [attainment] exist the words of the *Vedas* and of the *Smṛtis* as well as actions."[65] For Śaṃkara, therefore, the *śruti* texts and some later scriptures contained infallible knowledge – the identification of *Ātman* and Brahman: "It is indeed declared to us in the *Śruti* that knowledge is the notion of the oneness [of *Ātman* and *Brahman*] and nescience is the notion of the difference [of *Ātman* and *Brahman*]. Therefore knowledge is affirmed in the scripture with all vigor."[66] As so many of the orthodox schools of thought, Advaita Vedānta accepted the scriptures as revealed to ancient seers through direct experience – not by Brahman, either *nirguṇa* or *saguṇa* – but as authorless, timeless Truths that the seers cognized at the beginning of each world phase. For one locked into the ways of the world and the desire for some things and aversion for others, Śaṃkara said: "The scripture gradually removes his ignorance concerning this matter."[67] Yet ritual actions were regarded by him as merely supportive to the primary teaching of the *nirguṇa* Brahman and the identity of Brahman and *Ātman*. Such a denial of the primary importance of *Vedic* ritual as the means to liberation was, as Atmananda commented, one of "the boldest steps taken by Sankara".[68] Once again, we find the dual views of the enlightened and unenlightened, the primary teaching that leads to enlightenment, and the supportive teaching for the unenlightened. And it has to be said, I think, that the *Vedas*, timeless as they were believed to be, were part of the phenomenal world that Śaṃkara tried to place in an unreal category. Śaṃkara accepted the *Veda* as revealed Truth, but as a means to ultimate Reality that was still part of the apparent world only.

The key to all *śruti* for Śaṃkara lay in the words of the *Chāndogya Upaniṣad* 6:8:7, *tat tvam asi*, "That you are". These words, which identify the innermost Self with Brahman, are analysed at length by Śaṃkara. Eric Lott considers Śaṃkara's interpretation of such key texts of the scriptures to be "probably the most subtle aspect of his system",[69] and there is certainly much penetrating commentary to be found in Śaṃkara's exposition of such texts. As I said earlier, most other teachings in the *Veda* Śaṃkara believed to be subordinate to this central statement. They were supportive texts that would assist in the growth of knowledge by making ultimate Truth initially easier to understand. In the last event, however, it would be the experience within that would transcend all knowledge for Brahman-realization. Thus, *Vedic* revelation supplied the initial impetus for the disciple.

Cleverly, Śaṃkara interpreted *Upaniṣadic* texts that appeared to separate Brahman from the self, or that spoke of Brahman as having qualities, as the *Vedic* method of "false attribution" in order to offset incorrect knowledge. So if the self is depicted as something that can be "attained", this is only to demonstrate that it cannot be realized apart from knowledge. Or if the Absolute is referred to as a "Knower", this demonstrates that only the Absolute is worth knowing, and so on.[70] In other words, supportive material in the *Veda* was concerned with the means of assisting the experience of ultimate knowledge itself. It would depend on one's level of consciousness just what would be absorbed, and what left behind. Either way, Śaṃkara endorsed the *Veda* as the best possible means of knowledge. Although the *Veda* did not always portray the truth, it was the best preparation for it, but once liberation was attained, the *Veda* was rendered useless. Ultimately, no words could ever describe the Absolute, but the *Veda* could speak of Its existence in negative terms and still point in Its direction through language appropriate for those still bound by nescience. It was particularly those parts of the *Veda* that referred to Brahman in negative terms that Śaṃkara accepted – the *nirguṇa* Absolute, devoid of all qualities. "The Absolute is that in which there is no particularity. There is no name, no form, no action, no distinction, no genus, no quality. It is through these determinations alone that speech proceeds, and not one of them belongs to the Absolute. So the latter cannot be taught by sentences of the pattern 'This is so-and-so.'"[71] Wilhelm Halbfass demonstrated well how Śaṃkara viewed the *Veda* "as a complex, differentiated structure of discourse, speaking at different levels and with different voices.[72]

Avidyā is error in knowledge by which the nature of one particular thing is superimposed on another. It is, thus, "illegitimate transference".[73] In Śaṃkara's words: "It is the false appearance in one place of what has previously been seen at another place, of the nature of a memory".[74] So just as the qualities of silver are erroneously superimposed on a shell, so that the shell is mistakenly believed to be silver, or a rope appears to be a snake, or a post appears to be a man, the empirical, ordinary self and all its experiences are superimposed on the *Ātman*. Thus, the real nature of the *Ātman* is obscured. Error, or superimposition of the qualities of one thing onto another, is the ignorance, nescience, *avidyā*, that is endemic to life. It is a lack of discrimination between what is real and what is unreal. Nescience colours all – all knowledge in ordinary existence – simply because only the *Ātman* as pure Consciousness is real. When there is consciousness *of* something, *of* an object, this can only be because superimposition occurs. Only the Absolute exists, and is One without a second: there can be no duality of subject *and object*, no experience of any object in the liberated state. The Advaitin who finds himself in *avidyā*, says Arvind Sharma, "seeks to understand its nature, to describe its operation, and to overcome it: he cannot tell us why it, or the mental processes which constitute it, is there in the first place. With respect to its ontological source, *avidyā* must necessarily be unintelligible."[75]

The self

Each individual consists of a physical body, a subtle body, vital breath or air, five organs of action, five senses, and the *antaḥ-karaṇa*, the intellect, ego and mind.[76] As far as Śaṃkara was concerned, these are all aspects of the self that exist only because of *avidyā*, ignorance. The *real* Self is the *Ātman*. And since it is passive Consciousness, the *Ātman*, the real Self, is never born, is never bound, and never dies – a point emphasized by the *Bhagavad Gītā*. Like the Absolute that it is, it is not subject to any modifications at all. It is pure Being, Existence-*ness*. It is Brahman of the *tat tvam asi* of the *Chāndogya Upaniṣad* affirmed. There is, then, a Self and a not-self: one is Reality and the other appearance. AnthonyAlston writes of these: "From failure to apprehend the true nature of the Self arises, by way of unwitting superimposition or projection, a not-self. And then comes that 'failure to discriminate' (aviveka) the Self from the not-self which is the proximate cause of our self-identification with the body and mind and thus of our painful experiences in the realm of saṃsāra".[77] In Śaṃkara's words: "The notions 'oneself' and 'one's own' are indeed falsely constructed [upon *Ātman*] through nescience. When there is [the knowledge of] the oneness of *Ātman*, these notions certainly do not exist. If the seed does not exist, whence shall the fruit arise?"[78]

It is Brahman as *Ātman* that is the real essence of all things, so all Selves are identical, a point so often iterated in the *Upaniṣads*.[79] It is only through ignorance that the illusion of the diversity of forms in existence, and the diversity between one individual and another, are present. As *Ātman* the Self pervades all things as pure Existence, pure Being. What constitutes the Self is really Consciousness – that factor that unites all aspects of an individual – and it is Consciousness that, for Advaita, is not an attribute of the self, but the real *essence* of the self. The true Self is characterized by *pure* Consciousness, whereas the unreal, empirical self, is characterized by consciousness that is subject to ignorance and illusion. But this inferior consciousness can only exist by reason of the pure Being of *Ātman* as pure Consciousness by which ordinary consciousness can exist through false superimposition of it on pure Consciousness. Sinha writes: "Transcendental consciousness is to be conceived as the foundation behind the conscious life, beyond which there can be no further background – at least within the realm of personal experience."[80] Consciousness, then, is the essence of the real Self and the means of existence for the empirical self. Consciousness that is the essence of the self for Advaita is that which is not dependent on any objects for its manifestation, but which makes possible the consciousness of objects that characterizes the empirical self.

Thus, similar to much *Upaniṣadic* thought, the individual, empirical self that we ordinarily know is not the real Self, for it is changeable, finite and illusory in comparison to the *Ātman*. The *Ātman* is merely the passive observer. The *Ātman* is not at all involved in the experiences of the empirical self, even though it is present in every reincarnation. It merely observes – just like the passive bird in the analogy of the two birds that we saw in the last chapter – and is the "innermost nucleus"[81] of all cognition. All the reactions of the empirical self to the world that create a fluctuating consciousness, are, as far as Śaṃkara was concerned, illusory perceptions of reality. Joseph Milne's comment here is apt: "Thus the personal self cannot hold steady in any certain knowledge of itself, but changes with different states and experiences. It cannot settle on any fixed relation with the world, but is agitated by the ever-changing impressions of the senses and the never-ending stream of desires and aversions that arise from this."[82] The *real* Self is devoid of subject–object differentiation, devoid of perceptions that are unreal, and aware only of its own self-luminosity that runs through all things. The self – whether empirical or real – can never be an object, for it is consciousness that reveals objects and it cannot itself be an object of itself. And if consciousness *were* to be an object, then it would require something else to make it an object, and that would require something else, and so on *ad infinitum*. The self-luminous and independent nature of pure Consciousness means that any knowledge is dependent on it.

This self that is so involved in the world is the *jīva*. It is the self that transmigrates and that is involved with the world in every way; it is the thinking and egoistic self. Śaṃkara depicted it as a sad self:

> But those who take part in the round of transmigration revolve round the midst of ignorance, of thick darkness, swaddled in the bonds of a thousand longings for sons and cattle and worldly goods. Thinking themselves to be wise and to be great experts in the secular and sacred sciences, they pursue a crooked and devious course. Lacking true discrimination, they wander about afflicted by old age, death and disease, like a large crowd of blind people being led by others as blind along a rocky road leading to a great disaster.[83]

These words of Śaṃkara vividly depict the bound self that is unaware of its true nature. It is an apparent, material self that is difficult to escape.

Differences between individuals occur because pure Consciousness is seemingly sullied by the specific nature of the ignorance of the individual. Like the moon or the sun reflected on water, which are really separate from it, they appear to take on the character of the water as moving or still, as rippled, murky, or clear, and so on. Potter describes such reflection analogies as "the most complex and sophisticated of the models offered by Śaṃkara and his contemporaries" to explain the apparent differences between the selves and the divine.[84] But the particularly good analogy often cited is that of the *jīva* being like space in a jar. This space is really no different to the space in other things, and no different to the space outside it. But the *jīva* ignorantly sees itself as different, and sees Brahman as confined in various forms like the space. When the jar disappears, like ignorance, the space inside becomes the space outside – which it always was – just as the self becomes the pure Existence and Consciousness that it has always been. No modification of the original space has taken place at all, just as no modification of Brahman takes place for the illusions of the world.

The *jiva* lives life after life forgetful of its true nature as Brahman, and is constantly involved in the world and relates all things to its own ego – owning things, liking things, disliking things, and experiencing appropriate joys and sorrows. It treats others as different and as beings to be liked or disliked or indifferent to, and thus the veil of ignorance prevents *Ātman*-realization. However, the egoistic self can only exist because of the pure Consciousness of *cit*. The pure Consciousness is there all the time which, it seems to me, must always lend to the self a degree of Reality even if that combines with the unreality of ignorance. Past memories and past *karmic* dispositions are stored by the self, surrounding the *Ātman* layer by layer, and the veil that obscures it is constantly thickened. Deussen poignantly remarked: "No man, whatever he may do, can get out of his own Self; everything in the world can only arouse our interest, nay, only exists for us, in so far as, affecting us, it enters the sphere of our 'I,' and so, as it were, becomes a part of us."[85]

In line with the *Taittirīya Upaniṣad*, Advaita accepted "five sheaths" or "five selves", that make up what we know as the self. Symbolically, these are like five layers of an onion. They are, first, the gross physical body (*anna-maya-kośa*), pervaded within by the second sheath or layer, its subtle replica as vital breath or energy (*prāṇa-maya-kośa*). The third is the subtler mind-self (*mano-maya-kośa*), the fourth, the even subtler "knowledge-self" (*vijñāna-maya-kośa*), and the fifth, the subtlest "bliss-self" (*ānanda-maya-kośa*). All these are composed of the elements (fire, air, water, earth and ether); they are all material, and non-conscious, though increasingly subtle. The true Self as pure Consciousness, as far as

Śaṃkara was concerned, transcends all five. Each of these selves lies within the former one, and the more adept the student, the more the inner selves will be experienced. The bliss of the inner self comes from treading the path of greater control of the mind, of following the *Veda*, and practising celibacy and meditation. Again, however, such detailed descriptors of the nature of the self speak volumes against any thought of their their non-existence.

Although the *Ātman* is passive and does not do anything, from the level of the ignorant self, it is said to be in three states – a thought put forward in the *Upaniṣads*, especially the *Māṇḍūkya*. These three states – waking, dreaming and deep sleep – were of particular interest to Śaṃkara because of the light they cast on the question of consciousness. The true pure Consciousness that is the natural state of the Self is known as *prājña*. Matter is superimposed on true Consciousness, and through nescience seems to exist in the dreaming and waking states. *Virāj* or *vaiśvānara* is *prājña* in the waking state, when the senses are focused externally. In the *Māṇḍūkya Upaniṣad* it was associated with the syllable *a* of the symbol *Aum/Oṃ*. *Taijasa* is *prājña* in the dreaming state, when subconscious impressions come to the surface in dreams, and the effects of *karma* are worked out. In the *Māṇḍūkya Upaniṣad* it was associated with the syllable *u* of the symbol *Aum*. Here, the senses are inactive; it is only the internal organ, the *antaḥ-karaṇa*, which consists of intellect, ego and mind, that is functioning, and that is creating the appearance of dualities. All perceptions in the dreaming state are erroneous perceptions. However, according to Śaṃkara, the *Ātman* is purer in this state than in the waking state, for it is not subject to the external sense stimuli and the desires and aversions that these involve, it is simply observing-consciousness. But both the waking state and the dreaming state are determined by past *karma*. If the external senses are withdrawn in the dreaming state, then this leaves only the light of pure Consciousness to view the dreams, via the intellect. Śaṃkara maintained that consciousness in dreams is no different from consciousness in the waking state. In the latter, like the former, it is merely witnessing. This renders all perception as imaginary and illusory.

Prajñā (wisdom), *avyākṛta* (unmanifest) or *tamas* (darkness) are the terms given to the *Ātman* in deep sleep, when even the *antaḥ-karaṇa* is not operating. In the *Māṇḍūkya Upaniṣad* it was associated with the syllable *m* of the symbol *Aum*. It is a state in which there is total non-perception. The *Ātman* here is "a mass of mere consciousness"[86] with no sense stimuli and no activity of the intellect, mind or ego. All is still, and there can be no emotions, no experience of happiness, pain or sorrow – just consciousness. Śaṃkara believed that in this stage of dreamless sleep, the individual ceases to exist and becomes identical with the Self of all. He said: "And this same soul, embraced by its own Self in the form of Consciousness in its real natural state of transcendent Light, becomes a perfect unity, the Self of all, with no internal differentiation, and knows no other object outside itself, and no distinction within itself, such as 'This am I, happy or miserable (or whatever the case may be).'"[87]

This state of deepest sleep, then, is the closest the individual can come to the enlightened *Ātman*. The Self is united with pure Being. We might note here, with Indich, this hierarchy "based on increasing degrees of interiorization or unification of modified consciousness within itself".[88] But, even though the purity of it underpins deep sleep, as also, the dreaming and waking states,[89] a metaphorical "seed" of nescience remains. The *Ātman* is coalesced with nescience. Once the individual moves again into the dreaming or waking states, this "seed" will permit the subconscious impressions to influence the mind once again. The mind is simply not ready for the enlightened experience, and the Self will fall from its true nature. Thus, Śaṃkara also equated the state of deep sleep with darkness and ignorance. This is seen in his following words: "That which is called deep sleep is darkness or ignorance (*ajñāna*), the seed of sleeping and waking awareness. It ought to be completely burnt up by Self-knowledge like a burnt seed that does not mature. That seed, called *māyā*, evolves into three states that succeed each other over and over. The self, the locus of *māyā*, though without change and single, appears as many like reflections in the water."[90]

The only constant factor between waking, dreaming and deep sleep states is the unifying *reflected* Consciousness that is supplied by the *Ātman* that is Brahman. Beyond these three states is *turya* (*turīya*), Śaṃkara's fourth state, the final, enlightened Reality. It is the stage of spiritual intuition and knowledge of the Absolute and of the Self as that Absolute. It is consciousness of the Absolute unlike the state of dreamless sleep where the Self is at one with the Absolute, but has no consciousness of the fact. It is a knowledge that is final, eternal and infinite. Reality perceived here shows the former states of waking, dream and dreamless sleep to be unreal, though the real Self, *prājña*, remains the same through these three states.

The nature of the self in Advaita is, thus, a complex of three aspects, the real Self, the *Ātman*; the *jīvātman* that is the *Ātman* limited by a false conjoining of it with the empirically conscious self associated with experiential existence; and the *antaḥ-karaṇa*, which is the sum total of all experiences of the past, and is the cause of the reincarnating self. It is an *upādhi*, a limiting adjunct of the self. These last two aspects composing an individual are superimposed on the true self, the *Ātman*, and thus consciousness experiences joys, sorrows, suffering and the bondage of reincarnation, and identifies with the illusory phenomena of existence. *Ātman* and matter are *mutually* superimposed. Again, the idea here resonates with Sāṃkhya philosophy. Overcoming this superimposition – caused by ignorance, and overcome by knowledge – is the key to liberation. All the entities that Consciousness reflects are its external adjuncts (*upādhis*). Memory and subconscious impressions feed the ordinary self with reinforcements of previous desires, aversions, attachments and fears. Through nescience the self feels "I am happy, sad, intelligent" and so on. All these factors are but mind-functions, rooted in apparent matter, but not reality. Puligandla writes: "The mind can grasp neither itself nor reality. It can only function by drawing distinctions, and for it to grasp itself it should function without drawing distinctions – a self contradiction. In a word, the mind cannot catch itself, just as a knife which cuts everything cannot cut itself. The mind can't grasp reality, because reality wholly transcends the realm of the mind – the realm of distinctions."[91]

All these attributes drawn up in the mind are assigned to the self and superimposed on the *Ātman* that is the real Self, by means of the Consciousness that is *Ātman*. But *that* Self has *no* attributes, and it can never be known as an object, only intuitively realized. In the words of Vivekananda: "That Self cannot be known; in vain we try to know It. Were It knowable, It would not be what It is; for It is the eternal Subject. Knowledge is a limitation; knowledge is an objectification. It is the eternal Subject of everything, the eternal Witness of this universe – your own Self. Knowledge is, as it were, a lower step, a degeneration. We are that eternal Subject already; how can we know it?"[92] This pure Subject is

Reality. It is the real Self that is Brahman. The self that we know is merely an apparent self invented by the material mind. Raphael depicts the other end of the scale from Vivekananda's words above, when he writes: "In our mind we can conjure up an ideal, a passion, etc., and identify with it to such an extent as to forget that we are individuals above and beyond passions and ideas. We can dream while wide awake . . . and identify with our dreams to such a degree that we lose our identity. This happens to the majority of people; in fact, they are not persons but teachers, politicians, tradesmen, fathers, mothers, children etc.; they are everything and anything but entities aware of their true and profound reality."[93]

So any characteristics given to the Self are the results of erroneous superimposition. All its pain, suffering, joy and sensations are the result of false identification with the intellect and ego. Humorously, Śaṃkara stated: "Whoever wishes to characterize the nature of the Self in this way is like one wishing to roll up the sky like a piece of leather and climb up on it as if it were a step. He is like one hoping to find the tracks of fish in the water or of birds in the sky."[94] The Self can never be known by the mind, it can only be realized at liberation. Thus, it would be impossible to claim "I know the Absolute" – a point reminiscent of my final sentence of the last chapter, chapter 3. That is something that can only be experienced when ignorance is removed. It is like finding you are wearing something you have been searching for, or like ten people crossing a river and the leader finding only nine at the other side – for he forgets to count himself. "Here, within our own Self, we gain an infallible guide to the absolute Being which we are seeking."[95]

Is there, then, any distinction between selves and matter? Mysore Hiriyanna afforded *jīvas* a greater level of reality than the world. After all, it is selves that reflect the Consciousness that is *Ātman*. He wrote: "We cannot therefore say that the individual self is false (*mithyā*), as we may that the world is false."[96] But *Ātman* is the essence of all things, from Brahmā to a blade of grass. To say that the ultimate essence of *jīvas* is different from the ultimate essence of matter is to create a duality. What constitutes *jīvas* is the materiality of the intellect, ego and mind. But there can be no difference between the *Ātman* of the self and that in a blade of grass, or any material object, otherwise non-duality is compromised.

Ultimately, then, Śaṃkara's view of the self is, again, twofold – the enlightened self that is real, and the unenlightened self that is only apparent. And Śaṃkara has to work with the latter in order, ultimately, to transcend it for the former. This gets to the centre of the way Śaṃkara taught, something brought out fully in Satchidānandendra's analysis of the method of Vedānta. He wrote: "Whatever characteristics are attributed to the Self as a means to awaken the student to ultimate reality are always finally denied. This is the heart of the method."[97] Deussen called Śaṃkara's view of the two selves – the Self and the not-self – the "double fundamental view of the Vedānta".[98] The view of the liberated Self he refers to as the "esoteric" doctrine, and of the empirical self the "exoteric" doctrine.[99] It is the "exoteric" view that permits the plurality of selves in the world. And yet, as I see it, while Cause as Brahman and effect as Self are identical, what of the finite self in which the true Self is embodied? It is difficult to see it as anything other than an effect – albeit from the lower Brahman as cause – but something a good deal more than "apparent". Keith Ward is most apt when he says: "There is no reality independent of Brahman; so there is really no alternative than to say that Brahman is both wholly free of all contact and change; and also manifests itself in various forms, known by the ignorant and termed limiting adjuncts of its essential being. But this is to erect a vast dualism at the heart of a doctrine which is committed above all to non-dualism at any price."[100] We are left wondering why there should be a finite self at all, especially a finite self that is nothing like its creator – *saguṇa* or *nirguṇa* Brahman. Thus, it seems to me that it is difficult to avoid the suspicion that a dual perspective, as noted earlier, runs through Śaṃkara's philosophy of world, knowledge and self. We now need to see how it is worked out in relation to causality.

Causality

Vedānta accepts the theory of *sat-kārya-vāda*, the belief that only the cause is real, *sat*, and any apparent effects, *kārya*, exist only in the cause. In this case, no transformation occurs, and nothing new comes into being: the pot is still the clay from which it originated, just as the world is still Brahman as Cause. This is really *sat-kāraṇa-vāda* (*kārana* meaning "cause"), the belief that cause alone exists and is real, while any effects do not really exist and are illusory. The modifications of the cause are therefore of the nature of appearance only, or illusory, and termed *vivarta*. Śaṃkara related cause and effect completely so that they are identical and non-dual. For Advaita, it is impossible to identify the real nature of something without referring to its cause; thus the pot can only really be known in terms of the clay of which it is composed. The plurality of effects we see as the phenomenal world are only apparent manifestations of their single, unitary Cause and so they have no ultimate Reality.

An effect, then, is really its cause, and if this is the case, then nothing new has come into being. Moreover, even if we take into account an efficient cause of something, like the potter who turns clay into the pot, the potter does not make anything new; the pot still remains identifiable by its clayness, and is therefore no different from its cause. "We never build anew; we simply rearrange", said Vivekananda.[101] Consciousness that is Brahman and *Ātman* underpins the perceptions we have of the world by reflecting Consciousness in the intellect–mind complex, *antaḥ-karana*, of the empirical self. Brahman is the non-transforming basis of the world of appearance. This, too, is *vivarta*, a cause producing effects without undergoing any real change. Brahman changes neither wholly nor partially and, as Deussen neatly put it: "A transformation resting merely on words can alter nothing in the indivisibility of the Existent."[102]

The theory of *vivarta-vāda*, the belief that the world we see is but a false appearance and illusory, is unique to Advaita Vedānta. Śaṃkara described it thus:

> For pairs of opposites, like heat and cold and their causes, are not found to be real when critically examined through (perception, inference and other) recognized means of knowledge. For they are modifications and every modification is subject to change. Every formed object, like a pot, is unreal because, when it is examined through the eye, nothing is found apart from the clay or other material cause. And similarly every other modification is unreal because it is not found to be anything over and above the

> causal substance from which it is composed. Moreover, it is not apprehended at all before its production or after its destruction. Even the material cause itself, clay, together with its own material cause, are not found to be anything over and above the causal substances from which *they* are composed, and are hence unreal.[103]

From the standpoint of non-duality, the enlightened view, Śaṃkara had no choice but to deny that effects are non-different from their causes, otherwise the duality of cause and effect would obtain, and non-duality would be compromised. Similarly, there can be no whole and parts. Thus, the Absolute could not really emanate into the parts that form the world, "that which is partless and unborn (like the Absolute) cannot undergo real change or modification in any way whatever", he said.[104] But from the viewpoint of nescience, the unenlightened view, Śaṃkara had to accept causality to explain the relationship between causes and their effects in the empirical world in which we live. As Alston points out, positing no causality at all would be of little help to the, as yet, unenlightened disciple: "What he then needs is not a negation of causality but a rationally defensible theory of causality which will enable him to accept and make sense of the Vedic texts at the level of ordinary subject–object experience, while at the same time leaving the window open looking out onto the vistas of infinity in which causality is finally transcended."[105]

The dual perspective of an enlightened and unenlightened view is also applicable to the creation and dissolution of the universe as much as to the ordinary world of forms that we know, because it is something that is accepted only by the unenlightened. Creation is an *apparent* and not real evolution of the world from Brahman. Brahman as Cause does not change, and the world as effect always remains grounded in the Cause. The *apparent* changes are the illusory power of *māyā*, but in so far as the world is experienced as one of effects – as one with objects like selves and pots – *māyā* has a creative power to manifest itself in all things from the subtle to the gross to all those who are not enlightened to the Reality behind it. Cause and effect are one, so there is no difference between Brahman and the world of effects, but the effects as we mistakenly know them – the pot devoid of its causal substance of clay – are superimposed incorrectly on their cause. So the forms of things are given differentiated reality. The link that unites all things as their essence is missed for the illusory effects. In other words, Brahman as the true Cause is overlooked, and through ignorance, *ajñāna* or *avidyā*, all appearances in the world are given reality.

Śaṃkara's theory of creation solves one of the major difficulties that was highlighted in the discussion concerning the nature of reality in the introductory paragraph to this chapter. The difficulty is how to relate a world of change and finitude to the Absolute, ultimate Reality that is unchanging and infinite. Once it is claimed that the world emanates forth from Brahman then it has to be conceded that *part* of Brahman, the world, is changeable. This is somewhat contradictory and also inimical to the concept of the absolute, permanent Cause. And yet, if the world with all its finitude exists separately from Brahman, then the nature of Brahman is limited or, to really maintain its *absolute* nature, Brahman must be both change and permanence. Śaṃkara solves all these difficulties through the theory of *sat-kāraṇa-vāda*. The world of change is not real; it only appears so through ignorance. There are no changes, for the effects are the same as their cause and are permanent; the changes are apparent and not real. And the world does not exist separately from

Brahman: it is, in its essence, identical to Brahman, it is an apparent effect that inheres in its cause and is identical to its cause. Once Brahman is identified with the world – either wholly or partially – then the permanent and unchanging nature of Brahman is compromised. Śaṃkara's theory of causality being one of apparent and not real modification from cause to effect, avoids this difficulty.

All this does not really explain how the world of forms – apparent or otherwise – actually takes shape for each and every individual, and why the possibility of so many apparent effects, unreal as they may be, can be present. In the *Upaniṣads* it is clear that the world *does* come forth from Brahman, but from the *saguṇa* Brahman not the *nirguṇa* Brahman. It is only the *saguṇa* Brahman that can be the *Ground* of the world. And it is *saguṇa* Brahman that is the material and efficient cause of all, as well as of *māyā*. This would seem to offer the world a substantial degree of reality. As noted above, to overcome the difficulty *māyā* is the power of illusion and ignorance in creation that, after Śaṃkara, came to be credited to Brahman. So while Brahman does not actually change, *māyā* is the power that is within Brahman just like the power to burn is inherent in fire. In this case, creation is not an independent or dependent effect of Brahman, it is Brahman with a veil of ignorance thrown over it to make it appear as diverse effects. The difficulties of the projection of *māyā* into creation are manifold, and have resulted in various explanations in Vedānta as a whole, particularly if *māyā* is connected with the *nirguṇa* Brahman.

So whereas the *Upaniṣads* tend to present creation as an emanation of the Absolute, Brahman, Śaṃkara could not bring himself to link the world so intimately with the divine in the sense of a finite and impermanent world emanating from the eternal Brahman. The concept of an Absolute that was active in a world of suffering and change was impossible for Śaṃkara. And yet, since the average individual – even the disciples of Śaṃkara – was far from the end of the spiritual journey, positing a Creator of the world had some value for those still within the bounds of an egoistic existence. As Alston points out, "the conception of the Absolute as the Creator and Controller of the world, endowed with omniscience, omnipotence, compassion and other superabundant excellencies, is for most people the best that is available".[106] So Śaṃkara had two concepts of creation: first, the enlightened view, that it does not exist at all, it has never happened; and secondly, that for those entrapped in nescience, there is no harm in accepting the divine as a Creator and Sustainer of the world. It is only the liberated one who continues to live in what Alston terms "a kind of twilight existence" until death.[107] Creation here exists only in so far as the enlightened one has a physical body that encases the true Self that is Brahman. All else ceases to have effect on what is now a Reality that transcends "creation". So Śaṃkara wrote of creation, of duality, of an omnipresent God, and of the world of varied effects that rise from the single Absolute of Brahman – all of which is ultimately unreal when intuitive knowledge reveals the *Ātman* as Brahman. And it has to be said, I think, that Śaṃkara wrote *extensively* of the world of nescience and of the unreal God that creates and sustains it.

These concepts are taught "as a preliminary device to help induce the mind to understand the unity and sole reality of the Self."[108] In considering the *Upaniṣadic* texts, Śaṃkara believed those passages that taught of the creation-through-emanation theory, were deliberately directed to those who, in their world of nescience, could only think in terms of causality. The higher wisdom of Brahman as separate from the world, as non-Creator and

Consciousness only, the identity of Brahman and *Ātman*, and the illusory nature of all else, were aspects of the *Upaniṣads* pertinent to *ultimate* and non-dual Reality. Only the liberated *Ātman* could experience this higher Reality. It is also from the viewpoint of nescience that Śaṃkara depicted Brahman as he who metes out the respective rewards and punishments according to the *karmic* merit and demerit of each individual. But since that *karma*, too, is illusory, the Absolute remains the inactive pure Consiousness at all times, experienced only by the liberated, but believed to be the controller of the world and all that is in it by those still bound by nescience. Any good and evil can exist only at the empirical level: at the ultimate level of the *nirguṇa* Brahman, in the same way as all differentials, they cannot obtain. Evil is, thus, a facet of creation and cannot exist beyond it. The acceptance of these two aspects of Brahman neatly reflects the dichotomy of the cosmic, *saguṇa*, and acosmic, *nirguṇa*, views of Brahman in the *Upaniṣads*, but Śaṃkara's attempts to solve it are not wholly successful. He gave so much space to the world of dualities that it is difficult to see how he could ultimately deny it. He even posited a very tangible theory of creation that fitted rather badly, it seems to me, into his dominant theory of the world as illusion. This is thoroughly evident in Śaṃkara's explanation of reincarnation.[109]

The collective *karmas* of all individuals – the myriad impressions built up by a humanity trapped in nescience – are what cause the particular nature of the next world appearance. The power of ignorance to produce this is *śakti*. Through nescience an individual has a misconceived perception of causes and effects, and a relational desire for certain effects and an aversion for others. The world of appearances does not disappear when I am not perceiving it myself, for it exists for the effects of the *karmas* of other individuals also. But it remains an apparent plurality that is particularly difficult to explain away, especially considering the amount of space the Advaitin affords it in discussion. Individual *karma*, and the transmigration necessitated by it, are determined by the subconscious impressions (*saṃskāras*) and habits (*vāsaṇās*) that are built up over countless past lives, all carried forward to the next life by the subtle body, the *liṅga-śarīra*. Śaṃkara followed much of the traditional *Upaniṣadic* view of the cause–effect process that brings about reincarnation, with a post-death "northern path" for those who have knowledge of Brahman and a "southern path" for those who have followed *Vedic* rituals carefully, but who do not have knowledge of Brahman. The subtle bodies of those who are destined to return to earth are of those who reach the moon, pass through ether, air, smoke, mist, cloud and rain, back to the earth. This is the reverse order to their ascent to the moon after death. The subtle body is no larger than a grain of rice and, as such, its fate on the earth is a hazardous one. It may take a long time before it is ingested by an animal or human, is passed into the blood and semen, and is then reborn with a physical body. The newly-born is not starting anew in character, type of birth, birth circumstances, and so on. All these factors, and those that befall it in life, will be determined by past *karma*, specifically *prārabdha-karma*, *karma* that is already on its way.[110] But *karma* of any kind belongs to the world of illusory appearances and the supposed cause–effect processes that that world conjures up. *Karma* is simply a pragmatic reasoning to make sense of the world and an idea that will be contradicted by the higher knowledge of Brahman. Yet, paradoxically, as creation itself, it is without beginning and is eternal, and according to Arvind Sharma, it is the *saguṇa* Brahman as Īśvara that "supervises the workings of *karma* through various lives".[111]

The cause and effect process that results in transmigration has nothing to do with the *Ātman*. It only *seems* as if the self is born time and time again, and that it experiences the joys and woes of existence. In reality the cause–effect process also does not exist, but through ignorance, nescience, we experience ourselves as mortal beings with all the trappings that mortality brings. Ultimately, the Absolute remains *neti neti*, "not this, not this", neither manifest nor unmanifest, always beyond all dualities. Bearing in mind the Advaita view of causality as a particular kind of *sat-kārya-vāda* whereby effects are non-different from their causes, true modifications of the cause into effects cannot occur. The diversity that seems to exist in all creation, cannot have any reality, for in Śaṃkara's words, "this pluralistic universe, consisting of experiencers and their objects of experience, is nothing other than the Absolute".[112]

The concept of God

Unsurprisingly, from what we have seen above, Śaṃkara wrote of two concepts of God, the concept held by the liberated Self, and that held by the non-liberated. As far as he was concerned, this reflected the teachings of the *Upaniṣads* where two kinds of Brahman were dealt with, the *nirguṇa* Brahman without attributes, the "higher Brahman", and the *saguṇa* Brahman, the "lower Brahman", who has attributes and is that from which the whole world comes forth. As *nirguṇa*, Brahman is the ultimate Reality and essence that pervades existence: It is *sat* and *cit*.[113] Anything beyond this is unreal. Śaṃkara's supreme Brahman, the higher Brahman or *Para-Brahman*, is the *nirguṇa* Brahman about which nothing can logically be conceptualized: no distinctions can be made about It: It is therefore indeterminate. Even descriptions such as infinite, pure Consciousness, ultimate Reality, and so on, cannot in any way depict this totally transcendent Absolute. Assigning attributes or qualities would only serve to limit It in some way. It is, thus, non-predicable in every sense. However, it is an utter denial of any qualities for Brahman that is not without its critics. Lott writes: "There is no denying the determination with which Sankara sets out to protect the absolute nature of the knowledge of Brahman. The skill and the consistency with which he maintains its transcendent nature is impressive. The question is, however, whether this does not result in a loss of viability as a theological descriptive method. He can allow no statement about that supreme Being to stand without radically stripping it of all those positive meanings normally associated with such statements."[114] This is perfectly true, but Śaṃkara counteracts negative statement of Brahman with the fully describable Īśvara.

Thus, in contrast to the *nirguṇa* Brahman is the *saguṇa* aspect of Brahman. It is the *saguṇa* Brahman who is equated with the ocean, the Ground from which the changing waves that form its surface exist. But, always, it is the *nirguṇa* Brahman that is the *ultimate* Reality, and it is that which the Self really is. As Arvind Sharma puts it, "Advaita accepts one God as the ultimate *empirical* reality, but not as the ultimate *absolute* reality".[115] Only in the latter case are the waves the ocean, not extensions of it. It is the *saguṇa* aspect of Brahman that becomes Īśvara, "Lord", or "God", and is the perspective of God held by the empirical self. As such, it is a perspective that must be seen only through the veil of ignorance that is the characteristic of all knowledge other than Brahman-realization. As Chandradhar

Sharma said, "the moment we speak of Brahman, He ceases to be Brahman and becomes Īshvara".[116] This is because being *saguṇa*, Īśvara has qualities. These are qualities normally associated with supreme divinity – omniscience, omnipotence, omnipresence, Creator, Sustainer, Dissolver. But, as I see it, the distinction between the *nirguṇa* and *saguṇa* Brahman is very much a blurred one, especially since Śaṃkara seems to give qualities to the *nirguṇa* Brahman in his commentary on the *Brahma-Sūtras*. If the *saguṇa* Brahman is in any way related to the *nirguṇa* Brahman then *nirguṇa* is describable in part and ultimately responsible for the world, its causes and effects and the whole appearance of *māyā*. Positing *saguṇa* Brahman as an aspect of Brahman[117] involves the *nirguṇa* Brahman in the world vicariously. Īśvara is superior to ordinary selves but must be Brahman according to the *tat tvam asi* concept, so it seems his function must be of the realm of appearance, but not his essence. Īśvara can be the focus of worship but, in so far as it is ignorance that sustains the view of him, when liberation occurs, Īśvara will cease to exist. Īśvara, then, is only *apparent*, like all the other illusory phenomena in the universe. Radhakrishnan put this rather neatly when he wrote: "Transcendental absolutism becomes when it passes through the will of man's mind an empirical theism, which is true until true knowledge arises, even as dream states are true until awakening occurs."[118] In some ways, then, Īśvara is identifiable with the empirical self, for both are identified with *māyā*.

When he wrote of the *saguṇa* form of Brahman, Śaṃkara stated that the *ātman* (of the empirical self) and Brahman are dual, "the Lord is something more than the embodied soul if the latter is considered *qua* embodied",[119] because he was writing for those who are still bound by nescience. Any differentiation at all – whether between worldly phenomena or between Brahman and *Ātman* – is ignorant perception. It is only when he wrote of the *nirguṇa* Brahman that he wrote of the non-duality of all things and identified the *Ātman* as Brahman. "Brahman cast through the moulds of logic is Īśvara", wrote Radhakrishnan: "It is the best image of the truth possible under our present conditions of knowledge."[120] And in Śaṃkara's own words: "(The Absolute is that which ultimately has to be known.) So, in order to show that it exists, it is first spoken of in its false form set up by adjuncts, and fancifully referred to as if it had knowable qualities in the words 'with hands and feet everywhere.' For there is the saying of those who know the tradition (sampradāya-vid) 'That which cannot be expressed (in its true form directly) is expressed (indirectly) through false attribution and subsequent denial.'"[121] It is scriptures that provide knowledge of the omnipotent, omnipresent and omniscient God, the cause of the universe, as much as the indescribable Brahman.

Īśvara is thus intimately connected with *māyā* and is as unreal as *māyā*. As Dasgupta pointed out, "he is but a phenomenal being; he may be better, purer, and much more powerful than we, but yet he is as much phenomenal as any of us. The highest truth is the self, the reality, the Brahman, and both jīva and Īśvara are but illusory impositions on it."[122] Īśvara is like the role of a magician or actor on stage. The real person is not the one that we see and the degree to which we identify with the roles is the degree to which we are ignorant of the real nature of the magician and the actor. Thus, to the discerning, Īśvara lacks any reality. If we want to view the magician as real, or Īśvara as real, or the rope as a real snake, then, bound by our own ignorance, we can do so. But Reality is not affected by such ignorance. The magician is really someone else, and neither Īśvara nor the rope are really what we think they are just because we see them so. Brahman is not a Creator, the quality of being such is not a part of the *nirguṇa* essence of Brahman: the apparent association of creation with Brahman is only the result of our illusion and ignorance.

It is not difficult to see that a *nirguṇa* Brahman is removed from any taint of involvement in the *karmic* world. Only at the relative level of reality can good and evil obtain, and Īśvara be said to be responsible for both. But at the point where all dualities cease to exist – Brahman-realization – there can be no good or evil. In any case, at the empirical level it is the *karmas* of individuals that bring about resulting good or evil. So, in the long run, divinity is removed from evil (or good), at both the relative and absolute levels.

Despite the relative unreality of Īśvara, he serves the purpose of directing the steps of the individual to the higher planes of the evolution of the self. He is "an empirical postulate which is practically useful", as Radhakrishnan put it,[123] who points the way forward to the more ultimate level of Reality and is a means to the ultimate goal of liberation. So Śaṃkara was not totally non-theistic in his approach to that goal: he recognized the role of Īśvara, and even of many deities, in the progressive path to *mokṣa*. Arvind Sharma makes the point that *saguṇa* Brahman "is an objectification of spiritual experience. It is the experience that, although negated by *nirguṇa* Brahman, yet complements *nirguṇa* Brahman-experience and, because it takes up and harmonizes everything within itself, makes possible the affirmation of the spirituality or intrinsic value of all modes of being."[124] To Śaṃkara, the pre-eminent deity was Viṣṇu, whom he preferred to call Nārāyaṇa or Vāsudeva. Thus, he did not eschew the vast *smṛti* literature that dealt with the God Viṣṇu. Deities such as Viṣṇu, in particular his *avatāras* of Rāma and Kṛṣṇa, are an important focus for those on the path to liberation. Frequently, too, Śaṃkara equated Viṣṇu with the Absolute, but he wrote of deities other than Viṣṇu who are finite and transient, and every one is ultimately illusory.[125] The great creator God Brahmā, also called Hiraṇya-garbha and Prajāpati, is the world-soul, the divine being at the apex of all divinity and humanity. While the distinction between Īśvara and Brahmā is sometimes blurred in respect of their functions, Brahmā seems to have been equated by Śaṃkara with the Cosmic Intellect, consisting of the totality of past experiences of all beings. This brings about a certain identity between all beings, and an interconnectedness of all experiences.[126] But Brahmā is still part of the illusory fabric of the world, though posited as the active creator by those bound by nescience. From this nescient point of view, Brahmā also reflects the Consciousness of the Absolute, and is thus able to function in his own specific way as creator.

If there is a divine creator, and creation is an illusory appearance of effects, then it follows that God is also the creator of *māyā* – an illusory creator creating an illusory world. Dandekar called *māyā* "the potency imagined of *brahman* for cosmological purpose",[127] and Hiriyanna depicted it as "a mere accessory to Īśvara" in his role of creation, a "self-consciousness or self-determination".[128] An elaborate theory of Īśvara's role in creation and control of *māyā* seems, therefore, somewhat contrived, even if it is the empirical world itself that assigns to Īśvara the potency to create it, and Brahman ever remains *nirguṇa*, pure Consciousness and pure Essence. But it is certainly the *saguṇa* Brahman that Śaṃkara depicts as the efficient and material cause of the world – a magical creator creating a magical world of appearances. Īśvara is depicted as creating the world through his *līlā*, divine "sport" or "play". This is done, as we would say, "just for the hell of it", without any motive whatsoever and without any connection between what is created and the cause–effect processes that happen within it. It is a clever philosophical device – though to me a very unsatisfactory one – but Arvind Sharma writes: "By conceiving of Īśvara's activity as *līlā*, the Advaitin is able to place Īśvara as well as the world under *māyā* and thereby retain the unqualified Reality of Brahman."[129] Sharma thinks it is a sound concept since he says "treating it as a natural expression of God's existence, as breathing is of human existence, seems philosophically more sound. It has no motive because it is automatic – or natural to God".[130] *Līlā*, however, remains for me a thoroughly nebulous concept when posited in any aspect of Hinduism.

It is the acceptance of the *saguṇa* aspect of Brahman – albeit from the view of ignorance – and the many words that are used to portray his character, his involvement in the world process, his grace to his devotees, and so on, that belies the Advaitin standpoint of the world as only apparent. It is all very well to give analogies of a rope that appears to be a snake or, even more appropriately, that of the image in a mirror that is taken to be real, but to waste so many words on the snake and the mirror image, is illogical. Potter states: "What is difficult to comprehend from the standpoint of ordinary theism is that the Advaitin can say all this about God and yet view Him as conditioned by ignorance. Brahman is the Supreme, the texts say, and yet in the same breath they affirm that He is not only not the Highest, His properties are unreal, false attributions of our ignorant superimpositions."[131]

Thus, the Advaitin, it seems to me, is open to a good deal of valid criticism concerning the world of illusion in which he lives so enthusiastically. And as Potter further remarks: "Whatever the uninitiated may make of this apparently ambivalent attitude to the deity, it is undeniable that some, including Śaṃkara, are able to work up a fervent devotional attitude toward God despite His involvement with ignorance."[132] Ultimately, the Absolute does not act, does not change, does not exercise power but even Śaṃkara himself focuses readily on the *saguṇa* God. It is small wonder that later Advaitins found the issue of Īśvara, to use Chandradhar Sharma's phrase, "a taxing problem".[133]

Liberation

Liberation is what results when the involvement of the *jīva* in the illusory world ceases and pure Consciousness shines through. Potter puts the Advaita position on liberation succinctly in the following words: "The Advaita view is simple to state and devastating in its implications. Liberation is nothing more nor less than being, knowing and experiencing one's true Self. In this disarming statement we can find the key to many of the Advaita teachings."[134] Liberation is not a change from an unenlightened state to an enlightened one. It is simply the removal of the misconceptions about reality; a different perspective of reality that is not coloured by error. The Self that knows itself as the Absolute is the same Self that is the essence of the ordinary self; it is just obscured. Thus, Śaṃkara stated: "There is no real distinction between a (supposed) liberated and a (supposed) non-liberated state, for the Self is ever identical."[135] So liberation cannot be reached, found or acquired. It is not a result of some action. Nothing happens to the *Ātman* at liberation. It is as it always has been. Śaṃkara said: "It is also unreasonable that [final release] is a change of state [in *Ātman*], since [It] is changeless. If there were change [in *Ātman*, [It] would have parts; consequently [It] would perish, like a jar, etc."[136] Śaṃkara said that when nescience disappears and the Self becomes liberated, "empirical existence just disappears, swallowed up in the Self, like the squall of wind accompanying a stroke of lightning that vanishes into the sky, or the fire that sinks down into the burnt-out fuel".[137]

As far as the means to liberation are concerned, the life of the monk is the ideal according to Śaṃkara: "The true discipline is to become a monk and give up the three desires for a son, wealth and a 'world' (after death) and then to cultivate the qualities of wisdom . . . child-like simplicity and sagehood (mauna). Psychological defects like attachment, aversion, infatuation and the like have to be ironed out. The monk must know from the beginning what he has to reject, what he has to know, what he has to cultivate and what he has to eliminate, as this is the means to success."[138] The candidate for the path to liberation will have, then, a discerning nature in favour of what is more spiritual and be prepared to renounce sensual desires and display qualities of calmness and tranquillity, self-control, dispassion, forbearance, mind-focus and faith.

In accepting *Vedic* and some *smṛti* testimony, Śaṃkara believed that the first stage on the pathway to liberation is *hearing* (*śravaṇa*) the words of the *Vedānta* under the supervision of a *guru*. While Śaṃkara conceded that *śruti* ritualism is essential for those on the lower slopes to liberation, and potential disciples of his would certainly be expected to be well versed in walking the path of *Vedic* morality and ritual, such ritualism is activity, and all activity is of the nature of illusion, not of the Consciousness that is Brahman. For this reason, action could not ultimately procure liberation. But tradition endorsed *dharmic* activity in obedience to *Vedic* injunctions, and this must involve ritual activity. There are occasions, then, when Śaṃkara is prescriptive about the means to liberation, as Mayeda notes in his analysis of Śaṃkara's *Upadeśasāhasrī* 1:17, 21–3. Here, Śaṃkara advocates restraint, non-violence, truthfulness, non-theft, continence, non-possessions, austerities, concentration, bodily emaciation, and performance of obligatory *Vedic* duties.[139] Critical study of the four "great sayings", *mahā-vākyas*, of the *Upaniṣads* and, of course, Advaita interpretations of important texts, is essential.

Non-active, intuitive knowledge is the ultimate key by which freedom becomes possible. But as a preparation for the path to *mokṣa*, and for final liberation of the Self, knowledge of the *Veda* is considered essential, and this certainly necessitates action. *Brāhmins* are expected to maintain their class duties and those relevant to their stage of life, and it would be expected that in this, or a former, life the obligatory rituals and duties as laid down in the *Vedas* are maintained, as well as avoidance of prohibited actions, and observance of any optional duties that promote selflessness. Such a path leaves one without fruitive *karma*. Yet knowledge of Brahman and Its identity with *Ātman* remains the key to liberation. It is knowledge at the deepest levels of the self, and can only come about when activity ceases, even if that activity is obedience to *Vedic* injunctions, moral action, or ethically necessary action. In Śaṃkara's words: "Whoever sees *Ātman* as devoid of duties remaining [undone], devoid of action itself and of the result of the action, and free from the notions "mine" and "myself," he [really] sees [the truth]."[140]

The next stage in the journey is reflective thinking about what has been taught (*manana*), and the third stage is meditative contemplation. It is an internalizing of what has been learned. Śaṃkara saw meditation, *upāsana*, as an important part of the *Veda* and seems to have differentiated it from both ritual and knowledge.[141] It is meditation on the Absolute in its associated forms of particular deities – a practice that was believed to bring about liberation gradually – that was specifically taken up by Śaṃkara. Since the Absolute cannot be accessed directly through such meditation, the finite forms of the Absolute (albeit illusory) provide an appropriate intermediate focus. The advantage of such meditation is that, after death, the practitioner can enter the abode of the deity on whom he has focused, there to await the end of the aeon, when he will become Brahman and transmigrate no more. While recognizing that meditation on a finite form of a deity is still an action undertaken from the point of nescience, its ultimate result, according to Śaṃkara, is a transcendence of nescience to become Brahman. He stated: "Such meditations (Upāsanas) contribute to the final understanding of the metaphysical truth by purifying the mind, and are in this sense auxiliaries to knowledge of non-duality: and because they offer a definite conception for the mind to hold on to they are easy to practise."[142] Thus, a gradual path and clearly one that accepts and adheres to *Vedic* injunctions to liberation seems to have been accepted by Śaṃkara as well as a path that leads to the heaven of Hiraṇya-garbha/Brahmā. Śaṃkara said: "The unenlightened man is eligible for the ritual laid down in the Veda, which may be performed with or without accompanying symbolic meditations and which varies according to caste and stage of life. On this path (i.e. of ritual) he may rise higher and higher from the condition of man up to that of Hiraṇyagarbha. If, however, he ignores the injunctions and prohibitions of the Veda and acts merely according to his natural inclinations he will sink from the human level to that of vegetation."[143] The real point of meditation is put clearly by Alston:

> In Advaita teaching there is ultimately no duality. All deities, therefore, are reducible in the end to the non-dual Self. In their own true nature, they are identical with the true nature of the person meditating on them. It is therefore possible for a meditator to reach through meditation an intuitive awareness of his identity with the deity on whom he is meditating, and that awareness may have different degrees of intensity, ranging from a full sense of identity to a mere sense of proximity, according to the degree of intensity with which the meditative path is pursued.[144]

Meditation that informs the gradual path, however, is surpassed by that which is more directly intuitive, the third of Śaṃkara's stages on the pathway to liberation. It is *nididhyāsana* "deep" or "sustained meditation". It is "fixing the mental gaze on the principle of reality to determine its true nature, like one examining a jewel".[145] It is associated with the higher Brahman. *Upāsana*, on the other hand, is "maintaining a stream of identical images of which the form is (not dictated by one's knowledge of any reality but) prescribed in the Veda",[146] and is associated with the lower, *saguṇa* Brahman. Some of Śaṃkara's own writings, as exemplified in the *Upadeśasāhasrī*, were clearly used for meditation, and reflect the striving for intuitive discernment through meditation on the Supreme Self (*adhyātma yoga*). The following, sensitively translated by Alston, is an example:

> I am the Absolute, the all, ever pure, ever enlightened. I am unborn and am everywhere beyond decay, indestructible and immortal. In all beings there is no other

> knower but me. I distribute the rewards of merit and demerit.[147] I am the Witness and illuminer, eternal, non-dual, without empirical qualities. I am neither being nor non-being nor being and non-being combined. I am the Alone, the Transcendent. I am that eternal Witness in whom there are neither day nor night, neither dawn nor dusk. Like the ether in being subtle and free from all form, I am one without a second. I am the non-dual Absolute, void even of the ether.[148]

In the *Upadeśasāhasrī*, Śaṃkara says that the means to liberation should only be taught to one with faith and desire, and,

> if he is dispassionate toward all things non-eternal which are attained by means [other than knowledge]; if he has abandoned the desire for sons, wealth, and worlds and reached the state of a *paramahaṃsa* wandering ascetic; if he is endowed with tranquility, self-control, compassion, and so forth; if he is possessed of the qualities of a pupil which are well known from the scriptures; if he is a Brahmin who is [internally and externally] pure; if he approaches his teacher in the prescribed manner; if his caste, profession, behavior, knowledge [of the *Veda*], and family have been examined.[149]

The importance of intuitive, meditative knowledge in Advaita Vedānta is critical. Deussen stated, "liberation consists only in Knowledge, but in Knowledge of a special kind, in that there is no question of an object which investigation could discover and contemplate, but only of that which can never be an object, because in every cognition it is the subject of cognition".[150] To embark on the path to liberation the disciple will need to cultivate knowledge that can differentiate between the real and the non-real. He will need to be detached from all the experiences that occur in the physical body, both in the present and in the future. He will need to have the equanimity that comes from having been an adept in all the required moral restraints, and he will be thoroughly focused on liberation. It is not that there is an increasing knowledge, as much as a "desuperimposition" process, as Indich terms it.[151]

The liberated person, the *jīvan-mukta*, is sometimes equated, as far as Śaṃkara was concerned, with the *saṃnyāsin*, one at the fourth and final stage of life.[152] If the two are equated, then it seems that the *jīvan-mukta* can either lose the Self in Brahman, or as a *saṃnyāsin*, turn towards a world that is no longer characterized by perspectives of life that are dual. The goal of liberation does not exclude *egoless* action, and the *mukta* is capable of service to others through such action. Śaṃkara followed the *Bhagavad Gītā* in his emphasis on the kind of actions that are devoid of thought of either success or failure, but that are performed without attachment. Indeed, Śaṃkara himself travelled widely in India teaching and founding monasteries. Only when actions are selfless and performed without attachment to their results can they bear no fruitive *karma*. Interestingly, Śaṃkara does not seem to exclude women from the liberated state. He said: "If there should be some few souls, whether they be men or women, who acquire a fixed conviction about the existence of the unborn, all-homogeneous principle of reality, they alone will be the people of true metaphysical knowledge."[153] Śaṃkara accepted that those of lower castes and even outcastes (as they were then termed) could attain to liberation through the gradual path – though probably because they had had experience of the *Veda* in a previous life.

Advaita, then, accepts the concept of *jīvan-mukti*, the belief that liberation can occur whilst still confined to the physical body. While after death there will be no *karma* left to render another birth necessary, the *prarābdha-karma* that created the present life will still have some *saṃskāras*, latent impressions, from past actions, that need to work themselves out. But there will be no more fruitive *karma* for the liberated one who is devoid of egoistic identity and who no longer relates to the sensory world. Any *karma* in formation will be burnt up and eradicated, since the liberated Self is no longer connected with it, and has acquired the kind of knowledge that destroys formative *karma*. The *jīvan-mukta*, the liberated one, is no longer an agent or experiencer of the world but, remarkably, the world of appearances is still in view!

Śaṃkara described liberation as the non-rebirth of the mind. It is what happens, writes Loy, "when the mind stops trying to grasp its own tail".[154] The liberated mind is not subject to sensory impressions; it is still. "It is eternal, identical in all states, featureless and without subject–object duality", said Śaṃkara in his commentary on the *Gauḍapāda-kārikā* 4:77.[155] The *jīvan-mukta* enjoys blissful pleasure in the remaining days of what have been long journeys in countless reincarnated lives. He becomes the all-pervading Absolute, living in a state of total bliss that is totally divorced from the world of matter and the senses that perceive it. He experiences everything as his own Self. Any actions that he performs are *inactions* in so far as they are not performed by a self, and there is no attachment to actions or the fruits of them. Actions of the liberated one do not *belong* to anyone. The dualities of life have disappeared; pain and pleasure, gold or a piece of earth, are the same. It is as if he were disembodied, though he still has a physical body. He sees all beings and all things as his own Self, and that Self and all beings as the Absolute. In his commentary on the *Bṛhadāraṇyaka Upaniṣad*, Śaṃkara stated:

> Since this glory of the Brahmin (who has realized the Self) is unconnected with action and transcendent in nature, it follows that one who has this realization becomes "peaceful" (śānta), which means desisting from the activities of the external senses, "controlled" (dānta), which means above the thirsts of the mind, "withdrawn" (uparata), which means a renunciate (saṃnyāsin) who has given up all desires, "ascetic" (titikṣu), which means able and willing to bear extremes of the pairs of opposites such as heat and cold, "concentrated" (samāhita), which means concentrated in one-pointedness after withdrawing from all movement of senses or mind.[156]

To the *jīvan-mukta* there is no more identity with the physical self or the physical world as such: the illusion of it will have vanished, and all that remains is *Ātman* Consciousness. While active service to others is still maintained, the *mukta* will continue only so long as is necessary for the final working out of *karma* – *prārabda-karma*, that which is already on its way – and then, once the physical body is left, will become *videha-mukti*. Notably, again, the physical world of appearance does not actually evaporate. Liberation, then, is the dispelling of ignorance, the ridding of illusions that veil Truth. It is what Dasgupta termed "the dissociation of the self from the subjective psychosis and the world."[157] The ignorance of the world, its illusory nature, however, has to continue, for it is beginningless and timeless, just as consciousness is. But the liberated Self is divorced from it, having realized the higher Reality that is Brahman, and having experienced the bliss of pure Consciousness that is the Essence of all selves and the universe. In Śaṃkara's words: "There is no need for taking active steps to achieve peace (liberation) in the Self. All souls are eternally at rest, unborn, and completely withdrawn by nature, homogeneous and non-different from one another. That is, the Self, as a metaphysical principle, is unborn, homogeneous and pure, and hence there is no need to *produce* the state of blessed abstraction or liberation. Action can have no effect on that which is eternally of the same nature."[158]

Concluding remarks

Much has been written about Śaṃkara's legacy to Indian philosophy, some negatively, and much positively. Undoubtedly, his contribution is considerable, indeed, to the extent that he has been depicted by one writer as "an epoch-making reformer of the Vedānta school of philosophy".[159] This is especially true in that Śaṃkara was faithful to the *Upaniṣadic* concept of a totally transcendent Absolute that is Brahman. It is this that informs all Vedānta inquiry, whether that inquiry remains monistic or diversifies into more qualified monism or dualistic panentheism. While other schools diminished the concept of deity, Vedānta schools enhanced it to its ultimate levels, and it is to Śaṃkara that such a trend partly owes its foundation. By positing a dual perspective of reality in which the inferior was sublatable/contradicted, Śaṃkara attempted to unite the disparate trends of the non-dual absolutism and the dualistic theism of the *Upaniṣads*. Some measure of success must be granted given the influence of Advaita up to, and including, the present day.

Regarding the prevailing influence of Advaita, Ninian Smart commented that: "Śankara's metaphysics is *par excellence* the theology of modern Hinduism as presented to the West; and is the most vigorous and dominant doctrine among Hindu intellectuals."[160] There are a number of possible reasons for such an appeal. To begin with, Śaṃkara relates primarily to the bound, empirical self. Radhakrishnan wrote of him: "Religion for Śaṃkara is not doctrine or ceremony, but life and experience. It starts with the soul's sense of the infinite and ends with its becoming the infinite,"[161] – a remarkably all-embracing, almost universalist perspective. As Radhakrishnan also pointed out: "In Śaṃkara we find one of the greatest expounders of the comprehensive and tolerant character of the Hindu religion, which is ever ready to assimilate alien faiths. This attitude of toleration was neither a survival of superstition nor a means of compromise, but an essential part of his practical philosophy. He recognised the limitations of all formulas and refused to compress the Almighty within them."[162] Such a view was later echoed by Ninian Smart.[163] There is also a definite attractiveness in the idea that all is ultimately divine, and ultimately equal. In the last resort, seeing all others as one's own self must lead to the ultimate kind of altruism, "for a true elimination of delusion will also eliminate all those self-centred ways of thinking that motivate selfish behavior".[164]

As far as his philosophy is concerned, Śaṃkara has been described as "the most remarkable rationalist India has ever produced".[165] But it has to be said that it is his denial of reality and, therefore, the absence of any *real* focus of devotion, that suggests an ultimately limiting aspect of the concept of deity for the devotee. And some have appended to this a lack of emphasis on moral requirement and ethical values. Mayeda is one, however, who defends Śaṃkara against such an accusation. He makes the valid point that: "Śaṅkara is primarily concerned with the salvation of people who are suffering from transmigratory existence here in the present world and not with the establishment of a consistent philosophical system. . . . Śaṅkara's view of ethics may be vague or self-contradictory, but this is because its real aim is the highest possible effectiveness in leading his pupils to the final goal."[166] In positing Reality that is ultimately non-dual, morality has to transcend the self. As Deussen poignantly said, "in truth morality lies beyond Egotism, but therefore also beyond causality and consequently beyond comprehension".[167]

In examining Śaṃkara's theories, it seems that he owed a considerable debt to the school of Sāṃkhya for his main theory of the mutual superimposition of *Ātman* on the world, and the world on *Ātman*. I shall be examining this system of belief in the following chapter. The motif of superimposition is repeated as the basis of all his other theories. Potter justifiably writes: "Listening to an Advaitin is deliciously, or irritatingly, repetitive, depending on one's receptivity to the message."[168] But Gerald Larson is highly critical of Śaṃkara's borrowing of the concepts of others. He writes: "Vedānta, stripped of its scripture-based monistic *brahman-atman*, is in many ways a warmed-over Sāṃkhya ontology and epistemology spooned up with the philosophical methodology of the old negative dialectic of the Mādhyamika Buddhists."[169] But it is the major differences from Sāṃkhya that makes Śaṃkara's work so valuable – the identity of all Selves as one *Ātman* that is Brahman, rather than the plurality and isolation of the individual *puruṣas* of Sāṃkhya, as we are about to explore, which left no room for the divine, as well as Śaṃkara's challenges to the reality of phenomenal existence. Yet the charge that Śaṃkara was a synthesizer and copyist is partially justified. He owed a considerable debt to other philosophical systems for major concepts, even if, as Isayeva observes, "he bore full responsibility for the specific way in which these blocks were fitted into the balanced structure of Advaita".[170] Nevertheless, despite the intellectual depths and complexities of his ideas, Śaṃkara's system of philosophy became the major one throughout India, the one most written about and most commented on.

It is the lack of a *real* world, and the mysteries of ignorance, *avidyā*, and the power of illusion, *māyā*, that are problematic areas for Śaṃkara, and were pursued by his successors. The same questions with which Śaṃkara dealt – the relation between Brahman and the self, and between Brahman and the world – were taken up by other Vedāntins who posited different answers. A few of these will occupy some space in the remaining chapters of this book. Sinari thinks that Śaṃkara "sidetracks" the issue of the relationship between Brahman and the finite world,[171] and there is a pronounced measure of truth in this, since the linking factor of *māyā* remains ever mysterious. As far as I can see, Śaṃkara rejects relationship between the two by a theory of two distinct realities that pervade his philosophy – the enlightened and unenlightened perspectives of what reality is. The unenlightened view is always devoid of proper reality. It is a dual view that is evident in all his themes:

- liberation and bondage
- higher knowledge and lower knowledge

- Reality and appearance
- Brahman and Īśvara
- cause only and the cause–effect processes.

But while he accepted such dualities at the level of the empirical world, he then denied them in order to transcend the world and keep Reality non-dual.

Sometimes criticized for its cold metaphysics, there is certainly warmth in the presenting of Advaita Vedānta by its more modern proponents. Vivekananda thus got to the heart of Śaṃkara's teaching when he said: "The highest heaven, therefore, is in our own souls; the greatest temple of worship is the human soul, greater than all heavens, says Vedānta; for in no heaven, anywhere, can we understand Reality as distinctly and clearly as in this life, in your own soul."[172]

5

Influential Theories:
Sāṃkhya and Classical Yoga

In the last chapter, chapter 4, I explored one strand of the philosophical system, or *darśana* (literally a "seeing", "vision of"), known as Advaita, one of the six orthodox schools of Hindu philosophy. What I want to do now is examine two others, Sāṃkhya and Yoga. These are very much interrelated, as we shall see, but there is some advantage in dealing with them separately in their classical formats, beginning first with Sāṃkhya.

Sāṃkhya

While Sāṃkhya today is scarcely evident as a practising school[1] it has had considerable influence on Hindu and, indeed, Indian philosophical thought. It is not an easy school to study because of its variety of interpretation and its contradictory commentarial teachings. Furthermore, its beginnings do not stem from a single tradition or even homogeneous traditions. It is not, says Gerald Larson, "a monolithic system stemming from ancient times . . . One finds, rather, a kind of slowly growing organism which has assimilated a variety of traditions over a period of centuries".[2] Its roots stem back to ancient times, making it in some senses the oldest of the schools,[3] though Sāṃkhya as an independent system did not obtain until much later. It is this, independent, school – known as *classical Sāṃkhya* – on which I am concentrating in the first half of this chapter.

Background to the school

The term *sāṃkhya* is usually taken to mean "enumeration" or "number". Since this can also mean "calculation" or "summing up of", *sāṃkhya* can mean the enumeration of the principles found in material existence, for which it is so well known, or it can also have a more philosophical meaning of calculating, reasoning, analysing and discriminating in a more reflective sense. Indeed, the term probably had a variety of meanings.

But while the most consistent one refers to its enumeration of the factors that compose the world of matter and experience, the idea of discrimination is crucial to the philosophy of Sāṃkhya because the summation of its knowledge lies in the utter discrimination between Self and matter – the characteristic dualism of the school. Its purpose is the soteriological one of liberating the Self from suffering, and yet classical Sāṃkhya is an atheistic system. Sāṃkhya pins its soteriology on three important principles – an unmanifest and a manifest material world, *avyakta* and *vyakta* respectively, and a pure subject or knower, *puruṣa* or *jña* – Sāṃkhya's term for *ātman*. Knowledge is key for it provides a way of release from the sufferings of life by an alteration in one's perspective of it. The major fundamental work of classical Sāṃkhya, the *Sāṃkhya-Kārikā*, begins with the statement that suffering is characteristic of all existence, that Sāṃkhya is the way to overcome it, and that the means to overcome it is knowledge; rather reminiscent of the Buddha's *Four Noble Truths*. Both Sāṃkhya and Buddhism saw the root cause of suffering as ignorance, and both rejected the Absolute, Brahman.

It is possible to analyse Sāṃkhya as a distinct school of thought, but it is frequently to be found conjoined with the school of Yoga. The usual differentiation between the two – if somewhat oversimplified – is based on the acceptance that while Sāṃkhya is concerned with theory and knowledge Yoga accepts most of its tenets and concentrates on practice. Yoga is also theistic as opposed to the atheistic stance of Sāṃkhya. Such distinctions are generally more one of emphasis than of basic doctrine, and the similarities between the two *darśanas* are sufficient to find them combined into one school.[4] Nevertheless, a long spell of association was broken by a period of classical separation, but both were probably closely complementary to each other in their evolution.[5]

Just as Advaita based its theories on the *Upaniṣads*, Sāṃkhya did so, too.[6] *Vedāntic* ideas of creation emanating from one source, and the importance of overcoming ignorance through knowledge, for example, are concepts likely to have been attractive to Sāṃkhya proponents. The *Kaṭha*, *Śvetāśvatara* and *Praśna Upaniṣads*, in particular, contain many concepts that are important to Sāṃkhya teaching, though the implications are more applicable to what Larson terms "a kind of undifferentiated *sāṃkhyayoga*".[7] The technical terms to be used by Sāṃkhya proper were certainly in place from an early period.[8] The *Sāṃkhya-Kārikā*, "Verses on Sāṃkhya" – a *kārikā* being a short verse unit of about two lines – was the culmination of varied traditions.[9] The *Sāṃkhya-Kārikā* systematized ideas of a number of traditions and schools (the latter in a very minor sense) into a coherent system. What emerged, as Larson points out, "is a derivative and composite system, a product of speculations from a wide variety of contexts, both orthodox and heterodox."[10] Classical Sāṃkhya extends from about the first century CE to the tenth, with a later resurgence from the fourteenth to fifteenth centuries.

Main proponents and commentators

There are no texts at all that emerge from pre-classical Sāṃkhya, and it is, therefore, the *Sāṃkhya-Kārikā* that emerges as the foundational and authoritative text. It was compiled by Īśvara-Kṛṣṇa, and has become the most important source for the study of this school, though tradition generally assigns the founding of the school of Sāṃkhya to a legendary sage called Kapila. Īśvara-Kṛṣṇa's work may have been summative rather than foundational in presenting the views of the school. His dates vary: Surendranath Dasgupta favoured a date of around 200 CE[11] while Larson considered a much later date of somewhere between 300 and 500 CE[12] narrowing this down to about 350–450 CE, probably nearer to the former.[13] What we have with Īśvara-Kṛṣṇa's *Sāṃkhya-Kārikā* is an explicit separation of Sāṃkhya as a distinct school from Yoga. At this point it is characterized by independently defined doctrines, and specific terminology. Of the important commentators on the *Kārikā* I should single out Gauḍapāda's *Sāṃkhya-Kārikā-Bhāṣya*, from about the sixth century, Vijñana Bhikṣu's *Sāṃkhya-Pravacana-Bhāṣya* and Vācaspati Miśra's *Sāṃkhya-Tattva-Kaumudi* of about the ninth or tenth centuries.

The *Sāṃkhya-Kārikā* is composed of seventy-two verses or short sections. It is thus a very short text. It is set out poetically and, unlike more formal *sūtras*, makes use of similes and metaphors to portray ideas. Karl Potter and Gerald Larson write: "If the term 'darśana' is to be taken in its original sense as an 'intuitive seeing' that nurtures a quiet wisdom and invites ongoing thoughtful meditation, then surely the *Sāṃkhyakārikā* must stand as one of the most remarkable productions of its class, far removed, on one level, from the laconic *sūtra* style that glories in saying as little as possible and presupposing everything, and even further removed, on another level, from the frequently petty and tedious quibbling of Indian philosophy."[14]

We might, with Śaṃkara, be right in criticizing the school as very *unorthodox* in its rejection of the major doctrine of orthodox *Brāhminism*, the concept of Brahman. The Sāṃkhya conception of the true Self was of a *puruṣa* that is a distinct soul suspended in its own timeless essence and separate from all other souls. It is a far cry from the unifying *ātman* of the *Vedānta*. There are similarities with the concept of *ātman* in that *puruṣa* is also an egoless consciousness that is in reality free from the *karmic* effects of existence, and is not really bound to *saṃsāra*. But each *puruṣa* is distinct, and there is absolutely no monistic identity of it with anything. Śaṃkara's criticism of this school as rejecting Brahman – and, therefore, as having no grounds for orthodoxy – is somewhat apt, despite the fact that Sāṃkhya claims to base its teachings on *Vedic* authority. Such a claim, to Śaṃkara, was anathema.

Reality: The Sāṃkhya view of the world

The Sāṃkhya view of the world is essentially dualistic, but in that it accepts the reality of all things that we perceive in the world, it is generally believed to be realistic. It is its dualism that is the most important factor and the two components of this dualism are considered to be totally separate. They are, on the one hand, *puruṣas*, the true Selves of pure consciousness, each being a *jña*, or "knower", and on the other, both unmanifest (*avyakta*) and manifest (*vyakta*) material, unconscious existence called *prakṛti*. The dualism of self and the world is not unknown to *Upaniṣadic* thought, the Self being equitable with ultimate Reality and the world being a lower level of reality. But the dualism of Sāṃkhya sees no unity to the ultimate reality of all Selves. It does, however, accept the unity of the material world, of *prakṛti*. While there is a certain interaction between *puruṣas* and *prakṛti* – a critical issue that will need examination below – these two aspects remain dual. Reality is thus divided into two – non-material, inactive consciousness, and material unconsciousness that is both potentially active and really active. Sāṃkhya metaphysics, then, for most analysts, can be termed dualistic realism. There is, however, a suggestion by one writer, Mikel Burley, that the Sāṃkhya and Yoga systems are not realist at all. Burley finds the *prakṛtic* evolutes to be capacities, potentials for *experience* of gross matter *in the mind*, in other words, experiential possibilities in the *puruṣas*: such a theory would make the evolutes idealist and not realist. Burley writes: "Indeed, I have found nothing to indicate that these systems are incompatible with idealism; and if my view that the modes of manifest *prakṛti* can be best understood as constituents of experience is correct, then there is no reason to suppose that any mind-independent correlates of experienced phenomena are postulated by Sāṃkhya-Yoga."[15] Burley's view is not mainstream but it is an interesting one that would serve to answer some of the problematic areas of Sāṃkhya metaphysics, but his view is a minority one, and is not the one that I am presenting in this chapter.

Prakṛti[16]

It is *prakṛti* that constitutes the whole theory of evolution in the Sāṃkhya system. In its basic state the whole world is a totally unconscious, unmanifest potentiality. As will be seen when the concept of the self is examined later, it is the *proximity* of the *puruṣas* that causes this unmanifest potentiality to evolve into its manifest form. In its unmanifest state *prakṛti* can also be termed *pradhāna* and *avyakta*. Both refer to the primordial source of all existence, that from which all emerges. All things in existence inhere in this ultimate cause of *prakṛti*, are unified by it, and will return to it. Knut Jacobsen puts this superbly: "*Prakṛti* expresses the unity and interdependence of the worlds of gross and subtle matter. It denotes the innate nature of living beings, the world's innate nature, and the material world in its totality. It therefore expresses the correlation of the micro- and macro- cosmos. It is the creative stuff of the world, the generative principle, that from which the world is produced, and that into which it will dissolve, in the eternal rhythm of death and rebirth, withdrawal and manifestation."[17] So really, manifest existence – despite its apparent differentiation – is a unity, just like all things made of clay are different in appearance but are ultimately of the same substance. Whereas *prakṛti* and *puruṣas* form a distinct duality, and *puruṣas* are plural, *prakṛti* is the one aspect of Sāmkhya metaphysics that is unified. There is no transcendent deity or Absolute that is given the function of a First Cause from which all emanates, there is nothing conscious that creates the world through idea, volition, or as material cause. The world simply evolves from an unmanifest state of *prakṛti*.

There are, therefore, two forms of *prakṛti*. *Avyakta* is unformed *prakṛti*, often termed *mūla-prakṛti*, and is the substratum of evolution, but is non-creative in its unmanifest form. The creative and created aspect of *prakṛti* is *vyakta*. It is this manifest aspect of *prakṛti* that is the effect of *avyakta*, though it is worth noting that manifest *prakṛti* cannot and does not exist without the *puruṣas*: without them, it can only be unmanifest potential that must be co-eternal with the *puruṣas*. As an effect, it infers its cause, but this cause, *avyakta* or *mūla-prakṛti*, is itself uncaused. *Avyakta*, then, though unmanifest, contains within it as the first cause the *potential* for everything in existence: all the effects are held in an unmanifest state in *mūla-prakṛti*. The one thing, however, that the *mūla-prakṛti* cannot contain potential for are the *puruṣas*; these must always be separate.

Avyakta is uncreated and unmanifest but dynamically so, for the potential for existence is held in three constituents called *guṇas*. These will be examined in detail below, but in this context it is necessary to point out that there are three basic kinds of *guṇas*. They are *sattva* the subtle substance of intelligence, light and evolution; *rajas* the subtle substance of energy and activity; and *tamas* the subtle substance of mass and materiality. It is the many possible combinations of such *guṇas* that will produce the material world. And I think it is important to point out at this stage that most commentators and writers consider the *guṇas* to be *substances*, that is to say, they inform *matter*. In the state of unmanifest *prakṛti*, that of *avyakta*, these *guṇas* are dynamically vibrant, but in total equilibrium – an equilibrium that cancels out each of the others so that one cannot dominate. Dasgupta said of this state of the *guṇas*: "This is a state which is so absolutely devoid of all characteristics that it is absolutely incoherent, indeterminate, and indefinite. It is a qualitiless simple homogeneity. It is a state of being which is as it were non-being. . . . This is a state which cannot be said either to exist or to non-exist for it serves no purpose, but it is hypothetically the mother of all things. This is however the earliest stage, by the breaking of which, later on, all modifications take place."[18] The "modifications" to which Dasgupta referred are the *tattvas*, literally "thatnesses", the evolutes that emerge from the *mūla-prakṛti*. And it is a disturbance, a quiddity, in the *guṇas* that brings this about. What causes this disturbance, though in a passive way, is the sheer proximity of the many Selves, the *puruṣas*. It is the activity *guṇa* of *rajas* that is the first to be disturbed by the proximity of the *puruṣas* and, in turn, *rajas* disturbs the other *guṇas* of *sattva* and *tamas*. As a result of this disturbance the *guṇas* are able to combine into the differentiated material entities that compose the world: evolution begins. Importantly, as Knut Jacobsen puts it: "*Prakṛti* is a mutating absolute principle. Movement is inherent in it, and no agent is necessary at any stage to move it."[19]

Evolution takes place from subtle cosmic evolutes to grosser psychical/physical ones in beings. The subtle psychical ones are intellect (*buddhi*), ego (*ahaṃkara*), mind (*manas*), and ten organs of sense. Bridging the psychical and the physical are five subtle *tanmātras* from which evolve five gross, physical elements, the *mahā-bhūtas*. From the moment the *guṇas* are disturbed, *prakṛti* begins to produce its evolutes until twenty-three *tattvas* or principles have evolved all the way from the subtle to the gross. The twenty-five principles of the Sāṃkhya system, then, are as follows: *puruṣas* as the independent and separate principle are the first, and are differentiated from all the others. The other twenty-four principles are all *prakṛtic*. The second one is unmanifest *prakṛti* from which evolution begins. The third and fourth – the first two manifest aspects – proceed "vertically", *buddhi*, intellect, first, from which evolves *ahaṃkāra*, ego. These are initially cosmic but will also inform the human self.

1 Puruṣas *2* **Unmanifest *Prakṛti***
(primordial matter)

3 ***Buddhi/mahāt-buddhi****
(intellect)

4 ahaṃkāra*
(egoity)

From the ego, *ahaṃkāra*, evolve "horizontally" and simultaneously, the mind or *manas*; five capacities for sense, the *buddhīndriyas*; five capacities for action, the *karmendriyas*; and five subtle elements, the *tanmātras*. These, then, are as follows:

5 manas	***6–10 buddhīndriyas***	***11–15 karmendriyas***	***16–20 tanmātras***
	hearing	***speaking (mouth)***	***sound****
	feeling	***grasping (hands)***	***touch****
	seeing	***walking (feet)***	***form****
	tasting	***excreting (anus)***	***taste****
	smelling	***generating (genitals)***	***smell****

The five gross elements, the *mahā-bhūtas*, evolve directly from the *tanmātras*:

21–25 mahā-bhūtas
ether (akāśa) associated with sound
air or wind associated with touch
fire associated with form
water associated with taste
earth associated with smell

* = created and creative in nature.

Unlike the unmanifest aspect of *prakṛti*, *avyakta*, the manifest aspect of *vyakta* according to the *Kārikā*, is caused, finite, non-pervasive, active, plural, supported, mergent, composite, and dependent.[20] Limitations of space in this chapter preclude a discussion of *all* the evolutes of *prakṛti*[21] but I want to concentrate on three very important ones, *buddhi*, *ahaṃkāra* and *manas*, for these constitute the *antaḥ-karaṇa* (*citta* in the *Yoga-Sūtras*), the thinking aspect of a human being. Most important to note is that they are *matter* and incapable of consciousness that can only be sourced from the spiritual *puruṣas*. These three *tattvas* have both a cosmic character in that they precede the possibilities for gross matter, but also they materialize in the human being. Thus, most accept a cosmological and psychological dual function of the evolution of *prakṛti*.[22]

Buddhi or *mahat*

Buddhi or *mahat*[23] is the first of the evolutes to emerge from unmanifest *prakṛti*. Its synonym *mahat*, meaning "great one", suggests its pre-eminence among all the *tattvas* and its function as the cosmic intelligence and awareness from which everything else emerges.[24] In a sense, then, it is an all-pervasive cosmic principle that becomes more specifically defined as *buddhi* or "intellect" in individuals. Derived from the Sanskrit root *budh*, "to be aware of", the main characteristic of *buddhi* is *sattvic* reflective discrimination. And since all creation emerges after it, it has the potential to discern all that is created: it is in this sense that it is *mahat*.

It is in the human being that *buddhi* functions as that which enables the individual to ascertain, discriminate and differentiate. In essence it is a *sattvic* principle, having arisen mainly from the *sattvic guṇas* of the *avyakta*. So in the human being, it can lead potentially to qualities that are good, that promote the evolution of the self to liberation, that are *dharmic* and that facilitate true knowledge, *jñāna*. Conversely, the *buddhi* of the human being also includes *tamas* and *rajas* causing orientation towards ignorance and to attachment to the world. The *buddhi* contains eight[25] such possible *bhāvas* or dispositions and it is these that will determine the life of the individual. The four that are related to *sattva* are *dharma*, *jñāna*, *vairāgya* and *aiśvarya* – what is right, true knowledge, non-attachment and power respectively. Four *tamasic bhāvas* are the opposites of these. The Sāṃkhya conception of the *buddhi*, then, covers the whole realm of human emotion and activity – all possible combinations of human disposition. It is the gene-house of experience.

Only one *bhāva*, *jñāna*, "knowledge", is the medium for liberation. All other *bhāvas* lead the individual to rebirth. It is the *bhāvas* that determine how a person will behave in respect of past *karma*. They are therefore predisposed to operate in conjunction with *karma*, the *sattvic* person behaving in one way and those disposed to other *guṇas* in other ways. The *bhāvas*, then, are closely associated with the transmigrating, subtle body, the *liṅga-śarīra* as it is called. They will dictate those drives and dispositions applicable to each individual as a result of past actions, causing the particular composition and personality of each one in the present existence. So though the *buddhi* is essentially *sattvic*, when it is individualized in each person, affected by *rajasic* and *tamasic karmic* residues, and by *rajas* as the dominant *guṇa* of all human life, its *sattvic* nature is temporarily minimized; reality becomes blurred by *karmic* involvement with life. Importantly, such *karma* can only accrue to the *buddhi* and not to the Self, the *puruṣa*, which is always a separate reality.

Despite the fact that it is the *buddhi* that carries *karmic* dispositions, it is *always* unconscious matter. But what each *buddhi* can do is reflect the consciousness of an individual *puruṣa* by which it *seems* itself to be conscious and intelligent. It *seems* to be a subject and not an object, and it *seems* to be the true Self. The greater the predominance of *sattvic* dispositions in the *buddhi*, the more able the individual will be to gain the kind of knowledge that overcomes this misapprehension about the real nature of the *buddhi*. Importantly, too, *buddhi* always *precedes* ego, *ahaṃkāra*, and, indeed, the entire gross world. This suggests that it is impersonal in its natural state, when it is not reacting with the ego and the mind. It can transcend the phenomenal world and the desires and aversions of the egoistic self.

Puruṣa, in witnessing *prakṛti* in the form of *buddhi*, sees itself as *buddhi*, just as *buddhi*, in reflecting *puruṣa*, seems to be pure consciousness and the real Self. Since it is the *buddhi* that is capable of being predominantly *sattvic*, and therefore of the quality of light, it has the capacity to reflect the *puruṣa* in a way that gross matter – which has minimal *sattvic* content – does not. And since the *buddhi* is the direct evolute of unmanifest *prakṛti* it has within it the potential for all knowledge. When knowledge takes place, the *puruṣa* illuminates the *buddhi* with consciousness in respect of the particular cognition, and the ego and the mind – the later evolutes of *buddhi* – co-operate to bring about the relational and differentiating processes that we use in our view of the world around us. For the most part the *buddhi* is involved with the phenomenal world and the objects that fill it. It becomes modified to suit the form of an object conveyed to it from the senses via the mind, and *transforms* itself into the necessary forms. When *puruṣa* informs it with consciousness, experience results.

Ahaṃkāra

Ahaṃkāra, or ego, evolves directly and vertically from *buddhi*. Like *buddhi*, the ego is material and unconscious. The word *ahaṃkāra* is probably a composite of two words, *kāra* meaning "acting", "making" or "working", with the addition of the prefix *ahaṃ* meaning "I"; but it is a difficult word to translate. The *Kārikā* does not tell us a great deal about it, other than to say that it is the source of individuation and in beings is the source of both self-awareness and self-conceit. Sri Garib Weerasinghe describes it as "the uniform apperceptive mass as yet without any definite personal experience but with an obscure feeling of being Ahaṃ or 'I'".[26] In reality, the ego is unconscious and material; it imagines itself otherwise, considering itself to be the real agent of all actions, desires and aversions. It is associated with "me" and "mine", it owns things and people, makes choices, acts for its own ends and relates to the whole world from its own egocentrism. In developing from the *buddhi*, the particular balance of *guṇas* in the *ahaṃkāra* will match the same kind of balance of *guṇas* associated with the *bhāvas*, the dispositions, of the *buddhi*. It is *karma* that will dictate these predispositions. In other words, each human being creates for him or her self the *guṇic* dispositions of the intellect that predispose him or her to a particular type of ego in the next existence. All this is part of the cause–effect process. *Ahaṃkāra* is the "I-ness"[27] by which *puruṣas* become enmeshed in the activities of *prakṛti* – and each becomes differently enmeshed: the world-picture that each *puruṣa* "sees" is different – dependent on dispositional tendencies of the intellect, as well as the individual impressions that affect the ego. It is *ahaṃkāra* that creates subject and object, desire and aversion, and responds to sense perceptions of the external world. Notably, the whole strata for the manifest world stems from the *ahaṃkāra*, with the exception of the final *mahā-bhūtas*. As such, as Edwin Bryant points out so well, *ahaṃkāra* is "the critical midpoint in the choice between material world or the pure *puruṣa*".[28] Why does egoity occur here before anything exists? Burley's theory of idealism means that egoity provides "the conditions necessary for perceptual experience" rather than some cosmic "I-ness"; the "factors internal to the instigation of experience".[29] It is a tantalizingly interesting point that would explain why ego should be so near the apex of the order of emergence of *tattvas*.

Manas

From the *ahaṃkāra* emerge the *manas*, the *indriyas* and the *tanmātras*. The *manas*, the mind, derived from Sanskrit *man*, "to think", is that which constructs and arranges the sense impressions that reach it from the senses and the organs of action, the *indriyas*. It performs an analytic function, providing sensible explanations of the sense data that it organizes, and its functioning feeds both the ego and the intellect, and links the two. Again, it is *prakṛtic* material, finite and unconscious. It is, in fact, an *indriya*, a sense organ, but in that it is connected so intimately with the higher subtle evolutes of intellect and ego, it is often classed with these two as an "internal organ", while the other *indriyas* are the "external organs". The mind is a sense that is of the nature of both the sense organs and the organs of action because, as the *Kārikā* states: "It is characterized by reflection (or synthesis or construction) and it is a sense because it is similar (to the senses)."[30]

Since the mind is composite in Sāṃkhya, it is capable of synthesizing many different senses at the same time. It interprets all the perceptions of the senses, which will remain at the indeterminate level of knowledge until the mind synthesizes them. The ego then reacts to the determinate knowledge that the mind has presented and such reaction may be positive or negative or even neutral. But the *guṇic* dispositions of the ego will determine to a great extent just how the ego will react to the sense stimuli conveyed to it by the mind. The role of the intellect is in the level of choice about the conveyed impressions, and it is the intellect, therefore, that provides the resulting volitional activity of mind or body. *Buddhi*, *ahaṃkāra* and *manas*, then, are collectively the "internal organ" or *antaḥ-karaṇa* (Yoga, *citta*).

The *prakṛtic* evolutes make up a subtle body, the *liṅga-śarīra*, that transmigrates, permanently accompanied by the *puruṣa* through its respective reincarnations – indeed, until the *puruṣa* separates from *prakṛti* in the enlightened state. Since each *liṅga* is dependent on its own particular combination of *guṇas*, it will differ from others, in addition to being different in each existence as a result of the *karmic* residues that have been built up. The *liṅga*, then, is what supplies our personality, our particular character and the happinesses and sorrows of life. It also dictates where life will be – in plant, animal, human, divine or hellish realms. The subtle body is the only means by which the dispositional tendencies can find an outlet, tendencies built up by the gross elements, the *mahā-bhūtas*, that form the physical world and that are normally found to be pleasurable, painful or neutral. The nature of the individual is already set by the *bhāvas* of the intellect and the appropriate *guṇic* make-up of the ego: it is *karmically* predetermined, or genetically coded in today's terminology.

Thus we have the Sāṃkhya theory of evolution. It is not difficult to see that its perception of reality is, despite the designation of Sāṃkhya as orthodox, a total rejection of Brahman as the ultimate Reality and cause of manifest existence. Śāṃkara, in particular, criticized the idea of a first cause as *avyakta* that was itself unconscious. And since Śāṃkara was very orthodox, the positing of a first cause that rejected *śruti* authority and its clear acceptance of Brahman was anathema. Sarvepalli Radhakrishnan wrote of *prakṛti*: "It is the symbol of the never-resting, active world stress. It goes on acting unconsciously, without regard to any thought-out plan, working for ends which it does not understand."[31] But, as will be seen below, it does have a purpose in relation to the *puruṣas* that become so involved in the *guṇic* interplay of which it consists.

The *guṇas*

The word *guṇa* means "thread" or "cord", and in Sāṃkhya it aptly refers to the three threads, strands or constituents, *sattva*, *tamas* and *rajas*, that make up the unity of unmanifest and manifest existence, though the word can have several nuances of meaning.[32] In normal usage in Hinduism the *guṇas* are *qualities*; however, Sāṃkhya seems to view the *guṇas* as *substances*, even though, if they are, they are subtle substances, more like essences. The *guṇas* are the cosmic components of all manifest existence, and even in the unmanifest state of *prakṛti* they are indestructible potentialities. Each entity in existence is composed of them in some proportion in the same way as a rope is composed of its respective strands. They are the basic constituents present in the unmanifest *prakṛti* that are transformed into the increasingly differentiated evolutes of manifest *prakṛti*. Since they serve to bind individuals to material existence, and are also the substances that create happiness, pain and dullness, the analogy of a rope that ties the individual to the world is an apt one.[33] The three *guṇas* inform each entity in existence with varying proportions that account for the differentiation of matter. They are completely dependent on each other, and account for the interconnectedness of all things in the universe and, reciprocally, the interconnectedness accounts for the evolution of all things from primal, unmanifest *guṇas*. The *Sāṃkhya-Kārikā* states: "The *guṇas*, whose natures are pleasure, pain and indifference, (serve to) manifest, activate and limit. They successively dominate, support, activate, and interact with one another."[34] Each entity in existence has a predominant *guṇa* giving it its more general characteristic, but all three are present in everything which, again, accounts for the unity and interconnectedness of existence.

Sattva

Sattva, from Sanskrit *as*, "to be", is "beingness", and is purity, light, goodness; it is connected with pleasure and happiness and is buoyant and shining. It is associated with whiteness, permits striving forward, and is inimical to darkness and ignorance. Because it is light, it is the most subtle of the *guṇas*, and characterizes the inhabitants of the heavenly world. The *sattvic guṇa* is of the nature of discernment, that is to say, of reflective determination. As the first of the evolutes to become manifest and essentially *sattvic*, *buddhi* has all the potential for discernment in whatever direction its predispositions will take it. But it is the *sattvic* element of it with its pure, reflective perception, that is the only means of liberation.

Tamas

The *tamas guṇa* is opposite in nature to *sattva*. *Tamas* is characterized by dullness and indifference, by restraint, obstruction and heaviness. Its restraining aspect opposes activity of the *rajas guṇa*, so it opposes all movement, rhythm, activity of the mind, and promotes ignorance, bewilderment and confusion. It is a *guṇa* associated with darkness and negativity. When we are sleepy, drowsy and lazy, we are *tamasic*. *Tamas* has more to do with materiality and is the *guṇa* that predominantly composes the *tanmātras* and *mahā-bhūtas* of *prakṛti* – the subtle and gross elements of life respectively. So if the individual is preoccupied with the *tamasic* elements of life he or she is a long way from the *sattvic* thought processes that lead to liberation, and is enveloped in ignorance. It is a *guṇa* that characterizes the sub-human realm in particular. Whereas *sattva* is associated with joy, pleasure and happiness in life, *tamas* is associated with the kind of inertia that is the potential for pain and sorrow. The particular blend of sorrow and happiness in life was as evident to the ancient mind as it is to the modern one. It often seems that the moment one seems to relish a time of happiness, life brings the sorrows from around the corner very quickly! But the converse does not seem to be quite the case even for the most positive of people. Sāṃkhya answers this paradox of life from the perspective of the *guṇas*. *Sattva*, being light and very subtle, is barely evident in gross matter; whereas *tamas* is present in every evolute of *prakṛti* but particularly in the whole of the physical world in which the human being is involved. Thus, *tamas* pervades the world at all levels and makes life proportionately more inert, and more sorrowful than happy.

Rajas

Rajas (from Skt. *rañj* "to redden", "to colour"), is involved with action, movement and stimulation, with energy and passion. It is that force or essence that compels and drives action rather than being action *per se*. *Rajas* is an aggressive *guṇa* and is therefore associated with redness. "It is on account of rajas that fire spreads, the wind blows, the senses follow their objects and the mind becomes restless,"[35] wrote Satischandra Chatterjee and Dhirendramohan Datta. While *tamas* leads to pain through ignorance, *rajas is* pain, suffering, *duḥkha*, and since it is the stimulator of the other two types of *guṇic* substances, which cannot operate without it, it is present in every single evolute of life in some degree, and characterizes the human race in general. *Rajas*, according to the *Sāṃkhya-Kārikā*, characterizes worldly creation "from Brahmā down to a blade of grass".[36] This is another reason why pain and sorrow are proportionately greater than happiness and joy; indeed, with *two guṇas* operating to cause pain and suffering, the happiness in life can be very little and always tinged with sorrow.[37]

The three *guṇas* are, in their unmanifest state, the *mūla-prakṛti*. Here, the *guṇas* are in equilibrium, but in this state, they are still dynamic, still changing, but *homogeneously* so, only in themselves. It is only when evolution begins that they interact *heterogeneously* with each other. Then, they pervade the entire *vyakta* or manifest evolutes of *prakṛti*, constantly in co-operation, opposition and tension with each other, resulting in all kinds of collocations and modifications, and this causes the multiplicity of differentiation that obtains in the world. What results will depend on the predominance of one *guṇa* over the others. Because of the interplay of the *guṇas* there is continual transformation and change in all existence, in all *prakṛti*. And yet, while subject to change in the world of matter, the *guṇas* are eternal substances which, when not manifest, simply reside in unmanifest equilibrium. It is the *guṇas* that provide the unity of the Sāṃkhya system, for it is these that inform both unmanifest and manifest *prakṛti*. In terms of experience for each *buddhi*, they will create happy and satisfying, uncomfortable or confusing experiences. But they are unconscious matter and completely separate from the *puruṣas*, though as will be seen below, they "function for the sake of the *puruṣa* like a lamp",[38] as the *Kārikā* says.

Each being is a composite of the three kinds of *guṇic* substances at a different number of levels – intellect, ego, mind, and subtle and physical bodies. The *guṇas*, then, "mingle, combine and strive in every fibre of our being",[39] said Radhakrishnan. Transcending the *guṇas* to become *nirguṇa*, and of the nature of the *ātman*, was the goal of much *Upaniṣadic* thought, and for Sāṃkhya the goal is similar, with the exception that its *puruṣas* are many, not one.

Knowledge

Before examining the nature of the Self – the other aspect of the Sāṃkhya duality – it is necessary to pause here to examine the theory of knowledge. Sāṃkhya ideas of valid knowledge are somewhat different to those of the other schools of philosophical thought, because the mind, the intellect and the senses that apprehend objects of knowledge are all part of the unconscious material *prakṛti*. The only *conscious* elements in any valid knowledge are the *puruṣas*. It is the *reflection* of the *puruṣas* in the intellect (*buddhi*), that allows any form of knowledge to occur – and it is only because the *puruṣas* are reflected in the intellect that anything can be known. Why this should happen in the first place is no more explained by Sāṃkhya than it is in any other Hindu or Indian school. It is just accepted that the ignorance that is the opposite of knowledge has always, eternally, existed.

For knowledge to occur, first the senses are excited by an object. This is indeterminate perception. The *manas* then shifts the perception to the determinate level and channels the object (or inferred sign) to the *buddhi*. The *buddhi* becomes modified to correspond with the form or mode (*vṛtti*) of the object, and the *ahaṃkāra*, the ego, relates the perception to "I-ness". The *puruṣa* reflected in the *buddhi* illuminates the form or mode, and lends consciousness to the intellect, ego and mind. Then, the fatal mistake occurs. The *puruṣa* identifies itself with the "I" of ego and becomes enmeshed in the results of knowledge – worldly activity. While direct perception is accepted by Sāṃkhya as a valid means of knowledge, much of what Sāṃkhya teaches is inferred, mediate knowledge; its positing of *puruṣas* and *prakṛti* both falling into this category. So it is possible to have inferred knowledge of something that is not perceived, like fire, from something that is perceived, like smoke. Since the two critical principles that supply the Sāṃkhya dualism – *puruṣa* and *prakṛti* – are ultimately unmanifest and, therefore, imperceptible, they can only be known through the means of inference. Thus, inference is the superior means of knowledge. Sāṃkhya also accepts reliable authority, *śabda* or *āptavacana*, as valid knowledge. Īśvara-Kṛṣṇa did not stress the importance of the *Vedas*, of worship of God, or of concomitant rituals: it was later Sāṃkhya tradition that felt the obligation to accept *Vedic* authority. Here, the *Veda* was accepted as not composed by human hand and, therefore, as self-valid.

The Self: *Puruṣas*

We must turn now to examine the second fundamental aspect of reality – *puruṣa*, Sāṃkhya's term for *ātman*.[40] Each *puruṣa* is pure consciousness, and this is a pure consciousness that is not subject to change, is permanent, is inactive, and is pure subjectivity, "something like a mirror without any reflection in it or a light that illuminates nothing",[41] Weerasinghe writes. Each *puruṣa* or Self is not an effect of anything; it is uncaused and therefore eternal, and it is devoid of *guṇas*. The self that we think we know – that which is active, impermanent, subject to change, and the one that experiences pleasures, pains, joys and sorrows – is not the real Self. It is a reflection and superimposition of a material, *prakṛtic* combination of *guṇas* on the pure *puruṣa*, so that the two cannot be distinguished. It is the separation of the two that brings about liberation from *saṃsāra*. *Puruṣas* are all different and individual when trapped by *prakṛti*, but despite being pure consciousness, they have no sense of "I"; they are not *personal*. The personal self that we experience is the result of the three *material* aspects of *prakṛti* – intellect, ego and mind, *buddhi*, *ahaṃkāra* and *manas* respectively. And these three material components of *prakṛti* will reflect, or superimpose themselves on, the pure consciousness of the *puruṣa* in different ways – in fact, in as many ways as there are individuals: thus, there are many *puruṣas*. It seemed reasonable to assume that given multiple different births and deaths of beings, varied activities in different times and the varying collocations of the *guṇas* in each individual, that there must be a separate *puruṣa* for each being.

Each *puruṣa* is the *jña*, or "knower"; that is to say it is the pure subject by which all the objectivity of the material world can be known.[42] Lloyd Pflueger described it as "the uncharacterizable mystery behind all awareness".[43] Yet it is itself separate from knowledge. Knowledge, intellect, ego and the mind cannot exist without the pure consciousness of each *puruṣa*, but the Self is not really connected in any way with the emotions, the self-identity, or the personality that is each human being. Within the process of knowledge, if the *puruṣa* comes to accept itself as having knowledge, it becomes bound, as Radhakrishnan so poignantly said: "Losing the peace of eternity, it enters the unrest of time."[44] *Puruṣas* cannot know themselves, and they have no volition, so cannot decide to act or to think; they cannot reflect on themselves for they are simply consciousness without content.

The idea of the Self as pure consciousness is far from alien to *Upaniṣadic* conceptions of the *ātman* and the idea of the egoistic self as the source of suffering in the *saṃsāric* cycle. The world in the context of both the *Upaniṣadic* concept of *ātman* and the Sāṃkhya concept of *puruṣa* is that which ensnares the real Self and obscures what is ultimate and permanent in life. Sāṃkhya is, thus, not too wide of the orthodox mark in its evaluation and identity of the true Self. It is the multiplicity of Selves rather than the unity of essence of the Self that is the major departure from *Upaniṣadic* thought. The consciousness of *puruṣa* is necessary for the evolution of the unconscious matter of existence, and yet it is the opposite of material existence. And while *puruṣas* are necessary for material existence to come into being, they cannot be said to be the cause of it since they are neither causes nor caused. The *Kārikā* says of the real Self that it is a witness (of *prakṛti*); it is isolated and free; it is indifferent to the world; it is a spectator that simply views the world; and it is inactive.[45]

The self that we normally know, then, and the self that is subject to *karma* and *saṃsāra*, does not really exist. It is just a material conglomeration that acquires a false and transient consciousness that is not its own through ignorance of the real Self, *puruṣa*. *Puruṣas* are reflected in the world, just as the moon is reflected in water, but they are not of the world at all. And just as the ignorant see the moon in the water and believe that it is really there, so the ignorant in life experience the reflected *puruṣa* in the intellect of the egoistic self and believe that the transient self is the real Self.

The entire psychical and physical self that we ordinarily experience in life, then, is totally material. It is subject to change and to transience, to rebirth and to death, in a way that the real Self is not. After each life, the subtle body, the *liṅga-śarīra*, will be composed of the *karmic* dispositional residues that will dictate the nature of the next life. The *liṅga*, then, is a "permanent annexe"[46] to each self, transmigrating according to the nature of the dispositions of the intellect. So it is the subtle body, the *liṅga-śarīra* that carries all the ingredients for each reincarnating self. The subtle body is primeval, emerging with the initial manifestations of *prakṛti*. It is permanent, though dispositionally changeable, and is connected with a particular *puruṣa* for its entire transmigratory experiences. This inseparable connection remains until the *puruṣa* knows itself as free. The *Sāṃkhya-Kārikā* graphically describes the associated relation between the *puruṣa* and the subtle body: "This subtle entity, motivated for the sake of the *puruṣa*, appears like a player (who assumes many roles) by means of its association with efficient causes and effects (i.e., by means of its association with the *bhāvas*) and because of its association with the power of *prakṛti*."[47] Problematically, the *puruṣas* do not appear to be any different from each other than numerically so and, as Sharma rightly comments: "Numerical pluralism is sheer nonsense."[48] Without difference in essence, the characterless consciousness of each *puruṣa* cannot really differ from the next one. This makes Sāṃkhya's move away from a unity of liberated Selves a very difficult issue.

The interaction of *puruṣas* and *prakṛti*

As has been seen, *Prakṛti* is an unconscious material principle that cyclically evolves into an equally unconscious material universe, and then involves. But, as Chatterjee and Datta pertinently pointed out with reference to Sāṃkhya: "It is not the dance of blind atoms, nor the push and pull of mechanical forces which produce a world to no purpose."[49] The whole purpose of *prakṛti* is to serve the *puruṣas*,[50] and thus *prakṛti* is a uniquely Indian teleological principle or, perhaps, "quasi-teleological" to use Hiriyanna's term,[51] because it is not consciously teleological. Yet it is perhaps this area of the interaction between the two aspects of the Sāṃkhya dualism that is its most problematic one. It is the *relation*, the *proximity* between *puruṣas* and *prakṛti* (and I believe it is important to remember that *puruṣas* are plural in this context), that causes the process of evolution to take place. What, then, causes involution, when all *prakṛti* returns to its unmanifest state? Are the *puruṣas* no longer in proximity? And if they are not, then what causes this spatial change, for they are inactive in themselves? Accordingly, any suggestion that *prakṛti* is guided by *puruṣas* in some way, makes the *puruṣas* active and not passive, and it is difficult to avoid the suggestion that the proximity of the *puruṣas* is causal. Any suggestion that *puruṣa* and *prakṛti must* interact is nonsense, for matter has no spirit and consciousness, and spirit has no efficient action.[52] Without interaction there is no point to evolution, or even no evolution at all. On this point, Radhakrishnan's following words were more than pertinent: "If an error of judgment had not thrust the *puruṣa* into the playhouse, and if our deluded minds had not watched the performance of *prakṛti*, there would be no action of *prakṛti* at all."[53]

Even more of a paradox is the apparent accumulation of *karma* by the Selves. Since they alone are capable of experience, only they can react to the material world in positive, negative and indifferent ways. Sharma comments: "Poor Puruṣa suffers for no fault of its own. Prakṛti performs actions and Puruṣa has to reap their fruits good or bad. And Prakṛti knows how to make delicious dishes, but not to enjoy them!"[54] But reaction is action, and it could be claimed that there is a dimension of the Selves that is not pure, inactive consciousness, but is active consciousness, otherwise it cannot be the recipient of fruitive *karma*. Presumably it is the *collective karmas* of seemingly bound *puruṣas* that create the proximity that brings about the evolution of matter, and the same *collective karmas* that cause manifest *prakṛti* to return to the unmanifest state.[55] Either way, it is difficult to maintain that the Selves are not in some way the cause of these processes, particularly if it is all for their own ends. On the other hand, if it is claimed that *prakṛti* has a teleological purpose that is aimed at liberating the Selves then this can only be an *unconscious* purpose, since it is all matter. It is difficult to accept how unconscious matter can itself decide to evolve into manifest form for the sake of a totally separate principle that it cannot really know, especially if all knowledge is of material nature and objective.[56] And yet, the way *prakṛti* is in any one evolutionary process must be determined by the *guṇic* necessities engendered by the *puruṣas'* involvement in the previous evolutionary world-process. *Prakṛti*, then, is conditioned by the needs of *puruṣas* and the *karmic* natures they have built up. It does not evolve without a blueprint for its nature; it can only evolve the way it is meant to. In this sense it really is unconsciously quasi-teleological.

The purpose of *prakṛti* is to provide the objective knowledge that will enable each Self to realize its true state, preventing it from thinking that the reflection in the mirror is real. Essentially it is the *buddhi* of each individual that is capable of this liberating knowledge for the *puruṣa*, just as it is the evolute that is able to reflect the real Self. *Puruṣa* is the knower that appropriates the knowledge supplied by the *buddhi*. The separation of knower and knowledge, of subject and object, is the reverse step that the *buddhi* has to present to the *puruṣa*. However, it should be impossible for the *buddhi* to infer the presence of *puruṣa*, since what is objective cannot infer what is subjective. It is nonsense to claim that the material object can ever have knowledge of the subject.[57] However, the Self becomes liberated through the knowledge it can have of itself in *prakṛti*; it can *witness* the knowledge that is the truth. So between *prakṛti* and *puruṣa*, there is what Frauwallner termed "a reciprocal dependence, a tie of mutual interest".[58] The two separate aspects of *puruṣa* and *buddhi* have enough similarity to become so incorrectly superimposed one on the other, that reality is blurred. It is the separation of this reality into its accurate dualities that is the whole goal of Sāṃkhya, and that amounts to the liberation of the Self in *mukti*.

These are difficult aspects of Sāṃkhya philosophy, particularly the attempt to assign some kind of blind purpose to unconscious matter on the one hand, and to suggest that something that is already separate and pure consciousness can be trapped in such unconscious matter on the other. It seems futile for *prakṛti* to be purposefully (and yet unconsciously) operating for the freedom of that which is already free. Radhakrishnan justifiably commented that "The sāṃkhya cannot get across the ditch which it has dug between the subject and the object."[59] Indeed, without a third principle that causes the proximity of the *puruṣas* and *prakṛti* for the process of evolution, and that pulls apart such proximity for cosmic dissolution or *pralaya*, it is difficult to see what creates the proximity in the first place. It is also difficult to see what causes the interdependence, if neither aspects of the duality are causal to the other: some designer or efficient cause to make it all so seems exigent. The dualism of Sāṃkhya is certainly compromised by the interdependency of the two principles and, as Hiriyanna pointed out, "puruṣa, were it not for its association with *prakṛti*, would be hardly distinguishable from nothing".[60]

Causality

Causation is an extremely important concept in Sāṃkhya philosophy, because the theory of the unitary nature of all evolution is dependent on it. Sāṃkhya posits the theory of *sat-kārya-vāda*, the view that all effects exist latently in their causes; in other words effects exist even before they are manifest. The term *sat-kārya-vāda* – similar to that of Advaita Vedānta in the last chapter – can be broken down into *sat*, meaning "true", "real", or "existent", *kārya* meaning "effect", and *vāda* meaning "theory". Nothing new can come into being; everything exists potentially in its cause. As Dasgupta said, "just a little loosening of the barrier which was standing in the way of the happening of such a change of arrangement will produce the desired new collocation – the effect."[61] So when an effect comes into being, there is no *material* change, only a modification of the material. Despite periods of quiescence when the *guṇas* of *prakṛti* are in equilibrium in *avyakta*, the process of collocations of cause and effect is beginningless and endless. Evolution and involution follow each other in eternal cycles. *Prakṛti* is, therefore, termed *pradhāna* "primordial matter", that from which all effects emerge, and to which they will return. There is no creation as such for there is no real beginning, no ultimate dissolution, only perpetual transformation to effects and return to cause.

The interrelation and uniformity of things in the world are put down to the interaction of the manifest *guṇas* in the immediate sense, and the presence of the same *guṇas* in the non-interactive unmanifest state – the first cause. Verse 14 of the *Sāṃkhya-Kārikā* states that: "The unmanifest is . . . established because of the *guṇa*-nature in the cause of the effect (or because the effect has the same qualities as the cause)."[62] *Mūla-prakṛti* is the cause (*kāraṇa*) of all the effects (*kārya*) of existence. All that happens when evolution unfolds is that the pre-existent effects are transformed into their manifest forms. But the obvious question here is what is the agent for such transformation: after all, we need a potter to transform clay into a clay effect?[63] Such transformations of cause to effect are, for Sāṃkhya, *real* changes, unlike as we saw with the school of Advaita Vedānta where *sat-kārya-vāda* meant transformations from cause to effect that are only *apparent*, the cause not really being transformed at all. But for Sāṃkhya, all the effects are parts of *one*, unified whole, a whole that is divided into parts or, a cause that is transformed into effects. The eternal existence of the *guṇas* and their constant interdependence maintains the whole.

There is no conscious first cause, only the material and unconscious first cause of *prakṛti* in its state of *avyakta*. Presumably the *puruṣas* would have to be as much conscious of, and a witness to, unmanifest *prakṛti* as of its manifest evolutes, otherwise they would be at sometimes conscious of objects and at other times not conscious of them, and therefore changeable. The difficulty is, as was raised above, that if the *puruṣas* affect the *avyakta* to promote creation, how, then, do they affect creation to cause *pralaya*, dissolution, when evolution ceases and there is a movement backwards until the *guṇas* return to their unmanifest state? Latent *karmas* of the *puruṣas* are believed to be held in the unmanifest state of *prakṛti*, that is to say, all the different *buddhis* containing reflected *puruṣas* that have been trapped in the world through their misconceptions of, and involvement in, it are suspended. So how can they then affect the *avyakta* to cause creation without some kind of change or activity in themselves? The *puruṣas* are conscious but only witnesses; they cannot *do* anything. What happens to the *puruṣas* during involved unmanifest *avyakta*? Sāṃkhya gives us no answer here. Radhakrishnan wrote of the effect of *puruṣas* on involution: "When the desires of all *puruṣas* require that there should be a temporary cessation of all experience, *prakṛti* returns to its quiescent state."[64] But, again, this belies the so-called passivity of the *puruṣas*, and overtly presents them as the conscious cause of involution. Yet it is really the only logical outcome to the question of what causes involution.

The absence of God

Classical Sāṃkhya is an atheistic system, possibly influenced by Buddhism and Jainism, though beyond the classical Sāṃkhya of the *Kārikā* there were certainly theistic strands, and these may have been more typical.[65] Yoga, on the other hand is theistic, and the combined Sāṃkhya-Yoga usually supports a theistic stance, as exemplified in the *Bhagavad Gītā*. This is not to say that classical Sāṃkhya rejected all ideas of Hindu gods. Indeed, the deities of Hinduism were accepted, but they were simply redundant in a school of thought that saw knowledge alone as the means to liberation, and that accepted an unconscious material first principle that was the cause of all things. Gods were demoted from the spiritual to the material – caught by their respective *puruṣas* in the materiality of existence, albeit a divine one. There was no room for a transcendent Absolute, and no need for it,[66] though a more overt linking of just one *Puruṣa* with the unmanifest aspect of *prakṛti* was probable in pre-classical Sāṃkhya.[67] The emphasis on knowledge meant that it would be impossible for Sāṃkhya to accept that knowledge could ever be of a transcendent God. Knowledge occurs only when the *buddhi* formulates an object for the *puruṣa* as subject to see. And it could not formulate an imperceptible, inconceivable God.

The resulting denial of a concept of Brahman in classical Sāṃkhya, however, was a considerable departure from *Vedāntic* thought and was a clear rejection of theism and monistic absolutism. Brahman was rejected because what is permanent and unchanging cannot be the cause of what is constantly impermanent and changing. What is the point, Sāṃkhya claimed, of a totally transcendent Absolute that is beyond all action and non-action, and is completely unmanifest. How could this Brahman involve itself in material manifestation? And if it did, for what purpose? Why would such an Absolute create a world full of evil and suffering? Then, too, as far as the individual self is concerned, if it were partly or wholly that Absolute it must have some divine powers. But we know that individuals do not have such powers. And if the individual self is non-divine and simply created by God, then why would God want to create something that is finite and subject to destruction? Thus Sāṃkhya's dualism saw no need for a transcendent deity to which the universe owed its existence, and which provided the rationale for liberation. *Prakṛti* could operate by itself, and knowledge could prove to each *puruṣa* that it is, in reality, already free.

Liberation

Given the material nature of every component of the human being, most claim that it is certainly real. It is real in that it is a collocation of *guṇas* at all its composite levels, but it is unreal in respect of its false consciousness of itself as a subjective agent in the *prakṛtic* world. It is this latter aspect that is the *avidyā*, *ajñāna*, the "non-knowledge" or ignorance that binds the *puruṣa* to the world, for it is the reflection of the *puruṣa* in the *buddhi* that creates this individual and unreal self. It is the failure of the *puruṣa* to see itself as separate from material existence and separate from experience that is the root of *ajñāna*. It is too intimately connected with the *buddhi* to see the truth, and it is ignorance of this truth that causes the self to suffer or, rather, causes the individual *puruṣa* as the subjective consciousness to be the one who experiences suffering. It is the non-discrimination (*aviveka*) of itself as separate that is the problem and which causes the binding of the real Self to a material world. Discriminative knowledge (*viveka-jñāna*) of the separation of the two is therefore essential.

The means to freedom of the Self are referred to in verse 51 of the *Sāṃkhya-Kārikā* as eight spiritual attainments or perfections: "The eight perfections are proper reasoning, oral instruction, study, removal of the three kinds of suffering, friendly discussion and generosity."[68] Knowledge that transcends worldly knowledge is, according to the second verse of the *Sāṃkhya-Kārikā*, "the (discriminative) knowledge of the manifest (*vyakta*), the unmanifest (*avyakta*) and the knowing one (or knower – i.e., *puruṣa*)."[69] It occurs with loss of "I-awareness", and with release of the Self from the *buddhi* and the evolutes that emerge from it. What sets the Self free is the Self itself; matter cannot do this but the Self in conjunction with matter can. The *puruṣa* sees what the *buddhi* presents to it: its involvement or detachment from the material world is, as a result, its own affair. Separate the reflection between the two and there is no suffering, no positive and negative responses.

The liberated *puruṣa* is in a state of *kaivalya*, total isolation, passivity, aloneness, suspended in its own eternity. There is total dissociation from *prakṛti* and total isolation from all other Selves – "translucent emptiness", as Larson terms it [70] – in which consciousness lacks even the witnessing of *prakṛti*. This is the Sāṃkhya *mokṣa* or *mukti*, total liberation. It is the revelation of the *puruṣa* as it has really always been. According to the *Sāṃkhya-Kārikā*: "No one therefore, is bound; no one released, likewise no one transmigrates. (Only) *prakṛti* in its various forms transmigrates, is bound and is released."[71] In reality nothing has changed in the nature of *puruṣa*: it has always been free, always eternal and always separate from the *prakṛtic* world. Now it becomes totally isolated. But this isolation was a perspective of liberation that was not without its critics past and present: "The grandeur of the soul, in Kapila's system", wrote John Davies, "is unreal and useless. It has no moral elevation. It knows nothing of virtue and vice as connected with itself. It has no purpose beyond itself. It directs in some undefined degree, but it never condescends to work, either for itself or for others. It has no sympathy. Its highest state is one of perfect abstraction from matter and from other souls; a self-contained life, wherein no breath of emotion ever breaks in on the placid surface."[72] It is a "most uninspiring"[73] end to the trials and tribulations of poor *puruṣa*. There is a problem too, as noted earlier, in the natures of this plurality of Selves. Why should they be plural? What is it that makes them so? Hiriyanna justifiably commented: "In their liberated state there is absolutely no difference; and to postulate numerical difference between entities, when there is no distinction whatever in their intrinsic nature, seems unwarranted."[74]

The lack of differentiation between the *puruṣas* is also surprising in that *mokṣa* is not something that can only be realized after death, for Sāṃkhya recognizes that one can be a *jīvan-mukta*, one liberated while still in the body, awaiting *kaivalya* after death. Here we have a liberated but seemingly differentiated *puruṣa* still engaged with physical and subtle bodies that are different from all others. A *jīvan-mukta* is accepted because of the *prārabdha-karma* that is already on its way, but no new fruitive *karma* is formed. The *buddhi* has seen the light of the *puruṣa* and is the cause of its release, but past impressions are the causes that compel the free *puruṣa* to dwell until death, reflected in the physical body. When death occurs, the Self becomes free from all matter, free from all sense of "I", free from all happiness, sorrow, joy and pain. The Self becomes empty of subjective awareness of matter, suspended in its own timeless, and spaceless essence.

Notwithstanding the problematic areas of Sāṃkhya metaphysics, it has left its mark on Indian philosophy. The whole *prakṛtic* nature of manifest existence was widely adopted, especially the essential active constituents of thought – *buddhi*, intellect; *ahaṃkāra*, ego; and *manas*, mind – collectively, the *antaḥ-karaṇa*. The theory of *guṇas* still informs much Hindu thought, though their natures vacillate between substances and qualities.

Classical Yoga

Background to the school

Classical, Raja (Royal), Yoga is associated with Patañjali, who lived sometime in the second or third centuries CE, though his dates are very uncertain. His Yoga is a practically orientated philosophical view, *darśana*, presented in *sūtra* form – short statements using minimal words.[75] Patañjali compiled the classic text of the school, the *Yoga-Sūtras*, which is dated to about the first to second centuries CE, and was underpinned by the philosophy of Sāṃkhya. In its broadest sense *yoga* has been a varied phenomenon in Indian practice from the earliest times and has become allied to different perspectives of Hinduism as much as to the other schools of philosophy in one form or another. In this same, broad, sense, *yoga* is a philosophy for the living of one's life in its practical dimension. Yoga in its narrower sense of a specific school of practice is by no means to be undertaken by the faint-hearted and unmotivated. In most of its aspects, *yoga* perceives that the Self that is real in the deeper levels of our consciousness transcends the empirical self that we know, and it provides the practical means for its realization. It is thus pervasive in Hinduism. Classical Yoga is not so practically orientated that it must rely completely on Sāṃkhya for its underlying metaphysics for it offers a thorough understanding of the nature of the mind, particularly the way in which the mind impedes or impels each individual on the spiritual quest – that is the legacy of Yoga, even today.

The ultimate goal of Yoga is the cessation, *nirodha*, of the "modifications", *vṛtti* (from Skt. *vṛt* "to turn, move, revolve"), that constitute the mental functioning of the mind, *citta*. *Vṛttis* are literally "whirls", a word that provides a very graphic image of the human mind, and the thoughts that whirl into the mind in day-to-day life, even in dreams. The fifteenth-century commentator on the *Yoga-Sūtras*, Vijñana Bhikṣu, compared *vṛttis* to the flames of a fire or waves on the sea. Taking up his metaphors, Bryant refers to the "never-ending but ever-changing temporary forms and permutations produced by the constant flux of the tides, undercurrents, and eddies of the *citta*".[76] Combining these three Sanskrit terms, then, we have the Yoga goal of *citta-vṛtti-nirodha* which, in Patañjali's words, means "the restriction of the fluctuations of mind-stuff",[77] and can only be achieved by immense discipline of the mind. This is essentially what the word *yoga* as a concept means, being both an aim and a practice. In general, the word is associated with the kind of discipline of the mind that takes place in meditative practices on the one hand, and through austere practices, on the other. The actual meaning of the word is derived from Sanskrit *yuj* "to yoke", "to bind together", and this is suggestive of yoking the senses so that the "fluctuations of mind-stuff" are stilled,[78] though theistic strands would have encompassed the yoking of the self to God. To the extent that one is able to still the mind, there will be a corresponding transcending of the senses and the usual mind patterns. This brings about what Karel Werner has described as a very different perspective of being and existence: "The whole personality becomes transformed and can function in a new dimension hitherto unknown or inaccessible to it. Knowledge is widened, deepened and increased and there is a sense of communion with the infinite or with the essence of all things or with reality as a whole."[79]

But the sense of communion – indeed any sense at all – is completely quelled in the classical expression of Yoga, when the mind becomes totally still. Here, personality is lost along with all sense of duality and objectivity. The Sāṃkhya goal of *kaivalya*, isolation of the Self in its pure consciousness, is the ultimate goal of classical Yoga, and it is therefore something of a "science" that sets about providing a technical means for the achievement of its goal. The aim, then, is the silence of the mind. This, as Ravi Ravindra depicts it "is the prerequisite condition for the mind to be able to reflect accurately the objective reality without introducing its own subjective distortions. Yoga does not create this reality, which is above the mind, but only prepares the mind to apprehend it, by assisting in the transformation of the mind – from an ordinary mind full of noise, like a whole army of frenzied and drunken monkeys – to a still mind."[80] Classical Yoga reflects the long and diverse prehistory of *yoga* and the many inquiries into the depths of spiritual consciousness behind ordinary mortal thought. As such, classical Yoga is only one dimension of *yoga*. However, it is an important one that serves to systematize a variety of trends that had been present in the centuries before the advent of Patañjali's work, a "cluster of interconnected and cross-fertilizing variants of meditational *yoga*", as Bryant describes it.[81] Patañjali wrote at a time when Yoga traditions had infiltrated many aspects of orthodox and unorthodox Indian society and it is likely that the techniques included in the *Yoga-Sūtras* were already in place before he compiled his text.[82] Although Patañjali's system of Yoga is very closely allied to the philosophy of Sāṃkhya, there are differences, particularly considering Yoga's acceptance of a divine being, and of a theistic, devotional approach to that being, which I shall examine in due course. But it is not necessary to discuss the same twenty-five principles of Sāṃkhya in the context of Yoga, since there are no real differences. However, Yoga has different terminology for the evolutes of *prakṛti*,[83] and *puruṣa* is termed "the seer", *draṣṭṛ*, and *prakṛti* "that seen", *dṛśya*. Important to note, too, is that Yoga emphasized mind control, rather than solely emphasizing intellectual discernment, as did Sāṃkhya.[84] Yoga aims at a practical means for liberation in addition to a theoretical philosophy, and it uses the philosophy for its praxis. It is in this sense that it provides complementary teaching to that of Sāṃkhya. From major texts of the time as the *Mahābhārata* (12:304:1–4) and the *Bhagavad Gītā* (5:2 and 4–5) it seems, however, that Sāṃkhya and Yoga were regarded as the same.

From what has been said it is obvious that Patañjali was not the founder of Yoga; he was simply one who drew together a number of important threads into a composite philosophical and practical system. As Sāṃkhya, Yoga begins with the fundamental life condition of the suffering and disharmony of each individual and with what Werner terms "the solitude and self-enclosedness of the human heart".[85] As Sāṃkhya, then, classical Yoga aims to direct the Self to the point at which its distinction from material existence – and that includes intellect, mind and ego – is realized, and the *puruṣa* is liberated into pure, isolated consciousness. Classical Yoga aims at presenting the means by which the individual is able to transcend the functions of mind and ego that bind the Self to the world of matter.

Although associated with the school of classical Yoga and the compiler of the foundational *Sūtras* of the school, Patañjali was neither a founder nor an innovator, nor was his school the only form of Yoga in the wider Indian and Hindu landscape. It was simply the one that predominated. Yet Surendranath Dasgupta described his *Sūtras* as "a masterly and systematic compilation, supplemented with certain original contributions".[86] What he did was to present in his *Yoga-Sūtras* a very systematic and succinct account of the practice of Yoga – "a codifier of what was best in the Yoga practice and knowledge of his time", writes Werner.[87] But we know little of him.[88] Patañjali's *Yoga-Sūtras* is a collection of short aphorisms easily committed to memory and conducive, therefore, to oral transmission but, since many of the aphorisms are obscure, it is necessary to learn them with the aid of a teacher. Since each of the *sūtras* composing the work is cursory, explanation has been left to the commentators, and their commentaries, *bhāṣyas*, are essential to the understanding of the text,[89] though it is important to bear in mind that each commentator probably had his own philosophical agenda in approaching the text,[90] and there are also many differing translations of the *Yoga-Sūtras*. The major commentators that I shall be mentioning in the following pages are Vyāsa from the fourth or fifth centuries,[91] Vācaspati Miśra of the ninth century and Vijñana Bhikṣu from the fifteenth century, though there were others, including the famous Advaitist, Śaṃkara.

General features of the school

Patañjali says in his *Yoga-Sūtras* 2:15 that to a discriminating mind everything involved in *prakṛti* is characterized by suffering – a tenet that Bryant considers to be the heart of the whole text.[92] Suffering, *duḥkha*, is particularly evident because all in life, even happiness, is subject to *guṇic* fluctuations and cannot be permanent. The *sūtra* is reminiscent of the first of the *Four Noble Truths* of Buddhism and was a fundamental tenet of Sāṃkhya, too. The answer to the problem of suffering is *yogic* practice, a practice that "becomes firmly established when it has been cultivated uninterruptedly and with devotion over a prolonged period of time", says the *Yoga-Sūtras*.[93] In emphasizing practice, classical Yoga turns its attention to the analysis of the mind – one that, I believe, holds as good for modern times as for the centuries past. In holding the fluctuations of the mind in check, the *Yoga-Sūtras* recommends concentration on one single object, what is termed *ekāgra*.[94] It is concentration on a single object as opposed to the normal mind fluctuations of multiple perceptions and thoughts. So until the final stages of *yogic* practice, classical Yoga does not suggest that the mind is emptied, but that it is controlled by single-object concentration. If the focus of the mind can be maintained on just one thing, then all the other thoughts are constrained, and all the stimuli that promote such thoughts will remain unnoticed. Breathing is particularly important in promoting such concentration with emphasis on the inhalation, retention and exhalation of the breath.

Two principles in particular are important in Yoga: *viveka*, which is "discriminative discernment", and *vairāgya*, which is "detachment", "dispassion", "renunciation". According to Vācaspati Miśra, renunciation of desires is not the aim: rather, *indifference* to desires is what the *yogin* should achieve. *Viveka* refers to the kind of discernment that enables the distinction between the consciousness of *puruṣa* and the materiality of *prakṛti* to be realized, and the true and permanent nature of the former, as opposed to the impermanent, finite and changeable nature of the latter. All the thoughts that invade the mind as a result of sense perceptions serve to promote a personality that, in constant reaction to these sense stimuli, becomes tied to the world of matter. It is the desires and aversions of the individual in response to such stimuli that are *karmic* and that bind the individual to the process of rebirth. *Vairāgya*, then, is non-desire, non-passion, dis-passion, and suggests the training of the mind to restrain it from reacting to the stimuli of the world. Reflecting almost exactly the Buddhist *brahma-vihāras*, *sūtra* 1:33 says: "By cultivating an attitude of friendship toward those who are happy, compassion toward those in distress, joy toward those who are virtuous, and equanimity toward those who are nonvirtuous, lucidity arises in the mind."[95] Closely connected with the strenuous exertion to free the mind of all desires is the asceticism associated with Yoga – hunger, thirst, cold, heat, standing or sitting for long periods, immobilization and fasting.

Reality: The view of the world in classical Yoga

In the fourth *pāda* of the *Yoga-Sūtras* Patañjali tells us that: "The that-ness of a thing is due to a singleness of mutation."[96] This is to say that each entity in the phenomenal world is a particular combination of the three substances accepted by Sāṃkhya, the *guṇas* of *sattva*, *rajas* and *tamas*. Since these three *guṇas* are eternal, they lend reality to the phenomenal world, even if that reality is a changeable one in terms of the coming together and breaking apart of the various combinations of the *guṇas*. So, as Sāṃkhya, Yoga accepts the realism of the world, along with the same division of reality into the pure consciousness of the *puruṣas* on the one hand, and the unified *prakṛtic* matter on the other. Throughout this entire *prakṛtic* scheme are the changing collocations of the three *guṇas*, except in the unmanifest state, where they are as much real but do not interact. Reality, then, is *prakṛtic* reality as much as the reality of the other dual principle, *puruṣa*. The nearer mind functioning comes to this fact – that is to say, represents matter truly – the more the mind is dislodged from involvement with *prakṛti*. It is the beginningless conjunction, *saṃyoga*, between *puruṣa* and *prakṛti* that causes all the ignorance and suffering of each being, which will continue until they separate. Importantly, *prakṛtic* matter is not dependent on *puruṣas* for its own reality: it exists, irrespective of any liberated *puruṣas*.[97]

It is exactly because the *guṇic* reality is a changing one, and because each individual is a codified blend of *guṇic* dispositions that are different from all other individuals, that each individual perspective of reality is different. As Jacobsen puts it, "the experience of reality is conditioned by the capacity of the species of the experiencer as well as by individual capacities. Reality, as humans experience it, is conditioned by our nature",[98] and the senses by which we view the world "are narrow portholes allowing us a fragmentary and deformed glimpse of the reality outside".[99] Inevitably, then, the human mind is trapped in its own specific kind of reality, programmed to be receptive to certain stimuli and to repel others according to the individual *guṇic* composition of its higher subtle faculties of intellect and ego. Inevitably, too, there can be no true perception by anyone other than the liberated *yogin*, so all perspectives of reality, other than the liberated one, are false: empirical truth is always tainted. And since *prakṛti* is without beginning and without end, human bondage, the *karma* that produces it, and the ignorance that sustains it, will always be characteristic phenomena of manifest *prakṛti*. Thus, *stilling* the mind, *controlling* it, are the only possible solutions to a myopic, ignorant and individual perspective of reality. The *yogin* has to still the mind in order to view matter as it really is.

Knowledge

In the main, Yoga has the same Sāṃkhya view of knowledge as critical to the dissociation between *puruṣa* and *prakṛti*. The only knower is the pure consciousness, or pure awareness, of the *puruṣa* of the individual. Yoga accepts the extraordinary knowledge that states of *samādhi*, the ultimate meditative state, can bring; knowledge of subtle levels of *prakṛti* that could never be known via the ordinary means of knowledge. The process of acquiring *discriminating* knowledge (*viveka-khyāti*) is essential to the *yogin*. It involves a regression from ordinary perception through the senses, to the deeper knowledge of the subtle evolutes of *prakṛti* – a journey of knowledge of ever finer *prakṛtic* evolutes. This is an important point to which I shall return later. The *yogin* has to understand thoroughly the true nature of *prakṛti* but, as Jacobsen succinctly puts it, "the purpose of understanding matter in Sāṃkhya and Yoga is not to use matter, but to get rid of it".[100]

Three valid means of knowledge are accepted by Yoga – perception, inference and testimony. Knowledge takes place as a modification of the mind complex when it has been affected by some external thing through the channel of the sense organs. The mind becomes subject to modifications in order to come into a state of balance with the object. This process is direct and immediate, but the *yogin* has to transcend all the sense stimuli of ordinary perception for extra-ordinary perception that penetrates directly to the subtler states of *prakṛti*. Eventually, the *yogin* reaches that finely subtle state of *sattvic* knowledge pertinent only to the intellect, *buddhi*. Such *yogic* perception that is extraneous to the senses is not subject to *karmic* results.

It is the modifications of the mind that bind the *puruṣa* to the world of matter. For instead of being a mere observer of an object, the *puruṣa* becomes involved with it. It lends consciousness to predications that are made about the object – it is this or that, it is something to be liked or disliked, it is a source of pain or joy, and so on. Thus, objects are not perceived as they are, but are reacted to. It is this reaction and the subsequent modifications of the mind in the perceptive process that have to be controlled. Instead of perceiving external gross objects, the *yogin* attempts to perceive the essence of them, the subtle *tanmātras*. Then, without any subsequent reaction related to such objects, they remain such as they are – *prakṛtic* matter, and no more. Classical Yoga also accepted inferential knowledge (when things are always related, as smoke and fire), and verbal and scriptural testimony, though both were deemed inferior to the extraordinary perception of a *yogin*. Error in perception occurs when the mind fluctuations, or modifications of the mind, do not come into a state of balance with the object of perception.[101]

Citta

In the Sāṃkhya analysis of *prakṛti*, as we have seen, three "inner" evolutes are initially present. The first is *buddhi* or "intellect", the second is *ahaṃkāra* or "ego", and the third, along with the organs of sense and activity, is *manas* or "mind". While Yoga accepts the twenty-five principles of Sāṃkhya, it is a school that prefers the use of *citta* to refer to the mind: indeed, *citta* is derived from Sanskrit *cit*, "to think", "focus the mind on". But in many cases, it seems this term *citta* covers also the principles of *buddhi* and *ahaṃkāra* – this last termed *asmitā* in the *Yoga-Sūtras*. *Citta* in the Yoga system is "mind-stuff",[102] that is to say, all that goes on in the substance of the mind, the sophisticated organ of sense.[103] But since the *buddhi*, the intellect, synthesizes the mind-stuff, there is a certain overlap in the use of the term *citta* as bridging the two. And since the ego is that which relates so readily to the objects conveyed by the sense organs to the mind, then mind-stuff is intimately connected with that also. Gaspar Koelman, therefore, defines *citta* as "mind-complex", and considers that the term is akin to *manas* when it is linked more with the physical aspects of the functioning of the mind, and is akin to *buddhi* when it is more concerned with the psychical aspects. He considers that the term *citta* covers the three aspects of intellect, ego and mind because it refers to the individualized thinking and experiential self. It is, he says, "individualized cognitive nature with its set of incommunicable experiences, dispositions and inclinations. It is the whole individual psychical and psychological and moral prakritic individual."[104] Larson, too, is definitive that *citta* is the collective term for intellect, egoity and mind.[105] But Yoga primarily focuses on *mind* in particular, intellect being drawn into the mind functioning. If anything, Yoga *citta* is Sāṃkhya's *manas*, though encompassing the necessary intellect and egoism for efficient functioning.

Citta, then, refers to the psychological individual that is motivated by his or her dispositional intellect and ego, and that thinks and synthesizes sense impressions in his or her own unique way. The term *citta* is, thus, a very comprehensive one, and it is one that may be synonymous with *manas* in some contexts and with *buddhi* or *ahaṃkāra* in others, and sometimes may refer to all three. In what follows, I shall use the term *citta* to refer to the collective functioning of intellect, ego and mind. This corresponds to the Sāṃkhya *antaḥkaraṇa* that combines the three. It is highly likely that Patañjali understood the term *citta* in this way, though some writers will disagree.[106] Incorporating the three aspects of intellect, ego and mind, the *citta* acts as the medium between *prakṛti* and *puruṣa*. With justification, I think, Bryant sees *citta* as "perhaps the most important entity in *yoga* practice".[107]

If, however, *citta* is mind-stuff, then it has the potential to be the mind that is free of the fluctuations that pervade it – the still mind-stuff, the substratum of the intellect, ego and mind that is like an empty screen on which no images are placed. It is only in this sense that *citta* has the potential to be like the Sāṃkhya *mahāt-buddhi*, the pure *sattvic* intellect that is unrelated to either ego or mind. The whole purpose of Yoga is to restrain the fluctuations of the mind so that it becomes still in this way. Then, being *sattvic*, the *citta* is better positioned to discriminate between spirit and matter, *puruṣa* and *prakṛti*. But in ordinary life the *citta* is disposed to react according to its own combination of *karmic guṇas*. It reacts to the stimuli that invade the senses and cannot be still. It is "an arena of conflicting forces",[108] "bubbling in a hundred places with disturbing visions excited by uncontrolled emotion or worrying thought".[109] It classifies everything into categories of pleasure (*sattva*), pain (*rajas*) and indifference (*tamas*), and so reinforces the *karma* of its nature. But really, the *citta* is pure substance, as is all that takes place in it, and it is only the pure Self, the *puruṣa*, that lends it a sense of subjective consciousness that it can reflect but never be. The *citta* is dependent on both *puruṣa* for its proximity to give it a false consciousness, and on *prakṛti* that fills its substance with sense impressions from the gross world of physical forms; it could not exist in the ordinary sense without both. Conversely, the *puruṣa* sees the images of the world in the *citta* with all the fluctuations of the *vṛttis* and finds its pure consciousness involved with them in the same way as distorted reflections in a dusty mirror. With borrowed consciousness from the *puruṣa*, the *citta* sees itself as an "I" – an "I" mostly involved with *rajasic* and *tamasic* dispositions. *Rajas* and *tamas* spur the *vṛttis* into constant fluctuations. By encouraging *sattvic vṛttis* through discrimination and control of the mind, the detrimental *vṛttis* caused by the other two *guṇas* can be curbed. Once the mind fluctuations cease, then the *citta* is simply just aware of *prakṛtic* existence, and it no longer *reacts* to it. It is then in a position to perceive the reality of the separation of the *puruṣa* from the world of matter or, to put it more appropriately, the *puruṣa* is simply reflected in the *citta* as its pure Self, as pure consciousness, and as totally separate from the *prakṛtic* world of matter.

The eight *aṇgas* of Yoga (*Aṣṭāṅga Yoga*)

To turn, now, to the practices by which the goal of liberation is achieved, it has to be asked, how much is the aim to turn away from life entirely? There are those who see the accomplished *yogin* as having an aversion to involvement or participation in life, preferring the route of harsh ascetic practice and isolation. It is perhaps the more common view of the *yogin* – one deep in meditation without care for the world. Others are more sceptical about such traditional views of withdrawal, and have a view of the *yogin* as a more compassionate being. A point of Feuerstein's is worth noting here. He observes, "the yogin to whom conditioned existence becomes transparent and who is able to discern the subtle workings of, and relationships in, nature, does not display a fanatic thirst for life, but rather refrains from getting too much involved in its enticing-dangerous play".[110] But the real point of *yogic* practice is to withdraw the senses from *karmic* mind fluctuations that lead to increased bondage. The *controlled* mind should have no fear of falling into the "enticing-dangerous play" of ordinary *prakṛtic* existence. Practice, *abhyāsa*, is the important ingredient on the pathway to discriminating liberation. However, in 2:1, Patañjali advocates *kriyā-yoga*, the path of disciplined action as good practice. It involves self-discipline, study and probably chanting of scriptures, and devotion to Īśvara, God. Perhaps in line with the same kind of teaching in the *Gītā*, Patañjali was offering an alternative pathway for people of different dispositions. The path of action in the *Gītā* involved removal of the ego by dedicating all actions to God, and that seems to be the thought of this *sūtra*. Bryant thinks devotion to God in *kriyā-yoga* was mandatory.[111] But it is likely that Patañjali's path of action was a much more ascetic one than Kṛṣṇa advocated in the *Gītā*,[112] though Shyam Ranganathan is of the view that Patañjali endorsed moral *dharma*, and therefore *dharmic* action and life, throughout his text.[113]

The practical dimension of classical Yoga is formulated into eight progressive *aṅgas*, a word meaning "parts", "limbs" or "individuals". It is worth noting that they do not represent the major part of the *Yoga-Sūtras*, only one section of it, despite being frequently, and mistakenly, considered as the sole contribution of Patañjali. The *aṅgas* deal with the outer body and response to life as much as the inner spiritual individual. They are the means by which the final discipline of Yoga can be realized, and provide a technique for release of the Self from *prakṛtic* existence. These eight *aṅgas*[114] are *yama*, which is restraint; *niyama*, discipline; *āsana* bodily postures;[115] *prāṇāyāma*, which is rhythmic control of respiration; *pratyāhāra*, which is the withdrawing of the senses from the external world of sense stimuli; *dhāraṇā*, focused concentration and attention; *dhyāna*, meditation; *samādhi*, which is deep and unified concentration and the medium for liberation. *Dhāraṇā*, *dhyāna*, and *samādhi* are more directly concerned with Yoga, the former five being external aids to it.[116] While I do not want to concentrate on the external aids, which I have documented elsewhere[117] the final three stages need some mention.

The final stages of the pathway to liberation begin with *pratyāhāra*, the withdrawing of the senses from the sense stimuli of the environment. As one commentator, Vyāsa, put it in his commentary on Patañjali's *Sūtras*: "Just as when the king-bee flies up, the bees fly up after him; and when he settles down, they settle down after him. So when the mind-stuff is restricted, the organs are restricted."[118] Here, the goal of *citta-vṛtti-nirodha* is assisted by reaching a stage where focus is one-pointed, just one undeviating *vṛtti* present in the mind. Fixing the mind on *one* object – gross at first and then subtle – empties the mind. The senses are brought back into the mind instead of out into the world, providing knowledge of objects at a different level – not the outward *form* of the objects, but the inner *essences* of them.

With the withdrawal of the senses we find the first control of the mind that is foundational for the more intensive practices that come with the last three *aṅgas*: *dhāraṇā*, *dhyāna*, and *samādhi*. It is these last three stages that are most important, and they are collectively given the name *saṃyama*. They are linked by single-pointed contemplation, concentration and meditation, so they really form three parts of one process to the ultimate stages of *samādhi*. Further, their boundaries merge as the *yogin* moves from one stage to the next, so there is no clear demarcation between each one. It is a question of the depth of practice that makes one stage glide into the next. During these stages, we have the real one-pointedness of Yoga, *ekāgra*, "a motionless meditation, a silent collecting together of the mind's powers".[119]

Samādhi, sometimes translated as "enstasis", and meaning "settling down",[120] is the last of the eight *aṅgas* and itself consists of several stages that merge into each other, so that there is no abrupt change from one to another, just a deepening of the experience and an intensification of the process. But each stage is purer and subtler than the previous one, and the mind becomes more and more refined until the purely *sattvic buddhi* enables the *puruṣa* to see its reflection as an independent spiritual being that is separated from matter, and aware only of itself. The world of *guṇas* no longer enslaves the *puruṣa*. When this final goal of *kaivalya* is realized, all latent past *karma* is destroyed, and the *yogin* lives in the world as a *jīvan-mukta*, one liberated while still confined to the physical body.

The final stages of *samādhi* are accompanied by the ability of the *yogin* to manipulate *prakṛtic* matter at its subtle levels to bring about supernatural powers. Patañjali devotes his third set of *sūtras* to this aspect and lists the kinds of mystical skills that can be acquired when the *yogin* can "influence or rearrange the evolutes emerging from macronature as the universal mind", as Bryant put it.[121] *Yogins* can thus acquire knowledge of the past and future (3:16); have knowledge of the speech of all creatures (3:17); of previous births (3:18); of the minds of others (3:19); make themselves invisible (3:21); know the nature of one's death (3:22); and many, many more mystical skills. But they hinder that final releasing *samādhi*.

The self

The liberated Self is that which is separate from suffering and reincarnation, and is beyond the mind–body unity that we normally know. Strictly speaking, there is no other self at all, but we all experience an ordinary *jīva*, the ordinary personality that exists in the causal network of life. It exists only because the *puruṣa* becomes so intimately involved with *prakṛti*. In so far as the self functioning in the world can have no experience or knowledge at all without the ongoing presence of *puruṣa*, the self might be said to be a composite of both *puruṣa* and *prakṛti*. Because the *puruṣa* cannot separate itself from *prakṛti* it believes that *it* is initiating and reacting to all the mind fluctuations of the *citta*. And so it becomes involved in the world of choices, desires and aversions, in a world of birth, decay and death, in a world of suffering, sorrow and joys – in short, it becomes the empirical self, a *jīva*, that does not really exist. For every fluctuation or modification of the *citta*, there is an involvement of the *puruṣa*, for it is reflected in the whole mind process and cannot free itself from it.

In ordinary existence the self is subject to what are termed *kleśas*, "afflictions" or "hindrances", and there are five of them, all influenced by the *rajas* and *tamas guṇas*. Their nature is indicated by the Sanskrit root *kliś*, "to inflict pain", "to torment", "to trouble". Whicher calls them "the motivational matrix of the unenlightened mind".[122] The first is ignorance, *avidyā*, of the true nature of existence. It is *undifferentiated consciousness*, that is to say the inability to see consciousness as pure and separate from matter. Whicher describes it as a "congenital infection located within our psychophysical being".[123] It is also the inability to recognize impermanence in all life and to see what is impure. It is the undifferentiated consciousness that believes itself to succeed or fail, that owns things, that likes and dislikes, and so on. *Avidyā* is a fundamental misconception, a misidentification, of Reality.

The second *kleśa*, *asmitā*, is the false identification of the Self with the material mind, intellect and ego, and is closely linked to the first. It produces what we call personality, and the failure to recognize that the Self is separate from the thinking process perpetuates that personality. The third *kleśa* is *rāga*, which is the attachment to, and desire for, pleasurable things and happiness. The fourth is the opposite of *rāga*, *dveṣa*, which is the aversion to anything painful in life, the disposition that causes anxiety about so many things. The fifth is clinging to life, visually, the fear of death, *abhiniveśa*. This, said both Vyāsa and Vācaspati Miśra, occurs because, while the living being can have no real experience of death in this life, the fear of it comes from the experience of it in past lives. It creates the will to live, the will to avoid that which is the ultimate in pain – death.[124] The common denominator of the five *kleśas* is the ignorance that maintains them, so that the first *kleśa* of *avidyā* underpins the other four, and is responsible for all erroneous perception. Without the afflictions, moreover, there will be no self-assertive "I" that relates to the world in terms of I, me and mine.[125]

Karma

Karma is critical to Yoga because it is that which impedes discriminative knowledge. The *kleśas* bring it about, just as *karma* instigates the *kleśas*. It is the cause of the ignorant self, and it is what subjects *puruṣa* to bondage in the world of matter. We are, then, thoroughly responsible for what we are, for how we behave and for what befalls us in life. The intricate balance between *karma*, the subconscious impressions (*saṃskāras*) that are left in the memory and subconscious as residues of human living, and the forming of habits (*vāsaṇās*) in each individual, are critical to the Yoga system, and we need to examine each in turn, beginning with *karma*.

There are three kinds of *karma*. ***Prārabdha-karma*** is *karma* that has already been accumulated and is beginning to take effect in the present life, or is waiting to come to fruition in the present life. It will already have determined the nature of the physical and mental person in the present existence. It cannot usually be changed, only used up. ***Sañcita-karma*** is *karma* that is beginning to mature from past or present life. It is in the process of being formed and has not yet produced any effects, nor will it in the present existence. ***Āgāmi-karma*** is *karma* that is being formed now in the present existence and still has to mature.

Karma acquired through thought is ***mānasa-karma*** "mental action/reaction". More active *karma* of speech and physical action is ***vāhya-karma***. All action is black, white, or black and white. Black *karmas* are evil ones and are *adharmic*. White *karmas* are meritorious and are associated with those who practise austerities, who study and meditate. When carried out by advanced *yogins*, they are wholly *sattvic*, for the *guṇas* of *rajas* and *tamas* will be quiescent through practice of *samādhi*. Black and white *karmas* are both good and bad, and are the kinds of actions of ordinary individuals. Being thoroughly *guṇic*, any good actions of such people may be *sattvic*, but never wholly so, for they must contain some elements of *rajas* and *tamas*. Equally so, evil, *tamasic*, acts can never be wholly evil but must contain elements of the other two *guṇas*. The balance between good and bad actions produces the particular nature, or *karmāśaya*, of an individual, as human, or animal, for example.[126] Those who perform all actions for God, for Īśvara, so having no actions of their own, and therefore having no fruits of their actions, are said to have neither black nor white *karma*. Those in the final phases of *samādhi* will also have no black or white *karma*, nothing that might cause the need to be reborn.

All actions inform two kinds of *karma* in an individual. Actions undertaken through individual free will, through personal effort, form ***puruṣa-kāra-karma***. Unconscious, innate actions form ***adṛṣṭa-phala-karma***. The way in which an individual acts, thinks and speaks will depend a good deal on the innate tendencies – the coded genetics of character, temperament, propensities and dispositions. This is ***adṛṣṭa-phala-karma*** operating. But each individual also has the free will to counteract his or her natural tendencies – the *guṇic* combinations that make up each person. Although it will be difficult to offset the experiences due in each life that are the effects of previous causative actions, free will permits some degree of control over the manifestation of such effects.[127] *Prakṛtic* materiality, as Jacobsen puts it, "can flow into any form".[128] Thus, each thing that exists, whether plant, creature or human, carries the *guṇic* potentiality to be something else in existence. And as Jacobsen also notes, all living beings physically consist of the same gross elements. The possibilities for rebirth are, therefore, countless. And whatever rebirth occurs, the physical body – whether human or animal – is given the mind and senses appropriate to it by the *prakṛtic* order of things, that is to say, the nature of causes created by that individual or creature in past experiences. But having at least some free will to affect the future life is essential to the liberating process.

Saṃskāras

Why is it that we cannot still our minds for anything more than brief moments? And if we could, through constant practice, would we then become liberated? Is that all we would have to do? What prevents a simple affirmative answer here are the complexities of the human subconscious. While consciousness in the sense of mind fluctuations may be suspended for a short (usually very short) time in ordinary existence, it is from what Mircea Eliade termed "the immense reserves of latencies in the subconscious"[129] that new activity is immediately relayed to the mind. The subconscious is a dark, unknown world that is stocked full of the residues of past experiences of countless lives, and is continually being replenished by present consciousness. The subconscious was graphically described by Dasgupta as a "treasure house which is also a work house".[130] It is this lower world of the subconscious that normally lies beyond our control and yet influences the way we think and the way we behave as human beings.

All actions leave subtle, but dynamic and latent, impressions in the self. They are the "latencies" of which Eliade wrote above. Every *vṛtti*, fluctuation of the mind, leaves an imprint, and all such imprints are stored in the mind as *saṃskāras*. Some will remain deeply and subliminally latent while others will surface into the mind to influence its present state. It is these that are called *saṃskāras* and they feed the faculty of memory. Feuerstein calls them "subliminal-activators",[131] and "a vast, inexhaustible pool of stimuli".[132] The impressions are stored in the mind following any experience or memory activity that we have. In many ways they are difficult to separate from the self, because they inform so much of each individual's character, behaviour and outlook on life. In psychological terms, they condition action, thought and speech. F. W. J. Humphries compares the *saṃskāras* with the Freudian *id*, "that repository of chaotic instinctive drives which have to be lived with and controlled if civilization is to survive".[133] *Saṃskāras* gather homogeneously deep in the self. Every time the mind is active or recalls a memory it creates further *saṃskāras* and it is the five afflictions that will dictate the kinds of memories an individual will wish to recall.[134]

Saṃskāras are not only effects of actions, but are also causative in that they condition the self in each rebirth. At death, the prominent *saṃskāras* will be in place ready to be imprinted into the *citta* of a new form, determining its exact nature, birth and life environments. Even when the world is absorbed back into its unmanifest state, latent *saṃskāras* are held in potential to take form in a new being as manifest existence unfolds once again. In ordinary humans, where ignorance prevails, the mental activity of each individual will be informed by these subconscious impressions rising to the surface consciousness, and will lead to related actions in the present life. Immediately, other impressions of the same type are sown back into the subconscious, and older ones are reinforced. There is thus a continuous cycle of subconscious impressions conditioning all actions, speech, thoughts and habits, and these in turn build up more of the same kinds of subconscious impressions. Rebirth is inevitable. The continual building up of impressions will result in the energy necessary for continued lives, the energy that feeds ignorance and attachment to egoistic identity and the world of matter. At the end of each life the balance of negative/positive *saṃskāras* will dictate the kind of character an individual will have in the next life.

Vāsaṇās

While the term *vāsaṇās* is sometimes used as a synonym for *saṃskāras*, it is likely that there is a difference between the two, for *vāsaṇās* are more passive and latent in the mind.[135] They are the deep-rooted habits, the traits and tendencies brought about by *saṃskāras* that gather together homogeneously to form them, so that "the mind is pervaded all over with them like knots of a fishing net".[136] Feuerstein calls them "subliminal traces".[137] *Vāsaṇās* are acquired from the experiences of *all* previous existences. They form our core genetic make-up that provides our essential natures and are almost unchangeable in ordinary circumstances. Such deep subconscious habits or traits, as we know so well, are very difficult to counteract. Here, then, is the reason why we are unable to still the mind, why we are more subject to the dictates of our minds than we are able to exercise control of them. The human being is bound by the particularities of the mind's subconscious characteristics that will cause him or her to act and react in certain ways. This, in turn, reinforces and builds up the same or similar characteristics. It is in such a way that the human being is bound. All the time new impressions are forming new *vāsaṇās*, collecting together in like-with-like fashion, building on previous impressions – in short, formulating the person of the future. Memory reinforces the impressions, for the memory of a particular happiness or a particular sorrow will feed the *karmic* accumulation of the same related impressions. And it is the fluctuations, the *vṛttis*, of the mind that perpetuate the memories and impressions. In this manner, the Self is trapped in *prakṛti* until it can discriminate between knowledge that is binding it to the world, and the knower, *puruṣa*, that is separate from all knowledge.

In Sāṃkhya an individual is a coded entity with a psyche that exists by reason of the particular distribution of dispositions in the intellect. Similarly, in Yoga, the pre-coded character of each individual is also accepted – a character coded by that individual's own actions in previous existence(s). It is the *mind* that is the medium by which such a pre-coded character is formed, and is the means by which it can be changed for the future.[138] However, the emphasis is on mind control in classical Yoga, and its praxis for overcoming the limitations of the mind far outweigh anything Sāṃkhya had to offer.

Karmāśaya

The collective *saṃskāras* of a particular type – accumulated from actions in all kinds of different places, different times, and in different births – will form the *karmāśaya*, the "potential energy", as Āraṇya defined it,[139] which will become a specific *karmic* effect as one individual. There is, so to speak, a thread that unites similar residues of actions into a connected cause or causes and this thread will, one day, in one particular birth, come to full fruition when sufficient strength of cause has accumulated. It is this *karmāśaya* that will determine the particular and unique kind of life an entity will have – human or animal, for example – as well as the time of that life and the pleasurable and painful experiences in it. Āraṇya described it as "the aggregate of manifold latencies of Karma";[140] in other words, an aggregate of *saṃskāras*. Some *karmāśaya* comes to fruition in a present life, some in a future life, and some in the very distant future. Even death is no chance event, for the *karmāśaya* of the present existence will determine the length of life and the death that will end it. Then the particular nature and balance of other *karmāśaya* will determine the nature of a being in the next existence.

Vāsanās that stretch back through countless previous lives stimulate *karmāśaya*. The term "potential energy" used by Āraṇya above, is an apt one, for it is a dynamic energy that is subject to continual change through the activities of the mind. Changing the *karmāśaya* in an attempt to alter the patterns of the next existence is no easy task. Since we usually follow our individual natures in our response to the world in which we live, there is a tendency for the potential energy of the *karmāśaya* to be *reinforced* rather than changed, though all the time, it is being modified by present activity. But the complex matrix of *karmic* causes that result in *karmāśaya* stretch back over countless lifetimes – even to those in animal form – and are being slowly modelled and formulated to account for just one particular life. So because *karmas* are constantly being built up, they will not ripen fully for a long time. It is as if each individual fills many vessels with the residues of myriad actions. Only when a vessel is full of the same propensities and characteristics will it brim over into fruitive effect in the life of the individual.

From all that has been said here on the nature of *saṃskāras*, *vāsanās*, *karma*, and *karmāśaya*, it is obvious that stilling the mind is not going to prevent the subconscious from presenting images and thoughts to it, nor will it overcome the accumulated impressions of innumerable lifetimes. What, then, can the *yogin* do? How can liberation of the *puruṣa* be secured when an individual carries within the baggage of lifetimes of causes that are continually being formulated into effects? The *yogin*, too, is subject to subconscious impressions, but through discriminative knowledge and not ignorance, is able to tread a different path from that of ordinary mortals. The *yogin* begins with the five afflictions, the *kleśas*. The effects of the afflictions, the *saṃskāras*, are like seeds that will eventually ripen in the fruits of new actions and new experiences. So as long as the *yogin* refrains from being subject to the afflictions, no reinforcing or new negative and *karmic*-producing *saṃskāras* are generated. Constant effort, *abhyāsa*, will be needed to control the mind-fluctuations, *vṛttis*.[141] Any formative *saṃskāras* should be of the nature that build up discriminative knowledge: it is these that will burn up the negative ones, like roasted seeds.

The *yogin*, then, fills the subconscious with positive impressions stemming from truer knowledge and from calmness and stillness of mind. Then, the impressions already in the subconscious will undergo change, and will become weaker when counteracted by the newer ones. If, and when, they rise to the conscious level, they will do so in a form that enhances and not impedes the *yogin's* progress. Through effort, gradually there is less and less in the subconscious to form effects of actions. In promoting a mind that is dispassionate, in ridding the self of desires, aversions and ego-identity, fruitive *karma* is burnt up. "As a wheel set in motion keeps on rotating for some time out of its own inertia, so also the Karma of such a person having started fructifying, gradually becomes attenuated and then vanishes for ever."[142] In *sūtra* 1:50, Patañjali says that positive *saṃskāras* inhibit others from emerging, thus transforming the *citta* into wise and *sattvic* states that create positive cycles in the fall and rise of *saṃskāras* to the mind.

As to the rest of humankind, we are how our minds work, and it would appear that we are trapped in our own natures, bound by our archetypal tendencies as much as by our present actions rooted in lifetimes of habits. But it must not be forgotten that Yoga is a soteriological school. It does not suggest that human beings are doomed to be trapped in their own *karmic* personalities for endless lifetimes. Āraṇya made the pertinent point that: "A storm in the sea is not caused by an individual's Karma but the decision to sail or not to sail in such a storm lies with him alone."[143] Āraṇya's words are indicative that no one should sit back and accept the way he or she is and what befalls one in life. *Karma* is what we make of it. Yoga accepts that it is essential to strive to overcome the mental forces that bind the Self to perpetuated ignorance of the kind that impedes soteriological progress.

Causality

The *sat-kārya-vāda* theory of causality of Sāṃkhya – the theory that effects inhere in their causes – is critical to the praxis of the Yoga school and its many branches. Just as the ultimate subtle cause of manifest existence causes evolutes to emerge from the subtle to the gross, so the *yogin* reverses the process in practice and deconstructs himself, refining the mind from attraction to the gross world, to concentration on the subtler stages of *prakṛtic* evolution. The *yogin* learns to settle concentration in pure egoity. Once this is accomplished the mind is no longer subject to the fluctuations stimulated by the outward, gross world: it has transcended gross matter and is still. From there, the *buddhi* – the intellect that holds the key to discriminating knowledge of the separation of *puruṣa* and *prakṛti*, knower and knowable, subject and object – will be the highest plane to which the *yogin* can aspire with the exception of liberation itself. The process of reversal from gross to subtle could not occur if effects were not real transformations of their causes. Cause and effect are of the same nature and simultaneously existent in both latent and manifest forms. This is called *pariṇāma-vāda.*[144] However, the ultimate state of liberation transcends all cause and effect and all the by-products of *guṇic* interaction, including unmanifest *prakṛti* itself.

The concept of God

From an examination of the *Yoga-Sūtras* of Patañjali, it would seem that the concept of God, Īśvara, does not play a major role, despite the characteristic theism of the school in general. Indeed, Radhakrishnan wrote very disparagingly of the concept, "we cannot help saying that the Yoga philosophy introduced the conception of God just to be in the fashion and catch the mind of the public".[145] Yoga is a practical rather than a theoretical *darśana*, and God, therefore, serves a practical purpose as an object of *yogic* concentration. But it is also evident that there are other means of concentration than Īśvara, and so it is difficult to claim a major role for the concept of God in Yoga. In fact, as Koelman remarks: "It is striking how the mention of the *Iśvara* in the Yoga Sutras is quite casual."[146] In his view, devotion to God serves not the function of submission to, and adoration of him, but only as a focus for single-mindedness – a means to still the fluctuations of the *citta*. And he therefore suggests that the theistic sections of the *Sūtras* could very well be taken out without any detriment to the overall coherence of the teaching.[147]

While there are only five *sūtras* that deal explicitly with Īśvara, and only eight in all,[148] Bryant thinks quite the opposite to the above and considers Patañjali to have been a Vaiṣṇava devotee. As is the case with many other such texts, Patañjali's *Yoga-Sūtras* begins with a dedication to a personal deity – here Vāsudeva, a patronymic of Kṛṣṇa. The commentators, too, seem to have wanted a greater role for Īśvara as the agent for liberation. Vijñana Bhikṣu, indeed, projected knowledge of Īśvara as of primary importance. When Patañjali compiled his *Yoga-Sūtras*, devotional Hinduism was prolific, especially amongst Vaiṣṇava sects and he was certainly influenced by the theistic *Gītā* but his aim as *practice* as opposed to theology may have resulted in less emphasis on Īśvara as a thoroughly theistic God – one, Bryant thinks, that would have been identified as Śiva, Viṣṇu or Kṛṣṇa.[149] Pflueger believes that the theism "is among the very oldest threads of this classical tapestry".[150]

It would also seem that devotion to God is the best means of concentration.[151] For God is more than an object of concentration, and is the Supreme Lord, Īśvara, that is able to assist in the ridding of obstacles on the path to liberation of his devotee, in particular, the hindrances, the *kleśas*, so the commentators tell us. This, then, renders single-pointed focus on God as rather different from the same kind of focus on any other object, and there was a tendency in later Yoga to emphasize this theistic path. But such thoughts do not feature in the *Yoga-Sūtras* itself. Yet the idea proposed by both Feuerstein[152] and Eliade,[153] that some vision of Īśvara was part of *yogic* mystical experience, and that it is here that the God of Yoga has its origins, is certainly possible. Furthermore, when Patañjali advocated study (*svādhyāya*) in 2:44, he surely meant study of the scriptures and recitation of *mantras*. He explicitly stated here that it would bring about a connection with the deity of one's choice, one's *iṣṭa-devatā*. Bryant believes that Patañjali "must be using *devatā* to refer to the established forms of Īśvara evidenced on the mainstream theistic landscape of his time", in other words major rather than minor deities.[154] And in the following *sūtra*, 2:45, Patañjali says that perfect *samādhi* comes from surrender to God. Perhaps Bryant is right in suggesting that Patañjali believed devotion to Īśvara is the best path, in line with what Kṛṣṇa had to say in the *Gītā* (12:2 and 3–5).[155]

Focus on the divine, even if it is not pervasive in Yoga, lends the school a definite orthodoxy in its support of *śruti* testimony to a Supreme Being. The school of Yoga, as most Indian schools of philosophy, accepts the existence of minor gods who are fellow travellers in *saṃsāra*, albeit having reached a plane of existence that surpasses, temporarily, the earthly one. But, when their good *karma* – which is what has placed them in a heavenly realm – has been exhausted, then they will return to the *status quo* of life in human form. In contrast, Īśvara transcends such *karmic* existence as the Supreme Self that is purely *sattvic* and that is beyond the world of matter.

There is no sense of Īśvara being an omnipotent creator or material cause of the universe. Yoga does not abandon the concept of the evolution of the world from unconscious matter, *prakṛti*. Īśvara is a purely *sattvic puruṣa*,[156] one that has never been bound in *prakṛti* like all other Selves. As such, Īśvara stands as an inspiration to the *yogin*, the Supreme *Puruṣa*, superior to all other *puruṣas* because he has been, and always will be, eternally free from the *kleśas* that cause fruitive *karma*.[157] He is the God of theistic Yoga, the eternal Perfect Being who has unsurpassed omniscience, omnipotence and omnipresence.[158] Therefore, unlike the liberated Selves, God, especially in the developed views of the commentators, is able to exercise a permanent control over the world of *prakṛti*, directing its course by sheer will, controlling the cause–effect processes and individual *karmas*. It is he that is the source of the wisdom of the *Veda* and who has imparted that wisdom to the ancient sages, so the *Yoga-Sūtras* states (1:26), and it is he who is expressed in the mystical syllable of *Oṃ*. *Oṃ* became both a symbol of Īśvara and a focus of concentration.[159] For all that, Pflueger insists that the *Yoga-Sūtras*' view of Īśvara is "the impersonal *puruṣa*, the mysterious principle which illuminates all yogins, and all things".[160]

It is a perception of the divine that gave credence both to Īśvara himself as divine and omnipotent, and to the scriptures, the *śāstras*, of which he came to be known as the source and which, as a result, were regarded by the Yoga school as absolute Truth. But Koelman sensibly argues that the God of Yoga must have need of the *prakṛtic* world of matter in order for consciousness to function in it. This would necessitate an intellect, mind and ego by which to have such involvement, and by which a recognition of his self as affecting the world can be known. Even though the purely *sattvic* nature of God means there is no element of either *rajas* or *tamas* to cause an imbalance in his perfection, Koelman argues that God must have a *prakṛtic* body in order to exercise guidance, compassion, to impart knowledge, and to communicate with the world.[161] Pflueger, on the other hand, finds Īśvara "the *totally other* to *prakṛti*"[162] and the *Yoga-Sūtras* certainly seems to say that Īśvara is a "special" *puruṣa* (1:24), though Vyāsa seemed to have accepted Īśvara as a blend of both *puruṣa* and *prakṛti*. And if God has a body – albeit a subtle, *sattvic* one – he, too, must be dependent on the duality of *puruṣa* supplying consciousness and *prakṛtic* reflective analysis and all material characteristics. Moreover, Īśvara is eternally in contact with matter albeit *sattvic*:

Richa Clements justifiably asks, therefore, whether he can be a real *puruṣa* when permanently united with matter.[163]

What we have here, then, are many of the characteristics of a theistic divine being, one to whom devotees are able to relate and focus their attention. Yoga is, therefore, basically theistic, and it would be difficult to argue otherwise in view of the clear statements of devotion to God as a means for liberation. But it should be remembered that it was left to Patañjali's commentators to provide the anthropomorphic descriptions of Īśvara by which he became a devotional focus. It is also wise to remember that Yoga is allied with the atheistic system of Sāṃkhya, and that fact in some measure limits an all-out theism. Theistic devotion is *one* means to liberation, as was stated above, but it is by no means the only one. There is no suggestion that *kaivalya* as a goal of isolation of the Self is ever compromised to allow fusion with God or even awareness of God in the liberated state. God is only a *means* by which the *yogin* is aided to final liberation in the functioning world of *prakṛti*, and a supreme example of what the *yogin* can achieve. And yet, the eternal nature of Īśvara, his distinction from *prakṛti* and *puruṣas*, really posits him as a separate, twenty-sixth category, but the *Yoga-Sūtras* does not accede to such a possibility, leaving Īśvara firmly in the category of *puruṣa* alone. Perhaps Pflueger is right in his view of Īśvara as an impersonal "salvific meditative bridge between ordinary consciousness and pure consciousness".[164]

The God of Yoga does not cause the world to be as a material cause. *Prakṛti* still operates in its cycles of evolution and involution. But later developments in Yoga solve at least one problematic area of Sāṃkhya philosophy. For God becomes the agent that causes the proximity of *puruṣas* to *prakṛti* that enables the world to evolve as an instrumental cause. It is also God who dissociates them so that the evolutes of *prakṛti* will break down into their primal unmanifest state. At least this explains why two principles that are unrelated to each other can so affect each other, and it also explains why a process of increasing evolution should suddenly cease and dissolve.[165] The relationship between causes and their effects – the unseen and mysterious power called *adṛṣṭa* that operates to make one, particular effect emerge from a particular cause and no other – is seen as under the power of Īśvara. And this is so, not only of the cosmos itself, but also in relation to the cause–effect principle that governs individual life – *karma*. God, then, becomes the director of *adṛṣṭa* at all levels, and directs it in favour of the liberation of the Selves. However, theodicy is not a problem for the God of Yoga, for evil is part of *prakṛtic* matter and God is independent of all *prakṛti*.

It is as a focus of meditative devotion, however, that Īśvara is important in this tradition of classical Yoga. For if God is pure *sattva* in his operative sense in the world of matter, then each Self, each *puruṣa*, is more intimately similar to God than to any other object of concentration, whether gross or subtle. Yoga came to accept that God is of service to the *yogin* in aiding his journey, even to the extent of causing a leap in practice on what would normally be a progressive path through his grace. God is seen as the *ultimate* Self, the Self at its greatest limits, and as such is the "archetypal yogin",[166] or "the image of the living guru".[167] Īśvara is a deity for *yogins* only, and is thus relevant only to one on the *yogic* path. Eliade thus diminished his status considerably when he wrote: "All in all, Īśvara is only an archetype of the yogin – a macroyogin; very probably a patron of certain yogic sects."[168] A completely opposite view, however, is posited by Feuerstein, who writes, "any attempt to exorcise this concept would amount to a crippling of both the theoretical superstructure and the practical substructure of Yoga".[169] Bryant, too, argues forcefully against such an idea.[170]

Unlike Sāṃkhya, then, Yoga is a theistic tradition, though it will depend considerably on its different branches how far that theism is taken; later tradition, especially, took a firmer theistic stance. Considering the emphasis on orthodox scripture it is difficult to see how any so-called orthodox school could deny existence to some sort of transcendent divine being, particularly an impersonal Absolute. The God of Yoga comes nowhere near both of these and often seems something of an appendage to the tradition. The concept of God in Yoga was sufficiently weak to allow all sorts of speculation in the commentarial literature concerning his nature and role.

Liberation

Liberation for the *yogin* is the realization of the freedom of an individual *puruṣa* from the *prakṛtic* world in which it became entangled. Importantly, the *puruṣa* is *always* free; it has never been bound, but its close association with *buddhi* when that *buddhi* is world focused, makes it seem so. However, Patañjali says little about liberation. Despite the remote nature of the final goal of Yoga, and the innumerable lifetimes that the Self remains bound by its own involvement with matter, the journey to the final goal is a positive, if arduous, one. It is a journey that sees constant effort to control the mind, and it is the mind that is the locus for the changes necessary to facilitate liberation. This is Yoga's positive message. The more the *yogin* can remain in *samādhi*, the more ordinary states of knowledge become transcended for the wisdom of true knowledge. In the pure *sattvic* state of the mind, a particular balance between the *sattva* of the *buddhi* and *puruṣa* occurs. It is this that is the impetus for liberation, as *sūtra* 3:55 tells us: "When the purity of the intellect is equal to that of the *puruṣa, kaivalya* liberation ensues."[171] Here, discriminative knowledge prevents any further misidentification. Liberation, *kaivalya*, has been realized, and the *puruṣa* is in its natural nature of aloneness or, as Bryant says "not-connected-with-anything-else-ness".[172]

The liberated *yogin* is sometimes termed a *mukta-kusāla*. He has no "I". His actions do not belong to him any more than worldly objects or people. The *puruṣa* that he is remains separate from all *prakṛtic* existence. What can be known is no longer of relevance to the liberated *puruṣa*: it no longer needs knowledge of the world, and it no longer wants involvement with *prakṛti*.[173] Complete annihilation of the subconscious impressions, the *saṃskāras*, has occurred, so there is no fruitive *karma* remaining. Any *karmic* forces already in motion may still occur, like a potter's wheel that continues to turn when the potter has ceased, but the *yogin* is not in the *prakṛtic* world to notice and no new *karma* is generated. There is nothing left of the *guṇic*, empirical self; it has been absorbed back into unmanifest *prakṛti*, leaving the *puruṣa* alone. But *prakṛti* only ceases to be for the single *puruṣa*, whose objective *prakṛtic* constituents have dissolved into their unmanifest cause. For all other bound *puruṣas*, *prakṛti* continues – and will eternally do so. Just one tiny fraction of *prakṛti* ceases to be in its manifest form. The Self that never really was bound, that never really changed, is now free.

However, so many problems remain. A rather difficult issue is posited by Patañjali in 2:18, where he says that *prakṛti* exists for the purpose of providing not just sense experience for *puruṣas* but also liberation. The *Sāṃkhya-Kārikā* said the same (17, 21, 31).[174] Without some agency how can *prakṛti* or *puruṣa* become bound together or separated? Bryant assigns free will to the *puruṣas* in order to overcome this problem,[175] and Whicher qualifies the radical dualism between *puruṣas* and *prakṛti* to solve the issue in another way.[176] The acceptance of a *jīvan-mukta*, one who has become liberated while still alive, still having a physical body, is hardly consonant with the total divorce from matter that liberation posits. The *Yoga-Sūtras* itself does not seem to suggest such a possibility but the commentators allow for it. The theory is an oddity. My own inclination here is to maintain the strict duality of *puruṣa* and *prakṛti*, and to lay the developed concept of *jīvan-mukti* at the feet of tradition – much as Feuerstein[177] and T. S. Rukmani[178] suggest. The attractive view of Whicher is of a liberated *yogin* that *engages* altruistically in the world though remaining unaffected by *guṇic* changes and *karmic* residues, rather like the *bodhisattvas* of Mahayana Buddhism.[179] Indeed, in one *sūtra*, Patañjali advocates cultivating friendship, compassion, joy and equanimity – the same as the *brahma-vihāras* of Buddhism: these are outgoing attitudes to the world. And yet, a major tenet of Sāṃkhya and Yoga is that it is the conjunction, *saṃyoga*, between *puruṣas* and *prakṛti*, seers and seen, that makes the world possible. Remove conjunction for a *puruṣa* and there should be no world to be seen: there really can be no object when *puruṣa* is enlightened to self-awareness in *kaivalya* which, after all, is "aloneness".

The *kaivalya* of the *puruṣa* endorses fundamental dualism and upholds what seems to be a goal of cessation of all mind activity (*citta-vṛtti-nirodha*). It is doubtful whether Patañjali had the conception of a world-engaged liberated *yogin* in mind, even if tradition has overlaid his perception with a more attractive picture of such a *yogin* with emotions, feelings and thoughts, "vital, creative, thoughtful, empathetic, balanced, happy, and wise".[180] Ranganathan also believes that Patañjali's view of *puruṣas* was as active agents.[181] It must be remembered, too, that there is much in the nature of Yoga that advocates withdrawal from the world of matter while on the long path to the final goal. As Eliade noted, the liberated *yogin* has achieved the final goal through techniques that are deliberately "antisocial" and "antihuman".[182] He considered Yoga to be an opposition to life,[183] not an altruistic engagement in it. It is unlikely that the goal would reverse the trends to be found in praxis. And as Feuerstein points out, once liberation takes place, "the *yogin* in fact ceases to exist as a human being. His body may live on for a period of time, though in a state of catalepsy, and before long goes the way of all finite things".[184] Thus, attractive as Whicher's thesis is, my own view is that Patañjali's *citta-vṛtti-nirodha* referred to a *complete* cessation of all mind activity – a separation of mind from spirit after, not before, death.[185]

But is there just one, universal *puruṣa*, or are there a plurality of them? Feuerstein points out that "qualitatively there is no difference between the Selves (*puruṣas*) and the one Self (*ātman*) of Śaṅkara".[186] Without individuality for the *puruṣas* there seems little point in their separation. Some suggest that Patañjali did not advocate a plurality of *puruṣas*,[187] but if this was the case, then it is surprising that Patañjali did not make more of what was to be a Supreme Self, or even to project Īśvara to this end. But, to cite the Sāṃkhya argument, positing a single *Puruṣa* would not explain the differences in experiences of multiple Selves. Nor would Whicher's view of liberated Selves being active in the world be tenable. For if there were just one Self – albeit free of matter and in control of mind fluctuations – there could be no difference between one liberated *yogin* and another: they would have the same mind functioning, the same feelings and the same thoughts.

Vijñana Bhikṣu believed that *puruṣas* did not lose their individuality in liberation even if they are one in having the same essence.[188] Pflueger thinks that *puruṣas* are beyond number in the same way that they are beyond any other categorization: he believes pure consciousness can only be just that and that *puruṣa* itself must be a non-dual principle.[189]

Concluding remarks

How, then, should Patañjali be assessed? Is his work merely a contrived patchwork of bits and pieces from earlier sources as some suggest?[190] And if so, does this diminish his achievement? Thomas Berry claimed that, "the work of Patañjali deserves all the praise lavished on it, for it is in truth one of the masterworks of the spiritual history of man".[191] Perhaps the truth lies somewhere in between these two extremes. Certainly, as Berry also points out concerning Patañjali's work: "It is so universal in its basic outline that it has proved wonderfully adaptable to the various religious movements in India throughout the centuries that have found spiritual support in the Yoga tradition."[192] For the most part, it must be said that Patañjali's contribution to Yoga is inestimable. Eliade rightly claimed: "Patañjali's *Yoga-sūtras* are the result of an enormous effort not only to bring together and classify a series of ascetic practices and contemplative formulas that India had known from time immemorial, but also to validate them from a theoretical point of view by establishing their bases, justifying them, and incorporating them into a philosophy."[193]

It is to Patañjali's credit that Yoga is a living tradition that is still handed down by the great (and not so great) *gurus*. While Sāṃkhya had critics sufficient to make it obsolete as a system of practised belief, Yoga has never suffered from this; very much, I think, because Yoga subordinated Sāṃkhya metaphysics to clear praxis. The fact that it is a word understood – admittedly not as it should be – by those westerners far removed from knowledge of Indian history or philosophy, shows how far Yoga has spread its influence in time and location. And whatever the philosophical tenets held by Indians, they accord the utmost respect to the *yogins* of the Indian culture. These *yogins* have climbed to the summit of Reality and have left behind the foothills of ignorance. Others may find different paths to the summit, but it is still the *yogins* who are living examples of the fact that such ultimate Reality is realizable in mortal state. To me, the brilliance of Yoga lies in the extraordinary analysis of the conscious and subconscious mind, of the way in which beings are trapped by their own natures, entrenching patterns of thought and behaviour. Patañjali, Freud and Jung would have had much to share in mind analysis and while Jung did not think Yoga suitable for the West, he was considerably influenced by it.[194]. But Yoga does not leave each being tragically trapped: it offers a remarkably sound reasoning for why we are as we are, providing at the same time, a means of release – albeit a tough one.

In contrast to Sāṃkhya, Patañjali's Yoga is "essentially psychological, warm and dynamic".[195] And there is an ethos to Yoga that counterbalances the turmoil of life. Radhakrishnan put this well:

> We discern in the Yoga those cardinal conceptions of Hindu thought, such as the supremacy of the psychic over the physical, the exaltation of silence and solitude,

> meditation and ecstasy, and the indifference to outer conditions, which make the traditional Hindu attitude to life appear so strange and fantastic to the modern mind. It is, however, conceded, by many who are acquainted with it, that it is a necessary corrective to our present mentality, overburdened with external things and estranged from the true life of spirit by humdrum toil, material greed and sensual excitement.[196]

The fact that forms of Yoga are becoming so popular in the western world is indicative of the strength Yoga contains to offer a variety of paths to searching souls in modern life.

6

Devotional Hinduism

The *Bhagavad Gītā*

The *Bhagavad Gītā* is *The Song of the Lord* (*Bhagavad* "Lord" and *Gītā* "Song"), where the Lord here is Kṛṣṇa, God on Earth. He is Brahman in its ultimate manifest form, close to humanity, born on Earth with a childhood, adolescence, maturity and lordship to which human beings can readily relate. I have dealt extensively with the *Gītā* in another text[1] and have introduced it in the context of *Scriptures* in Volume I,[2] so I do not want to repeat that material here in the introduction to this chapter. However, a few points are necessary. The *Gītā*, dated to somewhere around the second century BCE or earlier, is a tiny part of the very long *Mahābhārata* and recounts Kṛṣṇa's words to Arjuna, one of the five Pāṇḍava brothers who are at war with their hundred cousins over their rightful succession to the kingdom of Bharata. After all attempts at reconciliation fail, a great battle is about to commence and Arjuna asks his chariot driver, Kṛṣṇa, to take him to the middle of the battlefield. There he pauses and sees opposing him members of his own family – great teachers and warriors that he has known so well – and he becomes deeply saddened at engaging in a fratricidal war and will not fight. It is at this crucial point when he and Kṛṣṇa are centred physically and mentally between two armies and two pathways that Kṛṣṇa begins his profound teaching.

Kṛṣṇa and Arjuna are both *Kṣatriyas*, nobles and warriors, and so we would expect some kind of shift from the *Brāhmin* focus on Brahman to a religious outlook that is more world focused. More than this, Kṛṣṇa is an expression of the devotional trends in religion, religion of the heart that spoke to the sections of the wider populace. Such devotional fervour gained so much ground that the priests recognized the need to embrace it into orthodoxy. The *Gītā* does not, however, depart wholesale from orthodox praxis, and rather than single out one religious pathway it incorporates many. But since Kṛṣṇa is the central character of the text, God on Earth, we cannot head too far from the devotional stance as important. Yet, Kṛṣṇa does not confine his nature to the anthropomorphic being he is in the *Mahābhārata* and the *Gītā*, for he projects into his teaching of Arjuna higher levels of his being that encompass the manifest and unmanifest Brahman. It is these concepts of what Kṛṣṇa is with which I want to begin, and my whole approach here will be a thematic one, engaging with what I consider to be the key concepts of, and the major pathways to, God. Nevertheless, I do not think that the *Gītā* offers an exclusive pathway to God: indeed, it has a somewhat synthesizing approach to different stances at many points and it seems to me that is partly because it has many levels in its understanding of God.

The concept of God

As was seen in chapter 3, the *Upaniṣads* contained belief in an ultimate Reality, an Absolute that is the Source of all and that is termed Brahman. For the most part, Brahman was indescribable but equated monistically with the innermost essence, the *ātman*, experienced deep within the self. The concept of God here is one of an "It" that is beyond the conceptions of human logic and imagination. Brahman transcends all the dualities and differentiation of existence and is *neti neti*, "not this, not this", in other words, It is beyond all opposites – light and darkness, good and evil, male and female.

Kṛṣṇa as *nirguṇa* Brahman

The *Bhagavad Gītā* takes up the full force of the *Vedāntic* concept of a *nirguṇa* Brahman, Brahman that is without *guṇas*, devoid of qualities, beyond all manifestation, and it is this concept of Kṛṣṇa as the *nirguṇa* Brahman with which I want to deal first. Being beyond all descriptors, the *nirguṇa* Brahman is given negative terms – *un*-manifest; *in*-conceivable; *in*-explicable; *un*-changeable; *im*-movable; *im*-perishable. When Kṛṣṇa is designated as the Unmanifest, *Avyakta*, this is not the unmanifest of Sāṃkhya, the *mūla-prakṛti*, for he says "beyond this unmanifest there is another Eternal Unmanifest Existent, who is not destroyed even when all other beings are destroyed" (8:20). In 2:25 of the *Gītā*, Kṛṣṇa describes the Self also as unmanifest (*avyakta*, similar to the Sāṃkhya use of the term), inconceivable (*acintya*) and unchangeable (*avikārya*), and this makes the Self, the *ātman*, of the same nature as Brahman, though not, as far as I am concerned, monistically so, as we shall see below. In 2:18, the *ātman* is given other terms that are given to Brahman – indestructible (*avināśī*), eternal (*nitya*), unborn (*aja*), and imperishable (*avyaya*) and, additionally, in 2:24 as all-pervading (*sarva-gata*), stable (*sthāṇu*), immovable (*acala*), and ancient, eternal (*sanātana*). The particular brilliance of the *Gītā* is that it does not exclude devotion to this *nirguṇa* aspect of Brahman. In 12:3 we find the words: "But those who truly worship the Imperishable, the Indefinable, the Unmanifest, the Omnipresent, the Unthinkable, the Unchangeable, the Immovable, the Eternal . . .", in other words the *nirguṇa* Brahman, will obtain Kṛṣṇa, though he says that it is the harder pathway.

The syllable *Oṃ*, the very sound of the cosmos, is generally recognized as being a symbol of the *nirguṇa* Brahman, of the Imperishable, *Akṣara*, this last term being a synonym of *Oṃ* in that it can mean "syllable". The sound vibration of *Oṃ* is the Absolute Brahman, and Kṛṣṇa identifies himself with this as *nirguṇa* Brahman emphatically in 9:17 and also in 8:13 when he says ". . . thus uttering *Oṃ*, the one-syllabled Brahman, remembering me [Kṛṣṇa], he who departs, leaving the body, attains the supreme goal". Again, in 7:8, Kṛṣṇa says he is the "primeval sound", and in 10:25, Kṛṣṇa again identifies himself as the "one syllable", *eka akṣara*, that is *Oṃ*, the symbol of the Unmanifest. Brahman is established unequivocally as the "Imperishable, the Supreme" in 8:3, Imperishable here being, once again, *Akṣara*. As Krishna Prem put it, "beyond all and alone stands the Supreme Eternal, the Imperishable *Brahman*, dark in utter mystery, the Root of all that is, was, or shall ever be".[3] The Imperishable, or *nirguṇa* Brahman is, it seems, known by "knowers of the *Veda*" (8:11); in other words, by the path of knowledge. *Akṣara* is explicitly identified with the Unmanifest, *Avyakta*, in 8:21 and Kṛṣṇa calls this "my supreme abode", to know of which is the ultimate goal. Then, too, in 7:24, Kṛṣṇa explicitly refers to himself as the Unmanifest. He also says: "Nothing is higher than me" (7:7) and given his identification of himself as *nirguṇa* Brahman these words blur the distinction between Kṛṣṇa and the ultimate indescribable Absolute.

Śaṃkara's commentary on the *Gītā* interpreted it wholly as monistic and it is easy to see that an *advaitist* view could be gleaned from the verses that point to a *nirguṇa* Brahman. Kṛṣṇa even refers to those who attain "unity" with him (14:2), and Śaṃkara saw this certainly as *identity*.[4] But the word for unity here, *sadarmya*, is more of a "likeness with" or "similarity to". Aurobindo translated the term as "become of like nature and law of being with Me" or, better, "that putting on of the divine nature".[5] J. A. B. van Buitenen made the point here that at dissolution beings "do not disappear as *persons*, but continue to exist with their unimpaired memory and full awareness of themselves".[6] It is an interesting comment that supports the dualism between God and human that seems to be the message of the *Gītā*. The final verse of chapter 17 states: "*Oṃ*, *Tat*, *Sat*; this has been declared the threefold designation of Brahman." *Tat*, "*That*", is reminiscent of the *tat tvam asi*, "*That* you are" of the *Chāndogya Upaniṣad* (6:8–16), where it indicates the non-dual total identification of the inner *ātman* with the *nirguṇa* Brahman, and *Sat* is Truth, Reality. But there is nothing in the *Gītā*'s verse to point to a monistic identity of *ātman* with Brahman. The spirit of the *Gītā* is, in my view, one of a dualism between God and human: *nirguṇa* Brahman pervades all of the cosmos as its Source but is, ultimately, greater than what is created. It is beyond unmanifest *prakṛti* and all that exists when *prakṛti* is manifested – a panentheistic rather than a monistic view, whereby the *nirguṇa* Brahman is unaffected by the whole of the manifest cosmos – ultimately, Kṛṣṇa as *nirguṇa* Brahman exists when nothing else does. This does not preclude the unity of all *prakṛti* or even the unity of all selves.

One verse, 6:29, seems almost to have a classic statement of monism: it says: "One whose self is integrated by *yoga* sees the *ātman* as dwelling in all beings and all beings in the *ātman*. One sees the same everywhere." Śaṃkara's comment "he sees that the Self and Brahman (the Absolute) are one"[7] seems justified in that the verse reflects the *Īśā Upaniṣad* 6–7, where the sense is almost identical and is more certainly monistic. But the spirit of the *Gītā* is panentheistic, though accepting – as I think is the case in this verse – a unity and interconnection of all by way of the *ātman*. There is no explicit statement in this verse that the unity it suggests is with the *nirguṇa* Brahman. Brahman is, also, so often depicted as the *Source* of all, a Source that exists when all else does not. Notice, then, the dualism that obtains when the final goal is reached in the following verse (18:54): "Brahman-become, of serene self, he neither grieves nor desires; the same to all beings, he obtains supreme *devotion* to me." *Devotion* I have highlighted because it is so explicitly dualistic and theistic. Seeing the same *ātman* in others as in one's own self, in my view, is a unity that cannot be pressed as far as identity with Brahman in the *Gītā*. The unity comes from seeing the essence of Brahman in all things: "The wise see the same in a learned and humble *Brāhmin*, a cow, an elephant, a dog and even an outcaste" (5:18). In Gandhi's words: "Ganga water in separate vessels is Ganga water after all",[8] or, as Veeraswamy Krishnaraj more philosophically puts it, "there is a metaphysical unity in empirical diversity".[9] Similarly, the dualism is very evident in 6:30–31: "He who sees me everywhere and sees all in me does not become lost to me and I do not become lost to him", also in verse 31, a verse that Robert Zaehner described as "the climax of the chapter":[10] "Whoever worships me as abiding in all beings, remaining established in unity, whatever his mode of life, that *yogin* abides in me also."

The *nirguṇa* Brahman is neither *sat*, "being", "manifestation", nor *asat*, "non-being" or "non-manifestation" as opposites (13:12), because it transcends both and is truly the *neti neti* of the *Vedānta*. And yet the world is pervaded by *nirguṇa* Brahman as "*That*" (2:17): "*That*" is described as Supreme, as the *ātman*, and as that into which *yogins* project their intellect and in which they are established (5:17). "*That*" in 13:15 is said to be; "Outside and within beings, the unmoving and also the moving; because of its subtlety, "*That*" is incomprehensible, and "*That*" is far and near." Moreover, *Oṃ*, *Tat* and *Sat* are in one place (17:23) "declared the threefold designation of Brahman". In this case, Brahman as *Sat* is Truth, Reality and Being in their ultimate sense, though the word also has the more mundane meaning of good and praiseworthy in the *Gītā* and is also used of best *yogic* praxis (17:26–7).

The panentheism of the *nirguṇa* Brahman is explicit in 9:4, where Kṛṣṇa says: "All this world is pervaded by me in my unmanifest form. All beings exist in me but I do not exist in them." *I do not exist in them* means that the *nirguṇa* Brahman is not dependent on beings for continued existence, but they are dependent on Brahman: the thought reflects the *Īśā Upaniṣad* 5.[11] As we shall see presently, it will be the manifestation of the *nirguṇa* Brahman in *saguṇa* form that is the medium of the pervasive manifestations and energies of the divine but "there is no being, moving or unmoving, that can exist without me", Kṛṣṇa says in 10:39. Importantly, the *nirguṇa* Brahman as the ultimate Source of all unites all manifestation as one. 13:30 tells us: "When he sees the whole variety of beings resting in the One and radiating out from that alone, then he becomes Brahman." The idea of *radiating out* here is reminiscent of the etymology of the word "Brahman" as expanding out or bursting forth, blowing out.[12] The *nirguṇa* Brahman is like the centre of a circle from which radiates out every possible point on that circle both on its circumference, beyond it and within it.

Verse 7:5 speaks of a lower and higher *prakṛti* probably as two complementary natures of Kṛṣṇa, lower as the manifest world and higher as the *nirguṇa* Brahman that is the Source of manifestation and the life-element of the universe. Everything would be a minute particle of the manifested divine energy and nature, a wave on an infinite ocean, but never the ocean itself. And there are many instances, including much of chapters 7 and 10 of the *Gītā* that depict Kṛṣṇa as Brahman and as the essence of all things. But the intimacy of the *nirguṇa* Brahman with what is manifest does not, in fact, involve Brahman in the world of action: "The Lord[13] does not create agency or actions for this world: he does not create union with fruits of actions. One's nature leads to action" (5:14). In total stillness and passivity and separate from activity, the *nirguṇa* Brahman does not dictate the actions of human beings or the results of actions, just as the still passive *ātman* of each being does not act at all.

Kṛṣṇa as *saguṇa* Brahman

While the *nirguṇa* Brahman is well attested in the *Gītā*, it is especially the *saguṇa* aspect of Brahman with which Kṛṣṇa is mostly associated. As *saguṇa*, "with qualities", Kṛṣṇa is brought nearer to his devotees as a God more than a transcendent Absolute. Peppered throughout the *Gītā* are names for Kṛṣṇa that reflect his *saguṇa* aspect. Arjuna calls Kṛṣṇa Acyuta, "Immortal, Immovable", "One who has not fallen"; Ananta, "Infinite, Endless"; Arisūdana, "Destroyer of enemies"; Hṛṣīkeśa, "Lord of the senses"; Janārdana, "Liberator of men" or "Giver of rewards" (or perhaps "One worshipped for prosperity and freedom"). The titles "Lord" and "God" are most relevant for the *saguṇa* concept of God. In 11:37 and 38, Arjuna refers to Kṛṣṇa as Mahātma, "Great Soul": he is also called the Primal Cause; Infinite Being; Lord/God of gods; Lord/Source of beings; Ruler of the world; Abode of the universe; that which is supreme; Primal God; Ancient/Eternal Puruṣa; and is said to be resplendent and to possess infinite forms. Arjuna has a spiritual journey to undertake in the *Gītā* and he gradually comes to recognize his friend and companion Kṛṣṇa as Brahman itself; a realization explicit in 10:12, where Arjuna says: "You are the supreme Brahman, the supreme Abode, the supreme Purifier, the eternal divine Puruṣa, the primeval God, the Unborn, the Omnipresent." These are all epithets of the *saguṇa* Brahman. In 11:18, Kṛṣṇa is described by Arjuna as "the imperishable protector of eternal *dharma*", and this is a protector that pervades the whole universe. That protection is such that Kṛṣṇa takes *saguṇa* – and, indeed, anthropomorphic – form, whenever there is a decline of *dharma* and a rise in *adharma*: then, says Kṛṣṇa, "I manifest myself" (4:7). The *saguṇa* form of God, then, is the *manifestation* of what is ultimately the Unmanifest, *nirguṇa* Brahman.

The *saguṇa* Brahman can take a multitude of forms and has a multitude of qualities. A whole chapter of the *Gītā* is devoted to manifestations, *vibhūtis*, "divine glories" or "powers" that are the ubiquitous[14] manifestations of Brahman in all existence, especially in the sense of Brahman being the essence that underpins everything by the merest fraction of his self. Vimala Thakar sensitively describes this powerful word *vibhūti* as "the capacity, the faculty, the energy to permeate something which emanates out of you, though you retain your uniqueness and individuality at the same time. To be immanent and transcendent at the same time is called *vibhuti* in this chapter. It is a beautiful word."[15] It is, indeed, a beautiful and powerful word in that it encapsulates the ability of divinity to permeate all creation and yet transcend it, not be bound by it in any way, and to remain inexplicably and indescribably greater than it. The *vibhūtis* are the manifest forms of the Unmanifest and there is no end to them, Kṛṣṇa says in 10:40 – many forms, "by hundreds and by thousands, of various kinds, divine, and of various colours and shapes" (11:5). Prem wrote magnificently of this verse:

> "but all the splendours of the cosmic depths, their mind-annihilating magnitudes of time and space, symbol to all men of Eternal Law and Beauty, are but a moment of the *Mighty Atman*; infinities ranged on the shoulders of infinities; a wondrous hierarchy of living spiritual Powers where each is each and each is All and all dance forth in ecstacy the Cosmic Harmony. Vast beyond thought as is this spiritual realm, this flaming Cosmos of Divine Ideas, yet still beyond lies Tat, the One Eternal, the *Parabrahman*, Rootless Root of all".[16]

Then, in chapter 11, Arjuna is permitted to have a vision of the Universal or Cosmic Form of Kṛṣṇa. This is the *viśva-rūpa*, the manifest *saguṇa* form of Brahman as the great God Kṛṣṇa. In this tremendous vision, all the multiplicity of forms in the universe converge into that one Universal Form: Arjuna will see two forms, first the benign vision of Kṛṣṇa manifest as Īśvara, "Lord", and then the terrible universal aspect, Kṛṣṇa with thousands of arms, eyes, mouths.[17]

Critical to the *saguṇa* aspect of Brahman as Kṛṣṇa is the fact that a describable God can be praised, worshipped and offered devotion as a God who supports all of humanity. He is Father, Mother, Ordainer, Grandfather of the world, he says in 9:17, and in the following verse, Kṛṣṇa says: "I am the Goal, the Supporter, the Lord, the Witness, the Abode, the Shelter, the Friend, the Origin, the Dissolution, the Foundation, the Treasure-house and the Imperishable Seed". *Witness* here is the classic passive observer of all, the *ātman* of the *Upaniṣads* and Advaita Vedānta, and the *puruṣa* of Sāṃkhya-Yoga. While the *saguṇa* Brahman is more readily describable as God, he does not act. He remains the imperishable Lord, Īśvara, who is a superior, eternal Puruṣa called the Supreme Self, the *Param-Ātman*. In chapter 15, Kṛṣṇa speaks of a perishable *puruṣa*, the *jīvātman* or ordinary self; then of the *puruṣa* that is the imperishable *ātman* of all beings and that is his essence in all; and further, in verse 18, Kṛṣṇa says that he transcends both as the *Puruṣottama*, the "Supreme Person" – a thoroughly panentheistic transcendence of Kṛṣṇa beyond all phenomena but especially beyond the *ātman* in all that is but a fraction of himself.

The relationship between the *nirguṇa* and *saguṇa* Brahman – while often blurred in the *Gītā*, making each difficult to determine at times – is a unified one, attractively conveyed by Thakar: "The inter-locked nature of the manifest with the unmanifest cannot be separated. The very existence of the manifest and the unmanifest depend upon each other. The manifest declares the unmanifest as its essence, and the unmanifest declares that the variety of the manifest world, the diversity, is contained in emptiness. The one declares the existence of the other. Diversity decorates unity, and unity breathes into the expression of diversity."[18] Chapter 9 of the *Gītā* deals with both the *nirguṇa* and *saguṇa* natures of Brahman. As the *saguṇa* Brahman, Kṛṣṇa depicts his lower nature as all *prakṛti*, though he is not affected by it in any way because, at the same time, he is the *nirguṇa* Brahman that exists when all *prakṛti* disappears and is in no way limited in, defined in, or dependent on, manifest existence. Kṛṣṇa as *saguṇa* Brahman is the personal God but also pervades the entire world as its essence and as the *Ātman* of all things. Thus, as Śaṃkara put it, beings "are what they are in virtue of Me, the Self, underlying them all".[19] The relationship between the *nirguṇa* and *saguṇa* aspects is expressed in one verse where Kṛṣṇa says: "Know action to have arisen from Brahman and Brahman to have arisen from the Imperishable. Therefore, all-pervading Brahman is eternally established in *yajña*" (3:15). The first Brahman from whom action arises, and the "all-pervading Brahman" are likely to be the *saguṇa* Brahman, whereas it is the "Imperishable" – again, *Akṣara* – that is the *nirguṇa* Brahman.

The title "Lord", Īśvara, for Kṛṣṇa is endemic in the *Gītā*. It is a title for the personalized Brahman in both *saguṇa* form as manifest Creator, Sustainer and Dissolver, and also as humanized Kṛṣṇa. Importantly, Kṛṣṇa in anthropomorphic form is identical in nature to both the *saguṇa* and *nirguṇa* Brahman. Kṛṣṇa says as much in 9:11: "The deluded disregard me assumed in human form, not knowing my higher nature as the Lord of Beings." Here, Kṛṣṇa is *Maheśvara*, "Great Lord" and, elsewhere, we find him given the epithets *Mahā-yogeśvara*, "Great Lord of Yoga" and *Yogeśvara*; *Loka-Maheśvara*, "Great Lord of the Worlds"; *Parameśvara*, "Supreme Lord"; and *Viśveśvara*, "Lord of the Universe". Kṛṣṇa is also Lord (*prabhu*) of all *yajñas*, sacrifices.

Kṛṣṇa in anthropomorphic form

While many of the *saguṇa* forms of Brahman may be anthropomorphic, it is Kṛṣṇa in human form that is the epitome of anthropomorphism. Later Hinduism was to develop the concept of *avatāras*, the "descents" of the great deity Viṣṇu into various forms in order to restore the balance of good in the world. Kṛṣṇa is one such descent, but it is doubtful whether the full extent of the doctrine of *avatāras* was in existence at the time of the composition of the *Gītā* [20] and Viṣṇu barely features in such a sense throughout the text: indeed, he is mentioned only a few times.[21] Nevertheless, the rationale for the concept is there clearly in that expressive verse noted above: "Whenever there is a decline of *dharma* . . . and a rise of *adharma*, then I manifest myself" (4:7). But, as Rohit Mehta pointed out, there is no diminution of Brahman, just as the sun is in no way diminished by its rays: the descent is like a tiny particle of divinity in the manifest world.[22] In the *Gītā*, Kṛṣṇa is present to restore the balance of good epitomized by the five Pāṇḍava brothers against their evil relatives, the hundred sons of Dhṛtarāṣṭra. He is in definite human form, a *Kṣatriya*, very much a warrior, chieftain and hero, and we have only glimpses of his divinity in the *Mahābhārata* in which the *Gītā* is set. Indeed, when Arjuna learns the true nature of Kṛṣṇa as divine, he becomes only too aware of his over-familiar friendship with Kṛṣṇa as a human, his playful "Hiya Kṛṣṇa . . ." and irreverent fun with one whom he thought to be a mere mortal: for such past behaviour he begs forgiveness (11:41–2). Even gods and anti-gods seem not to know who Kṛṣṇa really is (10:14). But the human identity of Kṛṣṇa is crucial for the development of devotional theism. The *Gītā* does not deal with Kṛṣṇa's birth, babyhood, adolescence, and life and death, which were developments to come. Nevertheless, the *Gītā* in a way becomes central to the lasting theology of Kṛṣṇa as an expression of Brahman by defining his divinity and lordship, his roles as Creator, Sustainer, Protector, and yet the closeness of God to human. In the descent of God in human form as Kṛṣṇa, we have an overt synthesis of God and human, of divine eternity with manifest time, of God as subject and the world as object, and of spirit with material existence. That union is always present; it is just made more explicit through the concept of God in human form. The *Gītā* permits the rise of popular religion to great metaphysical heights, while retaining its popular, very visual, God.

Kṛṣṇa's anthropomorphic character is reflected in some of his names, such as Keśiniṣūdhana, "Slayer of Keśi" and Keśava, "Destroyer of Keśi" (or "One who has long hair"). Similarly, he is called Madhusūdana, "Slayer of Madhu" and Mādhava "Descendant of Madhu" or "Lord of fortune". His human form is referred to in the patronym for him, Vāsudeva, "Son of Vāsudeva". However, in the battle that will follow, Kṛṣṇa is Arjuna's charioteer in a war in which he will remain neutral and passive as the *nirguṇa* Brahman.

Kṛṣṇa as the personal God beyond the *nirguṇa* Brahman?

The main message of the *Upaniṣads* is of a *nirguṇa* Brahman with which the deepest part of the self, the *ātman*, is identical and, also, a *saguṇa* God such as Rudra, or the *Person* in the later *Śvetāśvatara Upaniṣad*, with whom a personal relationship is possible – monism and theism respectively. However, the *Upaniṣads*, as was seen in chapter 3, have far from consistent concepts and we witness there developing ideas as much as fully evolved theories. The *Kaṭha Upaniṣad* (3:11) hints at a "person" beyond the unmanifest: "Higher than the immense self is the unmanifest; Higher than the unmanifest is the person; Higher than the person there's nothing at all; That is the goal, that's the highest state." Patrick Olivelle's translation with lower case for self, unmanifest and person suggests that Olivelle does not accept the unmanifest here as Brahman, which his note to the verse also supports.[23] Verses 7–8 of the *Upaniṣad* are a little more specific: "Higher than the senses is the mind; Higher than the mind is the essence; Higher than the essence is the immense self; Higher than the immense is the unmanifest. Higher than the unmanifest is the person, pervading all and without marks. Knowing him, a man is freed, and attains immortality."[24] *If* there is any suggestion that there is a personal God *beyond* Brahman it is not clearly articulated in the *Upaniṣads*, and it would have to rest on very limited extracts, such as this one. What *is* evident is a personal God *as* Brahman in the theistic *Upaniṣads*.

Since the *Gītā* stresses devotion as a means to God and a means to final release from the confines of a perpetual round of births and deaths, God must always remain *personal* for the emancipated one, but I do not think we have to project such a personal God beyond the totally transcendent Brahman: the two aspects of deity, the personal and the transcendent, are not mutually exclusive and without total identity with Brahman – which, it seems to me, the *Gītā* does not suggest – there must be aspects of divinity that are beyond the devotee at liberation. What is clear is that the *Gītā*'s concept of God is a lofty one: Kṛṣṇa is a personal God of great depth and metaphysical heights. The highest metaphysical concept of deity in the Hindu tradition up to the time of the *Gītā* had been the *nirguṇa*, incomprehensible Brahman about which nothing could be claimed, except to posit it as the unmanifest Source of all that is manifest, even of the dissolved unmanifest phases of the universe. Kṛṣṇa in the *Gītā* is both this Source and the personal God. The reference to "another Eternal Unmanifest Existent" that is "beyond this unmanifest" and "who is not destroyed even when all other beings are destroyed" in 8:20, I have taken to be the Unmanifest, the *nirguṇa* Brahman that is beyond the unmanifest state of the world, who is there when the world is not as the uncaused cause and underpins the cycles of manifestation and dissolution. Thus, the suggestion of Robert Zaehner, that the Eternal Unmanifest Existent is the *personal* Kṛṣṇa, making Brahman the penultimate not the ultimate goal,[25] to me, is not viable. What is important in the verse is the causative link between what is manifest existence and the Unmanifest Brahman as its ultimate cause. Ithamar Theodor, too, accepts Kṛṣṇa as a personal God beyond Brahman, referring increasingly throughout his text to the "Supreme Person", even though the *Gītā* uses the expression with more caution.[26] "Brahman rests upon Kṛṣṇa himself", Theodor says,[27] which is perhaps why he rejects any concept of a *nirguṇa* Brahman in his analysis of the *Gītā*.[28]

Another critical and more complex verse in this context is 14:27 which says: "For, indeed, I am the abode of Brahman, the Immortal, the Imperishable and eternal *Dharma* and absolute happiness." The word for *abode* in the text is *pratiṣṭhā* and it is variously translated. It certainly could mean "foundation", which is something of a problem for much other content of the *Gītā* if Kṛṣṇa is saying that he is the foundation of Brahman. Some commentators insist that it cannot mean "abode".[29] Richard Gotshalk believes that the term should be taken to mean Kṛṣṇa as the incarnation, the *place* (*pratiṣṭhā*) "where the power dwells (particularly for the purpose of approaching human beings and receiving worship and devotion from them".[30] "Embodiment", then, might be an appropriate synonym. Indeed, *pratiṣṭhā* can mean "gross matter", "earth",[31] suggesting Kṛṣṇa as materialized Brahman. There is a certain blurring of the impersonal and personal Brahman at times in the *Gītā* and Kṛṣṇa may be referring to himself as the abode/source/foundation of the manifest Brahman that is lower *prakṛti*. In summation, it seems to me that there is no clear evidence at all to suggest that Kṛṣṇa is the personal God *beyond* the *nirguṇa* Brahman: rather, he *is* Brahman in its *nirguṇa*, *saguṇa*, and human form.

Creation

It is the *saguṇa* aspect of Brahman that is responsible for the creation and dissolution of the world and when the *saguṇa* aspect of Brahman is withdrawn, it is the *nirguṇa* aspect that provides the changeless, permanent, eternal "It" that is the passive force and abode of potential manifestation. Kṛṣṇa is referred to as such an abode a number of times, and in 8:21 he says: "What is called the Unmanifest and Imperishable, [they] say it is that highest goal, having reached which, they do not return. That is my supreme abode." It is to the Unmanifest, the *nirguṇa* Brahman, the Imperishable, *Akṣara*, to which we have to look for the ultimate Source of creation, what Sarvepalli Radhakrishnan termed "the immutable [*avyaya*] centre of endless mobility",[32] for only the *nirguṇa* Brahman exists when manifestation is present or absent. It alone has the latent potential for existence. If we cast our minds back to the previous chapter on Sāṃkhya and Yoga, we have a similar idea of cycles of an unmanifest source, *avyakta*, from which manifestation, *vyakta*, in the form of the *guṇas* of *prakṛti*, emerges. The *Gītā* seems to have accepted in the main the Sāṃkhya theory of the evolutes of *prakṛti*[33] along with these *guṇas* as the components of manifest reality. The *Gītā*'s view of creation is that: "Beings are unmanifest in the beginning, manifest in their interim state and unmanifest again in the end" (2:28). The Sāṃkhya idea is present also in the following verse: "At the coming of the day, all that is manifest proceeds from the unmanifest. At the coming of the night, indeed, it is dissolved in that which is called the unmanifest" (8:18). Day and night here are creation and dissolution respectively. Whatever is dissolved – the body, the world, the universe – is absorbed into an unmanifest state with its essences nothing but seed-like potentiality, latencies for newly creative energies; seeds in the darkness of an unmanifested reality.

While the cycles of unmanifest > manifest > unmanifest are clearly evident in the *Gītā* and probably reflect ideas that were gaining ground by the exponents of Sāṃkhya, the *Gītā* does not lose sight of *Vedāntic* concepts of Brahman – both *nirguṇa* and *saguṇa*. We do not know whether developing Sāṃkhya had any concept of Brahman as creator of the world cycles, but any elements of Sāṃkhya in the *Gītā* are absolutely inferior to Brahman as the Originator, Controller, Sustainer and Dissolver of the universe. Indeed, the total distinction between Spirit and matter advocated in Sāṃkhya is absent in the *Gītā*. Zaehner put this succinctly when he wrote: "The Sāṃkhya system sought neatly to divide time from eternity, the phenomenal from the Absolute: what the Gītā sets out to do is to bring the two together again in a more or less coherent whole – to bring religion back to the Upanishads for which the supreme Principle is not a static monad but a dynamic reality which is at the same time eternally at rest."[34] It is the *saguṇa*, manifest, aspect of Brahman that appears to act in creation: at the same time, the unmanifest, *nirguṇa* aspect remains passive and inactive but informs all. Either way, while the Creator of the *guṇas* and of the cause–effect processes of *karma*, Kṛṣṇa remains passive and so does not actively predetermine or predestine causes and their results. As Arjuna's spiritual journey evolves in the Gītā, he comes to recognize Kṛṣṇa as controlling the origin and dissolution of beings (11:2). Kṛṣṇa's control of *prakṛti* is evident in 9:7 where he says: "All beings . . . go into my *prakṛti* at the end of the aeon. At the beginning of an aeon, I send them forth again." The manifest and unmanifest aspects of *prakṛti* are part of the *saguna* Brahman. Whereas Sāṃkhya posited the complete separation of spirit and matter, *puruṣa* and *prakṛti*, Puruṣa in the *Gītā* is Brahman and *prakṛti* is the manifestation of Brahman so that the two are inseparable; two apparent dualities that are united as one. The *Upaniṣads* supported, in the main, an emanationist view of creation as emitted from Brahman as Source: the *Gītā* has the same concept. In 7:6 Kṛṣṇa says: "Know that this is the womb of all beings. Thus, I am also the Source and dissolution of the whole universe", the "womb" aptly described by Prem as "a dark matrix full of unlimited potentialities".[35] *Nirguṇa* Brahman is the ultimate Source, the *womb*, being the potential of all that is manifest, followed by its manifestation then dissolution when all is absorbed back into the unmanifest womb. And Kṛṣṇa says in the following verse, 7:7: "Nothing is higher than me . . . in me all this is strung like clusters of pearls on a thread." Here, Brahman is the connecting thread, hidden by the pearls on it, unseen by the world, but is the same throughout all things and makes coherent manifestation possible. *Prakṛti* belongs to the being of Brahman: "Having animated my own *prakṛti*, I send forth again and again this multitude of beings, all helpless by the force of *prakṛti*" (9:8). Yet, Brahman remains passive and inactive leaving *prakṛtic* force and its collocations of *guṇas* to assemble into changing realities.

In an important verse, 4:6, Kṛṣṇa says: "Being unborn, also imperishable Ātman, and being Lord of all beings, controlling my own *prakṛti* , I come into being by my own *māyā*." Here, Kṛṣṇa speaks of his *prakṛti*, manifest creation, linking himself with manifest existence in an important way. Kṛṣṇa has clear ownership of *prakṛti* which, though ever-changing because of the *guṇas*, is bestowed a certain degree of empirical reality in which Kṛṣṇa becomes tangible – *by my own māyā*, he says. *Māyā* usually means "illusion" or "magical power", but here it means the divine power of empirical existence in comparison to *ultimate* Reality, and is synonymous with *prakṛti*. There is no sense here in the *Gītā* of *māyā* being non-reality and illusion in the sense of that in Advaita Vedānta: the *Gītā* is more truly *Vedāntic* in tone, unifying both manifest and unmanifest reality. *Māyā* is, thus, more of a "power of projection", as Rohit Mehta put it,[36] or, for Srinivasa Murthy, "supernatural power", reflecting perhaps its *Vedic* usage.[37] Kṛṣṇa refers specifically in 7:14 to "this divine *māyā* of mine, made of *guṇas*", again making *māyā* the equivalent of *prakṛti*, and therefore it is not unreal in any way. The presence of the *ātman* in all things, as will be seen below, will also ensure a reality to the world. And yet, *māyā* serves to distance Kṛṣṇa or Brahman from all action, even though "Īśvara dwells in the hearts of all beings . . . causing all beings by his *māyā* to whir as if mounted on a machine" (18:61). Īśvara is the means by which *prakṛti* operates because of his creative power, *māyā*, but Kṛṣṇa does not engage in action, in the same way that he drives Arjuna's chariot but carries no weapons and does not wage war himself. Kṛṣṇa causes all but is the detached observer of it: "And these actions do not bind me . . . like one sitting indifferent, unattached in those actions" (9:9). So *māyā* is the workings of *prakṛti*, also referred to as *yoga-māyā*, but while emanating from Brahman and incapable of being without Brahman, *prakṛti* can only operate with Brahman as the passive witness, rather as *prakṛti* in the Sāṃkhya scheme of things can only operate through the proximity and passive involvement of the *puruṣas*. The *Gītā*, however, unifies God and matter, though the key to liberation will remain the differentiation between Puruṣa as Brahman, the *Kṣetrajña*, or Knower of the field, as Kṛṣṇa says throughout chapter 13, and *prakṛti* as the world of changing *guṇas*, the *kṣetra* or "field" of manifestation. Kṛṣṇa speaks of those who are "deprived of knowledge by *māyā*" (7:15); in other words, they are too deluded by *prakṛti*. The ability to see the relationship and discriminate between the two is the ability to see the universe as it really is and this is what liberation is all about.

Prakṛti as the manifestation of Brahman not only unifies reality itself but also unites manifest reality with Brahman. Liberation is also about the recognition of this unity as much as differentiation through knowledge of their respective natures, seeing the permanent, unchanging Reality in the impermanent, changing *prakṛti*. Thus, Kṛṣṇa says: "He sees, who sees the Supreme Lord existing the same in all beings, the Imperishable in the perishable" (13:27). Similarly, when Kṛṣṇa gives Arjuna divine vision so that the latter can see the divine forms of Kṛṣṇa, Kṛṣṇa shows him "this whole universe existing in one, with the moving and unmoving in my body" (11:7). Aurobindo saw this as "the keynote, the central significance. It is the vision of the One in the Many and the Many in the One."[38] Nevertheless, while Kṛṣṇa is manifest in *prakṛti* and *ātman* he transcends both, being greater than his own essence in all beings and all things. *Prakṛti* operates because it gains potential from Brahman: "By me as supervisor, *prakṛti* produces the moving and the unmoving; by this cause . . . the world revolves", Kṛṣṇa says in 9:10. Thus, we should view Kṛṣṇa as the ultimate Cause as *nirguṇa* Brahman, and the effect that is *prakṛti* as manifest, *saguṇa* Brahman. And that effect is the *All*, as Arjuna comes to recognize finally when he sees the *vibhūtis*, the manifestations, of Kṛṣṇa; so he says: "Hail to you before, also to you behind, hail to you on every side even. O All! Infinite in power, infinite in strength, you pervade all and therefore are all" (11:40). However, lest this should lead one to assume a pantheism for the *Gītā*, Kṛṣṇa as *nirguṇa* Brahman always exists, whether the cosmos is manifest or unmanifest. Kṛṣṇa pervades creation and supports it until it is dissolved. Then it is held latent until he brings forth creation again and the ancient energy streams forth (15:4) – a process that is without beginning and end. Maharishi Mahesh Yogi attractively depicted the fact that Kṛṣṇa is greater than what he creates by saying "he is the ocean of life, while time rises and falls as the tide on the surface of the ocean. Although the tidal waves draw on the depths they can never fathom the unfathomable abyss . . . The life of man is like a wave which rises up to see – it can see so far and no more."[39] Chapter 10 makes it very clear that Kṛṣṇa is the Source of all that is created – not just tangible things but intangible aspects such as intellect, patience, fear and fearlessness: nothing exists except by the sustaining energy of Kṛṣṇa. And commenting on the statement in 7:12, where all natures stem from Kṛṣṇa (though he says "but I am not in them; they are in me"), Mehta wrote: "And so while Reality is immanent, it is at the same time transcendent. The Formless cannot be caught in the Form, the Transcendent cannot be imprisoned in the Immanent. The Creator is more than his Creation; He is immanent in his creation but only as the musician is immanent in his music. The music, however beautiful it may be cannot contain the musician. While the music resides in the musician, the musician does not reside in the music."[40]

While *prakṛti* is real, and there is an interconnection between manifest existence and unmanifest, ultimate Reality as Brahman, the world of phenomena is nevertheless a lesser or partial reality because it is changeable and impermanent: this will include the body and mind, as we shall see below, but not the *ātman* that is the permanent and unchangeable part of the self that is also partially – though not wholly in the *Gītā* – equated with Brahman and, therefore, with Kṛṣṇa. The crucial difference between the lesser reality of the world and ordinary knowledge of things, and the deep experience of the ultimate Reality that is Kṛṣṇa as Brahman is what Arjuna desperately needs in order to pick up his bow and fight. As long as he is focused on ordinary reality and knowledge, he will remain lost. All through the *Gītā*, Kṛṣṇa is leading Arjuna to deeper levels of reality. As Mehta put it: "The mind freed from the dust of knowledge is like a quiet lake into which is reflected the Wisdom of the Ages",[41] and Kṛṣṇa has much to teach Arjuna before such a point is reached.

The Self: *Ātman*

The *Gītā*'s perspective of the self corresponds finely to the *Vedāntic* view of a *karmic*, impermanent, changeable and transmigrating self that has in its depths the essence that is Brahman as its permanent, unchanging and eternal Self. But *ātman* and Brahman in the *Gītā* are not monistically identical; they are dualistically relational. While enough has been said in earlier chapters about the nature of Brahman and *ātman*, Kṛṣṇa's teaching about the self is critical to Arjuna's plight, and it is these aspects with which I want to deal here. It would seem from the outset and throughout chapter 1 of the *Gītā* that Arjuna views the self as the body and mental faculties: all the concerns he has about fighting revolve around this fact, he is, thus, absorbed in *prakṛti*. Kṛṣṇa's teaching begins in chapter 2 of the text. He tells Arjuna that the wise do not grieve for the living or the dead (v. 11) for the Self will never cease to exist. The true Self of each individual existed in the past and will continue to do so in the future, irrespective of their deaths on the battlefield (v. 12). The body may change from one life to the next, but the Self[42] that accompanies it does not (v. 13). Then Kṛṣṇa explains that it is "contacts of the senses with objects" creating choices between dualities in life, that create the problem. Such dualities – cold and heat, pleasure and pain" come and go and are therefore impermanent (v. 14). The one who does not react to such dualities and remains passive to them rises beyond them, unruffled by the dualities of *prakṛti*

(v. 15). Death is inevitable for all beings but it is only the body that dies. If Arjuna can function dispassionately from the point of the inner, passive Self, he will be beyond the influence of action, become a non-agent, free from egoistic involvement and, therefore, be beyond *karmic* effects. Since the indestructible Self cannot be slain by Arjuna's arrows, there is no reason why he should not fight. Kṛṣṇa's argument is that: "Anyone who believes this (embodied Self) is the slayer or who thinks this is the slain, both do not know. It slays not, nor is slain. It is never born and never dies. Not at any time having come to be will it come to be again. Unborn, eternal, permanent, ageless, it is not slain when the body is slain" (vv. 19–20).

As a *Kṣatriya*, a warrior, it is Arjuna's duty to fight and, as a warrior, he will gain Heaven as tradition held, if he were to die fighting but vanquished. But it is *how* he engages in the war that interests Kṛṣṇa and his advice is: "Making pleasure and pain, gain and loss, victory and defeat the same, engage yourself for battle: then you will not incur evil" (v. 38). So it is right that Arjuna should fight but from a state of equanimity, perfectly poised between defeat or victory just as he and Kṛṣṇa are poised at the mid-point of the two armies. Satya Agarwal suggests that personal *dharma* and equanimity in all activity are harmonized in this verse in a way that could be considered a basic, new teaching in the *Gītā*.[43] Indeed, we have the core teaching of right action without desire for results articulated clearly in this verse. The point here is the absence of egoistic involvement, of *desire* for victory and *aversion* to fighting. Desire and aversion "like thieves on the road", according to Śaṃkara,[44] are the major dualities that involve an individual in the *prakṛtic* world, the world of *guṇas*, and Kṛṣṇa says: "When a man casts off all the desires of the mind . . . satisfied in the *ātman*, within the self, then he is said to be one of steady wisdom" (v. 55). Any action undertaken in this state of equilibrium is *detached* action not action attached to something in the phenomenal world.

Another angle to Kṛṣṇa's argument occurs in 4:35, where he tells Arjuna that knowledge will enable him to "see all beings in your *ātman* and also in me". Arjuna can be free from dualities of conflicting forces, free from delusion, by the realization of the interconnection of all existence that the *ātman* provides and the *ātman* as united with Kṛṣṇa. Such unity is pertinent to both the relative and the absolute and is a removal of the veil of *prakṛti*, though it should be remembered that the *Gītā* also differentiates between manifest creation and Brahman, for Brahman is always greater. Perhaps this is evident in Kṛṣṇa's words in 10:20: "I am the *Ātman* . . . existing in the hearts of all beings: I am also the beginning, the middle and the end of all beings." Radhakrishnan commenting on Kṛṣṇa's *vibhūtis* wrote: "The world is a living whole, a vast interconnectedness, a cosmic harmony inspired and sustained by the One Supreme."[45] Kṛṣṇa says a similar thing in 10:32: "Among creations, I am the beginning and the end and also the middle", suggestive of the control of creation and dissolution as well as the sustaining of what is created: such is never said of the *ātman* of a being. That existence of Kṛṣṇa in the heart of each being is as a passive witness rather as the *puruṣas* of Sāṃkhya. Action can only be part of the *guṇas* of *prakṛti* as Kṛṣṇa says in 13:29: "He sees, who sees all actions performed by *prakṛti* alone, and the *ātman* as the non-doer."

The *Gītā*'s view of the ordinary self reflects the traditional concepts outlined in Sāṃkhya and Yoga, the developing ideas of the *Upaniṣads* and Advaita Vedānta. There may be hints of Buddhist influence in verses that emphasize the loss of desires and ego as the key to liberation: "That man attains peace who, abandoning all desires, moves about free from longing, without ownership, without ego", Kṛṣṇa says in 2:71, but such a thought is thoroughly consonant with *Vedāntic* teaching as well as Sāṃkhya-Yoga. However, the influential Sāṃkhya theory of the three *guṇas* of *sattva*, *rajas* and *tamas*, is clearly present in the *Gītā*. In 3:27, Kṛṣṇa says: "In all cases, actions are performed by the *guṇas* of *prakṛti*. One whose mind is deluded by egoism thus thinks, 'I am the doer'". The ego (*ahaṃkāra*), assumes authorship, ownership and causation of all that takes place, and becomes bound to the results of actions, mistaking the *prakṛtic* world (or the "field", the *kṣetra*, as it is called in chapter 13), for the ultimately real instead of the *ātman* that is part of Brahman. Buddhist influence seems clear in verses 8 and 9 of chapter 23 where Kṛṣṇa stresses the path to freedom involves " . . . detachment from sense objects and absence of egoism also, perception of the evils of birth, death, old age, sickness and pain, non-attachment, non-entanglement with son, wife, home and the like, and constant even-consciousness in the attainment of the desirable and undesirable . . .". One is reminded here of the Buddha's visions of old age, sickness and death in his early search for enlightenment and his abandonment of his family in that search. And the answer to Arjuna's problem is exactly this lack of detachment and egoistic involvement: "He who is free from the notion of egoism, whose intellect is not tainted, even though he slays these worlds, he does not kill, he is not bound" (18:17). In other words, no retributive *karma* will accrue to Arjuna in the battle as long as he is desireless and egoless, fighting in a state of perfect equilibrium, engaged only in the passive, still *ātman*. But Kṛṣṇa warns: "If, having taken refuge in egoism, you think 'I will not fight', vain is this your resolve; your nature will compel you" (18:59). Arjuna has been thinking in terms of results of his actions that will involve him in consequential *karma*. Additionally, his nature as a *Kṣatriya* is such that he has to fight; he cannot hide from his *dharma*, what is right for him.

The *jīva*, the ordinary self in Sāṃkhya and Yoga is pure matter, totally separate from spirit, *puruṣa*, and is illusory, or at most a lesser reality in Advaita Vedānta. The *Gītā* suggests a more intimate relationship between Kṛṣṇa and the ordinary self. While it exists, the *jīvātman* is part of *prakṛti*, and *prakṛti* is inseparable from Brahman for it is caused by Brahman as its Source. Thus, Brahman becomes the individual life-element of each being.[46] Nevertheless, the *jīvātman* is the active agent that becomes bound up in egoism, desires and aversions, and the *Gītā* points to desire (*kāma*), anger (*krodha*) and greed (*lobha*) as three characteristics that are displayed by the egoistic self: the passive *ātman* has no part in such natures. Kṛṣṇa has depicted desire and anger as the deadliest of enemies (3:37–41), but they can take no hold of the one who "is anchored to eternal silence as a ship is anchored to the sea bed".[47] The mixture of *guṇas* in an individual will dictate his or her nature with one predominant that will determine the core personality. In modern terms, it is a reductionist theory that makes behaviour dependent on intrinsic make-up that will even influence the kind of faith one has (17:2). Zaehner termed such *prakṛtic* make-up "that parcel of the whole material cosmos which has attached itself to his individual self".[48] Chapter 14 of the *Gītā* describes the various natures of the *sattvic*, *rajasic* and *tamasic* individuals, describing how each binds individuals in the *prakṛtic* world. Even *sattva*, associated with light, joy, evolutionary knowledge and happiness can bind one if *sattvic* goodness is desired (14:6), though elsewhere, Kṛṣṇa tells Arjuna to be without the three *guṇas* but to be "ever remaining in *sattva*" (2:45), perhaps here meaning "truth" or "purity", indicative of purity in equilibrium or purity in mastering the self. The aim is to transcend the dualities of existence and retain equilibrium in honour and dishonour, with friend and foe. Such advice is certainly pertinent to Arjuna's position. He is anxious about killing his friends in the opposing army and even his foes, who are his family. With equanimity, he will be able to fight, and by abandoning all undertakings for the purpose of results, he will be able to act, anchored in the passivity of the *ātman*. Eknath Easwaran said of the inactivity of the inner Self: "The Self abides in the inner chamber of the heart, always at peace, whatever forces of prakriti may storm outside. The illumined man or woman maintains a joyful evenness of mind in happiness and sorrow."[49] The *jīvātman*, however, is destined to wander from life to life in perpetual death and rebirth, bound by its own egoism, its own desires, pleasures, attachments and aversions, according to its *guṇic* make-up, perpetually in a state of delusion and confusion (*moha*) about reality and perpetually reaping the results of its past actions in a world that is constantly changing and thoroughly impermanent.

Dharma

The battle that is about to take place is at Kurukṣetra on the "Field of Dharma", a large plain owned by the Kurus and is a place of pilgrimage up to the present time. It is fitting that it is *dharma* that has brought events to the point of war and *dharma* that is about to be worked out. Fundamentally, *dharma* means "what is right" but it has a number of meanings in the *Mahābhārata* as a whole. Coming from the root *dhri* "to support", it has the idea of inner sustaining of something as its basic essence; that which sustains, holds, keeps something right. Thus, *dharma* can extend to the essence of duty, law, class, social norms, ritual, and to the cosmos itself. *Dharma* represents the way things should be in all these different dimensions and is fundamental to the evolution of the individual, of society and of every part of life. Its opposite is *adharma*, the breakdown of what is right, and the *raison d'être* for Kṛṣṇa being incarnate on Earth.

In the first chapter, Arjuna raises a pertinent point regarding *dharma* – it is wrong to kill: "What pleasure would there be for us having slain the sons of Dhṛtarāṣṭra . . .? Evil alone would take hold of us having killed these wicked people" (1:36). To Arjuna, at this point, to kill is evil and can only result in evil: it is a negative act that can only produce negative effects. He adds another argument about *dharma*, "in the destruction of a family, ancient family *dharmas* perish. With the destruction of these *dharmas* the whole family is overcome by *adharma*" (1:40). With the destruction of many members of a family, he thinks, there will be no traditions about *dharma* to be handed on and the normal rhythms of life will break down, leading to corruption of women, the breakdown of class rules (v. 41) and birth and cast family traditions (v. 43), and neglect of ancestors and religious rites (v. 42). But there is a further issue here. Arjuna is a *Kṣatriya*, a warrior and leader of men, and it is his *dharma* to fight if necessary, to protect society and to uphold *dharma*. He is poised between expectant *adharma* and his own *dharma* – with a penchant for the former that depresses him. Alan Jacobs describes Arjuna's depression rather aptly as "Hamlet's disease", the kind of mind oppression that paralyzes action,[50] so Kṛṣṇa shocks him by accusing him of being "un-Āryan-like" (2:2), in other words, failing in his noble class *dharma* as an Āryan warrior. Many may sympathize with Arjuna, but at this stage he is not sufficiently evolved to see the bigger picture: he is thinking from the point of view of attachment, from aversion, from an egoistic "I", and with a confusion that is a profound disturbance of normal reasoning. It is in such a state that he surrenders to Kṛṣṇa for his guidance.

Arjuna has a *sva-dharma*, an "own *dharma*", a personal path to follow as his duty that is in many ways an instrument of the divine to ensure and maintain the appropriate balance of positive forces in the cosmos – a higher *dharma* that is the *sanātana*, "eternal" *dharma*. Kṛṣṇa describes the war to come as "righteous warfare" (2:33). But to fight, Arjuna has to abandon the "I", the egoism, the weighing up of victory or defeat, the good or evil of the act of war. So Kṛṣṇa says: "Making pleasure and pain, gain and loss, victory and defeat the same, engage yourself for battle: then you will not incur evil" (2:38). It is this word *same*, (Skt. *sama*), that is important here and the verse is a major key to the understanding of the *Gītā*. When all is the same there is equanimity between all opposites: there are no dualities, and gain and loss are ultimately one and the same thing. Arjuna must abandon thoughts of such dualities for equanimity. Subsequently, Kṛṣṇa will lead Arjuna to knowledge of the *ātman* but here in this verse we have a core teaching of the *Gītā* – right action without desire for results. It is at this point that Kṛṣṇa begins his teaching about the *prakṛtic guṇas* and the need to transcend them along with all pairs of opposites.

The importance of following one's own *dharma* is epitomized in the well-known verse, 3:35: "Better one's own *dharma* devoid of merit, than the well-discharged *dharma* of another. Death in one's own *dharma* is better; the *dharma* of another is fraught with danger." Arjuna had at one point thought it would be better to beg for food as a wandering ascetic, but this would be to turn his back on his own *sva-dharma*, and that would be a personal retrograde step rather than an evolutionary one. And late in the text, Kṛṣṇa says to Arjuna: "One should not abandon the duty for which one was born . . . even if defective" (18:48). The natural patterns of existence are upheld by the powerful force of *dharma*, but if *adharma* occurs in any exaggerated sense, the path of evolution is distorted and society declines. Then Kṛṣṇa becomes manifest on Earth to redress that balance and Arjuna is his instrument. As Kṛṣṇa says: "For the protection of the good and for the destruction of the wicked, for the firm establishment of *dharma* I am born in every epoch" (4:8): he is "the imperishable protector of eternal *dharma*" (11:18). In chapter 11, where Kṛṣṇa permits Arjuna a vision of his universal form, something depicted by one writer as "the most tremendous vision in religious literature",[51] Kṛṣṇa says that time has grown full and the fate of the warriors in the battle has already been decided. The complicated network of causes and effects, of *karma*, both individual and collective, and the imbalance between *dharma* and *adharma* are such that the particular conditions in time have come to fruition and the time is right to put an end to the imbalance between evil and good. Thus, Arjuna must fight because it is his *dharma* to do so, and Kṛṣṇa says to him: "If, having taken refuge in egoism, you think 'I will not fight', vain is this your resolve; your nature will compel you. Bound by your own *karma*, born of your own nature . . . that which from delusion you wish not to do, helpless, you will surely do" (18:59–60). In the same chapter, chapter 18, Kṛṣṇa endorses and describes the duties of each of the four classes (18:42–4), which in 4:13 he says that he created. *Dharmic* duty, then, is part of the fabric of creation and it must be obeyed, though without desire for results, without attachment, and focused on the *ātman* within.

There are times in the *Gītā* when Kṛṣṇa is critical of the *Vedas*. In 9:20–21, for example, he says that those who know them can only reach Heaven from where, when their good merit is used up, they will return to the mortal state. But at the end of chapter 16, he endorses the scriptures as sources of *dharma*. However, here he uses the term *śāstras* not *Vedas* as "the authority determining what ought to be done and ought not to be done. Knowing what is said in the ordinance of the *śāstras* you should perform it here" (16:24). This suggests that scripture dictates what is right or wrong, but the use of *śāstras* rather than *Vedas* widens the scope of teaching on *dharma* by including *smṛti* ("remembered") scriptures that are separate from the *Vedas*. Nevertheless, Kṛṣṇa says of actions ordained by scripture that they have to be conducted with equanimity: "Action that is ordained, free from attachment, done without passion or with hatred, by one not desirous of the fruit, that is declared to be *sattvic*" (18:23). It is a verse particularly pertinent to Arjuna who must carry out his personal *dharma* as the scriptures ordain but in a state of detached action that is not result orientated, *not desirous of the fruit*. Arvind Sharma pertinently says: "The attitude of the *Gītā* to the Vedas is like that of a wayfarer towards a raft – which is to be used while crossing but is to be abandoned after the crossing has been made. For one who has had self-realization the Vedas are not binding, but for one like Arjuna who is not a realized soul they are."[52] Even where Kṛṣṇa endorses *Vedic* ritual as in 9:16–17, he identifies himself with every facet of that ritual: only those who understand that each aspect of the ritual and the *Vedas* themselves *are* Kṛṣṇa, are reaching him through such praxis.

Paths to God: *Yoga*

The path to Brahman in the *Vedānta*, in Advaita Vedānta and in Sāṃkhya was one of knowledge and a path of inaction – renunciation of actions – that was promoted also by the Buddhists and Jains. Such inaction is withdrawal from the world and was contrasted with the *Vedic* ritualism that focused on action, *karman*, for worldly results and life with the gods after death. The *Gītā* is faithful to the path of knowledge of Brahman but does not promote either renunciation of action or action for results: instead, it accepts action as essential, but action that is not tainted by any desire for results *at all* – a different synthesis of knowledge and action. Such a synthesis underpins the *Gītā*'s discussion of *yoga*, and of the related paths of knowledge, action and devotion.

The *Gītā* is replete with references to the practice and theory of *yoga* as a path to liberation and describes many of the practices associated with *yoga* – breathing, concentration, meditation and control of the senses. The word *yoga* is derived from the Sanskrit root *yuj*, "to bind together", "to yoke", "to harness". Such yoking in the *Gītā* is meant in the sense of yoking oneself to the divine but it is not confined to the traditional views of *yoga* as a process of deepening meditative stages. The essential message of the Yoga of the *Gītā* is the *yoga* of the renunciation of the fruits of actions and the desire for results, goals, rewards – even if such results of actions are good. Such *yogic* renunciation is applied to knowledge, to all actions, and to devotion, which makes it wider in appeal and open to all irrespective of gender, class or caste. Aurobindo made the rather relevant point that "the yoga of the *Gītā* is a large, flexible and many-sided system with various elements, which are all successfully harmonized by a sort of natural and living assimilation".[53] In 2:39, Kṛṣṇa tells Arjuna that he will explain to him the "integrated wisdom" by which he will "cast off the bonds of *karma*." *Integrated* here is *yukta* and *wisdom* is *buddhi*, the discriminating factor in mental processes. The state of the *buddhi* will dictate the character of the being, so if it is subject to desires and aversions and the results of actions, it will accumulate *karma* and necessitate rebirth. If, however, the *buddhi* can be purified so as to be pure wisdom, pure intellect, it will be detached from desires, aversions, goals, egoism and *karmic* results. We saw a very similar idea in the Sāṃkhya-Yoga of the previous chapter. Such a detached, *integrated, buddhi* is essential whether the focus is on knowledge, actions or devotion and can be said, I think, to be the kernel of the Yoga of the *Gītā*. Kṛṣṇa states as much in verse 48 of the same chapter, chapter 2: "Act steadfast in *yoga* . . . having abandoned attachment, being the same in success and failure: this equanimity is called Yoga." When the mind is poised in a state of perfect equilibrium, is placid and calm, *yoga* is taking place.

Yoga is a state of one-pointed, single-minded (2:41) intellect, "a motionless meditation, a silent collecting of the mind's powers".[54] It is *samādhi*, the highest meditative state (2:44), a consciousness characterized by "steady intellect" (2:53) and that is "satisfied in the *ātman*" (2:55). From 2:47 to the end of that chapter, Kṛṣṇa describes the being with steady intellect who is without desires, attachments, longings and who "entirely withdraws his senses from sense objects, like a tortoise withdraws its limbs" (2:58). Otherwise, "the mind that follows the wandering senses has its wisdom carried away like the wind carries away a boat on water" (2:67). The expression *yoga-yukta*, "integrated in *yoga*" appears repeatedly in the text to depict not just one on the pathway to liberation but also one who is liberated, synonymous with "the *ātman* integrated in the Yoga of Brahman" (5:21), and "integrated in the *yoga* of renunciation" (9:28), both pointing to renunciation of the fruits of actions.

This Yoga, Kṛṣṇa says in the opening few verses of chapter 4, is an imperishable and ancient Yoga that had been given by him to ancient sages and handed down in succession, and such Yoga does not exclude the traditional practices that were to be systemized later by Patañjali: "Excluding all external contacts and [fixing] the gaze between the eyebrows, making equal the outgoing and incoming breaths moving within the nostrils, with senses, mind and intellect controlled, the sage, having liberation as his supreme goal, who is free from desire, fear and anger, he truly is liberated for ever" (5:27–8). Chapter 6 is devoted to *Dhyāna-Yoga*, the "Yoga of Meditation": the opening verse iterates the core message of the *Gītā* that true *yogins* act without dependence on the fruits of actions and in verse 2 Kṛṣṇa says: "Know that which is called *yoga* . . . as *saṃnyāsa*. Truly, no one becomes a *yogin* who has not renounced *saṃkalpa* [intention]." Mehta aptly commented here: "Yoga is concerned with Action, not with reaction or with mere activity. Action in terms of Yoga arises from the Ground of Inaction, a negative state where all mentation has come to an end."[55] It is renunciation of *saṃkalpa*, intentions in the mind, that brings this about. The *saṃnyāsin* epitomized ascetic wanderers devoted to inaction and total focus on the divine. The *Gītā* rather favours *tyāga*, which also means "renunciation" and, while occasionally synonymous with *saṃyāsa*, is also used more specifically in the text, especially in chapter 18, of renunciation of the fruits of action. Kṛṣṇa can be critical of ascetic praxis at times, but here in 5:2 it is *saṃkalpa* that is the important issue for it is "determination", "will", "intention" or "purpose" – all indicative of the egoistic thought behind an action that is undertaken for a specific outcome – and verse 4 makes it clear that if *saṃkalpa* is renounced then so is attachment to sense objects or actions. The *ātman* as the "friend of the self" (v. 6) is the means by which attachment to the fruits of actions can be abandoned: it is the *yoga* of the *ātman* (v. 19). Krishnaraj comments attractively on this verse: "There are no thoughts wafting in and out; the wind has died down; the thoughts have died down; there is that little steady flame of the Self; there is oneness, stillness, absolute freedom."[56] Later, in chapter 6, Kṛṣṇa explains how the *yogin* should formally practice, where that practice should be and the accompanying bodily posture, and just as in classical Yoga Īśvara was a focus for the *yogin*, so Kṛṣṇa says the *yogin* should be thinking on him (v. 14). A clearly articulated definition of what the *yogin* should do is to be found in verses 24 and 25 of chapter 6: "Having abandoned without reserve all desires born of *saṃkalpa* and by the mind completely restraining all the senses on every side, little by little let him gain quietude by the intellect held firm. Having made the mind fixed in the *ātman* let him not think of anything." Such praxis, Kṛṣṇa says, will bring "contact with Brahman" (v. 28), enabling the *yogin* to know and be established in Brahman (5:20).

The outcome of true *yogic* praxis is to be able to recognize the *ātman* everywhere, an experience that unifies all creation and the Self with Brahman, though not, in my view, non-dualistically: "Whoever sees things everywhere as the same as his Self, Arjuna, whether pleasure or pain, he is regarded as the highest *yogin*" (6:32). But it needs constant practice, *abhyāsa*, and constant non-attachment, *vairāgya*, to bring about a one-pointed and single-minded intellect. Many times Kṛṣṇa offers himself as the focus of *yogic* praxis. In verses 6–8 of chapter 12 Kṛṣṇa says: "But whoever worships me, renouncing all actions in me, regarding me as supreme, meditating on me with single-minded *yoga* , for them whose thoughts are set on me, ere long . . . I become the deliverer from the ocean of mortal *saṃsāra*. Fix the mind on me only, place the intellect in me. Without doubt, you will live in me alone hereafter." One is reminded of Mahatma Gandhi's words here: "To love God means to be free from attachment to any work."[57] The message is of exclusive devotion to Kṛṣṇa, the deliverer of his devotees. The Yoga of the *Gītā* is one that centres on the divine and the *yogin* focused on Kṛṣṇa merges with him: "Of all *yogins*, whoever worships me endued with faith, with the inner *ātman* merged in me, he is deemed by me to be integrated in the Self" (6:47). Hill's comment on this verse is important and he was critical of commentators who misinterpreted the *Gītā* here: "They do not realize that the superiority of the true *yogin* consists in the combination in himself of all those elements which up to the time of the Bhagavadgītā had been too severely separated; and especially in the addition of devotion, *bhakti*, as the most essential element of all."[58] Indeed, when Kṛṣṇa tells Arjuna to remember him and fight (8:7), Theodor believes the ensuing battle is "a kind of a *yoga* practice, involving sense restraint, mental control and an inner meditation on Kṛṣṇa".[59]

How, then, does Kṛṣṇa's teaching on *yoga* help Arjuna in his despondency? Indeed, in 2:54, Arjuna asks Kṛṣṇa this when he wishes to hear of the sage of steady intellect. It is Arjuna's state of mind, intellect and ego that has to change in order for him to become such a sage himself. For the *yogin* this would take constant practice, endeavour and repetition to bring the three under control,[60] but Arjuna's need is more urgent. So Kṛṣṇa tells him he has to be firm, still, steady and immovable, *acala*, in his inner self by fixing his mind on the passive *ātman* within so that he is settled in stillness. When he is of steady thought with a mind that cannot be shaken, controlling his thoughts so that he is without attachment to anything in the world of senses because his own senses are restrained, without dualities, without the *guṇas*, he will acquire the intuitive wisdom that will enable him to act from a state that will view all beings – friends and enemies – as the same. In such a state of settled wisdom, with senses restrained, his being will be integrated, *yukta*, because he will have realized the *ātman*: "When the perfectly controlled consciousness rests only in the *ātman*, without longing, without desires, then is one said to be *yukta*" (6:18). Arjuna should, thus, aim at being integrated in the Self, in the *ātman*, with a one-pointed, single-minded intellect. Thus: "he who is free from the notion of egoism, whose intellect is not tainted, even though he slays these worlds, he does not kill, he is not bound", Kṛṣṇa tells Arjuna (18:17). Arjuna can engage in the battle provided he has this untainted *buddhi* without fear of reaping adverse *karma*, indeed, any *karma* at all. And again in 18:49: "He whose intellect is everywhere unattached, who has subdued his self, whose desires have fled, by renunciation he attains the supreme perfection of freedom from *karma*." So Kṛṣṇa tells Arjuna he can "take refuge in *yoga*" (4:42) for he, Kṛṣṇa, is the giver of the *yoga* of intellect, "the integration of the soul" as Zaehner translated it,[61] to those who are integrated (10:10). But Kṛṣṇa does not advise Arjuna to tread the path of asceticism, *tapas*, the often adopted life of the *yogin*, and is critical of those who abuse their bodies with crippling austerities, even categorizing those who do so as demonic (17:5–6), and as *tamasic* (17:19). He also says that the true *yogin* is superior to those who practise *tapas* (6:46) though, as we shall see, he will not object to the "austerity of knowledge" (4:10) or that practised by steadfast men who do not desire the fruits of their actions (17:17): it is the *kind* of *tapas* that is important and relevant to the pursuit of *yoga* and that is mainly desireless action or fervent devotion.

Jñana-mārga: The path of knowledge

At the close of each chapter of the *Gītā*, the contents are described as having presented Brahma-*vidyā*, "knowledge or science of Brahman", and "the teaching of *Yoga*" through dialogue between Kṛṣṇa and Arjuna. Each of the chapters is a *Yoga* and so each is entitled "The *Yoga* of . . .", the knowledge in the chapters being of Sāṃkhya; Action, Knowledge; Renunciation; Meditation; Knowledge and Realization; the Imperishable Brahman, Royal Knowledge and Royal Mystery; Manifestation; the Vision of the Universal Form; Devotion; the Differentiation of the *Kṣetra* and the *Kṣetrajña*; the Differentiation of the Three *Guṇas*; the Supreme *Puruṣa*; the Differentiation of the Divine and the Demonic; the Differentiation of the Threefold Faith; Liberation and Renunciation – eighteen chapters in all, each supplying knowledge of its title though with much material that overlaps between chapters. Clearly, the Yoga of the *Gītā* is not just about practice but is fundamentally rooted in knowledge.

Knowledge is *jñāna* and is the deep intuitive knowledge, wisdom and understanding that brings experience of *ātman* and of Brahman. Knowledge as a pathway to God is, therefore an important feature of Hinduism and was the way accepted by the non-dualism of Advaita Vedānta and by Sāṃkhya and was important enough for each of the philosophical schools to set out means by which true knowledge can take place. The *Gītā* depicts it as a path that is only for the few, because it is steep and very difficult. For developing Sāṃkhya, the *jñāna-mārga*, the "path of knowledge", meant the renunciation of *all* actions in order to concentrate on inner knowledge, and while the author of the *Gītā* is tolerant of such a way to Brahman, it favours disciplined *activity* alongside knowledge, even if both ways achieve the same end. We find Kṛṣṇa in 12:4 saying of those who concentrate on the path of knowledge and focus on the *nirguṇa* Brahman, "... having restrained all the senses, even-minded everywhere, rejoicers in the welfare of all beings, they also obtain me", so while one has controlled his senses and is the same in joy or sorrow, he is not passive in that there is concern for the welfare of others. On the path of knowledge, concentration, meditation and suspension of the senses to all except the inner *ātman* are the means, and Kṛṣṇa says much to endorse such praxis as we saw above. It is more the suspension of activity with which he takes issue: indeed, such a means to ultimate knowledge would hardly suit Arjuna's current position. Renunciation of the fruits of actions was what Kṛṣṇa advocated, not the renunciation of action *per se*. Satischandra Chatterjee and Dhirendramohan Datta, among others, pointed out that the discipline of *yoga* and the principle of renunciation often encouraged the acquisition of positive traits that were in many ways world-affirming, for example the development of compassion and generosity.[62] The *Gītā* certainly endorses such engaged *yoga* rather than total renunciation and its practice of austerities as exclusive means of developing the spiritual at the expense of the physical. Control of the self is easier when it is withdrawn from the world than when it is bombarded by the sense stimuli of daily existence.

Kṛṣṇa tells Arjuna in 3:3: "In this world, the twofold path previously told by me, sinless one, was the *jñāna-yoga* of the Sāṃkhyas and the *karma-yoga* of the *yogins*", so he identifies himself with both and legitimizes both. In chapter 4, Kṛṣṇa outlines many different pathways, different *yajñas*, as he terms them, all of which are legitimate means to Brahman. True knowledge can be a fire that burns up desires and reduces all *karma* to ashes, so the *Gītā* endorses being established in knowledge: that knowledge is of the *ātman*, which, once known, obliterates any delusion. Even the sins of "the most evil of all people" can be obliterated "by the raft of knowledge" (4:36). And yet he says: "All action in its entirety culminates in knowledge" (4:33), which rather suggests that knowledge *and action* are necessary: this would certainly be pertinent to Arjuna's position. But knowledge is clearly extolled by Kṛṣṇa: "Truly", he says, "there is nothing here as pure as knowledge. In time, he who is perfected in *yoga* finds that in his own *ātman*. The man of faith, devoted, having restrained the senses, obtains knowledge. Having obtained knowledge he goes rapidly to supreme peace" (4:38–9). And again, in 5:16: "But those whose ignorance is destroyed by knowledge of the *ātman*, their knowledge, like the sun, reveals "*That*" Supreme." Clearly, knowledge of the *ātman* is the key to liberation.[63] Thus, the *jñānin* is highly praised by Kṛṣṇa, who says that "the *jñānin*, ever integrated, devoted to the One, excels. Truly, I am exceedingly dear to the *jñānin* and he is dear to me ... the *jñānin*, in my opinion, is my very *Ātman*. He is integrated in the *Ātman* and is truly established in me, the supreme goal" (7:17–18).

Chapter 7 of the *Gītā* deals with knowledge and realization, *jñāna* and *vijñāna* respectively. The object of both is God, Brahman, *jñāna* being the understanding of the nature of God in this chapter and *vijñāna* carrying a greater intensity of meaning; it is the *realization* and *experience* of the very *essence* of God in all things. Mehta usefully saw *jñāna* as quantitative and *vijñāna* as qualitative, the quantitative being a gradual process and the qualitative a sudden awakening, with the latter a perception of the whole.[64] But in chapter 7 Kṛṣṇa combines the two as necessary for liberation (v. 2). Then, in chapter 13, Kṛṣṇa describes true knowledge as knowledge of himself as the *Kṣetrajña*, the "Knower of the Field", and the *kṣetrajña* as the *ātman*, and what he and the *ātman* witness or know is all of *prakṛti*, the *kṣetra*, the "field". Kṛṣṇa, however, is the knower of knowers and of whatever can be known. Knowledge of the *ātman* will make an individual a knower, *kṣetrajña*, that will enable differentiation between *prakṛti* and its impermanent world of the senses and the ultimate Reality that is Brahman. So chapter 13 ends with the statement: "Those who, by the eye of knowledge know the distinction between the *kṣetra* and the *kṣetrajña* and liberation from *prakṛti* of being, they go to the Supreme" (v. 34). The ability to understand all existence as unified by Brahman is critical and is the highest *sattvic* knowledge: "That knowledge by which one sees the imperishable Reality in all beings, undivided in the divided, know that as *sattvic*" the text has in 18:20, a verse that Zaehner described as "the *Gītā*'s consistent metaphysical doctrine".[65]

The inimical inhibitors of knowledge are desire, delusion, ignorance, slavery to the senses, ignorance of the *guṇas*, and the binding of the *guṇas* on personality, *karma*, and also the *māyā* that is *prakṛti*. In chapter 18, Kṛṣṇa explains how knowledge, the actions that stem from it concerning the objects of knowledge, and the agent who carries out action are all related to the *guṇas*: the more *sattvic* the knowledge, the more one will be able to see Reality as a unified whole and the highest knowledge that is Brahman. As far as Arjuna is concerned, he has to overcome his thinking in terms of opposites, so Kṛṣṇa says to him: "The *Vedas* deal with the three *guṇas*. Be without these attributes, Arjuna, without the pairs of opposites, ever remaining in *sattva*, free from acquisition and preservation, established in the Self" (2:45). It is the *guṇas* that create the desire to differentiate between this and that – in Arjuna's case between fighting and abstention from fighting, what he thinks is evil and good. These dualities cannot be reconciled from the point of view of matter, but they can be reconciled from the point where all dualities dissolve and are harmonized. Dualities, *pairs of opposites*, are manifestations of time and space. If they can be transcended, then the true Self that is beyond time and space can be experienced, concomitant with Kṛṣṇa, with Brahman. Then, Arjuna will be free from the relative field of opposites and, in being free, whatever he gains or loses will be of no consequence to him. Aurobindo called this state "spiritual impersonality".[66] Being without dualities means being even-minded, and not being a slave to desire and aversion – choices between one thing and another and all the various shades in between, which delude the senses. The knowledge that has been imparted to Arjuna by Kṛṣṇa is that he should fix his mind on the *ātman*, conquer any attachment to sense objects so that he can act egolessly detached, stay anchored in the Self, repel desires, be free from the pairs of opposites, and correct the deluded perspective of reality as consisting only of *prakṛti* and the three *guṇas*. The result of such a state of knowledge is the ability to see the oneness, the unity of all things with a one-pointed, single-minded intellect. The *ātman* that is in all unites all since Kṛṣṇa abides in all beings. In chapter 11, when Arjuna sees the universal form of Kṛṣṇa: "There, in the body of the God of Gods, [Arjuna] saw the whole universe, divided into groups, existing as one" (v. 13). Some translators bring out the unity more forcefully here. Thus, Lars Martin Fosse translates as "united in its infinite diversity".[67] So Kṛṣṇa tells Arjuna that by knowledge "you will see all beings in your *ātman* and also in me" (4:35).

The renunciation, *tyāga*, normally associated with the path of knowledge and the *jñāna-yogin* is not the abandonment of action but of the fruits of actions and the desire for certain outcomes. This is certainly the *jñāna-yoga* of the *Gītā*, where action *per se* is not renounced, only the results of it, and is deemed by Kṛṣṇa to be better than knowledge alone and better than *yogic* meditational praxis (12:12). Arjuna needs *detached* action, action undertaken dispassionately, but to avoid action is not viable. *Pure* knowledge found in the *ātman* will enable such dispassionate action.

Karma-mārga: The path of detached action

As was seen in earlier chapters, the law of cause and effect, *karma*, suggests that a person has to be reincarnated in order to reap the results – negative and positive – of the accumulation of all his or her actions in life. And since physical and mental actions are taking place in every waking moment of life, the effects that have to bear fruit necessitate countless lifetimes. So at death it is only the body that ceases to exist, while the subtle accumulated *karma* of one's existence in the present and past lives continues into the next. Each *jīvātman*, then, creates for itself its specific personality in the next existence and the sorrows and joys that are the fruits of its actions in past existence(s). *Karman* is literally just "action" and meant ritual action for specific results in *Vedic* sacrificial ritual. Such ritual action is mentioned many times in the *Gītā* and Kṛṣṇa is sometimes critical of it as results orientated and *karma* producing. *Karma* also occurs with other nuances of meaning in the text but its most important usage is as action *and reaction*, cause and effect, that is to say action that is connected to a result, to a consequence of action, and it is in this sense that the results of actions accrue to an individual.

The path of action in the *Gītā* thoroughly upholds the necessity for action, but this action is not that of simply following scriptural injunctions. And Kṛṣṇa has been critical of the inaction of the renouncer who, after all, has to have an aversion to action, and that is sure to reap *karma* just as much as desire. Rather, *karma-yoga* of the *Gītā* is an expanded view of action as undertaken without initial desire and, importantly, without any desire for effects. This the *Gītā* terms "inaction in action and action in inaction" (4:18), "anchored to the silence of the inner Being" as Maharishi Mahesh Yogi put it,[68] but it also involves wisdom, knowledge, in order to acquire the right perspective of reality that allows egoless action. The combination of the two culminates in the true *yogin* of the *Gītā* as opposed to the *yogin* who withdraws from the world and tries not to act at all. It is a complementary combination of the *jñāna* of Sāṃkhya and the *karma*, practice, of Yoga. Nevertheless, there are those who would favour one or the other: Śaṃkara, of course, favoured the former, seeing *karma-yoga* as "for the ignorant only".[69] Renunciation of all action, the pathway of the *saṃnyāsin*, is still a legitimate way, but Kṛṣṇa says: "Both renunciation and *karma-yoga* lead to the highest good but of these two, the *karma-yoga* is superior to renunciation of action" (5:2). It is the action in inaction aspect of *karma-yoga* that makes it superior – acting from the equilibrium of the still passive *ātman.* In Mehta's words: "The flower of Wisdom can bloom only in a mind that is utterly silent, and it is only the wise that know what Right Action is."[70] Such action in inaction is an *inner* renunciation of the fruits of action, enabling outer action to continue. As Theodor put it: "This interesting reconciliation of the two otherwise contradictory ideals, offers a system which intertwines social responsibility and action in the world, with a deep sense of spirituality and relinquishment of worldly attachments."[71]

The *karma-yoga* of the *Gītā* has two dimensions: *action should be done without a view to results* and *one should not be attached to the action.* To attempt to lessen the importance of *karma-yoga* in the *Gītā* would be perverse. No solution can occur for Arjuna, the warrior about to go to war, that does not include action: but the *Gītā* synthesizes such action not only with knowledge, *jñāna*, but also with devotion, as we shall see below in the case of the latter. In chapter 2, Kṛṣṇa seemed to Arjuna to have favoured *jñāna-yoga* and at the beginning of chapter 3, which is devoted to *karma-yoga*, Arjuna asks Kṛṣṇa why on earth he should act so terribly in the coming war if Kṛṣṇa thinks knowledge is superior? Arjuna cannot at this point deepen his consciousness to the point where he is rooted in the *ātman*, where differentiation evaporates into equilibrium. As Kṛṣṇa says: "he who knows this indestructible, eternal, unborn, imperishable . . . whom does he cause to be slain? Whom does he slay?" (2:21). To be established in the consciousness of the inner Self is to be beyond the influence of actions and to become a non-agent: no desires or results of actions are thought of at this deep level in the Self. Action is a feature of *prakṛti* alone; the *ātman* is the passive and non-active observer only. In a classic statement of one of the central tenets in the Gītā, Kṛṣṇa says: "In action only you are right not at any time in its fruits. Let not the fruits of action be the motive nor attachment to inaction" (2:47).[72] Arjuna is attached to inaction, *akarma*, at the moment and is attached also to the fruits of his actions. To dispel such attachment, Arjuna will need to become "steadfast in *yoga*" (2:48), a *karma-yogin.* Once integrated in his inner Self – which is what *yoga* seeks to achieve – Arjuna will be able to engage in the field of action, being disciplined and egoless.

Unless rooted in the *ātman*, action is impossible to avoid: even if the body is inactive, the mind is not because, says Kṛṣṇa: "No one remains even for a moment without performing action, for all are helplessly made to act by the *guṇas* born of *prakṛti*" (3:5). Action, change and flux is the nature of *prakṛti*; we eat, breathe, sleep, and all is action and "even maintenance of the body would not be possible with inaction" (3:8). But to perform action free from attachment is, Kṛṣṇa says, to attain the Supreme (3:19), otherwise: "One whose mind is deluded by egoism thus thinks, 'I am the doer'" (3:27). Kṛṣṇa adds, too, another dimension that combines *karma-yoga* with focus on himself: "Renouncing all actions in me," he says, "with the consciousness centred in the intrinsic *ātman*, free from hope, free from ownership, having become free from fever, fight!" (3:30). The focus on Kṛṣṇa here is reminiscent of the theistic contemplation of Īśvara that we saw in classical Yoga in the previous chapter. But Kṛṣṇa, as we shall see when we turn to *bhakti* and the devotional path below, will have a much more intimate relationship with those who renounce actions in him.

In one verse (3:20), Kṛṣṇa says "you should perform only having in view the welfare of the world (*loka-saṃgraha*)". While it looks at first glance that such words advocate results of actions, the thought is more that desireless actions should be undertaken within the world scene and not separated from it – a point advanced by those who extol the *karma-yoga* pathway over any other. And again, in 3:25, Kṛṣṇa says: "As the ignorant act attached to action . . . so the wise should act unattached, wishing the welfare of the world." Selfless action is the message of this verse, and if acting *unattached*, yet *wishing* world welfare is somewhat incongruous, Bina Gupta is probably right when she points out: "The larger the goal one entertains, the lesser would be the concern for the agent's own fortune and fame."[73] The message of the *Gītā*, as we saw above, is to be *integrated* (*yukta*), steady and anchored in the *ātman* so that one is not swayed by sense stimuli and remains free from attachments to the results of actions: "Having abandoned attachment to the fruits of action, ever content, depending on nothing, even engaged in action, he does not do anything. Without hope, with consciousness and self controlled, having abandoned all possessions, doing merely bodily action, he incurs no sin. Content with what comes to him by chance, free from dualities, free from envy, even-minded in success and failure and though acting, not bound" (4:20–22). *Karma* will not bind the one who renounces fruits of actions according to the Yoga of the *Gītā*. The *karma-yoga* path, then, is far-reaching in its expansion out to the welfare of the world – a concept that in Radhakrishnan's view was suggestive of the unity of the world and the interconnectedness of society.[74]

It is from Brahman that *prakṛti* receives the power of manifestation and action and from whom the constantly changing *guṇas* bring about causes and effects, and yet, "these actions do not bind me", Kṛṣṇa says in 9:9, "like one sitting indifferent, unattached in those actions". Beings, too, must aim to achieve the same kind of indifferent and unattached action that is not results based, but it is difficult to be involved in the world and always act without desires and aversions for specific results. So, importantly, Kṛṣṇa offers focus on himself in actions, "be intent on actions for me", he says, "by doing actions for me you will also attain perfection" (12:10). In this way, actions are performed only by *prakṛti* while the *ātman* remains separate as the non-doer because it is focused on Kṛṣṇa who, though the source of *prakṛti*, ever remains still and passive: "But he who rejoices only in the *ātman*, who is satisfied in the *ātman*, the man contented only in his *ātman* does not have anything to do", Kṛṣṇa says (3:17). Chidbhavananda wrote: "The river is active until it reaches the ocean. On merging in it its functioning is over. Likewise the functioning of the mind is over in its being resolved in Atman. Bliss is the characteristic of Atman. The mind which is set in the Self is therefore ever satisfied, pacified and blissful. The finale of all activities is for the mind to rest in the Atman."[75] In such a state of peace, actions cannot bind one, and Kṛṣṇa says: "Actions do not taint me: nor have I desire in the fruit of action. He who knows me thus is not bound by actions" (4:14): to know the *ātman* is to know Kṛṣṇa and Brahman and if actions are focused there they are focused in passivity not in the *prakṛtic* world of actions. In chapter 18, Kṛṣṇa says that even when undertaking actions involved with *yajña*, sacrifice, the act of giving, *dāna*, or renunciation, *tyāga* – necessary undertakings according to Kṛṣṇa – they should be carried out by "renouncing attachment and fruits" (18:6). He tells Arjuna that self-control and renouncing the fruits of actions are "my Yoga" (12:11). But focus on Kṛṣṇa is the epitome of the *karma-yoga* path in the *Gītā*: "Mentally renouncing all actions in me, having me as the highest goal, resorting to *buddhi-yoga*, always have your thoughts fixed on me" (18:57),[76] Kṛṣṇa tells Arjuna. When all actions are resigned in Kṛṣṇa, there can be no sense of ego, of "I", as the agent of actions or their consequences. The egoistic *jīvātman* is then lost and without attachment to actions and their results, no fruitive *karma* can be reaped: the individual has crossed beyond the *guṇas*. Kṛṣṇa says in 9:27: "Whatever you do, whatever you eat, whatever you offer in sacrifice, whatever you give, whatever austerity you practise . . . do that as an offering to me." Chidbhavananda said here: "The panacea for all evils of earthly life is presented here. To change the secular into the sacred is the only way to metamorphose the human into the divine."[77] In similar vein, Gandhi said: "To love God means to be free from attachment to any work."[78]

Bhakti-mārga: The path of devotion

Despite the fact that Śaṃkara interpreted the entire text of the *Gītā* as advocating first and foremost the path of knowledge and the identity of the *ātman* with Brahman, the very fact that Kṛṣṇa is manifest on Earth with a *personal* relationship with Arjuna belies a monistic understanding of the *Gītā*. Phrases such as "he comes to me" in 4:9, where Kṛṣṇa is speaking of the one with true knowledge of his nature, express the dualism between God and human, the drop merging into the ocean, but not becoming the ocean itself. Other phrases that Kṛṣṇa uses suggest the same – "absorbed in me, taking refuge in me" (4:10), "you shall come to me, liberated" (9:28), "my devotee . . . enters into my being" (13:18) – and a wonderfully clear personal dualism occurs in 6:30, where Kṛṣṇa says: "He who sees me everywhere and sees all in me does not become lost to me and I do not become lost to him." Thus, even though the individual self is transcended to reveal pure *ātman*, identical to all others in essence, the *ātman* is only a part of God not the whole of God: God is not lost, nor does he vanish at liberation; he continues to be experienced. In 7:17, Kṛṣṇa says "I am exceedingly dear to the *jñānin* and he is dear to me", which expresses the dual relationship that is to be found even on the path of knowledge as well as in *bhakti*, "loving devotion", not just from man to God, but from God to man also. It is a verse that blends *jñāna* with *bhakti* rather well.

The word *bhakti* comes from the Sanskrit *bhaj*, "to serve" or "to worship" and *bhakti* as the path of devotion is immensely important in the *Gītā* because it is not exclusive and so is open to women and to all classes regardless of birth providing the devotee takes refuge in Kṛṣṇa. *Bhakti* is of the nature of supreme love, of longing, surrender, trust and adoration; it involves the whole being. For devotion to God to obtain there can be no question of identity with God. The theme of *bhakti* develops with increasing momentum as the *Gītā* proceeds, especially from 6:30 on. Here is a doctrine of salvation and a salvific God, faith in whom can give hope for an end to the cycle of continued births and deaths. And this is not a God that is distant and remote but one that descends to live among humankind, one to whom praise and offerings can be given and one who is believed to *respond* with love to his devotee. Kṛṣṇa does not claim that other paths – knowledge, ritual, worship of other deities – are wrong, but he says that the Supreme "is truly attainable by exclusive *bhakti*" (8:22). He speaks of "single-minded *bhakti*" by which he is able to be known and even seen in his cosmic form (11:54). The reciprocal relationship between man and God is found in 9:29 where Kṛṣṇa says "whoever worships me with *bhakti* they are in me and I am in them". Notably, however, God is always greater than all: "Also, whatever being is manifest, prosperous or powerful, know that to be a manifestation of only a fragment of my splendour" (10:41). The individual always remains dualistically related to God but God is always greater, irrespective of how beautiful, powerful, glorious or god-like an entity may appear. Kṛṣṇa speaks of the undeluded, all-knowing individual who "worships me with his whole being" (15:19). In a verse that combines *jñāna* and *bhakti* rather well Kṛṣṇa says: "And whoever studies this sacred dialogue of ours, by him I shall have been worshipped by *jñāna-yoga*" (18:70). The key word here is *dialogue*, the two-way instruction of the teacher and the questioning of the pupil indicative of the dual relationship between Arjuna and Kṛṣṇa, man and God. Clearly, knowledge, *jñāna*, can be combined with *bhakti*, and the *yogin* whose senses are restrained and who is integrated "should sit intent on me", Kṛṣṇa says in 2:61, and "thinking on me, integrated" in 6:14.

Kṛṣṇa also infuses the path of the *karma-yogin* with *bhakti*: "But for men of virtuous actions, whose evil is at an end, they are liberated from the delusion of the pairs of opposites, worship me, steadfast in vows" (7:28). And in the final verse of chapter 11 (v. 55), Kṛṣṇa says: "He who does actions for me, who looks on me as the Supreme, who is devoted to me, is freed from attachment, is without enmity towards all creatures; he comes to me." Even Śaṃkara justifiably described this verse as "the essential teaching of the whole Gita-sastra".[79] With the mind and intellect fixed on Kṛṣṇa alone, Arjuna will be able to fight.

Bhakti involves a willingness to surrender to God and Arjuna does just that in 2:7 where he recognizes that his nature is afflicted with pity for those he has to fight. He is profoundly confused about *dharma* and he asks Kṛṣṇa as a disciple to teach him what is right: he *surrenders* to Kṛṣṇa. "Taking refuge" in Kṛṣṇa is another way of expressing such surrender, as Kṛṣṇa says to Arjuna in 18:66, "take refuge in me alone" and on many other occasions.[80] Taking refuge in Kṛṣṇa is said to enable an individual to transcend the *māyā* of *prakṛti* (7:14). Moreover, it is often stated in the text that it is by Kṛṣṇa's grace that men are liberated. The idea is hinted at in many verses as, for example, when Kṛṣṇa says he will aid those on the path to him who are devoted to him (9:22), even if the person is evil but offers Kṛṣṇa exclusive devotion (9:30). And when Arjuna realizes the true nature of his friend, he bows and prostrates before Kṛṣṇa imploring forgiveness, the word here being *prasāda*, "grace" (11:44). Indeed, it is by the grace of Kṛṣṇa that Arjuna is permitted to have an experience of his cosmic form (11:53). The word "grace", *prasāda*, is used explicitly by Kṛṣṇa in 18:56 of those on the path of *karma-yoga*: "Continually doing all actions taking refuge in me, by my grace he obtains the eternal, imperishable abode". The same grace is offered to Arjuna in 18:58 where Arjuna is told that if he fixes his thought on Kṛṣṇa, by that divine grace he will overcome all obstacles, and in verse 62, Kṛṣṇa says that grace will give Arjuna supreme peace and the eternal abode. Finally, at the close of the text in verse 73, Arjuna's delusion is destroyed and he recognizes that his freedom from doubts and regained memory of what is right is due to the grace of Kṛṣṇa.

Faith, *śraddhā*, is also a facet of *bhakti*. Kṛṣṇa says: "Those who constantly practise this teaching of mine, full of faith, not contentious, they are also freed from actions" (3:31). To be free of actions here means to be capable of detached action and, therefore, freed from fruitive *karma*. Faith, then, is not confined to *bhakti* but is expected from the *karma-yogin* and also the *jñāna-yogin*: "Of all *yogins*, whoever worships me endued with faith, with the inner *ātman* merged in me, he is deemed by me to be integrated in the Self" (6:47). The verse is an explicit statement of theism, of the dualism between God and human and combines *bhakti* with *jñāna-yoga* very well. With some justification, Theodor considers it to be "no doubt one of the *Bhagavad Gītā*'s peaks".[81] Faith, said Radhakrishnan, "is the aspiration of the soul to gain wisdom. It is the reflection in the empirical self of the wisdom that dwells in the deepest levels of our being."[82] In one place (4:39) Kṛṣṇa suggests that faith even precedes knowledge. It seems, too, that devotion may well follow knowledge, for Kṛṣṇa says: "I am the Source of all, from me everything evolves. Understanding this, the wise worship me full of affection" (10:8). Here, *full of affection* expresses an intensity of focus on the divine. It is an expression variously translated – "full-filled with warm affection",[83] "immersed in devotion",[84] "endowed with faith",[85] "filled full with love"[86] – all of which are strong indicators of *bhakti*. Indeed, whatever the choice of religious worship, Kṛṣṇa enhances and strengthens that worship (7:21). "He, steadfast in that faith, engages in worship of it and truly obtains from that those desires really ordained by me" (verse 22). Thus, if deities are solicited for help in the fulfilment of desires, it is actually Kṛṣṇa that is the source of that fulfilment, though faith is, again, a prerequisite. In fact, Kṛṣṇa says that if devotees worship other gods full of faith in those gods, they are really worshipping him, though by the wrong method (9:23) and: "In whatever way men approach me, so do I reward them", Kṛṣṇa says in 4:11. It seems that whatever path is chosen, faith is crucially important: "Those who, fixing the mind on me", says Kṛṣṇa, "ever steadfast, worship me, endowed with supreme faith, these I consider are the most steadfast" (12:2). Faith is, thus, inextricably woven with *bhakti* and Kṛṣṇa says: "Truly, whoever follows this immortal *dharma*, as declared, endued with faith, regarding me as supreme, devotees – they are exceedingly dear to me". This statement in 12:20 is explicit in its expression of *bhakti* and the reciprocal relationship between human and divine that it entails. Chapter 17 of the *Gītā* relates faith to the three *guṇas* and says that each individual's type of faith is dependent on the nature of that individual, so the faith a person has, its degree of intensity, quality, and resulting actions, will be related to the inner personality. A *rajasic* individual, for example, is hardly likely to have the faith or life-style of the mystic, and will be prone to a religious path that will focus on rewards of actions: faith and personality are inextricably linked. Even austerities, *tapas*, are related to the *guṇas* in this chapter, as well as giving, *dāna*. As Aurobindo said: "We create our own truth of existence in our own action of mind and life, which is another way of saying that we create our own selves, are our own makers."[87]

The intense devotion that epitomizes *bhakti* is encapsulated in some of the most beautiful phrases. Kṛṣṇa says to Arjuna "you are my devotee and friend" in a verse (4:3) in which he tells Arjuna that his words are a "supreme secret", a phrase that enhances the closeness and intimacy of God and man. Debroy aptly annotates "kindred soul" for friend here.[88] In chapter 12, which is devoted to *bhakti-yoga*, Kṛṣṇa speaks of those who are dear to him and those who are *exceedingly* dear are said to be ones who follow his immortal *dharma*, who have faith, who regard him as supreme and who are devotees (12:20). Where an individual sees Kṛṣṇa in all things, Kṛṣṇa says that person "does not become lost to me and I do not become lost to him" (6:30). The exquisite and well-known verse: "Whoever offers to me with devotion, a leaf, a flower, fruit, water, that I accept, offered with *bhakti* by the pure-minded" (9:26) lifts the normal understanding of religious rituals of the time to a whole new level that incorporated the simpler, natural expressions. And the following verse that says that every action should be done as an offering to Kṛṣṇa serves to "change the secular into the sacred" and "to metamorphose the human into the divine" as Chidbhavananda put it.[89] "Fill your mind with me, be devoted to me, sacrifice to me, bow down to me alone", Kṛṣṇa tells Arjuna, "then you shall come to me" (9:34). And then, in what seems to me the most exquisitely beautiful words in the *Gītā* to epitomize the personal relationship between God and man, Kṛṣṇa says to Arjuna: "Hear again my supreme word, most secret of all: you are beloved by me" (18:64). Here is the heart of the theism of the *Gītā*. This love of God for the devotee is presented as the *supreme* or highest utterance: it is tantamount to saying "I love you dearly", and is one of the most beautiful statements of Kṛṣṇa in the *Gītā*. The answer to Arjuna's problem is clear from Kṛṣṇa's words in the following two verses: "Fix your mind on me, be devoted to me, sacrifice to me, pay homage to me, then, in truth I promise you, you will come to me, for you are dear to me. Renounce all *dharmas*; take refuge in me alone. I will liberate you from all evils; grieve not." And, more specific to the situation, Kṛṣṇa says: "Therefore, at all times, remember me and fight. With mind and intellect fixed on me alone, you will no doubt come to me" (8:7).

Liberation

I think it is critical to note that the paths I have stranded out for the reader are not mutually exclusive by any means, and so many times Kṛṣṇa unites two or more pathways for Arjuna. It seems the blend of knowledge and non-attached actions that are devoted to Kṛṣṇa is the ideal, but not the sole means to liberation, *mokṣa*. To lose the egoistic perceptions of the world, the dualities which that perception engenders, and the desires and aversions that create ego, were the goals of *Upaniṣadic* thought. It is a *liberation*, a *release*, "the supreme perfection" (18:19), from all that restricts, binds, and holds humans in ignorance and cycles of death and rebirth. The term for such liberation is *mokṣa*. The early *Vedic* idea of liberation was that at the end of one existence, the souls of the good would be recompensed in Heaven and those of the evil in a somewhat underdeveloped Hell. The later idea of reincarnation is sometimes combined with this concept, so that an individual is believed to go on experiencing the results of *karmic* action accumulated in life in the context of some heavenly or hellish abode, only then to be reborn in order to reap the fruits of other positive and negative *karma*. The *Gītā* accepts this composite view even for the gods who, when their good *karma* is exhausted will be reborn in the land of mortals. Liberation for them, as for any mortal, is to be devoid of any *karma* at all. Kṛṣṇa seems to say, too, that those who conduct *Vedic* ritual with desires for results will have only Heaven as the final goal (2:43, 45; 3:11, 12; 9:20, 21).

From what we have already seen of the pathways to liberation, Kṛṣṇa's teaching to Arjuna is that he must operate in the world in an egoless way. As the point at the centre of a circle is equidistant from all points on the circumference, so the liberated being is equally poised between all dualities of life, observing all, actively engaged in all, but not from the level of desire for one thing rather than another, or preference for this as opposed to that. But what is certain is that the *Gītā* is against renunciation of all action *per se*. A measure of knowledge is necessary to understand that all matter is impermanent, and that the sensory reactions to it need to be stilled; and Kṛṣṇa says that it is the one "who is the same in pleasure and pain, wise, he is fit for immortality" (2:15). To be immortal is to rise above the ever-changing phenomenal world and to be neither this not that – the *neti neti* of the *Upaniṣads* – and so unruffled by dualities. To abandon the fruits of action is again and again the message of the *Gītā* and it is this that brings liberation, no matter which pathway one has chosen. Once the mind is controlled the individual can be egoless, "satisfied in the *ātman*" (2:55) and "settled in stillness" (2:70).

Throughout the *Gītā*, liberation is associated with Brahman many times. It is described as "the state of Brahman" and "Brahma-*nirvana*" (2:72). *Nirvana* is a Buddhist rather than a Hindu term and many see the expression as a direct borrowing from Buddhism,[90] but *state of Brahman* (*Brahmi-sthiti*) is thoroughly Hindu.[91] In 4:24 we find the words, "Brahman will be attained only by him who is absorbed in action that is Brahman". Those who perform true, egoless sacrifice, "go to the eternal Brahman" (4:31), or are "fit for becoming Brahman" (18:53), as is a sage integrated in *yoga* who "quickly goes to Brahman" (5:6). We find expressions such as "knowing Brahman" and "established in Brahman" (5:20), "integrated in the Yoga of Brahman" (5:21) to describe the liberated state, and again in 5:24, we find "Brahma-*nirvana*" alongside "Brahman become" (also in 6:27). 5:24 has been described as "the crest of the teaching" on renunciation"[92] and says: "One who has happiness within, who rejoices within also, one who is illuminated within, that *yogin* attains Brahma-*nirvana* and is Brahman become."[93] "Brahma-*nirvana*" occurs again in verses 25 and also in 26, where it is said to exist "on all sides for those who have realized the *ātman*". At times, it is said of the liberated one that "he becomes Brahman", or "one may obtain Brahman" (18:50), but I do not think this is meant in a monistic sense. In 13:30 we find: "When he sees the whole variety of beings resting in the One and radiating out from that alone, then he becomes Brahman". The sense here is more of identity with the *ātman* as a result of which one sees the same *ātman* in all things and all beings and, so, becomes in unity with Brahman. Later in the same chapter it is said "they go to the Supreme" (verse 34). Dualism is maintained with the personal Kṛṣṇa as the focus, as in 14:26, where Kṛṣṇa says: "And who serves me with unswerving *bhakti-yoga*, and crosses beyond these *guṇas*, is fit for becoming Brahman." The synonymy between Brahman and Kṛṣṇa as the goal of liberation is brought out admirably in 18:54 and 55: "Brahman become, of serene self, he neither grieves nor desires; the same to all beings, he obtains supreme devotion to me. By devotion he knows me, what and who in truth I am: then, having known me in truth, he enters me forthwith." Knowledge of Brahman here involves knowledge of the *nirguṇa* and *saguṇa* Brahman and realization of the *ātman* – *what and who in truth I am. Enters me* is in the dual sense; there will always be a differentiation between the devotee and Brahman and individuality is retained, even if the ego is lost. The *ātman* is not the totality of Brahman but can become panentheistically at one with it.

On occasion, the Brahman of the final goal seems to be the *nirguṇa* Brahman: "But those whose ignorance is destroyed by knowledge of the *ātman*, their knowledge, like the sun, reveals "*That*" Supreme" (5:16). Similarly in the following verse, 17, which we have met earlier, the avoidance of the actual word "Brahman" seems to imply the *nirguṇa* Brahman as the state of liberation: "With their intellect in "*That*", their *ātman* in "*That*", established in "*That*", with "*That*" for their supreme goal, those whose sins have been dispelled by knowledge go, not again returning." But Kṛṣṇa also says that: "Those who strive for liberation from old age and death, having taken refuge in me, know completely that Brahman, the intrinsic *ātman* and all action" (7:29). This verse states quite clearly that Brahman can be *completely* known, suggestive of an understanding of ultimate Truth for those who engage in action that is non-attached and non-fruitive. Kṛṣṇa has already said earlier in 7:21–3 that he is the force behind all worship, whatever form that takes and, here, he is the means and refuge by which his higher Self as Brahman can be known. Kṛṣṇa calls himself the "Supreme Resplendent Puruṣa" and says that whoever meditates on him with integrated thought through practising *yoga*, will go to him (8:8, 10) and reach "that imperishable goal" (15:5).

More personally, the theism of the *Gītā* is epitomized in such times when Kṛṣṇa says the liberated one "comes to me" (4:9), with a clear dualism between man and God. Other similar phrases are found: "absorbed in me" (4:10), "the peace abiding in me that culminates in *nirvana*" (6:15), and since Kṛṣṇa says he abides in all beings he should be worshipped as such. The *yogin* who does this, Kṛṣṇa says, "abides in me also" (6:31). The very fact that Kṛṣṇa uses the word "worship" in association with liberation is indicative of the dual, personal relationship with God that liberation brings. He speaks of those *yogins* that worship him with faith, "with the inner *ātman* merged in me" (6:47), expressive of the thorough theism that pervades the *Gītā*. While worshippers of gods go to the gods, Kṛṣṇa tells Arjuna, "my devotees go to me" (7:23; 9:25, 28). Indeed, the state one is in death was believed to dictate the birth conditions and environment of the next existence, and Kṛṣṇa says: "And whoever goes forth at the time of death, leaves the body remembering only me, he attains my state of being, there is, here, no doubt" (8:5). Since the mind is usually unclear at death and incapable of directing its own thoughts, little control of the last moments is inevitable. If God is not the centre of thought during life, he is unlikely to be so in death. The aim for those wishing liberation is to think of nothing else but Kṛṣṇa, constantly remembering him (8:14): once having attained Kṛṣṇa there is no more rebirth (8:14, 15). For those whose thoughts are set on him, Kṛṣṇa says, "I become the deliverer from the ocean of mortal *saṃsāra*" (12:7), and what is attained Kṛṣṇa depicts as, "the supreme primeval abode" (8:28), "my supreme abode" (15:6), "the supreme goal" (16:22) and, Kṛṣṇa says, "he attains to my being" (14:19). Liberation into Kṛṣṇa's abode is open to all his devotees: "Indeed . . . those who take refuge in me, even those of an inferior birth – women, *Vaiśyas*, and also *Śūdras* – they also attain the supreme goal" (9:32). This quite exceptional verse bars no one from either the path to liberation or liberation itself. Women and low-class Hindus were deemed to have a *guṇic* make-up without any *sattva* and inferior births because of past *karma*: despite the *Gītā* being predominantly concerned with the high-class male, this particular verse is sensitively notable. The *Gītā* opens its religion to all in perhaps the most important expression of theism and what devotion to Kṛṣṇa as a personal God can mean – "you will come to me", Kṛṣṇa says, "for you are dear to me" (18:65).

The *Gītā* implies that liberation from the endless round of rebirths and from suffering in the world is brought about not by one path in particular but by their complementary, or even independent, nature. Knowledge is needed, desireless actions are also needed, as is devotion to God. The overall message, however, is that it is essential to give up attachment to the fruits of actions, but not actions *per se*. But we should never lose sight of the pragmatic context of the *Gītā*, and that is the dilemma of a warrior who is despondent at having to engage in a fratricidal war that is not of his own choosing. Knowledge will help to answer his dilemma, but ultimately he must *act*. Arvind Sharma makes this point when he says of apparent contradictions in the *Gītā*: "They arise because Kṛṣṇa uses as many points of view as he can to convince Arjuna to fight, and in such a situation these points of view may be contradictory. What is required is that they should all converge (on the issue at hand), not that they should merge."[94] Of course, such a view would depend on whether the focus of the author was on Kṛṣṇa's teaching pegged onto Arjuna's dilemma, or *vice versa*. But as Sharma later states, the *Gītā* not only presents one of the paths of *karma*, *jñāna*, or *bhakti* as pre-eminent at different points, but may synthesize two at one point and another two elsewhere, or treat different ones as ancillary to a third only for the third to be itself ancillary at another part of the text.[95]

The colophons at the end of each chapter describe the *Gītā* as a *śāstra*, a teaching or science about Yoga, but we cannot pin it down to one precise aspect of *yoga*. We can only accept that the *Gītā* deals with many dimensions of it and leaves the individual to choose the best path. For Arjuna, that will surely be an active one that does not concentrate on the results of that action, through sacrificing action to Kṛṣṇa. So there is no need for Arjuna to deny the world, but just to have the right knowledge about it; not to be attached to its transience or to what one wishes to gain from it. Focus on God assists any pathway, but this is by no means emphasized in the earlier chapters of the *Gītā* and we find now knowledge, *jñāna*, now action without desire for results, *karma-yoga*, coming to the fore. Then, too, we could argue for liberation encompassing oneness with the *nirguṇa* Brahman without attributes or encompassing the more personal, *saguṇa*, Brahman who is describable. Nevertheless, the emancipated Self is at one with the universe but not obliterated by it. That Self has an expansion of knowledge that encompasses the universe and all other Selves and the nature of God as the Source of all matter and spirit. Such is "having become Brahman" or "attaining Brahma-*nirvana*". Becoming Brahman is suggestive of unity or identification with Brahman, and if the *Gītā* does not shy away from such an idea, its overall theology only suggests partial unity and identity, never full monistic fusion.

Sprinkled throughout the *Gita* are to be found descriptors of the liberated state as an eternal abode of bliss, perfection and peace. There is no sense of an obliteration of experience that prevents such supreme states being realizable – again, pointing to a dual relationship between God and human. To be liberated is to come to Kṛṣṇa who is Brahman, to enter his being, reaching the highest realm where all is calm, all is peace. "The marks of such a man are balance and steadfastness of judgement, clearness of vision, independence of external things, and utter satisfaction in the Self."[96] The liberated Self rises beyond nature, knowing that Self as separate from it. Pleasure and pain and all such pairs of opposites are experienced with equanimity; all things are the same and the liberated one acts in the world without thought of gain or reward, in total equilibrium.

7

Devotional Hinduism
The Rise of Vaiṣṇava *Bhakti* in Medieval India

For many Hindus, divinity is not some remote transcendent abstraction but is intimately present in the universe, in the world itself and in every creature and being that inhabits it. God is present in the abundant natural phenomena from the stars and planets to the tiny seeds concealed within plants, flowers and trees that give form to our planet. Difficult ascetic pathways to an indescribable Absolute have little part to play where God is believed to be immediately present, everywhere, and easily approachable. "Indeed", writes Frederick Smith, "reason and doctrine, the recipients of much greater literary and analytical attention, are rarely the pulsating heart of religion."[1] The key to such an easier pathway is *devotion*, devotion that is inclusively fluid and available for anyone regardless of gender and caste. Devotion here is far deeper than its English term suggests. In Hinduism, it is *bhakti*, and while this is an all-encompassing term with wide and subtle interpretations dependent on different sects, as we saw in the previous chapters it generally embodies a depth that transcends ideas of devotion in the sense of normative religious praxis: *bhakti* connotes a depth of love that necessitates total surrender of the self.

The meaning of *bhakti*

Bhakti is derived from the Sanskrit root *bhaj*[2] which has wide connotations of, for example, to share, divide, apportion, receive, participate in, experience, be part of. *Bhaj* can also mean to love, be devoted to, choose, serve, adore, honour, worship, and the like. Putting the two together suggests that the abstract noun *bhakti* can mean adoration or, as I prefer, loving devotion, but the two meanings of *bhaj* are suggestive of a reciprocity in the meaning of *bhakti* and a two-way loving devotion as there was in the *Gītā* between God and human, human and God. *Participation* is an attractive nuance of meaning alongside loving devotion and it seems to me it depicts rather well the power of *bhakti* to experience the love of God as much as to offer love to God. Additionally, the ideas of sharing and participation are suggestive of communal congregation and of the coming together of groups of people in order to offer love to God and experience his love in return but, at the same time, there is much that is *personal* and *individual* about the *bhakti* experience. Adding all these ideas together, Mariasusai Dhavamony defines *bhakti* as "mutual participation and communion between God and man in love and surrender".[3] Karen Pechilis Prentiss, as many, has taken up the term participation as the meaning of *bhakti* because she says: "Participation signifies the bhaktas' relationship with God; it is a premise of their poetry that they can participate in God by singing of God, by saying God's name, and in other ways."[4] As we shall see below, her words are certainly born out in the songs of the medieval poets.

Despite attempts to define *bhakti*, different sects and individual poets had different ideas as to what constituted devotion in terms of praxis. Just as love takes many expressions in the human realm so, too, it varies in its religious expressions. *Bhakti* is endemic in popular religion but it is also subject to time, place, occasion and tradition. Diversity is part of its essence because manifestations of the divine are infinitely diverse, and the way in which the divine is conceived of will colour the nature of the approach of the devotee. Texts such as the *Bhāgavata Purāṇa* even list different types of *bhakti*.[5] The many poet–saints who inspired the *bhakti* movements were themselves influenced by varied and eclectic mixtures of traditions that ranged from the *Vedas* to folk religion and even Buddhism, Jainism and Islam. These varied expressions of *bhakti* will become clear later in the chapter.

Nirguṇa and *saguṇa bhakti*

While *bhakti* is mainly a personal approach to a personal God it may also be deep devotion to an impersonal Brahman, much along the lines of Advaita Vedānta in some cases. Such is *nirguṇa bhakti*; *nirguṇa*, as we saw in earlier chapters, being the divine "without attributes". Many great saints, or *sants* in North India were *nirguṇa bhaktas* – famous names from about the fifteenth century such as Ravidās, the low-caste poet, Guru Nanak of Sikhism, Kabir, and Nāmdev. These *sants* composed and sang devotional songs to an impersonal Absolute, though not without using the more devotional term "God" at times. Kabir, for example, called God by Viṣṇu's names of Rāma and Hari. Their approach to the divine was more mystical, esoteric and inward focused. Occasionally, *nirguṇa bhaktas* incorporated asceticism and renunciation into their perspective of devotion. The tensions between the transcendent absence and accessible presence of God have amounted on occasion to what Rachel Fell McDermot describes as "emotional upheavals"[6] and we shall often find an overlap between *nirguṇa* and *saguṇa* concepts of deity.

Space does not permit me to peruse *nirguṇa bhakti* and it is *saguṇa bhakti* that I want to take up in this chapter, that is to say, the conception of the divine as *saguṇa*, "with attributes". Here is the God that can be described, anthropomorphized, loved, intimately worshipped, adored and participated in. Essentially, the *saguṇa* God is a personal God who, in one form or another, comes close to his devotees. There is an *intimacy* between God and devotee, for God is believed to love his devotee to the extent that the devotee loves him. Such devotion is monotheistic because other divine beings, while mainly accepted, become merely the mythical backdrop to the divine object of intense devotion. There is no fusion of God and soul here and separate existence for each devotee is maintained: Creator is always greater than created, but is intimately there with each devotee, who remains always dependent on his or her Creator. But it is a Creator that is richly presented in mythology, rich in personality and present locally as much as cosmically. It seems to me that some kind of personal devotion to the divine has been endemic throughout the long pre-history and history of Indian religious praxis, perhaps not monotheistically, but the expression of devotion between individual and the divine is probably the most natural in religious feeling.

Bhakti became integral to religious devotion and, as we shall see below when I examine the poetry of the medieval saints, the content draws heavily on daily life, thus reaching out to all individuals. Individuals could come together and share their lives in communal devotion, united by singing devotional songs that had meaning for both individual and group. Importantly, the use of the vernacular by *bhakti* poets meant that religious expression was grounded in local language. In Prentiss' words: "Through the use of regional languages, the author is localized in a language and in a place where the language is spoken. Bhakti is represented to be as natural as a mother tongue; just as no one lacks a first language, no one is incapable of bhakti. By implication, God is also in that place, inside us or near us, for bhakti is a theology of participation in God and the ability to reach God, whether God is imagined as nirguṇa or saguṇa."[7] *Bhakti*, thus, is expressed in local traditions that are close to ordinary people, that they can understand and in which they can participate. Dhavamony describes it as "the warp and woof of popular Hinduism, for it underlies, and to a greater or lesser extent inspires, popular worship."[8] *Bhakti* reached out to ordinary people and made them the centre of devotional religion not peripheral observers. Prentiss describes *bhakti* as "a theology of embodiment" in that "the range of human experiences is religiously significant if grounded in the experience of God".[9] *Bhakti* transformed religious praxis from external observed ritual to personal and communal participation and love of God in all life's experiences.

The origins of *bhakti*

There is no clear opinion as to when exactly *bhakti* movements began. Some suggest the first or second century CE[10] but it is in the medieval period from about the sixth to the twelfth centuries that major *bhakti* movements became conspicuously evident, especially in the South of India in the Tamil lands. However, *bhakti* was certainly evident earlier and extended later, flourishing long after the twelfth century. Most suggest that it originated in the South in Tamil Nadu where two outstanding factors characterised it: first, the use of the vernacular and, secondly, monotheistic devotion which, I think, are at least two indicators of some sort of *terminus post quem* for its positive beginnings. If *bhakti* were to be defined simply as devotion to a personal God, there is certainly evidence of such in parts of the *Ṛg Veda*. In the *Śvetāśvatara Upaniṣad*, especially, we find evidence of a personal God of grace (*prasāda*), to whom self-surrender is advocated, the final verse of chapter six speaking of a man who has the deepest love (*bhakti*) for God (6:23): indeed, it is in the *Upaniṣads* that the word *bhakti* occurs for the first time and, to use Dhavamony's expression, the *Śvetāśvatara* "stands at the door"[11] of the *bhakti* movements. Both the *Kaṭha* and the *Muṇḍaka Upaniṣads* have a doctrine of the grace of God.[12] When used in the epics, the *Mahābhārata* and the

Rāmāyaṇa, *bhakti* is used to portray the love of a devotee for God *and*, at times, the love of God for the devotee, this latter being an important dimension and characteristic of medieval *bhakti*. And yet, in the *Mahābhārata* one does not gain the impression of *bhakti* as a valid or superior pathway to God as opposed to more orthodox ones. It is in the *Bhagavad Gītā* that *bhakti* is presented as a legitimate, easier, less orthodox and often superior pathway to a personal God who loves his devotees. And God in the *Gītā* is in human form as Kṛṣṇa, thoroughly anthropomorphized, the relationship between him and man, Arjuna, epitomizing the intimacy of God and his devotee. Nevertheless, to cite John Koller's wise words, "in important ways the Gītā has provided the foundation of religious devotionalism for the last twenty-two hundred years. But, again, this does not establish the beginnings of devotionalism".[13] And yet, while *Vedic* devotion was mainly propitiatory, aimed at rewards for devotion, and was obedient to orthodox praxis, the *Gītā* offered *bhakti* not just as a pathway but also as a final goal and opened that pathway outside orthodox classes and gender.

In the North, one devotional religion that informed the rise of *bhakti* was the monotheistic Bhāgavata cult, with Bhagavān as the personal God of grace and compassion whose devotees were as dear to him as he was to his devotees. The Bhāgavata religion in the North may have been present as early as the third century BCE,[14] and paved the way for worship of Viṣṇu and especially of Kṛṣṇa. The rise of Viṣṇu and of Kṛṣṇa as his most important *avatāra* began in the North perhaps before the fifth century.[15] But it was not here that *bhakti* first gained ground. Despite earlier manifestations of devotion, the characteristics of medieval *bhakti* run far deeper in the individual and communal psyches. True *bhakti* movements began in the Tamil South, perhaps springing from the indigenous Dravidian elements that were less inspired by the orthodoxy of the North. Orthodox devotion was recorded in the Sanskrit texts, but *bhakti* devotional hymns in the South retained the vernacular Tamil language and thoroughly Tamil contexts of place and time and of temple and shrine. In the South, it is Śiva who was the predominant personal God and when true *bhakti* arose, its eventual spread – century by century and territory by territory – was such that it characterized popular religious expression throughout all India, not as one movement but as multiple expressions of devotion to God, whether that was Śiva, Kṛṣṇa or Rāma or, indeed, though less so, the Mother Goddess: regional movements had their own preferred names for the God of their choice. What began as devotion in the regional language of Tamil led the way to devotional hymns in other vernacular languages throughout India. Śiva remained the deity most popular in the South, while in the North, Kṛṣṇa was favoured. A great many sects or *saṃpradāyas* developed, some of which I shall mention below, and the founders of those sects, the hymns they sang and the stories they told of their chosen God are widely celebrated in temples, iconographic art and festivals to the present day.

Characteristics of *saguṇa bhakti*

Bhakti became distinguished from ordinary devotion in so many ways. To begin with, it transformed the whole being into one focused entirely on God. Devotion became wholehearted and whole-minded. Love between parent and child, between lovers, servants and their masters and teacher and pupil were ways in which devotion could be normally understood and these examples from daily life were transformed into devotion to God and used to describe the love one has for God. It was not new to refer to God as a father or friend but now, God-intoxicated devotional love took on a whole new meaning. In short, in whatever way one understood love and devotion it was transferred to God in such a way as to be totally disinterested and *guṇa*-less, where the mind was totally God-focused and the self was surrendered. Any other kind of devotion was secondary and probably motivated by desires. And yet, true *bhakti* was mostly rooted in folk religion, local dialects, local understandings of divine myths and could contain songs composed or sung by illiterate devotees: the paramount nature of it was intense love of God to the exclusion of worldly desires, but *bhakti* was not removed from the sorrows and vicissitudes of the world. The concept of a highly personalized and anthropomorphized God stimulated the growth of images at temples and shrines, perpetuated the myths about the favoured divine being, and permitted patterns of devotional worship that were participatory and meaningful to the ordinary individual. Devotees could listen to tales of their God, chant his name and his attributes, remember him, offer service to him, worship him and dedicate themselves to him. In short, the ways in which a devotee could approach his or her God were natural without need for austerities, renunciation of the world, recitation of Sanskrit scriptures – many of which were forbidden to some – and complex prescribed ritual. Devotees did not want to become God, they just wanted to love God and they could do this in non-institutionalized and spontaneous ways. A. K. Ramanujan put the point superbly when he said: "The emphasis has shifted from hearing to speaking, from watching to dancing, from a passive to an active mode; from a religion and a poetry of the esoteric few to a religion and a poetry of anyone who can speak."[16]

Bhakti was and is not world-denying even if it should be self-less. Noticeably, even the desire for liberation, *mokṣa*, is absent from the mind of the true devotee. *Bhakti* is existential in that its literature deals with the difficulties of life: most of the concerns of ordinary life find space in the compositions of its founder poets. Such poets often led normal lives, were married and familiar with the cultural milieus in which they lived. Focused on God as they were, they retained their householder station and sang about their doubts, sorrows, lack of money, family problems and common life situations. *Bhakti* has a positive view of life in which the divine is thoroughly present: there is no need to renounce life for an inner, meditative knowledge of God when he is readily available to his devotees in his temples and images. Detachment from the world is not essential in *saguṇa bhakti*. The *Gītā* had recommended active involvement in the world in selfless, egoless action through abandonment of the fruits of actions, and medieval *bhakti* has the same kind of message: the world is the real creation of God and is not to be denied but embraced, for divinity is everywhere. The world provides abundant opportunities for the devotee to cultivate qualities such as selflessness, humility, harmlessness, truthfulness, compassion and so on. As R. N. Vyas puts it: "Bhakti is a transforming experience because a God-orientated attitude is produced in a devotee that brings about a complete change in the attitude of the latter towards the world."[17] Similarly, while selfish desires are lost through concentration on God, the "I" that offers devotion and service to God is certainly not lost. The dual relationship between God and devotee is immensely necessary in *bhakti*. As Lee Siegel says of the erotic *bhakti* movement in Bengal, "the sense of 'I' and 'mine' could be sanctified if one could say

'*I* worship and love Kṛṣṇa, longing for him to be *mine*".[18] Actions *should* be done for God, and it is such actions that will bring liberation: devotion is exteriorized through spontaneous temple and shrine worship, festivals and processions.

Love, *prema*, is at the heart of *bhakti* – love of the individual for God and of God for the individual. The duality of a loving relationship always has at heart the *personal* God. Govind Pande asserted that: "The quest for love thus necessarily assumes the personal reality of godhead and the immortality of the human person. Humanity for God and immortality for man are possibilities essential to the religion of love."[19] Pande's words are of immense importance, for the love relationship between God and human in *bhakti* extends eternally. That love, *prema*, is perfect devotion, something Nancy Martin says "is mediated through the body, experienced through the senses, with devotees employing metaphors of sight, sound, taste, smell, and touch. They even speak sometimes as if they were God, losing all awareness of themselves as separate, in an experience akin to possession by the divine beloved".[20] Such relationship, then, may even sometimes feel like union of lover and beloved because it transcends the self as we shall see later when I examine Vaiṣṇava *bhakti* specifically. Love pervades *bhakti*, which is why the devotion featured in *Vedic* texts is so different, because love is barely mentioned in earlier institutionalized texts:[21] the *Gītā* is the first remarkable exception. Mutual love is the medium through which God and human communicate in *bhakti*.

Whereas knowledge had always been an important ingredient of the pathway to liberation, it is often subordinated to love in *bhakti*. The *gopīs* who so loved Kṛṣṇa were simple milkmaids for whom complete devotion alone was all that was needed. Yet, the *Gītā* often saw devotion and knowledge as concomitant and many proponents of *bhakti* also saw knowledge as important. The difference between Kṛṣṇa as Lord in the *Gītā* and Kṛṣṇa as the amorous youth in the *Bhāgavata Purāṇa* perhaps reflects the respective view of knowledge and love. Love and devotion are *emotional* feelings but they need not be bereft of intellectual or philosophical knowledge. Yet, according to Wendy Doniger O'Flaherty, emotional *bhakti* can serve to suspend reason in cases where myth becomes irrational,[22] and there were many times when the proponents of *bhakti* such as poet–saints included irrational myths in their compositions. While there is always a certain tension between emotion and intellect in *bhakti* it was not usually a problem for the *bhakti* poets because they had a personal, describable deity to whom they were devoted on the emotional side, but whom they regarded as the all-powerful, omniscient Creator, Sustainer and Dissolver on the intellectual side. I think *bhakti* here portrays the balanced human who is neither all intellect nor all emotion but a natural blend of both. But there are times when the poets revealed thorough emotional outbursts in a kind of devotion described rather well by Vyas: "Devotion is a region where the surging emotions, feelings and sentiments rush spontaneously to touch the feet of the Lord in a spirit of blissful dedication and fragrant self-surrender."[23] The *experience* of God is essential to *bhakti* and the practice of singing praises to God, *bhajans*, which are set to music and accompanied by dancing, feed the emotional experience of the divine. Emotional, too, is the profound feeling of separation and longing that occurs at times when the divine is felt to be absent, just as the *gopīs* pined desperately for Kṛṣṇa when he disappeared. This is love in separation, *viraha*, which features extensively in *bhakti* poetry.

Certain practices are almost unanimously accepted in *bhakti*. I am listing here some that are outlined in the *Bhāgavata Purāṇa* and concern Viṣṇu but can be extended, too, to Śaiva practices. They are:

- Listening to stories about God, about his attributes and actions, so inclining the mind towards God. Such hearing is called *śravaṇa*.
- Recitation of the name of God, called *nāmā-japa*, is a key characteristic of individual and communal *bhakti* and focuses the mind meditatively on God. The essence of God and of his name are believed to be identical. Such repetition is superbly indicative of the non-institutionalized nature of *bhakti* because it can be undertaken in any place at any time provided it is done so with devotion. Becoming attached to the name of God means that one is less attached to the world.
- Remembrance, *smaraṇa*, is indicative of remembering aspects of God – his form, his attire, his beauty or even, in the case of Śiva, his grotesque images.
- Veneration of the feet of God occurs again and again in the hymns of the *bhakti* poets. It is a very interesting symbol, I think, for it exemplifies the emotional need to reach God, but at the same time, is suggestive of God as being far cosmically greater, far superior to the devotee. To be at God's feet is to secure not just refuge but also God's grace.
- Worship, *pūjā*, results in a massive impetus to the iconography of deities and the sacred places that house them. It also simplifies the process of approaching God and makes it a natural expression not a ritualistic observance. The *Bhāgavata Purāṇa* particularly emphasizes the establishment of images of God, permanent temples to house him and pleasant flower gardens to be used for processions and festivals. This text also speaks of the cleansing and anointing of the images and their circumambulation as well as the need for simple gifts given with full devotion. Faith, devotion and simplicity are the characteristics of true *pūjā*. In theory, such different methods of worship opened up a whole new way of approaching the divine.
- Prostration is also a means of showing humility towards God.
- Becoming a servant for God is expressive of surrendering the self to God, surrendering one's mind, actions and heart in utter devotion. Surrender is *prapatti*, a concept that denotes the utter helplessness of the devotee and the dependence he or she has on God. *Prapatti* means that one takes refuge in God, surrendering every action and its results to God. As such, it is one of the most important concepts of *bhakti*.
- Taking refuge in the Lord, *śaraṇa*, is a key characteristic of a *bhakta*. It epitomizes the need of the devotee to seek refuge at times of despair – often despair at feeling separated from God but also at times of great distress in life.
- *Kīrtan* is the communal chanting, singing and dancing before God. Stephen Slawek notes the antiquity of the word and its former non-musical meaning but, as he says, *kīrtan* "is associated with a musical setting of a text that glorifies a deity".[24] It sometimes overlaps with the term *bhajan* but what is really important about *kīrtan* is that it is practised by small groups of people. As Slawek comments: "The people who comprise these groups are among the anonymous masses of

India and usually know little of India's classical traditions of music. The musical materials of these kīrtans are drawn from regional folk music or mass-mediated popular songs."[25]

A true *bhakta* is replete with excellent qualities and so is able to engage altruistically and beneficently in society, being kind and compassionate to all. Indeed, the *Bhāgavata Purāṇa* lists many such qualities.[26] But, however hard a devotee may try, however much he or she may be devoted to God, it is always through God's *grace* that communion between the two can occur. We shall see this again and again in the works of the poet–saints.

As *bhakti* spread and movements arose in different locales, the importance of a teacher, a *guru*, became essential. Disciples attached themselves to one *guru* or another to the extent that particular schools, traditions, sects or *saṃpradāyas* – each devoted to a specific deity – emerged, and teachings were handed down from generation to generation. *Gurus* had realized God and, therefore, were in a position to teach those they initiated into the *saṃpradāya*. In some traditions, the *guru* was, and is still, venerated as God, as an incarnation of God or, at the very least, the representative of God. As such, the *guru* can offer grace to a devotee. Service offered to a *guru* is service offered to God. Such *gurus* are not necessarily *Brāhmins* but can belong to any class or caste: what matters is their *quality* of devotion. Such emphasis on the quality of devotion led *bhakti* along unorthodox pathways. *Brāhmin* supremacy counted for nothing and occasionally, high-caste individuals found themselves sitting at the feet of low-caste men or women or even untouchables. Then, too, experience of God in *bhakti* came spontaneously not as a result of orthodox praxis. As we shall see below, many of the saint–poets abandoned any kind of conventional norms.

Despite a considerable degree of unorthodoxy, there were occasionally disputes between the different *bhakti* traditions and there was intense exclusivity in relation to Buddhism and Jainism in southern India, even to the extent of violence. But one could be a *bhakta* irrespective of class or caste, gender or religious affiliation: universality and catholicity were hallmarks of *bhakti* traditions. *Bhakti* annihilated barriers, so becoming a means to God for all. And there was a genuine belief in the equal presence of the divine in all beings. Saral Jhingran expresses this so well when she writes: "Nowhere in Hinduism is this vision of one Self in all presented so forcefully and its practical implications accepted so honestly as in the *Bhakti* tradition. Perhaps it is so because this vision is affirmed in it, not at the theoretical level, but at the experiential level. God's indwelling all and the perception of all as divine are an integral part of the God experience that is sought to be achieved through devotion."[27] But *bhakti* has never eliminated caste discrimination in India and in many cases did not care to attempt to. Wendy Doniger's acerbic remark is rather apt, I think, when she says that "*bhakti* merely created another, alternative system that lived alongside the Brahmin imaginary, a system in which caste injustices were often noted, occasionally challenged, and rarely mitigated".[28] In the period of the growth of the *bhakti* traditions, however, devotees came together to eat and worship regardless of caste and gender but, inevitably, each tradition in a way became a caste itself. It is not unusual for low-caste devotees to be denied access to some temples even today and as traditions grew, they became more particular about food protocols and caste distinctions. We shall meet some women *bhaktas* below who completely defied the strict rules for women and as much as I would like to say that greater equality for women emerged as a result, it did not. Nor did it emerge as a result of male devotees having to approach God as if they were females in the *bhakti* traditions, something I shall be taking up further below. And yet, as Karen Pechilis so neatly says: "The voices of bhakti span many bodies, regions and genres, but the voices of the saints emphasize bhakti's own point of origination – the human heart. Bhakti's vitality is in its popular accessibility; it can be validly claimed as an identity by anyone."[29]

What of the final goal, liberation, in *bhakti* traditions? There is less to say of this because it was not seen as much different from the means, the path, to God as total dedication and devotion to God. This would not cease at the point of liberation but would continue. The only difference would be that the long periods of painful separation from God would disappear and there would be no need for rebirth in any form whatsoever. Blissful experience at the feet of God in his Heaven from where singing of praises and service to God with unceasing devotion continue as the ultimate aim: in short, the means to God and the goal merged as one. Perfect devotion, *para-bhakti*, brings direct experience of God that never ceased.

The *Bhakti-Sūtras*

At the beginning of the second millennium CE, two outstanding philosophers compiled separate *Sūtras* that became standard works on *bhakti*. These two were Śāṇḍilya and Nārada,[30] the former being slightly earlier in date than the latter. Both men emphasized emotional love of God. Śāṇḍilya's *Bhakti Sūtras* placed *bhakti* as far superior to the paths of knowledge, action or disciplined pathways incorporating *yoga*. His view of *bhakti* was one of total attachment to and affection for God. He believed that *bhakti* was superior because it was inclusive and not just a religion for the literate upper classes. Nārada also believed *bhakti* to be the best and highest means of approaching God. He also accepted that the lowest individual could attain perfection, immortality and perfect peace, all of which are experienceable but indescribable. The *bhakta* was expected to surrender his or her self completely to God to the extent of being intoxicated with God's presence – so much so that the effect may be to burst into song, cry spontaneously but, certainly, be overwhelmed by joy. Nevertheless, it was through divine compassion that the devotee was accepted by God, for God chooses his devotees and sews the seed of devotion within them. Attachment to God was the key factor in Nārada's *Bhakti Sūtras* and that involved attachment to service to God; attachment as of a parent or wife; attachment to the attributes and majesty of God; attachment to remembering God at all times, and so on. Nārada seems to have eschewed much of orthodox ritual and certainly any class or caste distinctions.

Poet–saints

The poet–saints of medieval Hinduism were the means by which God entered the hearts of ordinary people. Such poets were, to use S. N. Bhavasar's phrases, "an open book of spirituality, the living example of the Life Divine". And, as he goes on to say, the poets were ordinary people who used ordinary language, words, metres, images and events to describe the God they loved.[31] Their poems reached out to poor villagers as much as to wealthy nobles and kings. These poets *sang* their compositions to all who would listen, and singing praises to God (*bhajans*) or listening to them came to be regarded as a superior way of worship. Some poets travelled widely throughout their homeland; others were attached to a specific place. They were very diverse and ranged from those who were more orthodox to those who were thoroughly unorthodox. They came originally from the South but when *bhakti* fervour travelled North, poets sprang up there, too, until they represented all parts of India. It was these poets who *participated* in God by bringing ordinary daily life into the realm of devotion: the poems are full of experiential, existential thought. Prentiss thus describes such saints as "the primary embodiment of *bhakti*".[32] They sang of God with intense emotion and those who heard their songs were inspired to love God, getting caught up in that emotional fervour. Since the wave of poetic devotion began in the South in the Tamil lands it is worth looking briefly at the nature of this southern phenomenon.

Tamil poetry

It was in the Tamil lands of South India that diverse expressions of *bhakti* poetry emerged. The Tamil language evolved in different pathways to that of Sanskrit so we should expect differences between the two. The earliest Tamil poetry dates from the first to third centuries CE[33] or earlier[34] and it would be expected that later *bhakti* poetry reflected some of the earlier Tamil literary conventions. The early poems were written and collected together in a genre known as Caṅkam (Skt. Saṇgam) and was of two kinds, *puṟam* "exterior", which were poems of war and statesmanship and of heroes and heroines, and *akam*, "interior", which were poems of personal and reflective experience, of the heart, and of secular love between man and woman mainly written in the first person singular. It is easy to see that it was the latter that informed much of the later religious *bhakti* poetry. *Akam* (Skt. *aham*) poetry could often be erotic and certainly romantic – characteristics that were employed by the later *bhakti* poets to portray intense love of God, who was often portrayed as the lover of the devotee, but also as the mother, child and father. The use of eroticism in Tamil *bhakti* poetry was, at first, unique to the South, having acquired the genre from earlier traditions. Thus, V. Subramaniam writes: "To sum up, the great Tamil saints enjoyed the emotional intensity of their God experience in erotic terms because Tamil poetic conventions encouraged it and they transformed it into various other modes of identification."[35] But the *bhakti* poets were also influenced by *puṟam* conventions that enabled them to depict God in terms of kingship and rulership. Put bluntly, Doniger writes: "Some of the early Tamil poems praise the god just as they praise their patron king; you can substitute the word "god" wherever the word "hero" or "king" occurs in some of the early royal panegyrics, and *voilà*, you have a hymn of divine praise."[36] What is striking about Tamil poetry is the use of nature to express ideas: it uses birds, flowers, trees and the relationship between lovers as symbolic means to portray ideas with what George Hart III terms "the technique of suggestion".[37] Applied to Śaivism and Vaiṣṇavism in the Tamil lands, the poetry blossomed into devotional fervour and expressive outpourings of love for God. Again, it was the vernacular dialects in which the *bhakti* poems were composed and were designed to be sung and listened to: they probably reflect considerable oral traditions. We do not have any trace of vernacular *bhakti* works before the fifth or sixth centuries[38] but it was certainly in the South that they first emerged.

So it is mainly to *akam* influence that we should look for the origins of Tamil erotic poetry, and as Ramanujan pointed out: "Thus when saints both male and female address love poems to Krishna and Śiva and adopt such feminine personae as wife (*kāntā*), illicit lover (*parakīyā*), trysting woman (*abhisārikā*), even Rādhā herself, they are drawing on a long, rich history."[39] And elsewhere Ramanujan noted the synonymy between one meaning of *bhaj*, the root of *bhakti*, as "to share a body, to copulate, to unite", and the passionate intimacy of erotic, sexual relationships.[40] Two groups of poets will deserve space in this and the following chapter; Śaiva poets from the beginning of the sixth century to the beginning of the tenth I shall leave until the next chapter, leaving Vaiṣṇava poets from about the beginning of the seventh century to be the subject matter of the remainder of the present chapter. The importance of Tamil *bhakti* poetry cannot be overestimated. God became embodied not just in the person of the poet–saint but also in the poetry itself, which is why the poems became an integral part of shrine and temple worship. Norman Cutler put this so well when he said: "All who participate in the ritual performance of the saint's poem re-enact the saint's experience of communion with the deity."[41] In time, *Brāhmins* who moved South introduced Sanskrit to Tamil culture paving the way for traditions to spread northwards and intermixing the two languages even in vernacular dialects. Inevitably, some fusion of local Tamil and Āryan deities occurred but Subramaniam believes that there was always a feeling that Tamil literature was superior.[42] Doniger, however, refers to the diverse "cultural bricolage" that came to inform *bhakti* poetry[43] but we should remember that the poems were the personal religious experience of those who sang them and, whatever the eclectic mixture that eventually informed the written poems, it was really the experiential dimension of the originals that spoke to the people.

Vaiṣṇava *bhakti*

Vaiṣṇavism is concerned with the worship of Viṣṇu as supreme and because Viṣṇu descends in the form of *avatāras*, particularly in the form of Kṛṣṇa, Vaiṣṇava religion is almost wholly dominated by *bhakti*, unlike Śaivism, and the worship of Śiva. Viṣṇu is a personal God, as is any form that he takes. His various descents offer different aspects of deity for the purpose of different modes of approaches to him but Kṛṣṇa remains the most popular form. And Kṛṣṇa is special because he is intimately approachable through his own life as a baby, child, youthful lover and majestic Lord, and is related to in these forms. Many different devotional traditions or sects, *saṃpradāyas*, emerged – the Śṛī-Vaiṣṇavas of South India, the worship of Viṣṇu as Viṭhoba in Maharashtra and that of Rāma in the North are the ones with which I shall deal below. Kṛṣṇa's life as a child and youth took place in Vṛndavana, which became immensely significant in Śrī-Vaiṣṇavism. Vṛndavana is not a *tīrtha*, a "crossing place" from the mortal to the divine: it is, rather, a "singular sacred space", as Steven Gelberg describes it.[44] It is an *emotionally* spiritual place that, according to Gelberg, may be as much in the mind as in spatial reality.[45] Kṛṣṇa's descent to Vṛndavana brought

Heaven to Earth making the place synonymous with Kṛṣṇa and everything in it – animate and inanimate – divine: Vṛndavana represents a wonderful unified divinity of all its animals, insects, trees, plants and human dwellers. As Gelberg puts it: "Vrindaban is the spiritual world, the eternal home of the eternal soul – a place beyond the endless mutability and the chaotic vicissitudes of the temporary, perishable material world."[46] There, in Vṛndavana, emotional devotion, immersion in the love of God becomes tangible, beyond time and normal space where the devotee can experience "the deep, sustained, sustaining thrill to the soul touched by ultimate and absolute realities".[47] It is, Gelberg believes, as much able to be experienced in the mind as in reality, as "a state of mind, a mode of being, a sacred space that is at once nowhere and everywhere, a place in the heart and in the soul".[48]

One of the most important scriptures that informs Vaiṣṇava *bhakti* is the Sanskrit *Bhāgavata Purāṇa*. It is one of the latest of the *Purāṇas*, being dated to around the ninth century CE. Although the Kṛṣṇa legends are located in the North, the *Bhāgavata* was written in the Tamil lands of the South. This text delineates acts of devotion into primary devotion that is supreme single-minded, whole-hearted devotion to God and secondary acts such as listening to, and chanting of, God's name, remembering him and the like. Its tenth book is a favourite devotional part, but the whole text encompasses the life of Kṛṣṇa who is given a variety of names in the text. "More than a story", writes Martin, "this drama becomes map and mirror for divine-human love, an eternal drama in which each devotee has a role."[49] The divine-human love is depicted as the love of the *gopīs* for Kṛṣṇa but the *Bhāgavata* includes in its long text every possible kind of love relationship and stories of different *bhaktas*. The *Bhāgavata* also presents us with all the different means of *bhakti*. So many of the expressions of *bhakti* are articulated in its pages – the dedication of all actions of body, speech and mind to God in surrender at his feet; listening to stories about God; chanting God's name; worshipping God's images; liberation through erotic passion for Kṛṣṇa. The concept of God is of Kṛṣṇa as a romantic lover, a much humanized deity, and in whatever form he is worshipped he is conceived of monotheistically. It is especially the *rāsa-līlā*, the story of the *rāsa* circular dance where each *gopī* unites sexually and spiritually with Kṛṣṇa that inspired early Vaiṣṇava *bhakti*.[50] But, then, there is an agony of longing when the *gopīs* experience separation from Kṛṣṇa and the *Bhāgavata* presents this as the highest form of devotion.

We shall see many of these above aspects in the works of the poets, and the *Bhāgavata* reflects, too, the universality of *bhakti* that is open to all classes and castes, to women as well as men and to the distressed and ill including, too, *Śūdras* and untouchables, even demons and animals. However, there seems no conscious aim to overthrow orthodox class and stage-of-life *dharma*.[51] The key message is that nothing can prevent a true devotee from religious liberation. In this sense the *Bhāgavata* is a this-worldly scripture open to all, and more so because it advocates service at temples, in temple gardens and at shrines as devotional practice. Its proximate goals are easily attainable, for complete devotion to God naturally expresses itself in active ways – the nine ways highlighted above, as well as emotional ecstatic dancing, playing musical instruments and, indeed, merriment. In the words of Vyas: "The Bhagavata has thus tried to achieve a transformation of human tendencies through the soft, pleasant, and perfumed path of devotion" and he further notes the massive influence of this Vaiṣṇava text as a religious inspiration.[52]

Śrī-Vaiṣṇavism

The Vaiṣṇavism of the South in Tamil lands is known as Śrī-Vaiṣṇavism, a name given to those who worship Viṣṇu only and to a community of worshippers that may date to the ninth century or earlier.[53] Its roots lie in the ancient Bhāgavata religion that elevated Kṛṣṇa as the deity Vāsudeva, and in the Pāñcaratra tradition, a Vaiṣṇava sect dated to the first or third centuries BCE. Rāmānuja, in the eleventh to twelfth centuries, formulated the theology and philosophy of Śrī-Vaiṣṇavism into a consolidated movement. The female consort of Viṣṇu, Śrī, is accepted equally with her consort. As noted above, the cults of Viṣṇu originated in the North along with Kṛṣṇa as his major *avatāra* with the favoured name of Nārāyaṇa. In its southern expression, however, it became a more exaggerated emotional devotion characterized by intense love. In R. Meena's words, "when the fire of *bhakti* was waning in the north and was going to be nearly extinguished, it was the flames from the south that revitalized it".[54] As far as the literature of Śrī-Vaiṣṇavism is concerned, the tenth-century *Ācārya*, Nāthamuni – of whom, more below – is regarded as the formulator. The main literary tradition is the poetry of the *Ālvārs*, which I shall examine in detail below, and it was Nāthamuni who gathered this together in one scripture. However, the myths of the Sanskrit *Purāṇas* and the epics were very much part of Śrī-Vaiṣṇava religion, and the Sanskrit *Vedas* were also accepted as legitimate scripture resulting in what is termed the Tamil and Sanskrit "dual *Vedānta*".

Śrī-Vaiṣṇavism emphasizes self-surrender, *prapatti*, as a means to receiving the liberating grace of God. Liberation itself is characterized by life in Viṣṇu's Heaven, Vaikuṇṭha, and a continued relationship of love, service and devotion to God. The concept of God always remains an intimate, highly anthropomorphic one. It is Kṛṣṇa especially who embodies such a concept and who becomes more separated from the cosmically conceived Viṣṇu. The divine pair, Kṛṣṇa and Rādhā, are the focus of Śrī-Vaiṣṇavism with their love-play, exquisite beauty and joyful lives. Their relationship in Vrndavana, their passion, playfulness, unity, serenity and love games are at the centre of the concept of deity in Śrī-Vaiṣṇavism. Siegel puts this perfectly: "In the history of Kṛṣṇaism profane love, sensual, human longing, became clearly related to sacred love. Within the Kṛṣṇa-cults a love-mysticism, a love-symbolism, developed. The human and divine became inextricably interwoven in love, in *bhakti*, no longer *bhakti* simply as 'devotion', but *bhakti* as fervent, passionate love."[55] Rādhā became the perfect devotee in her passionate, sexual love for Kṛṣṇa: hers was the elicit love of a simple cowherd girl offering herself totally to a divine prince. Rādhā, as all the other *gopīs*, was spontaneous and uninhibited in her love for Kṛṣṇa: there were no barriers such as marriage, social convention or caste; even *Brāhmin* knowledge was presented as inferior to the intensity of passionate devotion to Kṛṣṇa by the *gopīs*. The goal of the Śrī-Vaiṣṇava worshipper, then, was, and is, to become as a *gopī* in his or her devotion to Kṛṣṇa, and for men, that means thinking as a female when approaching God, losing attachment to the world and to anything other than Kṛṣṇa. As we shall see below, at times the *bhakti* poets used the voice of a female to express their devotion to God, sometimes assuming themselves to be one of the *gopīs* and at other times, Rādhā herself. It was tantamount to saying that the female is the perfect medium for emotional intensity.

I shall turn now to explore this depth of devotional passion in the poets that expressed it. Richard Davis does not exaggerate when he writes that such vernacular poetry "is quite likely the richest library of devotion in world literature, distinguished not only by its religious intensity but also by the great variety of psychological states and emotional responses it explores".[56] Not only did the *bhakti* poets express immense emotion that stemmed from the devotion of rather ordinary and occasionally extraordinary lives, but they included in their poetry many of the myths associated with their deity, reinforcing the rich store of legends and divine exploits that are so vivid a part of Hinduism past and present. These myths are often dramatized, set to music, sung in poetic form and immortalized in annual festivals. Telling and listening to stories about the Gods has become a major part of religious praxis; part of the important "remembering" God.[57] In what follows, space does not permit me to deal at any length with the lives of the individual poets. Suffice it to say, while we have to depend on hagiographic accounts for the lives, miracles and encounters of the poets, the hagiographic stories are immensely important aspects of regular worship, especially since they tell of how love of God transcends class, caste and gender and how *anyone* may approach God if he or she is full of love for him.

The *Āḻvārs*

Vaiṣṇava and Śaiva *bhakti* movements were coterminous in southern India from about the sixth or early seventh century CE. Hitherto, Buddhism and Jainism vied for popularity and while it is often said that the Hindu poets sang them out of Tamil Nadu, neither of these heterodox religions was entirely eradicated by *bhakti*. Vaiṣṇava *bhakti* was founded by twelve *Āḻvārs* and Śaiva *bhakti* by sixty-three *Nāyaṇmārs*, these poets defining religious belief and praxis for centuries to the present day. *Āḻvār* means "one immersed"[58] in love of God, an immersion that brought intense intimacy with the divine fuelled by utter love and devotion. The twelve *Āḻvārs* came from all sections of society. They were Poykai, Pēy, Pūtam, Tiruppāṇ, Tirumaḻicai, Kulacēkaraṉ, Toṇṭaraṭipoṭi, Periyāḻvār, Āṇṭāḷ, Tirumaṅkai, Nammāḻvār and Maturakavi. Of the twelve, eight were *Brāhmins*, one was a *Kṣatriya*, two were *Śūdras* and one was an untouchable: one was a woman. They were probably thoroughly indigenous Tamil natives and from Dravidian stock. Pēy, Pūtam and Poykai were the earliest; they sometimes venerated Śiva as well as Viṣṇu, though mainly the latter. The remainder devoted their poems to Viṣṇu and sometimes to Kṛṣṇa (whom they called Māyōn) and Rāma. All the *Āḻvārs* were regarded as incarnations of Viṣṇu or of his accoutrements such as the mace, conch and so on. The impact of these poet–saints on Tamil religion was immense. They mostly travelled exhaustively, singing in market places, towns, villages, at shrines and temples and, as Ramanujan put it: "Their pilgrimages, their legends, and their hymns (which they sang by the thousand) literally mapped a sacred geography of the Tamil regions and fashioned a communal self-image that cut across class and caste."[59] They created what Ramanujan termed "a unified field" of sacred space, "mapping man's country onto god's kingdom".[60] They made *bhakti* popular and their songs became", to use Pande's words, "imperishable monuments of love divine.[61]

Although they sang in local dialects, the *Āḻvārs* were influenced by Sanskrit literature. There is no evidence for any rejection of the *Vedas* and S. M. Srinivasa Chari even believes that part of the purpose of the *Āḻvārs* was to promote *Vedānta* philosophy to the ordinary populace through the medium of Tamil.[62] If so, then it was the theistic *Upaniṣads* that influenced them and not non-dual philosophy. They were also thoroughly conversant with the many Sanskrit myths about Viṣṇu that were to be found in the epics and *Purāṇas*. Additionally, the *Pañcarātra Āgama*, the text hailed by the devotional sect of Bhāgavatas from about the second century CE as the scripture that was superior to the *Vedas*, also influenced the *Āḻvārs*. This scripture emphasized the grace of God, the "descents", *avatāras*, of God, and his presence in images. The later *Bhāgavata Purāṇa* is likely to have been influenced by much of the *Āḻvārs'* devotional poetry. Their theistic devotional beliefs were systematized by the great theologian and teacher Rāmānuja. We must not forget, too, the certain influence of earlier *akam* and *puṟam* Tamil poetic conventions, particularly the love poetry or the poems of heroines. One major difference, however, was the use of the first person singular in the poems of the *Āḻvārs* to express their relationship with God: this was a new departure.[63] But, for all these prior influences, the poetry of the *Āḻvārs* became the Tamil *Veda*. The poems were collected together by Nāthamuni (whom we shall meet again below), early in the tenth century into a composite work. This was comprised of twenty-four sections, the full work being called the *Nālāyira-divya-prabandham* "Four Thousand Divine Hymns", but called simply the *Prabandham*, which is currently the main prayer and hymn book of the Tamil Vaiṣṇavites.

Beliefs of the *Āḻvārs*

While the *Āḻvārs* accepted Viṣṇu as the supreme God, their poems also included Kṛṣṇa as well as Rāma but in such a way as to be thoroughly monotheistic, for Kṛṣṇa and Rāma were regarded as manifestations of Viṣṇu. Such manifestations catered for all possible aspects of deity from the transcendent God to the playful Kṛṣṇa: where local temples were devoted to a particular deity, this divine figure was subsumed under Viṣṇu and any other deity from scriptural myth was subordinated and created by Viṣṇu. The *Āḻvārs* are often described as God intoxicated, ecstatic when God is near and plagued with anguish when he is not. Their view of Viṣṇu as a transcendent deity was of an infinite, imperishable Creator of all beings and the Protector and Dissolver of the universe in its many cycles. All things were particles of his being and part of him resided in each heart but nevertheless he always transcended the whole of creation while he also pervaded it. However, as a God of love, knowledge and bliss in his essential nature, ever beyond human comprehension, through his grace he took on the form of an *avatāra* with attributes, and even pervaded his temple images in order for his devotees to become intimately close to him. It is in this way that Viṣṇu became a very personal God with whom his devotees could enter into a relationship, which is why the poets could write of that relationship in the first person singular. Their deity was usually a local one as Narayanan writes: "It is the local deity whose beauty entrances the *Āḻvār*; it is to this deity that he sends messages of love; it is this deity whom he addresses as a lover and with whom he seeks union. While Kṛṣṇa and, to a lesser extent, Rāma are the focus of a devotion that is simultaneously erotic and submissive, an overwhelming number of songs, where the *Āḻvār* assumes the role of 'heroine,' are addressed to Viṣṇu enshrined in a temple."[64] Such a focus on temple images meant that the *Āḻvārs* could describe the wonders of Viṣṇu's appearance, personality and attributes, as well as incorporating into their poetry the wondrous deeds of Viṣṇu immortalized in myths. They wanted a direct *vision* of Viṣṇu, which they believed could be granted by God through his grace, love, compassion, friendliness, generosity and accessibility – these being the main attributes that they ascribed to Viṣṇu. And because their songs portrayed their intimate relationship with God, their hymns became the means for others to know God also. They described Viṣṇu as sweet, as honey and nectar, depicting his apparel, his lotus feet, his lotus-petal eyes, his coral lips, his ornaments and weapons – all of which said to the listener that the poets *had* had a vision of God. It was especially the feet of God that symbolized the whole body of the divine and the *Āḻvārs* often spoke of devoting themselves to the feet of the deity. All such manifestations and attributes were the effects of the grace of a transcendent God who, in his essential nature has no such forms.

The manifestation that is most accessible is, of course, Kṛṣṇa and it was he to whom the *Āḻvārs* frequently related in their personal relationship with their God and that may be as Kṛṣṇa's mother, as one of the *gopīs* or, in the case of the only female *Āḻvār*, as his bride. In the Tamil poems of the *Āḻvārs*, the consort of Kṛṣṇa became his cousin, Nappinnai, rather than Rādhā and Kṛṣṇa's sporting with the cowherd girls was as much a feature of Tamil countryside as it was in Vrndavana. In these episodes, Kṛṣṇa was called "the darling", Kannan.[65] Even more accessible was the permanent presence of the deity in his temple and shrine icons, for God did this through his compassion and grace to make himself easily available for his devotees. The icons pervaded by God in this way were equivalent to his other *avatāras*. The importance of temples, especially Śrī-raṅgam, for the *Āḻvārs*, amounts to what Narayanan terms "a territorial theology" that is typical of Śrī-Vaiṣṇava tradition.[66] It was to the iconographic God within the temples that the *Āḻvārs* directed their hymns. They travelled from temple to temple singing their hymns and inspiring those who heard them to be devotees, too. There are said to be a hundred and eight holy places where they sang. For the *Āḻvārs*, singing to, and about, God was the central means of approaching God, "an end in itself, a salvation realized on this earth with the dawning of a golden age",[67] writes Narayanan. She appropriately entitles her book *The Way and the Goal*, because the singing of the poets' hymns and God's thousand names "are seen to be not just the *way* to immortal life but the *goal* itself":[68] singing was the way to reach the feet of God. It is easy to see the universality of such a pathway that required no special knowledge or social status: it was open to all.

As firmly in the Śrī-Vaiṣṇava tradition, the *Āḻvārs* also accepted Śrī as the inseparable consort of Viṣṇu. Many of the hymns refer to her as aiding the devotees to find God and as working with her divine husband, or even independently, to remove sins and grant liberation through her great compassion. Both Viṣṇu and Śrī have the power of conferring grace and removing any obstacles preventing the devotee from being liberated. The myths and divine deeds that accompany the pair are the *līlās* of God by which their glorious deeds are to be known either together or separately.

As to the nature of the self, the *Āḻvārs* believed it to be the property of God because it is a mode of God. God is, thus, its natural home and the true Self knows itself as utterly dependent on God, subordinate to God, and existing only to serve God. It is through total surrender, *prapatti*, to God that the individual is granted his grace. The world need not be abandoned but it should have no allure for a God-intoxicated soul who devotes every thought, word and action to God. Important was the feeling of helplessness so often portrayed in the hymns of the *Āḻvārs* that epitomized their self-surrender. What also is found is a sense of utter humility and self-deprecation in their hymns, and such feelings were often accompanied by a sense of separation from God. There was sadness in waiting for God and Nammāḻvār sighed into the night: "Evening has come: He has not". The tension between experience of the presence of God and then separation made the tales of the *gopīs'* love and longing for Kṛṣṇa all the more relevant to include in the hymns. Humility is also portrayed through the plea to reach the feet of God; that is to say, being able to touch the lowest point of the divine body, indicative of being a servant, but being able to be at the feet of God also represented intimate joy divorced from any separation. And that is exactly what liberation is; not union with God but communion and fellowship with him. The *Āḻvārs* were not focused on *mokṣa* but on continued devotion and service to God at his feet, ultimately to dwell in Vaikuṇṭha, the spiritual realm that belongs to Viṣṇu, never to be reborn and freed from all sin and suffering.

Before leaving this section, I think it prudent to look briefly at just three of the *Āḻvārs*, the most important of whom is Nammāḻvār. Periyāḻvār is also an important *Āḻvār* not least because he was also the adopted father of the only female *Āḻvār*, Āṇṭāḷ, who will also feature below. Generic beliefs of the *Āḻvārs* have been dealt with above so, here, I want to concentrate on the distinctive features of these three. Space does not permit an exploration of their hagiographic lives, so I shall concentrate on their respective approaches to the divine.

Nammāḻvār

Vaiṣṇavas hold Nammāḻvār in the highest esteem and he is the greatest of the *Āḻvārs*. His name means "Our Saint" or "Our Own *Āḻvār*". He was, in fact, the last of the *Āḻvārs* and the first of the *Ācāryas*, the great teachers, but he warrants consideration first in view of the immense respect held for him. His biographers say he was a *Śūdra*, of the *Veḷḷāla* caste, a fairly affluent farming group. He is mostly believed to have lived in the eighth or first half of the ninth century[69] and wrote four works of varying lengths but it is his longest work of over a thousand hymns, his *Tiruvāymoḻi*, "Holy Word" or "Holy Utterance", for which he is most famous: (*tiru* is the Tamil equivalent of *Śrī*). The hymns contained in this text form the core of the Tamil *Veda*, his four works sometimes being called the *Four Vedas*,[70] termed *veda* because they are believed to show the true meaning of the Sanskrit *Vedas* in a more accessible way for all people and because they are considered to be "revealed" by God to the poet and so timeless. God "made me over into himself and sang in Tamil his own songs through me", Nammāḻvār said.[71] Such accessibility is highlighted in his hymns when Nammāḻvār used the term "we" to refer to all his fellow worshippers of Viṣṇu: the saint wanted to rescue all beings and bring them to Viṣṇu, or Nārāyaṇa, as he often called him. The *Tiruvāymoḻi* thus has pride of place in Vaiṣṇava temple liturgy.

Nammālvār is reputed to have had visions of God and then spontaneously sang the poems. Emphatically monotheistic in their understanding of God, the hymns of the *Tiruvāymoli* reveal a concept of a God who is unsurpassable, as Reality that is ultimate and, as did so many of the *Ālvārs*, Nammālvār believed that the all-pervading God is he on whom every being depends, as the visible body is dependent on the invisible soul. Such a body–soul theory of the relationship between divine and human is an important one here, implying that the self is a property of, and dependent on, God, just as the body is on the soul. It is a central aspect of the later teaching of Rāmānuja, as we shall see. And as the body exists for the soul, and serves it, so God exists for the devotees whose role is to serve him. Viṣṇu was also a God that possessed personal attributes, a *saguṇa* God that had describable qualities. But Nammālvār did not lose sight of the transcendent reality of God:

> He is not male, not female, nor eunuch
> He cannot be seen: He is not existent nor non-existent,
> He assumes the form in which his devotees desire to see him:
> He is not of such form,
> It is extraordinarily difficult to speak of Him.[72]

God remained one but became the many of the universe, though he was not affected by changes and defects within the world. "You stand in all things", said Nammālvār of God, "and yet transcend them".[73] All paradoxes and dualities were present in Nammālvār's concept of God. Viṣṇu was goodness and sinfulness, poverty and wealth, heaven and hell, enmity and friendship, poison and nectar, memory and forgetfulness, existence and non-existence and yet was none of these things for he transcended them all. But most important was the immanent nature of God in every single entity, and that permitted the personal nature of the relationship between Viṣṇu and Nammālvār. This is beautifully portrayed in the *Tiruvāymoli*:

> All that I pray for now and forever is that You give me the hand of wisdom to reach Your Feet without the least delay. Fill my mind with Your Presence without any let-up and bid me to your eternal service. It does not at all matter to me whether at death I go to the Eternal Abode or to heaven or hell. Let me instead have the joy of being aware of You, without the least lapse. Let me joyfully worship you by thought, word and deed. Such is the fickleness of the mind that it may stray away even after You have brought me to Your Feet. So please ensure that I never depart from Your Feet.[74]

The revealed nature of the hymns that Nammālvār sang is clear in one hymn: "How can I ever forget my Father, my Lord? He makes Himself me. Faultlessly He sings (through me) His songs. He redeems me – who am a person of incomparable iniquity. He refines my nature. How indeed can I forget him when I witness His excellence in wandering in quest of me?"[75] Nammālvār's relationship with God was as a servant to a master. It was also an expression of ecstatic devotion that could take effect in the temples before the images of his beloved Viṣṇu. Nammālvār cried, sang and danced before God with the knowledge that God's presence was within his temple icon. In whatever form a devotee wished to concentrate on God, God would take that form to aid the devotee:

If you say he exists, he does,
his forms are these forms,
If you say he does not,
his formlessness
is of these nonforms.[76]

Because God was personal and could have attributes, Nammāḻvār was able to describe the appearance of his physical form, albeit that that was a spiritual divine body. Nammāḻvār also described the divine deeds of Viṣṇu and his hymns recount such miraculous deeds as Viṣṇu's creation of the world and Kṛṣṇa's lifting of the mountain above his devotees to protect them from the god Indra's deluge. The Goddess Lakṣmī, Śrī, who personifies compassion, was also included as inseparably and inalienably one with Viṣṇu in Nammāḻvār's concept of deity. She resided in Viṣṇu's chest, probably as the *Śrī-vatsa*, the curl of hair and, as other *Āḻvārs*, he believed she removed obstacles on the pathway to the divine just as Viṣṇu did.[77]

Love was a major theme of Nammāḻvār's hymns and the love between God and devotee was a reciprocal one. Similar to another *Āḻvār*, Tirumaṅgai, Nammāḻvār used the medium of erotic poetry to express a passionate relationship with God. In a poem addressed to Rāma, whom he calls Kākutstha, he spoke as if he were a cowherd girl desperately pining for her lover: "If my Kākutstha with his shining, angry bow does not come, I shall kill myself", he says.[78] And to Kṛṣṇa he wrote in the same way: "Give me the nectar of your mouth, and adorn my lowly head with your jewelled lotus hands."[79] Approaching God from the point of view of a woman enabled Nammāḻvār, as other poets, to express their longing for God. As the love-intoxicated *gopīs* drowned in the ecstasy of the touch of their lover, once apart the depth of yearning could not be born.[80] Nammāḻvār sometimes sang hymns as if he were the mother of a lovesick girl who pleaded with God to pity her daughter, or he sang as an intoxicated bride or a friend of a bride. Such love poetry was a particular feature of one of his other works, the *Tiruviruttam*, reflecting the old Tamil *akam* love poetry where poets used the medium of female voices to express love. In the *Tiruvāymoḻi* we find this following typical poem:

You're unfair, Kanna [Kṛṣṇa], you're unfair!
When you make love and embrace my full breasts,
a tidal wave of pleasure, unchecked by our union,
rises to the firmament, and soars beyond,
making my wits drown in a flood.
And then it recedes like a dream.
My passion permeates my inner life
and throbs in every cell of my body –
my soul cannot bear this burden.
If I am to be separated from you,
every time you go to graze cows,
I die.[81]

Nammāḻvār may have accepted *bhakti-yoga* as a means to God[82] but his emphasis on surrender, *prapatti*, at the feet of God and service to God seem the more favoured means to acquiring God's grace, which was essential for liberation. Importantly, God was the sole means to liberation *and* the goal itself: neither changed for a devotee who loved and surrendered the self to God. *Bhakti-yoga* would have been perceived as a harder, disciplined path of meditation and concentration on God, when the easier path of dedicating all words, thoughts and actions to God and chanting his names, were accessible to all and easily practised: *surrender* was really the key. Simple acts of offering flowers, incense, light and water with loving devotion to the images of Viṣṇu in the temples – actions far removed from disciplined *yoga* – were also part of his *bhakti*. Surrendering at the feet of God is taking refuge in him: "Oh Lord of the eternal souls," said Nammāḻvār, "Thou has vouchsafed unto me your feet as my sole refuge."[83] Refuge here is suggestive of the sense of God being the *only* means of grace and protection, and recognition of the soul's utter dependence on God. "O dark raincloud Kṛṣṇa without you I'm not: take me" said Nammāḻvār.[84] It is at the feet of God that surrender, devotion and service were the means by which God's refuge was given and his grace obtained and these actions themselves were liberation, *mokṣa*. "Lord in perpetual paradise let me be at your feet", said Nammāḻvār.[85]

Humility was a prominent dimension of nearly all the poet–saints. They often described themselves as lowly and Nammāḻvār's hymns suggest that he spoke not just for himself but for all lost souls who aspired to reach the feet of God. There is, thus, a universality about his hymns, he believed that all should be served by him even "if they have fallen below the four castes, (*sic*) which hold this society together, and are outcastes of the outcastes who have no trace of virtue".[86] If they were servants of servants of servants . . . he believed he should serve them: the humility of Nammāḻvār knew no bounds. His humility often emerged at points when he felt separated from God, when he was deeply dejected: "Devoid of merit, I am indeed a humble person and yet the evil in me looms large; you do not respond to my ardent appeal . . . I must have committed many sins and you do not, therefore, appear before this sinner though I beckon you often with melting heart and tearful eyes."[87]

The pain of separation, *viraha*, from God was balanced with expressions of union with him. "He and I and everything else mingled within him" he said in one hymn.[88] And again: "The Lord mingled with my soul which he chose as a lovely heaven."[89] In one hymn he described God as all around him and in every part of his body.[90] With great beauty he said of God he, "made me his own cool place in heaven and thought of me what I thought of him and became my own thoughts";[91] and, "he came down and filled my heart".[92] The union of which Nammāḻvār spoke was a union in the present, not one achieved at a distant point in a far off life through lives of continual practice of one or more of the paths of knowledge, works or devotion. *Bhakti* here was intense *loving* devotion that brought its ultimate goal in the here and now through the grace of God: "Even as I said, 'He became the master, took me as a servant,' he came to me happily, all grace."[93]

The legacy of Nammāḻvār is immense, especially since he gave God total ownership of his words, "he speaks in me this sweet poetry which I speak in my own words, and so my marvellous one now praises himself in his own words, my First One who before me spoke in his three forms".[94] His hymns are regularly sung in Vaiṣṇava temple liturgy and a ten-day festival honours him at the Srī-raṅgam Temple in what Nancy Ann Nayar refers to as a "direct communication of his own emotions". She writes: "So successful was he in this enterprise, that in the Śrīvaiṣṇava tradition the *gopī* came to be superseded by Nammāḻvār as the paradigmatic devotee, and the devotional goal largely shifted from that of experiencing the emotions of the *gopīs* to that of experiencing the emotions of Nammāḻvār himself."[95] He remains the greatest of the *Āḻvārs* and as Ramanujan so pertinently commented: "Anyone who reads his poems can see why: the poems are at once philosophic and poetic, direct in feeling yet intricate in design, single minded yet various in mood – wondering, mischievous, tender, joyous, subtly probing, often touching despair but never staying with it."[96]

Periyaḻvār and Āṇṭāḷ

Two other *Āḻvārs* worthy of mention here are Periyāḻvār (formerly Viṣṇucitta), "The Great Āḻvār" and Āṇṭāḷ. Periyāḻvār became the father of Āṇṭāḷ after he adopted her, calling her Kōtai. He never married but found Āṇṭāḷ abandoned in some *tulasī* bushes in his flower garden – the *tulasī* being a plant much associated with Viṣṇu. Periyāḻvār was an orthodox *Brāhmin* priest who officiated at one of Viṣṇu's temples. He wrote two works in poetic form, the *Tiruppallāṇḍu* and a much longer work the *Periyāḻvār Tirumoḻī*. While a devotee of Viṣṇu, Periyāḻvār's hymns were mainly devoted to Kṛṣṇa as a baby and young child. This was, at the time, the novel way in which Periyāḻvār preferred to relate to God mostly in the guise of Yaśodā, the foster-mother of Kṛṣṇa. His depictions of the baby and child Kṛṣṇa are enchanting, his words delighting in the baby antics of Kṛṣṇa and describing the baby's lovely smile, little white teeth, his chuckling laughter and the like. Periyāḻvār's exquisite hymns are often in the form of lullabies still sung in Tamil homes today. It is a remarkable way in which a devotee can pour out love for God. Narayanan comments: "In a sense, this is the ultimate paradox of the divine incarnation: the omnipotent Lord appears as a vulnerable child just to indulge and gratify the emotional *bhakti* of the devotee, who seeks to protect, jealously guard over, and serve his beloved."[97] It is a very natural and joyful approach to God, as are his hymns that tell of the antics and mischief of the young boy. But his hymns are by no means devoid of recognition of Viṣṇu whom he glorified as a transcendent God who is "forever and forever", very, very old, ageless and beginningless. He said he always had Viṣṇu in his mind: "I have placed you inside me and I have placed myself within you."[98]

Āṇṭāḷ is unique amongst the *Āḻvārs* because she was a woman, though such female poets were present from the first century to the seventeenth.[99] She came to be accepted as an incarnation of Bhū-devī, one of the consorts of Viṣṇu. Her name means "She Who Rules" and, indeed, she did rule in that she refused to obey social norms set for women and did not marry: she regarded herself as a bride of Kṛṣṇa. One of her two works, the *Tiruppāvai*, "Sacred Lady",[100] symbolized her ascent to Heaven to the mansion of Kṛṣṇa and her awakening of him to see her and the devotees she had brought with her. Some hymns here reflect the religious rite that a bride undergoes in autumn. They also recall the *gopīs'* longing for union with Kṛṣṇa, and Āṇṭāḷ internalized her love, devotion and longing in separation – this last, so typical of many of the poet–saints. It was always the bride of Kṛṣṇa that she longed to be (though she also sang to Rāma), and her hymns tell of her intense mental suffering in separation from him. Her poems are infused with a great amount of symbolism and depth so they have both literal and esoteric meanings. Because she was a woman, emotional love was considered natural for her; she did not have to adopt the role of a female as male poets did. Her approach to Kṛṣṇa was as a bride or a maiden that wanted physical union with him, so her poetry is often highly erotic. Dennis Hudson writes: "She addressed her own erotic desire (*kāma*) directly through liturgical action, first invoking it in her body, and then manipulating it to bring her face-to-face with Kṛṣṇa in her inner consciousness where he would take her to himself as the Self (*ātman*) at the center of her being. In the process, she created a poetry rich in the sensual pleasure of him as the only male in her erotic life."[101] Saroja Sundararajan says that texts such as this serve to give depth to the concept of God: "The basic or underlying theme of the *Tiruppāvai* is that the Lord must be thought of as the most adequate fulfilment of every power and faculty in us."[102] The other work of hers, *Nācciyār Tirumoḻi*, "The Sacred Words of the Lady", records her anguish and longing for her lover, Kṛṣṇa, but sings also of her complete surrender to God in order to receive his grace. Archana Venkatesan points out that Āntāl's desire in the *Nacciyār Tirumoḻi*, "is terrible, full-blown and unremitting. The experience of such a desire is essentially an isolating one, where there are neither friends nor companions to alleviate the suffering."[103] Venkatesan also sees violence in this text as the poet's "dominant means of expressing an impossible desire and the fleeting nature of her encounter with the divine".[104] "I waste away through the long endless years waiting for the day when he finally sends word", Āṇṭāḷ said.[105] Her erotic poems also feature in the *Nācciyār Tirumoḻi*:

> Oh clouds bearing lightning within your heart
> Tell Him who bears the Goddess of wealth on His chest
> How my young breasts yearn deeply everyday
> To clasp His golden chest in tight embrace.[106]

In this text, Āṇṭāḷ sings of sandcastles of white sand at the thresholds of homes that she asks Kṛṣṇa not to destroy. She sings as if she were one of the *gopīs* whose clothes Kṛṣṇa had stolen as a prank while they bathed. She begs a *kuyil* bird to take messages to her Lord because she aches to gaze on his golden feet. Viṣṇu's conch – intimate with his lips – is praised as fortunate. Bose has an interesting comment on such female poets when she writes: "To the woman mystic, poetry brings liberation from the constraints of social relations because it gives her a voice which, singing of divinity as it does, cannot be silenced by convention, and which thus lifts her above the gendered constructions of identity prescribed by conventional Hindu thought and practice."[107] I shall return to the subject of such social liberation in respect to other female *bhaktas* later. But Venkatesan points out that Āṇṭāḷ's status as one of the *Āḻvārs* is tenuous and that she is sometimes excluded from the list, despite the fact that the poet often ended her hymns by saying that those who sing them will have access to God.[108]

So Āṇṭāḷ's poems are universal and not class or caste bound. The very fact that she was a woman in natural opposition to gendered constraints opened her poetry to all.

She showed that total love of God and complete surrender to him were all that was needed, giving her songs a lasting legacy for temple and home ritual, complemented by the eight-syllabled *mantra*, *Om-namo-nārāyaṇāya*, "Hail to the abode of man", the "abode of man" being the divine Nārāyaṇa[109]. Āṇṭāḷ is portrayed in paintings and bronzes as a very beautiful young maiden and her hymn of marriage to Kṛṣṇa is sung today in Tamil Vaiṣṇava homes at the occasion of weddings.[110] Legend has it that she achieved union with Kṛṣṇa by merging with his icon in the great temple at Śrī-raṅgam.

The Śrī-Vaiṣṇava *Ācāryas*

The *Ācāryas* were great teachers: Śaṃkara-*ācārya* of the Advaita Vedānta school of thought is one example. The title, *ācārya*, is traditionally added to the names of great men but, here, I want to deal with the original Śrī-Vaiṣṇava *Ācāryas* who were very different from Śaṃkara. They were antagonistic to the monistic view of Brahman, favouring the personal God who is describable and has an abundance of attributes and manifestations. Some *Ācāryas* were contemporaries of the *Āḻvārs*, others came later, but the *Ācāryas* were different in that they based their teachings on both Sanskrit and Tamil scriptures and melded *bhakti* with established traditions of *jñāna* and *karma*. Since they were *Brāhmins*, they were far more orthodox than the *Āḻvārs* but they respected the teachings of the latter sufficiently to divinize them, creating associated cultic praxis along with regulations and dogmas. Given their orthodoxy, according to Nayar, the emotional relationship between Kṛṣṇa and the *gopīs* as a focus for devotion diminished somewhat.[111] Three *Ācāryas* deserve mention, Nāthamuni, Yāmuna and Vallabhā.

Nāthamuni (824–924), is renowned because he is said to have "rediscovered" the *Prabandham* of the *Āḻvārs*. He was a great scholar, well-versed in the Sanskrit scriptures and a *yogin*. He organized the works of the *Āḻvārs* into the "Four-Thousand Verses" that became the established *Prabandham* giving it the status of *Vedas* and promoting its recitation in temples and at festivals along with images of the *Āḻvārs* in temple shrines. His "dual *Vedānta*" – the Tamil poets of the *Āḻvārs* and the Sanskrit commentaries of Rāmānuja – became the scriptural foundation of all Śrī-Vaiṣṇavism, providing prayers, hymns, liturgies and doctrines. His concept of God was a dual one of devotee blessed by the grace of God who could find fellowship with God at liberation.

Yāmuna was the grandson of Nāthamuni and a staunch proponent of the Pāñcaratra scriptures and rituals. All his works were written in Sanskrit. It is easy to see the influence of the *Āḻvārs* on his beliefs. Śrī, Lakṣmī, he saw as important on the path to liberation: just as her consort, Viṣṇu, she was the fount of compassion. For Yāmuna, Lakṣmī was equal to her consort in every way. He had a thorough belief in the need for self-surrender to Viṣṇu but blended it with the kind of *bhakti-yoga* that we saw in the *Gītā*. His was a more disciplined *bhakti* than we have seen hitherto and included both *jñāna-* and *karma-yogas*, but since he never lost sight of love as the foundation it was a different *bhakti-yoga* that was really a *yoga* of love. He did not believe himself to be in the least way qualified to practise *bhakti-yoga* and could only offer himself to God in total surrender as an alternative. Thus, he sought refuge in, and surrendered to, God in the same way as the *Āḻvārs*, taking refuge at the feet of God as they did and recognizing that only God could provide protection through his grace: "I have committed thousands of sins", he said in his text, *The Jewel*, "I am helpless and come for refuge to your sacred feet. By your grace, make me yours."[112] He referred to God as a father and mother, dear as a son and loving as a friend. He believed that once a devotee took refuge in Nārāyaṇa, the Lord would not want to be separated from that devotee and would become very affectionate to him or her. Yāmuna's words are laced with feelings of unworthiness and self-deprecation yet, as Narayanan writes: "Love and a desire for service overflow through the humility of Yāmuna. He pleads for grace so that he can see the Lord, serve him, and have more *bhakti* toward him. Yāmuna has declared that he has no *bhakti*, and yet every line of *The Jewel* pulsates with love and a God-centeredness."[113] Siegel notes that the highest *bhakti* occurs not with union but in the fear of separation from God because it amplifies the love, making it more intense.[114] There was much in Yāmuna's concepts of God that was to influence Rāmānuja who brought to fruition many of the seeds that were laid down by Yāmuna.[115]

Vallabhā is dated later from about 1479–1531. His name means "Beloved" and he was believed by his *sampradāya*, of which he was the founder, to be an *avatāra* of Kṛṣṇa. He was a *Brāhmin* who believed souls (*jīvas*) and the world to be parts of Brahman like sparks from a fire, but mostly stressed total service, *sevā*, to Kṛṣṇa as the manifestation of Brahman. His *bhakti* of grace he saw as superior to other forms of *bhakti* or other paths of *karma* or *jñāna*. The *Bhāgavata Purāṇa* was for him the supreme revealed scripture that was second to no other, and the *gopīs* of Vrndavana were the highest example of devotion to God: their dual relationship and yet union with Kṛṣṇa exemplified the same kind of relationship in liberation that a devotee could enjoy through God's grace. His central tenet was the doctrine of the way of grace (*puṣṭi-mārga*), a doctrine and school of thought that has remained popular to the present day, especially since it is open to anyone irrespective of caste or gender. *Puṣṭi* is the freely given grace of God that is proffered without any cause of the devotee: just to be a devotee in the first place can only happen through God's grace. Kṛṣṇa will "play" with those whom he chooses, loving them and nurturing them until they enjoy the bliss of God – something far greater than realization of Brahman. Such was Kṛṣṇa's interactive *līlā* with his devotees. While Vallabhā advocated rejection of mundane thoughts about the world, just as the *gopīs* did, Vallabhā believed the world to be real as a partial manifestation of God. Kṛṣṇa he accepted as the Brahman of the *Upaniṣads*, a transcendent God who took on diverse and real manifestations but who had a higher, personal form. Therefore, Vallabhā eschewed any ascetic withdrawal from the world: he rather believed in the gradual realization of the true relationship of the self as a partial manifestation of God but explored through the householder stage of life and family religion. His beliefs gave considerable impetus to home ritual where devotion to images and singing of hymns became central,[116] but temple worship was also important and images of Kṛṣṇa were all accepted as full manifestations of him.

It is through personal interaction with Kṛṣṇa's images that devotees experience his *līlā*: he plays with them and they chat with him, attending to all his comforts and needs. There is a profound warmth and devotion in Vallabhā's *saṃpradāya*. Peter Bennet writes: "The generous offerings of *sevā*, made over with such loving care, presuppose that Kṛṣṇa *qua* image thrives on the attentions of his worshipers in the same way that an infant thrives on the loving and caring attentions of its mother."[117] Devotees sing *kīrtans* to images, dress and feed the images and regard them as the deity in reality. It was Vallabhā who articulated the four kinds of devotion to God through parental love, the love of a servant, the love of a friend and the love of a spouse. In the Vallabhā *sampradāya*, most favoured devotion to the child Kṛṣṇa, but Vallabhā believed Rādhā to be at one with Kṛṣṇa, and to epitomize the truest devotion, and so he advocated devotion to God in the female mode, though it seems he believed women should be born as male in order to emulate devotion of the *gopīs*![118] The pervasive concept of God as a refuge is encapsulated in the *mantra* of the Vallabhite tradition, *Śrī-kṛṣṇah-śaraṇaṃ-mama* "Śrī-Kṛṣṇa is my refuge". Descendants who are spiritual leaders of the tradition, *goswāmins*, are considered to be bodily incarnations of Kṛṣṇa and are honoured as divine by devotees. Today's Swaminarayan order that sprang from the Vallabhite tradition maintains the view that its religious leaders are gods, sometimes to the extent that their images are given central places in temples[119] where Kṛṣṇa is relegated to make way for a divinized human *guru*.[120]

Rāmānuja

The most famous *Ācārya* was the eleventh to twelfth-century theologian Rāmānuja (1075–1140 CE). His life was, in the main, centred at the great Tamil Temple of Śrī-raṅgam. Along with Śaṃkara, he is the greatest philosopher of the Vedānta tradition. Whereas Śaṃkara's philosophy was more rooted in *Upaniṣadic* thought, it might be claimed that Rāmānuja's was primarily rooted in the religion that was fully established in his day – Vaiṣṇavism, devotion to Viṣṇu. Indeed, it was the grafting of *Upaniṣadic* credence on the Vaiṣṇavism of his time for which Rāmānuja is so well known, and it is this that hallmarks a major contribution of his as a philosopher and theologian. Rāmānuja's philosophy is known as the school of Viśiṣṭādvaita generally translated as "qualified monism". *Advaita* means "not dual" and *viśiṣṭa* means "particularity", "distinctness", indicating what is qualified, or determinate. Viśiṣṭādvaita, then, is a composite term that is designed to suggest two things: first, *identity* and *non-duality* of the world and selves with the divine (*advaita*) and, secondly, a certain *difference* between the world, selves and the divine because there are differences of attributes that inform each entity. There is, thus, oneness and wholeness that is characterized by distinctiveness of all its modes – a theory that would have been unacceptable to Śaṃkara. And it is God that creates and sustains the whole unity of reality, because its interrelated parts are, in fact, the attributes of God himself. Unlike Śaṃkara's Brahman that is without attributes, Rāmānuja's Brahman has an abundance of characteristics and qualities – "particularities" – both in his own being and in the form of the whole universe that stems from him. Brahman is the underlying Reality that unites and sustains, but allows plurality. Everything is thus dependent on Brahman for its existence, is interrelated through Brahman, but has a certain independent reality from anything else. Such *inseparable relationship* between the whole and its qualities is termed *apṛthak-siddhi* – unity that contains inseparable, different and dependent attributes.

Rāmānuja's philosophy was formulated in accordance with the authority of the *Upaniṣads*, but the essence of the *Upaniṣadic* teaching was seen as *bhakti*, and as a dualistic monotheism between devotee and the divine. There was a clear purpose to bring together the philosophical and metaphysical teachings of the *Upaniṣads* on the one hand with, on the other, the powerful expression of loving devotion to a personal God that so characterized the *bhakti* movements. It was liberation through love, not just knowledge, and yet a deliberate attempt to formalize and systematize the powerful, emotive expression of devotion. What Rāmānuja did was to blend his philosophy with a thoroughly practical religious expression – what one writer terms "a very powerful correlation of theism and philosophy".[121] Rāmānuja was clearly influenced by the *Āḻvārs*, though he does not refer to them, but the close correlation between the fundamental beliefs of the *Āḻvārs* – particularly Nammāḻvār and Yāmuna – and the philosophy of Rāmānuja, suggests that he was certainly systematizing philosophical and religious ideas that had been long in currency.

According to tradition, Rāmānuja descended in direct line from the first *Ācārya*, Nāthamuni (900–950) and his grandson Yāmuna (966–1038) and became *the Ācārya* of the Śrī-Vaiṣṇava sect but it was particularly the ideas of Yāmuna that were more acceptable to Rāmānuja.[122] The ultimate Reality was Viṣṇu or, as the preferred name of the sect, Nārāyaṇa.[123] A good deal of anthropomorphic theism lifts Viśiṣṭādvaita from strict Vedānta philosophy to a level of workable devotion. What emerged as a result of Rāmānuja's work was a school that systematized a doctrine of devotion to, and grace from, a personal God. Ian Kesarcodi-Watson described Rāmānuja as "a *bhakta* to the core. This was his atmosphere, his family, his nature; the being he began with, not something he set out to absorb".[124] The writings that he produced amounted to his *Śrī-bhāṣya* on the *Vedānta-Sūtras* (*Brahma-Sūtras*) and eight other works, including a commentary on the *Bhagavad Gītā*, and the *Vedārtha-saṃgraha*, his "philosophical debut",[125] which forms the essence of his beliefs.

As to Rāmānuja's concept of God, Nārāyaṇa is the only *independent* Reality – the other two kinds of reality, world and selves, are dependent on God though independent from other selves and objects. Both world and selves are substances that have inseparable attributes. So each sentient (*cit*) or insentient (*acit*) object is differentiated from others by its own inseparable attributes. But every sentient or insentient object is itself an inseparable attribute of God. God controls and sustains the world but is beyond selves and the world for he exists in his own being beyond all other substances as the only eternal and self-dependent "Real": God is never an attribute of something else but he has attributes that depend on him. The example used by Rāmānuja and Viśiṣṭādvaita to explain the inseparability of substance and attribute is the soul and the body, the soul being the substance to which the body belongs, because the soul controls the body and not *vice versa*. It is a particular example of *apṛthak-siddhi* that is central to the philosophy of Viśiṣṭādvaita. The world and the selves that inhabit it are God's body, his attributes, standing in inseparable and organic relation to him – and thereby in unity with him – but remaining different from, and dependent on, him.[126] As we saw earlier, the body–soul concept was one taught by Nammāḻvār.[127] It is the subordination of the self to God that permits the personal devotion of the *bhakta* to the Lord, to Īśvara – and that is the *raison d'être* of Vaiṣṇava religion and worship.

The body–soul theory serves to depict the relationship between the One and the many – the One being Brahman, and the many being the plurality of the world, the One containing the many. It is a oneness characterized by internal diversity, in other words, Brahman with distinguishing characteristics. Selves and the world phenomena are all modes, the body, of God; to use Bhatt's expression, "moments in the life of God".[128] Rāmānuja made the world thoroughly real – the whole unfolding of Nature as the magical effects and attributes of God. He wrote, "this one Being has an infinite and wonderful variety of forms and still retains His uniformity in this infinite and immeasurable diversity".[129] There could never be complete *identity* between the self and God, as far as Rāmānuja was concerned. Yet, because God is the substance from which the self takes its whole being, there is an element of identity.

Rāmānuja's view of the divine stands clearly in the framework of theism. God is *accessible* to the devotee, though at the same time, he remains the Absolute of so much *Upaniṣadic* thought. This is a God, too, that has a spiritual "body" that lends itself to much anthropomorphic description. But, while pervading all, the utter transcendence of God is never compromised by the defects of the sentient and non-sentient attributes – the selves and matter – that are his body. According to Rāmānuja, God is "the material cause, the operative cause, the substratum, the controller and the principal of the entire phenomenal world of spiritual and non-spiritual entities".[130] As the Ground of all, then, there is a relational intimacy between Brahman and the attributes he generates and it is this intimacy that permits devotion to a describable God, a *saguṇa* God, with an abundance of marvellous qualities. Where Śaṃkara stripped Brahman of qualities, Rāmānuja expresses them in abundance, but he gives philosophic credence to the devotional movement by staying well within *Vedāntic* confines for his understanding of the concept of God. His God is one who could be the object of worship and a means to the liberation of the self. God reaches out to his devotee with compassion, grace, love that is forgiving, protection, and generosity. And God is everywhere: everything is intimately a part of Brahman. This was put beautifully by Rāmānuja: "The supreme wonder in nature is its being the garment of God. All that seems ugly, trivial, or insignificant, acquires a new dimension of this view. Nature and finite souls are packed with God and are suffused with the hues of the Divine. . . . God is not merely a marvel in Himself but also He moulds nature into a wondrous manifestation of Himself."[131] God is a describable, predicable deity. He has personhood and has many perfections such as Love, Beauty, Power and Goodness, and no imperfections. He has a supernal form, is male, and can be anthropomorphically depicted. He is the "Golden Person" of the *Chāndogya Upaniṣad* with a golden beard and golden hair, who is brilliant to the tips of his fingers (1:6:6), with eyes like a lotus flower (1:6:7). He lives in a divine abode and enjoys the pleasures that sense perception offers. But God's form is not of the same kind as human physical and *prakṛtic* form; it is a special, supernal form, which Rāmānuja graphically described:

> He who is always gloriously visible is the pre-eminent Person who dwells within the orbit of the sun. His splendour is like that of a colossal mountain of molten gold and His brilliance that of the rays of hundreds of thousands of suns. His long eyes are spotless like the petals of a lotus. . . . His eyes and His forehead and His nose are beautiful, His coral-like lips smile graciously, and His soft cheeks are beaming. His neck is as delicately shaped as a conch-shell and His bud-like divine ears, beautifully formed, hang down on His stalwart shoulders. His arms are thick, round and long and He is adorned with fingers that are reddened by nails of a most becoming reddish tinge.

> His body, with its slender waist and broad chest, is well-proportioned in all parts, and His shape is of an unutterably divine form. His colour is pleasing. His feet are as beautiful as budding lotuses. He wears a yellow robe that suits Him and he is adorned with immeasurable, marvelous, endless and divine ornaments – a spotless diadem, earrings, necklaces, . . . [132]

And so the descriptions continue. Rāmānuja was remarkably graphic and anthropomorphic about such characteristics of the divine.[133] Intimacy and union with his *bhaktas* is joy to God, and therefore his devotees experience his loving kindness, his mercy and his love. The supernatural bodily form of God is for the benefit of relational devotion between human and divine.

As the highest, transcendental Brahman, *para* Brahman, God manifests himself in four other forms. One of these is as Nārāyaṇa, Viṣṇu or Vāsudeva, the divine form that lives in the supernatural, pure *sattvic* realm of Vaikuṇṭha. Then, there is God in his creative, sustaining and dissolving role in the manifested world as his body, and his indwelling of all. Another form constitutes his *avatāras*; yet another, his presence in the sacred images in the special temples of his devotees. The physical representations of the divine are the visible presence of God in the realm of humankind. For Rāmānuja there is no question of this presence being an inferior reality of the nature of God, or a temporary, illusory one that would cease to exist when the devotee transcended the lower slopes of devotion and knowledge. Scripture attests to the reality of the divine form and it is this perspective of divine reality that was so essential to the heart of Vaiṣṇava religion in the richness of its thought and practice. In the evolution towards liberation, God's grace is effective in removing obstacles on the path. It is a *love* of God for the devotee and the reciprocal love of the devotee for God that promotes God's grace – a concept repeatedly stated in the *Bhagavad Gītā*. For Rāmānuja, a certain balance of *effort* on the part of the individual was necessary, along with *election* on the part of God. But the human effort involved is steeped in deep devotion and self-surrender to God. Ultimately, it is by God's grace that the law of *karma* operates, and yet God seeks to liberate the self from its bound state. Rāmānuja, then, does not remove God so far from human action that he becomes remote and impersonal: God becomes fully involved in the human world through his *avatāras* – a concept central to Vaiṣṇava religion. They arise from a compassionate desire of God to assist humankind and to perform miraculous acts in order to captivate humankind.

Rāmānuja's concept of liberation was a graphic one. Essentially, the self comes to know itself as the mode of God. There is absolutely no sense of complete identity with an impersonal Absolute. On the contrary, the personal nature of the relationship between the liberated Self and the divine is stressed concomitant with a conscious and blissful relationship with God that is dualistic and personal. But liberation is possible only through the grace of God. With a consciousness that is different from God's, the liberated soul is able to experience the joy and bliss that communion with God brings. But, in that the liberated soul is still an attribute of the divine, there is a certain identity between Brahman and the Self, particularly because of the inseparable relationship, *apṛthak-siddhi*, between the two. It is a very positive state of liberated existence; the omniscience attained through liberation permits the full comprehension of God by the soul. It is, then, a relational experience and not a fusion and identity.

It seems clear that Rāmānuja believed liberation was not for those who were unprepared, who lacked the *Vedic* knowledge that could prescribe correct ritual practice, meditation, and correct knowledge of Brahman. This, inevitably, included only twice-born classes, and excluded *Śūdras* and women, for whom study of the *Veda* was not permitted.[134] And it would have to be said that if God abides by the law of *karma* then each individual is different because of his or her relative merits or demerits. The *Śūdra*, having no access to the *Veda* because of *karmic* dispositions, would not be able, therefore, to acquire the prerequisites for release.[135] Nevertheless, Rāmānuja spoke out against class or caste pride as a hindrance to devotional faith: "All beings who worship God by bhakti – whether they be of an exalted or a humble class – will at their desire foregather in God as if they share his virtues, and God himself will dwell in them as if they were more exalted than He."[136] It seems, too, that Rāmānuja was not averse to eating with *Śūdras*.[137] But he never admitted that women should study the *Veda*, should be nuns, or should undertake devotional practice alongside men; he believed carrying out household duties was where their role in life should be.[138] In fact, he left his wife, whom he clearly did not like, but is reputed to have done so because she could not accept his lower-class associates. His teacher, in fact, was one such person. Ideas of universality and equality, then, did not overstep traditional boundaries in terms of scriptural tradition, but certainly departed from established norms in other areas. Essentially, for all classes, for rich and poor, it was possible to turn to the refuge of God in self-surrender, particularly in starting out on the path to liberation. But Rāmānuja favoured a measure of conservative acceptance of *Vedic* injunctions as essential for the path of liberation, though he seems to have been open to the use of other means for those not qualified to engage in the accepted tradition.

While the biographers of Rāmānuja are keen to illustrate his universality and brotherhood, it is likely that this may have been a somewhat intentional hagiographic portrayal.[139] But devotion is an approach to God that really needs no mediator, and it seems that for some, Rāmānuja encouraged the love of God through *bhakti* that was independent of scriptural prescriptiveness. All are fundamentally eligible for liberation, and all can set out on the path for it, progressing towards God in each birth. The initial steps on this path need not be the hearing of the *Veda* but, instead, the opening and surrendering of oneself to God. However, for those on the higher slopes, more prescriptive means were traditional and Julius Lipner puts forward the following pointed comment: "Clearly, at the very least Rāmānuja implies that the one ideally qualified (i.e. the *adhikārin*) for embarking on the path to salvation in the present life is a pious Śrī Vaiṣṇava male, belonging to one of the twice-born castes (*sic*), and duly initiated by the proper teacher into reflection upon the Vedas and into the performance of the ordained sacrifices."[140] The ideal devotee for Rāmānuja was the *bhakta* who was also a *jñānin*, one who had direct intuitive knowledge of the divine, intuitive knowledge synonymous with constant and continuous love of, and devotion to, God. This was not so much an emotional love, as one characterized by intuitive vision of divinity.[141] At the same time, the emotion of *bhakti* was, to a certain extent, blended within the established norms. As C. J. Bartley pertinently says: "Rāmānuja 'intellectualises' the emotional *bhakti* of the Āḻvārs and locates devotion in a context of necessary social and religious obligations."[142] There is an increasing knowledge of the nature of the self, of God, and of the inseparable relationship between the two. There is blissful realization of the self as the attribute of God, and an outpouring of love and devotion to God that is reciprocated by the grace of God, who loves his devotee.

It is God who has the final word in the process of liberation. For, while all humanity is loved by God, his devotees are particularly elected – something that was a theme in the *Bhagavad Gītā*. In Viśiṣṭadvaita, God is the ultimate means to *mokṣa* and favours his elect with the rewards appropriate to their righteous *karmic* activity, which is why observance of obligatory commands of the *Veda* was so important. God himself strives to bring the devotee to him – again, something that the *Gītā* stressed.[143] All human action needs the grace of God to succeed. In the words of Rāmānuja: "So when people have taken refuge in God, then his grace will facilitate all their activities: they will no more be subject to the misconception that ātman is non-ātman."[144] J. B. Carman writes, "intimate communion with God is not something that man can gain; not even the advanced devotee who yearns desperately for this communion can gain it by his own effort. Salvation is God's election and God's gift".[145] Rāmānuja himself stated: "For it is only He, who is omniscient, omnipotent, and very generous, who having been worshipped . . . is pleased to grant different forms of enjoyment and final emancipation, which consists in attaining His own essential nature."[146] Yet such grace does not offend the law of *karma*, and it is not proffered without being justly deserved. God's grace has to be earned, for God does not operate outside his own laws. God effectively remains the inner Ruler, the *antaryāmin*, by nodding his head in agreement to the fruition of appropriate effects for individual human causes: certainly for Rāmānuja the individual is expected to strive for liberation.

Released souls enjoy the bliss of the transcendental realm of God, the place of pure *sattva*. They can assume bodies that are composed of this transcendental material if they so wish, (and hence must be individual), but for the purpose of serving God in their enlightened state. *Mukti*, liberation, is a direct apprehension of God, and the knowledge of the self as inseparably related to God. It is a positive state of existence, of self-fulfilment, of communion with God. Knowledge is expanded to the point of omniscience in each soul. And Viśiṣṭādvaita makes no sense unless that knowledge is one that includes a *personal* identity for the soul. As each soul was individual in life, so it is logical for it to have particular characteristics that differentiate it from other souls in the state of liberation. But the point is never clear in Rāmānuja's works. It seems to me that, in line with substance–attribute relationalism, liberated Selves as substances are identical, but their attributes are different – again, identity qualified by difference. There is, too, a definite anthropomorphism about the nature of the Viśiṣṭādvaita afterlife, where souls dwell in a beautiful *sattvic* world with a visible God. It is something graphically described in Vaiṣṇava accounts – golden sunshine, gentle breezes, refreshing streams of water, trees laden with fruit, music, singing and feasting. There is a fellowship of liberated souls, each of the same nature of attributive knowledge and bliss, but subtly different from the next. And all are united in service to God: "The released soul becomes a piece of living poetry, beauteous in form, rhythmical in beats of living", writes Murthy.[147]

In combining traditional philosophy with Tamil devotion, Rāmānuja's contribution to the Vaiṣṇava religion was immense. He gave devotional religion scholastic and academic credence, and gave an enormous impetus to the Vaiṣṇava religion, establishing it firmly in the bounds of orthodoxy. Chandradhar Sharma wrote of Rāmānuja: "He has given us the best type of monotheism pregnant with immanentism. He has emphasized the religious side but not at the cost of the philosophical. His intense religious fervour and his bold logic make him one of the immortals in Indian Philosophy."[148] But it is the goal of Viśiṣṭādvaita that is its greatest legacy to Hinduism: "The end of knowledge is not an 'It', but first an 'I', the one who knows, and then finally the 'THOU', the Supreme Person in whom alone I find my fullness and fulfilment."[149]

The Śrī-Vaiṣṇava poets of Maharashtra

As we move North from the Tamil regions we come to Maharashtra in the central West of India and here in the thirteenth century we find the Vārkarīs, the Vaiṣṇava devotional worshippers of Viṭhobā or Viṭṭhal – their preferred names for Viṣṇu as Kṛṣṇa – whose main temple is in the southern area at Pandharpur, a place of pilgrimage – important to the Vārkarīs – in the past and present, near the border of Karnataka. In Karnataka, too, devotion to Viṭṭhal was characterized by devotional singing of *bhajans* in the local language that was easily understood by all, and recitation of the names of God. People of all castes and both genders were captivated by the devotional fervour in which they could participate. Nevertheless, the Vārkarīs were conservative in their acceptance of the orthodox traditions of class and stage-of-life *dharma*. Viṭhobā is an unusual deity in that he could sometimes be addressed as female as well as male and may at times be amalgamated with Śiva as well as Viṣṇu.[150] *Gurus*, too, receive veneration.

Of the many saints, *sants*,[151] five are renowned in the Maharashtra traditions. Jñāneśvar (1275–96), was a *Brāhmin*, who was the inspiration for the rise of *bhakti* movements in Maharashtra and whose concept of God was of a caring, affectionate, loving and friendly deity – the characteristics of deity favoured by the Maharashtra *sants* as opposed to the erotic Kṛṣṇa. Jñāneśvar's father had entered the fourth stage of life of total renunciation but then abandoned it, so he, Jñāneśvar and his siblings were regarded as outcastes. Jñāneśvar was the spiritual teacher of the great and most renowned *sant*, Nāmdev (1270–1300 or 1350). Nāmdev was a tailor, and is reputed to have written more than two thousand hymns – *ābhaṅgas* as the hymns of the Maharashtra *sants* were called. These dealt with the life of Kṛṣṇa. But if he concentrated on Kṛṣṇa at times, his hymns also have a characteristic blending of both the *nirguṇa* and *saguṇa* concepts of deity – the indescribable transcendent Absolute on the one hand and the personal God with attributes on the other. He, too, attracted people from all castes and introduced *kīrtans* into Maharashtra *bhakti*. Nāmdev approached God as a small child, as a cowherd boy. As Vidyut Aklujkar says: "He talks baby talk with God, plays games with God, quarrels with God, brags in front of God, and even sternly admonishes God."[152] He is, thus, known as God's "buddy". Nāmdev loved to describe the antics of Kṛṣṇa and his brothers, almost as if he were an eye-witness: "They pee and use their palms to smear the ground, then wipe their hands on their bellies", he wrote.[153]

Much later was Eknāth (1528/33– 1600), whose poems Aklujkar describes as "the most philosophically charged and socially potent of the Marathi *sant* poems."[154] Although he was an erudite *Brāhmin*, his hymns show that they were for the lower castes as much as the elite.

His philosophy, however, was firmly in the school of Advaita Vedānta but he still addressed Kṛṣṇa in his hymns as if he were playing games with the young God remembering that such frolicking of the cowherds was clearly casteless. Interestingly, Eknāth believed God's greatness to be possible only as a consequence of the love of his devotees. And yet, he spoke of his own complete helplessness and, as other saint–poets, the need to surrender to God, so typical of the Vaiṣnava path.

Tukārām

In early seventeenth-century Maharashtra, a great and famous poet was born – Tukārām, the Shakespeare of India. He had a short and difficult life but his devotional poetry has remained to make him one of India's best loved and most famous of poets. Tukārām was a *Śūdra*[155] and had many, many tribulations in the forty years that he lived, not least, the fierce opposition of the *Brāhmin* class against his religious expression. His parents died, famine caused the death of his first wife and his child, and his business as a trader went bankrupt. The only source of solace was at the shrine of Viṣṇu as Viṭṭhal/Viṭhobā, which he began to repair, taking up his ancestral religion of the Vārkarīs. In a dream he was given the *mantra* "Rāma-Kṛṣṇa-Hari" and was told to create *ābhaṅgas*, short poems, in praise of Viṭhobā. Tukārām was not at all thrilled with this idea and exercised great humility in singing to God, but attracted large numbers of followers. Having been given the *mantra* he stressed the chanting of the divine name as a way to God. His poetry shows his deep longing for experience of God and his equally deep understanding of human nature. His own tribulations and ordinary experiences were transferred into religious poetic spirituality in a language that remained close to village life.

Tukārām's poems were described by Dilip Chitre as "a massive jumbled collection of randomly scattered poems" without any chronological or thematic sequence.[156] Chitre did a superb service in translating selections of Tukārām's poetry thematically, and it is his work that I am mainly referring to here. Interestingly, Chitre described Tukārām's *bhakti* as a "middle way" between the excessive orthodoxy of the *Brāhmins* and folk religion.[157] Since the poems, as those of other Maharashtra poets, were in the local Marathi, as Chitre said: "They made language a form of shared religion and religion a shared language" leaving ordinary low-caste folk and women "thrilled by the heights their own language scaled and stirred by the depths it touched."[158] These were poems to God that held meaning for literate and illiterate hearers; poems that could be remembered and sung by all. Their context was often village or household life, the farming community, harvest time and the like. And Tukārām used the local names for Viṣṇu as Viṭhobā, Viṭṭhal and Pandarang.

Tukārām often felt the frustration of his task as a poet: "My caste is low; My origins humble. A little help from you Will go a long way", he says to God.[159] To write poems, he said, is tough without any experience of God. And yet he said: "This voice is not my own" for he believed it was God himself who created the poems.[160] But Tukārām criticized God: "In my eyes He is empty. He does not care If one starves To death"[161] and he wondered whether God even heard him. But he put himself in God's hands: "I am tired. You are my last stop, My final place of rest."[162] In a beautiful hymn before the image of Viṭhobā he said:

From now on
Let me remain in this trance
My sight, my mind
Tempted beyond time

I shall shut my life
To enclose His form
I shall feel Him in my body
To worship Him

He will enter my soul
And make it still
Peaking
Into an absolute spire

Says Tuka,
O my bonny Vithoba
Let me lie prostrate
At your feet.[163]

As with the southern poets, the idea of surrendering to God remained in the *bhakti* poetry of Maharashtra and, indeed, in that of Tukārām. He referred to himself as a dog lying at the door of his Lord, never leaving the feet of his master. To experience God's grace, surrender was essential. In one of his poems it is clear that he believed all suffering came from God – whether the meteorite that shatters one's home or a catastrophe that wipes one out – but when one is beyond all hope, the only refuge is God.[164] And few others suffered more than him. Even when he felt God was distant, he knew that God was with him at every moment, "fixed within him"; and as wicked and unjust as he felt, he just wished to lay his head upon the feet of his Lord. He *loved* God and cherished the dual relationship between himself and God that allowed that love to be. In a very interesting and charming hymn, Tukārām sang of the need for an anthropomorphized God and yet, he knew at the same time that God could never be so confined:

We fit You in a frame to worship You,
Though You contain the fourteen universes.
We display You to show our pleasure
Though You have no definition or form.
We sing songs addressed to You,
Though you are way beyond words.
We put garlands around your neck,
Though you are apart from all action.

Says Tuka, O God, become limited
To pay me a little attention.[165]

Tukārām reasoned, almost bargained with, and certainly questioned, God: "What sort of dumb God are you Who needs to be told what ought to be done?" he said.[166] And again he said of God: "Tukā says, you heartless man, you don't give a damn about yourself or anyone else."[167]

Some of Tukārām's poems were critical of social injustices. He castigated *Brāhmins* and was highly critical of caste conventions. He also intensely disliked those who set themselves up as *gurus*, "may his Guruhood end up in a creek of shit!", he wrote, "He has condemned his ancestors to Hell!"[168] As to the ascetic, he wittily said: "He must consume a lot of *bhang*, and opium, and tobacco; But his hallucinations are perpetual."[169] He also criticized Vedāntic *paṇḍits* and worshippers of the Mother Goddess.

For all his sufferings, Tukārām did find God and then he said: "I have no name Or form I am neither active Nor passive"; "Narayana has given me refuge All my feelings lie at His feet" and "I have dissolved God, the self, and the world To become one luminous being."[170] He also said: "I have compressed my space. I have no room for myself", and "We have become what is immutable and pure";[171] "My entire body is filled with Vitthal."[172] Yet he loved to be the servant of God his master more than anything and said he was happy not to be liberated. We do not know how he died, he simply left his friends and devotees and was never seen again, leaving only the tales about him and his hymns. These last have become the *kīrtans* that he advocated as a means to the grace of God for devotees. They are sung, recited and chanted today by the Vārkarīs and are known widely throughout India.

The fifth of the great Maharashtra saints was Rāmdās (1608–81). His name means "Servant of Rāma". As his name suggests, his chosen deity was Rāma but he also honoured Hanumān, the famous monkey general of the *Rāmāyaṇa*, as well as Bhavanī, the divine Mother and *śakti* force. In the temples he established, these three deities were honoured through *bhakti* and his followers came from both genders and all castes. More politically aware than the other Maharashtra saints, he sang to royalty as much as the general populace.

Women poets of Maharashtra

Maharashtra also had a number of important women *bhakta* poets who were devoted to Viṭhobā. It was very, very difficult for a woman to behave devotionally in the same way as men. Some, against all odds, left the safety of their guarded convention-driven lives to devote themselves to their chosen God. Others had to maintain their expected roles and, at the same time, express their devotion to God through remarkable devotional poetry. Muktābāī (*bāī*, "saint", is an honorific term added to a great woman's name), was the sister of Jñaneśvar, whom we met above, and so, as he, was an outcaste because their father had renounced *saṃnyāsa* and returned to his home. As an outcaste, Muktābāī did not marry but spent her time in devotion to God with her three brothers. Her poetry is full of natural imagery. Another female poet was Jānābāī who lived as a servant at the family home of

Nāmdev. She feminized the God Viṭhobā referring to him as her Mother. She brought God into her daily life as her aid in collecting cow dung, grinding grain, washing, and even removing lice,[173] such was her devotion. The female saint–poet Soyrabāī and her sister Nirmala were untouchables. The former was married to a saint and the latter may also have been married.[174] Soyrabāī's poems show how she felt that even though she was an untouchable she was able to offer God simple food: "I'll place a leaf before you and serve you family food", she said.[175] She knew, too, that: "The net of pollution is broken with the strength of the Name."[176] In one magnificent hymn she reflects on the unity of God with the enlightened soul:

> All colors have merged into one. The Lord of Color himself is immersed
> In that colour.
> When I saw the Lord of Pandhari, the I–you feeling also disappeared . . .
> You who have a body are not embodied . . .
> I who look and the looking itself are one, says Cokha's Mahari.

As the translator, Eleanor Zelliot says here, her poem merges the *saguṇa* and *nirguṇa* conceptions of God – the describable God with qualities on the one hand and the indescribable Absolute without qualities on the other.[177] Nirmala, too, had a developed concept of God. She surrendered to his feet, put her head in his lap, utterly giving herself up to God.

Another woman poet–saint was Bahiṇābāī, born in 1628 and so a contemporary of Tukārām in the seventeenth century: indeed, she became his initiated disciple. She bemoaned her fate as having been born a woman and denied access to the *Vedas*, the secret *Gāyatrī-Mantra* and other sacred *mantras*, or the right to chant *Oṃ*, and she bemoaned, too, the perspective of women as foolish and seductive, ready to bring harm to men and, indeed, she bemoaned the *punishment* of being a woman. Yet, she was a dutiful *Brāhmin* wife, a *pati-vratā*, despite being the subject of domestic violence. She wrote of the tension between obeying *Vedic* injunctions that had created the role of a subservient wife and her devotion to God. In her *ābhaṅgas*, her hymns that are still sung today in Maharashta by Vārkarīs, she comes across as an ordinary woman with the same difficulties as other married women but in her case she had to maintain her devotion despite opposition from her husband. Mary McGee aptly comments: "Bahiṇābāī's *abhaṅgas* often reveal the tension between Brahmanical elitism (symbolized by her husband) and the emotion-filled bhakti tradition (represented by herself)."[178] Since she was married at the age of five, her devotion to her God, Viṭhobā, was exceptional and by the time she was eleven, her devotion was very deep-rooted, even though she prayed fervently for some release from the violent beatings she received from her husband: she naturally questioned God as to why he did not help her. It was at this age that she became a disciple of the *Śūdra* Tukārām, whom she revered as much as her God Viṭhobā/Lord Viṭṭhal. Her domestic situation was alleviated somewhat when her husband fell ill and was sufficiently frightened to travel with Bahiṇābāī to the place where Tukārām lived to become his devotee, though her husband's violence was not totally assuaged.

Bahiṇābāī's concept of God seems to have been a non-dual one: perhaps that was why she could put up with her suffering since she believed that being devoted to God helped her to live as a true *bhakta* in prescribed service to her family and to God, both being ultimately one.[179] The Vārkarīs' religious outlook has always been that religion is as much to be fulfilled in the home as the temple and outwardly in the world as much as inwardly: caste *dharma* was maintained by the Vārkarīs. Bahiṇābāī's non-dualist view also made God and her *guru*, Tukārām, identical and in many of her hymns she refers to them both as her brother.[180] That non-dual view also led to her thinking that even her violent husband and Tukārām were, in fact, not different from one another.[181] So Bahiṇābāī supported the Advaitist view of the non-dual Brahman, the "That thou art" of the *Chāndogya Upaniṣad*, and the Advaita view that the world is *māyā* and unreal. Bahiṇābāī died at the age of seventy-two.

The Maharshtra saints, as their Tamil counterparts, saw complete surrender to God and service to God as the simple means of reaching his feet but the Maharashtra saints did not make such a simple pathway effective without combining surrender with established collective and personal *dharma*. Yet, while the external aspects of religion were upheld, the very fact that the hymns of the saints were in the Marathi tongue brought about a shift in the emphasis of religion from elitist expressions to ordinary simplicity that was appealing to the popular mind. The devotion of these saints was experiential and that was what they expressed in their hymns so that their experiences were passed on to the common man and woman. *Love* for God was the key to transcending worldly egocentricity and desires. God is to be found in the mundanity of life, in the home, in every being and within each self. *Gurus* are important in the Maharashtra tradition, sometimes being equated with God and sometimes being superior to God. Hence, the Maharashtra saints outlined here are of immense importance.

Northern Vaiṣṇava saints

Bhakti movements were probably present in northern India by the fourteenth century, reaching their peak in the fifteenth and sixteenth centuries. Vrindavana, especially Braj, was where Kṛṣṇa's life was cast and it was natural that it would be him on whom the northern *bhakti* poets focused. As those in the South, they composed their songs in local languages that attracted many devotees. The northern poets were more orthodox than their southern counterparts and many belonged to *Brāhmin* castes, though their devotees came from all areas of society, even untouchables.[182] In the religious context, caste did not matter, but in the social context it was rigidly supported by the northern poet–saints. The northern saints also differed from those in the southern lands in that they did not become divinized *gurus*, mainly because they delineated themselves very clearly from the God they worshipped.[183] I want to concentrate on three of the sixteenth-century northern saints, three great poets, Sūrdās (exact date uncertain), Tulsīdās (1532–1623), and a female, Mīrābāī (1498–1546). All three were *saguṇa bhaktas* and devotees of Viṣṇu in one form or another.

Sūrdās

This renowned Hindi poet Sūrdās is well-known throughout India. As so many of the poets, his life is obscured by what John Stratton Hawley describes as "centuries of encrustation and retouching".[184] Sūrdās was born in a village south of Delhi near Braj from where the Kṛṣṇa stories abound. He is said to have been blind, but there is much doubt concerning his blindness: references in his poems are vague and may refer to spiritual blindness.[185] It seems he had much contact with the *Ācārya* Vallabhā and his son, Viṭṭhalnāth. Vallabhā is said to have influenced his poetic repertoire on the nature and *līlā* of Kṛṣṇa. Leaving the life of the saint aside, I want to concentrate more on his poetry and his concept of God. Vallabhā, as we saw above, preferred to focus on Kṛṣṇa as a young child, and Sūrdās does, too. His poetic content includes much about Kṛṣṇa as very young with his naughtiness in stealing butter, his older life tending cows, and his interaction with the *gopīs*, especially the incident of Kṛṣṇa stealing their clothes.

Sūrdās wrote in Hindi with a desire to tell the story of the *Bhāgavata Purāṇa* in the local language of Braj to bring it into the experience of ordinary people and to inspire them to become devotees of Kṛṣṇa.[186] But his work was not a translation for he embellished stories to meld with his own concept of Kṛṣṇa resulting in some very original material. Sūrdās' great work was his *Sūr Sāgar*, the "Ocean (*sāgar*) of Sūr",[187] so named when additions of other contributors raised the work to mammoth size after his lifetime. S. M. Pandey and Norman Zide depict rather well the attractive reflection of daily life at the time of Sūrdās when they write: "These poems present dramatically the psychology of an Indian childhood, in the context of vividly presented scenes of village life, and depict the various rituals, festivals, customs, and manners of common people of medieval India in Braj."[188] Factors such as these were the inspiration for ordinary folk to approach God in a natural manner especially since the Kṛṣṇa whom they worshipped was presented in contexts of ordinary domestic life that they could understand. Sūrdās' poems are replete with spontaneity, naturalness and charming contexts: he presents Kṛṣṇa as a lovely, lovely child, drawing the listener into a relationship of delight in an exquisite young God.

Sūrdās was a *saguṇa bhakta* and in one poem, Kṛṣṇa sent a friend to preach *nirguṇa bhakti* to the *gopīs*. They would have none of it and ridiculed the messenger in one of Sūrdās' famous "bee" songs when the *gopīs* likened the messenger to a black bumblebee. Their God, Kṛṣṇa, was an approachable God with an abundance of qualities: they did not need knowledge to approach him, only total devotion, love and surrender of the self. Through the medium of the *bhajans*, the sung poems of Sūrdās, the devotee was brought close to the *saguṇa* God: "Song, for Sūr – singing to the Lord", writes John Stratton Hawley, "is as close as one can come to salvation."[189] Through the power of song at the feet of the Lord the devotee had direct access to Kṛṣṇa, was drawn into him through the poet's words and, at the same time, intimately remembered God. Most of Sūrdās' songs were devoted to Kṛṣṇa but some were directed to Rāma and even included Śiva. Sūrdās called God his friend and companion, the one who loves his devotee as his own no matter what the lowly or sinful state of the devotee: it was an all-encompassing message. While Sūrdās' poetry featured wonderfully attractive lengthy verses of Kṛṣṇa's birth and childhood, it also had its erotic themes. His erotic poetry sometimes had a play on Mūralī, Kṛṣṇa's female flute, and his intimate relationship with it, and he told also of Kṛṣṇa's dalliances with many lovers and his unfaithfulness to Rādhā. He included in his poems much of the love play between the *gopīs* and Kṛṣṇa and especially that between the latter and Rādhā.

Rādhā occupied an important place in the theology of Sūrdās and he paid significant and extended attention to her relationship with Kṛṣṇa. Later, she was to be presented as in unity with Kṛṣṇa, two aspects of the same divinity. But this more extensive treatment of Rādhā was an evolving one with additions to Sūrdās' earlier poems by later contributors. For Sūrdās, it was the depth of love that she had for Kṛṣṇa that was most important. In describing the love between the maidens and Kṛṣṇa, Sūrdās seemed to speak as if he was one of the lovelorn *gopīs*. The *gopīs* continually awaited the grace of Kṛṣṇa, not because they believe they deserved it but because their love was so intense they could think of nothing else. When they were united with Kṛṣṇa as in the dance of love, the *rāsa-līlā*, Sūrdās described the scene in great detail, but it is the following separation and longing, *viraha*, that showed the extent of their love: Sūrdās dealt with this theme extensively and movingly. Hawley comments on the early *Sūr Sāgar*, here, "the great text throbbed with poems of anger and despair, irony and complaint",[190] and in Hawley's excellent analysis of the hymns of Sūrdās, he considers these early *viraha* compositions to be Sūrdās' "major voice":[191] "No theme in the early *Sūr Sāgar* can rival *viraha* in prevalence or intensity."[192] The *gopīs* complain: "We've heard that love is a life-giving vine, but now, says Sūr, it bears poisonous fruit, And deprived of the light from Hari's lunar face the lotus of our hearts declines to bloom."[193] Focus on Kṛṣṇa was, thus, greater in his absence than in his presence.

Surrender to Kṛṣṇa came from true humility and awareness of one's inadequacies and sins. "Wearing the garment of lust and anger, on my neck a garland of sensuality. The ankle bells of delusion peal out sweet words of malice; envy sounds in my body in all kinds of beats",[194] were the words of Sūr Dās as a humble poet who could describe himself as the worst of sinners. In another poem he said: "All those other sinners are a flock of amateurs, but I have practised every day since birth", "And look", he said, "you've abandoned me, rescuing the rest!"[195] Sūrdās *expected* his Lord to save him otherwise Kṛṣṇa could be accused of not being fair! As we have seen with other poets, Sūrdās had the kind of intimacy with God that enabled him to be critical of Kṛṣṇa – but plaintively so. Such poems are full of sadness as well as anger and insult – in other words, they are spontaneously natural. It is surely such natural feeling that is a major reason why Sūrdās' songs are still sung in temples and homes all over India today, not just in those of the Vallabhā tradition. And in Hindi-speaking areas, the name given to a blind man is likely to be Sūrdās. The legends of Sūrdās have long outstripped reality but his hymns have remained the inspiration of a whole tradition and have given solace to multitudes of devotees throughout the centuries – an inspiration and a solace that is ongoing in present time.

Tulsīdās

Tulsīdās, ("Servant of the *tulasī*", *tulasī* being the sacred plant associated with Viṣṇu), came from a poor *Brāhmin* family, so he spent his early life in poverty and reflected on this in one of his hymns: "From childhood on, poor thing that I was, I went weeping, begging from door to door. To me the four great goals of life were four little grains of food."[196] Braj Sinha describes him as "probably the most powerful influence on the popular religiosity in the northern India".[197] Tulsīdās was a devotee of Rāma and is most famous for his version of Vālmīki's Sanskrit *Rāmāyaṇa* written in a Hindi dialect. It was a daring feat to produce a non-Sanskrit text based on the original orthodox tale and it is to Tulsīdās' famous *Rāma-carita-mānasa*, "The Sacred Lake of the Acts of Rāma", that we owe the conception of Rāma as a fully deified *avatāra* of Viṣṇu. Hagiographic legend overcomes the distinction between the two texts by claiming Tulsīdās as an *avatāra* of Vālmīki himself.[198]

Tulsīdās was a great exponent of *saguṇa bhakti*, though occasionally he travelled the path of knowledge but admitted it to be a tougher one. His God, Rāma, had an abundance of describable qualities. While he had some poems to Kṛṣṇa, Rāma was for him the supreme God and, given the character of Rāma as opposed to Kṛṣṇa, there is none of the erotic content in Tulsīdās' poetry that appears in Kṛṣṇa *bhakti*. Tulsīdās approached God as a servant to a master, his Lord, whose grace was necessary for liberation: "Say Ram, say Ram, say Ram, you fool! That name is your raft on the awful sea of life."[199] He also included Hanumān, the famous monkey-general from the *Rāmāyaṇa* as a deified being; a being that exemplified the ideal of a servant to his master. Rāma for Tulsīdās pervaded the whole world and was there to be served, not just as Rāma himself, but in the form of his devotees and all creatures. Although Rāma was an *avatāra* of Viṣṇu, Tulsīdās seemed to project Rāma as greater than Viṣṇu and as an *avatāra* of the Absolute Brahman. As such, the devotee could only be a fervent and loyal servant: "No one is so downtrodden – none more than I – and you are the one who lifts the heavy weight. You are all life, I am one life; you are the master and I the servant; You are mother and father, teacher and friend: in every connection my lot is relieved."[200] He had the sense of humility before God that was typical of many of the Hindu poets. While he did not lose sight of the formless, transcendent, unqualified nature of God, he believed the formless took on form through love for his devotees so easing the path to God regardless of the sinful nature of the devotee. Repetition of the name of God, he believed, linked the devotee with the formless and qualified God. But the perpetual supreme message of all the *bhakti* poets remained paramount, total surrender to God. Nancy Martin points out the theme of reconciliation in Tulsīdās' poems. She writes: "Within his telling of the tale, Tulsīdās seeks to cultivate deep devotion to Rāma but also to reconcile and integrate Vaiṣṇava and Śaiva devotion, *nirguṇ and saguṇ* perspectives, and *advaita* and *bhakti* religiosity."[201] The point illustrates the extensive learning and erudition of Tulsīdās and his grasp of orthodox philosophies as much as devotional texts.

Despite the all-encompassing nature of *bhakti*, Tulsīdās was rather orthodox in his views. He even claimed that *Śūdras* and women could be beaten, classing both alongside drums, cattle and fools, and he wrote about men being under the power of women, though also that all women should be looked on as mothers. He upheld the established social system and believed that *Brāhmins* should be venerated even if they were evil. *Gurus*, too, he elevated to a high status. And yet, whatever status one had, without devotion to God, it would be as nothing. Tulsīdās did not deny the reality of the world and was world affirming in that he stressed the need for social values in daily life underpinned by devotion to God. A life lived in the company of other devotees all being focused on God, singing God's glories, repeating God's name and surrendering to God were the means by which life should be lived according to Tulsīdās. Chanting of the name, *nāma-japa*, was considered by Tulsīdās to be the best means to the Lord since the name of Rāma was the equivalent of his essence.

So important is Tulsīdās' *Rāma-carita-mānasa* that it is recited at *Rām-līlās*, recitations of it that take up to a week or a month at annual festivals. These festivals are attended by pilgrims from all over India. What the *Mānasa* provided was not just a translation of the Sanskrit *Rāmāyaṇa* but an attractive embellishment of it that includes moral issues – so typical of Rāma the hero – and *emotion* that had immense appeal to the populace. People were able to approach God through a scripture that they themselves could sing and – even simpler – they could just chant the name of its God. In a more official way, the sect called the Rāmānandis founded by Rāmānanda, earlier in date than Tulsīdās, took up the poet's teachings as part of its fundamental theology. But unlike Rāmānanda, who came to be accepted as a form of the God, Rāmā, himself, Tulsīdās did not found an order, and it is likely that he never belonged to one.

Mīrābāī

Mīrābāī, born in about 1500, is surely the greatest of female medieval saints of northern India. She was a Hindi princess of the royal house of Merta in Marwar kingdom in northern Rajasthan. A marriage was arranged for her in 1516 with the prestigious and powerful Śisodiyā Rajput royal family from the southern kingdom of Mewar. She was a devotee of Lord Kṛṣṇa, whom she had adored since childhood, whom she liked to call "The Dark One", Shyām, and to whom she felt herself to be absolutely bodily and spiritually wedded. So to be wedded to an earthly man was anathema to her and she refused to consummate her marriage. Belonging to a high class and being female, Mīrā had no say in the life she was expected to live, but she defied everyone, met often with holy men, refused to worship the Mother Goddess and Śiva in her married home, and revolted against established norms in order to dedicate herself entirely to Kṛṣṇa. For this, she was heavily persecuted by her in-laws and attempts were even made to kill her. Rajasthan had (and still has) very strict codes of conduct for women and when her husband died she refused to become a *satī* and immolate herself on his funeral pyre. Mīrā became an ascetic wanderer, composing songs to Kṛṣṇa and dancing to her Lord. Much later in her life she reached Kṛṣṇa's final home in Dwaraka where she remained at one of his temples, becoming a famed *bhakta*. It is said that when her husband's family pursued her there, on entering the temple they found only her robe draped over the image of Kṛṣṇa as if she had merged with him. While Indian women are defined in relationship to men, Mīrā was never so. Parita Mukta has found that Mīrā today has become a regionally specific saint especially for subordinated classes of Saurashthra and Rajasthan.[202] But Mīrā's life story, though heavily embellished by hagiography with many variations, is very well known throughout all India: Mīrā has pan-Indian appeal because of her spiritual strength in the face of opposition.

Many of the poems, *padas*, accredited to Mīrā were probably composed in her name after she died and there is no corpus of poems that can be clearly ascertained as hers probably because she was never part of any established tradition, though this does not detract from the force of *bhakti*, nor from Mīrā herself in the legacy of her life to devotional Hinduism. As a *saguṇa bhakta*, Mīrā's concept of God was as a personal being with a full character and she was fond, especially, of Kṛṣṇa Giridhāra, Kṛṣṇa as he who lifted the mountain and held it above people as protection from Indra's deluge of rain: "Mine is the mountain-lifting Gopal", she said "there is no other."[203] Mīrā sang of Kṛṣṇa's large playful eyes and the darkness of his skin. Her approach to Kṛṣṇa was intimate at every turn: she implored him, scolded him, cried to him and sang and danced to him and sang at one point of flame twisting on flame to describe the intimacy of their relationship. Mandakranta Bose writes: "In her songs she sees herself in a relationship with Kṛṣṇa as a real entity whose presence is always actual, immediate and intimate, a familiar being whom she places in every kind of loving relationship of domesticity, including those of bride, friend and mother."[204] Mīrā wrote of her love:

> Let us go to a realm beyond going,
> Where death is afraid to go,
> Where the high-flying birds alight and play,
> Afloat in the full lake of love.
> There they gather – the good, the true –
> To strengthen an inner regimen,
> To focus on the dark form of the Lord
> And refine their minds like fire.
> Garbed in goodness – their ankle bells –
> They dance the dance of contentment
> And deck themselves with the sixteen signs
> Of beauty, and a golden crown –
> There where the love of the Dark One comes first
> And everything else is last.[205]

While Mīrā wrote of her Dark Lord as a husband, there was no eroticism in her poetry. If she gave him personality, she also recognized his greatness and majesty. She dreamt of her marriage to Kṛṣṇa but in her poems he was always absent and she experienced separation, *viraha*: "Having launched the boat of passion," she wrote, "You abandoned it on the sea of separation. Lord, where have you gone?"[206] This is so typical of all the poet–saints' experiences. It is her longing and searching quest to be in communion with Kṛṣṇa that was at the heart of her poetry. And she blended ascetic living with desired marital union – two incompatible concepts in orthodox Hinduism.[207] Andrew Schelling aptly writes that her poems "cut to the quick – amorous, hungry, full of ecstasy or tossed with despair". He says that "in her song she reanimates India's old tradition of love poetry, and recklessly sweeps it up into religious conviction".[208]

There are a few poems to Rāma amongst those attributed to Mīrā but it was Kṛṣṇa who was the centre of her world: "The dear Dark Lover is my breath, the root, the source of my life", she sang.[209] The world without Kṛṣṇa was but a temporary one, a phantasy of untruth. As Lindsey Harlan points out, Mīrā rejected the common idea that she should be a *pati-vratā*, serving with devotion a human husband: she became, instead, a *pati-vratā* of Kṛṣṇa.[210] "I will become the servant of your lotus feet", she said.[211] Mīrā pursued what Schelling describes as "a phosphorescent love affair" with Kṛṣṇa,[212] and a "feral passion".[213] Mīrā wrote:

O Unborn, Indestructible,
come to your beggar!
Finish her pain and touch her
with pleasure!
This coming and going will end,
says Mīrā
with me clasping your
  feet forever.[214]

Her experience of God was direct and non-institutionalized. As a Rajput princess, her normal life would have been confined to the courtyard of her home, but she left it to roam from temple to temple, singing and dancing to Kṛṣṇa. Her poems have much content that is mystical rather than erotic to depict her relationship with Kṛṣṇa, and Pandey and Zide are probably right to think her longed-for union with Kṛṣṇa was spiritual rather than physical.[215] Indeed, she says she will accompany Kṛṣṇa through the world, *yogi* and *yoginī* together.

Since Mīrā was female she easily adopted the role of one of the *gopīs* and she could be just as unconventional in her intimacy with Kṛṣṇa as the married wives who were beckoned by his flute. We must remember that male *bhaktas* had to become spiritually female in order to approach Kṛṣṇa. Some of Mīrā's *bhajans*, indeed, are sung only by men.[216] But Mīrā never had to imagine herself as female. She was unconventional in that she never belonged to any one tradition, *saṃpradāya*: that made her immensely popular with people of all castes and of both genders. She *lived* the fact that caste and gender were no barriers to *bhakti* and she *lived* the fact that devotion alone brought God's love and grace. As a woman, her songs sometimes reflected those of local women and must have had wide appeal for the ordinary female householder.

So what of the legacy of Mīrā as a woman for women who came after her? She was not a political creature and had no intention to liberate other women from their conventional roles. But her poems were a heavy challenge to the Rajput hierarchy and feudal power. Inevitably, the peasants and lower castes found her *bhajans* a delight to sing, and in this sense, they are still sung today. The Rajput opposition to Mīrā's songs both in her own time and today is considerable. Mukta found as much in her field research in Rajasthan.[217] It is not prudent to mention the name of Mīrā in some sections of Rajput society and many women are critical of Mīrā's abandoning of her husband. In some cases, the name Mīrā has become a term of abuse, though there are other Mīrās who take up the devotional life and are respected for doing so.[218] There has been some "Rajputizing" of Mīrā by Rajput women today, who make her actions accord with their notions of heroism and valour, but many reject her,[219] and regard her as having been insane.[220] In Rajasthan, therefore, Mīrā's songs are rarely heard in areas of Rajput-controlling power. Nevertheless, Lindsey Harlan's research suggests that some Rajput women in Rajasthan admire Mīrā as their famed ancestor but they still believe that she acted shamelessly.[221] Nancy Martin-Kershaw believes that Rajasthan historians presented Mīrā as a heroine and *ideal wife* by dismissing her social and religious unorthodoxy as folk legend.[222] In effect, Mīrā was "Rajputized" to accord with Rajput ideals and values.[223] This, notes Mukta, has allowed Mīrā to surface more recently in the Rajput community.[224] Often, however, the term for a female *bhakta*, *bhaktani*, is used as a derogatory term for a woman.

Despite attempts to sanitize Mīrā, it is amongst the poorer castes that she is hailed as a heroine. Because Mīrā did not belong to any *saṃpradāya* she could remain close to the people. As Mukta puts it: "Mira returns to this society and is alive within it not as a renouncer, and not simply as a bhakta either, but as one who lived a life close to the people".[225] It is the oppressed people who sing her sad songs in their fight against privilege and discrimination by the upper castes, gathering together after the toil of the day. Mukta describes it as the "evocation of a life" and a "common life" that serves to bind together the poor and oppressed.[226] Mukta evocatively writes:

> In this articulation, Mira does not emerge as a lone, isolated voice, but as the voice of the community gathered around, which is not just confined to one's immediate caste community. The community embraced through the bhajans stretches beyond the confines of the gathering, to take in all those who are known to share a common life of suffering. It is a class expression, which cuts across the divisions of caste, and in fact levels down the minute and complex differences which mark out one caste community from another. The poor are all brought together in the evocation of a common life.[227]

If social liberation for women did not ensue from Mīrā's life, spiritual liberation, the inner life of a woman certainly did. When women listen to Mīrā's *bhajans*, they can internalize and identify with her struggles against a patriarchal restrictive existence that most have to endure. At the very least, Mīrā showed that a woman's *bhakti* can equal that of a male. And as a widow expected to immolate herself on her husband's funeral pyre, Mīrā is an example to widows everywhere in her refusal to comply. Mīrā sang of the pain of widowhood and her opposition to it, giving widows the opportunity to articulate their own degraded states through her songs. But the pitiful plight and destitution of so many widows today is reflected with some ambivalence of praise and detestation in their being called Mīrābāīs. Mīrā sang, too, of the mendicant life she led and her songs were taken up by those who led the harsh life of an ascetic so dependent on others for sustenance. The name Mīrā is given to female composers of poetry, or those who sing and dance for God, as well as to those who live a life of devotion to God but, again, with some ambivalence of praise and criticism.

It is a travesty that the life of this great woman did not bequeath social change for women. Mīrā was never a victim as many women are and she gave physical and mental expression to her determination to follow her own course in life. Schelling graphically says: "Hers is the wildness of forest and field, backlane and market",[228] epitomizing rather well her appeal to the ordinary populace. Gandhi wrote of her as an inspiration for his political agendas and in modern times she has been celebrated in film and television, in the famous comic series of *Amar Chitra Katha*, in novels and dance dramas. In Vṛndavana in Braj, there is a little temple in which the shrine has Kṛṣṇa in the centre and Rādhā and Mīrā on either side. Her songs are still sung by the evening communities who need to express their discontent and articulate their emotions through her words. Mīrā's words are a means by which they can openly criticise their superiors. "The community of Mirabai", writes Mukta, "is essentially the community of bhajniks who, over the centuries, have provided a voice to the struggle for dignity, and hope of a better life. The community forged includes within it the community of all sufferers."[229]

My purpose in writing this chapter was to convey the intense warmth of devotional Hinduism especially in the poetry of its medieval proponents. Vaiṣṇava religion past and present is a vast study, particularly in view of the descent of the divine to live and breathe among human beings. Limits of space have not permitted me to explore many other sectarian Vaiṣṇava movements such as Gauḍīya Vaiṣṇavism and the massive contribution of the Bengali saint, Caitanya (1486–1533), in the founding of that sect. Gauḍiyā Vaiṣṇavism deserves a chapter in itself: it exemplifies the intensity of love of God in which many of the earlier expressions of *bhakti* were retained, enhanced, modified and extended to the present day in the well-known Hari Krishna movement. Suffice it to say that devotion to Kṛṣṇa and Rāma as personal Gods has diversified into multiple forms wherever the need has arisen to find new approaches, new pathways of exploration of the personal God who is ever manifest in a multiplicity of ways. In the next chapter, I want to turn to ways in which Śaiva devotionalism have emerged in Hinduism.

8

Devotional Hinduism
The Rise of Śaiva *Bhakti* in Medieval India

Śiva features prominently in southern India's Tamil Nadu, both in the medieval past and in the present. It was here that the famous *Naṭarāja* image originated as well as the symbol so much associated with Śiva, the *liṅga*. The more beneficent aspects of Śiva, too, seem to be prevalent in the South with the characteristics of goodness, love, kindness and graciousness expressed in the Tamil words for *bhakti*, *aṉpu* and *patti*, terms that suggest also surrender of the devotee to God. Śaiva *bhakti* emerged in the Tamil regions in the sixth century, spanning the Pallava dynasty from the sixth to eighth centuries and the Chola dynasty from the ninth to the twelfth centuries. Mariasusai Dhavamony's comment that "Tamil Śaivism is shot through with *bhakti* in every aspect of its life and doctrine"[1] summarizes rather well the potency of Śiva *bhakti* in the Tamil South. It was spread through the devotion and hymns of a number of saints who traversed the land singing of surrender to Śiva and it is these saints with whom I want to deal below: a word, first, on the nature of Śaiva *bhakti*.

Śaiva *bhakti*

The Śaiva poet–saints of the Tamil regions were called *Nāyaṉmārs*, "leaders" (sing. *Nāyaṉar*), or *Aḍiyārs*, "slaves". They represent Śiva-*bhakti* similar in expression to the Vaiṣṇava *bhakti* that was explored in the last chapter but developed into a much more philosophical Śaivism known as Śaiva-Siddhānta. The *Nāyaṉmārs* spanned the centuries from the seventh to the tenth but Śaivism has remained dominant in the South and more prolific than anywhere else in India. There were sixty-three *Nāyaṉmārs* and they consisted of seventeen *Brāhmins*, seven kings, four chieftains, four army chiefs, six *Vaiśyas*, thirteen *Veḷḷālas*, nine *Śudras*, four women and one untouchable.

The lives of the *Nāyaṉmārs* focused entirely on *bhakti* and *bhakti* was their goal and the means to their goal: it was liberation in itself, involving the knowledge of their utter dependence on God. For the *Nāyaṉmārs*, relationship with God was very much a servant–master one in which they submitted and surrendered themselves to God. Vaiṣṇavism had Kṛṣṇa as a focus and the tales of his amorous relationships with the *gopīs* promoted an equally amorous approach to God. Śaiva-*bhakti* was different in that there were no *avatāras* that could bring God quite so readily into the realm of ordinary life. The servant–master relationship, therefore, was the more natural one. Nevertheless, intimacy between devotee and God is very much evident in the hymns of these great poets. Their intense love of God was expressed experientially and emotionally and was grounded in ordinary life with its vicissitudes, toil and suffering. In the same way as the Vaiṣṇavas, they composed their hymns in their native Tamil language in a manner that elicited instant appeal. Love of God poured from the words of their songs as they wandered from place to place, village to village and temple to temple. They sang to Śiva in his localized forms in different shrines, so inspiring the local people to love and worship the form of Śiva residing in each respective shrine.

The poetry of the *Nāyaṉmārs* is stunningly beautiful, full of rich imagery taken from nature and overflowing with love of God. Indira Viswanathan Peterson points out that the Tamil of the hymns is not too distant from that spoken today so that they have become "the center of Tamil Śaiva experience". She also writes: "To this day, devotees directly consult the words of the saints for guidance in various situations, and sing them when they seek personal inspiration or comfort as well as devotional experience."[2] Occasionally, the *Nāyaṉmārs* showed exasperation in their search for God, expressing this by chiding, scolding, rebuking and even cursing God – signs not of irreverence but of the intimacy with which they communicated with Śiva. And yet, there is present also in their hymns an immense humility before God, concomitant with the need to surrender a sinful self completely to him. In the same way as the Vaiṣṇava poets, the *Nāyaṉmārs* saw the feet of the Lord as being the place where they wished to rest. As Peterson beautifully puts it: "The greatest affective value is attached to the Lord's feet, supreme symbol of his power and grace; these beautiful, flower-soft feet are the devotee's ultimate refuge, and his highest aim is to rest in their 'cool shade'."[3] To be at the Lord's feet is to be liberated: "Renouncing all my ties, I think only of your holy feet" wrote one *Nāyaṉār*, "Thinking of them, I have achieved the purpose of my birth."[4] "Brand me with the print of your flower-feet", said another *Nāyaṉār*.[5] I want to expand on such devotion by exploring the *bhakti* of five of the *Nāyaṉmārs*.

Kāraikkāl Ammaiyār

Kāraikkāl Ammaiyār was the first real Śaiva *bhakti* poet–saint, her hymns being the earliest example of Tamil hymns devoted exclusively to Śiva at a time when Śaivism was not yet pan-Indian. Her dates are variously given: somewhere between the fifth and seventh centuries is a wide estimate but most suggest mid-sixth century; Karen Pechilis, for example, suggesting about 550 CE.[6] Her name means "Mother from Karaikkal", Karaikkal being her native place of origin and Ammai being the name, according to legend, that Śiva gave her. Her earlier name may have been Punitavati, "Very Beautiful" but, if she was beautiful she was prepared to abandon her beauty in devotion to Śiva: indeed, just as she saw beauty beneath the grotesque forms of Śiva, she believed he would see the beauty of her devotion beneath her own external form. She asked Śiva to take away her beauty and replace it with a demonic form, a *pēy*: Śiva granted her wish. Kāraikkāl Ammaiyār was a *Vaiśya* and had been married. She balanced her domestic duties to her husband with her love of Śiva, but her devotion to Śiva became the greater of the two and was such that her husband released her from her marriage. Śiva became the sole focus of her life without any wish for something in return from the God. As Dhavamony comments: "This kind of pure love, discounting any return for the efforts made in loving God, is hardly met with elsewhere among the *bhakti* cults of India."[7] Love was the key to her *bhakti* and she believed that it would bring anyone to the feet of God.

Kāraikkāl Ammaiyār's poems were probably the earliest to have been written in the local Tamil language,[8] but she blended Tamil and Sanskrit with sophisticated effect, using Sanskrit, particularly, to describe the form of her God, Śiva. At the same time, she did not lose sight of the ordinary contexts of life and so appealed to her listeners. She may have been influenced by the Caṅkam *puṟam* poetry of the past with its concentration on heroic deeds, death, demons and the like,[9] since one genre of her poems was devoted to the cremation grounds and the ghouls and demons that inhabited them. Her poetry is replete with references to the myths of Śiva and to his visual iconography – both serving to deepen the listeners' knowledge of the God and as a means to him when they were heard. But, as Karen Pechilis notes, while the hagiographic account of her life is now well known in Tamil lands, her poems are rarely sung,[10] even though Kāraikkāl Ammaiyār told her hearers that those who sang her hymns would find their love of Śiva increased, "those who recite them will reach the lord with their inexhaustible love and praise, and undying devotion will be born", she said.[11] Her collections of hymns amount to three: *Sacred Linked Verses of Wonder* (*Aṟputat Tiruvantāti*), referred to as *Wonder*; *Sacred Garland of Double Gems* (*Tiruviraṭṭai Maṇimālai*), known simply as *Garland*; and *Sacred Decade of Verses on Tiruppatikam* (*Tiruvālaṅkāṭṭut Tiruppatikam*), known simply as *Decades*. The *Decades* concentrates on cremation grounds and the ghouls in the first part but includes the dancing Śiva in each section of the second. In the *Garland*, Kāraikkāl Ammaiyār speaks to herself so it is as if her listeners overhear her talk of God.

Kāraikkāl Ammaiyār's concept of God was one that combined a metaphysical conception with a mythical perception, intellectual and emotional:

> I thought of only One.
> I was focused on only One.
> I kept only One inside my heart.
> Look at this One!
> It is He who has Ganga on His head,
> A moonbeam in His hair,
> A radiant flame in his beautiful hand.
> I have become His slave.[12]

The metaphysical and yet iconographic ideas of Śiva are neatly juxtaposed and yet united in this skilful poem. Kāraikkāl Ammaiyār was fond of referring to the River Ganges tumbling from Śiva's hair and she also referred frequently to the permanent blue throat he acquired after drinking the deadly poison that appeared in the myth of the churning of the ocean by the gods and demons, "lord with the iridescent neck that turned black from poison in times of yore", she wrote in one poem.[13] Nevertheless, she seemed to penetrate beyond outward forms and reach the metaphysical truths behind them. Elaine Craddock says as much in the following comment: "Through her powerful poetry, Karaikkal Ammaiyar reveals that the horrific cremation ground is really the cosmos, and the terrifying form of Shiva performing his dance of destruction is really the most sublime and blissful experience of the Lord."[14] Kāraikkāl Ammaiyār makes death beautiful and points to the beauty of Śiva beyond his gruesome forms, what Craddock describes as a "beautiful embodiment of the rhythm of life, burning away our illusions with the fire in his hand".[15] She loved to think of Śiva dancing in the cremation grounds surrounded by female demons such as her. Kāraikkāl Ammaiyār's message was that a devotee should be a living offering to Śiva as she herself was.

The intimacy between Kāraikkāl Ammaiyār and Śiva is very evident from her poems: she had a very *personal* relationship with God and felt that she could question him. She asked him if Pārvatī, his consort, knew of his relationship with Gaṅgā, Mother Ganges, whose flow is broken by his matted hair, or why his lips are not as blue as his throat from the poison he drank? She worried for him about the snake he wears and advises him not to touch it. He had called her Ammai out of fondness and she sometimes referred to him as my father, *appā* or *endai*. But such intimacies do not belie the fact that Kāraikkāl Ammaiyār saw herself as the *servant* (Tam. *toṇṇtar* or *āḷ*) of Śiva: "we will never become servants of any other", she said.[16] And she wrote:

If we, his servants,
knowledgeably complain of our sorrows,
what is the reason that
the lord
    with the lustrous red body
    and the contrasting throat
who takes us as his servants
would neither hear nor listen to us?[17]

Later in the same text, she said: "I have taken refuge in him and live as a servant to the lord".[18] As Pechilis says: "Kāraikkāl Ammaiyār actively kept Śiva in her mind and heart by crafting poetic images of him that could serve for both contemplation and adoration at any time and in any place; they were a moveable feast."[19] The poet's descriptions of Śiva were vivid:

His body is as luminous as morning
His covering of ashes has the brilliance of noon
His matted locks are the colours of sunset
And his throat is like the deepest night.[20]

In such ways, she made an often grotesque and fearful God beautiful and wondrous.

We saw with all the Vaiṣṇava poet–saints that the grace of God was an essential feature of their concept of deity. The same belief is prevalent in Kāraikkāl Ammaiyār's hymns:

> Was it not by grace
> that I long ago achieved
> the precious status of servant
> to the lord who rules?
>
> It was indeed grace
> from the lord as majestic as a golden mountain
> that bears rivulets of the sacred Gaṅga
> like flames of streaming fire.[21]

She took refuge in her God and lived as his servant, believing that he resided in her heart and that her status of servant was a result of his grace. In *Wonder* she wrote:

> By grace the lord protects the entire world
> by grace he stops the cycle of rebirth
> by grace I clearly know eternal truth;
> grace is everything to me.[22]

It is only by the grace of God that he can be known, and for that grace to be proffered the devotee must love God with all his or her heart for the grace received will be in direct proportion to the love offered by the devotee. She told her listeners to pray to the lotus feet of God and desire him with a full and true love. Pechilis uses the expression "devotional subjectivity" to depict how embodiment in human form provides the medium for hymns of praise to Śiva.[23] Kāraikkāl Ammaiyār's aim was to reach the "sacred red feet", the "beautiful lotus-like feet" of Śiva; the divine feet with all the poets being indicative of the transcendent God who is greater than all and who is Creator, Sustainer and Dissolver of the whole universe. That important concept of surrender was also a feature of Kāraikkāl Ammaiyār's poetry: the refuge of God was there for those who were prepared to surrender themselves to him. Her surrender was absolute: the One, the Infinite and the ultimately unknowable Śiva possessed her. At the heart of the means to God, then, were love and surrender of the whole being as well as keeping God perpetually in the heart. She herself praised Śiva with "garlands of words", and adoration of his feet with garlands of flowers:

> If we reach
> our incomparable lord of wisdom
> by lovingly praising him with garlands of hymns
> and adorning his golden feet with ribbons of flowers
> how could the stain of our negative karma
> possibly affect us?[24]

The five-syllabled *mantra*, *Na-ma-Śi-va-ya*, was also an aid to reaching the feet of God.

Kāraikkāl Ammaiyār became an ascetic *pēy*, a ghoul or demon, rejecting her original beauty. Just as Śiva danced wildly in the cremation grounds she, too, wished to be like the God she so loved, seeing beyond his outward form to his inner beauty. She turned away from her own youthful beauty in complete renunciation, and depictions of her show her emaciated form. Her idea of liberation was a mystical one in which she would be enveloped in bliss, in the bright light of God, having swum across the terrible ocean of interminable *karmic* births. The legacy of this amazing woman is considerable in that she was the first to combine her poetry with musical form – a legacy that was to gain impetus with the poet–saints who followed her. North of Chennai is the Sacred Banyan Tree Forest where Kāraikkāl Ammaiyār is said to have spent the remainder of her days and in the Tiruvalankatu Temple she is to be found at the feet of Śiva singing her hymns to him accompanied by her cymbals. Bronze images of her are to be found in many temples of Tamil Nadu, the only *Nāyaṇār* to be portrayed *sitting* at the feet of God.

The *mūvar*

Three Śaiva *Nāyaṉmārs* of the seventh to ninth centuries[25] or perhaps the late sixth to the beginning of the eighth centuries,[26] were also great *Ācāryās*. They are known as "the three", the *mūvar*, and they were Sambandar (Tam. Campantar), Sundarar (Tam. Cuntarar), and Appar.[27] Sambandar and Appar are likely to have been contemporaries since Sundarar mentions them both in a much later work. They were very different in their concept of God and Vidya Dehejia cites a Tamil saying that has Śiva declaring: "My Appar sang of me; Sambandar sang of himself; Sundarar sang of women."[28] The hymns of the *mūvar* are recorded in the very popular *Tēvāram* (Skt. *Dēvāram*), the first seven books of the Tamil Śaiva canon of twelve books called the *Tirumuṟai*. The poems of the *Tēvāram* reflect some of the earlier classical Caṅkam (Skt. Saṇgam) poetry but have very subjective, experiential and personal depictions of Śiva.[29] There is not much influence of erotic *akam* poetry to be found in the *Tēvāram*, though, as Peterson shows, there is more of an influence of the Caṅkam *puṟam* tradition, with "poets expressing personal sentiment, praising a real God who manifests himself in particular places, and celebrating a particular community".[30] Thus, for the *mūvar*, Śiva was grounded not so much in emotional idealism but in real circumstances that permitted direct experience of God. So we have minimal erotic poetry in the hymns of the *mūvar*. The twelfth book of the *Tirumuṟai* is an additional biographical volume to the poets giving us an account of their lives. It is a hagiographic composition called the *Periya Purāṇam* and was composed by Cēkkiḻār in about the twelfth century. He referred to the hymns of the *mūvar* in the *Tēvāram* as the "Tamil *Veda*", and today devotees both at home, in temples, concert halls and festivals – indeed, wherever inspirational praise of Śiva occurs – sing the hymns of the *Tēvāram*.

The poetry of the *mūvar*, composed entirely in the Tamil language, was replete at every point with Śiva-*bhakti* bringing God into every aspect of life, every corner of the land. As Prentiss puts it: "In this way, they wove fragments of ancient and contemporary, esoteric and exoteric, mundane and sacred, and bits of realism and imagination together to create a cohesive discourse of bhakti."[31] And, elsewhere, Prentiss gives us animated, realistic pictures of Śiva *bhaktas*: "The hymns provide us with portraits of happy people at festivals, good servants of Śiva who wear the Śaiva marks in ashes on their foreheads, and people who worship Śiva with flowers and sandalwood paste; in a remarkable poem from Appar, agricultural labor is used as a metaphor for spiritual development that culminates in the bliss of Śiva."[32] Images such as this from everyday life and the world of ordinary folk provided an immense impetus to the popularity and spread of Śiva-*bhakti*. V. Subramaniam comments that the hymns of the *mūvar* "can be compared with the best nature poetry in Sangam Tamil literature".[33]

The concept of God of the *mūvar* was not of a fearsome, gruesome Śiva: they brought to the masses of the population instead a God who was close to them, a God to whom they could sing and dance. While they certainly attested to the transcendence of Śiva they also localized him, bringing him close. In many ways, they transferred the kind of vocabulary used to extol the kings of previous literature to Śiva the God and transferred to Śiva heroic profiles that linked him to specific locales,[34] evoking what Peterson describes as "a religion of love that is quintessentially Tamil in character: love of a Tamil king-hero-god whose presence and acts are 'placed' in beloved Tamil landscapes, love expressed through the images and animated with the spirit of a treasured classical literature".[35] Many of the poems of the *mūvar* depict Śiva's form, his accoutrements and attire. Sambandar portrays Śiva as a lute player who "came to me chanting sweet Tamil poems".[36] In bringing Śiva into personal and local focus, the *mūvar* made him a thorough Tamil God; with cosmic powers, yes, but at the same time intimately concerned with the problems and difficulties of his devotees. By bringing Śiva so close, every aspect of life was infused by him. Reciprocal love was the tie between God and devotee and that love was close enough for the *mūvar* to call Śiva father or mother. The God of the *mūvar* pervaded the entire universe, every being, every plant, everything in nature and everything celestial: he was Lord of all but also the Lord in all. In the many temples the *mūvar* saw Śiva as pervading his many images or his *liṅga*, his renowned symbol – a Lord as sweet as honey and nectar.

All three sang of Śiva in his form as Ardhanārīśvara, half male and half his consort Śrī. This image was, for the *mūvar*, a symbol of his auspiciousness and his great majesty but his female consort was not given any primary importance by all the *mūvar* and it was the transcendence and immanence of Śiva on whom they concentrated. I want to deal with the poetry of the three separately below, but a beautiful hymn of Appar's is so relevant here. He wrote:

> As wide earth, as fire and water,
> as sacrifice and wind that blows,
> as eternal moon and sun,
> as ether, as the eight-formed god,
> as cosmic good and evil, woman and man,
> all other forms, and his own form,
> and all these as himself,
> as yesterday and today and tomorrow,

the god of the long red hair stands,
O wonder!

As rock, as hill, as forest,
as river, as streams and small canals,
as salt marshes by the sea,
as grass, as bush, as plants and herbs,
as the city, as the one who smashed the three cities,
as the word, as meaning in the word,
as the stirring of all life,
as the places where life stirs,
as grain, as earth in which it grows, as the water that gives it life,
the Lord who blazed up as the great flame stands,
O wonder![37]

The three favoured the image of Śiva as *Naṭarāja*, Lord of the Dance. They also sang of him as a beggar and included many myths associated with the God in their hymns, particularly his victory over demons. By these means, they popularized Śiva's myths and images, entrenching the God in the hearts of the people throughout the Tamil lands.

The *mūvar* reached out to Śiva in a variety of ways simply because they saw him everywhere throughout the Tamil lands. He was present in temple images as much as in their own hearts and minds. Thus, their experience of Śiva was direct: wherever they experienced God they sang spontaneously of that communion. Prentiss points out the importance of such experience, "they not only communicated their experience as a present tense reality but also encouraged others to participate in the experience". And, as Prentiss goes on to say, their very lives were an experience of God and the stories about them were in themselves a means to God for those who focused on them.[38] During the singing of their hymns, they were at the feet of God, servants of God. Appar, in particular, epitomized the servile position at the feet of God: he was humble and self-deprecating before Śiva but he communed with him. It was the singing about such communion that brought devotees together to hear the hymns, making Tamil Śiva-*bhakti* a highly communal phenomenon. The *mūvar* were the eyes through which others could come to know Śiva and were examples of the devotional love of God in which devotees could participate. The *mūvar* sang of Śiva's exploits and linked him to specific locales by his myths as if he were a local hero as in *puṟam* poetry: a symbiotic relationship between Tamil lands and its people, and the God Śiva, resulted. Peterson notes how myths of the origins of local shrines were linked to Śiva and how tales of his wanderings as a beggar further linked him with the whole of the Tamil country.[39] Śiva was himself depicted as journeying to many of the major shrines and the *mūvar* praised the towns as much as the shrines within them where Śiva was believed to dwell. In this way, the *mūvar* and other *Nāyaṉmārs* built up a network of sacred places and landscapes that became important devotional centres. The *mūvar* also are said to have performed miracles that made them popular and enhanced Śiva worship.

If they reached out to Tamil people universally, declaring that love of, and devotion to, Śiva was all that was needed – and Appar included here lepers and outcastes – their catholicism did not stretch to Jains and Buddhists. In the same way as the *Āḻvārs*, the *mūvar* and other *Nāyaṉmārs* were antagonistic to Jainism and Buddhism and did their best to oust both. Securing the patronage of the Chola monarchs, they were partly successful in doing this: indeed, the famous Chidambaram Temple was set up under the Cholas as a centre for Śiva-*bhakti* worship. And at least for the *mūvar* and other *Nāyaṉmārs*, caste did not preclude a devotee from being a Śiva *bhakta*: devotees came together through their abundance of love for Śiva regardless of their social status.

Thus we have the beginnings and consolidation of Śiva-*bhakti* in the Tamil lands with the *mūvar* travelling widely to pilgrimage sites with their devotees and singing their hymns in the presence of Śiva at each place. They loved their land and so Śiva loved his land, too. As Peterson puts it: "Poet, God, king, and community are united by their love for the Tamil countryside."[40] Temples and shrines were particularly sacred and important to the *mūvar* and, as Peterson also very aptly says: "By unifying the many sacred places of Śiva through a network of pilgrimages and hymns, the three saints created a Śaiva 'sacred geography' for the Tamil land."[41] However, we need to be careful not to picture the temples and shrines of the time as elaborate affairs. Many of the Śiva shrines were in open spaces of forests, especially where there were sacred trees under which the Śiva *liṅga* would be placed. Proper structures were confined to a few towns.[42] Many of the iconic images of Śiva were constructed from the descriptions of the God in the *Āgamas*, the non-*Vedic* texts of the early Śaiva traditions, and when imperial temples were built, the hymns and life stories of the *mūvar* became an established part of the liturgy. Before leaving the *mūvar*, I want to look in a little more detail at their individual contributions to Śiva-*bhakti* beginning with Appar.

Appar

The date of Appar, the first of the *mūvar*, is variously given but, though elusive, is probably seventh century and Dehejia gives compelling evidence for his birth right at the end of the sixth century.[43] Peterson, however, places him much earlier and somewhere between 570 and 670, overlapping with Sambandar.[44] Appar's original name was Tirunāvukkarasu, but he was given the name Appar, "Father", by Sambandar. Appar was born into a wealthy non-*Brāhmin* upper class of *Veḷḷālas*, a caste that was fairly influential in religious affairs in supporting sacred sites. Śaivism was not his first choice of religion for before he converted to worship of Śiva he had been a prominent Jain. I have noted above that Appar accepted any who payed homage to Śiva even if they were lepers or outcastes, but to anyone else, he was thoroughly intolerant:

If men speak not His name in letters five [the Śiva *mantra*]
Nor e'er the fire-formed Śiva's praise repeat,
And never walk in reverence round His shrine,
And pluck no flowers for offering ere they eat,
If they for healing wear no sacred ash,
I'll tell you whereunto such men were born,

'Twas that foul plagues might torture them to death,
The death bring rebirths endlessly forlorn.[45]

His castigation and despising of the Buddhists and especially Jains – the "weak and filthy Jains" he said – was vitriolic and involved cruel imagery: though he himself had converted from Jainism, as the others of the *mūvar* he could not accept that Jains and Buddhists could ever be worshippers of Śiva or good Tamil citizens.[46]

The poetry of Appar showed some, if not wide, influence of *akam* conventions. He depicted a young woman madly in love with Śiva, for example, a woman who lost herself in Śiva so much that she forgot her own name with her head placed at the feet of the Lord. In a similar hymn, Appar wrote:

Once she heard his name,
then learned of his lovely form.
Then she heard of his excellent town,
and fell madly in love with him.
That same day she left her mother and father
and the proper ways of the world,
lost herself,
lost her good name.
This woman has joined the feet
of the Lord, her lover.[47]

Yet there are also places where he was critical of women as stumbling blocks to God, and he himself found it hard to resist running after women, describing himself as being trapped by their voluptuous looks, their young soft breasts and their slender waists.[48] A true devotee of Śiva would have to turn away from marriage and relationships with women. Indeed, it seems Appar did not have a good view of the world because it was inimical to love of God. Nevertheless, he called God mother, father and relative: "You are my father, my mother, my teacher. You are my lovng uncle and aunt; you are my fair lady, my rich treasure; you are my family, my relatives, my home."[49]

If there were such negative elements in the poetry of Appar, there was immense beauty in his concept of God. Śiva constituted the entire cosmos – began it, sustained it and ended it. Śiva was everything from darkness and light to the seed, sprout, root and flower of each plant including its colour and fragrance. Thus, Śiva was also the destroyer of rebirth and of the suffering of his devotees. Śiva was both beyond and within all. Appar's relationship with God was a servant–master one in which every action was done by him as a servant, a *toṇṭar*, for Śiva. But the search for God and the relationship with him was mainly an inner one that took place in the mind and the heart and when it did, it was accompanied by knowledge, *jñāna*, but not before love of God brought the devotee to that point: knowledge is not for the *bhakta* a path *per se*. Outward ritual – sacred bathing, pilgrimage, chanting of the *Vedas*, obeying religious prescriptions, fasting – he saw as useless without bringing Śiva into the mind with a profound depth of love and servitude. He said of Śiva: "O wealth, my treasure, honey, red flame of heavenly hosts that excels all lustre, embodied One, my kin, my flesh, heart within my flesh, image within my heart, my all-bestowing tree, my eye, image seen in that pupil, save me from the disease of the powerful *karma*."[50] The imagery with which Appar depicted his communion with Śiva was exquisite: "The *vīṇā*'s pure sound, the light of the evening moon, a gentle breeze, springtime sun, a pool humming with bees – like these in the shade at my Lord, my Father's feet."[51] At the same time, Appar's hymns reflected the inscrutable transcendence of Śiva:

> He is ever hard to find, but He lives in the thought of the good;
> He is the innermost secret of Scripture, inscrutable, unknowable;
> He is honey and milk and shining light. He is the king of the Devas,
> Immanent in Vishnu, in Brahmā, in flame and in wind,
> Yea in the mighty sounding sea and in the mountains.[52]

As with so many of the poet–saints of Vaiṣṇava and Śaiva faiths, the grace of God was the only means by which a devotee could come into his presence, in Appar's words, "be admitted into his grace". And that grace was given to devout devotees "who rise at dawn to bathe, to gather fresh flowers, and lovingly offer them in worship, lighting lamps and burning incense for the rite".[53] These were the simple acts of devotion that stood in contrast to the institutionalized rites that Appar criticized above but, at the same time, the internalizing of devotion was needed – offerings given with a deep personal and intense love of God. He said: "I do not know the beauties of Tamil language. I am not a poet. I am not capable of understanding your nature and yet you showered on me your love, bestowed affection like father and mother, showed me the path of righteousness, you followed me in every one of my actions, and made me your man."[54]

Singing of the poems was fundamentally important as a means to God, for they were replete with praise of God and some of Appar's hymns were so characterized by simplicity that they are still learned and sung by Tamil children.[55] Appar's poems also contain details of the process of worship, *pūjā*, in the temples, especially the important rite of bathing Śiva's image or *liṅga*, offerings of fragrant flower garlands and honey, and circumambulation of the image of Śiva at the same time as singing praises to him and dancing ecstatically before him. These acts, he said, should be performed daily. He seemed to favour particularly the five-faced, ten-armed image of Śiva. The *mantra Na-ma-Śi-vā-ya* was central to worship from the moment of waking to the end of the day:[56] true glory, Appar said, is to cry out loud, "Hail, Śiva hail!".

It was at the feet of God where Appar wished to be; there where Śiva's grace was ultimate and release from *karma* and rebirth achieved. Meditating on the feet of God was, therefore, part of the means to his grace and to reach his "beautiful, flower-fresh feet" was the means and the goal. But Appar was a humble, self-deprecating poet, conscious of his own sin and unworthiness:

> In right I have no power to live,
> Day after day I'm stained with sin;
> I read, but do not understand;
> I hold Thee not my heart within.
> O light, O flame, O first of all,

I wandered far that I might see,
Athihai Vīraṭṭānam's Lord,
Thy flower-like feet of purity.[57]

Appar tried to imprint God's feet in his mind: "What else can I think of except the sacred feet of my Lord?", he said. "What else can I see but the jewelled feet which I worship? O virtuous One, I come to your sacred feet!"[58] When God accepted his *bhakta* as a servant it was because the *bhakta* had surrendered to Śiva: grace and surrender became reciprocal and refuge found when they combined. Appar knew that Śiva was a God of boundless love and experienced immense personal sorrow that he could not always feel that love in his heart. Yet he seemed to have absolute faith in the grace of God that would redeem him.

Sambandar

When Appar was an old man, he heard of a child saint, Sambandar, and went to meet him. It was then that Sambandar called him "Father", Appar. The two travelled together through the Tamil lands, attracting followers and singing at the sacred places they visited. Sambandar's full name was Tiru-jñāna-Sambandar, "Man Connected with Divine Wisdom". He was a *Brāhmin* and from a young age, according to hagiographic accounts, travelled from village to village singing hymns in praise of God but, also, sang hymns in which he castigated the Jains and Buddhists. He is said to have been accompanied on the harp by a skilled untouchable husband-and-wife couple.

Sambandar's poetry reveals his love of nature and a happy approach to life. If Appar was ambivalent about the status of women, Sambandar was not: he praised their beauty and dignity, perhaps because he held Śiva's consort, Umā, in great esteem. Umā, or Pārvatī, features in most of his poems and he describes her movement as like that of a swan, her scarlet lips, her teeth like pearls, her smoothly curved stomach, her breasts like lotus buds, and so on. Clearly, he had none of Appar's restrained approaches. The following poem I have included because it epitomizes so well the poet's love of nature when he described the twin cities of Kutralam and Kurumbala:

The fragrant hills are rich with Vengai trees and groves
The lovely bee sings as if playing a harp in Kutralam.
The Lord dances here wearing the Konrai flowers.
Oh friends in worship! In this lovely city.

The lush Cenbaga creeper climbs up the Vengai tree
And bursts out into soft buds and rich bloom.
The plantains on one side are full of fruit
And sweet fruit hang a plenty on the branches of mango trees on the other side.

The monkey with its young ones comes here
And eats the ripe sweet fruits from the plantain and

The maidens with dark eyes gather the pearls from the streams
As they feed the parrots with fruits.

The lovely peacock with its peahen,
Dances in the garden with cool waters and blue lilies.
The bee mates with its lady, climbs the Kurunda tree and madly sings the tune of Sevvali.
The female monkey tastes the mango fruit first for ripeness and the male monkey eats it thereafter.

The male and the female elephants pluck the Vengai flower clusters
And bear them on their heads to worship the Lord.
The lone monkey jumps on the long bamboo and dances
And the huntsmen gather and clap in admiration.[59]

What a wonderful setting and exquisite imagery in which to place Śiva! As Dehejia sensitively puts it: "With song and rhythm the birds, bees and insects seem to participate in the paean to Siva."[60] Such a comment belies the oft-cited criticism of Sambandar's poetry that it lacks philosophy and religious expression. But Sambandar, it seems, saw God in nature and his devotion is clear in the depths of his vivid descriptions. His hymns were so well received that they did much to diminish the popularity of Jainism and Buddhism. The Jains suppressed the old *akam* poetry and also music, but Sambandar used both, some of his poems written as if he were a love-sick maiden pining for her lover. In such poems, messages were sent to Śiva with creatures of the forest and garden. Yet he referred to God as stealing his heart and addressed him intimately as a child would a father, in addition to the love-sick maiden. Singing and chanting of the Lord's name were fundamental acts of devotion for Sambandar. The same *mantra* of *Na-ma-Śi-vā-ya* extolled by Appar was taken up by Sambandar. In a rhyming translation, F. Kingsbury and G. P. Phillips translate a stanza that illustrates this:

Those who repeat it while love's tears outpour,
It gives them life, and guides them in the way.
'Tis the true substance of the Vedas four,
The Lord's great name, wherefore "Hail Śiva," say.[61]

Regrettably, Sambandar's poetic skills were so often directed against the Jains and he even asked for Śiva's grace in order to defeat these "rogues". In one hymn he says:

I will easily defeat those filthy Jain monks
who wander like elephants in rut,
and eat their food standing, embarrassing pious men,
and mutilate the good Sanskrit of the Āgama and mantra texts,
loudly declaiming in the corrupt Prakrit tongue.[62]

He railed against the Jains as evil, destructive, wicked and indecent and it is a sad reflection on the beauty of his poetry to know that Sambandar is reputed to have had eight-thousand Jains impaled alive. Nevertheless, Sambandar is worshipped widely in Śiva temples today in southern India and is honoured even more than Appar. But for true *bhaktas* there was release, and lest I give the impression that Sambandar's poetry lacks religious depth, the following hymn should remedy any negative impression:

> They will never be reborn,
> but will enter the highest state;
> they won't lose heart on earth,
> they won't suffer from hunger,
> nor endure the pain of disease.
> Those who know and learn to know the Lord
> have no use for heaven,
> for they belong to the feet
> of our Lord in Cāykkāṭu in Pukār
> whose long highways are lined with palaces.[63]

Sundarar

The third of the *mūvar* was Sundarar (Tam. Cuntarar), or Sundara-mūrti. His dates are somewhere in the late seventh and very early eighth century, late enough to be responsible for providing a full list of all the *Nāyaṉmārs*, including Kāraikkāl Ammaiyār, whom we met earlier, praising the hymns and lives of all sixty-two of them: he was added later as the last, making sixty-three in total. His name means "Beautiful One". He was a *Brāhmin* though far from strictly so since he is reputed to have married a woman from the *Veḷḷāla* caste and then, praying to Śiva for his aid, married a low-caste temple girl, perhaps a dancing girl or a weaver of flower garlands. He had a good deal of problems with both women, including financial worries, but since Śiva, too, had more than one consort, Sundarar felt he had something in common with his God! He abandoned his first wife for the second and Śiva is said to have punished him for doing so by making him blind. Sundarar was quite impudent about the fact, asking Śiva why he, as a God with three eyes, would want to do such an unbefitting thing as to deprive him of his two. And when Śiva restored his sight in one eye, Sundarar was rudely accusatory of Śiva in response. When he needed food, he asked Śiva to provide it. Nevertheless, his intimacy with God was a treasure of honest and spontaneous feeling and devotion. Dehejia describes his present-day images as "standing in defiant attitude with arms crossed against his chest", which "reflects his impudent personality rather than his saintly soul".[64] If he needed something – food, money, luxuries, a sword, a horse – he asked for worldly things from Śiva with a confidence that Śiva would grant his wish, and they materialized!

Despite Sundarar's cavalier attitude, his poetry is delightful. Dehejia captures it well: "he used simple, direct language, his verses are replete with both rhyme and rhythm and his words seem to bubble as they flow along".[65] And lest it seem that Sundarar was an arrogant, self-opinionated being, his poetry also showed that he felt himself unworthy and occasionally there was great beauty in his approach to God:

> You may not care for me, yet I'll call you my Lord.
> Even if I'll never be born again, I'll never forget you.
> Though you won't look at me, I will still see you,
> Though you won't love me, I'll still love you in my heart,
> and never stop singing the praise of your feet.[66]

He took refuge at the feet of God and asked Śiva to take him but at the same time was critical of God that he did not seem to listen. Yet he was only too aware of his own dreadful failings:

> I fritter my life away in lies,
> I'm neither a temple servant nor your devotee.
> You have not possessed me with your truth,
> nor given me hope for the future state.
> Even if I were your servant,
> you would ask nothing of me, give nothing,
> say nothing to me!
> Yet are you not my Master from former lives,
> O Lord who lives in Ōṇakāntaṉṟaḷi?[67]

Sundarar said that his heart melted for God but at the same time he treated God as an intimate companion, a friend that he could chide, tease and often be critical of. But there is no doubt at all that he had a profound love for Śiva. In fact, he has been called "the Lord's friend". He said:

> How can I live far away
> from my God in Ārūr?
> How can I bear to be parted
> from him whose glory was sweetly sung
> by two before me,
> the Lord with the forehead eye,
> the fruit of all learning,
> the god whom I love with all my heart?[68]

In other poems, Sundarar showed that his intimacy with God was reciprocal. The depth of his devotion was beautifully portrayed in the following hymn:

> O everlasting light burning bright,
> I thought only of you.
> You came to me,
> and have never left me since.

> Focus of all my thoughts,
> Lord who dwells in the holy Western shrine,
> Father, I will sing
> no one but you.

"I thought only of your feet", he continued.[69] Finally, he surrendered to Śiva and said he could no more deny him, God's grace ensued: "My Master who chose me, saved me from birth and death, and gave me grace," he wrote. And in another stanza of the same hymn:

> I have won over my Lord
> who wears the *konṟai* which blooms in the rains;
> I have won a heart that will never forget him.
> Once a sinner, I have now been raised
> to the birthless state – who is so fortunate as I?
> I behold my Lord with the dark throat and the gold earring,
> I sing of him, and will unite with him[70]

He said he was possessed by the Lord's lotus feet – that symbol of surrender and refuge: this colourful being was no less precious as a devotee to the God to whom he submitted himself. Immortalized iconographically, he is portrayed as a handsome youth, elegant, relaxed and exquisite, the friend of Śiva.

The importance of the *mūvar* is epitomized in Prentiss' term of "embodiment of *bhakti*"; their spiritual experiences of Śiva embodied him within their hearts and minds and their hymns sang out of that embodiment for those who wished to participate with them in worship of Śiva: "For all of the Tamil Śiva-bhakti agents, bhakti is a theology of embodiment that encourages active participation in the worship of Śiva and that values human experience. Bhakti became embodied, then, in the words, actions and images of agents who gave it distinctive representation, based on their engagement with their own historical contexts and rhetoric."[71] It is the being of the poet–saint that became the focus of *bhakti* and the medium by which the feet of God could be experienced as a refuge, and as love. The *mūvar* travelled the land, singing and giving service to Śiva so that those who followed them could participate and themselves become emotionally close to God. Sambandar described servants of God as "devotees who know how to weep, to dance and sing and rise, and again fall at the father's feet".[72] Sundarar says: "Dance, lovers of Śiva, become devotees of the Lord, crown yourselves with dust from his feet!"[73] And Appar said: "O devotees who have joined our group out of love, dance, weep, worship him, sing his feet, gather at Kuraṅkāṭuturai, place of our Lord!"[74] How spontaneous is such devotion! There are no prescriptive rituals, just an outpouring of love, though the *mūvar* were unanimous in stressing the importance of the *mantra*, *Na-ma-Śi-vā-ya*. If ritual was present in the *mūvar*'s response to God, it could never become mechanical but remained ecstatically emotional.[75] The *mūvar* made simple actions of cleaning and the like at temples means of devotion. Such ritual that existed amounted to care of the shrines, temples and deity enshrined in them, bathing the deity in milk and *ghī*, and weaving garlands for him. They sang of communal festivals and local legends, bringing Śiva into the heart of celebration in every community. And in the passage of time, the *mūvar* themselves became icons that were worshipped alongside Śiva and celebrated at festivals in the temples they once had visited and at others that grew up to celebrate their embodiment of God. The warmth of their devotion and the infectious emotion of it were powerful means that gave expression to Śiva-*bhakti* throughout the Tamil lands, not just in the historic context of their own time but for centuries to come and in the present day. I shall leave it to Appar to supply the last words here:

> Our sole duty is joyfully to sing
> the glory of him who manifests himself
> as the moving and the still,
> as earth, water, fire, wind and sky,
> as the small and the great,
> as hard to reach, yet easily attained
> by his lovers,
> as the highest reality, immeasurably great,
> as infinite Sadāśiva, as you and me.[76]

Māṇikka Vācakar

Often regarded as the greatest of the *Nāyaṉmārs*, Māṇikka Vācakar's poetic hymns express a depth of emotion that is unsurpassed by his fellow poets. He seemed to be able to reach right into the heart with great philosophical depth and yet encapsulate very natural contexts. He wanted people to be able to sing of God while they were performing daily tasks so some of his hymns are set in everyday experiences – grinding corn, picking flowers, swinging, and playing a hand-clapping game. His songs could be sung by all kinds of people, young and old and in whatever occupation. Other poems are intensely personal. Dehejia says he "drowns himself in spiritual rapture".[77] The richness and warmth of his hymns are immensely appealing today as much as in the genre of medieval poems of his time. This was brought home to me only recently by a *Brāhmin* consultant physician, Kartik Hariharan, now living and practising in South Wales in the United Kingdom, but born in southern India, though he was not a Tamil-speaking native. He is passionate about Māṇikka Vācakar's hymns, so much so that he learned Tamil in order to be able to read and understand the poems in their original language. But these facts are incidental to the deep, emotive expression in his eyes as he spoke of the way in which the poetry moved him almost to tears, of the profound spiritual depth that the poems conveyed, and of the exquisite beauty of the poet's remarkable hymns. Here, I feel, the written word will fall short in conveying the depth of spirituality in Kartik Hariharan's eyes as he spoke of the hymns he clearly loved so much.

The name Māṇikka Vācakar means "One Whose Speech is Rubies" or "Speaker of Gems". He was not really a *Nāyaṉār* because he lived later than Sundarar in the mid-ninth century, and it was Sundarar, as we saw above, who listed the sixty-three *Nāyaṉmārs*. However, he was added to "the three", the *mūvar*, to make "the four", the *nalvar*. He was clearly an erudite thinker, being conversant with the Sanskrit and Tamil Śaiva *Āgamas* and gave up his post as royal minister to devote his life to Śiva, mainly centred at Chidambaram. Māṇikka Vācakar's *Tirukkōvaiyār* reflects the erotic *akam* poetry, but his best-known work is the truly wonderful *Tiruvācakam*, "Sacred Utterance". A Tamil saying claims that if the heart is not melted by the *Tiruvācakam* nothing can melt it. This text forms the eighth section of the Tamil canon of scriptures. It has been described as a "spiritual biography" of the poet because it expresses the poet's emotions at different times of his life.[78] It shows the evolution of spiritual development in a deeply religious man and takes us through modes of great sadness, great affliction and yet also great ecstatic devotion to, and love of, Śiva. Māṇikka Vācakar was a mystical poet whose gems of hymns reached exquisite heights of religious expression. He sent messages of his love to Śiva by a humming bee or a cuckoo and he had a superb use of natural images to adorn his words:

> Now anigh Indra's East
> Draws the sun; dark flies apace
> At the dawn; and the sun
> Of the kindness in Thy face
> Riseth high'r, ever high'r
> As like fair flowers opening,
> Eyes unclose from their sleep,
> Eyes of Thee our beauteous king.[79]

Māṇikka Vācakar's poetry contains, as was the case with other poets, many of the myths featuring Śiva, so enhancing the devotees' recollections of the great God. Although he was a mystical poet, his concept of deity was very much of a personal God and he was against the Advaita tradition of an impersonal Brahman. Thus he could describe Śiva (Tam. Civan in his hymns) in detail and wrote much of the feet of Śiva, whom he often called King: "Victory to the foot of the King, who soothed my soul's unrest and made me His!"[80] He was always humble before the God he so loved and saw himself unworthy, having traversed many lives in many forms until he finally reached the feet of God and secured his grace:

> I came, attained the grace the "Brow-eyed" showed,
> Adored the beauteous foot by thought unreached.
> O Thou, Who fill'st the heaven, Who fill'st the earth, art manifested light,
> Transcending thought, Thou boundless One! Thy glory great
> I, man of evil "deeds" know not the way to praise!
> Grass was I, shrub was I, worm, tree,
> Full many a kind of beast, bird, snake,
> Stone, man, and demon. 'Midst Thy hosts I served.
> The form of mighty Asuras, ascetics, gods I bore.
> Within these immobile and mobile forms of life,
> In every species born, weary I've grown, great Lord![81]

Out of his grace for humankind, he believed Śiva took infinite forms and allowed his devotees to experience him as a familiar friend, and yet was the God that pervaded all and was ultimately incomprehensible:

> He is the Ancient One, Who creates the Creator of all;
> He is the God, Who preserves the Preserver of things created;
> He is God, Who destroys the Destroyer;
> But, thinking without thought, regards the things destroyed. . . .
> Day by day He to the sun its lustre gave.
> In the sacred moon He placed its coolness;
> Kindled in the mighty fire its heat;
> In the pure ether placed pervasive power;
> Endued the ambient wind with energy;
> To the streams that gleam in the shade their savour sweet,
> And to the expanded earth with its strength He gave;
> For ever and aye, me and millions other than me,
> All in their several cells hath he enclosed.[82]

In a list of forty epithets, Māṇikka Vācakar described Śiva as the essence of all things; the melody in the lute; that which was smaller than an atom yet incomparably great; male and female and yet neither. And yet, the poet said he had seen Śiva:

> See, even I have seen Him with my eyes!
> See, the ambrosial Fount, yielding abounding grace!
> Lo, I have seen His mercy might!
> See, His roseate Foot this earth hath trod!
> See Him, even I have known, the Blessed One!
> See, in grace He made me His!
> See, her His Spouse whose eyes are dark-blue lotus flowers!
> See, Her and Him together stand![83]

To Māṇikka Vācakar, Śiva was the essence that indwelled each being, could be personally known, and was inseparable from his devotees. He was the unseen light within the soul for he was immanent in all; yet he was beyond all, greater than all. But the essence of God himself was love, a perfect love that surpassed anything his devotees could offer and Śiva showed his love through his grace to his devotees. It was only through that grace that a devotee could enter fully into the conscious presence of Śiva in eternal bliss. Māṇikka Vācakar always presented himself as totally unworthy of God's grace. He said: "Thou cam'st in grace on this same earth, didst show Thy mighty feet to me who lay mere slave – meaner than any dog – essential grace more precious than a mother's love!"[84] And in a particularly beautiful hymn:

> Like flowing billows swell from out the sea of milk
> Within my soul He made deep waters rise,

Ambrosia surpassing speech filled every pore.
This is His gracious work!
In every body in this currish state
He filled me full with honied sweetness;
Ambrosial drops most marvellous
He caused throughout my being to distil.
With tender soul, as though He'd make me as Himself,
He formed for me a frame where grace might flow.[85]

Bhakti was the gift of God's grace in Māṇikka Vācakar's concept of God: *bhakti* was a divinizing of the self, so it was not something that developed unless God gave it. It was a reciprocal desire of the poet to be ruled by the love of God and for God to melt into his soul. At the same time, God's desire was to love the poet: they desired each other. The intense longing of Māṇikka Vācakar for the grace of God appeared again and again in his hymns. While there were times when he experienced the ecstasy of communion with God there were so many times when his emotional struggle to find God seemed to overwhelm him.

Māṇikka Vācakar's relationship with Śiva was mostly a servant–master one. He sang of being enslaved by the Lord, sometimes referring to himself as a dog. But he also referred to Śiva as his Father. As so many of the poet–saints, his aim was to reach the feet of God, that place of refuge: "I pray for love of Thine own jewelled Feet", he said.[86] He was seized by an overwhelming sense of his own unworthiness, of his sins, and his immense sorrow at not being able to love God fully and respond to God's love because of his own deep shortcomings. And he wrote of those shortcomings in great honesty, particularly as a slave to desires of all kinds. He pined and longed to be in the presence of Śiva: "When shall I see thy face?" he asked, and he spoke of his weariness and sadness. Occasionally, his frustration burst out into chiding remarks about Śiva, calling him a madman. But there was also a sense of continuous effort in praising and performance of worship rites in order to secure Śiva's grace. And he did secure the grace of Śiva: out of grace, Śiva offered himself to the poet, and Māṇikka Vācakar surrendered totally melting in the love of God, losing all his own egoism and desires and finding God's own essence to be within his soul. Kingsbury's and Phillips' rhyming translation is particularly attractive here:

Thou gav'st Thyself, Thou gained'st me;
Which did the better bargain drive?
Bliss found I in infinity;
But what didst Thou from me derive?
O Śiva, Perunduṛai's God,
My mind Thou tookest for Thy shrine:
My very body's Thine abode:
What can I give Thee, Lord, of mine?[87]

In a long poem, Māṇikka Vācakar described the moment of his awareness of receiving the grace of God. For a poet who expressed so many emotions so spontaneously and naturally, the words I have chosen here from the long hymn are exquisitely graphic:

Not ev'n in dreams thought I of other gods.
The One most precious Infinite to earth came down;
Nor did I greatness of the Sage superne contemn,
Who came in grace. Thus from the pair of sacred feet
Like shadow from its substance parting not,
Before, behind, at every point, to it I clung.
My inmost self in strong desire dissolved, I yearned;
Love's river overflowed its banks;
My senses all in Him were centred; "Lord!" I cried.
With stammering speech, and quivering frame
I clasped adoring hands; my heart expanding like a flower.
Eyes gleamed with joy and tears distilled.
His love that fails not day by day still burgeons forth![88]

The reciprocal love between God and devotee is so obvious here; a surrender of love one to the other, matured love on the part of the devotee, the grace of love from God. "You made me yours", Māṇikka Vācakar said to Śiva and he spoke of merging with God, merging with a *personal* God, though in mystic union.

Thus we have the four great poet–saints of Tamil Śaivism. In the same way as the *Āḻvārs*, their legacy, along with other *Nāyaṉmārs*, is very evident today in the arts, in song, dance, sculpture and architecture. Their hymns reflect the wide range of emotions from desperate anguish to ecstatic joy through which the soul passes in search of God.

Śaiva Siddhānta

Māṇikka Vācakar is the first of the mystical poets who stand at the beginning of a more philosophical approach to the divine, an approach termed Śaiva Siddhānta, which is the main form of Śaivism in South India. The monotheism that characterized Śiva-*bhakti* was and is the hallmark of Śaiva Siddhānta also; indeed, Tamil Śaivism was always strictly monotheistic with exclusive devotion to Śiva. *Siddhānta* means "conclusion" or "final view", and so is seen by many as the culmination of Śiva-*bhakti*. Underlying its philosophy were three eternal "reals" put forward in the Śaiva *Āgamas*: first God, who was Śiva (*Pati*); secondly the soul (*paśu*, Tam. *pacu*); thirdly, bondage (*pāśa*, Tam. *pācam*), but with a greater degree of dependence of souls and inanimate matter on God in the Śaiva Siddhānta school. Souls were inanimate and unconscious but by the energy, the *śakti*, of Śiva, they acquired consciousness: they also acquired the bondage of *karma* and incessant rebirths through impurities. Knowledge played a key role in overcoming such bondage and it was Śiva who granted it through his grace. So *bhakti* occurred only when Śiva granted the soul his grace and placed an individual on the path to liberation. Four stages of God's grace were perceived – that given for devotion through service, that given for worship, that given for spiritual discipline and, finally, the grace of Śiva that gave ultimate knowledge. The emphasis on knowledge is notable and that knowledge was of the true soul as inseparably united with God's grace (Tam. *aruḷ*). That grace gave the kind of divine wisdom that dissolved the impurities that had accumulated on the soul. There is an important difference here in that whereas *embodiment* could be said to be a key feature of Śiva-*bhakti*, that is to say, the devotee *embodied* the grace of God – often regardless of any sin – in Śaiva Siddhānta, as Prentiss says "the body represents that which is farthest from the true and pure nature of Śiva".[89]

The concept of deity in Śaiva Siddhānta was of a God who is distinct from souls on the one hand and unified with souls through his grace on the other. As in Śiva-*bhakti*, God remains the ultimate refuge and was always present in every individual and all things. The relationship between devotee and God was always one of servitude and surrender: it would be inconceivable in Śaiva Siddhānta for the kind of personal relationship to exist in which the devotee could chide Śiva or take liberties in approaching him. And yet, the fundamental essence of God was that of love and it was because of that immense love that he proffered his grace. It was because of his grace that Śiva created, sustained and dissolved the world. Given the more philosophical concept of God in Śaiva Siddhānta ritual was lifted to a more sophisticated level. The *liṅga* was considered the most subtle, whereas the iconic images of Śiva were believed to be more gross aspects suited to inferior worshippers. Prentiss notes the orthodoxy of the Śaiva Siddhānta tradition here: "Worshippers of Śiva were thus not all on the same religious path. Nor did they all have access to the higher path, for the Śaiva Siddhānta school's version of the appropriate body for the worship of Śiva was carefully and rigidly defined by both caste and privileged knowledge of ritual transformations."[90] As a result, there was less emphasis on the simple methods of devotion with service and offerings at temples. Although the earlier poet–saints of Śiva-*bhakti* were not devoid of mystical experience, especially Māṇikka Vācakar, mystical knowledge through God's grace became a central tenet of Śaiva Siddhānta. God's grace remained the ultimate key to the understanding of God. Dasgupta put this succinctly: "Just as a crystal reflects many colours under the sun's light and yet retains its own transparent character, so the energy or wisdom obtained as a grace of the Lord irradiates the soul and permeates the world. Without the mystic wisdom obtained through the grace of Śiva, no one can obtain real knowledge. The soul is unintelligent without Śiva. All the actions of souls are performed with the active guidance of Śiva, and even the perception of the senses as means of knowledge is owed to Śiva's grace".[91] But if Śiva was believed to be a transcendent, unknowable Supreme Absolute, he was yet immanent in every being and in all things, ready, by way of his grace, to open the heart of each soul to his reality, granting mystical understanding of his nature.

The Śaiva Siddhānta school accepted the lives of the *Nāyaṉmārs* as examples of beings who had direct experience of Śiva but it viewed its own *gurus* and philosophers as the means to reveal ultimate truth, so Peterson thinks the link between the *Nāyaṉmārs* and the Śaiva Siddhānta philosophers was a tenuous one.[92] *Gurus* became the heart of Tamil Śaiva Siddhānta: they were regarded as living manifestations of God's grace who could direct the spiritual pathway of those chosen. The ultimate goal of liberation, *mokṣa*, was distinctly a goal and not the same as the means to the goal in continued service to the Lord. The state of *mokṣa* was unclear since without consciousness and sense perceptions, what of Śiva could be known? It was clearly a mystical liberation.

The Śaiva Siddhānta scriptures include twenty-eight *Āgamas* dealing with philosophy and temple ritual. Although not *Vedic* texts, they are regarded as their equal and are written in both Sanskrit and Tamil. The four *Vedas* and *Upaniṣads* are also regarded as sacred to the school, as well as a number of *Śāstras* – fourteen major texts that were written in Tamil. These last, especially, emphasize the personal nature of Śiva with qualities of knowledge, grace and love. Notable, too, in the Śaiva Siddhānta scriptures was Umāpati's *Tirumuṟai*, which incorporated the hymns of the *mūvar* and the *Nāyaṉmārs*, including Māṇikka Vācakar and Kāraikkāl Ammaiyār. The *Āḻvārs* and *Nāyaṉmārs* were both influenced by *Āgamic* thought, especially since the Śaiva *Āgamas* understand the nature of Śiva to be one that bestows grace on account of his love. But there was a gradation of pathways to liberation found in the *Āgamas* that was accepted also in Śaiva Siddhānta. The lowest path was religious and moral conduct (*caryā*); then service in the worship of Śiva (*kriyā*); then meditation and concentration on Śiva (*yoga*) and, finally, knowledge (*jñāna*). The last two stages were not ones particularly stressed by any of the poet–saints and, given that many were not eligible for the higher stages, they did not deem themselves worthy or capable of doing anything except wholeheartedly devoting their minds and actions to God. We lose much of this in the more formalized approach of Śaiva Siddhānta as, also, in the *Āgamic* stress on knowledge as the final and only means to liberation through God's grace. Liberation for Śaiva Siddhānta was a mystical union on the one hand but a consciousness of the duality between God and being on the other. Dhavamony describes liberation thus: "It is a mysticism of divine immanence inasmuch as the self lays hold on God's presence and activity in its own essence and lives mystically united with him. It is also a mysticism of divine transcendence, inasmuch as the self realizes its utter dependence on God and lovingly surrenders to him."[93] The soul, thus, becomes united with God but retains its individuality, though knowing that it is totally dependent on God. Today, Śaiva Siddhānta remains the foremost tradition of Śaiva worship in Tamil Nadu.

Vīraśaivas/Liṅgāyatas

The Vīraśaivas or Liṅgāyatas believed that Śiva was the material cause of all, while the efficient cause, that which effected creation, was Śakti. Vīraśaiva means "militant or heroic śaivism or faith in Śiva".[94] It was a medieval sect founded in the twelfth century in South Indian Karnataka by Bāsavaṇṇa (ca. 1106–68). Although a *Brāhmin*, Bāsavaṇṇa was unorthodox in his views and refused to accept divisions by class or gender. As the name Liṅgāyatas suggests, they favoured the *liṅga* symbol of Śiva and still wear a small stone one around their necks enclosed in a little silver box. There was much that they came to reject – *Brāhminism*, class and caste, image worship, temples, the *Vedas*, rebirth, child marriage and prohibition of the remarriage of widows. To this day, the Vīraśaivas are associated with sustained efforts for social reform. A. K. Ramanujan graphically wrote: "The Vīraśaivas movement was a social upheaval by and for the poor, the low-caste and the outcaste against the rich and privileged; it was a rising of the unlettered against the literate pundit, flesh and blood against stone."[95] They also buried rather than cremated their dead because they believed fire and light as divine essences to be so pure that fire should not be used to dispose of the dead. Being intensely monotheistic they rejected all other gods and goddesses, especially local minor ones that they believed to be surrounded in superstition and untrue legend. They rejected animal sacrifice and, interestingly, accepted the doctrine of non-violence, *ahiṃsā*, in line with Buddhists and Jains, but they were in fierce opposition to the Jains of the day, who were politically powerful in the Karnataka region. Many Vīraśaivas were wandering mendicants, while others were monastic living in monasteries, or *maṭhas*.

The Vīraśaiva concept of deity was intensely monotheistic. Śiva was, for them, supreme. The overriding conception of Śiva was of a God of grace, *kṛpa*, a grace never earned or demanded but was willingly given by God. Ramanujan commented: "A mystical opportunist can only wait for It, be prepared to catch It as It passes. The grace of the Lord is nothing he can invoke or wheedle by prayer, rule, ritual, magical word or sacrificial offering."[96] Śiva was believed to reside within the temple of the body, so external temples were unnecessary. Neither were priests necessary as intermediaries between God and human; Śiva could be experientially felt and his grace directly given. The *personal* relationship between God and human – so typical of *bhakti* – characterized the Vīraśaiva concept of God. Thus, as with so many of the poets that we have seen in this and the previous chapter, God could be approached through the medium of lover, father, mother or master. *Gurus* came to be accepted as manifestations of Śiva and became of supreme importance.

Spontaneity characterized the Vīraśaivas' concept of approaches to Śiva as well as the great poetry that the poet–saints of the movement composed. And they came from all classes and castes; literate and illiterate men and women praised Śiva in their own native Dravidian language of Kannada so that their words were readily understood by all. Their poetry consists of *vacanas*, "sayings" or "lyrics" that addressed Śiva, and that expressed the kind of devotional *bhakti* with which this chapter has been so concerned. The *vacanas* were often mystical and contained symbolic language but, nevertheless, included images of everyday life and expressions familiar to ordinary folk. They also reflected the poets' human problems subjectively so that we have an understanding of the real nature of the poets and their tribulations as well as their beliefs. I want to turn, now, to the poetry of four of the greatest of the Vīraśaiva poets, Dāsimayya, Bāsavaṇṇa, Āllāmā and Mahādēvī Ākkā.[97]

The earliest of the *vacana* poets was probably Dēvara Dāsimayya somewhere in the tenth century.[98] He was a weaver and his personal pathway to God was through working. "The earth is your gift, the growing grain your gift, the blowing wind your gift", he said of the grace of Śiva whom he called Rāmanātha. He believed that Śiva created all, pervaded all and sustained all through his indwelling presence, yet mysteriously transcended all, being beyond the changes and transitory nature of things:

Whatever It was

that made this earth
the base,
the world its life,
the wind its pillar,
arranged the lotus and the moon,
and covered it all with folds
of sky with Itself inside,

to that Mystery
indifferent to differences,

to It I pray,
O Rāmanātha.[99]

Bāsavaṇṇa I have already mentioned above. He is said to have cast off his sacred thread, the symbol of his *Brāhmin* status, and left his home to devote himself to Śiva, whom he called "The Lord of the Meeting Rivers". While his devotion was not neglected, he also became minister to the king in Kalyana and, at the same time, became surrounded by devotees from far afield, so building the unorthodox Vīraśaiva community. But hostility to the unorthodox community caused not just opposition from the king but extremism on the part of some of the Vīraśaivas, and when these extremists assassinated the king, the Vīraśaivas were forced to flee from the area. Despite this event, Bāsavaṇṇa had laid firm foundations for the survival of the Vīraśaivas.

Bāsavaṇṇa believed God always to be with him. In one poem, he likened Śiva to a mother:

As a mother runs
close behind her child
with his hand on a cobra
or a fire,

the lord of the meeting rivers
stays with me
every step of the way
and looks after me.[100]

He was intensely monotheistic and said: "There is only one god. He is our Lord of the meeting Rivers".[101] And that Lord resided in the body:

Make of my body the beam of a lute
  of my head the sounding gourd
  of my nerves the strings
  of my fingers the plucking rods.

Clutch me close
  and play your thirty-two songs
  O lord of the meeting rivers![102]

He threw established constructs for the writing of poetry to the winds and said "I'll sing as I love", with the true spontaneity of a *bhakta.*

A different kind of poetry came from Mahādēvī Ākkā a female Vīraśaiva poet from Karnataka in the twelfth century. Her approach to Śiva, whom she called "My Lord as White as Jasmine", was more of an erotic approach. She spoke of Śiva as her husband:

My mind is my maid:
by her kindness I join
my Lord,
    my utterly beautiful Lord
    from the mountain peaks
    my lord as white as jasmine

and I will make Him
my good husband.[103]

As we have seen with some of the other poets of both Vaiṣṇava and Śaiva traditions, relating to God as a lover or as a bride is a means of expressing union between man and God or woman and God. Similar, too, is the juxtaposition of union with, and separation from, her Lord. She wrote:

I love the Handsome One:
    he has no death
    decay nor form
    no place or side
no end nor birthmarks.
I love him, O mother. Listen

I love the Beautiful One
    with no bond nor fear
    no clan no land
    no landmarks
    for his beauty.

So, my lord, white as jasmine, is my husband.[104]

Later in the same poem she says:

When he's away
I cannot wait
to get a glimpse of him.

Friend, when will I have it
both ways,
be with Him
yet not with Him,
my lord white as jasmine?[105]

Her Lord White as Jasmine, Mahādēvī Ākkā saw as her true husband: her temporal husband she eventually left and wandered wildly and widely in search of the God she so adored, sometimes in union with him and often separated from him. Her love exemplified the illicit love of a married woman – the kind of love used many times in traditional Indian love poetry to express love of God. As with other poets, too, especially those female poets we have seen above, separation often revealed a deeper longing and love, which is why she asked when she will have it "both ways". She is reputed to have abandoned not just her home but also her clothes and to have debated with saints such as Āllāmā so well that she was accepted into the community of Vīraśaiva saints. Mahādēvī Ākkā wove much natural imagery into her poetry, blending mystical ideas with simplicity of language. The Vīraśaivas accepted that God was present in the temple of the human body, so she said:

Like
  treasure hidden in the ground
  taste in the fruit
  gold in the rock
  oil in the seed

  the Absolute hidden away
  in the heart

  no one can know
  the ways of our Lord

white as jasmine.[106]

Mahādēvī used objects of nature to beg them to find her Lord:

O swarm of bees
O mango tree
O moonlight
O koilbird
I beg of you all
One
Favour:

  If you should see my lord anywhere
  My lord white as jasmine

Call out
And show him to me.[107]

Day and night she grieved madly for her Lord, lost, sick and without food, water and sleep. She gazed down the road to see if he would come and pined and grew lean when he didn't: "I'm like the lovebird with nothing in her embrace", she said.[108] In a very beautiful poem, she showed how she used nature to commune with her Lord:

Sunlight made visible
the whole length of a sky,
movement of wind,
leaf, flower, all six colours
on tree, bush and creeper:
all this
is the day's worship.

The light of moon, star and fire,
Lightnings and all things
That go by the name of light
Are the night's worship.

Night and day
in your worship
I forget myself

O lord white as jasmine.[109]

Mandakranta Bose says of this remarkable woman that she "metaphorizes the phases of human love as the phases of a mystical approach to the divine" and that she "had given voice to the widest imaginable range of human yearning for the divine in humanly understandable rhetoric in countless poems".[110]

The last Vīraśaiva poet that I want to mention briefly is Āllāmā Prabhu. Prabhu means "Master" and that is how the other Vīraśaiva saints looked on him. It was with him that Mahādēvī debated and it was he who recognized her devotion and invited her to join his group of devotees. He is reputed to have aided many to the state of liberation and Ramanujan depicts this so well: "To men living and dying in lust, he taught the divine copulation of yogic practice; to alchemists, he brought the magical inward drop of essence that transmuted the base metal of fear; to holy men living in the fearful world, exploiting trees for clothing, stripping root and branch in their hunger, drinking up river and lake in their thirst, Allama taught the spirit's sacrifice, converting them from the practice of animal sacrifice to the sacrifice of bestial self."[111] Āllāma's poetry stems from his inner union with God:

Light
devoured darkness.

I was alone
inside.

Shedding
the visible dark

I
was Your target

O Lord of Caves.[112]

He worshipped the Lord and lost the world, he said. Devotees who had united with Śiva, he said, could smell the wind, know the sap of fire, the taste of sunshine on the tongue and the lights that are in oneself.[113]

Kashmir Śaivism

Before concluding this chapter, I think it prudent to say a little about devotion that occured in non-dual traditions, that is to say, in traditions where the unity between God and world and God and human is complete. Kashmir Śaivism is an example. The songs of Utpaladeva (*circa*; 900–950), illustrate admirably how devotion infused such a non-dual concept of God. Utpaladeva's songs are to be found in his *Śivastotrāvalī* and here, despite the unity of each being with Śiva, devotion on a personal level still seemed to obtain. Thus, Utpaladeva said to Śiva:

Ardently I desire to behold
Your ever-blossoming face.
O Lord, may you appear to me,
Howsoever faintly,
Face to face.[114]

Devotion, indeed, pervaded Utpaladeva's songs and he wrote, too, of Śiva's devotion to his devotees and Śiva's grace: both he deemed essential for liberation of the devotee. The goal was *identity* with the pure Consciousness of Śiva but, at the same time, the ability to revel in the immanent aspects of Śiva. As Constantina Bailley says, *devotion* here was the means to Śiva but it was also the end goal; Utpaladeva made this clear:

"One should worship Śiva by becoming Śiva"
Is the old saying. But the devotees say,
"One should worship Śiva by becoming a devotee."
For they can recognize your essence as nondual,
Even when it is in bodily form.[115]

So devotion was not obliterated for, and by, unity. The devotion of Śiva himself was stressed in his unity with his consort and the same devotion in unity was projected to the God–human relationship:

Just as Devī,
Your most beloved, endless pool of bliss,

Is inseparable from you,
So may your devotion alone
Be inseparable from me.[116]

And again:

With my eyes closed
At the touch of your lotus feet,
May I rejoice,
Reeling with drunkenness
From the wine of your devotion.[117]

The whole of the fifteenth song of Utpaladeva's *Śivastotrāvalī* was dedicated to the immensity of Śiva's devotion and the wealth of it he gave to his devotees. In many ways it seemed that it was that devotion of Śiva that was the unifying factor of all, "devotion is inherent in all", Uptaladeva sang,[118] and devotion became the exclusive pathway to unity with God because it was exactly that which provided experience of the non-dual nature of all things:

When shall I enjoy the bounteous celebration
Of the rapture of devotion,
Where the elements of the objective world
Become filled with the bliss of consciousness?[119]

The "bliss of consciousness" here was the full realization that all was the pure Consciousness of Śiva. And yet, the intimacy of the relationship between Utpaladeva and Śiva was warmly brought out in his poetry; it was almost expressive of Śiva as an elusive lover, as the poet yearned for the devotion from his adored. As an example of his belief that devotion was the means and the goal he said:

Let me delight in the sweet, sublime
Bliss of your devotion,
Leaving behind not only base powers,
But liberation itself.[120]

The feet of the Lord was the motif that pervaded all of our poets' songs and Utpaladeva described the experience thus:

So cool is the nectar
From the touch of your lotus feet!
May that always stream through me,
Within and without.[121]

As with so many of the poets, despondency and suffering when he felt separated from God was evident, so that the touch of Śiva's lotus feet was not always present. Unity *in devotion* was his aim, but that did not preclude some perceptions of the physical forms of Śiva: the whole of the fourteenth song of the *Śivastotrāvalī*, for example, was a glorification of the physical accoutrements and being of Śiva. Utpaladeva also accepted Śiva's consort – Bhavānī/Parameśvarī/Devī/Gaurī – and he even called Śiva his father and Bhavanī, his mother.

I do not want to dwell further on Kashmir Śaivism, but it is important to include it because it demonstrates so well how even where the unity of the cosmos is posited and the relationship between human and divine is a non-dual one, personal devotion to a describable deity need not be excluded from the pathway to God. *Bhakti* movements have never subsided in India: instead they have deepened, diversified and innovated. But the contribution of the great poet–saints of both the Vaiṣṇava and Śaiva traditions has never been minimalized. Later in time than my terms of reference here, came devotional impetus for the Śakta sects, too, with the devotion of the Bengali Rāmprasād (1718–75), to the great Goddess, Kālī and Umā.[122] What the devotional movements did was to make Hinduism relevant to the ordinary folk by retaining use of the vernacular and, in most cases, making devotional religion inclusive of all castes and none, and to both genders. Such movements also gave a great impetus to temple and home ritual in methods that did not rely on orthodox scriptures. We can still see icons of *all* the *Āḻvārs* and *Nāyaṉmārs* in *all* the major Tamil temples and in homes, and there are annual festivals to honour them. Their songs have become established in liturgy – such was their impact on the hearts and minds of the people. Their songs even feature on radio and television. Parita Mukta offers a very pertinent point about *bhakti* here when she says, "it is a self-created reality which is profoundly and intimately personal even as it is socially circumscribed, enabling the self to regenerate its capacity to face, endure, and at times overcome the harshness of an unloved existence."[123] *Bhakti* illustrates that whatever the *external* constraints on the self, the mind, and its imaginings and devotions is a free medium for love of God. *Bhakti* traditions kept the myths of the deities alive but, as Rachel McDermott notes, *bhakti* has a "tendency to soften gods and goddesses, making them more mellow, personable, and pleasing in form and character".[124] It is an important point in that it aided the accessibility of each deity to the spiritual mind.

The medium of poetry and song to pour out love of God is a spontaneous overflow that is both intuitive and immediate: it reflects a *direct* experience of God without the need for any mediator, and it is this that makes it capable of universal participation: those who hear the songs of the poets share in the direct experience of God, or the pain of separation from him, of which they sing. As Vasudha Narayana points out, it is the participation in the emotions of the poets in which the present-day *bhakta* experiences God. He or she identifies with the stories of the saints in their passion, in their surrender to God, in their outpouring of ecstatic devotion.[125] It is sad that, while we have witnessed a good number of great female *bhakti* saints in the foregoing, their contribution to religion has been insufficient to do much for the liberation of women in Hinduism, but at least they showed that devotion is of the heart and mind and this cannot be stolen from them, whatever their external circumstances. Dilip Chitre described *bhakti*'s wide characteristics, finding them in many of the hymns of the poets and all of them in Tukārām's poetry: "The gamut of *Bhakti* poetry has amazing depth, width, and range: it is emotional, devotional; it is vivid, graphic, frank, direct; it is ironic, sarcastic, critical; it is colloquial, comic, absurd; it is imaginative, inventive, experimental; it is intense, angry, assertive and full of protest."[126] And in that wide gamut we find all the manifestations of our own emotional journeys, our own hopes, frustrations, denials, and explorations of the spiritual quest.

9
Diversity and Unity

So how does one conclude an introduction to a religion that is as complex as Hinduism? And are there any real conclusions suited to such a diverse phenomenon? One theme that seems to me to provide an answer is the search for an underlying unity as a deeper reality than the transient world in which we live, albeit that there are different views of the nature of unity. While it would be impossible to find unity in all the many examples of diversity and disparity in the broad spectrum of Hinduism, it is, I think, a good starting point and a relevant means of inquiry. For the serious student of Hinduism, to search for the real beneath the apparent, is to follow the pathways of many of Hinduism's sages, poets and philosophers. Empirical pluralistic diversity informs the entire world that we see. Our complex minds make distinctions between this and that and understand things by doing so, creating relative points of contact for the mind out of dualistic concepts of opposites – good and bad, light and dark and so on. The duality that particularly interested the great Hindu sages was that between one and many or, to be precise, *the* One and the many. What could possibly be the answer to a transient world of change, of death and decay? The response was to search for an intransient, eternal *One* that informed the *many* evident in the phenomenal world. Everything in the world is subject to becoming and dying: even the universe itself is posited as becoming and ceasing in endless cycles. And if there is a permanent One that is contrasted with the impermanent world in which we live, what is the relationship, if any, between the two? Does one make sense without the other? The search for some kind of unity between the One and the many was the main goal that informed the quest of most strands of Hinduism. Different responses emerged to the philosophical question but the search for some kind of unifying principle unites many of the differing pathways of that search.

I began this exploration of Hindu ideas with the Indus civilization that pre-dated historical Hinduism by many centuries. What possible unity could be found in cultures that have left us no records? I think it worth mentioning, however, that not only was diversity underpinned by a remarkable cultural civic unity, but there was an equally remarkable symbiosis between human, animal and deity that found expression in concrete form on seals and tablets. Humans could be part animal and *vice versa*, and deities part human and animal in what I termed a supernatural integration of the conceived worlds of human, animal, and divine.

As far back as *Vedic* times we find connecting of the One and the many to be part of the spiritual quest of the seers. William Mahony sensitively says that "Vedic seers recognized in the universe about them suggestions of a metaphysical pulse or cycle of being that resonates in the existential rhythms of life in the human world".[1] That pulse or rhythm could be felt by the seers and, in Mahony's view, they used the power of their imagination, to make that critical connection between the One and the many. As Mahony puts it "in the beginning was the One. Then, in a procreative yet fracturous process of differentiation, the One becomes the many, which at once veil and reveal their unified source. Finally, in a (re)constructive process that heals the brokenness of being, the many return to the One."[2] As we saw in chapter 2 in the context of *Vedic* religion, there was a blurring of the distinctions between the deities so that they became different expressions of One. The spiritual experiences of the *Vedic* seers were grounded in a rhythmic pulse that informed the whole universe; a cosmic, unifying law called *ṛta*. The unifying nature of *ṛta* was indicative of an interconnection of the totality of all things in the cosmos, what Mahony terms, "a seamless universe rather than a disjointed multiverse".[3] It was *ṛta* that set the foundation for a more explicit unity of microcosm and macrocosm in the concept of "the One", as Brahman. While the *Vedic* seers certainly accepted the reality of the world and its plurality of forms, their acceptance of the interconnection of all phenomena was a major step on the pathway towards a fuller unity. Thus, a few later hymns of the *Ṛg Veda* moved to posit a mysterious, indescribable transcendent beyond space and time from which everything emanated. Even at the level of sacrificial ritual, the interconnection of divine and human worlds was clearly fundamental, and sought to harmonize the two. A deity such as the multiform god of fire, Agni, was sufficiently ubiquitous to be a unifying and interconnecting force in the universe, uniting the divine and human worlds. This is a god that coalesced so many dualities in his own form, not least explicit as fire in its many forms, and implicit as the divine essence within it; and he vibrated between the two. A goddess such as Aditi was depicted as the womb of all, the great mother, from whom everything emanated, and the One to which all deities were reduced. The *Ṛg Veda* also made other attempts to unite all the gods as One in the Viśvedevas, the "All-gods". Clearly, there were many attempts in the four *Vedas* to move to a unifying principle that answered questions about the nature of ultimate Reality and its relation to the plurality of ordinary reality that we see around us.

It was the sages of the *Upaniṣads* who searched the depths of knowledge in a more concerted quest to discover some permanent Reality behind the plurality of the visible world and, in doing so, infused unity into the diversity they experienced. They posited a fundamental essence that, though indescribable, was intimately present in all, so making all souls in existence united with their Source, united with each other and united with the physical world in one Reality. Monism, *identity* of all with Brahman, was the main current of the *Upaniṣads*. Even where Brahman was posited as without qualities (*nirguṇa*), and yet with qualities (*saguṇa*), both appear to have been unified as two aspects of just one Reality, two sides of one coin. All the apparent dualities in the manifest universe were unified with their Cause – differentiations unified in what is undifferentiated. At the very least, the *Upaniṣads* expressed in different ways the *interconnection* between all manifestation: but the seers mainly searched for a Primal Cause from which the world emerged. In some cases they saw the world emanating from its Source like sparks from a fire. The same Reality was found to run through all things, intimately uniting macrocosm and microcosm, and projecting the inner Self out into cosmic identity with all.

For so much thought in Hinduism, unity is experienced when subject–object differentiation within the pluralistic involvement with life disappears and all dualities are lost for the experience of passive, unifying stillness. The positing of the ultimate Absolute as Brahman entrenched a more definitive belief in an indescribable "*That*", which gave unity to the apparent diversity of all life. The existence of Brahman as the substratum of all phenomena is the real unifying principle, and the only way to experience such unity within the self is to get rid of the self, to get rid of the mind-differentiation between this and that, which creates the dualities that obscure the unity of all things as Brahman. Indeed, loss of the egoistic self, which makes such unity possible, could be said to be a common denominator of so much Hindu thought. The experience of unity would be varied, but it was deep within the self that it could be found, so transcending the world of dualities and differences for a transcendental unity between a Self that was real and an ultimate Reality.

This leads us to one important view of unity and diversity with the development of the concept of an *ātman*, a Self deep within but overlaid with a multitude of egoistic inhibitors that were inimical to its realization. It was a concept that united not just the inner Self with the supreme Brahman, but the inner Self with that of others – a rather brilliant unifying principle. Advaita Vedānta, in particular, fused the *ātman* and Brahman in total identity, following along the lines of some of the *Upaniṣads*, especially the *Chāndogya*. Here, the ultimate Reality was without qualities, *nirguṇa*. It was a non-dual perspective that identified the *ātman* with Brahman but denied any reality to, and unity between, Brahman-*ātman* and an illusory world. Others had a different perspective of unity: while retaining the concept of a transcendent deity, Brahman was brought into the realm of human experience as a personal God that was describable and *with* qualities, *saguṇa*. Despite such a disparity between the non-dual, *nirguṇa* concept of deity and the dualistic personal God, Brahman mostly remained the One unifying factor behind the many. But it was dualistic movements that permitted a personal God that connected Brahman with the world that he created, sustained and dissolved in repetitive cycles. Here, the unity of God and selves, God and world and to some extent selves and world was made viable.

The orthodox Hindu philosophical schools of Advaita, Sāṃkhya and Yoga all sought for some kind of unity in the face of the pluralism of the many. Sāṃkhya and Yoga in contrast to Advaita unified the whole world of matter but separated it from all liberated Selves. Important in the unity of matter here were the three interdependent *guṇas* that are, in the main, accepted, though with some modifications, by many strands of Hinduism. Since they inform every entity in different collocations and varying proportions, they provide an interconnectedness throughout the entire cosmos, informing what is unmanifest when in equilibrium, and then all manifestation – including internal thought processes in each being – when evolution takes place. Here, all manifest effects are parts of one unified material whole. In Sāṃkhya and Yoga metaphysics, matter came into being from an undifferentiated primordial substance that evolved from subtle to gross differentiated material. It was a meticulously designed plan of creation that unified the whole of the phenomenal and material world including the mind, ego and consciousness of individuals, and was immensely influential in its theory of matter. But there was no unity for liberated selves: they were separated from unified matter in which they had become trapped, and separated from each other in the liberated state.

The *Bhagavad Gītā* took up many of the *Vedāntic* concepts, as well as those of Sāṃkhya and classical Yoga, but gave to them its own particular emphases. The answer to the relationship between the One and the many lay in Kṛṣṇa. As the One, Kṛṣṇa was the Unmanifest, *nirguṇa* Brahman and "*That*", which exists when there is nothing else. As *saguṇa* Brahman, Kṛṣṇa was the equivalent of Sāṃkhya's *avyakta*, unmanifest matter containing the potential for all that becomes manifest. And when that unmanifest potential becomes manifest, since it consists of Brahman, Brahman/Kṛṣṇa pervades every aspect of it as the Source and unifying essence that runs through all. The wise in the *Gītā* were said to recognize such sameness and unity in all the apparent empirical diversity of the world. As Vimala Thakar says: "Diversity decorates unity, and unity breathes into the expression of diversity."[4] Nevertheless, in the *Gītā*, Brahman transcended the unified cosmos, though existence was interconnected and harmonized by him and by the *ātman* that existed in all beings: "When he sees the whole variety of beings resting in the One and radiating out from that alone, then he becomes Brahman", the *Gītā* said of a liberated Self in 13:30: the same essence was within the *Brāhmin*, the dog, the blade of grass. In the *Gītā*, there was oneness in creation, unity behind the many – all intimately part of Brahman – but, ultimately, there was a duality between Brahman and creation. The *Gītā* did not separate spirit and matter but made all *prakṛti* Kṛṣṇa's own so that he was intimately united with his creation, though Brahman always transcended and was greater than the matter and the Selves that he created.

Since Kṛṣṇa was the embodiment of God in anthropomorphic form on Earth, it could hardly be denied that the *personal* God was essential to the concept of divinity in the *Gītā*. That personal conception of God is what informed the powerfully spiritual *bhakti* movements and philosophies. While some in the *bhakti* movements maintained a focus on the *nirguṇa* Brahman without qualities, albeit with what was also a personal, devotional approach at times, the proponents of the main *bhakti* movements in the form of poet–saints wanted, above all, to be united with God but to retain the duality that allowed their devotion to continue in the liberated state. For them, as for many in devotional Hinduism, they expressed a desire for *intimacy* with God, a continued *love* of God, an experience of the reciprocated love of God, and so the goal was the duality of a loving relationship, a union in love. While God remained the Source of all and so unified the many, the experiential dimension of being "at his feet" was a dual one, and a dual one that made loving devotion to God the primary means to liberation that continued in the state of liberation. It was an *emotional* relationship with a personal God, an experience of the grace of God and the surrendering of the self to take refuge in that grace in unity with the divine. Because God was manifest in the world he could take the form in which his devotees wished to see him, according to that great Āḻvār, Nammāḻvār, and yet the poet knew that God was really beyond all forms. Tukārām sang of experiencing God within his body so that he enclosed the form of God, though he, too, knew that God was undefinable and without form. The Śaiva *Nāyaṉār*, Appar, sang of God's manifestation in earth, fire water, the wind that blows, moon, sun, good and evil, man and woman, rock, hill and forest, rivers, streams, grasses, bushes, plants and herbs: he understood God to be manifest everywhere. The wonderful

Śaiva poet Māṇikka Vācakar sang of the God he so loved who filled Heaven and Earth with manifested light though he transcended all thought; yet he placed the coolness in the moon, energy in the wind, and honeyed sweetness in the soul. He believed God used his mind for a shrine and his body for a temple: like shadow to form, Māṇikka Vācakar was united with Śiva.

The eleventh to twelfth century Ācārya, Rāmānuja, took the devotional concept of a personal God, a *saguṇa* Brahman with an abundance of qualities, and infused Vaiṣṇava devotional movements with a philosophical foundation and orthodox credence. His answer to the One and the many was to make the many the "body" of God and inseparable from God in the same way as the body is inseparable from the soul in every being. While this was a unity between God and man in one way, it was also a duality in that there was identity but difference. God could be the only independent Reality and all else was conceived of as dependent reality, attributes of God, and dependent on God as Creator, Sustainer and Dissolver of the universe. Unity encompassed diversity by making all creation the manifested attributes of God, who moulded Nature into magnificent manifestations of himself.

My point in revisiting these philosophies is to show that unity does not necessarily mean identity, and for the many Hindu movements that accept a personal God, God can be involved in the world as an indwelling force but is not diminished by the transience, change and imperfections of the world: yet God unifies the world as his creation, just as he does with its dissolution and rebirth. What is created must ultimately cease to exist in a world of flux and transience but, equally so, what ceases to exist is born again, from the universe to the tiniest plant. Life is death and death is life and the cyclical rhythm of its manifestation and unmanifest states are part of the unity of the flow of things.

We need not stretch our minds back into the distant past in order to experience the unifying rhythm of a uniting force behind the universe. More recent poets expressed the idea so well as in William Blake's words:

> To see a World in a Grain of Sand
> And a Heaven in a Wild Flower
> Hold Infinity in the palm of your hand
> And Eternity in an hour.

Then there are William Wordsworth's exquisite lines from *Tintern Abbey*:

> And I have felt
> A presence that disturbs me with the joy
> Of elevated thoughts; a sense sublime
> Of something far more deeply interfused,
> Whose dwelling is the light of setting suns,
> And the round ocean, and the living air,
> And the blue sky, and in the mind of man:
> A motion and a spirit, that impels
> All thinking things, all objects of all thought,
> And rolls through all things.[5]

And in *The Prelude* Wordsworth wrote:

> . . . with bliss ineffable
> I felt the sentiment of Being spread
> O'er all that moves, and all that seemeth still;
> O'er all that, lost beyond the reach of thought
> And human knowledge, to the human eye
> Invisible, yet liveth to the heart;
> O'er all that leaps, and runs, and shouts, and sings,
> Or beats the gladsome air; o'er all that glides
> Beneath the wave, yea, in the wave itself,
> And mighty depth of waters.[6]

For such poets and, indeed, the *Vedic* poets, it is as if there is a unifying web that spans out uniting all of nature and the whole universe. In Blake's and Wordsworth's words we have superb examples of Mahony's "power of imagination" that he believes acted as a "fundamentally religious function" in the case of the *Vedic* seers. He writes: "Even in the uncertainty of existence, even in the changes and transformations of life, even in the ubiquity of death, the imagination saw or sought to see the reflections of a deeper, unified, and unifying harmony of being."[7] The poets past and present could and can do what most of us cannot and that is to put into words what is not empirical and what is transcendental.

At more external levels, Hinduism is an umbrella term that has accommodated a multiplicity of religious expressions throughout a long period of history and pre-history. The idea that Brahman can be manifested in myriad forms or no form at all unites the diversity of religious beliefs and practices: the deities of others alongside one's own can often be accommodated. The very fact that temples house a variety of deities exemplifies this, along with the nature of different deities responding to different needs of their devotees. Such accommodation is no less evident in ideas: the belief in the cycles of birth and death, *saṃsāra*, is maintained alongside the earlier belief in ancestors and Heaven and Hell. No paradox is seen here: Heaven and Hell are simply places to which the dead will go depending on their *karma*, in order to reap some of the positive or negative *karma* before rebirth. Thus, two rather disparate concepts have been united and accommodated. Alain Daniélou wrote: "The whole of Nature is but a symbol of a higher reality"[8] and, if this is so, everything in the manifest world is a symbol of its Source and, as such, is interrelated with everything else. There are a multiplicity of viewpoints and experiences of the nature of God within the vast complexity of the manifest world. Varied praxis informs the many dimensions of Hinduism and, whether tangible or conceptual, all are part of the whole of Nature. Daniélou argued rather well that polytheism with its multi-dimensional aspects of the divine may be nearer the reality of what must ultimately be beyond anything we can comprehend as "God", than any one single perspective. He said: "The more we can seize of the different aspects of the phenomenal world, often apparently contradictory, through which the Divine may be approached, the more we come to a general, a "real," insight into the mysterious entity we call "God."[9]

A whole chapter of the *Bhagavad Gītā* is devoted to the manifestations of Kṛṣṇa in the universe, the manifestations that, through his essence, unites the whole of creation though, again, since everything is but a part of him, the sum total of those parts are still but a single fragment of him. As Brahman, Kṛṣṇa is always greater than all that is manifest and yet he is present as the divine essence in all, as the infinitesimal spark that is but a fragment of total divinity. In the words of Sri Krishna Prem: "From that *Eternal Brahman* issue forth the *Mighty Atman*, great beyond all thought, and all the countless starry worlds that fill the wide immensities of space. Yet so vast is Its spaceless, timeless grandeur that all these wondrous emanated worlds are as a drop taken out of the ocean, leaving Its shores being ever full."[10]

Glossary of Sanskrit Terms

The following is a selective list of the Sanskrit terms most frequently used in the chapters. Sanskrit consonants carry the vowel '*a*' with them, which is why transliterated Sanskrit words have so many '*a*'s. This '*a*' is normally short and pronounced like the *u* in English b*u*t. Where this is not so, here, and with other vowels, diacritical marks can be added in transliteration to indicate a change of sound. Sanskrit also has a number of aspirated words with an '*h*' following the consonant. When these combinations of letters occur, the reader is advised to separate the two consonants in order to obtain a more accurate sound. For example, *artha*, "wealth, success" is pronounced as *art* plus *ha* but since there are no diacritical indicators on the '*a*'s, both are pronounced as *u* – *urt-hu*. Such diacritical marks on vowels also help to indicate where stress on syllables is in a word. A simplified list of pronunciation of letters is as follows:

a	pronounced as in b*u*t
ā	as in f*a*ther
c	as in *ch*at
e	as in f*e*ll
i	as in f*i*t
ī	as in f*ee*t
ḷ	as in fab*le*
o	as in g*o*
ṛ	as in fu*r*
u	as in p*u*t
ū	as in y*u*le
ai	as in *ai*sle
au	as in v*ow*
ṃ	is a nasalized sound as in French to*n*
ṅ	as in a*n*ger
ñ	as in pu*n*cher
ṣ and *ś*	approximately as in *sh*ip

ābhaṅgas	hymns of the Maharashtra poet–saints.
abhyāsa	constant effort and practice.

Ācāryas	great theologians, teachers and spiritual guides, also a title attached to their names.
acit	insentient matter.
adharma	what is not right and against the norms of society, religion and the universe; evil, the opposite of *dharma.*
adhyāsa	superimposition (of what is not real on what is Real).
Aditi	*Vedic* goddess.
Ādityas	the sons of Aditi who personify aspects of nature.
adṛṣṭa	the power that transforms a cause into a specific effect.
advaita	non-dual.
Advaita Vedānta	the school of non-dualism associated with Śaṃkara, and one of the six orthodox schools of Hindu philosophy.
Āgamas	"source" or "beginnings", what first came about: non-*Vedic* Śaiva scriptures bearing testimony to a personal deity.
Agni	*Vedic* god of fire.
ahaṃkāra	ego.
ahiṃsā	non-violence and abstention from injury and violence to any form of life.
ajñāna	ignorance.
akam	"interior" early Tamil poetry that was romantic, erotic and personally reflective.
akṣara	imperishable (of Brahman).
Alakṣmī	the inauspicious sister of the Goddess of Good Fortune, Lakṣmī; she brings misfortune.
Āḻvārs	"divers", devotional mystics who "dive" into the divine.
ananda	Bliss; the nature of Brahman and the pure Self.
aṅga	part; limb; individual.
antaḥ-kārana	"internal organ" consisting of intellect, ego and mind.
antaryāmin	the divine as inner controller of selves and the world.
apṛthak-siddhi	inseparability between a substance and its attributes, a whole and its parts.
apsaras	celestial nymphs.
Āraṇyakas	forest, wilderness writings; *Vedic śruti* scriptures containing much mystical thought that overlaps with and prefigures some *Vedāntic* concepts.
Ardhanārīśvara	iconic representation of Śiva as an androgyne, half female and half male.
Arjuna	one of the five Pāṇḍava brothers and the central human character of the *Bhagavad-Gītā.*
artha	wealth, success, social status.
Āryans	"nobles", the race of people said to have infiltrated northern India in the second millennium BCE.
āsana	bodily posture.
asat	non-existence, chaos, non-being.

āśramas	four stages of life – student, householder, forest dweller and renouncer.
asuras	demons, anti-gods.
Atharva Veda	one of the four *Vedas* that deals predominantly with incantations, spells and charms.
ātman	"self" but specifically the true Self that is the essence of all things and that is equated partially or wholly with Brahman.
avatāras	literally "descents", mainly of Viṣṇu in animal or human form.
avidyā	ignorance.
aviveka	non-discrimination.
avyakta	unmanifest matter; Kṛṣṇa as Unmanifest.
Bhagavad Gītā	sacred Hindu devotional epic poem.
bhajan(a)s	hymns and devotional songs in praise of a deity.
bhakti	loving devotion to a personal deity including reciprocal love of the deity.
-mārga	the path of loving devotion to God.
-yoga	the *yoga* of loving devotion to the divine.
para-	supreme loving devotion.
bhakta	a *bhakti* devotee.
bheda	difference.
abheda	non-difference.
bedhābheda	"different yet not different"; identity-in-difference.
bhūtas	spirits; in Sāṃkhya, gross elements.
Brahmā	one of the triad of Hindu Gods with Śiva and Viṣṇu and responsible for the action of creation.
Brahman	the divine Absolute of Hinduism.
Brāhmaṇas	commentaries on the *Vedas* and part of Sanskrit *śruti* scriptures that are textual manuals related to ritual.
Brahma-*nirvana*	liberation.
Brāhmins	members of the highest class of the four classes of Hindus.
buddhi	knowledge; intellect; consciousness; the discerning faculty.
-yoga	the *yoga* of intellect.
Caṅkam (Tam.)	Skt. Saṇgam, early Tamil poems.
chela	disciple.
cit	consciousness.
citta	mind.
citta-vṛtti-nirodha	cessation of the fluctuations of the mind.
citta-vṛttis	fluctuations of the mind.
dāna	giving.
darśan(a)	viewing, sight of, audience with: a philosophical system.
Dāsas/Dasyus	the term in the *Ṛg Veda* used for non-Āryans, aboriginal and indigenous people.

devas	gods.
Devī	Goddess.
-Māhātmya	important text extolling the Great Goddess.
Mahā-	Great Goddess.
dhāraṇā	focused concentration and attention.
dharma	what is right socially and religiously; duty.
sanātana-	eternal *dharma.*
sva-	one's "own" *dharma.*
varṇa-āśrama-	*dharma* pertaining to class and stage of life.
dhyana	meditation.
draṣṭṛ	one who sees.
dravya	substance.
dṛśya	what is seen.
ekāgra/ekagratā	one-pointedness of the mind.
gandharvas	half-human, half-animal creatures.
garbha-gṛha	"womb house", the shrine housing a deity.
Gāyatrī-Mantra	an important *mantra* from the *Ṛg Veda* that is chanted daily.
ghī	clarified butter which, as a product of the cow, is regarded as especially pure.
gopīs	"cowherdesses", especially those associated with Kṛṣṇa.
guṇas	three strands or qualities – *sattva*, *rajas* and *tamas* – that are existent in all things.
nirguṇa	having no *guṇas.*
saguṇa	with *guṇas.*
guru	a spiritual teacher.
Hiraṇya-garbha	one of the *Vedic* deities posited as the source of creation.
Indra	a *Vedic* deity.
Īśvara	"Lord", a term to depict Brahman with qualities and manifest form; God; supreme deity.
iṣṭa-devatā	a personal deity.
jīva	individual, living soul.
-ātman	the living being and the inner *ātman.*
jivan-mukta	one who is liberated, enlightened, while still alive.
jñāna	knowledge.
-kāṇḍa	knowledge portion of the *Vedas.*
-mārga	the path to liberation that involves knowledge.
jñānin	one having knowledge, wisdom or who is on the path of knowledge.
kaivalya	isolation, aloneness, the Sāṃkhya and classical Yoga state of liberation.

Kāla	ultimate Time that is beyond normal time.
Kāma	the god of love.
kāma	pleasure, especially sexual; desire.
Kapila	legendary founder of the school of Sāṃkhya.
kāraṇa	cause.
karma	"activity", "action"; ritual action; the law of cause and effect by which an individual gains merit or demerit according to good or bad actions.
-kāṇḍa	the ritual action portion of the *Vedas*.
-mārga	the path to liberation that involves ritual action or egoless action.
-yoga	the discipline of egoless action without desire for results.
prārabda-	*karma* that is on its way and cannot be avoided.
karmāśaya	the accumulated specific *karmic* effects that produce a distinct individual.
kārya	effect.
kauṣṭubha	the jewel in the necklace worn by Viṣṇu.
kavya	a poem.
kīrtaṇ(a)	ritual chanting in praise of a deity.
kleśas	afflictions or hindrances of the mind.
Kṣatriyas	the second highest class of Hindus, traditionally warriors, rulers and administrators.
kṣetra	the "field" of all manifestation.
Kṣetrajña	Brahman as "Knower of the field".
līlā	divine sport or play.
liṅga	phallic symbol associated with the God Śiva.
-śarīra	subtle body that carries *karmic* residues from one life to the next.
mahā-bhūtas	five gross physical elements of evolution of matter.
mahā-vākya	"great saying".
mantra	a part of scripture or name of a deity used for meditation or ritual.
Maruts	gods of the wind.
maṭhas	monasteries.
Mātṛkās	"Mothers", female powers emitted by the Great Goddess Durgā.
māyā	in *Vedic* texts, concealed, mysterious, extraordinary power; later, delusion; illusion.
mahā-	great delusion.
mithyā	illusory in the sense that it is not completely unreal nor is it real.
mokṣa/mukti	"release", liberation from the cycle of rebirths.
muni	a sage, seer.
Mūralī	Kṛṣṇa's female flute.
mūrti	image, embodiment, especially of a deity.
mūvar	the "three" famous Śaiva *Nāyaṉmārs*.

nāmā-japa	recitation of the name(s) of God.
Nārāyaṇa	another name for the deity Viṣṇu.
Naṭarāja	the cosmic dance of Śiva that brings about the dissolution of the universe.
Nāthamuni	devotional mystic, one of the most prominent of the Āḻvārs.
Nāyaṉmārs	"leaders", sixty-three Śaiva Tamil poets.
neti neti	"not this, not this" referring to the nature of Brahman as beyond dualities.
nirākāra	without form.
nirguṇa	without qualities.
nirodha	cessation.
Nirṛti	a destructive *Vedic* goddess.
nirvana	enlightenment, liberation.
nivṛtti	inactivity.
niyama	discipline.
Oṃ/Aum	the primordial sound from which all emerged; symbol of Brahman; a *mantra*.
Paśupati	"Lord of Creatures", one of the names of the deity Śiva.
pati-vratā	the vow of a married woman to live for her husband's happiness.
pēy	demon, ghoul.
pīpal	a sacred tree with heart-shaped leaves used as a design and in ritual from pre-historic times.
Prabandham	twenty-four poems of the Āḻvārs known as the Tamil *Veda*.
prājña	wisdom, knowledge.
prakṛti	nature, manifested matter.
mūlā-	primordial matter.
pralaya	dissolution of the universe.
prāṇa	breath.
prāṇāyama	rhythmic control of respiration.
prapatti	surrender to God.
prarābda-karma	*karma* that is already on its way and cannot be averted.
prasāda	the "grace" of a deity given as the remains of food or other offerings to a deity; the love of God to his devotees.
pratyāhara	withdrawing of the senses from the external world of sense stimuli.
prema	love.
pretas	ghosts.
Pṛthivī	*Ṛg Vedic* goddess.
pūjā	worship, veneration, reverence.
puṟam	early Tamil poetry that was "external" and concerned with statesmanship and heroes.
Purāṇas	"ancient tales"; a class of *smṛti* scriptures.
puruṣa	man; primal Being. Kṛṣṇa as the Supreme Self.

Puruṣa-sūkta	the *Ṛg Veda* hymn of a great sacrificial being from whom the cosmos and the four classes were made.
Puruṣottama	Kṛṣṇa as the Supreme Person.
puṣṭi-mārga	the way of grace extolled by the *ācārya* Vallabhā.
rajas	one of the three *guṇas* responsible for activity and energy in all life.
rāsa/ rāsa-līlā	circular dance.
ṛṣis	ancient *Vedic* seers.
ṛta	the *Vedic* cosmic, rhythmic power and law that makes everything such as it is, interconnects all and is the force behind cause and effect.
saguṇa	with qualities.
Śaiva Siddhānta	philosophical, mystical Tamil Śaivism.
sākāra	with form (of Brahman).
śākta	devotee of the Mother Goddess in the Śākta sect of Hindusim.
śakti	power, energy; the divine in female form.
samādhi	stilled consciousness and deep, meditative concentration.
saṃkalpa	intention.
Sāṃkhya	"enumeration", "calculation"; the name of one of the six Hindu schools of orthodox philosophy.
-Kārikā	foundational text of classical Sāṃkhya.
saṃnyāsa	renunciation; the final fourth stage of life.
saṃnyāsin	renouncer.
saṃpradāya	a sect or tradition.
saṃsāra	the cycle of births and deaths.
saṃskāras	life-cycle rites; subconscious impressions from many lives.
saṃyama	the combined three final stages of classical Yoga.
saṃyoga	conjunction.
śāstras	scriptures, teachings, laws, rule books.
sat/ satya	Existence, Being, Truth/ultimate Truth.
satī (the)	wife who immolates herself on her deceased husband's funeral pyre.
sat-kārya-vāda	belief that only the cause is real and that any effects inhere in that cause.
sattva	one of the three *guṇas*, associated with light, spiritual evolution, what is good, truth, wisdom.
sevā	service to God or *guru*.
smṛti	"remembered"; scripture that is not *Vedic* and that contains much devotional and popular material.
soma/ Soma	a *Vedic* hallucinatory drink that heightened consciousness, and also the name of a god.
śraddha	faith.
Śrī-vatsa	curl of golden hair on Viṣṇu's chest, equated with Lakṣmī.
śruti	revealed *Vedic* scriptures that are regarded as timeless and without human or divine authors.

strī-dharma	the *dharma* of a wife.
Śūdras	those of the lowest and fourth class of Hindus who are not twice born.
Sūr Sāgar	the "Ocean of Sūr", hymns accredited to the northern Vaiṣṇava saint, Sūrdās.
sūtras	law texts.
sva-bhāva	"own being", one's innate nature.
tamas	one of the three *guṇas* and associated with dullness and inertia in the cosmos.
tapas	"heat", ascetic austerities.
Tat	"*That*", referring to Brahman as the indescribable Absolute.
tat tvam asi	"That you are", a statement of identity of the *ātman* with Brahman.
tattvas	"thatnesses", the evolutes of manifestation.
Tevāram	Skt. *Dēvāram*, the first seven books of the Tamil Śaiva canon of twelve books.
Tirumuṟai	The twelve books comprising the Tamil Śaiva canon of scriptures.
Tiruvāymoḻi	"Holy Word", over a thousand hymns composed by Nammāḻvār.
tulasī	the basil plant associated with Viṣṇu.
turya/turīya	the deep, dreamless stage of sleep when the self reflects the Consciousness that is Brahman.
tyāga	renunciation, literally "ignoring".
upādhis	"limiting adjuncts" and apparent but not real manifestations.
upāsana	meditation.
vacanas	"sayings"; poetry of Vīraśaiva/Liṅgāyata South Indian Śaivism.
vairāgya	non-attachment.
Vaiśyas	the third of the four classes, generally associated with trade.
vānaprastha	forest dweller, the third of the four stages of life.
varṇa	class, colour, covering.
varṇa-āśrama-dharma	the *dharma* of class and stage of life.
vāṣanās	deep-rooted *karmic* habits accumulated over many lifetimes.
Vedānta	the end of the *Veda*; the *Upaniṣads*.
vibhūtis	ubiquitous manifest powers of Kṛṣṇa.
vidyā	knowledge.
parā-	higher.
aparā-	lower.
vijñāna	intuitive realization.
viraha	separation from God.
Viśiṣṭādvaita	the tradition of qualified non-dualism associated mainly with Rāmānuja.
Viśva-rupa	manifest *saguṇa* form of Kṛṣṇa.
vivarta	"appearance" only and not real.

viveka	discrimination.
vṛtti	modification in the mind.
vyakta	manifest matter.
yajña	sacrificial worship.
yakṣīs	female spirits of the earth and trees.
yama	restraint.
yoga	discipline.
kriyā-	the path of disciplined action.
yogin	a male practitioner of *yoga*.
yoginī	a female practitioner of *yoga*, especially in Tantrism.
yoni	the symbol of the female genital organ.
yukta	integrated.
yoga-	integrated in *yoga*.

Notes

Introduction

1 Brighton, Portland and Toronto: Sussex Academic Press, 2012.

2 Brighton, Sussex and Portland, Oregon: Sussex Academic Press, 2002.

3 Georg Feuerstein, *The Yoga-Sūtra of Patañjali: A new translation and commentary* (Rochester, Vermont: Inner Traditions International, 1989 reprint of 1979 Folkestone: Dawson edn), p. 12.

4 *Bṛhadāraṇyaka Upaniṣad* 1.3.28, translator Patrick Olivelle, *Upaniṣads* (Oxford and New York: Oxford University Press, 1996), pp. 12–13.

5 Alain Daniélou, *The Myths and Gods of India* (Rochester, Vermont: Inner Traditions International, 1991, first published 1964), p. 7.

6 *Ibid.*, p. 5.

Chapter 1 The Indus Civilization

1 Troy Wilson Organ, *Hinduism: Its historical development* (Woodbury, New York, London, Toronto: Barron's Educational Series, Inc. 1974), p. 42.

2 Rita P. Wright, *The Ancient Indus: Urbanism, economy, and society* (Cambridge: Cambridge University Press, 2010), p. 274.

3 Gregory L. Possehl, "Archaeological Terminology and the Harappan Civilization" in Braj Basi Lal and S. P. Gupta, eds., *Frontiers of the Indus Civilization* (New Delhi: I. M. Sharma of Books and Books, 1984), p. 29.

4 Jane R. McIntosh, *The Ancient Indus Valley: New perspectives* (Santa Barbara, California, Denver, Colorado, Oxford, England: ABC-CLIO, 2008), p. 55.

5 Asko Parpola, "Is the Indus Script Indeed Not a Writing System?", *Airāvati* 1(2008), p. 120.

6 *Ibid.*

7 Bridget and Raymond Allchin, *The Rise of Civilization in India and Pakistan* (Cambridge, New York, New Rochelle, Melbourne, Sydney: Cambridge University Press, 1988 reprint of 1982 edn), p. 95.

8 Possehl, "Archaeological Terminology and the Harappan Civilization", p. 28.

9 Dilip K. Chakrabarti, *The Archaeology of Ancient Indian Cities* (Delhi, Calcutta, Chennai, Mumbai: Oxford University Press, 1998), p. 29.

10 This Pass is the link between the Indus Valley and the Iranian plateau by way of Quetta and Kandahar.

11 Gregory Possehl, *The Indus Civilization: A contemporary perspective* (Lanham MD: Alta Mira Press, 2002), p. 34.

12 Chakrabarti, *The Archaeology of Ancient Indian Cities*, p. 28.
13 Braj Basi Lal, "Aryan Invasion of India: Perpetuation of a Myth" in Edwin Bryant and Laurie Patton, eds., *The Indo-Aryan Controversy: Evidence and inference in Indian history* (London and New York: Routledge, 2005), p. 58.
14 *Ibid.*
15 Dating differs considerably. Different styles of pottery aid in the dating of levels: each style is given its type name from the name of the site where it was first discovered, for example the Kot-Diji culture has the specific Kot-Diji pottery, Amri-Nal pottery belongs to a different culture and so on. The dates I have given here, with some adjustments, are those suggested by Wright, *The Ancient Indus*, p. 54. Period IB is dated *c.* 6000–5500 BCE and Period II 5500–4500 BCE by Jim G. Shaffer and Diane A. Lichstenstein, "South Asian Archaeology and the Myth of Indo-Aryan Invasions" in Bryant and Patton, eds., *The Indo-Aryan Controversy*, p. 82.
16 Irfan Habib, *Prehistory, The People's History of India 1* (New Delhi: Tulika Books, 2012 reprint of 2001 edn), p. 55.
17 Remains of cattle (the humped South-Asian zebu), sheep and goats are much smaller in build than their wild forbears and illustrate the extent of domestication. There were other communities that produced food in such a way in this early period of approximately 7000–5000 BCE, such as the Kili Ghul Mohammad phase in the Quetta Valley of Baluchistan: see Possehl, *The Indus Civilization*, p. 30. Sites such as Amri, Kalibangan, Lothal, Anjira, Siah Damb, and Rana Ghundai also bear witness to this early phase of proto-historical farming settlement, but Mehrgarh is probably the oldest known.
18 Pottery was made by moulding clay in a woven basket and so is known as basket-marked ware.
19 Wright, *The Ancient Indus*, p. 57.
20 *Ibid.*, p. 270.
21 Habib, *Prehistory*, p. 56.
22 Wright, *The Ancient Indus*, p. 72.
23 Kenoyer, *Ancient Cities of the Indus Valley Civilization* (Oxford and New York: Oxford University Press, 1998), p. 26.
24 Wright, *The Ancient Indus*, p. 320.
25 Kenoyer, *Ancient Cities of the Indus Valley Civilization*, p. 38.
26 Habib, *Prehistory*, p. 54.
27 Kenoyer, *Ancient Cities of the Indus Valley Civilization*, p. 16.
28 Wright, *The Ancient Indus*, p. 67.
29 Dilip K. Chakrabarti, *India an Archaeological History: Palaeolithic beginnings to early historic foundations* (New Delhi: Oxford University Press, 2013 reprint of 1999 edn), p. 123.
30 See for example, Wright, *The Ancient Indus*, p. 58.
31 *Ibid.*
32 Kenoyer, *Ancient Cities of the Indus Valley Civilization*, p. 16.
33 Possehl, *The Indus Civilization*, p. 180.
34 See Wright, *The Ancient Indus*, p. 63.
35 *Ṛg Veda* 75:1, 7, translator Ralph T. H. Griffith, *The Hymns of the Ṛgveda* (Delhi: Motilal Banarsidass Publishers Private Limited, 1991 reprint of 1973 revised edn), p. 587.
36 See Possehl, *The Indus Civilization*, p. 63 for a useful chart.
37 Lal, "Aryan Invasion of India", p. 51.
38 McIntosh, *The Ancient Indus Valley*, p. 254.
39 Possehl, *The Indus Civilization*, p. 5.

40 Possehl illustrates this point by noting that inhabitants at Mohenjo-daro and Lothal were different from those at other Indus sites, and skeleton remains from a cemetery at Harappa have close affinities with those at Mehrgarh Periods III and IV who existed well over a thousand years earlier, for example, *ibid.*, p. 175.

41 Probably Mediterraneans, Alpines, Proto-Australoids and Mongoloids.

42 Kenoyer, *Ancient Cities of the Indus Valley Civilization*, p. 26.

43 The Ghaggar-Hakra flowed in the Ghaggar of North-West India and the Hakra of Pakistan. It no longer flows as the mighty river it once was, but was the site of considerable clusters of Indus settlements.

44 The full civilization extended to the border between Pakistan and Iran at Sutkagen-dor; Baluchistan; the North-West Frontier; the Indus plains; the Punjab of India and Pakistan; the Haryana and Ganges Doab; parts of the Thar Desert of Rajasthan; Kutch; Saurashtra; and from the mountains of the Himalayas in the North, to the southern Arabian Sea, the latter providing an inlet and outlet for trade.

45 Possehl, *The Indus Civilization*, p. 63.

46 Wright thinks that these hunter-gatherer communities could provide such things as honey, wax, ivory, resin, wild silk, and fibres from plants that were used to make cord: see *The Ancient Indus*, p. 160.

47 Allchin and Allchin, *The Rise of Civilization in India and Pakistan*, p. 163.

48 *Ibid.*, p. 163.

49 Asko Parpola, *Deciphering the Indus Script* (Cambridge: Cambridge University Press, 1994), p. 184.

50 See Possehl, *The Indus Civilization*, p. 48 for details of these.

51 *Ibid.*, p. 50.

52 Wright, *The Ancient Indus Valley*, p. 390.

53 Parpola, "Is the Indus Script Indeed Not a Writing System", p. 121.

54 Braj Basi Lal, "The Indus Civilization" in A. L. Basham, ed., *A Cultural History of India* (Oxford, New York, Toronto, Delhi *et al.*: Oxford University Press, 1989 reprint of 1975 edn), p. 17.

55 See, for example, Irfan Habib, *The Indus Civilization, The People's History of India 2* (New Delhi: Tulika Books, 2011 reprint of 2002 edn), pp. 16 and 60–1, and Hermann Kulke and Dieter Rothermund, *A History of India* (Totowa, New Jersey: Barnes & Noble Books, 1986), pp. 29–30.

56 Smaller sites may have had no such streets at all and a more haphazard layout.

57 Sharri Clark, "Embodying Indus Life", http://www.harappa.com/figurines/print.html, accessed 5/5/2014.

58 See B. K. Thapar, "Six Decades of Indus Studies" in Lal and Gupta, eds., *Frontiers of the Indus Civilization*, pp. 14–15.

59 See my companion Volume I, *Hinduism Beliefs & Practices: Major deities and social structures* (Brighton, Chicago and Toronto: Sussex Academic Press, 2014), chapter 8.

60 Possehl, *The Indus Civilization*, p. 6.

61 Kenoyer, *Ancient Cities of the Indus Valley Civilization*, p. 44.

62 See Chakrabarti, *The Archaeology of Ancient Indian Cities*, p. 83.

63 Suggested, for example, by Kulke and Rothermund, *A History of India*, p. 26.

64 Possehl, *The Indus Civilization*, p. 65.

65 *Ibid.*, p. 66.

66 *Ibid.*, p. 185.

67 Probably more a great hall than a granary, see Possehl, *Ancient Cities of the Indus Valley Civilization*, pp. 64–5, though there is a similar structure at Lothal, which is more likely to be a granary or

warehouse, but signs of grain usage are conspicuously absent from many Indus buildings described as granaries.

68 Harappa may well have been a city as early as 2800 and 2600 BCE in the Kot Diji phase, see Kenoyer, *Ancient Cities of the Indus Valley Civilization*, p. 49.

69 Wright, *The Ancient Indus*, p. 110.

70 Possehl, *The Indus Civilization*, p. 66.

71 *Ibid.*, p. 135.

72 Parpola, "Is the Indus Script Indeed Not a Writing System?", pp. 117 and 122.

73 For example, Steve Farmer, Richard Sproat and Michael Witzel, "The Collapse of the Indus Script Thesis: The Myth of a Literate Harappan Civilization" in *Electronic Journal of Vedic Studies* 11, 2(2004), pp. 19–57.

74 Asko Parpola, *A Dravidian Solution to the Indus Script Problem*, Kalaignar M. Karunanidhi Classical Tamil Research Endowment Lecture World Classical Tamil Conference, 25-06-2010, p. 8.

75 Parpola, "Is the Indus Script Indeed Not a Writing System?", pp. 123–4. Parpola used a rebus system to relate one sign to different meanings with the same sound, for example, "road" and "rode". Thus, one sign could have a number of meanings.

76 Farmer, Sproat and Witzel, "The Collapse of the Indus Script Thesis", *passim.*

77 See Iravatham Mahadevan's analysis of the theory of Madhusudan Mishra that the Indus script is an early Sanskrit, and the former's critique of other hypotheses in "Aryan or Dravidian or Neither? A Study of Recent Attempts to Decipher the Indus Script (1995–2000)" in *Electronic Journal of Vedic Studies* 8, 1(2002), pp. 2–5 and *passim.*

78 Habib, *The Indus Civilization*, pp. 6 and 50.

79 In particular, Parpola links the Indus inscriptions to the Dravidian language of Brahui that is spoken by people today in Baluchistan and Afghanistan which, as has been pointed out earlier, was a major centre of Indus civilization settlements, *Deciphering the Indus Script*, p. 160. His view is that "the Dravidian family is the best match for Harappan among the known non-Aryan language families of long standing in South Asia", p. 169. Others are critical of the links with Brahui and, indeed, with Dravidian, see Lal, "Aryan Invasion of India: Perpetuation of a Myth" pp. 62–3.

80 Farmer, Sproat and Witzel, "The Collapse of the Indus Script Thesis", p. 26.

81 *Ibid.*, pp. 42–3.

82 Steve Farmer, "Mythological Functions of Indus Inscriptions", http://www.safarmer.com/downloads Conclusion #1, accessed 05/05/2014.

83 *Ibid.*, p. 34.

84 Kenoyer, *Ancient Cities of the Indus Valley Civilization*, p. 73.

85 Parpola, *A Dravidian Solution to the Indus Script Problem*, p. 14.

86 Farmer, "Mythological Functions of Indus Inscriptions", p. 14.

87 Kenoyer, *Ancient Cities of the Indus Valley Civilization*, p. 59.

88 For example, McIntosh, *The Ancient Indus Valley*, p. 84, and Michael Jansen, *Mohenjo-daro: City of wells and drains, water splendour 4500 years ago* (Bonn: Bergisch Gladbach Frontinus-Gesellschaft, 1993), p. 17.

89 Possehl, *The Indus Civilization*, p. 195.

90 See Braj Basi Lal, "Some Reflections on the Structural Remains at Kalibangan" in Lal and Gupta, eds., *Frontiers of the Indus Civilization*, p. 57.

91 See McIntosh, *The Ancient Indus Valley*, p. 85.

92 John Keay described them thus: "Pop-eyed, bat-eared, belted and sometimes mini-skirted, they

are usually of crude workmanship and grotesque mien." *A History of India* (London: HarperCollins, 2000), p. 14.

93 See, for example, Chakrabarti, *The Archaeology of Ancient Indian Cities*, p. 195.

94 If women carried things on their heads, and bone structure analyses suggest that they did, then those with such high hair styles or headdresses would have been obvious higher status and did not work.

95 Kenoyer, *Ancient Cities of the Indus Valley Civilization*, p. 111.

96 See Clark, "Embodying Indus Life", p. 1.

97 Thomas J. Hopkins, *The Hindu Religious Tradition* (Belmont, California: Wadsworth Publishing Company, 1971, p. 9.

98 For example, Possehl, see *The Indus Civilization*, p. 141 and Kenoyer, *Ancient Cities of the Indus Valley Civilization*, p. 111. Figurines from the Quetta Valley from the Zhob culture have often been described as mother-goddesses, but I do not think the figurines here are necessarily indicative of a singular mother-goddess either. In any case, the Zhob culture is now dated to well before the Mature Indus Period, see Lal, "Aryan Invasion of India", p. 57.

99 A. L. Basham, *The Wonder That Was India* (London: Sidgwick & Jackson, 1967 reprint of 1963 revised edn), p. 22.

100 Clark, "Embodying Indus Life", p. 4.

101 Some structures at Mohenjo-daro have been posited as possible temples, see for example, the comments of Allchin and Allchin, *The Rise of Civilization in India and Pakistan*, p. 213.

102 See, for example, McIntosh, *The Ancient Indus Valley*, p. 276, and Habib, *The Indus Civilization*, p. 42.

103 For example, Chakrabarti, *India*, p. 197.

104 For details and photographs of both, see Kenoyer, *Ancient Cities of the Indus Valley Civilization*, pp. 215 and 216.

105 Farmer, "Mythological Functions of Indus Inscriptions", p. 45.

106 Indeed, Asko Parpola thinks a headdress was once possible and that the trefoil design can be linked to the *Vedic* god Varuṇa's divine robe. Such facets would make the figure divine in Parpola's view, see his discussion on the trefoil motif, *Deciphering the Indus Script*, pp. 211–24.

107 Clark, "Embodying Indus Life", p. 6.

108 Kenoyer, *Ancient Cities of the Indus Valley Civilization*, p. 219, with photographs.

109 Possehl, *The Indus Civilization*, p. 122, with photograph.

110 Clark, "Embodying Indus Life", p. 5.

111 *Ibid.*, p. 9.

112 Nothing here is suggestive of links with the later Hindu *aśva-medha* horse sacrifice where the queen copulated, or symbolized copulation, with the horse before its sacrifice.

113 McIntosh, *The Ancient Indus Valley*, p. 339.

114 It is interesting that the bull is linked with *Vedic* gods, especially Indra, in the *Ṛg Veda*, but I am wary of making the leap between Indus religion and any synonymy with Āryan culture.

115 Kenoyer, *Ancient Cities of the Indus Valley Civilization*, p. 88, with photograph p. 194.

116 Chakrabarti, *India*, p. 195.

117 Lal, "Some Reflections on the Structural Remains at Kalibangan", p. 57.

118 See Kenoyer, Ancient Cities of the Indus Valley Civilization, p. 119, with photograph p. 104.

119 *Ibid.*, p. 86.

120 Farmer, "Mythological Functions of Indus Inscriptions", p. 16. Parpola suggests that the stand represents the sacrificial post, a prototype of which occurs on earlier pottery, showing animals tethered to trees. See Parpola, *Deciphering the Indus Script*, p. 21.

121 Kenoyer, *Ancient Cities of the Indus Valley Civilization*, pp. 87–8, with photographs pp. 188, 189 and figurine p. 220.
122 For example, *Ṛg Veda* 8:4:10. See Gautama V. Vajracharya, "Unicorns in Ancient India and Vedic Ritual" in *Electronic Journal of Vedic Studies* 17, 2(2010), pp. 135–47.
123 See Parpola, *Deciphering the Indus Script*, pp. 253–4, with photographs.
124 Wright, *The Ancient Indus*, p. 295, with photograph p. 292.
125 *Ibid.*, p. 290, with drawing p. 291.
126 *Ibid.*, p. 306.
127 Kenoyer, *Ancient Cities of the Indus Valley Civilization*, p. 106, with photographs.
128 Fowler, *Hinduism Beliefs & Practices, Volume I*, chapter 6.
129 The identification of female buffalo-horned deities with the Hindu Goddess Durgā is a leap in the dark, though it has been attempted by Alf Hiltebeitel, see "The Indus Valley 'Proto-Śiva', Reexamined through Reflections on the Goddess, the Buffalo, and the Symbolism of *vāhanas*", *Anthropos* 73(1978), pp. 767–97.
130 Farmer, "Mythological Functions of Indus Inscriptions", p. 32, with photographs.
131 *Ibid.*, p. 35, with photographs.
132 Allchin and Allchin, *The Rise of Civilization in India and Pakistan*, p. 164, with photograph.
133 *Ibid.*, p. 214.
134 Kenoyer, *Ancient Cities of the Indus Valley Civilization*, p. 112, with photograph, and on another seal, p. 192.
135 Hiltebeitel, see "The Indus Valley 'Proto-Śiva', Reexamined through Reflections on the Goddess, the Buffalo, and the Symbolism of *vāhanas*", *passim.*
136 Fowler, *Hinduism Beliefs & Practices, Volume I*, p. 119.
137 It is equally difficult to accept the view of Parpola who links the fish symbol on seal M-305 (where he accepts the figure as "Proto-Śiva") with the Hindu gods Enki, Varuṇa and Kāma. The star signs that occur in the horns of the figure on the seal he regards as signifiers of a deity: see Parpola, *Deciphering the Indus Script*, pp. 184–90. In particular, Parpola associates Śiva with the fish and notes the prevalence of fish in Hindu mythology such as in the tale of Viṣṇu's first *avatāra* (p. 190). He thinks, too, that it was fish that were indicated as offered in the U signs of the Indus inscriptions (*ibid.*). His arguments are highly detailed, but are succinctly summarized in his article "A Dravidian Solution to the Indus Script Problem", *passim*, and it would depend a good deal on the acceptance of the Indus characters as Dravidian based as to how far it is possible to link religious ideas in the Indus civilization with historical Hinduism. I am reticent to make generous connections between Indus and later Hindu deities.
138 Hiltebeitel, see "The Indus Valley 'Proto-Śiva', Reexamined through Reflections on the Goddess, the Buffalo, and the Symbolism of *vāhanas*", p. 769.
139 Farmer, "Mythological Functions of Indus Inscriptions", p. 20.
140 Srinivasan, "Unhinging Śiva from the Indus Civilization", p. 82.
141 *Ibid.*
142 Hiltebeitel, "The Indus Valley 'Proto-Śiva', Reexamined through Reflections on the Goddess, the Buffalo, and the Symbolism of *vāhanas*", p. 771.
143 Kenoyer, *Ancient Cities of the Indus Valley Civilization*, p. 113, with photograph and drawings.
144 Possehl, *The Indus Civilization*, p. 143.
145 Srinivasan, "Unhinging Śiva from the Indus Civilization", p. 83.
146 Wright, *The Ancient Indus*, p. 291.
147 Kenoyer, *Ancient Cities of the Indus Valley Civilization*, p. 106.
148 See Parpola, *Deciphering the Indus Script*, pp. 228 and 261 and Fowler, *Hinduism Beliefs & Practices, Volume I*, pp. 121–2.

149 See Parpola, *A Dravidian Solution to the Indus Script Problem*, p. 24.
150 Parpola deals extensively with the iconography of, and inscriptions on this seal in *Deciphering the Indus Script*, pp. 256–72 and particularly the signs of the inscription pp. 275–7.
151 *Ibid.*, pp. 263 and 270. Parpola, with lengthy argumentation, believes that this goddess is a Proto-Durgā, a goddess of victory and fertility: see his conclusions, pp. 271–2. Since the dot in the fish sign he sees as the *bindu*, *poṭṭu* or *tilaka* that married women put on their foreheads, Parpola considers the *tilaka* to be the third eye of Durgā, here on the Indus seal represented by the dot in the fish.
152 Clark, "Embodying Indus Life", p. 9.
153 *Ibid.*
154 Parpola, *Deciphering the Indus Script*, pp. 190–1.
155 *Ibid.*, p. 232. The fish sign with six strokes could mean six stars, the Pleiades or with seven stars, Ursa Major.
156 See Yu Knorozov, B. Volchok and N. Gurov, "Some Groups of Proto-Religious Inscriptions of the Harappans", in Lal and Gupta, eds., *Frontiers of the Indus Civilization*, pp. 169–71.
157 Wright, *The Ancient Indus Valley*, p. 289.
158 Parpola, *Deciphering the Indus Script*, p. 107.
159 See the article by George F. Dales, "Sex and Stone at Mohenjo-daro" in Lal and Gupta, eds., *Frontiers of the Indus Civilization*, pp. 109–15.
160 Fowler, *Hinduism Beliefs & Practices, Volume I*, pp. 112–13.
161 Kenoyer, *Ancient Cities of the Indus Valley Civilization*, p. 53.
162 See Parpola, *Deciphering the Indus Script*, p. 218, with photograph.
163 F. R. Allchin, "The Northern Limits of the Harappan Culture Zone", in Lal and Gupta, eds., *Frontiers of the Indus Civilization*, p. 58.
164 See Possehl, *The Indus Civilization*, p. 152.
165 *Ibid.*, p. 157.
166 McIntosh, *The Ancient Indus Valley*, p. 250.
167 Wright, *The Ancient Indus*, p. 265.
168 McIntosh, *The Ancient Indus Valley*, p. 296.
169 Kenoyer, *Ancient Cities of the Indus Valley Civilization*, p. 122.
170 McIntosh, *The Ancient Indus Valley*, p. 249.
171 Possehl, *The Indus Civilization*, p. 170.
172 McIntosh, *The Ancient Indus Valley*, p. 295.
173 Wright, *The Ancient Indus*, p. 267.
174 Possehl, *The Indus Civilization*, p. 173.
175 *Ibid.*, p. 167.
176 Possehl, *The Indus Civilization*, p. 174.
177 Jonathan Mark Kenoyer, "Culture Change during the Late Harappan Period at Harappa: New Insights on Vedic Aryan Issues", in Bryant and Patton, eds., *The Indo-Aryan Controversy*, p. 36.
178 *Ibid.*, p. 39.
179 *Ibid.*, p. 43.
180 Possehl, *The Indus Civilization*, p. 170.
181 Wright, *The Ancient Indus*, p. 266.
182 Possehl, *The Indus Civilization*, p. 171.
183 Kenoyer, "Culture Change during the Late Harappan Period at Harappa", p. 45.
184 See the design in Fig. 3.3 in Habib, *The Indus Civilization*, p. 86.
185 Possehl, *The Indus Civilization*. p. 244.

Chapter 2 The *Vedas*

1 Wendy Doniger, *The Hindus: An alternative history* (Oxford: Oxford University Press, 2010), p. 90.

2 Edwin F. Bryant, "Concluding Remarks" in Edwin F. Bryant and Laurie L. Patton, eds., *The Indo-Aryan Controversy: Evidence and inference in Indian history* (London and New York: Routledge, 2008, first published 2005), p. 475.

3 See Gregory L. Possehl, *The Indus Civilization: A contemporary perspective* (Lanham, Boulder, New York, Toronto, Plymouth: Altamira Press, 2002), p. 249.

4 Asko Parpola and Christian Carpelan, "The Cultural Counterparts to Proto-Indo-European, Proto-Uralic and Proto-Aryan: Matching the Dispersal and Contact Patterns in the Linguistic and Archaeological Record" in Bryant and Patton, eds., *The Indo-Aryan Controversy*, p. 122.

5 Parpola and Carpelan think this division occurred in about 1800 BCE, *ibid.*, p. 131.

6 See Michael Witzel and Steve Farmer, "Horseplay in Harappa: The Indus Valley Decipherment Hoax" in *Frontline* October 13 (2000), p. 11.

7 Michael Witzel, "The Home of the Aryans", www.people.fas.harvard.edu/~witzel/AryanHome.pdf, accessed June 2014.

8 Michael Witzel, "Autochthonous Aryans? The Evidence from Old Indian and Iranian Texts" in *Electronic Journal of Vedic Studies* 7–3 (2001), p. 68.

9 Michael Witzel, *The Languages of Harappa*, www.people.fas.harvard.edu~witzel/mwbib.htm, (February, 2000), p. 7.

10 *Ibid.*, p. 29.

11 Fritz Staal, *Discovering the Vedas: Origins, mantras, rituals, insights* (London, New Delhi: Penguin Books, 2008), p. 16.

12 Michael Witzel, "Indocentrism: Autochthonous Visions of Ancient India" in Bryant and Patton, eds., *The Indo-Aryan Controversy*, p. 346.

13 For example Bridget and Raymond Allchin, *The Rise of Civilization in India and Pakistan* (Cambridge, New York, New Rochelle, Melbourne, Sydney: Cambridge University Press, 1988 reprint of 1982 edn), p. 303.

14 See Jonathan Mark Kenoyer, "Cutlure Change during the Late Harappan Period at Harappa: New Insights on Vedic Aryan Issues" in Bryant and Patton, eds., *The Indo-Aryan Controversy*, p. 26.

15 Irfan Habib, *The Indus Civilization* (New Delhi: Tulika Books, 2011 reprint of 2002 edn), pp. 98–9.

16 Asko Parpola, *Deciphering the Indus Script* (Cambridge: Cambridge University Press, 1994), p. 145.

17 Staal, *Discovering the Vedas*, p. 16.

18 Asko Parpola, "A Dravidian Solution to the Indus Script Problem". Kalaignar M. Karunanidhi Classical Tamil Research Endowment Lecture World Classical Tamil Conference" 25-06-2010 (Tamilnadu: Central Institute of Classical Tamil, 2010), p. 10. This seems to be a revised date from Parpola's earlier dating of the BMAC to 1900–1700 for phase 1 and 1700–1500 for phase 2: see his *Deciphering the Indus Script*, p. 148.

19 Steve Farmer, "Mythological Functions of Indus Inscriptions: Eight Conclusions Arising from the Nonlinguistic Model of Indus Symbols", saf@safarmer.com, (8–10 May 2004), pp. 43–4.

20 So Witzel, "The Home of the Aryans", p. 5.

21 Parpola, *Deciphering the Indus Script*, p. 150.

22 Staal, *Discovering the Vedas*, p. 24.

23 Doniger, *The Hindus*, p. 47.

24 Satya Swarup Misra, "The Date of the Rigveda and the Aryan Migration: Fresh Linguistic Evidence" in Bryant and Patton, eds., *The Indo-Aryan Controversy*, pp. 224–5.

25 Vishal Agarwal, "On Perceiving Aryan Migrations in Vedic Ritual Texts" in *Puratattva* (Bulletin of the Indian Archaeological Society), 36 (2005–6), *passim*.
26 Braj Basi Lal, "Aryan Invasion of India: Perpetuation of a Myth" in Bryant and Patton, eds., *The Indo-Aryan Controversy*, pp. 60–1.
27 *Ibid.*, pp. 71–2.
28 Koenraad Elst, "Linguistic Aspects of the Aryan-Invasion Theory" in Bryant and Patton, eds., *The Indo-Aryan Controversy*, pp. 234–78 *passim*.
29 Edmund Leach, "Aryan Invasions over Four Millennia" in Nayanjot Lahiri, ed., *The Decline and Fall of the Indus Civilization* (Delhi: Permanent Black, 2000), p. 132.
30 Parpola, *Deciphering the Indus Script*, pp. 149–50.
31 See Hans Henrich Hock, "Philology and the Historical Interpretation of the Vedic Texts" in Bryant and Patton, eds., *The Indo-Aryan Controversy*, pp. 288–9.
32 See A. D. Pusalker, "The Relation of Harappan Culture with the *Rgveda*" in Lahiri, ed., *The Decline and Fall of the Indus Civilization*, p. 67, though the author believed when he wrote this in 1950 that the Āryans were autochthonous in India.
33 Witzel, "Indocentrism", p. 344.
34 Cerebral or retroflexive consonants such as ṭ ḍ ṇ ṛ ḷ and ṣ are not part of the Indo-European linguistic heritage but are unique to *Vedic* Sanskrit and later developments of the language. These unique sounds are more than likely to have been incorporated into Sanskrit from indigenous Dravidian.
35 Laurie L. Patton, "Introduction" in Bryant and Patton, eds., *The Indo-Aryan Controversy*, pp. 16–17.
36 Kenneth A. R. Kennedy, "Have Aryans been Identified in the Prehistoric Skeletal Record from South Asia? Biological Anthropology and Concepts of Ancient Races" in Lahiri, ed., *The Decline and Fall of the Indus Civilization*, p. 108.
37 Doniger, *The Hindus*, p. 83.
38 Witzel, *The Languages of Harappa*, p. 2.
39 See the article by Farmer and Witzel, "Horseplay in Harappa".
40 Lal, "Aryan Invasion of India" in Bryant and Patton, eds., *The Indo-Aryan Controversy*, pp. 69–71.
41 For example, Pusalker, "The Relation of the Harappan Culture with the *Rgveda*", p. 68 and Misra, "The Date of the Rigveda and the Aryan Migration", p. 187.
42 Edmund Leach, "Aryan Invasions over Four Millennia" in Lahiri, ed., *The Decline and Fall of the Indus Civilization*, pp. 124–5.
43 See Habib, *The Indus Civilization*, p. 73. The Buddha, who died about 480 BCE, certainly knew of the *Vedas* and the *Upaniṣads*, though late *Upaniṣads* post-date the Buddha.
44 Dates vary widely: Doniger suggests 1700–1500 BCE for the oral composition, see *The Hindus*, p. 85 and dates the written text of the *Ṛg Veda* from about 1200 BCE, see p. 9. In an earlier work of hers she dated the *Ṛg Veda* to around 1000 BCE, see her *Textual Sources for the Study of Hinduism* (Manchester: University Press, 1988), p. 1. Stephanie W. Jamison and Michael Witzel suggest 1500–500 BCE for the whole *Vedic* corpus, including the *Upaniṣads*, see their *Vedic Hinduism*, www.people.fas.harvard.edu/~witzel/vedica.pdf, (1992), p. 2, and they date the *Ṛg Veda* to somewhere between 1900 and 1100 BCE (p. 67, note 8). Witzel dates the *Ṛg Veda* up to the beginning of the Iron Age c. 1200 BCE, see "Languages of Harappa", p. 9, and argues for the bulk of the text as dated to c. 1450–1300 BCE (*ibid.*, p. 10). Gavin Flood dates the earliest hymns to 1200 BCE, see his *An Introduction to Hinduism* (Cambridge: Cambridge University Press, 1996), p. 37, and A. L. Basham between 1500 and 1000 BCE, see *The Wonder That Was India* (London: Sidgwick and Jackson, third revised edn reprinted 1982, first published 1954), p. 31. The much earlier Arthur Berriedale Keith gave a *terminus ante quem* as 800 BCE for the four *Vedas* as a whole

and a date for the *Ṛg Veda* as no earlier than 1200 or 1300 BCE, see *The Religion and Philosophy of the Veda and Upanishads, Part 1* (Delhi: Motilal Banarsidass Publishers Private Limited, 1998 reprint, first published 1925), p. 6. Irfan Habib and Vijay Kumar Thakur point out that the *Ṛg Veda* does not mention iron, which was used in India after 1000 BCE, thus suggesting a *terminus ante quem* for the text as before that date, see *The Vedic Age* (New Delhi: Tulika Books, 2009 reprint of 2004 second edn, first published 2003), p. 2.

45 Louis Renou, *Vedic India*, translated from the French by Philip Sprat (Delhi, Varanasi: Indological Book House, 1971), p. 2.

46 Ainslie T. Embree, *The Hindu Tradition: Readings in oriental thought* (New York: Vintage Books, 1972, first published 1966), p. 4.

47 Wilhelm Halbfass, *Tradition and Reflection: Explorations in Indian thought* (Albany, New York: State University of New York Press, 1991), p. 1.

48 *Ibid.*, p. 3.

49 William K. Mahony, *The Artful Universe: An introduction to the Vedic religious imagination* (Albany, New York: State University of New York Press, 1998), p. 5.

50 John M. Koller, *The Indian Way: An introduction to the philosophies and religions of India* (Upper Saddle River, New Jersey: Pearson Prentice Hall, second edn 2006, first published 1982), p. 24.

51 Doniger, *The Hindus*, p. 33.

52 Arthur Anthony Macdonell, *A Vedic Reader for Students* (Delhi: Motilal Banarsidass Publishers Private Limited, 1995 reprint, first published 1917), p. xiii.

53 See Witzel, *The Languages of Harappa*, p. 3.

54 Thomas J. Hopkins, *The Hindu Religious Tradition* (Belmont, California: Wadsworth Publishing Company, 1971), p. 20.

55 Mysore Hiriyanna, *Outlines of Indian Philosophy* (Delhi: Motilal Banarsidass Publishers Private Limited, 1993), p. 29.

56 John Keay, *India: A history* (London and India: HarperCollins, 2000), p. 30.

57 Macdonell, *A Vedic Reader for Students*, p. xi.

58 Sarvepalli Radhakrishnan and Charles A. Moore, eds, *A Sourcebook in Indian Philosophy* (Princeton, New Jersey: Princeton University Press, 1957), p. 4.

59 There is a change in the use of language in this late book with signs that some earlier language was becoming obsolete and newer expressions were being incorporated, see Macdonell, *A Vedic Reader for Students*, p. xvi.

60 Gautama, Viśvāmitra, Vāmadeva, Atri, Bharadvāja and Vasiṣṭha.

61 Macdonell, *A Vedic Reader for Students*, p. xiv.

62 Staal, *Discovering the Vedas*, pp. 107–8. Some chants have non-Indo-European names, some of which have been identified with BMAC words: see Staal's comment on p. 115.

63 *Ibid.*, pp. 116–17.

64 Again, Staal believed that some of the names and words of these chants originated in the BMAC, *ibid.*, p. 123.

65 Sarvepalli Radhakrishnan, *Indian Philosophy, Volume 1* (Delhi, Bombay, Calcutta, Madras: Oxford University Press, 1994 impression, first published 1923), p. 118.

66 Surendranath Dasgupta, *A History of Indian Philosophy, Volume 1* (Delhi, Varanasi, Patna, Bangalore, Madras: Motilal Banarsidass, 1988 reprint, first published 1922), p. 13.

67 Renou, *Vedic India*, p. 23.

68 Michael Witzel, "The Development of the Vedic Canon and its Schools: The Social and Political Milieu". Kleine Schriften von Michael Witzel, archive.ub.uni-heidelberg.de/savifadok/view/schriftenreihen/sr-8.html, no. 8, (1997), pp. 275–6.

69 Renou, *Vedic India*, p. 55.
70 See Witzel, "The Development of the Vedic Canon and its Schools", p. 294 for a concise outline.
71 Staal, *Discovering the Vedas*, p. 68.
72 *Ṛg Veda* 9:112:1–3, translator Wendy Doniger O'Flaherty, *The Rig Veda: An anthology* (Harmondsworth, England and New York: Penguin Books, 1983 reprint of 1981 edn), p. 235.
73 Dasgupta, *A History of Indian Philosophy, Volume 1*, p. 11.
74 Allchin and Allchin, *The Rise of Civilization in India and Pakistan*, p. 238.
75 *Ibid.*, p. 266.
76 *Ibid.*, p. 277.
77 *Ibid.* pp. 277–8.
78 See Witzel, *The Languages of Harappa*", pp. 17 and 18.
79 Witzel, " Aryan and non-Aryan Names in Vedic India", p. 45.
80 *Ibid.*, pp. 19–20.
81 Michael Witzel, "Inside the Texts, Beyond the Texts. New Approaches to the Study of the Vedas". Harvard Oriental Series, Opera Minora 2 (Cambridge, 1997), www.people.fas.harvard.edu/~witzel/mwbib.htm, p. 16.
82 Witzel, "Aryan and Non-Aryan Names in Vedic India", p. 33.
83 Staal, *Discovering the Vedas*, pp. 54–5.
84 Witzel, "Aryan and Non-Aryan Names in Vedic India", p. 20.
85 *Ṛg Veda* 3:38:4, translator Mahony, *The Artful Universe*, p. 33.
86 Jamison and Witzel, *Vedic Hinduism*, p. 82.
87 See Michael Witzel, "The Vedas: Texts, Language & Ritual", Proceedings of the Third International Vedic Workshop, Leiden, 2002, eds., Arlo Griffiths & Jan E. M. Houben (Groningen: Egbert Forstein, 2004), p. 616. www.ling.upenn.edu/~rnoyer/courses/51/witzel2002.pdf
88 Wendy Doniger O'Flaherty's translation of this hymn is particularly beautiful: see her *The Rig Veda*, p. 242–3, with notes.
89 Jamison and Witzel, *Vedic Hinduism*, p. 49.
90 Arthur Berriedale Keith, *The Religion and Philosophy of the Veda and Upanishads, Part 2* (Delhi: Motilal Banarsidass Publishers Private Limited, 1998 reprint of 1925 edn), p. 379.
91 Witzel, "The Development of the Vedic Canon and its Schools", p. 276.
92 For example, *Atharva Veda* 1:7, which includes: "Do thou, O Agni, bring hither the sorcerers bound; then let Indra with his thunderbolt crush in their heads". William Dwight Whitney, translator, *Atharva-Veda Samhita* Volumes 1 and 2 (Cambridge, Massachusetts: Harvard University, 1905), Volume 1, p. 8. See also 1:28, 2:11, 4:18, 4:20, 5:14, 8:3, 8:4, 8:5, 10:1.
93 Max Müller, *Hymns of the Atharva-Veda: Together with extracts from the ritual books and the commentaries*, translated by Maurice Bloomfield. Sacred Books of the East, vol. 42 (Delhi, Patna, Varanasi: Motilal Banarsidass, 1973 reprint, first published 1897), pp. xlv–xlvii.
94 See Witzel, "Aryan and Non-Aryan Names in Vedic India", pp. 16–17.
95 *Atharva Veda* 19:46, translator Whitney, *Atharva-Veda Samhita*, Volume 2, p. 973.
96 Doniger, *The Hindus*, p. 100.
97 See Keith, *The Religion and Philosophy of the Veda and Upanshads, Part 1*, p. 67.
98 For example 1:5, 1:6, 1:33, 3:13, 4:14, 6:23, 7:18, 19:2, 19:69.
99 Staal, *Discovering the Vedas*, p. 17.
100 Govind Chandra Pande, *Foundations of Indian Culture, Volume 1: Spiritual vision and symbolic forms in ancient India* (Delhi: Motilal Banarsidass Publishers Private Limited, 1995 reprint of 1984 edn), pp. 22–3.

101 Mahony, *The Artful Universe*, p. 12.
102 *Ṛg Veda* 3:39:1–2, translator Ralph T. H. Griffith, *The Hymns of the Ṛgveda* (Delhi: Motilal Banarsidass Publishers Private Limited, 1991 reprint of 1973 new revised edn), p. 183.
103 Mahoney, *The Artful Universe*, p. 94.
104 *Ibid.*, p. 218.
105 Radhakrishnan, *Indian Philosophy, Volume 1*, p. 73.
106 Compare English *right*, *rite*, *ritual*. There is a parallel concept in the *Avesta*, which suggests that *ṛta* originated in the Indo-Iranian milieu.
107 Mahony, *The Artful Universe*, p. 104.
108 *Ibid.*, p. 3.
109 Jamison and Witzel, *Vedic Hinduism*, p. 67.
110 See Sukumari Bhattacharji, *The Indian Theogony: Brahmā, Viṣṇu & Śiva* (New Delhi, London and New York: Penguin Books, 2000, first published 1970), p. 29.
111 *Ṛg Veda* 1:90:6–8.
112 Mahony, *The Artful Universe*, p. 2.
113 Translator Mahony, *ibid.*, p. 118.
114 Michael Witzel, "On Magical Thought in the Veda", Kleine Schriften von Michael Witzel, archive.ub.uni-heidelberg.de/savifadok/view/schriftenreihen/sr-8.html (1979) p. 6.
115 Mahony, *The Artful Universe*, p. 105.
116 See Keith, *The Religion and Philosophy of the Vedas and Upanishads, Part 2*, p. 403.
117 *Ibid.*, p. 422.
118 Translator O'Flaherty, *The Rig Veda*, p. 53.
119 Wendy Doniger, *On Hinduism* (Oxford and New York: Oxford University Press, 2014), p. 161.
120 Translator O'Flaherty, *The Rig Veda*, pp. 25–6 my upper case for One.
121 Keith, *The Religion and Philosophy of the Veda and Upanishads, Part 2*, pp. 435 and 437.
122 See, for example, *Ṛg Veda* 1:164:46; 10:114:5; 8:58 and the *Atharva Veda* 10:8:28 and 2:2:1–2. On occasion, a deity is depicted as the One, as in *Ṛg Veda* 1:154:4; 1:52:14; 8:37:3; 8:58.
123 Hiriyanna, *Outlines of Indian Philosophy*, pp. 42–3.
124 Koller, *The Indian Way*, pp. 40–1.
125 Jamison and Witzel, *Vedic Hinduism*, p. 33.
126 Robert Charles Zaehner, *Hinduism* (Oxford and New York: Oxford University Press, 1966 reprint of 1962 edn), p. 21.
127 Keith, *The Religion and Philosophy of the Veda and Upanishads, Part 1*, pp. 258–9.
128 Witzel, "On Magical Thought in the Veda", p. 6.
129 Keith, *The Religion and Philosophy of the Veda and Upanishads, Part 1*, p. 259.
130 Koller, *The Indian Way*, see also *Ṛg Veda* 10:130 for the likening of *yajña* to a loom.
131 Mahony, *The Artful Universe*, p. 140.
132 Compare, for example, *Vedic hotṛ* and Iranian *zaotar* as a type of chief priest.
133 The *Hotṛ* was responsible for the *Ṛg Veda*, the *Adhvaru* for the *Yajur Veda*, the *Udgātṛ* for the *Sāma Veda* and the *Brāhman* for the *Atharva Veda*. The *Brāhman* was responsible for overseeing the entire ritual.
134 For a clear but succinct account of the different priests and their respective roles see Hopkins, *The Hindu Religious Tradition*, pp. 28–30.
135 For a detailed account of sacrificial performance see Laurie L. Patton, "Veda and Upaniṣad" in Sushil Mittal and Gene Thursby, *The Hindu World* (London and New York: Routledge, 2007, first published 2004), pp. 40–44.
136 See Doniger, *The Hindus*, p. 152.
137 Mahony, *The Artful Universe*, p. 142.

138 Jeaneane Fowler, *Hinduism Beliefs & Practices, Volume I: Major deities and social structures* (Brighton, Chicago and Toronto: Sussex Academic Press, 2014), pp. 144–5.

139 Ajoy Kumar Lahiri, *Vedic Vṛtra* (Delhi, Varanasi, Patna, Madras: Motilal Banarsidass, 1984), p. 26. The root can also mean the exact opposite of sheltering, protecting, freeing and extending spatially, see Lahiri, pp. 71–2.

140 Keith, *The Religion and Philosophy of the Veda and Upanishads, Part 1*, p. 57.

141 David Kinsley, *Hindu Goddesses: Visions of the divine feminine in the Hindu religious tradition* (Delhi, Varanasi, Patna, Madras: Motilal Banarsidass, 1987, first published 1986), p. 8.

142 O'Flaherty, *The Rig Veda*, pp. 151–2.

143 There may be some distinction between Bṛhaspati and Brahmaṇaspati, the former being the one who offers prayers and represents priesthood as an abstraction, whereas the latter is more the abstraction of prayer: see Bhattacharji, *The Indian Theogony*, pp. 317–18.

144 See Fowler, *Hinduism Beliefs and Practices, Volume I*, pp. 35–6.

145 O'Flaherty, *The Rig Veda*, p. 29.

146 Hopkins, *The Hindu Religious Tradition*, p. 25.

147 In Volume I we saw that some temple designs were laid out according to the plan of a cosmic man. That idea begins here with Prajāpati: see Fowler, *Hinduism Beliefs and Practices, Volume I*, pp. 187–8.

148 Translator Mahony, *The Artful Universe*, p. 28.

149 See Fowler, *Hinduism Beliefs and Practices, Volume I*, chapters 5, 6 and 7 pp. 83–169.

150 Hiriyanna, *Outlines of Indian Philosophy*, p. 33.

151 Doniger, *The Hindus*, p. 128.

152 Translator O'Flaherty, *The Rig Veda*, p. 80.

153 Translator Griffith, *The Hymns of the Ṛgveda*, p. 192.

154 See Witzel, "The Vedas", p. 591.

155 See Fowler, *Hinduism Beliefs and Practices, Volume I*, pp. 83–9, and 142– 50.

156 Michael Witzel, "Vedas and Upaniṣads" in Gavin Flood, ed., *The Blackwell Companion to Hinduism* (Malden MA, Oxford and Victoria: Blackwell Publishing Limited, 2005 reprint of 2003 edn), p. 72.

157 Keay, *A History of India*, p. 23.

158 Bhattacharji, *The Indian Theogony*, p. 281.

159 Zaehner, *Hinduism*, p. 20.

160 Patton, "Veda and Upaniṣad", p. 42.

161 Doniger, *The Hindus*, p. 130.

162 Bhattacharji, *The Indian Theogony*, p. 24.

163 Or perhaps from Skt. *Vāri*, Avestan *vār*, "water", suggestive of a very early Indo-Iranian association with water: see Bhattarcharji, *The Indian Theogony*, pp. 43–4.

164 See Parpola, *Deciphering the Indus Script*, pp. 214–15.

165 *Ibid.*, p. 214.

166 See Bhattacharji, *The Indian Theogony*, p. 36.

167 Parpola, *Deciphering the Indus Script*, pp. 189–90, 214 and 215.

168 Bhattacharji, *The Indian Theogony*, p. 45.

169 See Fowler, *Hinduism Beliefs and Practices, Volume I*, pp. 85 and 87.

170 Zaehner, *Hinduism*, p. 25.

171 The *Ādityas* may well be synonymous with the Iranian Ameša Spenta of the *Avesta*, see Keith, *The Religion and Philosophy of the Veda and Upanishads, Part 1*, p. 34.

172 Ekendranath Ghosh, *Studies on Rigvedic Deities: Astronomical and meteorological* (New Delhi: Cosmo Publications, 1983), p. 23.

173 Whitney, translator, *Atharva-Veda Samhita*, Volume 1, pp. 211–13, though 4:38 is devoted to luck in gambling with the aid of an *apsara*, see pp. 214–16.
174 Tracy Pintchman, *The Rise of the Goddess in the Hindu Tradition* (Albany, New York: State University of New York Press, 1994), p. 19.
175 See Fowler, *Hinduism Beliefs and Practices, Volume I*, pp. 116–28.
176 Keay, *A History of India*, p. 30.
177 *Ṛg Veda* 7:77:1–2, translator Mahony, *The Artful Universe*, p. 20.
178 See Fowler, *Hinduism Beliefs and Practices, Volume I*, pp. 131–2.
179 Mahony, *ibid*, p. 37.
180 *Ibid.*
181 Kinsley, *Hindu Goddesses*, p. 12.
182 See Fowler, *Hinduism Beliefs and Practices, Volume I*, chapter 6 pp. 106–41.
183 Hiriyanna, *Outlines of Indian Philosophy*, p. 40.
184 *Ibid.*, p. 31.
185 Radhakrishnan, *Indian Philosophy, Volume 1*, p. 66.
186 Doniger, *The Hindus*, p. 99.

Chapter 3 *Vedānta*

1 *Bṛhad-āraṇyaka Upaniṣad* 1:3:28, translator Sarvepalli Radhakrishnan, *The Principal Upaniṣads* (New Delhi: Indus, 1994, first published 1953), p. 162.
2 Translator Patrick Olivelle, *Upaniṣads* (Oxford and New York: Oxford University Press, 1996), p. 120.
3 *Chāndogya Upaniṣad* chapters 1 and 2 *passim*, *ibid.*, pp. 98–118.
4 Thomas J. Hopkins, *The Hindu Religious Tradition* (Belmont, California: Wadsworth Publishing Company, 1971), p. 37.
5 "Absolute" is a somewhat westernized term but since it tends to suggest a non-definable ultimacy it is useful if used with caution. As Fritz Staal commented, it is a "somewhat opaque but convenient English translation of a principle that holds the universe together": see *Discovering the Vedas: Origins, mantras, rituals, insights* (London and New York: Penguin Books, 2008), p. 178.
6 Against this view see Surendranath Dasgupta, *A History of Indian Philosophy, Vol. 1* (Delhi, Varanasi, Patna, Bangalore, Madras: Motilal Banarsidass, 1988 reprint, first published 1922), p. 52, where he suggests that the fact that deities such as Viśvakarman and Hiraṇya-garbha as well as Puruṣa were not discussed and developed in the *Upaniṣads* indicates that the monotheistic trends of the *Vedas* were not taken up in them and that the *Upaniṣads* are more distinctively separate from the *Vedas*. This kind of reasoning tends to follow the acceptance of an incomplete monotheism in the *Vedic* period, a flowering of which might be expected in later thought. But we do not get a move to full-blown monotheism in the *Vedānta*; *Vedic* monotheism went as far as it needed to, the monism of the *Upaniṣads* was the outcome, not a developed monotheism.
7 Stephanie W. Jamison and Michael Witzel, *Vedic Hinduism*, www.people.fas.harvard.edu/~witzel/vedica.pdf (1992), p. 75.
8 For the fluctuating usage of this term, see the useful chapter, "The Upaniṣads – What are They?" in Daya Krishna, *Indian Philosophy: A counter perspective* (Delhi, Calcutta, Chennai, Mumbai: Oxford University Press, 1997, first published 1991), pp. 95–109.
9 Olivelle, *Upaniṣads*, p. xxxvi.
10 *Ibid.*, or earlier, see William K. Mahony, "Upaniṣads" in Mircia Eliade (ed.), *The Encyclopedia of Religion* (hereafter *ER*), (New York: Macmillan, 1987), vol. 15, p. 147.

11 Mysore Hiriyanna, *The Essentials of Indian Philosophy* (Delhi: Motilal Banarsidass Publishers Private Limited, 1995 Indian edn), p. 18.
12 Following Olivelle, *Upaniṣads*, pp. xxxvi–xxxvii.
13 R. N. Dandekar, "Vedānta" in *ER* vol. 15, p. 208.
14 Alain Daniélou, *The Myths and Gods of India*, (Rochester USA: Inner Traditions International, 1991 reprint of 1985 edn), p. 5. See also Alistair Shearer and Peter Russell, *The Upanishads* (New York: Harper and Row, 1978), p. 11.
15 Paul Deussen, *The Philosophy of the Upanishads* (New Delhi: Oriental Books Reprint Corporation, second edn 1979, first published 1906), pp. 10–15.
16 This might rather speak against Wendy Doniger's view that the authors of the *Upaniṣads* were reaching out towards a wider audience in a "more vernacular direction": see her *The Hindus: An alternative history* (Oxford: Oxford University Press, 2010), p. 167. In fact, if William K. Mahony is right, the earliest principal *Upaniṣads* were written in prose that was close to the difficult and archaic Sanskrit of the *Vedas*: see his *The Artful Universe: An introduction to the Vedic religious imagination* (Albany, New York: State University of New York Press, 1998), p. 151.
17 Although, again, Doniger believes the *Bṛhad-āraṇyaka Upaniṣad* is "far more accessible, conversational, reader friendly", *ibid.*
18 Dasgupta, *A History of Indian Philosophy, Vol. 1*, p. 43.
19 Mysore Hiriyanna, *Outlines of Indian Philosophy* (Delhi: Motilal Banarsidass Publishers Private Limited, 1993), p. 54.
20 Hiriyanna, *Essentials of Indian Philosophy*, p. 19.
21 Dasgupta, *A History of Indian Philosophy, Vol. 1*, p. 7.
22 Klaus K. Klostermaier, *A Survey of Hinduism* (Albany, New York: State University of New York Press, 1994), pp. 198–9.
23 Olivelle, *Upaniṣads*, p. lvi.
24 Laurie L. Patton, "Veda and Upaniṣad" in Sushil Mittal and Gene Thursby, *The Hindu World* (New York and London: Routledge, 2007, first published 2004), pp. 46–7: see *Chāndogya Upaniṣad* 8:2:1–10.
25 *Śvetāśvatara Upaniṣad* 4:10, translator Olivelle, *Upaniṣads*, p. 260.
26 Doniger, *The Hindus*, p. 174.
27 Given the importance of this concept, I am putting it in the upper case, *B*rahman, throughout, though it is fashionable to refer to it as *brahman*, or *the brahman*. I am using this last to refer to a prayer or sacred utterance. I am taking the liberty of putting *B*rahman in all citations and will indicate my upper case when doing so. It is important to recognize, however, that Brahman is not a *name* of any kind and that the neuter term is normally beyond any name or form. I believe its importance necessitates some mark in the written word.
28 Heinrich Zimmer, *Philosophies of India* (Princeton, New Jersey: Princeton University Press, 1989 reprint of 1969 edn), p. 75.
29 Edward Gough, *The Philosophy of the Upanishads: Ancient Indian metaphysics* (New Delhi: Cosmo, 1979), p. 38.
30 See, for example, Jan C. Heesterman, "Brahman" in *ER*, vol. 2, p. 295.
31 Zimmer, *Philosophies of India*, p. 79.
32 Doniger, *The Hindus*, p. 187.
33 *Bṛhad-āraṇyaka Upaniṣad* 3:8:11, translator Radhakrishnan, *The Principal Upaniṣads*, p. 233.
34 Īśā *Upaniṣad* verse 5, translator Olivelle, *Upaniṣads*, p. 249.
35 Radhakrishnan, *The Principal Upaniṣads*, p. 53.
36 *Taittirīya Upaniṣad* 3:1, translator Olivelle, *Upaniṣads*, p. 190.

37 *Kena Upaniṣad* 1:3, translator Olivelle, *ibid.*, p. 227.
38 Chandradhar Sharma, *A Critical Survey of Indian Philosophy* (Delhi: Motilal Banarsidass Publishers Private Limited,1994 reprint of 1960 edn), p. 29.
39 *Kaṭha Upaniṣad* 2:20, translator Olivelle, *Upaniṣads*, p. 237.
40 Olivelle, *Upaniṣads*, p. xxxvii.
41 Translator, Olivelle, *ibid.*, p. 249.
42 *Śvetāśvatara Upaniṣad* 4:2–3, translator Olivelle, *ibid.*, p. 259.
43 *Ibid.*, 6:7, p. 263.
44 *Ibid.*, 3:2:9, p. 276.
45 Radhakrishnan, *The Principal Upaniṣads*, p. 73. We might compare here the German *Atem*, "breath".
46 *Bṛhad-āraṇyaka Upaniṣad* 1:4:8, translator Olivelle, *Upaniṣads*, p. 15.
47 *Chāndogya Upaniṣad* 8:2–3, translator Olivelle, *ibid.*, p. 167.
48 *Bṛhad-āraṇyaka Upaniṣad* 4:4:13, translator Olivelle, *ibid.*, p. 66 (my upper case for "Self").
49 Paul Younger, *Introduction to Indian Religious Thought* (London: Darton, Longman & Todd, 1972), p. 90.
50 Radhakrishnan, *The Principal Upaniṣads*, p. 73.
51 *Śvetāśvatara Upaniṣad* 5:9, translator Olivelle, p. 262.
52 *Kaṭha Upaniṣad* 2:18, translator Olivelle, *ibid.*, p. 237.
53 Madeleine Biardeau, *Hinduism: The anthropology of a civilization*, translated from the French by Richard Nice (Delhi, Oxford and New York: Oxford University Press, 1992 reprint of 1989 edn, first published in French in 1981), p. 17.
54 Hiriyanna, *Outlines of Indian Philosophy*, p. 58.
55 For detailed analyses of terms such as monism, monotheism, pantheism and panentheism, see Jeaneane Fowler, *Perspectives of Reality: An introduction to the philosophy of Hinduism* (Brighton, Sussex and Portland, Oregon: Sussex Academic Press, 2002), chapter 1.
56 Translator Olivelle, *Upaniṣads*, p. 15.
57 See Olivelle, *ibid*, p. 297 for discussion of the word "Whole".
58 *Bṛhad-āraṇyaka Upaniṣad* 2:4:12, translator Olivelle, *ibid.*, p. 30.
59 Translator Olivelle, *ibid.*, p. 33 (my upper case for "Brahman" and "Self").
60 Wilhelm Halbfass, *On Being and What There Is: Classical Vaiśeṣika and the history of Indian ontology* (Albany, New York: State University of New York Press, 1992), p. 26.
61 *Chāndogya Upaniṣad* 6:1:3, translator Radhakrishnan, *The Principal Upaniṣads*, p. 446.
62 *Ibid.*, 6:12:2, 3, p. 462, my parentheses.
63 *Īśā Upaniṣad* verse 5, translator Olivelle, *Upaniṣads*, p. 249.
64 *Kaṭha Upaniṣad* 6:11, translator Olivelle, *ibid.*, p. 246.
65 The *Ṛg Veda* (10:16:5) refers to Agni sending the deceased to the Fathers and follows with: "Wearing new life let him increase his offspring: let him rejoin a body," translator Ralph T. H. Griffith, *The Hymns of the Ṛgveda* (Delhi: Motilal Banarsidass Publishers Private Limited, 1991 reprint of 1973 revised edn), p. 540. However, there is nothing here to suggest that this is a rebirth on Earth as opposed to a life in the hereafter.
66 Wilhelm Halbfass, "Karma, *Āpūrva*, and Natural Causes: Observations on the Growth and Limits of the Theory of *Saṃsāra*" in Wendy Doniger O'Flaherty, ed., *Karma and Rebirth in Classical Indian Traditions* (Berkeley, Los Angeles and London: University of California Press, 1980), pp. 268–9.
67 *Maitrī Upaniṣad* 1:4, translator Radhakrishnan, *The Principal Upaniṣads*, p. 797.
68 Arthur Berriedale Keith also notes the acquisition of merit in the afterlife through the giving

of gifts to priests, suggesting that good causes result in a good life and good merit: see *The Religion and Philosophy of the Veda and Upanishads, Part II* (Delhi: Motilal Banarsidass Publishers Private Limited, 1998 reprint of 1925 edn), pp. 250 and 478.

69 *Chāndogya Upaniṣad* 5:10:1–6, cf. *Bṛhad-āraṇyaka Upaniṣad* 6:2.

70 From a verb *kri*, "to do", cf. Latin *creo.*

71 *Śatapatha Brāhmaṇa* 6:2:2:27.

72 *Bṛhad-āraṇyaka Upaniṣad* 3:2:13, translator Olivelle, *Upaniṣads*, p. 38. Perhaps we should be wary of accepting this statement as referring to the doctrine of *karma* as it later became known if Herman Tull is right in believing that it should be associated with good or badly performed ritual and should not be separated from *Brāhmaṇic* ritual as most seem to do. He sees a ritual substratum to the developing doctrine of *karma* in the *Upaniṣads* and a continuation of ideas of *karma* from *Brāhmaṇas* to *Upaniṣads*: see Herman Wayne Tull, *The Vedic Origins of Karma: Cosmos as man in ancient Indian myth and ritual* (Albany, New York: State University of New York Press, 1989), pp. 2–3 and 31. Tull says: "The point that draws the Upanisadic karma doctrine out of the realm of ritual activity is simultaneously the point that leads back to the model of the sacrifice. For only when the activity of the sacrifice became equated with all activity, that is, with life itself, did the Upanisadic thinkers begin to envision a doctrine of the moral efficacy of all actions that actually were disconnected to the sacrifice." His view is that *Upaniṣadic* ideas of *karma* were the culmination of those in the *Brāhmaṇas* (p. 41). Keith believed that such rebirths mentioned in this verse are to those in the afterlife and refer to "higher beings" not man, see *The Religion and Philosophy of the Veda and Upanishads, Part II*, p. 574. Certainly, the latter part of the verse refers to ancestors, divine beings, Prajāpati. However, later in the same section of the *Bṛhad-āraṇyaka Upaniṣad* (verses 5 and 6) the doctrine of *karma* as it later became known is more clearly articulated.

73 *Bṛhad-āraṇyaka Upaniṣad* 4:4:3, translator Olivelle, *Upaniṣads*, p. 64.

74 *Chāndogya Upaniṣad* 5:10:7, translator Olivelle, *ibid.*, p. 142.

75 Younger, *Introduction to Indian Religious Thought*, p. 113.

76 *Ibid.*, p. 114.

77 See Keith, *The Religion and Philosophy of the Veda and Upanishads, Part II*, p. 580.

78 Doniger, *The Hindus*, p. 165.

79 Sharma, *A Critical Survey of Indian Philosophy*, p. 19.

80 Translator Olivelle, *Upaniṣads*, p. 275.

81 A. L. Herman, *A Brief Introduction to Hinduism: Religion, philosophy and ways of liberation* (Boulder, San Francisco, Oxford: Westview Press, 1991), p. 71.

82 *Kaṭha Upaniṣad*, 6:14, translator Olivelle, *Upaniṣads*, p. 246 (my upper case for "Brahman").

83 Translator Olivelle, *ibid.*, p. 30 (my upper case for "Self").

84 Translator Radhakrishnan, *The Principal Upaniṣads*, p. 689.

85 Translator Olivelle, *Upaniṣads*, p. 39 (my upper case for "Self").

86 Translator, Olivelle, *Upaniṣads*, p. 187.

87 *Muṇḍaka Upaniṣad* 1:1:7, translator Radhakrishnan, *The Principal Upaniṣads*, p. 673.

88 *Ibid.*, 2:1:1, p. 680.

89 John M. Koller and Patricia Joyce Koller, *Asian Philosophies* (Upper Saddle River, New Jersey: Prentice Hall, 1998), p. 24.

90 Robert Charles Zaehner, *Hinduism* (Oxford and New York: Oxford University Press, 1966 reprint of 1962 edn), p. 55.

91 Younger, *Introduction to Indian Religious Thought*, p. 101.

92 *Īśā Upaniṣad* 1:2, translator Radhakrishnan, *The Principal Upaniṣads*, p. 569.

93 *Chāndogya Upaniṣad* 2:21:4.
94 *Kaṭha Upaniṣad* 5:13, translator Olivelle, *Upaniṣads*, p. 244.
95 The term *mokṣa* is found only in the *Śvetāśvatara Upaniṣad* 6:16 and the *Maitrī* 6:20 and 30.
96 *Kaṭha Upaniṣad* 1:2:23.
97 Translator Olivelle, *Upaniṣads*, p. 220.
98 *Ibid.*, p. 276 (my upper case for "Brahman").
99 Zaehner, *Hinduism*, p. 60.

Chapter 4 Advaita Vedānta

1 Also called the *Vedānta-Sūtra* and *Uttara-Mīmāṃsā-Sūtra*.
2 See Karl. H. Potter, ed., *Encyclopedia of Indian Philosophies, Vol. III: Advaita Vedānta up to Śaṃkara and his pupils* (Delhi, Varanasi, Patna: Motilal Banarsidass, first Indian edn 1981), p. 6.
3 See Eliot Deutsch and Rohit Dalvi, eds., *The Essential Vedānta: A new source book of Advaita Vedānta* (Bloomington, Indiana: World Wisdom, 2004), p. 97.
4 *Ibid.*, p. 99.
5 For the nature of the conflict between Śaṃkara's theory of self/Self and that in Buddhism, see Brian Carr, "Sankara On Memory and the Continuity of the Self". *Religious Studies* 36, 4(2000), pp. 419–34. And for the influence of Buddhism on Gauḍapāda, an early Advaita precursor of Śaṃkara, see Richard King, "Early Advaita and Madhyamaka Buddhism: The Case of the *Gauḍapādī akārikā*". *International Journal of Hindu Studies* 2, 1 (1998), pp. 67–83.
6 For these, see Sengaku Mayeda, translator, *A Thousand Teachings: The Upadeśasāhasrī of Śankara* (Albany, New York: State University of New York Press, 1992) p. 3; Anthony John Alston, *Śaṃkara on the Absolute: A Śaṃkara source-book, Vol. 1* (London: Shanti Sadan, 1981 reprint of 1980 edn), p. 43; Potter, *Encyclopedia of Indian Philosophies, Vol. III*, p. 14; and Bradley Malkovsky, "The Personhood of Śaṃkara's *Para Brahman*". *Journal of Religion* 77(1997), p. 541.
7 For a more detailed analysis of the traditions about his life and works, see Natalia Isayeva, *Shankara and Indian Philosophy* (Albany, New York: State University of New York Press, 1993), pp. 69–104.
8 For his Vaiṣṇava background, see H. V. Sreenivasa Murthy, *Vaiṣṇavism of Śaṃkaradeva and Rāmānuja: A comparative study* (Delhi, Varanasi, Patna: Motilal Banarsidass, 1973).
9 Alston, *Śaṃkara on the Absolute*, p. 47. But see also the *Śivāndalaharī*, a long hymn in praise of Śiva that tradition ascribes to Śaṃkara, in T. M. P. Mahadevan, *The Hymns of Śaṅkara* (Delhi: Motilal Banarsidass, 1995 reprint of 1980 edn), pp. 84–171, and Arvind Sharma, *The Philosophy of Religion and Advaita Vedānta: A comparative study of religion and reason* (University Park, Pennsylvania: The Pennsylvania State University Press, 1995), p. 9.
10 See Vidyasankar Sundaresan, "Conflicting Hagiographies and History: The Place of Śankaravijaya Texts in Advaita Tradition". *International Journal of Hindu Studies* 4, 2(2000), pp. 109–84.
11 Atheism, indeed, is world affirming, accepting the plurality and independence of world forms one from another. Such concepts would be alien to the philosophy of Śaṃkara who sought to prove the unreality of all except Brahman. While a theistic deity as Īśvara is accepted as a means to elevate consciousness to its pure state, as we shall see, this more theistic conception of a divine being is as unreal as the rest of existence.
12 Mayeda, *A Thousand Teachings*, p. 6.
13 Rasvihary Das, *Introduction to Shankara* (Calcutta: Firma KLM Private Limited, 1983), p. xviii.
14 For Śaṃkara's views on rival schools, see Anthony John Alston, *Śaṃkara on Rival Views: A Śaṃkara source-book, Vol. 5* (London: Shanti Sadan, 1989).
15 Chandradhar Sharma, *The Advaita Tradition in Indian Philosophy: A Study of Advaita in Buddhism,*

Vedānta and Kāshmīra Shaivism (Delhi: Motilal Banarsidass, 1996), p. 273. Sharma notes that the terms *māyā*, *avidyā*, *ajñāna*, *adhyāsa*, *adhyāropa*, *anirvachanīya*, *vivarta*, *bhrānti*, *bhrama*, *nāma-rūpa*, *avyakta*, *akṣara*, *bījashakti*, *mula-prakṛti*, etc., are used synonymously, *ibid.*

16 For problems with this term "monism", see Joseph Milne's article "Advaita Vedānta and Typologies of Multiplicity and Unity: An Interpretation of Nondual Knowledge" in *International Journal of Hindu Studies* 1, 1(1997), pp. 165–88.

17 With some justification, David Loy comments, "perhaps the term Ātman should be rejected as superfluous, because it suggests another entity apart from Brahman". But, as he notes, "the two terms do serve a function, since they emphasize different aspects of the Absolute: Brahman, that is the ultimate reality which is the ground of all the universe; Ātman, that is my true nature". David Loy, *Non-Duality: A study in comparative philosophy* (New Haven and London: Yale University Press, 1988), p. 198. However, since we cannot assign "different aspects" to the non-dual Brahman, the difficulty of the two terms for the same essence is not removed.

18 Śaṃkara, *Upadeśasāhasrī* 1:13:18, translator Mayeda, *A Thousand Teachings*, p. 133.

19 *Ibid.*, 1:13:2, p. 132.

20 Debabrata Sinha, *Metaphysic of Experience in Advaita Vedānta: A phenomenological approach* (Delhi: Motilal Banarsidass, 1995 reprint of 1983 edn), p. 45.

21 The term *sublated* is a word that is now obsolete in ordinary senses though it is sometimes retained in logic meaning to contradict or disaffirm. I have decided not to use it in the remainder of the text given its wider obscurity unless in a direct quotation, and to use the perfectly adequate and intelligible *contradicted.*

22 R. N. Dandekar, "Vedānta" in Mircea Eliade ed., *The Encyclopedia of Religion* (hereafter *ER*, New York: Macmillan, 1987), vol. 15, p. 210.

23 Śaṃkara, *Upadeśasāhasrī* 1:10:1–3, translator Mayeda, *A Thousand Teachings*, p. 123.

24 See here Arvind Sharma, *Advaita Vedānta* (Honolulu: University of Honolulu Press, 1973, first published 1969), pp. 95–6.

25 William M. Indich, *Consciousness in Advaita Vedānta* (Delhi: Motilal Banarsidass, 1995 reprint of 1980 edn), *passim.*

26 Raphael, *The Pathway of Non-Duality: Advaitavada*, translated from the Italian by Kay McCarthy (Delhi: Motilal Banarsidass, 1992), p. 11.

27 Bina Gupta, *An Introduction to Indian Philosophy: Perspectives on reality, knowledge, and freedom* (New York and London: Routledge, 2012), p. 228.

28 Chandradhar Sharma, *The Advaita Tradition in Indian Philosophy*, p. 182.

29 However, Gupta is of the view that they can be contradicted by "empirical existents", see *An Introduction to Indian Philosophy*, p. 228.

30 Keith Ward, *Images of Eternity* (Oxford: Oneworld, 1993 edn first published 1987), p. 28.

31 Malkovsky, "The Personhood of Śaṃkara's *Para Brahman*", p. 545.

32 Ramakrishna Puligandla, *Fundamentals of Indian Philosophy* (London, Lanham, New York: University Press of America, 1985 second edn), p. 217.

33 Arvind Sharma, *Advaita Vedānta*, p. 53.

34 For example Sarvajnātmamuni in his *Saṃkṣepaśārīraka.*

35 Brian Carr, "Sankara and the Principle of Material Causation" in *Religious Studies* 35, 4(1999), p. 426.

36 Ward, *Images of Eternity*, p. 15.

37 Arvind Sharma, *Advaita Vedānta*, p. 30.

38 Carr, "Sankara and the Principle of Material Causation", p. 429.

39 *Ibid.*, p. 439.

40 Das, *Introduction to Shankara*, p. xxii.
41 Śaṃkara, *Brahmasūtrabhāṣya* 2:1:9, translator Anthony John Alston, *Śaṃkara on Creation: A Śaṃkara source-book, Vol. 2* (London: Shanti Sadan, 1980), p. 78.
42 Das, *Introduction to Shankara*, p. xxvi.
43 Gupta, *An Introduction to Indian Philosophy*, p. 231.
44 Potter, *Encyclopedia of Indian Philosophies, Vol. III*, p. 70.
45 Gupta, *An Introduction to Indian Philosophy*, p. 231.
46 Śaṃkara, *Upadeśasāhasrī* 1:17:20, translator Mayeda, *A Thousand Teachings*, p. 162.
47 Das, *Introduction to Shankara*, p. viii.
48 Sarvepalli Radhakrishnan, *Indian Philosophy, Vol. 2* (Delhi: Oxford University Press, 1994 impression, first published 1923), p. 575. Radhakrishnan believed that for Śaṃkara *avidyā* had an "objective reality", a positive character, and existed in gross and subtle form (*ibid.*, p. 582). But if this were so, it could only be from the perspective of ignorance. For Śaṃkara, *avidyā/māyā* cannot obtain at all once liberation reveals the *Ātman*.
49 Surendranath Dasgupta, *A History of Indian Philosophy, Vol. 1* (Delhi, Varanasi, Patna, Bangalore, Madras: Motilal Banarsidass, 1988 reprint, first published 1922), p. 440.
50 Vivekananda, *Jnana-Yoga* (New York: Ramakrishna-Vivekananda Center, 1982, first published 1955), p. 18.
51 Śaṃkara, *Upadeśasāhasrī* 1:6:3, translator Mayeda, *A Thousand Teachings*, p. 116.
52 For a full discussion of the theory of knowledge in Advaita Vedānta, see Jeaneane Fowler, *Perspectives of Reality: An introduction to the philosophy of Hinduism* (Brighton and Portland: Sussex Academic Press, 2002), pp. 255–62.
53 Deutsch and Dalvi, *The Essential Vedānta*, p. 95
54 Indich, *Consciousness in Advaita Vedānta*, p. 6.
55 Radhakrishnan, *Indian Philosophy, Vol. 2*, p. 519.
56 Potter, *Encyclopedia of Indian Philosophies, Vol. III*, p. 39.
57 Śaṃkara, *Upadeśasāhasrī* 1:13:25, translator Mayeda, *A Thousand Teachings*, p. 134.
58 Chandradhar Sharma, *The Advaita Tradition in Indian Philosophy*, p. 178.
59 Śaṃkara, *Upadeśasāhasrī* 1:15:27–9, translator Mayeda, *A Thousand Teachings*, pp. 144–5.
60 Chandradhar Sharma, *A Critical Survey of Indian Philosophy* (Delhi: Motilal Banarsidass Publishers Private Limited, 1994 reprint of 1960 edn), pp. 283–4.
61 Śaṃkara, *Upadeśasāhasrī* 1:13:25, translator Mayeda, *A Thousand Teachings*, p. 134.
62 Radhakrishnan, *Indian Philosophy, Vol. 2*, p. 507.
63 *Ibid.*, p. 509.
64 The other two, related, means of knowledge accepted by Śaṃkara were perception and inference. For a full discussion of these, see Fowler, *Perspectives of Reality*, pp. 258–62.
65 Śaṃkara, *Upadeśasāhasrī* 1:17:4, translator Mayeda, p. 160.
66 *Ibid.*, 1:17:21, p. 162.
67 *Ibid.*, 2:1:42, p. 226.
68 Swami Atmananda, *Sankara's Teachings in His Own Words* (Bombay: Bharatiya Vidya Bhawan, 1989), p. xxv.
69 Eric Lott, *Vedantic Approaches to God* (London and Basingstoke: The Macmillan Press Ltd, 1980), p. 72.
70 For this method of explanation followed by negation of supportive material in using the *Veda*, see Sri Swami Satchidānandendra, *The Method of the Vedanta: A critical account of the Advaita tradition*, translated by Anthony John Alston (Delhi: Motilal Banarsidass, first Indian edn 1997, first published 1989), pp. 41–7.

71 Śaṃkara, *Bṛhadāraṇyaka Upaniṣad Bhāṣya* 2:3:6, translator Alston, *Śaṃkara on the Absolute*, p. 141.

72 Wilhelm Halbfass, *Studies in Kumārila and Śaṅkara*: Studien zür Indologie und Iranistik Monograph 9 (Reinbeck: Orientalistische Fachpublikationen, 1983), p. 31.

73 Mysore Hiriyanna, *Outlines of Indian Philosophy* (Delhi: Motilal Banarsidass Publishers Private Limited, 1993), p. 351.

74 Śaṃkara, *Brahmasūtrabhāṣya* 1:1:1, translator Alston, *Śaṃkara on the Absolute*, p. 94.

75 Arvind Sharma, *Advaita Vedānta*, p. 85.

76 The following chapter dealing with Sāṃkhya will do much to explain Śaṃkara's understanding of this function in the self.

77 Alston, *Śaṃkara on the Absolute*, p. 63.

78 Śaṃkara, *Upadeśasāhasrī* 1:14:19, translator Mayeda, *A Thousand Teachings*, p. 138.

79 It might have been more logical to have dispensed with the term *Ātman* and retained only Brahman, for the use of *Ātman* implies Brahman individuated. Sinari maintains that the subsequent relation between *Ātman* and *jīva* is "not logically warranted", see Ramakant A. Sinari, *The Structure of Indian Thought* (Delhi, Bombay, Calcutta, Madras: Oxford University Press, 1984, first published 1970), p. 114, and the metaphysics would have been significantly clearer without the two terms. See also Loy's point above, note 17.

80 Sinha, *Metaphysic of Experience*, p. 54.

81 Paul Deussen, *The System of the Vedanta* (Delhi: Low Price Publications, 1995 reprint of 1912 edn), p. 324.

82 Milne, "Advaita Vedānta and Typologies of Multiplicity and Unity", p. 167.

83 Śaṃkara, *Kaṭha Upaniṣad Bhāṣya*, translator Anthony John Alston, *Śaṃkara on Discipleship: A Śaṃkara source-book, Vol. 5* (London: Shanti Sadan, 1989), p. 18.

84 Potter, *Encyclopedia of Indian Philosophies, Vol. III*, p. 84.

85 Deussen, *The System of the Vedanta*, p. 172.

86 Mayeda, *A Thousand Teachings*, p. 45.

87 Śaṃkara, *Bṛhadāraṇyaka Upaniṣad Bhāṣya* 4:3:21, translator Anthony John Alston, *Śaṃkara on the Soul* (London: Shanti Sadan, 1985 reprint of 1981 edn.), p. 128.

88 Indich, *Consciousness in Advaita Vedānta*, p. 62.

89 Indich again argues for a "radical discontinuity" between these stages of waking, dreaming, deep sleep and enlightenment, corresponding to the same "radical discontinuity" between the ultimate Reality that is the true Self and the reality of the phenomenal world: *ibid.*, p. 18. However, the same Consciousness that is *Ātman* is *reflected* in all states, and it is this that lends continuity. Nevertheless, it is difficult to posit pure Consciousness from three illusory states of consciousness and, as Indich later states: "Having established a radical distinction between reality and appearance, the one and the many, eternal rest and temporal change, the Advaitin's attempts to argue from the latter back to the former may be systematically instructive and spiritually edifying, but they cannot be logically conclusive": *ibid.*, p. 122.

90 Śaṃkara, *Upadeśasāhasrī* 2:17:26–7, translator Potter, *Encyclopedia of Indian Philosophies, Vol. III*, pp. 240–1.

91 Puligandla, *Fundamentals of Indian Philosophy*, p. 215.

92 Vivekananda, *Jnana-Yoga*, p. 16.

93 Raphael, *The Pathway of Non-Duality*, p. 60.

94 Śaṃkara, *Aitareya Upaniṣad Bhāṣya* 2:1:1, translator Alston, *Śaṃkara on the Absolute*, pp. 142–3.

95 Deussen, *The System of the Vedanta*, p. 135.

96 Mysore Hiriyanna, *Essentials of Indian Philosophy* (Delhi: Motilal Banarsidass, 1995), p. 157.

97 Satchidānandendra, *The Method of the Vedanta*, p. 111.

98 Deussen, *The System of the Vedanta*, p. 286.
99 *Ibid.*
100 Ward, *Images of Eternity*, p. 22.
101 Vivekananda, *Jnana-Yoga*, p. 59.
102 Deussen, *The System of the Vedanta*, p. 278.
103 Śaṃkara, *Bhagavadgītābhāṣya* 2:16, translator Alston, *Śaṃkara on the Absolute*, p. 189.
104 Śaṃkara, *Muṇḍaka Upaniṣad* and *Gauḍapādakārikābhāṣya* 3:19, translator Alston, *Śaṃkara on Creation*, p. 202.
105 Alston, *Śaṃkara on Creation*, p. 95.
106 *Ibid.*, p. 3
107 *Ibid.*, p. 6.
108 Satchidānandendra, *The Method of the Vedanta*, p. 75.
109 For fuller details of this, see Fowler, *Perspectives of Reality*, pp. 270–75.
110 For a full analysis of these processes see Potter, *Encyclopedia of Indian Philosophies, Vol. III*, pp. 23–7.
111 Arvind Sharma, *The Philosophy of Religion and Advaita Vedānta*, p. 162.
112 Śaṃkara, *Brahmasūtrabhāṣya* 2:1:14, translator Alston, *Śaṃkara on Creation*, p. 41.
113 Primarily, Śaṃkara depicted the Absolute as pure Consciousness, *cit*, secondarily as Truth, *sat*, and less frequently as Bliss, *ānanda*.
114 Lott, *Vedantic Approaches to God*, p. 75.
115 Arvind Sharma, *The Philosophy of Religion and Advaita Vedānta*, p. 2.
116 Chandradhar Sharma, *A Critical Survey of Indian Philosophy*, p. 280.
117 So Arvind Sharma, *The Philosophy of Religion and Advaita Vedānta*, p. 8.
118 Radhakrishnan, *Indian Philosophy, Vol. 2*, p. 519.
119 Śaṃkara, *Bhagavadgītābhāṣya* 3:4:8, translator Alston, *Śaṃkara on Creation*, p. 14.
120 Radhakrishnan, *Indian Philosophy, Vol. 2*, p. 540.
121 Śaṃkara, *Bhagavadgītābhāṣya* 13:12, translator Alston, *Śaṃkara on Discipleship*, p. 304. The quotation actually makes full sense without the intrusion of Alston's words in parentheses.
122 Dasgupta, *A History of Indian Philosophy, Vol. 1*, p. 477.
123 Radhakrishnan, *Indian Philosophy, Vol. 2*, p. 545.
124 Arvind Sharma, *Advaita Vedānta*, p. 14.
125 In his earlier life as a peripatetic teacher, one of the temples Śaṃkara built in the South was to the Goddess Sarasvatī, and in the North, he built one to Nārāyaṇa.
126 Alston, *Śaṃkara on the Soul*, p. 146.
127 Dandekar, "Vedānta" in *ER*, vol. 15, p. 210.
128 Hiriyanna, *Outlines of Indian Philosophy*, p. 365.
129 Arvind Sharma, *Advaita Vedānta*, p. 44.
130 Arvind Sharma, *The Philosophy of Religion and Advaita Vedānta*, p. 28.
131 Potter, *Encyclopedia of Indian Philosophies, Vol. III*, p. 77.
132 *Ibid.*, p. 78.
133 Chandradhar Sharma, *A Critical Survey of Indian Philosophy*, p. 281.
134 Potter, *Encyclopedia of Indian Philosophies, Vol. III*, p. 32.
135 Śaṃkara, *Bṛhadāraṇyaka Upaniṣad Bhāṣya* 4:4:6, translator Alston, *Śaṃkara on Enlightenment* (London: Shanti Sadan, 1989, p. 211.
136 Śaṃkara, *Upadeśasāhasrī* 1:16:63, translator Mayeda, *A Thousand Teachings*, p. 155.
137 Śaṃkara, *Chāndogya Upaniṣad Bhāṣya* 8:1:1, translator Anthony John Alston, *Śaṃkara on Enlightenment*, p. 22.
138 *Gauḍapādakārikābhāṣya* 4:93, translator Alston, *Śaṃkara on Enlightenment*, p. 288.

139 Mayeda, *A Thousand Teachings*, p. 88.
140 1:14:22, 23, translator Mayeda, *ibid.*, p. 138.
141 Alston, *Śaṃkara on Enlightenment*, p. 1.
142 Śaṃkara, *Chāndogya Upaniṣad Bhāṣya*, Introduction 1:1:1, translator Alston, *Śaṃkara on Enlightenment*, p. 8.
143 Śaṃkara, *Bṛhadāraṇyaka Upaniṣad Bhāṣya* 1:4:10, translator Alston, *Śaṃkara on Discipleship*, p. 18.
144 Alston, *Śaṃkara on Enlightenment*, p. 20.
145 Satchidānandendra, *The Method of the Vedanta*, p. 147.
146 *Ibid.*, p. 146.
147 The causative nature of the Absolute is so incongruous here.
148 Śaṃkara, *Upadeśasāhasrī* (verse) chapter 13, translator Alston, *Śaṃkara on Enlightenment*, p. 152.
149 Śaṃkara, *Upadeśasāhasrī* 2:1:2, translator Mayeda, *A Thousand Teachings*, p. 211.
150 Deussen, *The System of the Vedanta*, p. 409.
151 Indich, *Consciousness in Advaita Vedānta*, p. 16.
152 Although Radhakrishnan, for one, does not accept that Śaṃkara saw *saṃnyāsins* as *jīvan-muktas*. He believed they were simply better placed for intuitive realization of Brahman as *Ātman*: see *Indian Philosophy, Vol. 2*, p. 617.
153 Śaṃkara, *Gauḍapādakārikābhāṣya* 4:94, translator Alston, *Śaṃkara on Enlightenment*, p. 290.
154 Loy, *Non-Duality*, p. 242.
155 Translator Alston, *Śaṃkara on Enlightenment*, p. 285.
156 *Bṛhadāraṇyaka Upaniṣad Bhāṣya* 4:4:23, translator Alston, *ibid.*, p. 294.
157 Dasgupta, *A History of Indian Philosophy, Vol. 1*, p. 440.
158 Śaṃkara, *Gauḍapādakārikābhāṣya* 90, translator Alston, *Śaṃkara on the Soul*, p. 171.
159 Mayeda, *A Thousand Teachings*, p. 12.
160 Ninian Smart, *Doctrine and Argument in Indian Philosophy* (Leiden, New York, Köln: E. J. Brill, 1992), p. 87.
161 Radhakrishnan, *Indian Philosophy, Vol. 2*, p. 649.
162 *Ibid.*, p. 652.
163 Smart, *Doctrine and Argument in Indian Philosophy*, p. 91.
164 Loy, *Non-Duality*, p. 297.
165 Sinari, *The Structure of Indian Thought*, p. 107.
166 Mayeda, *A Thousand Teachings*, p. 94.
167 Deussen, *The System of the Vedanta*, p. 404.
168 Potter, *Encyclopedia of Indian Philosophies, Vol III*, p. 100.
169 Gerald Larson, in Gerald Larson and Ram Shankar Bhattacharya, eds., *Encyclopedia of Indian Philosophies, Vol. IV: Sāṃkhya* (Delhi, Varanasi, Patna, Madras: Motilal Banarsidass, 1987), p. 84.
170 Isayeva, *Shankara and Indian Philosophy*, p. 11.
171 Sinari, *The Structure of Indian Thought*, p. 112.
172 Vivekananda, *Jnana-Yoga*, p. 99.

Chapter 5 Influential Theories: Sāṃkhya and Classical Yoga

1 The modern scholar and ascetic Swami Hariharānanda Āraṇya who died in 1947 founded a monastery in Madhupur and was a follower of Sāṃkhya-Yoga.
2 Gerald J. Larson, *Classical Sāṃkhya: An interpretation of its history and meaning* (Delhi: Motilal Banarsidass, second, revised edn 1979, first published 1969), p. 154.
3 Erich Frauwallner, for example, suggests an early oral tradition: see *History of Indian Philosophy,*

Vol. 1: The philosophy of the Veda and of the epic, the Buddha and the Jina, the Sāṃkhya and the Classical Yoga System, translated from the original German by V. M. Bedekar (Delhi: Motilal Banarsidass, 1993 reprint of 1973 edn), p. 221.

4 Both Sāṃkhya and Yoga probably originated as rather general terms. Harzer suggests that at the beginning of the first millennium, "the names *Sāṃkhya* and *Yoga* might not refer at this time to philosophical schools. *Sāṃkhya* may be a name for any system of metaphysics, knowledge of which leads to liberation. *Yoga* may be a name for any system of meditative practices that lead to liberation": see E. Harzer, "Sāṃkhya" in Mircea Eliade, *The Encyclopedia of Religion* (New York: Macmillan, 1987), vol. 13, p. 49. But if there were times when both terms were used generally, the synonymy of ideas between the developing schools brought them together.

5 Mikel Burley is of the view that "they probably derived from a single source, but they represent moderately divergent streams flowing from that source": see *Classical Sāṃkhya and Yoga: An Indian metaphysics of experience* (London and New York: Routledge, 2007), p. 52.

6 For a full account of Sāṃkhya in the *Upaniṣads* see Arthur Berriedale Keith, *The Sāṃkhya System: A History of the Sāṃkhya Philosophy*, Kessinger Legacy Reprints series (Calcutta: Association Press and London, New York, Toronto, Melbourne, Bombay and Madras: Oxford University Press, first published 1918), pp. 5–19.

7 Larson, *Classical Sāṃkhya*, p. 99.

8 See, for example, the *Kaṭha* 1:3:10–11, and the later *Maitrī Upaniṣad* 6:10.

9 There may even have been an original text that is no longer extant. See Edwin F. Bryant, *The Yoga Sūtras of Patañjali: A new edition, translation, and commentary* (New York: North Point Press, 2009), p. xlviii.

10 Larson, *Classical Sāṃkhya*, p. 95.

11 Surendranath Dasgupta, *A History of Indian Philosophy, Vol. 1* (Delhi, Mumbai, Chennai, Calcutta, Bangalore, Varanasi, Patna, Pune: Motilal Banarsidass, 1997, first published 1922), p. 212.

12 Larson, *Classical Sāṃkhya*, p. 252.

13 Gerald Larson, "Introduction to the Philosophy of Sāṃkhya" in Gerald Larson and Ram Shankar Bhattacharya, eds., *Encyclopedia of Indian Philosophies, Vol. IV Sāṃkhya: A dualist tradition in Indian philosophy* (Delhi, Varanasi, Patna, Madras: Motilal Banarsidass, 1987), p. 19.

14 Karl H. Potter and Gerald J. Larson "*Sāṃkhyakārikā*" in *Encyclopedia of Indian Philosophies, Vol. IV, ibid.*, p. 150.

15 Burley, *Classical Sāṃkhya and Yoga*, p. 157.

16 For a very full analysis and discussion of the term, see Knut A. Jacobsen, *Prakṛti in Sāṃkhya-Yoga: Material principle, religious experience, ethical implications*, Asian Thought and Culture, Vol. 30 (New York, Washington D.C., Baltimore, Boston, Bern, Frankfurt am Main, Berlin, Vienna, Paris: Peter Lang, 1999), pp. 25–121.

17 *Ibid.*, p. 52.

18 Dasgupta, *A History of Indian Philosophy, Vol. 1*, p. 245.

19 Jacobsen, *Prakṛti in Sāṃkhya-Yoga*, p. 54.

20 *Sāṃkhya-Kārikā* 10, translator Larson, *Classical Sāṃkhya*, p. 259.

21 For a full discussion of these, see Jeaneane Fowler, *Perspectives of Reality: An introduction to the philosophy of Hinduism* (Brighton, Sussex and Portland, Oregon: Sussex Academic Press, 2002), pp. 166–80.

22 Burley maintains the controversial view here that any cosmogony of *prakṛti* is incoherent and so rejects it. He writes: "Prakṛti's manifestation provides the conscious subject not with a world, but with the categories through which, or in terms of which, a world is experienced. These manifest categories are not fully-formed objects; they are the conditions that make

objects possible for us": see *Classical Sāṃkhya and Yoga*, p. 157. Again, his theory would make the dualism of Sāṃkhya – spirit/*puruṣa* and matter/*prakṛti* confined to the internal world of experience of the *puruṣas*. It does seem that neither the *Sāṃkhya-Kārikā* nor the *Yoga-Sūtras* suggest any dual interpretation of the evolutes as cosmic and psychic: perhaps it is simply common sense to see them as such given their mapped progressions.

23 Weerasinghe terms *mahat* "the great germ of the universe" and sees the *Vedic* Hiraṇya-garbha, the "golden germ" from which all things spring (*Ṛg Veda* 10:21) as its older prototype. See Sri Garib M. Weerasinghe, *The Saṅkhya Philosophy: A critical evaluation of its origins and development*, Sri Garib Das Series, no. 167 (Delhi: Sri Satguru, 1993), pp. 155–9. A full discussion of the origins of the term *mahat* and its links to the Sāṃkhya concept can be found on pp. 159–68 of Weerasinghe's work.

24 Cf. *Ṛg Veda* 10:129.

25 In the *Sāṃkhya-Kārikā* 46–51, fifty *bhāvas* are indicated contrasting with the eight identified in 42–45 and 52.

26 Weerasinghe, *The Sāṅkhya Philosophy*, p. 169.

27 Cf. *Chāndogya Upaniṣad* 7:25:1.

28 Bryant, *The Yoga Sūtras of Patañjali*, p. li.

29 Burley, *Classical Sāṃkhya and Yoga*, p. 111.

30 *Sāṃkhya-Kārikā* 27, translator Larson, *Classical Sāṃkhya*, p. 264.

31 Sarvepalli Radhakrishnan, *Indian Philosophy, Vol. 2* (Delhi: Oxford University Press, 1994 impression, first published 1923), p. 262.

32 Larson provides a detailed account of these in "Introduction to the philosophy of Sāṃkhya", pp. 65–7.

33 Although the *Sāṃkhya-Kārikā* mentions just *three guṇas*, later Sāṃkhya came to accept an infinite number of *guṇic*-like substances that inform each of them. In this case it would be more accurate to speak of the *sattvic class* of *guṇas*, or the *rajas* and *tamas* classes of *guṇas*.

34 *Sāṃkhya-Kārikā* 12, translator Larson, *Classical Sāṃkhya*, p. 259.

35 Satischandra Chatterjee and Dhirendramohan Datta, *An Introduction to Indian Philosophy* (Calcutta: University of Calcutta, 1984), p. 261.

36 *Sāṃkhya-Kārikā* 54, translator Larson, *Classical Sāṃkhya*, p. 272.

37 The *Sāṃkhya-Kārikā* does not deal at all with inorganic matter though later theories on the *guṇas* extended their combinations to inanimate matter also.

38 *Sāṃkhya-Kārikā* 13, translator Larson, *Classical Sāṃkhya*, p. 260.

39 Radhakrishnan, *Indian Philosophy, Vol. 2*, p. 311.

40 Sāṃkhya's adoption of the term *puruṣa* was not new. It is an ancient term that generally referred to the mortal human being, but it came to be used as the ultimate essence of the being that is equated, either partially or wholly, with Brahman. As such, the term became synonymous with *ātman*, but this term was also at one time the general term for the ordinary human self.

41 Weerasinghe, *The Sāṅkhya Philosophy*, p. 227.

42 *Sūtra* 17 of the *Kārikā* gives five proofs for the existence of *puruṣas*, *viz.* matter exists for a being/*puruṣa*; everything is composed of the three *guṇas*, which are objects of knowledge needing a subject/*puruṣa*; coordination of experiences can only be via consciousness/*puruṣa*; material *prakṛti* cannot experience its own evolutes so there must be an intelligent experiencer/*puruṣa*; striving for liberation means there must be a subject that does this and that is *puruṣa*. This last is a problem since *puruṣa* is passive.

43 Lloyd W. Pflueger, "Person, Purity, and Power in the *Yogasūtra*" in Knut A. Jacobsen, ed., *Theory and Practice of Yoga: Essays in honour of Gerald James Larson* (Leiden, The Netherlands: Koninklijke Brill NV, 2005), p. 33.

44 Radhakrishnan, *Indian Philosophy, Vol. 2*, p. 286.
45 *Sāṃkhya-Kārikā* 19.
46 So, Mysore Hiriyanna, *Outlines of Indian Philosophy* (Delhi: Motilal Banarsidass, 1993 Indian edn), p. 293.
47 *Sāṃkhya-Kārikā* 42, translator Larson, *Classical Sāṃkhya*, p. 268.
48 Chandradhar Sharma, *A Critical Survey of Indian Philosophy* (Delhi: Motilal Banarsidass, 1994 reprint of 1960 edn), p. 168.
49 Chatterjee and Datta, *An Introduction to Indian Philosophy*, p. 273.
50 See *Sāṃkhya-Kārikā* 17, 21, 36, 63, 56, 58 and *Yoga-Sūtras* 2:18.
51 Hiriyanna, *Outlines of Indian Philosophy*, p. 273.
52 Sāṃkhya posits the conjunction of the two as like a blind man and a lame man, the former able to carry the latter until the destination is reached. But this will not do, since both are active material agents and not at all like the completely passive *puruṣas.*
53 Radhakrishnan, *Indian Philosophy, Vol. 2*, p. 329.
54 Sharma, *A Critical Survey of Indian Philosophy*, p. 166.
55 See Dasgupta, *A History of Indian Philosophy, Vol. 1*, pp. 247–8.
56 In fact, it would be impossible to infer the presence of *puruṣa* since what is objective and matter cannot infer what is subjective in knowledge: the material object can never know the spiritual subject.
57 Burley's idealism view of *prakṛtic* evolutes would actually solve the oddity of a material and unconscious *prakṛti* working towards the liberation of *puruṣas*, which is nonsensical. But if all is taking place in the mind of the *puruṣa* then a conscious process of "disidentifying with experience (or the constituents thereof)" can bring about the goal of liberation: see *Classical Sāṃkhya and Yoga*, p. 161.
58 Frauwallner, *History of Indian Philosophy, Vol. 1*, p. 297.
59 Radhakrishnan, *Indian Philosophy, Vol. 2*, p. 303.
60 Hiriyanna, *Outlines of Indian Philosophy*, p. 287.
61 Dasgupta, *A History of Indian Philosophy, Vol. 1*, p. 257.
62 Translator Larson, *Classical Sāṃkhya*, p. 260.
63 In Burley's view, only consciousness can effect such transformations – a point with which it would be difficult to disagree – but Burley takes the point further: "It would seem to be more plausible to say that *prakṛti* is not 'turned into' anything; it is merely the case that in the presence of consciousness *prakṛti* has an appearance, a form, and can thus be said to *manifest*, whereas in the absence of consciousness – that is, 'in itself' – *prakṛti* has no appearance, and remains unmanifest": *Classical Sāṃkhya and Yoga*, p. 94. Again, Burley would be solving a glaring problem in Sāṃkhya metaphysics but, again, the leap from *prakṛtic* matter to mind experience alone is one that is not generally accepted.
64 Radhakrishnan, *Indian Philosophy, Vol. 2*, p. 279.
65 See Burley, *Classical Sāṃkhya and Yoga*, p. 3.
66 Even if at an earlier stage *sāṃkhya* in general terms may have originally linked what later came to be individual *puruṣas* as one. It was the increasing emphasis on knowledge as the means to liberation that supplied the root cause for the move to atheism, but it is unlikely that it was either a consistent developmental shift or a regular one; the steps towards it are obscure.
67 See Larson, *Classical Sāṃkhya*, p. 104 and Dasgupta, *A History of Indian Philosophy, Vol. 1*, pp. 216–17.
68 Translator Larson, *Classical Sāṃkhya*, p. 271.
69 *Ibid.*, p. 256.
70 Larson, *Classical Sāṃkhya*, p. 205.

71 *Sāṃkhya-Kārikā* 62, translator Larson, *ibid.*, p. 274.
72 John Davies, *Hindu Philosophy: An exposition of the system of Kapila* (New Delhi: Cosmo Publications, 1981), p. 112.
73 So, Sharma, *A Critical Survey of Indian Philosophy*, p. 168.
74 Mysore Hiriyanna, *Essentials of Indian Philosophy* (Delhi: Motilal Banarsidass Publishers Private Limited, 1995 Indian edn), p. 115.
75 *Sūtra* means "thread" from the Skt. root *sū*. The English word *sew* is cognate.
76 Bryant, *The Yoga Sūtras of Patañjali*, p. 28. Patañjali stated that there are five kinds of *vṛtti* – right knowledge, error, imagination, sleep, and memory.
77 *Yoga-Sūtras* 1:2, translator James Haughton Woods, *The Yoga-System of Patañjali* (Delhi: Motilal Banarsidass, 1992 reprint of 1914 edn), 1:2.
78 In other schools, where union of the self with the Supreme Self as Brahman is accepted, the word is often translated as "to unite" or "to connect". This is less applicable to a dualist school that separates, not unifies, spirit and matter.
79 Karel Werner, *Yoga and Indian Philosophy* (Delhi: Motilal Banarsidass, 1989 reprint of 1977 edn), pp. 93–4.
80 Ravi Ravindra, "Yoga: The Royal Path to Freedom" in Krishna Sivaraman, ed., *Hindu Spirituality, Vol. 1: Vedas through Vedanta* (London: SCM, 1989), p. 177.
81 Bryant, *The Yoga Sūtras of Patañjali*, p. xxv.
82 See *ibid.*, p. xxiv.
83 The unmanifest *prakṛti* is generally termed *aliṅga*. The three *guṇas* in their unmanifest state and in their multifarious collocations of manifest existence are called *dṛśya* "the seeable" – in other words, all that *puruṣas* are capable of seeing. *Puruṣa*, then, is often known as the "seer", *draṣṭṛ*. The Sāṃkhya *mahāt-buddhi* is generally termed the Designator, the *liṅga-mātra*. The Sāṃkhya *ahaṃkāra*, pure I-ness, is termed *asmitāmātra*, but when this is transferred to I-ness in the sense of "I am", "me", it is sometimes simply termed *asmitā*, self-identity. Yoga groups the *asmitāmātra* (Sāṃkhya *ahaṃkāra*) and the five subtle elements (*tanmātras*) together as the six *aviśeṣas* or "non-particularized", "undifferentiated". *Manas*, the ten *indriyas* and the five gross elements are grouped together as the *viśeṣas*, the "particularized", "differentiated".
84 A good critique of those scholars who minimalize the nature of Yoga in comparison to Sāṃkhya can be found in Georg Feuerstein, *The Philosophy of Classical Yoga* (Rochester, Vermont: Inner Traditions International, 1996, first published 1980), pp. 109–20.
85 Werner, *Yoga and Indian Philosophy*, p. 94.
86 Surendranath N. Dasgupta, *Yoga Philosophy: In relation to other systems of Indian thought* (Delhi: Motilal Banarsidass, 1996, first published 1930), p. 51.
87 Werner, *Yoga and Indian Philosophy*, p. 131.
88 Although some have favoured identifying Patañjali with the grammarian Patañjali who lived in the second century BCE, there is much about such an identification that is problematic: see Woods, "Introduction" in *The Yoga-System of Patañjali*, pp. xiii–xxiii for a detailed analysis of the authorship and dating of the *Yoga-Sūtras*.
89 Bryant, in fact, says: "It cannot be overstated that Yoga philosophy is Patañjali's philosophy as understood and articulated by Vyāsa": *The Yoga Sūtras of Patañjali*, p. xl.
90 For a concise list of commentators see Burley, *Classical Sāṃkhya and Yoga*, pp. 30–1.
91 Not the Vyāsa who was an ancient sage and seer and reputed compiler of major texts. But by giving himself that ancient name, the commentator acquired considerable status.
92 Bryant, *The Yoga Sūtras of Patañjali*, p. 205.
93 *Yoga-Sūtras* 1:14, translator Bryant, *ibid.*, p. 49.

94 This object can be physical, such as the tip of the nose, the navel, the middle of the forehead, or subtle, like the *sattvic* substance of the "Lotus of the Heart", or the light within the head. It can be mental, such as a particular idea or thought. It can also be concentration on God, on Īśvara. Even an object perceived in a dream is a possible focus for concentration; in fact, in the early stages of *yogic* practice, any object one wishes is suitable.

95 *Yoga-Sūtras* 1:33, translator Bryant, The *Yoga Sūtras of Patañjali*, p. 128.

96 *Yoga-Sūtras* 4:14, translator Woods, *The Yoga-System of Patañjali*, p. 318. Cf. for a different translation that of Bryant: "The things [of the world] are objectively real, due to the uniformity of [the *guṇas* that underpin] all change." *The Yoga Sūtras of Patañjali*, p. 428.

97 Vyāsa had a humorous point here against the idealists, for he asked, if a person is only seen from the front, does that mean that he has no back since it isn't being perceived? And yet, Burley maintains idealism is fundamental to Sāṃkhya and Yoga. The "seen" that is *prakṛti* is dependent on the "seer" and he believes that without the seer/*puruṣa*, the seen/*prakṛti* cannot exist. Manifest objects, he claims, are "merely appearances *for us*": see *Classical Sāṃkhya and Yoga*, pp. 136 and 137.

98 Jacobsen, *Prakṛti in Sāṃkhya-Yoga*, p. 242.

99 Alain Daniélou, *Yoga: Mastering secrets of matter and the universe* (Rochester, Vermont: Inner Traditions International, 1991), p. 2.

100 Jacobsen, *Prakṛti in Sāṃkhya-Yoga*, p. 3.

101 Whenever we see something but fail to perceive it accurately, the mind's analysis and synthesis of the perception will not correspond to the real thing. Error, then, is perception that is incorrect. The real error lies in the lack of discrimination between the real Self of pure consciousness and the whole of *prakṛtic* matter, including any notions of the egoistic and thinking empirical self: this is ignorance, *avidyā*, and the root cause of bondage, suffering and rebirth.

102 "Mind-stuff" is a translation rejected by Feuerstein because it lacks the awareness supplied by the *puruṣa* in order to function: see *Philosophy of Classical Yoga*, p. 59. Elsewhere he calls the translation a *horrific* word: see *The Yoga-Sūtra of Patañjali: A new translation and commentary* (Rochester, Vermont: Inner Traditions International, 1989, first published 1979, p. 26). But his translation of *citta* as "consciousness" is misleading, as would be Larson's "awareness": see "Introduction to the Philosophy of Sāṃkhya" in Larson and Bhattacharya eds., *Encyclopedia of Indian Philosophies, Vol. IV*, p. 27, for this is the nature of *puruṣa* only.

103 The word actually has a wide number of meanings: see Ian Whicher, *The Integrity of the Yoga Darśana: A reconsideration of classical Yoga* (New Delhi: D. K. Printworld (P) Ltd., 2000, first published 1998), p. 91.

104 Gaspar M. Koelman, *Pātañjala Yoga: From related ego to absolute Self* (Poona: Papal Athenaeum, 1970), p. 101.

105 Larson, "Introduction to the Philosophy of Sāṃkhya" in Larson and Bhattacharya, eds., *Encyclopedia of Indian Philosophies, Vol. IV*, p. 26.

106 Dasgupta, for example, believed it is important to differentiate between the *citta* as the mind, and the intellect and ego. Each, he believed, has a separate role in the process of knowledge: see *Yoga Philosophy*, p. 265. This is true, but the total mind functioning must incorporate all three, not only in ordinary exixtence but in all the stages of *yogic* training.

107 Bryant, *The Yoga Sūtras of Patañjali*, p. 11.

108 Radhakrishnan, *Indian Philosophy, Vol. 2*, p. 349.

109 Ernest Wood, *Seven Schools of Yoga* (Wheaton, Illinois, Madras, London: The Theosophical Publishing House, 1988, first published 1976), p. 16.

110 Georg Feuerstein, "The Meaning of Suffering in Yoga" in Georg Feuerstein and Jeanine Miller, *The Essence of Yoga: Essays on the development of Yogic philosophy from Vedas to modern times* (Rochester, Vermont: Inner Traditions International, 1998), p. 87.

111 Bryant, *The Yoga Sūtras of Patañjali*, p. 171.

112 See Richard King, *Indian Philosophy: An introduction to Hindu and Buddhist thought* (Edinburgh: Edinburgh University Press, 1999), p. 69.

113 Shyam Ranganathan, *Patañjali's Yoga Sūtra* (New Delhi, New York and London: Penguin Books, 2008), p. 26.

114 For a full discussion of each of these, see Fowler, *Perspectives of Reality*, pp. 211–19.

115 The *Yoga-Sūtras*, the *Mahābhārata* , and the *Gītā* have little to say on this *aṅga*, despite its prolific association with *yoga* in the West.

116 Some readers may be surprised to find an absence of references to the *cakras* and to the power of *kuṇḍalini* – both commonly associated with Yoga in the western mind. However, while Patañjali certainly had knowledge of the *cakras*, no mention of *kuṇḍalini* occurs in the *Yoga-Sūtras*: it was a development of Tantric Yoga.

117 Fowler, *Perspectives of Reality*, pp. 211–15.

118 Commentary on 2:54, translator Woods, *The Yoga-System of Patañjali*, p. 197.

119 Jean Varenne, *Yoga and the Hindu Tradition*, translated from the French by Derek Coltman (Chicago and London: The University of Chicago Press, 1976, first published, 1973), p. 120.

120 Whicher, *The Integrity of the Yoga Darśana*, p. 29.

121 Bryant, *The Yoga Sūtras of Patañjali*, p. 326.

122 Whicher, *The Integrity of the Yoga Darśana*, p. 259.

123 *Ibid.*, p. 153.

124 Vācaspati Miśra's explanation and Vyāsa's comments on Patañjali's *Yoga-Sūtras* 2:9, translator Woods, p. 117.

125 Patañjali mentions inimical inhibitors that disturb the mind – disease, idleness, doubt, carelessness, sloth, lack of detachment, misapprehension, failure to attain a base for concentration, and instability. He also says in 2:11 that the states of mind brought about by the *kleśas* can be eliminated by meditation or, in 2:2, by *kriyā-yoga*, egoless action dedicated to God.

126 *Sattva* pulls the individual towards inner spirituality; *rajas* and *tamas* pull the individual outward to the world. It seems, according to Vyāsa, that good *karma* can destroy bad *karma* but not *vice versa*.

127 On this point, see Hariharānanda Āraṇya, *Yoga Philosophy of Patañjali* (Albany: State University of New York Press, 1981 revised edn, first published 1963), p. 426.

128 Jacobsen, *Prakṛti in Sāṃkhya-Yoga*, p. 64.

129 Mircea Eliade, *Yoga: Immortality and freedom*, Bollingen Series LVI, translated from French by Willard R. Trask (Princeton, New Jersey: Princeton University Press, 1990 reprint of 1970 edn, first published 1958), p. 42.

130 Dasgupta, *Yoga Philosophy*, p. 286.

131 For example in *The Philosophy of Classical Yoga*, p. 60 *et al.*

132 *Ibid.*, p. 67.

133 F. W. J. Humphries, "Yoga Philosophy and Jung" in Karel Werner, ed., *The Yogi and the Mystic: Studies in Indian and comparative mysticism* (Richmond, Surrey: Curzon Press, 1994, first published 1989), p. 142.

134 The term *saṃskāra* carries the nuance of purification in its meanings. Thus it is applicable to birth, marriage and death rites, as was seen in Volume I.

135 Dasgupta certainly equates the two: see *Yoga Philosophy*, pp. 324 and 325, but I think there is some measure in recognizing a difference in the nuances of meaning of the two terms, though perhaps not as definitive as others suggest, see Feuerstein, *The Philosophy of Classical Yoga*, p. 67.

136 Dasgupta, *Yoga Philosophy*, p. 324.

137 For example in *The Philosophy of Classical Yoga*, p. 21.

138 This suggests that a *liṅga-śarīra* as in Sāṃkhya is unnecessary.

139 Āraṇya, *Yoga Philosophy of Patañjali*, p. 428.

140 *Ibid.*

141 Such constant practice was emphasized, too, in the *Sāṃkhya-Kārikā* 64, where the outcome of practice involving the *tattvas* brings knowledge. Similarly, *Yoga-Sūtras* 1:32 emphasizes one-pointed concentration on a *tattva*. The aim of both is knowledge of the true nature of *puruṣa*.

142 Āraṇya, *Yoga Philosophy of Patañjali*, p. 440.

143 *Ibid.*, p. 442.

144 The same idea occurs in the third chapter of the *Kaṭha Upaniṣad*.

145 Radhakrishnan, *Indian Philosophy, Vol. 2*, p. 371.

146 Koelman, *Pātañjala Yoga*, p. 57.

147 *Ibid.*, p. 58.

148 1:23; 1:24; 1:25; 1:26; 1:27, 1:28; 1:29; 2:45.

149 Bryant, *The Yoga Sūtras of Patañjali*, p. 94.

150 Pflueger, "Person, Purity, and Power in the *Yoga Sūtra*", p. 31.

151 See Chatterjee and Datta, *An Introduction to Indian Philosophy*, p. 309 and *Yoga-Sūtras* 1:23.

152 Feuerstein, *The Philosophy of Classical Yoga*, p. 5.

153 Eliade, *Yoga*, p. 75.

154 Bryant, *The Yoga Sūtras of Patañjali*, pp. 274–5.

155 *Ibid.*, p. 281.

156 Both Vācaspati Miśra's and Vyāsa's commentaries on 1:24 of Patañjali's *Yoga-Sūtras* refer to Īśvara as wholly *sattvic*. This is because Īśvara has the excellence of perfection that is associated with the *sattvic guṇa*. In a way, Vācaspati Miśra tells us, the *sattvic* quality of God is an assumed one for the benefit of the world, rather like an actor who assumes a certain role but always knows his real identity. God's *sattvic* identity is therefore one that is not *prakṛtic* but is merely eternally adopted, and there is no question of this divine Being having any trace of the ignorance of his true nature that would bind him to the world.

157 This is somewhat problematic in that it serves to diminish the nature of the liberated *puruṣa* as totally separate from *prakṛti*. It is projecting something beyond *puruṣa* that *puruṣa* can never be, and to which it will always be inferior.

158 Burley, however, notes that the *sūtra* that states as such depicts Īśvara as the "seed" of all knowledge, indicative, he thinks, that the knowledge is "potential rather than actual". He thinks Īśvara is "a special instance of the generic category of selves" and can be equated with the "highest seer", whom he thinks is Kapila. His point is that any supposed theism in Yoga is not a reason to separate the Sāṃkhya and Yoga systems, especially if Kapila and Īśvara are identical: see *Classical Sāṃkhya and Yoga*, pp. 50 and 51.

159 *Sūtra* 1:27 designates Īśvara as *Oṃ* and Bryant further believes that Patañjali "is consciously equating the Upaniṣadic *Brahman* with this personal *Īśvara*, by means of the common denominator of *oṃ*": see *The Yoga Sūtras of Patañjali*, p. 106. Repetition of *Oṃ* and concentration on its meaning was recommended by Patañjali (1:28), and Bryant's point is that Patañjali as an orthodox scholar would be thoroughly conversant with its synonymy with Brahman. But meditation on the abstract *Oṃ* would have been far more subtle than on a personal deity

and Patañjali must have known this. Then, too, Patañjali does not overtly or in any way suggest the oneness of each *puruṣa* with Īśvara as Brahman, as did Vijñana Bhikṣu. There is nothing in the *Yoga-Sūtras* to suggest that Patañjali saw Īśvara and *puruṣas* as anything but separate.

160 Pflueger, "Person, Purity, and Power in the *Yoga Sūtra*", p. 57.

161 Koelman, *Pātañjala Yoga*, pp. 61–3. Vācaspati Miśra, too, seems to have raised the point that the nature of Īśvara is suggestive that he had a *citta*, though he wriggled out of the issue by saying that Īśvara involves himself with matter of his own free will, again, as an actor who takes on a role but in reality is someone else: see Bryant, *The Yoga Sūtras of Patañjali*, p. 67.

162 Pflueger, "Person, Purity, and Power in the *Yoga Sūtra*", p. 35.

163 Richa Pauranik Clements, "Being a Witness: Cross-Examining the Notion of Self in Śaṅkara's *Upadeśasāhasrī*, Īśvarakṛṣṇa's *Sāṃkhyakārikā*, and Patañjali's *Yogasūtra*" in Jacobsen, ed., *Theory and Practice of Yoga*, p. 92.

164 Pflueger, "Person, Purity, and Power in the *Yoga Sūtra*", p. 57.

165 This theory would make Īśvara the *efficient* cause of creation. Vijñana Bhikṣu certainly asserted such, linking Īśvara with Kṛṣṇa in the *Gītā*: see Bryant, *ibid.*, p. 156.

166 So, Whicher, *The Integrity of the Yoga Darśana*, p. 85.

167 Pflueger, "Person, Purity, and Power in the *Yoga Sūtra*", p. 57.

168 Eliade, *Yoga*, p. 75.

169 Feuerstein, *The Philosophy of Classical Yoga*, p. 13.

170 Bryant argues that such an idea is absent in the commentaries and in wider Indian usage: see *The Yoga Sūtras of Patañjali*, p. 88.

171 *Yoga-Sūtras* 3:55, translator Bryant, *The Yoga Sūtras of Patañjali*, p. 403.

172 Bryant, *The Yoga Sūtras of Patañjali*, p. 457.

173 It would seem, however, that the liberated *puruṣas*' self-awareness is not extended beyond itself to *prakṛti*, so we have the anomaly of ultimate knowledge that is limited in that it has no knowledge of the whole reality of *prakṛti* – a point perhaps supportive of Burley's view of the unreality of *prakṛti*.

174 Certainly, the purely *sattvic buddhi* has to convey to the *puruṣa* the discriminating fact that it is subtle matter and the *puruṣa* is separate from it: this is important *viveka*, discrimination, that brings about liberation.

175 Bryant, *The Yoga Sūtras of Patañjali*, p. 466.

176 Whicher qualifies the radical dualism normally taken to underpin Yoga, by what he terms the "responsible engagement" of spirit (*puruṣa*) with matter (*prakṛti*) in the liberated, yet embodied, state: see Whicher, *The Integrity of the Yoga Darśana*, p. 2. This means that, far from denying worldly involvement, the liberated *yogin* turns *to* the world in altruistic, moral engagement. Whicher accepts what he calls a "sattvification" of the mind, through positive modifications of it – in other words, a process of refining the mind away from the *kleśas* towards a more *sattvic* nature. Whicher's thesis makes sense when it is remembered that it is the *sattvic* nature of the *buddhi* that permits the discriminative knowledge of the different natures of *puruṣa* and *prakṛti* that is penultimate to liberation – a point well in line with Patañjali's thought: cf. *Yoga-Sūtras*, 3:55.

177 Feuerstein claims that the idea of *jīvan-mukti* is not evident in the *Yoga-Sūtras*, and that Vyāsa as the major commentator and an outsider to the school, imposed this alien concept on Patañjali's thought. Feuerstein writes, "whenever a liberated person takes on a body again, either composed of gross or subtle matter, he is no longer residing in freedom, but is again subject to the laws governing the machinery of the universe": see "The Essence of Yoga" in Feuerstein

and Miller, *The Essence of Yoga*, p. 47. Feuerstein's deduction is sensible, and is suggestive that the Yoga adept stops short of complete release from *prakṛti* while alive. If not, and the concept of *jīvan-mukti* is accepted, then the radical dualism of Sāṃkhya cannot be the basis and aim of Yoga praxis. But to deny *jīvan-mukti* to India's *yogins* runs counter to the now established tradition of the school and its tributaries.

178 T. S. Rukmani, "Revisiting the Jīvanmukti Question in Sāṃkhya in the Context of the *Sāṃkhyasūtra*" in Jacobsen, ed., *Theory and Practice of Yoga*", pp. 61–74.

179 Whicher's interpretations are interesting. He does not accept that suppression or restraint of the mind – let alone annihilation of the mind – are true interpretations of Yoga. He prefers to view the goal of Yoga as control over the *vṛttis* of the mind, not a complete annihilation of them. His view is that the mind of the *yogin* is not dissolved into the unmanifest state of *prakṛti* at the point of liberation. Only the *karmically* binding *vṛttis* are dissolved: see *The Integrity of the Yoga Darśana*, p. 157. He is against what he calls "an anaesthetization of human consciousness" (p. 158) at liberation in favour of "a state of utter lucidity or transparency of consciousness (mind) wherein no epistemological distortion can take place, yet *vṛttis* (e.g., valid cognition, memory, etc.) can still arise, can still function" (p. 157). It is the misapprehensions that the mind carries that have to be negated, not the mind itself (p. 161). So according to Whicher, *nirodha* is not the cessation of all the *vṛttis* of the mind. It is the cessation of the "empirical limitations", "restrictions", "suppressions" in the mind, and "the removal of the *kleśas* and karmic barriers only to reveal the full-blown nature of *puruṣa*" (p. 167). This means not aloneness in the sense of total separation of the *puruṣa* from *prakṛti*, but a *jīvan-mukta* that can operate in the world. Whicher's particularly attractive view of the liberated state – one transcending by far the Sāṃkhya view of the total isolation, aloneness and almost nonentity of each *puruṣa* – permits altruistic interaction with the world, counteracting the view of writers such as Radhakrishnan, who claimed that Yoga is an unethical system in *Indian Philosophy, Vol. 2*, p. 364. According to Whicher, "cessation results in our consciousness remaining unbound, nonenslaved, and transparent to things of a worldly nature while yet being thoroughly engaged in practical life": *The Integrity of the Yoga Darśana*, p. 172. Whicher's theory is that *prakṛti* goes on, but the liberated *puruṣa* simply observes, unaffected by the *guṇic* changes and the *vṛttis* of the mind. Thus, there is a *harmony* between *puruṣa* and *prakṛti* and not a separation of the two, and this is a harmony that permits world involvement. Whicher writes: "The yogin does not become a 'mind-less' (or 'body-less') being. Rather, the yogin is left with a transformed, fully sattvified mind which, due to its transparent nature, can function in the form of nonbinding *vṛttis* – whether of a cognitive or affective/emotive nature – thoughts, ideas, intentions, and so forth" (p. 281).

180 Whicher, *The Integrity of the Yoga Darśana*, p. 293.

181 Ranganathan, *Patañjali's Yoga Sūtra*, pp. 52–4.

182 Eliade, *Yoga*, p. 95.

183 *Ibid.*, p. 96.

184 Feuerstein, *The Yoga-Sūtra of Patañjali*, p. 142.

185 See also Gerald J. Larson, "*On* The integrity of the Yoga Darśana: *A review*". *International Journal of Hindu Studies*, 3 (1999), pp. 183–6, and Whicher's response to this "*On* The Integrity of the Yoga Darśana: *A Response to Larson's Review*" in the same volume, pp. 187–97. What Whicher depicts as the liberated *yogin* is more akin to what are termed *prakṛti-līnas*. These are almost-liberated beings who achieve a lower form of final (*asaṃprajñāta*) *samādhi*. This is called *prakṛti-laya*. It is the dissolution of the *prakṛtic* self into its causative state – the ultimate, unmanifest *prakṛti*.

186 Feuerstein, "The Essence of Yoga" in Feuerstein and Miller, *The Essence of Yoga*, p. 21.
187 See Whicher, *The Integrity of the Yoga Darśana*, p. 80 and Feuerstein, *The Philosophy of Classical Yoga*, p. 23.
188 See Bryant, *The Yoga Sūtras of Patañjali*, p. 228.
189 Pflueger, "Person, Purity, and Power in the *Yoga Sūtra*", p. 33.
190 For example, Fernando Tola and Carmen Dragonetti, *The Yogasūtras of Patañjali on Concentration of Mind*, translated by K. D. Prithipaul (Delhi: Motilal Banarsidass Publishers Private Limited,1991 reprint of 1987 edn), p. x.
191 Thomas Berry, *Religions of India: Hinduism, Yoga, Buddhism* (New York: Columbia University Press, 1996), pp. 88–9.
192 *Ibid.*, p. 89.
193 Eliade, *Yoga*, p. 7.
194 See the interesting article by Patrick Mahaffey, "Jung's Depth Psychology and Yoga Sādhana" in Jacobsen, ed., *Theory and Practice of Yoga*, pp. 385–407.
195 Vivian Worthington, *A History of Yoga* (London: Arkana, 1989, first published 1982), p. 88.
196 Radhakrishnan, *Indian Philosophy, Vol. 2*, p. 337.

Chapter 6 Devotional Hinduism: The *Bhagavad Gītā*

1 See Jeaneane Fowler, *The Bhagavad Gita: A text and commentary for students* (Eastbourne, Portland, Oregon and Thornhill, Ontario: Sussex Academic Press, 2012).
2 *Hinduism Beliefs and Practices: Major deities and social structures* (Eastbourne, Chicago, Ontario: Sussex Academic Press), 2014.
3 Sri Krishna Prem, *The Yoga of the Bhagavat Gita* (Shaftesbury, Dorset: Element Books, 1988), p. 68.
4 Sri Sankaracharya, *The Bhagavad Gita*, translated by Alladi Mahadeva Sastry (Madras: Samata Books, 1985 reprint of 1979 corrected edn), p. 379.
5 Sri Aurobindo, translator, *The Message of the Gita* (Pondicherry: Sri Aurobindo Ashram, 1993 fifth edn, first printed 1938), p. 211 and 211 note 1.
6 J. A. B. van Buitenen, translator, *The Bhagavad Gītā* (Rockport, Massachusetts, Shaftesbury, Dorset and Brisbane, Queensland: Element, 1997), p. 100 note 14:2.
7 Sankaracharya, *The Bhagavad Gita*, p. 198.
8 Mahendra Kulasretha, ed., Mahatma Gandhi, translator, *The Bhagavadgita: A book of ethics for all religions* (New Delhi: Lotus Press, 2008), p. 155.
9 Veeraswami Krishnaraj, translator, *The Bhagavad-Gita* (San Jose, New York, Lincoln, Shanghai: Writers Club Press, 2002), p. 107.
10 Robert Charles Zaehner, translator, *The Bhagavad-Gītā* (London, Oxford, New York: Oxford University Press, 1973, first published 1969), p. 219.
11 A difficulty in the connection between Kṛṣṇa and beings is found in verses 4, 5 and 6 of chapter 9, which are at first sight contradictory: "All this world is pervaded by me in my unmanifest form. All beings exist in me but I do not exist in them" (4). "Nor do beings exist in me; behold my divine Yoga – my Self bringing forth and supporting beings but not existing in beings" (5). "As the great wind moving everywhere always exists in the *ākāśa* [ether], so know thus, all beings exist in me" (6). In my view, verses 4, 5 and 6 can only be understood in relation to the *nirguṇa* and *saguṇa* Brahman. J. A. B. van Buitenen said something similar in relation to the word "exist" or "subsist" in verse 4: "Krsna works here with two meanings of *avyakta* he has just described: as the *avyakta* = *prakriti*, he is the domain of phenomenal life, in which all creatures have their being, so that 'they exist in me', *matsthāni*. But even as the lower *avyakta* he is not summed up by these creatures." And for the expression *do not exist in me* van Buitenen said, "as

the *Avyakta* beyond the lower *avyakta* God represents an order of being completely transcendent to the creatures": see J. A. B. van Buitenen, translator, *The Bhagavadgītā in the Mahābhārata* (Chicago and London: University of Chicago Press, 1981), p. 166 notes 1 and 2. The Ātman does, in fact, exist in all beings: Brahman pervades all manifest existence from Brahmā down to a blade of grass as the essence or Ātman within all, but only while manifestation exists. Beyond manifestation, the *nirguṇa* Brahman ever remains. The thought is rather like 7:12, where the whole of *prakṛtic* existence is said to be dependent on Brahman, but Brahman is in no way dependent on *prakṛti*. Verse 6 helps to make sense of verse 5 in that it refers to the wind that is transient as, likewise, is all manifest existence: Brahman is beyond this transience. So Brahman is the Source of and sustains all things but is not attached to them, does not "appropriate" them, as Vimala Thakar put it (see her *Insights into the Bhagavad Gita*, Delhi: Motilal Banarsidass Publishers Private Limited, 2005, p. 287), or is not "contained" by them (Aurobindo, *The Message of the Gita*, p. 145 note 1), and exists when the finite universe does not. Douglas Hill's comment was most accurate, "all beings dwell in Kṛiṣṇa (or Brahman) inasmuch as *prakṛiti* is his, but as his proper, or higher, nature is *ātman*, which is in reality quite unconnected with the work of *prakṛiti*, it is equally true that beings do not dwell in him, nor he in them": see W. Douglas P. Hill, translator, *The Bhagavad Gita: Translated from the Sanskrit with an introduction an argument and a commentary* (Oxford: Oxford University Press, 1966, first published 1928), p. 182 note 1. The point is that ultimately, the Unmanifest is beyond person, personality, divinity: it is absolute and ultimate and no-thing. It is in this sense, I think, that beings cannot exist in Brahman. It is the panentheism of the *Gītā* that helps to clarify the verses.

12 See Richard Gotshalk, translator, *Bhagavad Gītā* (Delhi: Motilal Banarsidass Publishers Private Limited, 1993 reprint of 1985 edn), p. 163 note 24.

13 "Lord" here is *prabhu*, which could also refer to the *lord* of the body in the sense of the *ātman* or *jīvātman*: see, for example, Bibek Debroy, translator, *The Bhagavad Gita* (London, New York, Toronto, New Delhi: Penguin Books, 2005), p. 283 note 19.

14 Van Buitenen preferred a translation "ubiquity" for *vibhūtis*. He wrote: "I find this rendering of *vibhūti* more helpful than 'power manifestation', etc. The root *bhū-* with preverb *vi* indicates a pervasive, ubiquitous display of appearances": see *The Bhagavadgītā in the Mahābhārata*, p. 167 note 2.

15 Thakar, *Insights into the Bhagavad Gita*, p. 313.

16 Prem, *The Yoga of the Bhagavat Gita*, p. 100.

17 Ithamar Theodor accepts that this vision is of Viṣṇu: see Ithamar Theodor, *Exploring the Bhagavad Gītā: Philosophy, structure and meaning* (Farnham, Surrey and Burlington, USA: Ashgate, 2010), pp. 95 and 106. Indeed, in the developed Vaiṣṇava doctrine of *avatāras* of Viṣṇu the connection between the two deities becomes firmly established. But I do not think it is a clearly articulated concept in the *Gītā*, being barely mentioned as such, with the exception of 11:24 and 30.

18 Thakar, *Insights into the Bhagavad Gita*, p. 78.

19 Sankaracharya, *The Bhagavad Gita*, p. 241.

20 See Fowler, *The Bhagavad Gita*, pp. xxiv–xxv.

21 In 10:21, Viṣṇu is mentioned as one of the *Ādityas*, though chapter 11 seems to imply that Kṛṣṇa is Viṣṇu, and he is explicitly referred to as such in 11:24 and 30. Given the importance of the later acceptance of Kṛṣṇa as an *avatāra* of Viṣṇu, these few instances are too minimal, I think, to be of any note.

22 Rohit Mehta, *From Mind to Super-Mind* (Delhi: Motilal Banarsidass Publishers Private Limited, 1995 reprint of 1972 edn), p. 45.

23 Patrick Olivelle, translator, *Upaniṣads* (Oxford and New York: Oxford University Press, 1996), pp. 239 and 380 note 12.
24 Translator Olivelle, *ibid.*, p. 245.
25 Zaehner, *The Bhagavad-Gītā*, pp. 267–9 and 269–70. While verse 22 will mention a supreme Puruṣa, we have no clear reason to project this beyond the Unmanifest Brahman or to isolate it from its context. Indeed, Zaehner himself found a certain "deliberate ambiguity" at this point of the *Gītā*, though he believed verse 22 resolves this with the exhortation to *bhakti* (p. 270). The exhortation in verse 22, as far as I can see, is focus on devotion as a means to Kṛṣṇa as the ultimate Unmanifest Brahman. The fact that verse 22 mentions a *supreme* Puruṣa that is attainable through *bhakti* is suggestive of a manifestation of Brahman as Kṛṣṇa, who is not *beyond* Brahman but Brahman manifest.
26 *Bhagavad Gītā* 5:29; 8:1, 4; 10:15; 11:3; 15:12, 15, 18, 19: see Theodor, *Exploring the Bhagavad Gītā*, *passim*.
27 *Ibid.*, pp. 113–15.
28 *Ibid.*, p. 107.
29 See Zaehner, *The Bhagavad-Gītā*, p. 358; Geoffrey Parrinder, translator, *The Bhagavad Gita* (Oxford: Oneworld, 1996 reprint of 1974 edn), p. 95; Franklin Edgerton, translator, *The Bhagavad Gītā* (Delhi: Motilal Banarsidass Publishers Private Limited, 1994), p. 49 and p. 49 note 28; Sri Aurobindo, *Essays on the Gita* (Pondicherry: Sri Aurobindo Ashram, 2000 third impression of 1996 ninth edn, first published between 1916 and 1920), p. 91.
30 Gotshalk, *Bhagavad Gītā*, p. 163 note 9.
31 John Grimes, *A Concise Dictionary of Indian Philosophy* (Albany, New York: State University of New York Press, 1989), p. 271.
32 Sarvepalli Radhakrishnan, translator, *The Bhagavadgita, with an Introductory Essay, Sanskrit Text, English Translation and Notes* (New York: Harper, 1973, first published 1948), p. 223, my parentheses.
33 Although a simplified system of just eight evolutes is to be found in 7:4 – the five elements along with intellect, ego and mind – 13:5, however, expands these evolutes more in line with the Sāṃkhya system.
34 Zaehner, *The Bhagavad-Gītā*, p. 187.
35 Prem, *The Yoga of the Bhagavat Gita*, p. 135.
36 Mehta, *From Mind to Super-Mind*, p. 46.
37 B. Srinivasa Murthy, translator, *The Bhagavad Gita* (Long Beach, California: Long Beach Publications, 1985), p. 52.
38 Aurobindo, *The Message of the Gita*, p. 174.
39 Maharishi Mahesh Yogi, translator, *The Bhagavad Gita: A new translation and commentary chapters 1–6* (London, Toronto, Los Angeles, Rishikesh, Frankfurt, Oslo, Geneva: International SRM Publications, 1967), p. 189.
40 Mehta, *From Mind to Super-Mind*, pp. 7–9.
41 *Ibid.*, p. 52.
42 Here and elsewhere in the *Gītā*, *dehin*, "Self" is a synonym of *ātman*. The *Gītā* sometimes uses another synonym for the Self, *śarīrin*.
43 Satya P. Agarwal, *The Social Role of the Gita: How and why* (Delhi: Motilal Banarsidass, 1998), p. 279.
44 Sankaracharya, *The Bhagavad Gita*, p. 112.
45 Radhakrishnan, *The Bhagavadgita, with an Introductory Essay, Sanskrit Text, English Translation and Notes*, p. 262.

46 The distinction between *jīvātman* and *ātman* was, however, less clear at the time the *Gītā* was written.
47 Maharishi Mahesh Yogi, *The Bhagavad Gita*, p. 271.
48 Zaehner, *The Bhagavad-Gītā*, p. 174.
49 Eknath Easwaran, translator, *The Bhagavad Gita* (Tomales, California: Nilgiri Press, 1985), p. 176.
50 Alan Jacobs, translator, *The Bhagavad Gita: A transcreation of The Song Celestial* (Winchester, UK and New York: O Books, 2003), pp. 12–13.
51 Geoffrey Parrinder, translator, *The Bhagavad Gita: A verse translation* (Oxford, England and Rockport, MA: Oneworld, 1996 reprint of 1974 edn), p. 72.
52 Arvind Sharma, *The Hindu Gītā: Ancient and classical interpretations of the Bhagavadgītā* (London: Duckworth, 1986), p. xxii.
53 Aurobindo, *Essays on the Gita*, p. 69.
54 Jean Varenne, *Yoga and the Hindu Tradition* (Chicago and London: University of Chicago Press, 1976, first published in French in 1973), p. 120.
55 Mehta, *From Mind to Super-Mind*, p. 62.
56 Krishnaraj, *The Bhagavad-Gita*, p. 120, my upper case for "Self".
57 Mahendra Kulasretha, ed., Mahatma Gandhi, translator, *The Bhagavadgita: A book of ethics for all religions*, p. 242.
58 Hill, *The Bhagavad Gita*, p. 163 note 2.
59 Theodor, *Exploring the Bhagavad Gītā*, p. 15.
60 Verses 51–3 of chapter 18 depict the constant effort necessary: "Integrated with a pure intellect, controlling the self by firmness, relinquishing sound and other sense objects, and abandoning attachment and aversion, living in solitude, eating lightly, speech, body and mind subdued, always engaged in meditation and *yoga*, taking refuge in detachment, having abandoned egoism, force, arrogance, desire, anger, covetousness, with no sense of 'mine', peaceful, he is fit for becoming Brahman."
61 Zaehner, *The Bhagavad-Gītā*, p. 294.
62 Satischandra Chatterjee and Dhirendramohan Datta, *An Introduction to Indian Philosophy* (Calcutta: University of Calcutta, 1984), pp. 21–2.
63 But Kṛṣṇa does in one place describe the *yogin* as superior "even to men of knowledge" (6:46). I take this to mean that the *yogin* who is devoted to the Yoga of the *Gītā*, that is to say, the renunciation of the fruits of actions through being integrated in the *ātman*, is superior to those who have knowledge but have not renounced desires for good results.
64 Mehta, *From Mind to Super-Mind*, p. 75.
65 Zaehner, *The Bhagavad-Gītā*, p. 389.
66 Aurobindo, *Essays on the Gita*, p. 181.
67 Lars Martin Fosse, translator, *The Bhagavad Gita* (Woodstock, New York: YogaVidya.com, 2007), p. 106.
68 Maharishi Mahesh Yogi, *The Bhagavad Gita*, p. 203.
69 Sankaracharya, *The Bhagavad Gita*, p. 96.
70 Mehta, *From Mind to Super-Mind*, p. 48.
71 Theodor, *Exploring the Bhagavad Gītā*, p. 5.
72 Van Buitenen suggested that in the case of avoiding action, Kṛṣṇa is steering a middle course between over-zealous *Vedic* ritualistic activity and the necessary maintenance of general traditional laws: see his *The Bhagavadgītā in the Mahābhārata*, p. 163. Indeed, such a view would be

consonant with Kṛṣṇa's earlier emphasis on obeying personal and class *dharma* on the one hand, and his criticism of the ritualists on the other.

73 Bina Gupta, *An Introduction to Indian Philosophy: Perspectives on reality, knowledge, and freedom* (New York and London: Routledge, 2012), p. 284.

74 Radhakrishnan, *The Bhagavadgita, with an Introductory Essay, Sanskrit Text, English Translation and Notes*, p. 139.

75 Swami Chidbhavananda, *The Bhagavad Gita* (Tamil Nadu: Sri Ramakrishna Tapovam, 1982), p. 237.

76 This last synthesizes the paths of action, knowledge and devotion rather well.

77 Chidbhavananda, *The Bhagavad Gita*, p. 515.

78 Gandhi, *The Bhagavad Gita*, p. 242.

79 Sankaracharya, *The Bhagavad Gita*, p. 301.

80 7:1, 14, 29; 9:32; 18:56, 62, 66.

81 Theodor, *Exploring the Bhagavad Gītā*, p. 67.

82 Radhakrishnan, *The Bhagavadgita, with an Introductory Essay, Sanskrit Text, English Translation and Notes*, pp. 171–2.

83 Zaehner, *The Bhagavad-Gita*, p. 294.

84 Debroy, *The Bhagavad Gita*, p. 143.

85 Murthy, *The Bhagavad Gita*, p. 88.

86 Hill, *The Bhagavad Gita*, p. 192.

87 Aurobindo, *The Message of the Gita*, p. 243 note 1.

88 Debroy, *The Bhagavad Gita*, p. 278 note 8.

89 Chidbhavananda, *The Bhagavad Gita*, p. 493.

90 See, for example, Zaehner, *The Bhagavad-Gītā*, p. 158; and Will J. Johnson, translator, *The Bhagavad Gita* (Oxford and New York: Oxford University Press, 1994), p. 84.

91 It is worth noting Zaehner's comment, however: "The Gītā starts by taking the Buddhist conception of liberation fully into account: it adopts much of its terminology and accepts its conclusions and ultimate goal (Nirvana), but it goes further than this in that it seeks to adopt the Buddhist ideal into its own essentially theistic framework." *The Bhagavad-Gītā*, p. 213.

92 Maharishi Mahesh Yogi, *The Bhagavad Gita*, p. 272.

93 Zaehner, again, considered the expression *Brahma-bhūta*, "Brahman become", to be a thoroughly Buddhist one because it occurs often in the Buddhist Pali canon but rarely in other Hindu literature. He wrote: "The phrase *brahma-bhūta* seems to have been taken on in the *Gītā* in its Buddhist sense of entering a form of existence which is unconditioned by space, time and causation, the very 'flavour' of Nirvana": see his *The Bhagavad-Gītā*, p. 214. In the Buddhist sense, *brahma-bhūta* means one who has reached enlightenment and, therefore, *nirvana*, and the Buddha himself is said to have become Brahman in the *Sanyutta Nikaya* 4:94–5.

94 Sharma, *The Hindu Gita*, p. xx.

95 *Ibid.*, p. xxiii.

96 Hill, *The Bhagavad Gītā*, p. 71.

Chapter 7 Devotional Hinduism: The Rise of Vaiṣṇava *Bhakti* in Medieval India

1 Frederick M. Smith, "Notes on the Development of Bhakti". *Journal of Vaishnava Studies* 6, 1(1998), p. 17.

2 Klostermaier notes the possibility of derivation from a root *bhañj*, "to separate": see Klaus K. Klostermaier, *A Survey of Hinduism* (Albany, New York: State University of New York Press, second edn 1994), p. 221. Separation from, and longing for, God are major features of much *bhakti*, particularly poetry, as we shall see below.

3 Mariasusai Dhavamony, *Love of God according to Śaiva Siddhānta: A study in the mysticism and theology of Śaivism* (Oxford: Clarendon Press, 1971), p. 337.
4 Karen Pechilis Prentiss, *The Embodiment of Bhakti* (New York and Oxford: Oxford University Press, 1999), p. 24.
5 For these different types, see R. N. Vyas, *Melody of Bhakti and Enlightenment* (New Delhi: Cosmo Publications, 1983), pp. 59–67.
6 Rachel Fell McDermott, *Mother of My Heart, Daughter of My Dreams: Kālī and Umā in the devotional poetry of Bengal* (Oxford and New York: Oxford University Press, 2001), p. 7.
7 Prentiss, *The Embodiment of Bhakti*, pp. 26–7.
8 Dhavamony, *Love of God according to Śaiva Siddhānta*, p. 1.
9 Prentiss, *The Embodiment of Bhakti*, p. 153.
10 For example David L. Lorenzen, "Bhakti" in Sushil Mittal and Gene Thursby, eds., *The Hindu World* (New York and London: Routledge, 2004), p. 185.
11 Dhavamony, *Love of God according to Śaiva Siddhānta*, p. 66.
12 There is some dispute as to whether the doctrine of grace appears in the *Kaṭha*, see Dhavamony, *ibid.*, pp. 63–5.
13 John M. Koller, *The Indian Way: An introduction to the philosophies and religions of India* (Upper Saddle River, New Jersey: Pearson Prentice Hall, second edn 2006, first published 1982), p. 202.
14 Dhavamony, *Love of God according to Śaiva Siddhānta*, p. 100.
15 See Govind Chandra Pande, *Foundations of Indian Culture, Vol 1: Spiritual vision and symbolic forms in ancient India* (Delhi: Motilal Banarsidass Publishers Private Limited, 1995 reprint of 1984 edn), p. 150.
16 A. K. Ramanujan*: Hymns for the Drowning: Poems for Viṣṇu by Nammāḻvār* (London and New York: Penguin Books, 1993, first published 1981), p. 135.
17 Vyas, *Melody of Bhakti and Enlightenment*, p. 57.
18 Lee Siegel, *Sacred and Profane Dimensions of Love in Indian Traditions as Exemplified in the* Gītāgovinda *of Jayadeva* (Delhi, Bombay, Calcutta, Madras: Oxford University Press, 1990, first published 1978), pp. 60–1.
19 Pande, *Foundations of Indian Culture, Vol. 1*, p. 142.
20 Nancy M. Martin, "North Indian Hindi Devotional Literature" in Gavin Flood, ed., *The Blackwell Companion to Hinduism* (Malden, MA, Oxford and Victoria: Blackwell Publishing, 2005 reprint of 2003 edn), pp. 183–4.
21 There is much to be said for N. Subrahmanian's point that fear not love was at the heart of much earlier religion: see "Bhaktism in Medieval Tamilnad" in N. N. Bhattacharyya, ed., *Medieval Bhakti Movements in India: Śrī Caitanya quincentenary commemoration volume* (New Delhi: Munshiram Manorhal Publishers Private Limited, 1999 edn, first published 1989), p. 180. Fear of the unknown and fear of what a temperamental deity might do, characterized much early *Vedic* religion.
22 Wendy Doniger O'Flaherty, *Śiva: The erotic ascetic* (Oxford, New York, Toronto, Melbourne: Oxford University Press, 1981), pp. 38–9.
23 Vyas, *Melody of Bhakti and Enlightenment*, p. 20.
24 Stephen Slawek, "The Definition of Kīrtan: An Historical and Geographical Perspective". *Journal of Vaishnava Studies* 4, 2(1996), p. 58.
25 *Ibid.*, p. 92.
26 *Bhāgavata Purāṇa*, 11:11:29–33.
27 Saral Jhingren, *Aspects of Hindu Morality* (Delhi: Motilal Banarsidass Publishers Private Limited, 1989), p. 155.
28 Wendy Doniger, *The Hindus: An alternative history* (Oxford: Oxford University Press, 2010 reprint of 2009 edn), p. 360.

29 Karen Pechilis, "Bhakti Traditions" in Jessica Frazier, ed., *The Continuum Companion to Hindu Studies* (London and New York: Continuum International Publishing Group, 2011), p. 118.
30 For a translation of Nārada's *Sūtras*, see Graham M. Schweig, "The Bhakti Sūtras of Nārada: The Concise Teachings of Nārada on the Nature and Experience of Devotion". *Journal of Vaishnava Studies* 6, 1(1998), pp. 141–52.
31 S. N. Bhavasar, "The Spiritual Contribution of Maharashtra Saints" in K. R. Sundararajan and Bithika Mukerji, eds., *Hindu Spirituality II: Postclassical and modern* (London: SCM Press Ltd, 1997), p. 23.
32 Prentiss, *The Embodiment of Bhakti*, p. 7.
33 George L. Hart III, *The Poems of Ancient Tamil: Their milieu and their Sanskrit counterparts* (Berkeley, Los Angeles and London: University of California Press, 1975), p. 9.
34 Mandakranta Bose suggests 100 BCE to 300 CE: see her *Women in the Hindu Tradition: Rules, roles and exceptions* (London and New York: Routledge, 2010), p. 130.
35 V. Subramaniam, "The Origins of Bhakti in Tamilnadu: A Transformation of Secular Romanticism to Emotional Identification with a Personal Deity" in Greg M. Bailey and Ian Kesarcodi-Watson, eds., *Bhakti Studies* (New Delhi: Sterling Publishers Private Limited, 1992), p. 37.
36 Doniger, *The Hindus*, p. 350.
37 Hart, *The Poems of Ancient Tamil*, pp. 161–9.
38 Lorenzen, "Bhakti", p. 195.
39 A. K. Ramanujan, "On Women Saints" in John Stratton Hawley and Donna Marie Wulff, *The Divine Consort: Rādhā and the Goddesses of India* (Delhi: Motilal Banarsidass Publishers Private Limited, 1995 reprint of 1984 edn), p. 316.
40 Ramanujan, *Hymns for the Drowning*, pp. 152–3.
41 Norman Cutler, "Tamil Hindu Literature" in Flood, ed., *The Blackwell Companion to Hinduism*, p. 149.
42 Subramaniam, "The Origins of Bhakti in Tamilnadu", p. 37.
43 Doniger, *The Hindus*, p. 344.
44 Steven J. Gelberg, "Vrindaban as Locus of Mystical Experience". *Journal of Vaishnava Studies* 1, 1(1992), p. 14.
45 *Ibid.*, p. 9. O. B. L. Kapoor says much the same thing: see "Vṛndāvana: The Highest Paradise". *Journal of Vaishnava Studies* 1, 1(1992), pp. 42–9.
46 Gelberg, "Vrindaban as Locus of Mystical Experience", p. 20.
47 *Ibid.*, p. 27.
48 *Ibid.*, p. 31.
49 Martin, "North Indian Hindi Devotional Literature", p. 191.
50 For the devotion of the *gopīs* in the *rāsa* see Eric Huberman, "The Parā-Bhakti of the Gopīs in the Rāsa-Līlā Pañcādhyāyī". *Journal of Vaishnava Studies* 6, 1(1998), pp. 153–82, and John Stratton Hawley, "Every Play a Play within a Play: The Rās Līlā Performances of Brindavan". *Journal of Vaishnava Studies* 1, 1(1992), pp. 146–65.
51 Lorenzen, "Bhakti", p. 194.
52 Vyas, *Melody of Bhakti and Enlightenment*, pp. 51–2.
53 Vasudha Narayanan, "Tamil Nadu: Weaving Garlands in Tamil: The Poetry of the *Alvars*" in Edwin F. Bryant, *Krishna: A sourcebook* (Oxford: Oxford University Press, 2007), p. 187.
54 R. Meena, "A Note on the Bhakti Movement in Tamilnad" in Bhattacharyya, ed., *Medieval Bhakti Movements in India*, p. 188.
55 Siegel, *Sacred and Profane Dimensions of Love in Indian Traditions as Exemplified in the* Gītagovinda *of Jayadeva*, p. 21.

56 Richard H. Davis, "Introduction: A Brief History of Religions in India" in Donald S. Lopez Jr., ed., *Religions of India in Practice* (Princeton, New Jersey: Princeton University Press, 1995), p. 40.

57 Hart comments, however, that there is little mythology in early Tamil literature unlike the Sanskrit myths of the North: "Thus the Tamil poets and their audience had become accustomed to seeing beneath the surface of every object and event; a sacred power that inhered in it and gave significance to it": *The Poems of Ancient Tamil*, pp. 192–3.

58 From a root *āḻ* meaning "to immerse, to dive, to sink, to be lowered, to be deep": see Ramanujan, *Hymns for the Drowning*, p. ix.

59 *Ibid.*, p. x.

60 *Ibid.*, p. 166.

61 Pande, *Foundations of Indian Culture, Vol. 1*, p. 153.

62 S. M. Srinivasa Chari, *Philosophy and Theistic Mysticism of the Āḻvārs* (Delhi: Motilal Banarsidass Publishers Private Limited, 1997), pp. 2–3. However, Colas suggests their literary skills and learning were of a sufficiently high level for them not to be directed to the populace: see Gérard Colas, "History of Vaiṣṇava Traditions: An Esquisse" in Flood, ed., *The Blackwell Companion to Hinduism*, p. 238.

63 Subramaniam, "The Origins of Bhakti in Tamilnadu", p. 21.

64 Vasudha Narayanan, *The Way and the Goal: Expressions of devotion in the early Śrī Vaiṣṇava tradition* (Washington, D. C.: Institute for Vaishnava Studies and Centre for the Study of World Religions, Harvard University, 1987), p. 39.

65 Narayanan, "Tamil Nadu: Weaving Garlands in Tamil", p. 190.

66 Narayanan, *The Way and the Goal*, p. 3.

67 *Ibid.*, p. 48.

68 *Ibid.*

69 Karen Pechilis, however, has dated him somewhere from the seventh to early eighth centuries: see *Interpreting Devotion: The poetry and legacy of a* bhakti *saint of India* (London and New York: Routledge, 2012), p. 12. For difficulties of an attempt to reconstruct something of Nammāḻvār's life from his *Tiruvāymoḻi* see Francis X. Clooney, S. J., "In Search of Nammāḻvār: Reflections on the Meeting Point of Traditional and Contemporary Scholarship". *Journal of Vaishnava Studies* 1, 2(1993), pp. 8–26.

70 See Chari, *Philosophy and Theistic Mysticism of the Āḻvārs*, p. 21.

71 *Tiruvāymoḻi* 7:9:1, translator Ramanujan, *Hymns for the Drowning*, p. 169.

72 *Tiruvāymoḻi* 2:5:10, translator V. A. Devasenapathi, "Exemplars in the Life of Grace: Māṇikkavācakar and Nammāḻvār" in Sundararajan and Mukerji, eds., *Hindu Spirituality II*, pp. 101–2.

73 *Tiruvāymoḻi* 8:5:10.

74 *Tiruvāymoḻi* 2:9:4–5, translator Devasenapathi, "Exemplars in the Life of Grace", p. 103.

75 *Tiruvāymoḻi* 7:9:1, *ibid.*, p. 106.

76 *Tiruvāymoḻi* 1:1:9, translator Narayanan, "Tamil Nadu: Weaving Garlands in Tamil", p. 200.

77 Two other consorts, Bhū-devī, the Goddess of Earth, and Nīlā-devī, a cowherd incarnation of Bhū-devī, are also associated with Viṣṇu in the poems of Nammāḻvār as they are with the other *Āḻvārs.*

78 *Tiruvāymoḻi* 5:4:3 translator Narayanan, *The Way and the Goal*, p. 41.

79 *Tiruvāymoḻi* 10:3:5, *ibid.*, p. 42.

80 *Tiruvāymoḻi* 10:3:2.

81 *Tiruvāymoḻi* 10:3:2, translator Narayanan, "Tamil Nadu: Weaving Garlands in Tamil", p. 194.

82 See Chari, *Philosophy and Theistic Mysticism of the Āḻvārs*, pp. 122, 124, 129–31, and 164.

83 *Tiruvāymoḻi* 5:7:10, translator Chari, *ibid.*, p. 132.
84 *Tiruvāymoḻi* 2:3:6, translator Ramanujan, *Hymns for the Drowning*, p. 25.
85 *Tiruvāymoḻi* 8:1:9, *ibid.*, p. 39.
86 *Tiruvāymoḻi* 3:7:9, translator Narayanan, *The Way and the Goal*, p. 52.
87 *Tiruvāymoḻi* 4:7:1 and 4, translator Chari, *Philosophy and Theistic Mysticism of the Āḻvārs*, p. 173.
88 *Tiruvāymoḻi* 2:3:1, translator Narayanan, *The Way and the Goal*, p. 45.
89 *Tiruvāymoḻi* 2:5:1, translator Chari, *Philosophy and Theistic Mysticism of the Āḻvārs*, p. 180.
90 *Tiruvāymoḻi* 1:9:1.
91 *Tiruvāymoḻi* 1:8:7, translator Ramanujan, *Hymns for the Drowning*, p. 50.
92 *Tiruvāymoḻi* 10:8:1, *ibid.*, p. 78.
93 *Tiruvāymoḻi* 5:1:10, *ibid.*, p. 83.
94 Nammāḻvār, *Tiruvāymoḻi* 7:9:2, translator Clooney, "In Search of Nammāḻvār", p. 17.
95 NancyAnn Nayar, "After the Āḻvārs: Kṛṣṇa and the *Gopīs* in the Śrīvaiṣṇava Tradition". In *Journal of Vaishnava Studies* 5, 4(1997), p. 212.
96 Ramanujan, *Hymns for the Drowning*, pp. x–xi.
97 Narayanan, *The Way and the Goal*, p. 31.
98 *Periyāḻvār Tirumoḻī* 5:4:5, translator Chari, *Philosophy and Theistic Mysticism of the Āḻvārs*, p. 153.
99 Bose, *Women in the Hindu Tradition*, p. 3.
100 For a translation of all Āṇṭāḷ's poems, see Vidya Dehijia, *Āṇṭāḷ and Her Path of Love* (Albany, New York: State University of New York Press, 1990). See also Archana Venkatesan, *The Secret Garland: Āṇṭāḷ's Tiruppāvai* and *Nācciyār Tirumoḻi* (Oxford and New York: Oxford University Press, 2010).
101 Dennis Hudson, "Āṇṭāḷ's Desire". *Journal of Vaishnava Studies* 4, 1(1995–6), p. 45.
102 P. T. Saroja Sundararajan, "The Spiritual Quest of Āṇḍāḷ" in Sundararajan and Mukerji, eds., *Hindu Spirituality II*, pp. 137–8.
103 Venkatesan, *The Secret Garland*, p. 12.
104 *Ibid.*, p. 13.
105 *Nācciyār Tirumoḻi* 8:8 translator Venkatesan, *ibid.*, p. 14.
106 *Nācciyār Tirumoḻi* 8, translator Subramaniam, "The Origins of Bhakti in Tamilnadu", p. 23.
107 Bose, *Women in the Hindu Tradition*, p. 8.
108 Venkatesan, *The Secret Garland*, p. 6.
109 See Hudson, "Āṇṭāḷ's Desire", p. 42. The influence of Āṇṭāḷ's poems on ritual liturgy is dealt with in detail in Venkatesan, *The Secret Garland*, pp. 33–6 and 39, and on the arts, pp. 36–8.
110 For celebration of Āṇṭāḷ related to her poems see Vasudha Narayanan, "Śrī Vaiṣṇava Festivals and Festivals Celebrated by Śrī Vaiṣṇavas: Distinctive and Cosmopolitan Identities". *Journal of Vaishnava Studies* 7, 2(1999), pp. 178–91.
111 Nayar, "After the Āḻvārs", *passim.*
112 Yāmuna, *The Jewel* 48, translator Narayanan, *The Way and the Goal*, p. 66.
113 Narayanan, *ibid.*, p. 67.
114 Siegel, *Sacred and Profane Dimensions of Love in Indian Traditions as Exemplified in the* Gītāgovinda *of Jayadeva*, p. 140.
115 See Jeaneane Fowler, *Perspectives of Reality: An introduction to the philosophy of Hinduism* (Brighton and Portland: Sussex Academic Press, 2002), p. 293.
116 See John Stratton Hawley, *Sūr Dās: Poet, singer, saint* (Delhi, Bombay, Calcutta, Madras, 1984), p. 6.
117 Peter Bennet, "Krishna's Own Form: Image Worship and Puṣṭi Mārga". *Journal of Vaishnava Studies* 1, 4(1993), p. 119.

118 *Ibid.*, p. 113.

119 See Chris J. Fuller, *The Camphor Flame: Popular Hinduism and society in India* (New Delhi, Harmondsworth, New York, Victoria, Ontario, Auckland: Viking, 1992), p. 174.

120 *Ibid.*, p. 177.

121 Karl H. Potter, *Presuppositions of India's Philosophies* (Delhi: Motilal Banarsidass, 1999 reprint of 1991 first Indian edn), p. 153.

122 Yāmuna set out to prove the existence of the true Self as separate from the body, as a knower, as conscious of itself, as the very "I-ness" to which consciousness, knowledge, experience and perception are related as qualities. And just as the world is the perceived object of the "I-ness" of the self, so the world is an effect of God, who perceives it with his intelligent, all-knowing attributes. Yāmuna posited three categories of what is real – selves, the material world, and God. Though he was never to meet Yāmuna, Rāmānuja did not find much to be critical of in his theories: but he was to take Yāmuna's ideas a far greater distance, and in many directions.

123 Bhatt, however, considers that Rāmānuja was not a Śrī Vaiṣṇavite, and that it was his followers who associated him thus. If this was the case, then it might explain the absence of any reference to the Āḻvars, though not the synonymy of ideas, nor the many references to Nārāyaṇa in Rāmānuja's works. See S. R. Bhatt, *Studies in Rāmānuja Vedānta* (New Delhi: Heritage Publishers, 1975), pp. 181 and 187–8. Chari's work on the Āḻvārs demonstrated well that these devotional mystics were not divorced from the philosophy of the *Vedānta*, and that, far from teaching only a devotional means to liberation of the self, they sought to teach *Vedānta* philosophy to the common person in his – or her – own language: see S. N. Srinivasa Chari, *Philosophy and Theistic Mysticism of the Āḻvārs* (Delhi: Motilal Banarsidass, 1997), pp. 2–3 and *passim*.

124 Subramaniam, "The Origins of Bhakti in Tamilnadu", pp. 13–15.

125 See Rāmānuja, *Vedārthasaṃgraha*, translator J. A. B. van Buitenen, *Rāmānuja's Vedārthasaṃgraha: Introduction, critical edition and annotated translation* (Poona: Deccan College Postgraduate and Research Institute, 1956), p. 30.

126 Rāmānuja defined a body, *śarīra*, as that which is controlled, supported, and for the purpose of a soul, a *śarīrin*. And since the world and the *jīvas* (selves or *ātmans*) are controlled, supported and used by God, then together they must also be a body – the body, *śarīra*, of God. This is an inseparable relationship, *apṛthak-siddhi*, between two substances, just as the body and soul inseparable relationship is between two substances. But the lesser substance becomes the attribute – the body of the soul, and the self of God, because soul and God provide the substratum for modifying change. Once the soul is withdrawn, the body cannot exist: indeed, what possible purpose could a body have without a soul? Similarly, once God is withdrawn, *jīvas* and the world also cease to exist, and have no purpose whatever without the God who controls, supports and has a purpose for them. Īśvara is the Soul of all.

127 The body–soul doctrine is the central doctrine of Rāmānuja's teaching, and of Viśiṣṭādvaita in general. The idea of the *jīva* being the property and glory of God, and that it exists in order to serve God, was one taught and accepted in Vaiṣṇava theology: see Chari, *Philosophy and Theistic Mysticism of the Āḻvārs*, pp. 116–17. Essentially for Rāmānuja, the body–soul doctrine solved two issues: first, the need to remove God from the world sufficiently to avoid compromising the divine nature and, secondly, the need to involve God sufficiently in the world for the human soul to remain in a personal relationship with the divine. Thus, the essence of God is the Supreme Soul and the efficient cause of all things, yet remains unchanged. It is the *body* of God – the world of *cit* and *acit* – that is concerned with change. And all is organically united as the body of Brahman.

128 Bhatt, *Studies in Rāmānuja Vedānta*, p. 53.

129 Rāmānuja, *Vedārthasaṃgraha* 82, translator van Buitenen, *Rāmānuja's Vedārthasaṃgraha*, p. 240.

130 Rāmānuja, *Vedārthasaṃgraha* 18, *ibid.*, p. 194.

131 From the introduction to the *Vedārthasaṃgraha*, translator H. V. Sreenivasa Murthy, *Vaiṣṇavism of Śaṃkaradeva and Rāmānuja* (Delhi, Varanasi, Patna: Motilal Banarsidass, 1973), p. 85.

132 Rāmānuja, *Vedārthasaṃgraha* 134, translator van Buitenen, *Rāmānuja's Vedārthasaṃgraha*, pp. 289–90.

133 Bhatt is one who is critical of this outright anthropomorphism with which Rāmānuja adorns his concept of God. He claims: "In this adulteration of anthropomorphism in the metaphysical truth Rāmānuja loses the severity of his metaphysical contemplation and gives vent to mythological fancy." He further comments that "such sentimental expressions are quite superfluous and unwarranted in his ontological set up": see Bhatt, *Studies in Rāmānuja Vedānta*, p. 54. There is a good measure of truth in Bhatt's words. Such anthropomorphism detracts from the concept of God rather than enhances it, opening up all kinds of problems in connection with the transcendent essence of divinity on the one hand, and the implications for theodicy on the other.

134 See Murthy, *Vaiṣṇavism of Śaṃkaradeva and Rāmānuja*, p. 151.

135 See also Bhatt, *Studies in Rāmānuja Vedānta*, p. 158.

136 Rāmānuja, *Gītābhāṣya* 9:29, translator J. A. B. van Buitenen, *Rāmānuja on the Bhagavadgītā: A condensed rendering of his Gītābhāṣya with copious notes and an introduction* (Delhi, Varanasi, Patna: Motilal Banarsidass, 1974 reprint of 1968 second edn), p. 120.

137 Murthy, *Vaiṣṇavism of Śaṃkaradeva and Rāmānuja*, p. 216.

138 *Ibid.*, p. 201.

139 See V. Rangacharya, "Historical Evolution of Śrī-Vaiṣṇavism in South India" in Haridas Bhattacharya, ed., *The Cultural Heritage of India, Vol. 4: The religions* (Calcutta: The Ramakrishna Mission Institute of Culture, 1956 revised edn, first published 1937), p. 176.

140 Julius J. Lipner, *The Face of Truth: A study of meaning and metaphysics in the Vedāntic theology of Rāmānuja* (Basingstoke, Hampshire and London: Macmillan, 1986), p. 104.

141 The tension between devotionalism and orthodoxy was one that was not solved in Śrī-Vaiṣṇavism and resulted in the fourteenth- and fifteenth-century division of the *sampradāya* into the Vaḍagalai (orthodox) and Tengalai (emotional devotional) schools: see Thomas J. Hopkins, "Orthodoxy vs. Devotionalism: Tension and Adjustment in the Vaiṣṇava Tradition". *Journal of Vaishnava Studies* 6, 1(1998), pp. 5–16.

142 C. J. Bartley, *The Theology of Rāmānuja: Realism and religion* (London and New York: Routledge, 2014, first published 2002), p. 79.

143 See, for example, 7:17 and 10:10.

144 Rāmānuja, *Gītābhāṣya* 15:5, translator van Buitenen, *Rāmānuja on the Bhagavadgītā*, p. 152.

145 J. B. Carman, *The Theology of Rāmānuja: An essay in interreligious understanding* (New Haven and London: Yale University Press, 1974), p. 85.

146 Rāmānuja, *Śrībhāṣya* 3:2:37, translator Carman, *ibid.*, p. 86.

147 Murthy, *Vaiṣṇavism of Śaṃkaradeva and Rāmānuja*, p. 125.

148 Chandradhar Sharma, *A Critical Survey of Indian Philosophy* (Delhi: Motilal Banarsidass, 1994 reprint of 1960 edn), pp. 366–7.

149 J. B. Chethimattam, *Consciousness and Reality: An Indian approach to metaphysics* (London: Chapman, 1971), p. 78.

150 Gavin Flood, *An Introduction to Hinduism* (Cambridge: Cambridge University Press, 1996), p. 144.

151 The Marathi word *sant* is derived from Skt. *sat* meaning "truth", "being", "purity".

152 Vidyut Aklujkar, "Maharashtra: Games with God: *Sakhya-bhakti* in Marathi *Sant* Poetry" in Bryant, ed., *Krishna*, p. 206.

153 Translator Aklujkar, *ibid.*, p. 211.
154 *Ibid.*, p. 214.
155 At that time in Maharashtra *Brāhmins* considered *any* other class of people to be *Śūdra*, effectively making only two classes.
156 Dilip Chitre, *Says Tuka: Selected poetry of Tukaram* (New Delhi, Harmondsworth, New York, Victoria, Toronto, Auckland: Penguin Books, 1991), p. viii.
157 *Ibid.*, p. xvi.
158 *Ibid.*, p. xvii.
159 Tukārām, translator Chitre, *Says Tuka*, p. 4. For reasons of space I have not reproduced some of the poems in their translated poetic lines here and below. Each new line is indicated with an initial letter written in the upper case.
160 *Ibid.*, p. 10.
161 *Ibid.*, p. 26.
162 *Ibid.*, p. 56.
163 *Ibid.*, p. 62.
164 See Chitre, *ibid.*, pp. 95–6.
165 Tukārām, translator Chitre, *ibid.*, p. 98.
166 *Ibid.*, p. 108.
167 Tukārām, *Ābhaṅga* 1,817, translator Vinay Dharwadker, "Poems of Tukārām" in Lopez, ed., *Religions of India in Practice*, p. 100.
168 Tukārām, translator Chitre, *Says Tuka*, p, 117.
169 *Ibid.*, p. 119.
170 *Ibid.*, pp. 182–3.
171 *Ibid.*, pp. 188–9.
172 *Ibid.*, p. 196.
173 Eleanor Zelliot, "Women Saints in Maharashtra" in Mandakrante Bose, ed., *Faces of the Feminine in Ancient, Medieval, and Modern India* (New York and Oxford: Oxford University Press, 2000), p. 194.
174 *Ibid.*
175 Translator Zelliot, *ibid.*, p, 195.
176 *Ibid.*, p. 196.
177 *Ibid.*
178 Mary McGee, "Bahiṇābāī: The Ordinary Life of an Exceptional Woman, or, the Exceptional Life of an Ordinary Woman" in Steven J. Rosen, ed., *Vaiṣṇavī: Women and the worship of Krishna* (Delhi: Motilal Banarsidass Publishers Private Limited, 1996), p. 140.
179 *Ibid.*, pp. 162–3.
180 *Ibid.*, p. 146.
181 *Ibid.*, p. 157.
182 Lorenzen, "*Bhakti*", pp. 199–200.
183 John Stratton Hawley and Mark Juergensmeyer, *Songs of the Saints of India* (New York and Oxford: Oxford University Press, 1988), p. 130.
184 Hawley, *Sūr Dās*, p. xi. For the complexities of the hagiography of the life of this poet, see Hawley and Juergensmeyer, *ibid.*, pp. 94–8.
185 See Hawley, *Sūr Dās*, pp. 29–32 and his "Why Sūrdās Went Blind". *Journal of Vaishnava Studies* 1, 2(1993), pp. 62–78.
186 John Stratton Hawley claims that Sūrdās "creates Braj for his hearers all over again": see "The Creation of Braj in the Poetry of Sūrdās". *Journal of Vaishnava Studies* 3, 1(1994–5), p. 5 and pp. 5–22 *passim*.

187 For the development of the *Sūr Sāgar* and the countless additions to the original by later contributors, see Hawley, *ibid.*, pp. 35–64.
188 S. M. Pandey and Norman Zide, "Sūrdās and his Krishna-*bhakti*" in Milton Singer, ed., *Krishna: Myths, rites, and attitudes* (Chicago and London: University of Chicago Press, 1966), p. 178.
189 Hawley, *Sūr Dās*, p. 163.
190 *Ibid.*, p. 49.
191 *Ibid.*, p. 50.
192 *Ibid.*, p. 93.
193 Sūrdās, *Sūr Sāgar* 3815, translator Hawley, *ibid.*, p. 95.
194 Sūrdās, *Sūr Sāgar*, translators Pandey and Zide, "Sūrdās and his Krishna-*bhakti*", p. 195.
195 Sūrdās, *Sūr Sāgar* 138, translator Hawley, *Sūr Dās*, p. 151.
196 From Tulsīdās, *Kavitavali* 7:23, translators Hawley and Juergensmeyer, *Songs of the Saints of India*, p. 163.
197 Braj Sinha, "Mīrābāī: The Rebel Saint" in Sundararajan and Mukerji eds., *Hindu Spirituality II*, p. 163.
198 For the developments of hagiographic accounts of Tulsīdās, see Phillip Lutgendorf, "The Quest for the Legendary Tulsīdās". *Journal of Vaishnava Studies* 1, 2(1993), pp. 79–101.
199 From Tulsīdās, *Vinaya Patrikā* 66, translators Hawley and Juergensmeyer, *Songs of the Saints of India*, p. 165.
200 *Ibid.*, 79, Hawley and Juergensmeyer, p. 169.
201 Martin, "North Indian Hindi Devotional Literature", p. 192.
202 Parita Mukta, *Upholding the Common Life: The community of Mirabai* (Delhi, Bombay, Calcutta, Madras: Oxford University Press, 1994), p. 12.
203 Translator, Nancy M. Martin, "Rajasthan: Mirabai and Her Poetry" in Bryant, ed., *Krishna*, p. 246.
204 Bose, *Women in the Hindu Tradition*, p. 125.
205 Mīrābāī, *Caturvedi* no. 193, translators Hawley and Juergensmeyer, *Songs of the Saints of India*, p. 140.
206 Translator Martin, "Rajasthan: Mirabai and Her Poetry", p. 250.
207 Hawley and Juergensmeyer make the point that Mīrā imagines herself as a female *yogi* and Kṛṣṇa as the absent, ascetic *yogi* and yet the marriage of the two is, "something whose possibility is simply disallowed by basic categories of Hindu thought. To become a yogi is to leave behind one's marriage and everything that goes with it – family, home, and all. Mira, however, would seem to create a new institution to answer her urges. In doing so, she once again confuses the realms that others hold apart, and once again her audacity seems to have to do with her gender": see Hawley and Juergensmeyer, *Songs of the Saints of India*, pp. 132–3.
208 Andrew Schelling, "Mīrābāī's Prem Bhakti Marg" in Rosen, ed., *Vaiṣṇavī*, p. 53.
209 Translator Martin, "Rajasthan: Mirabai and Her Poetry", p. 250.
210 Lindsey Harlan, "Abandoning Shame: Mīrā and the Margins of Marriage" in Lindsey Harlan and Paul B. Courtright, *From the Margins of Hindu Marriage: Essays on gender, religion, and culture* (New York and Oxford: Oxford University Press, 1995), p. 210.
211 Translator Martin, "Rajasthan: Mirabai and Her Poetry", p. 252.
212 Schelling, "Mīrābāī's Prem Bhakti Marg", p. 52.
213 *Ibid.*, p. 54.
214 Translator Schelling, *ibid.*, p. 55.
215 Pandey and Zide, "Sūrdās and his Kṛṣṇa-*bhakti*", p. 198.
216 Mukta, *Upholding the Common Life*, p. 167.
217 *Ibid.*, pp. 2, 69–70 and 178–81.

218 Nancy M. Martin, "Mīrābāī: Inscribed in Text, Embodied in Life" in Rosen, ed., *Vaiṣnavī*, p. 15.
219 Mukta, *Upholding the Common Life*, p. 15.
220 *Ibid.*, p. 181.
221 Harlan, "Abandoning Shame: Mīrā and the Margins of Marriage", p. 204.
222 Nancy Martin-Kershaw, "Mīrābai in the Academy and Politics of Identity" in Bose, *Faces of the Feminine in Ancient, Medieval, and Modern India*, p. 167.
223 *Ibid.*, p. 175.
224 Mukta, *Upholding the Common Life*, p. 15.
225 *Ibid.*, p. 95.
226 *Ibid.*, pp. 97–8.
227 *Ibid.*, pp. 99–100.
228 Schelling, "Mīrābāī's Prem Bhakti Marg", p. 58.
229 *Ibid.*, p. 105.

Chapter 8 Devotional Hinduism: The Rise of Śaiva *Bhakti* in Medieval India

1 Mariasusai Dhavamony, *Love of God according to Śaiva Siddhānta* (Oxford: Clarendon Press, 1971), p. 1.
2 Indira Viswanathan Peterson, *Poems to Śiva: The hymns of the Tamil saints* (Delhi: Motilal Banarsidass Publishers Private Limited, 1991, first published 1989 by Princeton University Press), pp. 58–9.
3 *Ibid.*, p. 205.
4 Sundarar, *Pāṇṭikkoṭumuṭi* VII.48, translator Peterson, *ibid.*, p. 220.
5 Appar, *Cattimuṟṟam* IV.97.1, translator Peterson, *ibid.*, p. 222.
6 Karen Pechilis, *Interpreting Devotion: The poetry and legacy of a female* bhakti *saint of India* (London and New York: Routledge, 2012), pp. 1 and 14.
7 Dhavamony, *Love of God according to Śaiva Siddhānta*, p. 134.
8 Pechilis, *Interpreting Devotion*, p. 2.
9 See Elaine Craddock, "The Anatomy of Devotion: The Life and Poetry of Karaikkal Ammaiyar" in Tracy Pintchman, ed., *Women's Lives, Women's Rituals in the Hindu Tradition* (Oxford: Oxford University Press, 2007), p. 138.
10 Pechilis, *Interpreting Devotion*, p. 2.
11 Kāraikkāl Ammaiyār *Wonder* 101, translator Pechilis, *ibid.*, p. 179.
12 *Wonder* 11, translator Craddock, "The Anatomy of Devotion", p. 137.
13 *Wonder* 6, translator Pechilis, *Interpreting Devotion*, p. 149.
14 Craddock, "The Anatomy of Devotion", p. 137.
15 *Ibid.*, p. 140.
16 *Wonder* 3, translator Pechilis, *Interpreting Devotion*, p. 150.
17 *Ibid.*, 4, p. 148.
18 *Ibid.*, 44, p. 160.
19 Pechilis, *ibid.*, p. 51.
20 *Wonder* 65, translator Pechilis, *ibid.*, p. 167.
21 *Wonder* 8, *ibid.*, p. 27.
22 *Wonder* 9, *ibid.*, p. 150.
23 Pechilis, *ibid.*, pp. 43, 139 and 141.
24 *Wonder* 87, *ibid.*, p. 36.
25 Karen Pechilis Prentiss, *Embodiment of Bhakti* (New York and Oxford: Oxford University Press, 1999), p. 9.

26 Peterson, *Poems toŚiva* , p. 3.
27 I have retained the Sanskrit version of the names here, partly because these are more frequently used than the Tamil and, also, because the Sanskrit more readily reflects their proper pronunciation.
28 Vidya Dehejia, *Slaves of the Lord: The path of the Tamil saints* (New Delhi: Munshiram Manoharlal Publishers Private Limited, 2002 reprint of 1988 edn), p. 69.
29 Peterson, *Poems to Śiva*, p. 31.
30 *Ibid.*, p. 33.
31 Prentiss, *Embodiment of Bhakti*, p. 52.
32 *Ibid.*, p. 61.
33 V. Subramaniam, "The Origins of Bhakti in Tamilnadu: A Transformation of Secular Romanticism to Emotional Identification with a Personal Deity" in Greg M. Bailey and Ian Kesarcody-Watson, eds., *Bhakti Studies* (New Delhi: Sterling Publishers Private Limited, 1992), p. 29.
34 Peterson, *Poems to Śiva*, p. 34.
35 *Ibid.*, p. 41.
36 Sambandar 1.73.8, translator Peterson, *ibid.*, p. 104.
37 Appar VI.308 verses 1 and 3, translator Peterson, *ibid.*, p. 113.
38 Prentiss, *Embodiment of Bhakti*, p. 141.
39 Peterson, *Poems to Śiva*, p. 35.
40 *Ibid.*, p. 40.
41 *Ibid.* p. 13.
42 See Dehejia, *Slaves of the Lord*, p. 30. For temples featured in the hymns of the *mūvar*, see Peterson, *Poems to Śiva*, pp. 149–79.
43 Dehejia, *Slaves of the Lord*, p. 37.
44 Peterson, *Poems to Śiva*, p. 19.
45 Appar 63, translators F. Kingsbury and G. P. Phillips, *Hymns of the Tamil Saivite Saints* 1921 at sacred-texts.com, http://sacred-texts.com/hin/htss/htss02.htm, p. 67 [11/12].
46 Prentiss, *The Embodiment of Bhakti*, p. 75.
47 Appar VI.239.7 *Ārur* (*Tiruvārūr*), translator Peterson, *Poems to Śiva*, p. 245.
48 See R. Nagaswamy, *Śiva-bhakti* (New Delhi: Navrang, 1989), tamilartsacademy.com/books/siva%20bhakti/preface.html, p. 4/15, accessed 24/11/2015.
49 Appar 2435, translator Dhavamony, *Love of God according to Śaiva Siddhānta*, p. 151.
50 *Ibid.*, 812, p. 345.
51 Appar V.204.1, translator Peterson, *Poems to Śiva*, p. 209.
52 Appar 60, translators Kingsbury and Phillips, *Hymns of the Tamil Saivite Saints*, p. 65.
53 Appar IV.31.4 *Kaṭavūr Vīraṭṭam*, translator Peterson, *Poems to Śiva*, p. 180.
54 Translator Nagaswamy, *Śiva-bhakti*, p. 11/15.
55 See Dehejia, *Slaves of the Lord*, pp. 38–9.
56 A detailed account of such worship can be found in Nagaswamy's *Śiva-bhakti*, chapter 15 pp. 7–9.
57 Appar 29, translators Kingsbury and Phillips, *Hymns of the Saivite Saints*, p. 44.
58 Appar 1092, translator Dhavamony, *Love of God according to Śaiva Siddhānta*, p. 155.
59 Sambandar, first and second *Tirumurai*, translator Subramaniam, "The Origins of Bhakti in Tamilnadu", p. 30.
60 Dehejia, *Slaves of the Lord*, p. 49.
61 *Hymns of the Tamil Saivite Saints*, p. 25.
62 Sambandar III.297 *Ālavāy*, translator Peterson, *Poems to Śiva*, p. 278.

63 Sambandar II.177.1 *Cāykkāṭu*, *ibid.*, p. 264.
64 Dehejia, *Slaves of the Lord*, p. x.
65 *Ibid.*, p. 54.
66 Sundarar VII.15 *Nāṭṭiyattāṉkuṭi*, translator Peterson, *Poems to Śiva*, p. 229.
67 Sundarar VII.5 *Ōṇakāntanraḷi*, *ibid.*, p. 235.
68 Sundarar VII.51 *Ārūr (Tiruvārūr)*, *ibid.*, p. 306.
69 Sundarar VII.21 *Kacci Mēṟṟaḷi*, *ibid.*, p. 240.
70 Sundarar VII.58 *Kaḻumalam*, *ibid.*, p. 241.
71 Prentiss, *The Embodiment of Bhakti*, pp. 10–11.
72 Sambandar I.35.3 *Viḻiḻalai*, translator Peterson, *Poems to Śiva*, p. 257.
73 Sundarar VII.22.3 *Paḻamaṇṇippaṭikkarai*, translator Peterson, *ibid.*, p. 258.
74 Appar V.177.8 *Kuraṅkātuturai*, translator Peterson, *ibid.*
75 Peterson thinks that such ecstatic dimensions stemmed from purely Tamil earlier praxis such as communal dancing in devotion to the Tamil god Murukaṉ: see *ibid.*, p. 43.
76 Appar VI.312 *Maṟumāṟṟat Tirut Tāṇṭakam*, translator Peterson, *ibid.*, p. 295.
77 Dehejia, *Slaves of the Lord*, p. 65.
78 Surendranath Dasgupta, *A History of Indian Philosophy, Vol. V: The southern schools of Śaivism* (Delhi, Varanasi, Patna, Bangalore, Madras: Motilal Banarsidass, 1988 reprint of first Indian edn, first published 1922), p. 158.
79 Translators Kingsbury and Phillips, *Hymns of the Tamil Saivite Saints*, p. 113.
80 *Tiruvācakam*, 1 (line 6), translator Rev. G. U. Pope, *Tiruvācagam or Sacred Utterances of the Tamil Poet, Saint and Sage Māṇikka Vācakar* (Oxford: Clarendon Press, 1900), now available at http://www.shaivam.org/siddhanta/thivapop.htm, accessed 09/07/2015, I.6, p. 3.
81 *Ibid.*, 21–31, pp. 3–4.
82 *Ibid.*, 13–28, p. 12.
83 *Ibid.*, 58–65, p. 13.
84 *Ibid.*, II.59–61, p. 5.
85 *Ibid.*, III. 168–77, p. 17.
86 *Ibid.*, V decad VIII. lxxiv, p. 44.
87 Translators Kingsbury and Phillips, *Hymns of the Tamil Saivite Saints*, p. 12/15.
88 *Tiruvācakam* II.74–86, translator Pope, p. 19.
89 Prentiss, *The Embodiment of Bhakti*, p. 121.
90 *Ibid.*, p. 116.
91 Dasgupta, *A History of Indian Philosophy, Vol. V*, p. 153.
92 Peterson, *Poems to Śiva*, p. 53.
93 Dhavamony, *Love of God according to Śaiva Siddhanta*, p. 326.
94 A. K. Ramanujan, *Speaking of Śiva* (London and New York: Penguin Books, 1973), p. 11.
95 *Ibid.*, p. 21.
96 *Ibid.*, p. 32.
97 Ramanujan's *Speaking of Śiva* is a major source for these four great Vīraśaiva poets and it is his translations of their poetry in the main that I shall be using in what follows.
98 Ramanujan, *ibid.*, p. 91.
99 Dāsimayya 87, translator Ramanujan, *ibid.*, p. 103.
100 Bāsavaṇṇa 70, *ibid.*, p. 71.
101 Bāsavaṇṇa 563, *ibid.*, p. 28.
102 Bāsavaṇṇa 500, *ibid.*, p. 38.
103 Mahādēviyakka 328, *ibid.*, p. 50.

104 *Ibid.*, 283, p. 134.
105 *Ibid.*, 324, p. 140.
106 Mahādēvī Ākkā 2, *ibid.*, p. 115.
107 *Ibid.*, 74, p. 122.
108 *Ibid.*, 323, p. 140.
109 *Ibid*, 131, p. 130.
110 Mandakranta Bose, *Women in the Hindu Tradition: Rules, roles and exceptions* (London and New York: Routledge, 2010), p. 121.
111 Ramanujan, *Speaking of Śiva*, p. 147.
112 Āllāmā 675, *ibid.*, p. 164.
113 *Ibid.*, 616, p. 162.
114 Utpaladeva, *Śivastotrāvalī* 4.16, translator Constantina Rhodes Bailly, *Shaiva Devotional Songs of Kashmir: A study of Utpaladeva's* Shivastotravali (Albany, New York: State University of New York Press, 1987), p. 13.
115 *Ibid.*, 1.14, pp. 22–3.
116 *Ibid.*, 1.9, p. 30.
117 *Ibid.*, 5.5, pp. 48–9.
118 *Ibid.*, 1.7, p. 30.
119 *Ibid.*, 9.5, p. 59.
120 *Ibid.*, 16.4, p. 88.
121 *Ibid.*, 5.11, p. 49.
122 For devotional poems from the mid-eighteenth century to the present day in the Śākta tradition, see Rachel Fell McDermott, *Mother of My Heart, Daughter of My Dreams: Kālī and Umā in the devotional poetry of Bengal* (Oxford and New York: Oxford University Press, 2001).
123 Parita Mukta, *Upholding the Common Life: The community of Mirabai* (Delhi, Bombay, Calcutta, Madras: Oxford University Press, 1994), p. 214.
124 McDermott, *Mother of My Heart, Daughter of My Dreams*, p. 7.
125 Vasudha Narayanan, *The Way and the Goal: Expressions of devotion in the early Śrī Vaiṣṇava tradition* (Washington: Institute for Vaishnava Studies Washington, D.C. and Centre for the Study of World Religions Harvard University, 1987), p. 150.
126 Dilip Chitre, *Says Tuka: Selected poetry of Tukaram* (New Delhi, Harmondsworh, New York: Penguin Books, 1991), p. xvii.

Chapter 9 Diversity and Unity

1 William K. Mahony, *The Artful Universe: An introduction to the Vedic religious imagination* (Albany, New York: State University of New York Press, 1998), p. 223.
2 *Ibid.*
3 *Ibid.*, p. 2.
4 Vimala Thakar, *Insights into the Bhagavad Gita* (Delhi: Motilal Banarsidass Publishers Private Limited, 2005), p. 78.
5 "Lines Composed a Few Miles above Tintern Abbey, on Revisiting the Banks of the Wye during a Tour", from *The Works of William Wordsworth* (The Wordsworth Poetry Library, Hertfordshire: Wordsworth Editions Limited, 1994), p. 207.
6 "The Prelude": Book 2, lines 400–409, *ibid.*, p. 648.
7 Mahony, *The Artful Universe*, p. 230.
8 Alain Daniélou, *The Myths and Gods of India* (Rochester, Vermont: Inner Traditions International, 1991 reprint of 1985 edn), p. 4.

9 *Ibid.*, p. 5.

10 Sri Krishna Prem, *The Yoga of the Bhagavat Gita* (Shaftesbury, Dorset: Element Books, 1988), p. 101.

Further Reading

General sources that inform the chapters of this volume are two recent ones by Wendy Doniger, *On Hinduism* (Oxford and New York: Oxford University Press, 2014) and *The Hindus: An alternative history* (Oxford and New York: Oxford University Press, 2010, first published 2009).

Sources on the **Indus civilization** are numerous, but few deal with religious aspects *per se*. Nevertheless, there are some excellent texts that may have a chapter on religion as Rita P. Wright's *The Ancient Indus: Urbanism, economy, and society*, published in Cambridge by Cambridge University Press in 2010. This is a book that gives balanced assessments alongside detailed information with a whole chapter devoted to "Models for Indus Religious Ideologies". A chapter on religion in the Indus civilization is also to be found in the late Gregory L. Possehl's *The Indus Civilization: A contemporary perspective*, which was published in 2002 in Lanham MD by Alta Mira Press and has the advantage of having good diagrams, photographs and drawings. For a historical survey of the Harappan civilization from the early discoveries of the city of Harappa in the nineteenth century, see by the same author, *Indus Age: The beginnings* (New Delhi: Oxford University Press, 1999). Jonathan Mark Kenoyer's 1998 work, *Ancient Cities of the Indus Valley Civilization* published in Oxford by Oxford University Press in conjunction with the American Institute of Pakistan Studies also contains a chapter on "Religious Art and Symbols". Aspects of religious culture are not confined to single chapters in these three sources but can be gleaned throughout the whole texts. Kenoyer's book has a very useful "Catalogue" at the end, where he lists over two hundred photographs of artefacts from the Indus civilization with a description of each and its provenance. Jane R. McIntosh's *The Ancient Indus Valley: New perspectives* published in Santa Barbara, California, Denver, Colorado and Oxford, England by ABC-CLIO in 2008 is a very comprehensive book about the Indus civilization, but has remarkably few references, despite its length.

The signs or, for some, script of the Indus civilization have been extensively studied and deciphered in relation to Dravidian by the Finnish scholar Asko Parpola. His mammoth work, *Deciphering the Indus Script* (Cambridge: Cambridge University Press, 1994) is a minefield of detail, especially for those who wish to find links between the Indus religion and later historic Hinduism. There is a plethora of detailed argumentation in this work, along with diagrammatic and pictorial support for the author's views. However, shorter accounts of Parpola's views may suit the reader better, for example, his article in *Airāvati* 1(2008), pp. 111–31, entitled "Is the Indus Script Indeed Not a Writing System?", which is available online, as well as his paper *A Dravidian Solution to the Indus Script Problem*, given at the Kalaignar M. Karunandhi Classical Tamil Research Endowment Lecture World Classical Tamil Conference delivered on 25th June, 2010. An opposite stance that denies any presence of a script is taken by Steve Farmer, Richard Sproat and Michael Witzel in their article "The Collapse of the Indus Script Thesis: The Myth of a Literate Harappan Civilization", which is available online in the *Electronic Journal of Vedic Studies* 11 2(2004), pp. 19–57. Steve Farmer has a number of articles online that the reader may find very useful: these can be found on the internet under Steve Farmer Article Downloads, http://www.safarmer.com/downloads. A wide selection of articles can also be found at http://www.harappa.com, including photographic material with accompanying script by Mark Kenoyer. Kenoyer's article, "Ancient Indus: Introduction", published in 1996 can be found at www.harappa.com/har/har1.html. Sharri Clark has listed Indus figurines in her "Embodying Indus Life: Terracotta Figurines from Harappa", www.harappa.com/figurines/index.html. Bridget and Raymond Allchin's *The Rise of Civilization in India and Pakistan* (Cambridge, New York, New Rochelle, Melbourne, Sydney: Cambridge University Press, 1988 reprint of 1982 edn) is still a much respected work, though the connection between some aspects of the Indus civilization and later Hinduism are more suspect in today's academic circles. Two books that deal more extensively with archaeological details are Dilip K. Chakrabarti's *India: An archaeological survey – Palaeolithic beginnings to early historical foundations* (New Delhi: Oxford University Press, 1999), and his *The Archaeology of Ancient Indian Cities* (Delhi, Calcutta, Chennai, Mumbai: Oxford University Press, 1998). For the demise of the Indus civilization, an edited work by Nayanjot Lahiri, *The Decline and Fall of the Indus Civilization* has a range of articles that present the various views on the subject both past and present. It is published by Parmanent Black and Orient Longman (New Delhi, 2000).

The beginnings of historical Hinduism with the ***Vedas*** are supported with a number of excellent **primary texts**. Standard works here are R. T. H. Griffith's, *The Hymns of the Ṛg Veda* (Delhi: Motilal Banarsidass Publishers Private Limited, 1991 reprint of 1973 revised edn) and Wendy Doniger O'Flaherty's *The Rig Veda: An anthology* (Harmondsworth: Penguin Books, 1981). Dwight William Whitney translated *The Atharva Veda*, which was edited by C. R. Lanman. There are two volumes to this, both having extensive notes. They form volumes 7 and 8 of the Harvard Oriental Series published by Harvard University Press (Cambridge, Massachusetts). While an old translation published in 1905, the volumes were reprinted in Delhi by Motilal Banarsidass in 1962. Extracts from the *Vedas* can be found in Sarvepalli Radhakrishnan and Charles A. Moore, eds, *A Sourcebook in Indian Philosophy* published in Princeton, New Jersey by Princeton University Press in 1957.

Sources on the *Vedas* are prolific and there is now an increasing number of works on the origins of the Āryans. Edwin F. Bryant and Laurie L. Patton's edited work, *The Indo-Aryan Contoroversy: Evidence and inference in Indian History* is an excellent work that delivers contrasting perspectives by a number of authors on the controversy surrounding the origin of the Āryans. Michael Witzel has a number of articles on the origins of the Āryans at www.people.fas.harvard.edu/~witzel. He has combined with Stephanie W. Jamison to produce *Vedic Hinduism*, which is available online at www.people.fas.harvard.edu/~witzel/vedica.pdf1992. Lahiri's edited work noted above is also of relevance here. Edwin Bryant's, *The Quest for the Origins of Vedic Culture: The Indo-Aryan Migration Debate* (New York: Oxford University Press, 2001) covers all aspects of the Indo-Āryan debate from philological, linguistic and archaeological evidence as well as the modern implications of those theories. George Erdosy's edited work, *The Indo-Aryans of Ancient South Asia: Language, material culture, and ethnicity* published in 1995 in Berlin by Walter de Gruyter is Volume 1 in the Indian Philology and South Asian Studies edited by Albrecht Wezler and Michael Witzel. It examines the relative theories surrounding the origins of the Āryans along with the archaeological and historical evidence.

Sound general sources on the *Vedas* include Fritz Staal's *Discovering the Vedas: Origins, mantras, rituals, insights* (London, New Delhi: Penguin Books, 2008) as well as a book that is particularly philosophical and reflective by William K. Mahony, *The Artful Universe: An introduction to the Vedic religious imagination* in the SUNY Series in Hindu Studies. It was published in New York in 1998 by the State University of New York Press. Vedic deities are studied intensely in an old source that is still apposite here: this is Louis Renou's *Vedic India*, which is translated from French by Philip Sprat (Delhi, Varanasi: Indological Book House, 1971). Another, older, source but one that studies *Vedic* deities in detail is Arthur Berriedale Keiths's *The Religion and Philosophy of the Veda and Upanishads*. The work is in two volumes, the first of which is relevant for this topic and was published in 1925 but reprinted several times, the latest being 1998. It is published in Delhi by Motilal Banarsidass Publishers Private Limited.

There are a number of **primary sources on the *Upaniṣads***. I have used the fairly recent 1996 translation of the principal *Upaniṣads* by Patrick Olivelle, *Upaniṣads* (Oxford and New York: Oxford University Press), as well as the older translation by Sarvepalli Radhakrishnan, *The Principal Upaniṣads* (New Delhi: Indus, 1994, first published 1953). Useful commentary on the verses of each *Upaniṣad* is provided in this latter text as well as transliterated Sanskrit for each verse and, as in Olivelle's work, a lengthy introduction. For terms such as monism, pantheism, panentheism and the nuances of meanings these imply, see my *Perspectives of Reality: An introduction to the philosophy of Hinduism* (Brighton, Sussex and Portland, Oregon: Sussex Academic Press, 2002), chapter 1, on "Types of Belief". Older primary and secondary sources on the *Upaniṣads* are numerous and chapters on them feature widely in general books on Hinduism.

I have not included all six of the orthodox Hindu **systems of philosophy** in this book, only four – two schools of Vedānta; Advaita, and the theistic school of Rāmānuja in the context of Vaiṣṇava devotion in chapter 7, and Sāṃkhya and classical Yoga. My *Perspectives of Reality* mentioned above deals with all six for the interested reader, and Bina Gupta's *An Introduction to Indian Philosophy: Perspectives on reality, knowledge, and freedom* (New York and London: Routledge, 2012), does the same. **Primary sources** on Advaita Vedānta are numerous. The reader may find A. J. Alston's series, *Śaṃkara Source-Books*, very useful in that they are thematically grouped. Alston's translations of Śaṃkara's works, all published by Shanti Sadan (London), are Volume I, *Śaṃkara on the Absolute* (1981 reprint of 1980 edn); Volume II, *Śaṃkara on Creation* (1983); Volume III, *Śaṃkara on the Soul* (1985 reprint of 1981 edn); Volume IV, *Śaṃkara on Rival Views* (1989); Volume V, *Śaṃkara on Discipleship* (1989); Volume VI, *Śaṃkara on Enlightenment* (1989). These are the dates of publications of those volumes that I have but later reprints are likely to be available. Eliot Deutsch and Rohit Dalvi are editors of selections of texts on Advaita Vedānta in *The Essential Vedānta: A New Source Book of Advaita Vedānta* (Bloomington, Indiana: World Wisdom, 2004). Sengaku Mayeda has translated the *Upadeśasāhasrī* of Śaṃkara in *A Thousand Teachings: The Upadeśasāhasrī of Śānkara*, which was published in 1992 in Albany, New York by the State University of New York Press. Primary source extracts for the orthodox systems with which I have dealt in this book can be found in Sarvepalli Radhakrishnan and Charles A. Moore, eds., *A Sourcebook in Indian Philosophy*, published in Princeton, New Jersey by Princeton University Press (1989 reprint of 1957 edn). A sound **secondary source** is Arvind Sharma's *Advaita Vedānta* (Honolulu: University of Honolulu Press, 1973, first published 1969). The *Encyclopedia of Indian Philosophies, Vol. III: Advaita Vedānta up to Śaṃkara and his pupils* edited by Karl H. Potter is a standard work. I have the first Indian edition of 1981, published by Motilal Banarsidass (Delhi, Varanasi, Patna). A sound **secondary source for Rāmānuja's philosophy** is Julius Lipner's *The Face of Truth: A study of meaning and metaphysics in the Vedāntic Theology of Rāmānuja* (Basingstoke and London: Macmillan, 1986). Eric Lott deals with both Vedānta and the Viśiṣṭadvaita of Rāmānuja in his 1980 work *Vedantic Approaches to God* published in the USA by Harper & Row Publishers Inc. Barnes and Noble Import Division, and elsewhere by The Macmillan Press Limited (London and Basingstoke).

There are a number of **primary sources for Sāṃkhya and Yoga**. For the former, Gerald James Larson's *Classical Sāṃkhya: An interpretation of its history and meaning* is the foremost. The edition I used is the second revised edition of 1979 published in Delhi by Motilal Banarsidass. The book was first published in 1969. In addition, Gerald Larson and Ram Shankar Bhattacharya are editors of the extensive and comprehensive *Encyclopedia of Indian Philosophies Vol. IV Sāṃkhya: A dualist tradition in Indian philosophy* (Delhi, Varanasi, Patna, Madras: Motilal Banarsidass, 1987), in which Karl H. Potter and Gerald Larson have a translation of the *Sāṃkhya-Kārikā*. Edwin F. Bryant's translation of the *Yoga-Sūtras* is recent, clear and excellent. He gives the Sanskrit text for each verse followed by a transliteration and translation, and then a lengthy commentary in *The Yoga Sūtras of Patañjali: A new edition, translation, and commentary*. It was published in New York by North Point Press in 2009. A much older translation of the *Yoga-Sūtras*, but a very good one, was by James Haughton Woods in *The Yoga-System of Patañjali*. I used the 1992 reprint of the 1914 edition published in Delhi by Motilal Banarsidass. Georg Feuerstein is also a leading expert on classical Yoga with a number of works including *The Yoga-Sūtra of Patañjali: A new translation and commentary* 1989, first published 1979) and *The Philosophy of Classical Yoga* (1996, first published 1980). Both are published in Rochester, Vermont by Inner Traditions International. Feuerstein has also combined with Jeanine Miller to produce *The Essence of Yoga: Essays on the development of Yogic philosophy from Vedas to modern times*, with the same publishers in 1999.

Erich Frauwallner has a number of excellent texts. His *History of Indian Philosophy, Vol.*

1: The philosophy of the Veda and of the epic, the Buddha and the Jina, the Sāṃkhya and the classical Yoga system is translated from the original German by V. M. Bedekar (Delhi: Motilal Banarsidass, 1993 reprint of 1973 edn). Knut A. Jacobsen's work on Sāṃkhya is standard. Entitled *Prakṛti in Sāṃkhya-Yoga: Material principle, religious experience, ethical implications*, it was published in 1999 by Peter Lang (New York, Washington D.C., Baltimore, Boston, Bern, Frankfurt am Main, Berlin, Vienna, Paris). Gaspar M. Koelman's *Pātañjala Yoga: From related ego to absolute Self* (Poona: Papal Athenaeum, 1970) is also an invaluable work. More divergent interpretations of Sāṃkhya and Yoga are to be found in Mikel Burley's controversial, idealist view in *Classical Sāṃkhya and Yoga: An Indian metaphysics of experience* (London and New York: Routledge, 2007), and Ian Whicher's interesting work on classical Yoga in *The Integrity of the Yoga Darśana: A reconsideration of classical Yoga* published in New Delhi by D. K. Printworld (P) in 2000: it was first published in 1998. For Yoga in its wider contexts, Knut Jacobsen is editor of a comprehensive work, *Theory and Practice of Yoga: Essays in honour of Gerald James Larson* (Leiden, The Netherlands: Koninklijke Brill NV, 2005).

The standard Sanskrit text of the ***Bhagavad Gītā*** accepted today is that edited by S. K. Belvalkar as volume 7 of the *Mahābhārata.* This standard text was the one used by Śaṃkara, and the reader who wishes to use his commentary on the *Gītā* with the actual Sanskrit text would do well to obtain Alladi Mahadeva Sastry's translation of Śaṃkara's work, *The Bhagavad Gita: With the commentary of Sri Sankaracharya.* This was first published in 1897 and the edition I have used is the 1985 reprint of the 1979 corrected and reprinted 1977 edition, published in Madras by Samata Books. A more recent edition was produced in 1998 by Arcana Publishing.

The chapter on the *Gītā* in this present book has been sourced from my 2012 work, *The Bhagavad Gita: A text and commentary for students* (Brighton, Portland and Toronto: Sussex Academic Press) which, as its title suggests, supplies a verse by verse translation and a commentary on each verse. There are a number of recently published works that will supply the Sanskrit text along with a translation. Bibek Debroy has a Sanskrit text and translation with useful notes to the text in *The Bhagavad Gita* (London, New York, Toronto, Paris: Penguin Books, 2005), as does Lars Martin Fosse's very recent *The Bhagavad Gita* (Woodstock, New York: YogaVidya.com) in 2007. Swami Chidbhavananda's *The Bhagavad Gita* (Tamil Nadu: Sri Ramakrishna Tapovam, 1982 reprint of 1951 edn) has a useful arrangement of each verse in the Sanskrit script, a transliteration of the verse, a word-by-word translation of the Sanskrit, an English translation and then a commentary. A much older translation that gives the Sanskrit script, English translation and very full notes, is that of W. Douglas P. Hill. His work, first published in 1928 and reproduced at Oxford by Oxford University Press in 1966, is entitled *The Bhagavad Gītā: Translated from the Sanskrit with an introduction an argument and a commentary.* While an older source, it is an eminent one. Another older source, but an important one, is Sarvepalli Radhakrishnan's translation, which, as its title suggests, is very full – *The Bhagavadgītā, with an Introductory Essay, Sanskrit Text, English Translation and Notes.* It was published in London by George Allen & Unwin in 1948 and more recently in New York, by Harper in 1973.

Maharishi Mahesh Yogi did an extensive commentary of the first six chapters of the *Gita* that is interspersed with his teaching on transcendental meditation. This text provides the Sanskrit script with a translation and is *The Bhagavad Gita: A new translation and commentary, chapters 1–6* (London, Frankfurt, Oslo, Geneva, Toronto, Los Angeles, Rishikesh: International SRM Publications, 1967). The Sanskrit script with a translation and an extensive commentary was also provided by Sri Aurobindo in *The Message of the Gita*, published at the Sri Aurobindo Ashram in Pondicherry and edited by Anilbaran Roy. It was first published in 1938 with a later edition in 1993. Highly respected is Franklin Edgerton's *The Bhagavad Gītā*,first published in Cambridge in 1944 and brought out in an Indian edition in 1994 by Motilal Banarsidass Publishers Private Limited, in Delhi. Edgerton provided a transliterated Sanskrit text and a verse translation with extensive notes and very full chapters on themes that arise in the *Gītā*.

For an academic source that deals with the technicalities of the Sanskrit along with a commentary, Robert Charles Zaehner's *The Bhagavad-Gītā* is still hailed as a standard work. This text, published by Oxford University Press (London, Oxford and New York, 1973 reprint of 1969 Clarendon Press edition) supplies transliterated Sanskrit. For specifically a translation without a commentary, easily obtained is Will J. Johnson's *The Bhagavad Gita: A new translation*, published by Oxford University Press (Oxford and New York, 1994). George Thompson has also produced a very recent translation in 2008, *The Bhagavad Gita: A new translation* published in New York by North Point Press, and even more recent is Gavin Flood's and Charles Martin's *The Bhagavad Gita: A new translation* (New York and London: W. W. Norton & Company, 2012). While needing more stringent editing, Ithamar Theodor's *Exploring the Bhagavad Gītā: Philosophy, structure and meaning*, first published in 2010 and reprinted in 2012 by Ashgate (Farnham, Surrey and Burlington, USA) has a translation and commentary and an interesting interpretation of the *Gītā*.

Richard Gotshalk's translation is very sound, as are his extensive notes to the translation, if rather oddly arranged, making it difficult for the reader to access several pages at once. The translation and notes, however, are well worth the effort. The work is published by Motilal Banarsidass Publishers Private Limited in Delhi and the first 1985 edition was reprinted in 1993. Older translations include the English translation of J. A. B. van Buitenen, *The Bhagavad Gītā* (Rockport, Massachusetts, Shaftesbury, Dorset and Brisbane, Queensland: Element, 1997), which has useful notes to the translation, and his lengthier *The Bhagavadgītā in the Mahābhārata: Text and translation* (Chicago and London: University of Chicago Press, 1981) which, as its title suggests, has a transliteration of the Sanskrit text.

Of **secondary sources on the *Gītā***, Vimala Thakar's *Insights into the Bhagavad Gita*, now in an Indian edition of 2005 (Delhi: Motilal Banarsidass Publishers Private Limited) is, as the title suggests, "insightful" and a thoughtful perception of the *Gītā*. Rohit Mehta also provided a powerful philosophical commentary on the *Gītā* entitled *From Mind to Super-Mind: A commentary on the Bhagavad Gita.* This was first published in 1966, but there is a 1995 reprint of the 1972 edition published in Delhi by Motilal Banarsidass. Sri Krishna Prem's *The Yoga of the Bhagavat Gita* published in Shaftesbury, Dorset by Element Books in 1988 also provides a comprehensive commentary on the *Gita*. Sri Aurobindo's *Essays on the Gita* is a lengthy work that he wrote for the monthly review, *Arya*, between 1916 and 1918. In 1922, Aurobindo revised these essays to form a book, now in its third impression of 2000 and produced by the Aurobindo Ashram at Pondicherry.

For **devotional Hinduism** there are now a considerable number of studies of the great poet–saints of the Vaiṣṇava and Śaiva traditions. Among those that are particularly recommended is Vidya Dehejia's *Slaves of the Lord: The path of the Tamil saints* (New Delhi: Munshiram Manoharlal, 1988). This is a beautiful book that brings many of the poet–saints to life by not being inhibited about the use of the hagiographic accounts of them. The work also contains excellent extensive iconographic photography that enhances the material exquisitely. Some sources dealing with individual poets also need mention here. I found Parita Mukta's *Upholding the Common Life: The community of Mirabai* (Delhi: Oxford University Press, 1994), to be an excellent source that brings Mira to life not only in her historical milieu but in the wider context of her legacy. The work contains a particularly valuable analysis of Mira's *bhajans* in their social context with interpretation from Mukta's extensive fieldwork. Karen Pechilis Prentiss' *The Embodiment of Bhakti* (New York and Oxford: Oxford University Press, 1999) lifts *bhakti* from its stereotyped definitions of the past and places it in its rightful diverse settings with, at its heart, its embodiment in the human individual poets on the one hand, concomitant with, on the other, their influence on communal devotion. For the hymns of Nammāḻvār, A. K. Ramanujan's *Hymns for the Drowning: Poems for Viṣṇu by Nammāḻvār* is a standard work published by Penguin Books (London and New York, 1993, first published 1981). The works of Vaiṣṇava poets are also translated by Vasudha Narayanan in her *The Way and the Goal: Expressions of devotion in the early Śrī Vaiṣṇava tradition* published in 1987 by the Institute for Vaishnava Studies Washington D.C. and the Center for the Study of World Religions Harvard University. John Stratton Hawley has translated the poems of Sūr Dās in *Sūr Dās: Poet, singer, saint* (Seattle: University of Washington Press, 1984), and for those interested in the *nirguṇa sants* as well as the northern *saguṇa* saints, Hawley has combined with Mark Juergensmeyer, as translators in *Songs of the Saints of India* (New York: Oxford University Press, 1988). A work that draws out the mystical thought of the *Āḻvārs*, as its title suggests, is S. M. Srinivasa Chari's *Philosophy and Theistic Mysticism of the Āḻvārs* (Delhi: Motilal Banarsidass Publishers Private Limited, 1997). Dilip Chitre translated a selection of Tukārām's poetry in a useful thematic arrangement in his *Says Tuka: Selected poetry of Tukaram* (New Delhi: Penguin, 1991). Āṇṭāḷ's poems have been translated by Vidya Dehejia, *Āṇṭāḷ and Her Path of Love* (Albany, New York: State University of New York Press, 1990), and more recently by Archana Venkatesan, *The Secret Garland: Āṇṭāḷ's Tiruppāvai and Nācciyar Tirumoḻi* (Oxford and New York: Oxford University Press 2010).

An older work but a useful one on Śaiva devotional poets is Mariasusai Dhavamony's *Love of God according to Śaiva Siddhānta: A study in the mysticism and theology of Śaivism* (Oxford: Clarendon Press, 1971). A superb book that deals thoroughly with the three earliest *Nāyaṉmārs* of the Tamil Śaiva tradition and the nature of their poetry is Indira Viswanathan Peterson's *Poems to Śiva: The hymns of the Tamil saints* (Delhi: Motilal Banarsidass Publishers Private Limited, 1991, first published 1989 by Princeton University Press). The hymns of Kāraikkāl Ammaiyār are to be found translated in an excellent work by Karen Pechilis, *Interpreting Devotion: The poetry and legacy of a female bhakti saint of India* (London and New York: Routledge, 2012). A. K. Ramanujan has translations of four of the Kannada-speaking poets dealt with in chapter 8 in *Speaking of Śiva* (London and New York: Penguin Books, 1973).

Finally, the magnificent *Tiruvācakam* composed by the great Śaiva poet–saint Māṇikka Vācakar is now available online at http://www.shaivam.org/siddhanta/thivapop.htm. This is the Reverend G. U. Pope's translation entitled *Tiruvācakam or Sacred Utterances of the Tamil Poet, Saint and Sage Māṇikka Vācakar*, published in Oxford at the Clarendon Press in 1900. It is an old work but a complete translation and a beautiful one.

Index

Brāhmaṇas, 47, 59, 63, 66, 83, 86, 89, 98, 98–9, 99, 103, 301, 324 *note* 72
Brahmaṇaspati (n. pr. div.), 65, 68, 75, 320 *note* 143 *see also* Bṛhaspati
Brahma-Sūtras, 110, 114, 118, 135, 241
Brāhmins, 50, 53, 70, 85, 86, 100, 102, 138, 140, 141, 184, 187, 223, 226, 229, 238, 247, 249, 250, 251, 254, 282, 295, 301
Braj (n. pr. loc.), 251, 252, 258
breath/breathing, 83, 88, 89, 94, 98, 101, 166, 170, 200, 201; of life/vital, 88, 93, 94, 107 *see also prāṇa*
Bṛhaspati (n. pr. div.), 65, 126, 320 *note* 143 *see also* Brahmaṇaspati
Bronze Age, 8, 17, 20, 46
buddhi, 149, 150, **150–2**, 152, 153, 154, 155, 156, 159, 160, 161, 161–2, 162, 163, 167, **168–9**, 171, 176, 180, 201, 203, 301, 338 *note* 176; *-yoga* 208–9, 301; *mahāt-* 149, 169 *see also* intellect
buddhīndriyas, 150
Buddhism, 111, 143, 146, 161, 165, 166, 181, 196–7, 197, 200, 213, 217, 223, 229, 268, 269, 271, 283, 325 *note* 5, 344 *note* 93
buffalo, 16, 26, 27, 28, 29, 30, 31, 32, 51, 52, 70, 312 *note* 114
bull, 7, 16, 27, 28, 29, 30, 31, 32, 51, 52, 70, 312 *note* 114
burial customs, 9, 39; at Mehrgarh, **10–11**; in Indus civilization, 20, 36, **36–8**, 39; burial urns/pots, 37–8, 39, 43; fractional, 38, 39; *Vedic*, 59

Caitanya (n. pr. m.), 259
Caṅkam (Tam.)/Saṇgam (Skt.) poetry, 225, 262, 265, 301
caste, 139, 140, 200–1, 216, 223, 224, 227, 228, 229, 237, 239, 244, 246, 246–7, 247, 249, 251, 257, 258, 268, 281, 282, 283, 290
cause/causality, 50, 58, 60, 61, 62, 81, 100, 112, 115, 119, 129, **130–4**, 135, 143, 144, 148, 148–9, 157, 158, 159, **159–61**, 161, 163, 173, 175, 191, 194, 197, 293; efficient, 104, 118, 130, 132, 136, 159, 179, 282, 349 *note* 127; material, 104, 118, 131, 132, 136, 242, 282; ultimate, 88, 90, 91; *and* effect, 49, 60, 61, 70, 71, 72, 77, 80, 81, 88, 90, 91, 91–2, 93, 99, 100, 112, 117, 118, 118–19, 119, 122–3, 129, **130–4**, 135, 136–7, 148–9, 152, **159–61**, 174, 175, **176–7**, 178, 179, 193, 194, 199, 206, 208, 245
Cēkkiḻār (Tam. n. pr. m.), 265
celibacy, 106, 127
cemeteries, Harappan, **36–8**; Cemetery R-37, 36, 37; Cemetery H, 36, 38–9, 43
Chalcolithic cultures 8, 9, 11
change, 57, 88, 90, 91, 107, 108, 114, 115, 116, 119, 125, 129–30, 130, 131, 132, 155, 156, 157, 158, 160, 161, 166, 167, 175, 193, 194, 195, 198, 207, 208, 283, 292, 296, 297, 349 *notes* 126 *and* 127; social, 258
Chanhu-daro (n. pr. loc.), 28, 30
chanting/chants, 48, 49, 58, 65, 83, 170, 220, 222, 227, 235, 247, 249, 254, 255, 269, 272, 317 *note* 64
chariots, 44, 45, 55
charms, 53, 54, 83
chelas/śiṣyas, 84, 105, 301
Chidambaram Temple, 268, 276–7
Cholistan (n. pr. loc.), 7, 15, 17
circumambulation, 222, 270
cit, 94, 108, 116, 120, 126, 134, 241, 301
citta, 150, 153, 163, **168–9**, 170, 171, 174, 176, 177, 301, 335 *note* 106, 338 *note* 161; *-vṛttis*, 156, 163, 169, 170, 173, 174, 176, 307, 339 *note* 179; *-vṛtti-nirodha*, 163–4, 170, 181, 301
class, 55, 65, 100, 198, 198–9, 199, 200–1, 209, 214, 223, 224, 227, 229, 237, 244, 246, 282, 283, 343 *note* 72, 351 *note* 155; duties of, 138; subordinated, 155
communion/communal devotion, 217, 218, 223, 226, 229, 243, 245, 256, 258, 259, 267, 270, 279